Justus Doolittle

Social Life of the Chinese

A Daguerrotype of Daily Life in China

Justus Doolittle

Social Life of the Chinese
A Daguerrotype of Daily Life in China

ISBN/EAN: 9783742848765

Manufactured in Europe, USA, Canada, Australia, Japa

Cover: Foto ©Thomas Meinert / pixelio.de

Manufactured and distributed by brebook publishing software
(www.brebook.com)

Justus Doolittle

Social Life of the Chinese

GENTLEMAN RIDING IN A SEDAN, WITH A SERVANT ON FOOT.

MANDARIN SAVING THE SUN WHEN ECLIPSED.

SOCIAL LIFE OF THE CHINESE.

A DAGUERREOTYPE OF DAILY LIFE IN CHINA.

BY THE

REV. JUSTUS DOOLITTLE,

Fourteen Years Missionary at Fuhchau.

EDITED AND REVISED

BY THE REV. PAXTON HOOD.

FAC-SIMILE OF A HONG KONG CENT.

With One Hundred and Fifty Illustrations.

LONDON:

SAMPSON LOW, SON, AND MARSTON,

MILTON HOUSE, LUDGATE HILL.

1868.

PREFACE.

The Author of this work introduced it to his readers, when first published, by the following prefatory remarks :—

"The reader is invited to the perusal of an original work on the inner life of the most ancient and populous, but least understood and appreciated of nations. In it an attempt is made to describe many of their singular customs and opinions relating to almost all subjects of interest, and also to give their own explanation of the origin or the *rationale* of some of them. If an undue colouring or prominence has been given to any custom, or a false statement has been made in regard to any subject, no one will regret it more sincerely than the Author.

"Nearly two-thirds of the contents of these volumes appeared in 1861-64 in the *China Mail*, a newspaper published at Hong Kong, in anonymous letters, headed 'Jottings about the Chinese.' On the writer's temporarily returning to his native land last year, some of the oldest and most intelligent residents in China, both American and English, strongly recommended the republication of the letters they had seen in a permanent form, in order to supply a manifest want in the books already accessible relating to the Chinese, viz. DETAILED AND RELIABLE INFORMATION CONCERNING THEIR SOCIAL AND RELIGIOUS PRACTICES AND SENTIMENTS. The published and the unpublished 'Jottings'

accordingly have been re-arranged, abridged, and thrown into
the form of chapters. Only three or four chapters—those at
the commencement and the close—have been written in this
country. If circumstances had favoured, a more extensive
pruning of words, phrases, and sentences could have been made
to advantage. As the work appears, it makes no pretensions to
a high literary style, but is a simple and unpolished account of
some of the most singular, interesting, and important phases
of Chinese life and manners."

That which Mr. Doolittle appears to have regretted his inability to do, the Editor has attempted, and the only merit he
claims is that of a rigid revision of the material of the work :
the Editor is not aware that a single fact of the slightest importance has been omitted. The possessor of the present volume
may feel confident that he has Mr. Doolittle's work entire, for,
indeed, the original may be truly said to have been cumbered
by innumerable, most needless repetitions and prolixities, not
adding to, but rather detracting from, the value of the work ;
further, the Editor has to say, that he has no share in the style
and composition of the work, he has confined himself exclusively
to the task of excision ; and the entire language, with exceptions
so slight and inconsiderable as not to be worth mentioning, is
the Author's. For the notes the Editor is responsible ; they are
inserted, for the most part from travellers, where it seemed likely
they might add some illustration to the text. It is, perhaps, the
most complete and interesting work on the domestic life of the
Chinese hitherto published ; it is, in fact, a volume of Chinese
folk-lore, and in no other work will the reader find so complete
and entertaining a description of the manners and customs of
the mysterious people of the great empire. Matters of history,
ethnology, and geography, or topography, do not find any or
much mention in the work ; it is simply an interesting accumu.

lation of particulars of folk-lore, an astonishing account of the usages of paganism. The reader will no doubt be amused, not less than amazed, to find that deities worshipped among us, only subjectively, such as the god of the kitchen, the god of ancestry, the god of wealth, have in China a real objective worship, with immense paraphernalia of rites, ceremonies, services, and costly temples;* indeed, the whole practice of Chinese devotion, a huge and fearfully ridiculous coil of practices which seem to leave no moment of the year, or the life, free from some service of shamanism or fetichism, illustrates how paganism grows in the human mind. Perhaps the reader will notice the family-likeness of cultured and educated paganism everywhere, and in all ages, in the tendency of those peoples "whose understandings are darkened;" who, "alienated from God," have not liked to retain God in their knowledge, but clothe every fancy and bewildering dream of the mind with some shape "made like to corruptible man, birds, beasts, or creeping things." † This Chinese folk-lore only repeats what we are able to discover in the idolatry of pagan Rome, or to decipher among the tombs of Etruria, or Nineveh, or Egypt. The amusing unconsciousness of the religious business is very remarkable; and that men should deliberately kneel down and adore the "kitchen god," of whom the Apostle's language is true, "their god is their belly," perhaps seems very strange; but, indeed, the adoration is quite as fervent, although not so objective, in our European kingdoms. The honest reader will often say, as he follows the Author through some

* While they have the still more questionable morality implied in the god of thieves.
† In China they worship not only the monkey, and the tiger, and the fox,—who seems to be, singularly enough, the tutelary genius of law and trade,—but the pig has also his apotheosis, and they possess a god of swine.

ridiculous details, "How like this is to ourselves!" On other
matters, the most absurd practices will seem to point to collateral
connexions of this people with the great stem of the human family.
This is indeed the value attaching to all that we call folk-lore; the
superstition or the strange story may be interesting to children,
to the philosopher they have a deeper meaning, more profound,
perhaps, than "Slaukenbergius's nose." "Ah, brother Shandy,"
said Uncle Toby, "depend upon it, wise men don't talk about
noses for nothing;" the which profound reflection may be made
when a philosopher entertains his readers with ghost stories,
superstition, legends, absurd manners and customs. The reader
of this volume will find little that is elevating, but plenty of
material interesting, entertaining, and suggestive; their idea of
the world of spirits, while colouring all their religious and
domestic usages, and making in one sense a world of souls, un-
doubted enough to them, are of the meanest kind, even degrading,
and in many particulars not unlike the table-rapping ideas so
singularly growing up, in the midst of our intelligence and
refinement; their popular superstitions are innumerable, and
their worship of the "*measure*" grows out of a queer historical
incident, mentioned in its place in the following pages, which
reads like one of Grimm's fairy stories. Omens associated with
particular animals are as common with the Chinese as in our
Northern superstitions; in fact, in the folk-lore of the Chinese,
we find many traces of superstitions not unlike those which have
formed a part of our own treasures in that way, and still hold a
place in many a Welsh and English village: thus the voice of
the owl is universally heard with dread, and is regarded as the
harbinger of death, is constantly spoken of as a devil under the
guise of a bird, or as a constable from the dark land. Cats are
not liked better than they are by our own sailors, and one
coming into a household is invariably regarded as a sign of

approaching poverty; and the coming of a dog is as surely a sign of prosperity; the crowing of the cock is a sure sign of something unusual about to happen in the family.

The flight of swallows is watched, and where they build their nest good luck is sure to follow. The magpie is regarded very much as with ourselves in popular superstition, although the Chinese have a proverb, which says of this bird that its voice is good, but its heart bad. The crow gives to them a cry as ominous as its ancient "cras, cras, cras;" with them the cry is "ka, ka, ka;" and whoever hears this, may be sure that in the work in which he is engaged he will not be successful. Fortune-telling is common with them, and its methods of divining or prognosticating are very like the well-known usages of old, or even modern times with us. The calculation of the year, month, day, and hour of the birth; the inspection of the physiognomy, the examination of the palms of the hands, the shuffling of pieces of paper, and the use of money,—in all these ideas and customs, among a people so thoroughly secluded and shut away from intercourse with other nations, perhaps the student will see, as in their singular passion for flying kites, and the practice with many of walking on stilts, the indications of some ancient ethnological relationships; affinities, perhaps, throwing out a clue where even language, and more obvious characteristics, fail.

Thus, also, superstitions concerning thunder and lightning, and their great national absurdity of praying for rain, finds its analogy among the rude and ignorant tribes of Africa and America, with their institutions of rain-makers. The Chinese move in a region or groove of fixed ideas; thought seems quite unawakened, mind hampered and bound like their women's feet. The "Inner Land," the "Flowery Country," as the Chinaman delights, in his natural egotism, to call his empire, is covered

with schools and scholars; up to their mark, it is the most
universally educated nation on the earth. Learning is very
highly honoured, but it is a learning which has run in the
grooves, as we said above, of the most fixed of fixed ideas, and
most of them ludicrous and even contemptible; days and
seasons bring their festivities and joyous usages and observances,
but marriages and funerals are surrounded by elaborate customs,
which in their routine seem to make the one as painful and
grim and melancholy as the other. The spirits of the dead are
regarded from the fixed idea point of view; they are supposed
to be able to take breakfast and dinner, and remembering that
decapitation is the national punishment of China, a thoughtful
tenderness considers what multitudes of headless spirits are in
the world of souls, and these, having neither mouth nor teeth,
are provided for in the food and sacrifices which are placed
before them. Mr. Doolittle's work, reciting all these particulars,
and following them out into too refining a detail of description,
which we have attempted to curtail, we regard as a far from
unimportant contribution to ethnological speculation. ·

Who the Chinese are, is one of the most interesting questions concerning the peoples of our race; they seem to dwell
among themselves, and have no relations; we suppose we
do not go too far in saying their language is the greatest
mystery in all philology. Their antiquity, while not so great as
for a long time supposed, undoubtedly traces back some centuries beyond the commencement of the Christian era. The
characteristic of their civilization, as Professor Neumann has
said, is that it has no history; and in harmony with this it is
that they seem never to have had great ideas,—that is, spiritual
ideas. Their civilization is a vast scheme concerned solely with
temporal good: a North American Indian of the old savage
tribes, a wild old Saxon of the days of the Edda, had far

greater conceptions than ever entered the thought of the Chinese; their religious ideas are pre-eminently wretched; they have all the misery and repulsiveness of paganism, with few of those grand glimpses which sometimes illuminated the dark nights of other races or peoples. Professor Neumann again says, "They have had no prophets, no immense minds, who in the splendour of their poetry have shed some immortal coruscations over the gloom." Mr. Doolittle refers to the theory, to our thought a most absurd one, though he seems to look upon it leniently, and more than half believingly, of the possibility of their relationship to, or descent from, the Jews; the idea is not worth a refutation, but in the absence of all positive information, what may be called their folk-lore becomes important testimony—their traditions, proverbs, superstitions, and social practices; these, with them, as with other peoples, become like the crests or heraldic marks which, where there has been no possibility of tampering with Doctors' Commons, guide to national affinities.

With these few, we trust not unnecessary, preliminary remarks as to the nature and value of the book, and the Editor's share in it, which is of a thoroughly negative character, it is left in the hands of the reader.

CONTENTS.

LIST OF ILLUSTRATIONS.

b

EXPLANATION OF TERMS.

Cangue.—A heavy wooden collar, three or four feet in diameter, put upon the neck of a culprit for a specified time, and thus exposed in the street as a punishment.

Cash.—The only Chinese coin in use, made of copper or brass. Modern cash have four Chinese characters upon the obverse. Two of these are the title of the emperor during whose reign it was coined. The other characters imply that the coin is current everywhere. It has a square hole in the centre, used for stringing it. Coins of the present dynasty have the name of the mint where they were coined in Manchu characters on the reverse.

Censer.—Utensil used for holding incense while burning before the object of worship, generally made of brass, iron, or earthenware.

Chopsticks.—Small pieces of bamboo, six or eight inches long, and as large as a penholder, usually square, painted or unpainted, used in eating, instead of knives and forks. Sometimes they are made of ivory or bone. They are held in the right hand between thumb and forefinger.

Classics.—Term applied to the writings of Confucius, Mencius, and other ancient Chinese. Also applied to the formulas and contents of Buddhist and Tauist books.

Compradore.—Chinese head manager. Steward for household matters.

Congee.—Rice porridge, or thick gruel made by boiling rice soft in water.

Coolie.—Common house labourer, porter, or sedan-bearer. One who does coarse and heavy work.

Cue.—Braided tress of long hair, growing from the crown of the head, and dangling down the back.

Go-between.—Agent or middle person, either male or female, employed in the transaction of important business.

Go-down.—Usually a one-storied building where goods are kept. A warehouse.

Hong.—The building used for offices or counting-rooms, or where sales and purchases are made. Sometimes goods are stored in them. The term is occasionally applied to dwelling-houses.

Li.—Chinese mile, equal to about one third of an English mile.

Mandarin.—Common name among foreigners for Chinese officers. A word of Portuguese origin.

Mock Clothing.—Sheets of paper on which rude pictures of various kinds of clothing have been stamped. Also sheets of paper of various colours, representing materials for clothing, as pieces of silk, satins, and cotton goods. By the potency of a charm this paper is believed to become clothing, or materials for clothing, and may be used by those for whom it is designed in the world of spirits.

Mock Money.—Sheets of paper of various sizes, having tinfoil pasted upon them. If the tinfoil is coloured yellow, it represents gold ; if uncoloured, silver. Coarse paper, having holes in it, represents cash. Pieces of pasteboard, in size and appearance like Carolus dollars, with tinfoil on their sides, represent silver dollars. These are believed to become, when burned in idolatrous worship, silver, gold, cash, or dollars, according to colour and shape, which may be used by the divinity or the deceased person for whom they are designed.

Sumshu, or *Chinese Wine.*—Common name for Chinese distilled spirits or whisky, made usually out of rice, millet, or potatoes. The word wine is frequently used in speaking of this whisky.

Sedan.—A portable chair or seat, usually covered, and borne on the shoulders of two or more men by means of poles fastened to the sides.

Sycee.—Lumps or ingots of silver, weighing five, ten, twenty-five, or fifty taels, more or less.

Tablet.—Wooden or stone representative of the dead. An ancestral tablet represents one or more ancestors, according to its inscription and shape, and is made of wood.

Tael.—An ounce and a third of silver, value about one dollar and one third.

Tepaou.—A village or neighbourhood officer, performing, in part, the duties of a policeman.

Tiffin.—Lunch, or slight repast between breakfast and dinner.

Yamun.—The official residence of mandarins.

INDEX.

INTRODUCTION.

CHINESE LIFE IN FUHCHAU.

FUHCHAU, as the name of the city is known among foreigners, being according to the Mandarin pronunciation; Hokchiu, as known to its inhabitants, according to the local pronunciation—the "Happy Region"—is the capital of the province of Fuhkien. It is situated about thirty-five miles from the mouth of the river Min, and two and a half miles from its northern bank, in a valley fifteen miles in diameter from north to south. Its longitude is 119° 20' East, and latitude 26° 5' North, a little farther south than the most southern point of Florida. Of the five ports opened to foreign trade and residence at the close of the Opium War, by treaties made in 1842-1844 between China and England, France, and the United States, Fuhchau occupies the central position, being situated between Amoy on the south and Ningpo on the north, and about equally distant from Canton and Shanghai.

Fuhchau is a walled city, having seven massive gates, which are shut at nightfall and opened at daybreak. Over each of the gates are high towers, overlooking and commanding the approach to them. At intervals on the walls are built small guard-houses. The walls are from twenty to twenty-five feet high, and from twelve to twenty feet wide, composed of earth and stones. The inner and outer surfaces are faced with stone or brick, and the top is paved with granite flag-stones. The circuit of the walls is about seven miles, and can be traversed on the top on foot, or in sedan-chairs, affording a variety of novel and interesting views in quick succession. Outside of each gate are suburbs. The southern suburb, known to the Chinese under the general name of Nantai, extends southwards towards Amoy nearly four miles. Outside of the east, west, and south-western gates there are also extensive suburbs. The suburbs outside of the three most

B

northern gates, two of which lie on the eastern side of the city, are far less extensive and important than the other four.

The population of the city and suburbs has never been certainly ascertained. The inhabitants of the seven suburbs are believed to be as numerous as the inhabitants of the city itself. The population of both has been estimated by residents and visitors at all figures, from 600,000 to 1,250,000. Including people dwelling in boats, who are quite numerous, it probably would not be far out of the way to say that the population amounts to 1,000,000.

Like Canton, Fuhchau is a city of the first rank, being not only the capital of Fuh-kien province and the residence of its governor, but also the official and actual residence of a viceroy, or governor-general, whose jurisdiction extends over Fuh-kien and Chekiang, its adjacent northern province. The word *fu*, sometimes affixed to its name, as Fuhchau-fu, indicates that it is the chief city of a prefecture or department, and, so considered, it has the same rank as Ningpo. It is also the residence of two district magistrates, the boundary-line of whose districts passes through the city from north to south. Besides, it is the residence of a large number of civil and military officers of high grade. Among them are the Tartar general, who is of the same rank as the viceroy, the provincial criminal judge, the provincial treasurer, the commissioners of the salt and the provision departments for the whole province, and the literary chancellor. It is the political, literary, and commercial centre of a province, whose area is over 53,000 square miles, and whose population over 25,000,000. There are always at this city a large number of expectants of office of high grade awaiting their actual appointments. Numerous gentry reside here, who have retired from office in other parts of the empire.

It is a great literary centre, the official residence of the imperial commissioner, the literary chancellor, and many men of high literary attainments in a Chinese sense; all of the literary graduates of the first degree over the province of Fuh-kien must appear at Fuhchau twice every five years to compete in the provincial examination hall for the second degree, if they desire to compete for that degree at all. Usually six or eight thousand of the educated talent of the whole province assemble here on these interesting and exciting occasions.

Legitimate foreign trade at Fuhchau was insignificant until 1853. The opium trade had been extensively carried on for several years previous to that period by means of receiving-ships stationed near the mouth of the Min. In 1853, Fuhchau came suddenly into importance as a market for black teas, mainly through the enterprise of Messrs. Russell and Co., an American firm. In that year fourteen foreign vessels arrived at Fuhchau, and in 1856 one hundred and forty-eight vessels. A few statistics will show the rapid growth of the tea trade at this place. The exports of tea to foreign countries in the year 1856-7, from April 30th, from Canton, was 21,359,865 lbs.; from Shanghai, 36,919,064 lbs.; and from Fuhchau, 34,019,000 lbs. ; and that only three years after the trade was commenced at the latter port. During the tea season, the quantity sent from Fuhchau was nearly one million pounds more than the combined amount sent from Canton and Shanghai. During the same period, Canton sent to Great Britain 41,586,000 lbs. ; Shanghai sent 12,331,000 lbs. ; Fuhchau sent 36,085,000 lbs., or about two-thirds as much as both Shanghai and Canton. In the tea season, 1863-4, ending with May 31st, Fuhchau sent to Great Britain 43,500,000 lbs. ; to Australia, 8,300,000 lbs. ; and to the United States, 7,000,000 lbs. ; in all amounting to more than fifty-eight millions of pounds. From these data the relative commercial importance of Fuhchau is easily seen. It has become by rapid strides one of the most important of the consular ports in China for the purchase of black teas. Yet it was currently reported in 1850-51, that the English Government seriously contemplated giving it up, or at least exchanging it for some other port whenever an opportunity should occur, because it had no commercial importance.

In the year ending December 31st, 1863, the imports into Fuhchau from foreign lands amounted to over ten and a half millions of dollars. Of this sum, the value of the opium imported was over five millions. Unlike Shanghai and Canton, it furnishes no silk for exportation.

It has a large trade with other ports on the sea-coast by means of native craft, as well as in foreign vessels, giving and receiving some of the luxuries and the necessaries of life. Frequently rice is imported in large quantities from Formosa and from Siam. Timber and paper is brought down the Min from the upper or western portions of the province, and taken to various ports north and south ; and it annually exports large quantities of dried and preserved fruits.

While the high native officials, civil and military, live within the city, the foreign consuls, vice-consuls, and interpreters reside

two and a half miles outside the city, on the hill near the south
bank of the Min. No foreign merchant lives in the city, nor is
there any foreign hong or store inside the walls. The principal
native wholesale merchants do their business in the immense
suburbs surrounding the Great Temple Hill. The principal
native banks are also in the southern suburbs.

In the eastern and southern sections of the city is the residence of Manchu Tartars, subject, not to Chinese, but to Tartar
officers. A few Chinese live scattered about in the sections
originally given up to the Tartar population. The Manchus
number at present probably between ten and fifteen thousand.
All of the males professedly belong to the army, though the
number of those who actually receive pay as soldiers is said to
be limited to one thousand. When any of their number dies,
another Tartar takes his place on the roll of soldiers, and succeeds
to his salary and perquisites. These soldiers are not called away
from Fuhchau to serve in the army, but remain at home, assisting, when called upon, to guard and keep the city. They spend
their time principally in the practice of archery, horsemanship,
and shooting at a mark with matchlock guns. Until late years,
none of them engaged in any business for the sake of gain ;
poverty has driven a few to open shops, but as a class they are
indolent, ignorant, and proud.

They have the reputation of being overbearing and insolent
toward the Chinese—a natural and almost inevitable consequence
of their relative positions. They are the masters and the lords ;
the Chinese are subjects. The Manchu and the Chinese men shave
their heads and braid their cues alike ; the former having obliged
the latter nearly two hundred years ago to adopt the Manchurian
national costume of dressing their hair. The Manchu ladies do
not compress their feet as do the upper class of Chinese ladies at
this place, and in this respect compare favourably with them.
They are of a large frame, more noble in appearance, and more
independent in action, than are the Chinese females. The same
remark is true of the Manchu men compared with the Chinese
men. The two races are not allowed to intermarry.

The Tartars here are descendants of a colony of Tartars who
came from Peking by the will of the Emperor in the early part
of the present dynasty. They may be always relied upon by
the Peking Government as faithful to it under all circumstances.
In the result of a successful rebellion against the Government, in
case they should not be able to make their escape to the land of
their forefathers, an extremely doubtful event, they would all

lose not only their salaries and their property, but also their heads, for no successful rebel emperor would allow any of the Tartars to live in the country.

Foreign vessels of large tonnage anchor about ten miles below the city of Fuhchau, at Pagoda Anchorage, so called on account of a pagoda built on a hill on an island in the vicinity. Above that anchorage the water is too shallow for large vessels to endeavour to proceed with safety. Here the mail steamers, which arrive usually at least once in two weeks, come to anchor, sending the mails up to town in a small but well-manned boat. Not unfrequently are there twenty-five or thirty sailing vessels and steamers of several different nationalities to be found at Pagoda Anchorage, discharging and receiving their cargoes, where thirteen years ago there was not one foreign vessel. The vessels lie in the middle of the Min, and their cargoes are transferred into lighters, which ply between the town and the anchorage.

The entrance to the river is marked by bold peaks and high land. Foreign pilots usually take the charge of vessels until they have fairly entered the river, when they yield to native pilots, who navigate them until they reach Pagoda Anchorage. The banks of the Min are lined by lofty hills, generally destitute of thrifty trees, but terraced and cultivated to their tops, presenting in the spring and summer an interesting and unique appearance. The charming and romantic scenery has been thought by European travellers to resemble the scenery of Switzerland in its picturesqueness and grandeur. Americans are more frequently reminded by it of the Highlands of the Hudson.

The Min having separated into two parts six or eight miles above Fuhchau, the branches unite not far above the anchorage, and their waters flow together into the ocean. The city of Fuhchau lies to the north of the northern branch. The southern branch passes nearly parallel with the northern, the two forming a narrow and fertile island, fifteen or sixteen miles in length, and three or four miles in width in its broadest part.

Following up the northern branch of the river from the Pagoda Anchorage, about half-way to Fuhchau, on the right hand, is the mountain called Kushan, or Drum Mountain. Its peak is about half a mile high. A large and celebrated Buddhist monastery is situated half-way up the mountain, a favourite place of resort with some foreigners and Chinese in the hot summer months. The temperature at the monastery

is sometimes eight or ten degrees lower than in the city in the
valley below. The monastery takes its name, the "Bubbling
Fountain," from a spring of clear cold water in its vicinity.
Several score of Buddhist priests are usually found at the
monastery, where they spend their time in studying the rituals
of their order, and in the performance of the regular religious
rites and ceremonies. The landscape of the valley of the Min,
viewed on a clear summer's day from the top of the mountain
or from its side, is very fine, consisting of numerous small
streams and canals running in all directions, several scores of
hamlets dotting the country, and rice-fields in a high state of
cultivation.

Soon after passing Kushan, proceeding up the river, two
lofty pagodas become visible, three or four miles distant, situated
on the right hand, and inside the city, near the southern gate.
A lofty watch-tower marks the extreme northern angle of the
city. The foreign hongs and the flag-staffs of the English,
American, and other consuls, gradually become more and more
distinct, lying principally on the left hand, on the southern
bank of the Min. The hongs and residences of foreign merchants,
missionaries, and officials, being built in foreign style, afford a
pleasing and striking contrast to the shops and houses of the
Chinese. From some parts of the river opposite the city, the
brick chapel belonging to the Methodist Mission, and the stone
church where a chaplain of the Church of England officiates,
can be readily recognised by their belfries.

In the Min, abreast of the city, is a small, densely-populated
island, called Chung Chau by foreign merchants, and Tong
Chiu by the natives, i.e. "Middle Island." * It is connected

* "We passed several floating islands, those curious productions of Chinese
ingenuity, which no other people seem even to have thought of. These
floating islands are enormous rafts, generally constructed of bamboos,
which resist the decomposing influence of the water for a long time.
Upon the raft is laid a tolerably thick bed of vegetable soil; and, thanks
to the patient labours of a few families of aquatic agriculturists, the
astonished traveller beholds a whole colony lying on the surface of the
water,—pretty houses with their gardens, as well as fields and plantations of
every sort. The inhabitants of these floating farms appear to enjoy peace
and abundance. During the leisure time that is not employed in the
culture of their rice-fields, they employ themselves in fishing, which is at
the same time a pastime and a source of profit; and, often after gathering
a crop of grain from the surface of the lake, they cast their nets and bring
up a harvest of fish from its depths, for these waters teem with creatures
fit for the use of man. Many birds, particularly swallows and pigeons,
build their nests in these floating islands, and enliven the peaceful and

with the northern bank of the river by the celebrated "Bridge of Ten Thousand Ages," or the Big Bridge. This bridge is reported to have been built eight hundred years ago, and is about one quarter of a mile long, and thirteen or fourteen feet wide. It has nearly forty solid buttresses, situated at unequal distances from each other, shaped like a wedge at the upper and lower ends, and built of hewn granite. Immense stones, some of them nearly three feet square and forty-five feet long, extend from buttress to buttress, acting as sleepers. Above these stone sleepers a granite platform is made. On the sides of the bridge are strong stone railings, the stone rails being morticed into large stone pillars or posts. Until eight or nine years ago the top of the bridge was partly taken up with shops. The whole of the bridge is devoted to the use of passengers, and the conveyance of merchandise to and fro. The bridge connecting Middle Island with the south bank of the river, called the "Bridge in front of the (salt) Granaries," is built in a similar manner, but is only about one-fourth as long as the Big Bridge. Lighters and other boats which have movable masts pass under the Big Bridge, but the junks from Ningpo, Amoy, and other places, which come up the river, anchor below these bridges and Middle Island. There are no ferry-boats which ply regularly between the north and south banks of the Min, though there are numerous boats which can be hired for a few cents whenever necessary to cross the river above and below the bridges. From

poetic solitude. Towards the middle of the lake we met one of these islands on its way to take up a fresh position. It moved very slowly, though there was a great deal of wind, and large sails were attached to the houses as well as to each corner of the island : the inhabitants, men, women, and children, lent their strength to aid its progress, by working at large oars ; but their efforts did not seem materially to increase the speed at which they moved. However, these peculiar mariners do not probably trouble themselves about delay, as they are sure of sleeping on land, at whatever pace they may go. Their migrations are often without any apparent motive. Like the Mongols in the vast prairies, they wander at will ; but, more fortunate than these latter, they have constructed for themselves a little solitude in the midst of civilization, and unite the charms of nomadic life to the advantages of a sedentary abode. These floating islands are to be found on all the great lakes of China, and at first sight present an enchanting picture of happiness and plenty, whilst it is impossible not to admire the ingenious industry of these Chinese, so singular in all their proceedings. But when you consider the cause of their construction, the labour, and patience necessary for their creation, for people unable to find a corner of the solid earth on which to establish themselves, the smiling picture assumes a darker tint, and the mind endeavours vainly to penetrate the future of a race so numerous that the land will no longer hold it, and which has sought a resting-place on the surface of the waters."—Huc's *Chinese Empire*, vol. ii. pp. 100, 101.

early dawn until nightfall these bridges are usually thronged by
travellers on foot or in sedans, and by coolies carrying produce
and merchandise back and forth.

To the north-west, and distant six or seven miles across the
Min, is another celebrated stone bridge, called sometimes the
" Bridge of the Cloudy Hills." That and the Big Bridge are
built in a similar manner. The scenery in its vicinity is
mountainous and interesting.

The foreign residents live principally on the hill near the
southern bank of the Min. Standing on that hill, and looking
toward the east, north, and west, the scenery is beautiful. To
the eastward, looming up five or six miles distant, is " Drum
Mountain." Nearer is the river, with its multitude of junks
and boats. As one glances in a more northern direction, parts
of the city come within range. In it the white pagoda and the
watch-tower are prominent objects. Between the city and the
river, apparently about midway, may be seen the roof and belfry
of a brick church belonging to the Mission of the American
Board. In the city Black Rock Hill is conspicuous, and nearer,
in the suburbs, are seen Great Temple Hill and several spacious
foreign hongs. To the north-west and the west the numerous
boats on the river and the distant hills present a diversified and
striking appearance.

From the top of the Great Temple Hill, looking toward the
south, the prospect is also fine. Probably there is not a better
standpoint in the suburbs than that hill for taking a view of
the most prominent objects to be seen in the valley of the Min :
the river, spread out to the west, south, and east, covered with
its countless boats, the bridges on each side of Middle Island,
with their passing throng, foreign hongs, the British consulate,
flag-staffs and flags of various nationalities, &c. In the distance
to the southward, the hills called the Five Tigers, and other
ranges, add variety and picturesqueness to the scenery. To the
east and to the west are highly-cultivated plains, villages, canals,
&c. On the north the city is seen much more distinctly than
from the hill on the southern bank of the river.

Fuhchau contains within its walls three principal hills, two
in its southern and one in its northern quarter. On account of
these hills it is sometimes called in writing and in books the
Three Hills. It is also frequently styled the City of Banians,
or the Banian City, on account of the great number of mock
banian-trees which are growing everywhere in the city and
vicinity. The branches of this species of banian seldom extend

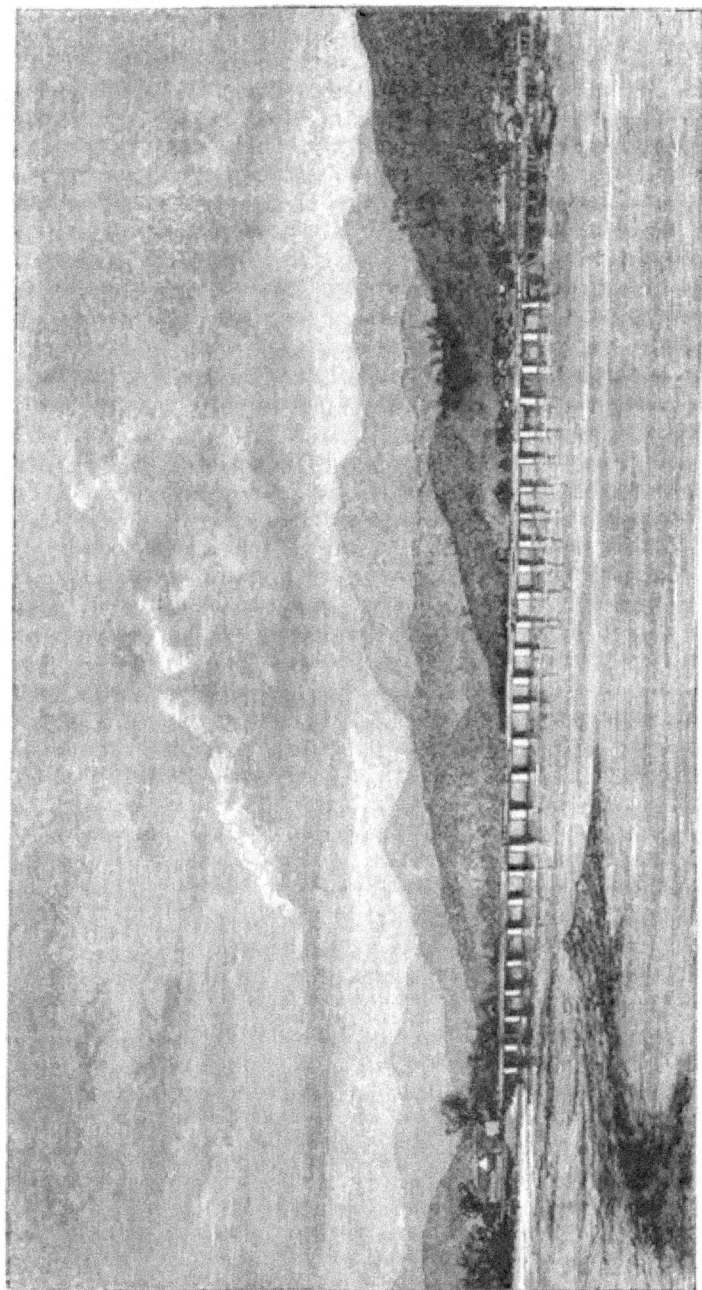

BRIDGE OF THE CLOUDY HILLS,
Seven miles north-west of the "Bridge of Ten Thousand Ages."

to the ground and take root.   The pendent branches look so much like whiskers that the common name for them among the Chinese is the Whiskers of the Banian.   They hang down several feet from the main horizontal branches, and swing back and forth in the breeze.   A single tree with its outstretched branches sometimes shades a space of ground from one hundred to one hundred and fifty feet in diameter.

The streets of the suburbs and the city are narrow and filthy.*

---

* The Rev. George Smith gives a very vivid description of the varied animation of the streets of one of the great cities of China: "As the visitor pursues his course, narrow lanes still continue to succeed each other, and the conviction is gradually impressed on the mind, that such is the general character of the streets of the city.   Along these busy traders, mechanics, barbers, vendors, and porters, make their way; while occasionally the abrupt tones of vociferating coolies remind the traveller that some materials of bulky dimensions are on their transit, and suggest the expediency of keeping at a distance, to avoid collision.   Now and then the monotony of the scene is relieved by some portly mandarin, or merchant of the higher class, borne in a sedan-chair on the shoulders of two, or sometimes four men.   Yet, with all this hurry and din, there seldom occurs any accident or interruption of good nature.   On the river the same order and regularity prevail.   Though probably there are not fewer than 200,000 denizens of the river, whose hereditary domains are the watery element that supports their little dwelling, yet harmony and good feeling are conspicuous in the accommodating manner they make way for each other.   The aquatic tribes of the human species show a most philosophic spirit of equanimity, and contrive, in this way, to strip daily life of many of its little troubles; while the fortitude and patience with which the occasional injury or destruction of their boat is borne, is remarkable. To return to the streets of the suburbs, the same spirit of contented adaptation to external things is everywhere discernible, and it is difficult which to regard with most surprise, the narrow abodes of the one, or the little boats which serve as family residences to the other.   There is something of romance in the effect of Chinese streets.   On either side there are shops decked out with native ware, furniture, and manufactures of various kinds. These are adorned by pillars of sign-boards, rising perpendicularly, and inscribed from top to bottom with the various kinds of saleable articles which may be had within.   Native artists seem to have lavished their ingenuity on several of these inscriptions, and, by their caligraphy, to give some idea of the superiority of the commodities for sale.   Many of those sign-boards contain some fictitious emblem, adopted as the name of the shop, similar to the practice prevalent in London two centuries ago. Sometimes no fewer than eight or ten blind beggars find their way into a shop, and there remain, singing a melancholy dirge-like strain, and most perseveringly beating together two pieces of wood, till the weary shopman at length takes compassion on them, and provides for the quiet of his shop by giving a copper cash to each ; on receiving which they depart, and repeat the same experiment elsewhere.   The streets abound with these blind beggars, who are seldom treated with indignity.   A kindly indulgence is extended to them, and they enjoy a prescriptive right of levying
a copper

They oftentimes are not as wide as a medium-sized side-walk in European or American cities. Some of the principal streets in places are so narrow that two sedans cannot pass each other. One must seek a wide spot and stop while the other passes along. Shopkeepers are in the practice of taking up part of the street in front of their establishments with their movable sign-boards, which are over a foot wide, placed in a perpendicular position, making the street actually allotted to the public so much the narrower. The eaves of the stores and native hongs are so arranged that, in case of rain, the water falls down in the middle of the street. There are no eave-troughs in use. It is impossible in a hard shower for one to pass through the streets, even with an umbrella, and escape a thorough wetting.

There are no glass windows in the fronts or sides of shops and stores in Fuhchau. The front part of stores, &c. is constructed of upright movable boards fitted into grooves in two pieces of timber, one fastened on or near the door-sill, and one put at the top of the front of the room. At night they are slipped into the grooves, and fastened securely on the inside. In the morning they are taken down, letting the passer-by see all that is transacted in the store, and furnishing all the light that is needed. In storms the wind oftentimes blows the rain into the establishment; in cold weather the clerks and customers are exposed to chilling draughts of wind. Usually the whole front sides of the shops,

a copper cash from every shop or house they enter. It is said that this furnishes a liberal means of livelihood to an immense number of blind persons, who, in many instances, are banded together in companies and societies subject to a code of rules, on breach of which the transgressor is expelled the community, and loses his guild. In every little open space there are crowds of travelling doctors, haranguing the multitude on the wonderful powers and healing virtues of the medicines which they expose for sale. Close by, some cunning fortune-teller may be seen, with crafty looks, explaining to some awe-stricken simpleton his future destiny in life, from a number of books arranged before him, and consulted with due solemnity. In another part, some tame birds are exhibiting their clever feats, in singling out from amongst a thousand others a piece of paper inclosing a coin, and then receiving a grain of millet as a reward of their cleverness. At a little distance are some fruit stalls, at which old and young are making purchases, throwing lots for the quantity they are to receive. Near these again are noisy gangs of people, pursuing a less equivocal course of gambling, and evincing, by their excited looks and clamours, the intensity of their interest in the issue. In another part may be seen disposed the apparatus of some Chinese tonsor, who is performing his skilful vocation on the crown of some fellow-countryman unable to command the attendance of the artist at a house of his own."—*Narrative of a Visit to the Consular Cities of China,* by Rev. GEORGE SMITH.

Black Rock Hill
(in the city).

Church of American Board
(in the suburbs).

White Pagoda
(in the city).

Hill of the Nine Genii
(in the city).

VIEW OF THE SOUTHERN SUBURBS OF FUHCHAU,
From a hill on the southern bank of the river.

facing the street, except a passage-way to the back, is occupied by a counter about four feet high.

The streets are paved with granite flag-stones. The hills in the street, ascended and descended by means of a flight of stone steps, prevent, even if the streets were wide enough, the use of wheeled vehicles. Merchandise, furniture, &c. are carried to and

GENTLEMAN RIDING IN A SEDAN, WITH A SERVANT ON FOOT.

fro through the streets by coolies. If the load is about a hundred pounds' weight, or less, and can be divided into two equal parts, not too bulky, each part is slung by means of ropes on the ends of a carrying-pole, four or five feet long, which is placed across the shoulder of the coolie. Bulky and heavy articles, too bulky and too heavy to be thus carried by one man, are slung upon the centre of a strong carrying-pole, six or more feet in length. The ends of the pole are placed upon the shoulders of two or more men, sometimes eight or sixteen, and the load carried between them.

The roads in the country, like the streets, are narrow, and not adapted to travelling or transporting merchandise in carts or

wagons. Oftentimes they are paved with granite, and only wide
enough for two to walk abreast with ease and safety. Every
five or ten li, on the most travelled roads, there are rest-houses,
where the tired traveller or coolie may stop and refresh himself.
There are no toll-gates in this section of the empire.

Travelling on land is performed, if not on foot, in very literal
carriages—Sedan Chairs, carried, in the case of a civilian,
by two or three men. Officers of a certain grade may have four
bearers. Those of the highest rank may have eight bearers.
Military officers of a low rank, and a class of interpreters or
assistants of high civil mandarins, sometimes ride through the
streets on ponies, but the common people never ride on horseback. In case a horse is rode through the crowded streets, a
boy or the groom precedes, crying out "Horse!" "Horse!" and
clears the way, else various accidents would often occur.

The hills in the vicinity of the city and suburbs of Fuhchau
are devoted principally to burying the dead, the valleys and the
level land to the residences of the living. Foreigners prefer to
reside in elevated and airy positions, as on the sides or the
summits of hills, but the Chinese reserve these situations for the
sepulchres of their honoured dead. The graves of the poor
Chinese are made much at random on the hills, on spots where
they succeed in securing the privilege of digging them; while
the sites for the graves of the wealthy are determined by the
nice rules of the art of geomancy, *à la Chinois*, having especial
reference to the future good fortunes of the families of the living.
No dead body may be buried inside the city, nor may a corpse
be carried into any of the gates of the city. It may not enter
the city on any consideration, no matter how high the rank of
the deceased, or how influential and respected his family. The
most fashionable form for a grave and its surroundings, considered as a whole, is the horse-shoe pattern, from its general
resemblance to a horse-shoe. It is also called sometimes the
Omega grave, from its resemblance to the Greek letter Omega.
The rich spend a large sum of money in erecting the grave-
stones, and in embellishing the sides and the front of the grave.
In the case of high officers, there are often large granite images
of a pair of horses, sheep, and other animals, arranged some
distance in front of the spot on which the corpse is buried.
One of each kind of animal is placed on the right and left hand
sides, corresponding to each other. Occasionally there are two
granite images of statues of men, arranged in like manner.
These granite images, some of which are larger than life, seem

to take the place of pillars and monuments, so common in the West, in connexion with the tombs of the distinguished dead.

The first Protestant Mission at Fuhchau was established by a missionary of the American Board of Commissioners for Foreign Missions in January 1847. The Mission has averaged three or four families since its commencement. In April 1856, occurred the first baptism of a Chinaman at this city in connexion with Protestant Missions. In May 1857, a brick church, called the " Church of the Saviour," built on the main street in the southern suburbs, and about one mile from the Big Bridge, was dedicated to the worship of God. Its first native church, consisting of four members, was organized in October of the same year. In May 1863, a church of seven members was formed at Chang-loh, distant seventeen miles from the city. In June of the same year a church of nine members was organized in the city of Fuhchau, having been dismissed from the church in the suburbs to form the church in the city. For the first ten years of this Mission's existence only one was baptized. During the next five years, twenty-two members were received into the first church formed. During the next two years twenty-three persons were baptized. Between 1853 and 1858 a small boarding-school, i.e. a school where the pupils were boarded, clothed, and educated at the expense of the Mission, was sustained in this Mission. Among the pupils were four or five young men, who are now employed as native helpers, and three girls, all of whom became church members, and two of whom are wives of two of the native helpers. There are at present a training-school for native helpers, a small boarding-school for boys, and a small boarding-school for girls connected with the Mission. It employs six or seven native helpers, and three or four country stations are occupied by it. Part of the members of this Mission live at Pouasang, not far from the Church of the Saviour, and part live in the city, on a hill not far from the White Pagoda, in houses built and owned by the American Board.

The Mission of the Methodist Episcopal Church was established in the fall of 1847. It has had an average number of four or five families. In 1857 it baptized the first convert in connexion with its labours. In August 1856, a brick church, called the "Church of the True God," the first substantial church building erected at Fuhchau by Protestant Missions, was dedicated to the worship of God. In the winter of the same year another brick church, on the south bank of the Min, was finished and dedicated, called the "Church of Heavenly Rest."

c

In the fall of 1864 this Mission erected a commodious brick church on East Street, in the city. Its members reside principally on the hill on which the Church of Heavenly Rest is built. One family lives at a country station ten or twelve miles from Fuhchau. This Mission has received great and signal encouragement in several country villages and farming districts, as well as in the city and suburbs. It has some eight or ten country stations, which are more or less regularly visited by the

PAGODA.

foreign missionaries, and where native helpers are appointed to preach regularly. It has a flourishing boys' boarding-school, and a flourishing girls' boarding-school, and a printing-press. At the close of 1863 there were twenty-six probationary members of its native churches, and ninety-nine in full communion. It employs ten or twelve native helpers. It has established a system of regular quarterly meetings, and an annual conference in conformity with the discipline of the Methodist Episcopal Church.

The English Church Missionary Society established a Mission at Fuhchau in the spring of 1850. It has met with many reverses, and has not averaged two families. Its members have always resided within the city on Black Rock Hill. It has two large chapels, located on South and on Back Streets, two of the most important streets in the city. It employs two or three native helpers, and has ten or fifteen baptized Chinese under its care and instruction.

Many of the small chapels, and some of the large church buildings, in connexion with these three Missions, whether in the city, or in the suburbs, or at the country stations, are opened daily for preaching in Chinese. All who please to come in are welcomed.

All these Missions have in former years distributed, in large numbers, tracts and parts of the Scriptures prepared in the general language of the country. (A considerable number prepared in the local dialect, have also been published.) The Methodist Mission in 1864 completed the translation and publication of the New Testament in the local dialect.

In some years, at the regular literary examinations of candidates for the first and for the second degree at Fuhchau, large numbers of volumes and tracts have been distributed among the competitors—in 1859, about nine thousand graduates of the first degree, from all parts of the province, including the island of Formosa, assembled at this place to compete for the second degree. The English and some of the American missionaries distributed to the competitors about seven thousand tracts and volumes, besides two thousand copies of portions of the Bible. Only a few out of this immense crowd refused to accept the books ; the vast majority seemed glad to obtain them.

In 1850, two missionaries, sent by the Swedish Missionary Society, arrived at this place, intending to establish a Mission ; but the untimely death of one, the result of an attack by pirates on the Min, near Kinpai Pass, in the fall of the same year, frustrated the enterprise. In 1852 his associate left China for his native land.

There is a small community of native Mohammedans at Fuhchau. In the western and north-western parts of the empire they are very numerous and powerful. The resident priest, who lives on the premises on which the mosque is built, is reported

c 2

to come from the western portion of China. These premises are
on the west side of the main street in the city, running north
and south, not far from the South Gate. On tablets put over
the principal door and posts of the mosque are gilt inscriptions
in Arabic. The Calendar, or list of days when fasts are observed
or worship is performed, usually contains a few sentences in
Chinese, which speak of several worthies mentioned in the Old
Testament. Very little is known by the common people about
the Mohammedans and their worship or creed.

Near the South Gate, outside the city, is a Roman Catholic
church. The number of native converts to Romanism living
in the city and suburbs is not known, but it has been vaguely
estimated at several thousands. Some of the boat population are
Roman Catholics. Worship is conducted statedly on the Sabbath ; but the Sabbath is not observed as a day of rest from
labour, and there is nothing in the general conduct of the
Chinese Catholics which distinguishes them from the pagans
among whom they live. They do not worship the ancestral
tablets in their houses.

Usually one or more European priests reside on the premises
connected with the church. They dress in Chinese costume,
shaving the head and braiding the cue. The priests and the
Chinese Catholics shun the acquaintance of Protestant missionaries and converts connected with Protestant Missions, and are
very wary and silent in regard to matters which concern the
Roman Catholic Mission. A boarding-school for boys is sustained on the Mission premises. Some or all of the pupils are
trained thoroughly in the doctrines and practices of the Roman
Church, preparatory to entering on the functions of the Romish
priesthood. Near the church is a new and convenient building,
erected expressly, a few years ago, for the purpose of saving alive
and bringing up the little girls found deserted by their parents,
or who should be brought there by them. There is a very
appropriate inscription, in large Chinese characters, over the
front door of this asylum, saying, " When thy father and thy
mother forsake thee, the Lord will take thee up." This institution is under the oversight of several nuns, or Sisters of
Mercy, from Manilla. It is reported as being in a flourishing
state.

The church is well built. It has an inscription in large gilt
characters upon its front, implying that it is erected in accordance with the especial permission of the emperor. Upon its
roof is a large cross, which may be seen from a considerable

distance. No seats are provided in the church for the worshippers, but mats on which they kneel. The men use one side of the church and the women the other. Near the pulpit or altar is an image or picture of Mary, and an image of the Saviour on the Cross, and on the walls are numerous pictures of Romish saints. A tablet to the emperor, having upon it the usual inscription which is applied only to him, several years ago was to be seen near the altar, in such a position that when the worshippers bowed toward the altar, and the images and pictures near it, they necessarily also bowed toward the tablet.

The Roman Catholic priests here operate secretly. Perhaps they labour principally among the descendants of Roman Catholics of former generations. During about two hundred years there have been native Romanists at this place. Sometimes they have been severely persecuted by the Government, and some have remained faithful to their professions through all their trials, and have brought up their children in the Romish faith.

The doors of the church are not open to all Chinese who desire to attend the worship, as all the Protestant missionaries open the doors of their chapels and churches to the public. Only members of the Romish community, or those who are properly introduced, are permitted to enter the church and remain during service. The foreign priests or their native assistants hold no public preaching service where their doctrines are explained and enforced.

They do not distribute the Bible, or even religious tracts, to the public now-a-days. It is doubtful whether they have made a complete translation of the Bible into Chinese for the study of the native priests or for their own use. They have a large variety of tracts and books. Some of them were prepared over two hundred years ago by converts in high stations at court. The catechisms and books used in schools by their catechumens and converts are like those we know nearer home; in the Catechism the second commandment is expunged from the Decalogue, and, to make up the requisite number, the tenth is divided into two.

Only one public distribution of Roman Catholic books is known as having occurred at this place between 1850 and 1863. Among the books which were given away on that occasion was one which had a singular stamp or imprint of six Chinese characters in red ink. These characters, taken in connexion with other characters in red ink also stamped upon the book, informed the reader that *the religion of the Lord of Heaven was different*

from the religion of the kingdom of the Flowery Flag. It is necessary to explain that the distinctive name in China for the Roman Catholic religion is the "religion of the Lord of Heaven," while the common name for the United States of America is the " kingdom of the Flowery Flag," a term derived doubtless from the unique appearance of the stars and stripes of the national flag. The meaning intended to be conveyed by the imprints was that Romanism was different from Protestantism. It would seem that the Romanists had been aroused, by the zeal of Protestant missionaries in distributing books, to an unwonted exhibition of zeal in the distribution of Roman Catholic books. But, in order to *protest* against Protestantism, and not knowing any better name to give it than the name denoting the nationality of the greatest number of Protestant missionaries at Fuhchau, they caused some or all of the books given away on the occasion referred to to be stamped in a prominent place, and in a colour which would attract attention, with a sentence meaning *that the religion of Heaven's Lord was not the same as the American religion !*

There are many points of similarity between Roman Catholicism and Chinese Buddhism. The common people here do not discover many points of dissimilarity between the lives of the converts to Romanism and the native adherents of Buddhism. The prominent points of similarity are the vows of celibacy, monastic seclusion, monastic habit, holy water, counting beads, fasting, forbidden meats, masses for the dead, worship of relics, canonization of saints, use of incense and candles, bell and book, purgatory—from which prayers and ceremonies deliver—use of a dead language, and pretension to miracles.

Huc, the Lazarist, seems pleased with this striking similarity, and says, *Buddhism has an admixture of truth with holy Church.*

Premare, another distinguished Romanist, says, *the devil has imitated Mother Church to scandalize her.*

Protestants ask, Has not Romanism borrowed from paganism ?

CHAPTER I.

AGRICULTURAL AND DOMESTIC MATTERS.

THE Chinese at Fuhchau are shorter than the generality of foreigners, mild in character, and timid in appearance. They are not as turbulent, bloodthirsty, and daring as are the Chinese of some of the more southern sections of the empire. They indulge oftentimes in angry scolding and violent quarrelling in the streets, but seldom come to earnest blows. They are proud and self-relying, and look with disdain, as do other Chinese, on foreigners. They are in the habit of applying diminutive and derogatory expressions to them : none so bad, however, as *"fanqui"*—" foreign devil"—formerly used so constantly at Canton. The most common epithet applied at Fuhchau to foreigners is *"Huang kiang"*—" foreign children." They, almost without exception, have black hair and eyes ; and, noticing the fact that most foreigners have hair and eyes not of the same colour, frequently express this difference by calling them red-haired and blue-eyed, though their hair may be white and eyes grey. Foreigners all belong to the kingdom of red-haired people, while the Chinese style themselves men of the " black-haired race."

The houses of the Chinese are usually one story high, and built of wood. Few substantial brick dwelling-houses are seen. The covering is earthen tiles burned in kilns. The flooring of most houses among the poorer classes is made of a cement composed of clay, sand, and lime, and is hard and smooth when properly prepared, or it is simply the earth pounded down. The wooden floors, even in the better kind of houses, are very poor, uneven, and unplaned. No carpets are used, and seldom is matting spread upon the flooring. Oftentimes there is no ceiling overhead, the room extending to the roof. A large number of families live in boats, about twenty or twenty-five feet long, and about six or eight feet wide. Here children are born, brought up, marry, and die.

Dwelling-houses usually have wooden windows, no glass being used even in wealthy families. Sometimes windows having a kind of semi-transparent shell ingeniously arranged in rows are found. When light is needed, the wooden windows are opened either partially or wholly. They are also opened for purposes of ventilation in the summer season.

The houses have no fireplaces, furnaces, or stoves. The doors and windows are poorly adapted to cold weather, not being fitted tightly. The Chinese at Fuhchau simply put on more garments than usual in the winter, the number being graduated by the intensity of the cold. In the absence of artificial means for heating their rooms, the people frequently carry around with them a portable furnace, containing embers of coals, with which they warm themselves from time to time.

At Fuhchau ice is very rarely seen, even as thin as a knife-blade. Frosty mornings seldom occur. Snow-storms are exceedingly uncommon. In February 1864, snow fell two or three inches deep, and remained on the surrounding hills for several days,—an event which had not taken place before, it was said, for thirty-eight years. Hail-storms are not so uncommon as snow-storms. The heat in the shade, in the hottest months of summer, seldom exceeds 96° Fahrenheit. August and September are oftentimes felt to be the most oppressive months, on account of the long-continued heat previously experienced. Rain falls in all seasons of the year, though more falls in the spring than the fall. Usually in April or May there is a freshet, covering the rice-fields in the vicinity, and flooding the ground on which many houses are built. When it comes late in the season, it is apt to damage or destroy the rice crop, causing much suffering among the poor.

The soil of the valley of the Min is very fertile, and is kept in a state of excellent tillage. Night-soil is hoarded in the city and suburbs by the Chinese with the greatest care. It is sold to persons who transport it into the surrounding country for use as manure. On some low lands two crops of rice and one of wheat are annually produced. From many gardens at least six or eight crops of vegetables are grown year after year. Two crops of the Irish or foreign potato, on the same land, can be cultivated, one coming to maturity in December, and the other in April.

Rice, of which there are several varieties, wheat, and sweet potatoes, are the most common crops. Barley, tobacco, and beans are produced in considerable quantities. A kind of sugar-cane, propagated by slips, and making inferior brown sugar, is also grown extensively.*

Fruits are plenty during all the year, but they are picked before ripe, very frequently when quite green, so that, as a general remark, they are not well flavoured. At the close of the season for each species, ripe fruits are found in market. They are often brought on men's shoulders a great distance in baskets, and if picked only when ripe they would spoil, or be very badly damaged, before they could reach the market. There are no railroads by which ripe fruit and other produce can be trans-ported without injury and with speed; nor are steamers avail-able for transporting fruit, &c. except between a very few places along the sea-coast. Junks and sailing vessels are usually too slow and uncertain a mode of conveyance for fruit, unless picked before fully ripe. Peaches, plums, pears, and several varieties of the orange, abound in their season. One kind of orange, which is called the Mandarin orange, has a loose jacket or skin, and the inside is divided into ten or twelve lobes. There are no lemons, cherries, or currants raised at Fuhchau, and no berries of any kind, as strawberry, gooseberry, whortleberry, blackberry, raspberry, &c. The pine-apple, plantain, cocoa-nut, mango, and a fine variety of pumelo, are brought from Formosa or Amoy. Native pumelos, shaddocks, pomegranates, the arbutus, the guava, persimmon, grapes of an inferior quality, the pipi, lichi, the lungan, or the dragon's eyes, are abundant, but no good apples. Large quantities of oranges, ginger, and various

---

* The so-called Chinese sugar-cane, or sorghum, is grown very extensively in Northern China, and is known among foreigners as a kind of millet—*the Barbadoes Millet.* The Chinese name for it is *Kauliang.* It is propa-gated—like broom-corn, which it resembles in some respects—by its seeds, which grow on the top of its stalks. The Chinese do not press the juice from its stalks for the purpose of manufacturing molasses or sugar, and they manifest surprise when informed that such a use is made of it in the United States. They make a coarse kind of bread from the flour of the seeds of the kauliang, eaten principally by the poorer classes. The best kind of Chinese whisky, oftentimes called Chinese wine, is distilled from the seeds. The stalks are used for fuel, for lathing in the partitions of houses, for slight and temporary fences, &c. Numerous and immense fuel-yards, consisting entirely of the dried stalks of the kauliang, are formed at Tientsin and many other cities in the north of China. During a few years past many inquiries have been made in regard to the manner in which the Chinese manufacture sugar and molasses out of the sorghum, but such information is vainly sought of them, for they never manufacture such articles from its stalks.

kinds of fruit and vegetables are preserved in sugar, and exported to other parts of China.   Bamboo-shoots for food are also
cured and sent away.   Water-melons, squashes, onions and
garlics, turnips, carrots, cabbages, lettuce, cucumbers, and a
variety of vegetables not cultivated in the United States or in
Great Britain, are produced in large quantities, and sold at
reasonable prices ; but no musk-melon, nor beets, nor tomatoes
of a large species.   A very small kind of tomato, about the size
of a small cherry, called " snake's eggs," not used as food by the
Chinese, is found growing wild.   Ground-nuts, or pea-nuts, are
extensively cultivated.   The art of grafting is considerably
practised, but fruit is not cultivated as carefully as in the West.

The Chinese at Fuhchau live principally on rice, fish, and
vegetables.   They never use bread at their meals.   Wheat-flour
is used for making various kinds of luncheon cakes.   The
most common meats are pork, the flesh of the mountain goat,
and the flesh of the domesticated buffalo or water-ox, and the
cow ; ducks, geese, chickens, and fish from salt and from fresh
water.   There is never any veal or mutton in market.   They
never salt down beef or pork.   Fuhchau bacon and hams are
celebrated in Eastern and Southern Asia.   It is considered a
hardship, and a mark of excessive poverty, to eat potatoes except
as luncheon.   Immense quantities of the sweet potato are grated
into coarse slips and dried in the sun for use as food among the
poor in case rice cannot be procured.   This dried potato is called
potato-rice.   Oysters abound in the winter, and are very cheap,
the usual price of clear oysters being between five and six cents
per pound.   Shrimps, crabs, and clams are plentiful.   Little
wild game can be obtained at any season of the year.   In the
winter, pheasants, in small numbers, are brought from the
country to sell, having been shot or entrapped upon the hills.

The Chinese at their meals usually have several small dishes
of vegetables, fish, &c. prepared, besides a large quantity of
boiled or steamed rice put in a vessel by itself.   Each person
helps himself to the rice, putting some, by means of a ladle or
large spoon, into a bowl.   The bowl, held in the left hand, is
brought near the chin, whence, by the use of a pair of chopsticks, taken between the thumb and fore and middle fingers,
the rice is shovelled or pushed into the mouth from time to time.
Whenever any vegetable or fish, &c. is desired, a morsel is taken,
by a dexterous use of the chopsticks, from the common dish
which contains the article, and conveyed to the mouth.   The
chopsticks are not used separately, one in each hand.   An

earthen spoon is sometimes used to dip out the gravy or liquor from the dish of vegetables or fish, but knives and forks are never used at mealtime.

Husband and wife and adult children oftentimes eat at the same table and at the same time, if there are no strangers or guests present; in such a case, females do not appear at the table with males. On festive occasions, when friends are invited to dinner, the men eat by themselves, and the women by themselves. Ladies and gentlemen, if unacquainted, are not formally introduced to each other when invited to a feast at the same house, nor do they converse or promenade together. The ladies keep by themselves in the inner apartments, while the gentlemen remain in the reception-room, or public hall, or library. Persons of different sex, even those who are acquainted or related, are not allowed to mingle together on public or festive occasions. Husband and wife never walk side by side or arm in arm in the streets. Sometimes a small-footed woman is seen walking in public leaning on the shoulder of her son. Dancing is unknown.

The common beverage of the Chinese is a weak decoction of black tea—according to common fame they never use green tea. At Fuhchau, the use of cold water as a drink is regarded by the natives as decidedly unhealthy, and most would prefer to thirst for a long time rather than drink it, though they might venture to rinse their mouth or wet their lips with water. A drink of hot or warm water would be greatly preferred to a drink of cold water. The poorest of the poor must have their tea, regarding it not so much a luxury as a necessity. They never use milk or sugar, but always take it clear, and as hot as they can drink it. They prepare it, not by steeping, but by pouring boiling water, or water which has boiled, upon the tea, letting it stand a few minutes, usually covered over. It is considered essential, on receiving a call from a friend or stranger, to offer him some hot tea as soon after he enters as possible, and usually he is also invited to smoke a whiff of tobacco. Unless the tea should be forthcoming, the host would be regarded as destitute of good manners, and unaccustomed to the usages of polite society.

The tea-shrub resembles, in some respects, the low species of whortleberry, being allowed to grow usually only about a foot and a half high. Some compare the tea-shrub to the currant-bush; but the currant grows too high and is too bushy to justify the comparison, according to our observation. The tea-shrub would grow much higher than what we saw, if allowed to do so.

It was kept low by picking the higher leaves and breaking off the highest branches. A high shrub would be in danger of damage from the heavy storms of wind, which are quite common amid the hills, and, besides, the leaves would not be as valuable as the leaves of a small shrub.

The tea-seeds should be planted in the tenth Chinese month (corresponding to November), and the plants are then ready for transplanting by the following autumn. They are transplanted from three to five together, in rows from three to five feet apart each way, in much the same manner as Indian corn is planted in America. In about four years the plants are large enough to spare some of their leaves without serious detriment. The plantations are not manured, but are kept free from weeds. The plant blossoms about the tenth month, producing a white flower, in appearance and size much like the flower of the orange. The seeds form in a pod, each pod containing three tea-seeds about as large as a small bean.

We were informed that only two kinds of tea, Congou and Oolong, were usually made from these tea plantations, differing from each other only in consequence of being manufactured in different ways.*

The leaves of a medium size are carefully plucked, principally by women and children. The largest leaves are usually left on the shrub, in order to catch the dew. If all were picked at once, there would be danger of killing or of greatly injuring the shrub. A thrifty clump will annually furnish from three to five ounces of leaves, and a smart picker can gather in a day eight or ten pounds of green leaves. There are three seasons for picking the leaves, viz. in the third, fifth, and eighth Chinese months, when each shrub is picked over, at intervals of ten or

* "There are few sights," says Mr. Fortune, "more pleasing than a Chinese family in the interior engaged in gathering the tea-leaves, or indeed in any of their other agricultural pursuits. There is the old man, patriarch-like, directing his descendants—many of whom are in their youth and prime, while others are in their childhood—in the labours of the field. He stands in the midst of them, bowed down with age. But to the honour of the Chinese, as a nation, he is always looked up to by all with pride and affection, and his old age and grey hairs are honoured, revered, and loved. When, after the labours of the day are over, they return to their humble and happy homes, their fare consists chiefly of rice, fish, and vegetables, which they enjoy with great zest, and are happy and contented. I really believe that there is no country in the world where the agricultural population are better off than they are in the North of China. Labour with them is a pleasure, for its fruits are eaten by themselves, and the rod of the oppressor is unfelt and unknown."—*Wanderings in China*, p. 202.

fifteen days, two or three times or more, according to its thriftiness, and the demand in market for the dried leaf. If there is no prospect of selling the tea at a profit, the leaf is not picked. A pound of green leaves makes only about three or four ounces of tea. The first picking is the best, and commands the highest price.

The following, we were informed, is the method of preparing Congou:—

1. The leaves are exposed in the sun or in an airy place. The object of this is not to dry them, but only to *wilt* them slowly and thoroughly.

2. A quantity of the leaves thus wilted are put into a shallow vessel, usually made of the splints of the bamboo, and trodden down together for a considerable time, until all the fibres and stems of the leaves are broken. The object is simply to break the stiff parts or fibres. Men, barefooted, are employed to do this work, because the Chinese do not appear to have found out a more convenient, expeditious, and effective method of attaining the object in view.

3. These leaves are then rolled in a particular manner by the hands of the operator. The object is solely to cause them to take a round or spiral form. If not rolled in this way, they would remain flat, a shape not adapted to the foreign market. While lying on the vessel, the hands, spread out, are passed around for some time in a circular manner, parallel to the bottom of the vessel, lightly touching the leaves.

4. They are now placed in a heap to heat for half an hour or longer, until they become of a reddish appearance.

5. The leaves are then spread out in the sun, or in a light and airy place, and left to dry. They must be thoroughly dried, else they would mould, and become unfit for the foreign market.

6. The leaf is next sold to the agents of foreigners or to native dealers, who take it away and expend a great deal of labour upon it before it is shipped to foreign countries. It is sifted in coarse sieves, and picked over several times, in order to separate the different qualities, to remove the stems, the large or flat leaves, &c. The large leaves are put by themselves, and the small by themselves. It is dried several times over slow fires in iron pans, in order to prevent its spoiling through moisture, according to circumstances, as the weather, length of time on hand, &c. seem to require.

The process of preparing Oolong tea differs in some particulars from the method of preparing Congou.

The fresh leaves are dried for a short time only, not until they are wilted, but only until all the dew, or water, or external dampness, is gone.

Instead of being dried in the sun, they are dried in an iron vessel over a small, steady fire. They are kept in motion by the hand to prevent any scorching, or crisping, or burning. They are not perfectly, but only about half dried.

They are trodden by barefooted men, rolled with the hand, and dried in the sun or air, and afterwards sifted, sorted, and fired in iron pans, as the leaf for making Congou was served.

PLOUGHING WITH THE DOMESTICATED BUFFALO.

In the suburbs of Fuhchau there are many establishments where large numbers of young men, women, and children are industriously employed during the tea season in sifting and sorting the leaves. Women and children earn from three to six cents per day, according to their skill and celerity, boarding themselves; while the young men receive from five to eight cents, besides their board, per day.

These facts, and others which might be added, show that tea can never be cultivated in Western or European countries to advantage. The high rate of wages in the United States, even if it would grow in the southern part of the country, would forbid the extensive and profitable cultivation of the tea-shrub. The same amount of capital, industry, and labour, employed in any of the common trades and occupations in that land, would be far more lucrative. Tea could not be offorred, if raised in America, at less than four or five times the cost per pound at which it can be offorred obtained from China.

The fields are cultivated by means of the plough and the harrow, drawn by the water-ox or domesticated buffalo, and by the hoe and light pickaxe. The use of the spade and the wheelbarrow is unknown. Women of the large or natural-

CARRYING BUNDLES OF GRAIN.

footed class and men work at farming together. Such women also carry burdens in the same manner as men. Only one beast, guided by a rope tied to a ring in its nose, is used in ploughing. The common plough is simple and light, turning a narrow and shallow furrow. Rice, wheat, &c. are always reaped by the sickle or bill-hook. There are no cradles or machines for cutting grain, nor are there any machines used for threshing grain.

When it is necessary to transport the bundles from one part of the field to another for any purpose, they are carried in the

usual manner of carrying other articles, by a pole laid across the
shoulder, never on carts or wagons.   Rice and wheat are usually
threshed by beating on a frame of slats ; sometimes by flails on
the hard ground.   A man takes a small quantity of the un-
threshed grain in both hands, and strikes it forcibly upon the
slats until the grain is beaten out, when the straw is thrown
aside, and another
quantity is taken and
beaten in the same
way.   The grain is
winnowed by throw-
ing it up into the
wind, or by a rudely-
constructed fanning-
mill, worked by a
crank, in general ap-
pearance very much
like Western fanning-
mills, *minus* sieves.
The modern fanning-
mills used in the
United States, un-
doubtedly, are only
improved Chinese fan-
ning-mills.

The hull is removed
from rice by a kind
of mill, turned by
hand, consisting of
two parts.   The upper
part, which is not

THRESHING GRAIN.

very heavy, is made to move slowly around upon the lower by
a man pushing and pulling upon the handle.   One end of the
handle is suspended by a cord attached to something in the top
of the room.   By simply pulling and pushing this handle in a
certain way, the upper part revolves.   The rice, unhulled, is put
upon the upper part, and passes through a hole down to the
surfaces, which touch and rub against each other.   The rice
comes out from the side and falls into a basket.   What is not
perfectly hulled by this process is then pounded in a large stone
mortar.   This operation always removes the last of the hulls
from the rice.

The mills for grinding wheat are very rude and poor.   Some

of them are turned by water, especially in hilly sections of the country, where there are small rapid streams. In cities and villages the motive power usually is a blindfolded buffalo, which is fastened to a pole connecting with the upper millstone. The animal, by walking around in a circle, the centre of which is the mill, causes the upper stone to revolve. The grain requires to be passed through the mill several times before the flour is fine enough for baking purposes. It is then sifted by hand, and is ready for use. Oftentimes the flour is very gritty, owing

HULLING RICE.

to a poor quality of stones, or to the bad manner in which they are repaired or fitted to each other.

There are no fences, or walls, or hedges dividing the fields. Boundaries between rice-fields are usually marked by a small raised pathway. Cattle, when let out to graze on the hills, are always kept from wandering far, and from destroying the crops in the vicinity, by boys or girls watching and tending them. There are no meadows where grass is cut for making hay; the scythe is unknown. The grass is wild. There is no

D

clover, or any of the various species of herds' grass cultivated. Cattle, in the winter, are kept principally on wheat and rice straw. Horses are not kept by farmers for use in the fields, or for riding or driving, the domesticated buffalo and a smaller kind of cattle being used exclusively for tilling the ground. Only officials of Government employ horses.

Irrigation is generally, in this vicinity, performed by means of an endless chain-pump. One end of the box in which the chain (or rather rope) and its buckets pass is placed at an angle

IRRIGATION BY MEANS OF AN ENDLESS CHAIN-PUMP.

of forty-five degrees, more or less, with the river, canal, or pond whence water is to be brought upon the neighbouring fields. This box is open on the top and both ends, and made very strong and light, one man carrying the whole apparatus with ease on his shoulders. The chain, with its buckets, passes over a horizontal shaft, which is supported by two perpendicular posts. One or more persons, steadying themselves by leaning upon a horizontal pole four or five feet higher than the shaft, and by walking or stepping briskly on short radiating arms, cause it to revolve on its axis, bringing up the water, which pours out of the upper end of the box. The faster the men walk or stop, the greater the quantity of water pumped up. The water, in little streams, is made to run wherever desired. The low rice-fields are usually kept flooded with water one or two months before and after the rice-plants are transplanted.

Between the Min and the city, on each side of the main street, are numerous artificial ponds, used as reservoirs for raising fresh fish. The eggs or spawn are obtained from Kiangsi, the province joining Fuhkien on the west. The fish, when young, are fed on a very singular vegetable which grows on the surface of the water, and multiplies during the nighttime with almost incredible rapidity. The large fish consume immense quantities of a certain long coarse grass, which grows wild in wet places or by the margin of the ponds. This is thrown into the ponds, where the fish eat it at their pleasure. The water is drawn or pumped off generally once a year, and the fish, when the water becomes low, are caught by nets. At the last, when nets cannot be used, men, women, and children wade in the mud and mire, and pick out the remainder of the fish, large and small. These fish-ponds are usually very profitable. In some years the annual freshet is so high as to overflow the ponds, when the fish escape, unless they are kept in by a kind of wicker-work made of bamboo splints, or by nets surrounding the ponds. Oftentimes large quantities of the rich mud found in the ponds when the water is drawn off are taken and spread on the neighbouring fields as manure. The removal of the mud serves to make the ponds capable of holding more water and raising more fish.

In the suburbs on the south bank of the Min, duck eggs are hatched by artificial heat, early in the spring, in immense quantities. Ducklings only a few days old are hawked about the streets for sale. Large numbers are taken to the country, where they are tended in droves by boys and girls. Oftentimes a boat, with several hundred half-grown ducks, is propelled from spot to spot along the banks of the river, or the canals which intersect the valley in all directions. When the person in charge wishes to feed his ducks, he lets them out of the boat by means of a plank extending from its edge to the shore. The ducks are trained to walk the plank to and from the shore at the will of their keeper. The ducks thrive upon the small, living, nameless creatures which abound on the shores of creeks and canals, and

D 2

which burrow in the mud, coming out at low water in immense numbers.*

At full tide, the bridges across the Min at Fuhchau may often be seen crowded with men viewing the feats of the tame fishing cormorants. These birds look at a distance about the size of a goose, and are of a dark, dirty colour. The fisherman who has charge of them stands upon a raft about two and a half feet wide, and fifteen or twenty feet long, made out of five large bamboos of similar size and shape, firmly fastened together. It is very light, and is propelled by a paddle. A basket is placed on it to contain the fish when caught. Each raft has three or four

* Chinese stolidity and stupidity contrast very curiously with Chinese ingenuity ; innumerable notes from various travellers might be given illustrating the last, as Mr. Doolittle's work illustrates the first in a remarkable manner. Mr. Fortune gives a very entertaining account of a visit to an old farmer, famous for hatching ducks ; and Dr. Lockhart, describing the singular process, says, " In the vicinity of most of the cities are large establishments for the hatching of ducks. These houses comprise a suite of long, low rooms, with several offices attached. The country people, in the spring and summer months, bring large quantities of eggs, which are purchased at a very cheap rate. These are put in flat baskets in a sort of fireplace made of brick and plaster, opened at the top but closed below, much like the recess of a boiler. Below the open space is a very small charcoal fire to warm the mass of brick. When the place is warm enough the basket of eggs is lodged within, and covered over with a thick plaited straw pad, to retain the heat, and after a day or two the basket is removed to another similar recess, which is slightly warmer. The eggs are turned over once each day, and carefully excluded from air, cold, or wind. After the required number of days, close upon the time of production, they are taken out of the baskets and laid side by side on a large table. This table is about thirty feet long by about fifteen wide, and covered with cotton wadding. When the eggs, to the number of 1,000 or more, are arranged, they are covered with a thin cloth, and over this one or more thick cotton quilts are placed. The removal of these, as soon as the ducklings are found ready to break their shells, reveals an extraordinary scene. In all directions the little creatures are working themselves free, causing a curious crackling from the breaking of the shells. An attendant watches the table day and night to remove them as they emerge, all folded up and apparently very weak, but speedily scrambling over the other eggs. They are removed to a basket in a warmer room, and fed by and by with flour and water. In a day or two their down has grown sufficiently to cover them, when they are sold to persons who come from the neighbourhood periodically to buy them. The price for a young duck is thirty cash, or about a penny ; the drakes sell for a little less, not being considered so useful as the other sex. These establishments, which require great care, are well conducted, and are profitable to the proprietors, though these occasionally suffer great loss from sudden changes of weather ; a cold northerly wind kills the ducklings in great numbers. The process is carried on only during the spring and summer, and the house is used only as a lodging-house for the rest of the year." --Dr. LOCKHART, Medical Missionary in China, pp. 99, 100.

cormorants connected with it. When not fishing, they crouch down stupidly on the raft.

The fisherman, when he wishes to make a cormorant fish, pushes or throws it off the raft into the water. If it is not

FISHING WITH CORMORANTS.

disposed at once to dive and seek for fish, he beats the water with his paddle, or sometimes strikes the bird, so that it is glad to dive and get out of his reach. When it has caught a fish it rises to the surface, holding it in its mouth, and apparently striving to swallow it. A string tied loosely around its neck, or a metallic ring, effectually prevents swallowing, except, perhaps, in the case of very small fish. It usually swims directly for the raft; the fisherman, on seeing the prize, paddles towards it with all speed, lest it should escape from the bird. Sometimes the fish is a large one, and there is evidently a struggle between it and the cormorant. The fisherman, when near enough, dexterously passes a net-like bag, fastened to the end of a pole, over the two, and draws them both on the raft. He then forces the fish from the grasp of the bird, and, as if to reward the latter for its success, gives it a mouthful of food, which it is enabled to swallow on his raising the ring from the lower part of its neck. The bird, if apparently tired out, is allowed to rest a while on the raft, and then it is pushed off again into the water, and made to dive and hunt for fish as before.

Sometimes the cormorant, from imperfect training, swims away from the raft with the fish it has caught. In such a case, the fisherman pursues and speedily overtakes the truant. Sometimes, it is reported, two or three cormorants assist in securing a large and powerful fish. Oftentimes two quarrel together for the fish one has taken, or one pursues the other for the fish in its mouth. At such times the interest of the spectators on the bridge increases to noisy shouting. The bird is provided with a sort of pouch or large throat, in which the small fish are entirely concealed, while the head or the tail of the larger fish protrudes from its mouth.

It is only at or near full tide that these birds are successful in catching fish under and near the bridges. Then the water is deep and comparatively still, and the fish seem to abound in the vicinity more than at low tide. At such times there are frequently several rafts with cormorants fishing near the bridges. The skill of the fisherman in propelling his craft, and the success of the bird in catching the fish, are attested by the delighted curiosity and animated interest of the spectators.

The fuel of the Chinese at Fuhchau is principally a kind of stunted fir or pine. It is brought down the Min in boats, sawed into sticks about twenty inches long, and done up in small bundles. Charcoal made out of hard wood is also brought down the river in large quantities. An inferior kind of stone coal is also procured here. The timber used in building houses and junks, a light and soft wood, somewhat resembles fir or pine. Several kinds of hard wood are used in cabinet work.

Among them is the camphor, but no maple, walnut, beech, or oak.

There are several kinds of vegetable oils in common use, but no mineral oil or gas. A good quality for burning is made out of pea-nuts. Another kind, simply called "vegetable oil," is manufactured from the seeds of a vegetable having yellow flowers, much resembling, when in blossom and at a short distance, the common mustard. Another oil, called tea-oil, the best kind for burning in lamps, is made from the seeds or kernels which grow on a species of tree. These three kinds of oil are much used in cooking by the people, taking the place of butter or lard. Vegetable tallow is made from the seeds or kernels which grow in clusters on another kind of tree, called the tallow-tree. The seeds are gathered in the fall. This tallow is found in market in large cakes weighing fifty or sixty pounds, and looks much like animal tallow; it is hardened by white wax. This wax is a very hard substance, brought from the western or north-western provinces. In cold weather, some of the vegetable tallow and some of the vegetable oils are mixed together in order to make candles. It is believed that the use of candles manufactured from the fat of the water-ox or buffalo would be offensive to the object worshipped, because the buffalo is regarded as a meritorious animal. It is said, also, that the odour arising from the burning of candles made of animal fat would be repugnant to the gods. The milk of the buffalo is not used for making butter or cheese, nor as an article of food. This animal is raised solely for its invaluable services in ploughing and harrowing the land. The butter made from its milk is white, and less palatable and rich than our fresh golden butter.

Fuhchau does not contain any great and elaborate works of art. It has but few public buildings, and these are mostly temples. The prefectural Temple to Confucius, not far from the south gate, in the city; the Emperor's Temple, near the west gate; the Municipal Temple, not far from the centre of the city, and near the Treasurer's Office; the Tauist temple to the "Pearly Emperor, Supreme Ruler," on the Hill of the Nine Genii, near the White Pagoda; a new temple built by traders from the western part of the province, situated a short distance north of Great Temple Hill; the Temple to the Goddess of Sailors, built by native merchants from Ningpo, in the surburbs on the south bank of the river; and the celebrated Buddhist Monastery on Drum Mountain, are among those which repay a visit. In some of these are fine specimens of Chinese carving in stone, especially in the Temple to the Sailors' Goddess. Curiosity Street, a little to the west of the viceroy's yamun, is often visited by foreigners, where are a large number of shops which have for sale costly curiosities. Among these are curious and fantastic objects cut out of roots of trees, and articles in bronze. A small quantity of lacquered-ware, of exquisite workmanship, and held at extremely high prices, is made at this place. Of late years, various curiosities or objects made out of a kind of soft stone, principally of a reddish colour, commonly called soap-stone, are manufactured and sold to foreigners. Among these may be mentioned sets of dinner and fruit plates, miniature pagodas from one to several feet high, miniature honorary portals to the memory of virtuous widows, about two feet high, miniature graves of the horse-shoe or Omega pattern, and a large variety of vases. Some thirty or forty kinds of charcoal birds, of delicate workmanship, shaped and painted so as to represent living birds, have a ready sale among foreign visitors. Great skill is exhibited in making these birds out of charcoal : many of them look as natural as life. Outside of one of the gates on the north-east side of the city are a number of hot springs. Many Chinese resort thither to bathe for scrofulous affections. Private bathing-rooms near by are to be had for a few cash. In one of the springs, which is walled up with stone, are frequently seen a dozen men crowded together, the water coming to their arm-pits. On Black Rock Hill, in the city, and on Great Temple Hill, in the southern suburbs, are altars to Heaven and Earth, where high mandarins are required to burn incense in honour of Heaven and Earth twice per annum, and where crowds assemble on the ninth day of the ninth month to fly kites. On the altar on the Great Temple Hill is a stone, in appearance very much like common granite, said to have fallen down from the skies. It has several holes drilled on its upper surface, which are used to hold incense. If it is a meteoric stone, which is doubtful, its original shape has been changed more or less, for it is now nearly round, and has evidently been under the tools of the stonecutter.

There are no asylums for the lunatic, the deaf and dumb, or for the blind, &c. at Fuhchau ; but, according to the wishes of the emperor, who is regarded as the father and mother of his subjects, the very destitute blind, poor and aged widows, and the crippled and the maimed who are without means of support, are entitled to a monthly stipend from the provincial treasury. Such is said to be the theory. In fact, however, of late years, owing to the emptiness of the treasury, and the squeezing customs which prevail in connexion with the payment of money from the treasury, very little money actually reaches those whom the emperor would relieve and befriend. Much trouble and delay are experienced by those who desire to have their names recorded on the list of imperial beneficiaries. The clerks and the underlings of the yamun where they should apply have the reputation of treating applicants for this benefaction with such insult and cruelty that few now-a-days apply for the purpose of having their names recorded there. In the summer of 1861, it was reported that over three hundred blind, crippled, and aged persons, in connexion with a kind of poorhouse located in the northern part of the city, received every one or two months five hundred cash each from Government, and a smaller number received a less amount.

Very little machinery is used in the manufacture of articles. There are no saw-mills, nor printing-presses, nor factories where cloth is made. There are a few foundries where ploughshares and the common vessels for cooking are cast. Almost everything is done by manual labour. Copper or iron wire is drawn by hand; needles are made by hand out of wire; logs are sawn into boards by cross-cut saws propelled back and forth in a horizontal direction by men; the dust out of which incense is prepared, used in immense quantities annually, is filed or rasped off from blocks of fragrant wood by hand. Paper, made out of the pulp of tender young bamboos, is manufactured by manual labour. Excepting some coarse kinds, the fine bamboo paper found in market here is prepared in the country one and two hundred miles to the westward of Fuhchau. Iron nails, and brass or copper utensils, axes, chisels, &c. are beaten out by hand. Notwithstanding the uncouth and unpolished appearance their tools present, many of them are of excellent quality.

The wages of the common people are low. Carpenters and masons obtain from twenty to thirty cents per day, boarding themselves. Hired men and women, who do coarse work in the fields or in houses as servants, generally receive from four to six dollars per month, and they board themselves. If their employers board them, they get from one to three dollars per month. Clerks and accountants receive from ten to thirty dollars per annum, with their board. School-teachers often obtain only from thirty to sixty dollars, besides small presents from their pupils, per annum. Literary men who are poor, and who fail of acquiring Government employment, are frequently glad to teach school at almost a nominal price. Food, clothing, and rents are cheap, and yet the poor of all classes are enabled to support themselves only by great industry and frugality.

Women who compress their feet, if poor, engage in various indoor employments to provide a living. Many of them are employed by needle manufacturers to drill, file, polish, and sharpen needles. Others take in needlework from clothing stores. Some are skilful in silk embroidery. A large number spend almost all their lives in pasting tinfoil upon bamboo paper for superstitious uses as mock money. The wages females receive for work done at their homes vary largely, owing to different degrees of skill and speed.

Handbills, books, &c. are stereotyped on wood, and then printed by hand. An exact fac-simile of the sheet or the page desired is first made on very thin bamboo paper by the use of the hair pencil and black ink. This is then pasted, with the written side down, on a smooth block of hard wood. The paper, or most of the paper, is now carefully rubbed off, having been moistened, leaving the characters and punctuation in black ink traced on the block. This is a process requiring considerable skill, lest the characters should be partially or wholly erased. The space taken up by the white portions of the block is cut out, an eighth of an inch deep, by small sharp knives, leaving the parts of the block occupied by black lines or dots. The printing from this block is performed by first slightly and evenly wetting the characters with Chinese printing-ink, by means of a damp brush ; and then a sheet of paper, placed on the block, is pressed down on all its surface lightly and quickly by a dry brush passed to and fro several times. The sheet is then removed, and forms the hand-bill or a page of the book. Good printing requires experience, and care, and skill, or the block will be unevenly inked, in which case some of the characters on the page will be darker or blacker than others. If too much force is used, the paper will be torn by the passage of the dry brush over it. Chinese printing-ink is usually made out of common soot and the water in which rice has been boiled. Books never have stiff pasteboard or leather covers, but are stitched. The beginning is at the right-hand side of the book, and the end comes where in an English book is the beginning. The characters are placed in columns, and read from top to bottom, beginning with the right-hand column and pro-ceeding toward the left. The paper is printed only on one side. The name of the book, the number of the section or chapter, and the paging are put in the centre of the sheet, and come on the outer edge of the leaf, where the sheet is folded. The notes, if any, are placed on the top of the page, and separated from the text by a line. The title-page usually contains the number of the year of the reign of the emperor when the book was published, marking its date.

The Chinese language is not alphabetical, nor does the acquisition of one character afford a reliable clue to the sound, use, or meaning of another. It is principally monosyllabic. Each character represents an idea, or is the name of a thing. The characters are composed of a few different-shaped strokes, and are distinguished by the relative positions of these strokes. These strokes are not used in the composition of a character, as letters are used in the formation of an English word. The form of the characters is arbitrary, and the number of characters very great. A knowledge of three or four thousand is sufficient for the reading of most books. The pronunciation of the characters is difficult to foreigners, from the fact that certain tones of voice, and in many cases certain aspirated or guttural modulations, are necessary to be carefully observed. The tones may be illustrated thus : a character represented in English by the letters *s-i-n-g*, if pronounced in an even, level, and slow tone of voice, would mean *heart ;* another character, represented by the same English letters, with a tonal mark, if pronounced in a sharp, quick, and angry tone of voice, would mean *spirit* or *god.* The aspirated modulations referred to may be illustrated thus : a character represented in English by the letters *t-i-e-n-g*, if pronounced in an even and slow tone of voice, would mean *mad* or *crazy ;* another character, represented in English by the same letters, with a mark indicating that it should be aspirated, when pronounced in the same even and slow tone, but *aspirated*, would mean *heaven.* The printed or written language is intelligible to educated Chinese in all parts of the empire, just as the numerals 1, 2, 3, 4, 5, &c. are understood all over Europe ; while the spoken language has many dialects, often differing widely from each other, so that men living in different prefectures of the same province are oftentimes unable to understand each other unless they have made their dialects a particular study. Besides the number of the dialects, many of the characters have several different meanings, according to the breathing or the tone with which they are pronounced, or the connexion in which they occur in a printed or spoken sentence, just as the word *p-r-e-s-e-n-t* has two different meanings according as it is a noun or verb. Many characters, too, having precisely the same sound, are written differently, and are very different in

signification, just as the words *rite, wright, right,* and *write* differ
in meaning, though pronounced alike.   Many of the characters
or words, when pronounced according to the book or classical
style, are different from the pronunciation given by the people
in conversation : *e.g.* the character for voice, according to the
classical style, is called *s-i-n-g,* but it becomes *s-i-a-n-g* in the
dialect of the people.

COUNTRY SCENE NEAR FUHCHAU.

CHAPTER II.

BETROTHAL in China is a matter with which the parties most deeply concerned have generally little to do. Their parents or guardians employ a go-between, or match-maker between the families. The proverb says, " Without a go-between, a betrothal cannot be effected."

The negotiation is generally commenced by the family to which the boy or the young man belongs. The go-between is furnished with a card stating the ancestral name, and the eight characters which denote the hour, day, month, and year of birth of the candidate for matrimony. This card he takes to the family indicated, and tenders a proposal of marriage in regard to a daughter in behalf of a son of the party employing him. If the parents or guardians of the girl, after instituting inquiries about the family making it, are willing to entertain the proposal, they consult a fortune-teller, who decides, after considering the eight characters which indicate the time of the birth of the parties, whether the betrothal would be fitting and auspicious. If a favourable decision is made, the go-between is furnished with a similar card ; the same consultation of a fortune-teller follows. If this fortune-teller pronounces favourably, and the two families agree in regard to the details of the marriage, a formal assent is made to the betrothment. If for the space of three days, while the betrothal is under consideration in each of the families, after the card having the eight characters has been received from the other family, anything reckoned unlucky—such as breaking a bowl or the losing of an article—should occur, the negotiation would be broken off at once, and the card would be returned to the party which sent it. The card during this time is usually placed under the censer standing in front of the ancestral tablets belonging to the family. When it is deposited there, incense and candles are lighted before these tablets.

The betrothal is not binding on the parties until a kind of pasteboard card has been interchanged between them. This, resembling a book-cover, consists of two pieces of pasteboard. The outside of it is covered with red paper. On this red paper is pasted a likeness of a dragon or a phœnix, according as it is designed for the boy or the girl, the dragon or the phœnix being made out of gilt paper. This cover-like piece of pasteboard shuts down on the other part. They are connected together by a paper pasted on one edge of both, somewhat as the two parts of a book-cover are fastened together. Their inner surfaces are covered over neatly by a piece of red paper.

The family of the bridegroom provides two of these cards, one having a gilt dragon on it and the other a gilt phœnix. On the inside of the former, the ancestral and given name of the boy's father, his own given name, and the characters which denote the precise time of his birth, the name of the go-between, and a few other particulars, are neatly written. There are also provided two long and large threads of red silk and four large needles. Two of these needles are threaded upon one of the silk threads, one needle being at each end of the thread, and then the needles are stuck in a particular manner into the inside of that card on the outside of which is the image of a dragon. The other card left blank, the other two needles and the other red silk thread, together with the card already filled out with particulars relating to the family to which the lad belongs, and its needles and threads attached, are taken by the go-between to the family to which the girl belongs. This card is then filled out with particulars relating to the family of the girl, corresponding to the particulars already recorded in the other. The thread and needles are also similarly stuck into the card having the phœnix on its outside. When this has been done it is sent back to the family of the boy, which carefully keeps it as evidence of his engagement in marriage ; the card having the dragon on it, and relating to the boy, being retained and preserved by the family of the girl as proof of her betrothal. The writing on each of these documents is performed in front of the ancestral tablets of the family to which it relates, incense and candles having been lighted and placed in the customary positions before them.

These cards having been thus exchanged by the families, the betrothment is consummated and legal. After this, neither party may break the engagement without the gravest of reasons.

Then presents are sent to the family to which the girl belongs; a pair of silver or gold wristlets, and for her family various articles of food, as pigs' feet, a pair of fowls, two fish, &c. When they send back to the family to which the boy belongs the engagement card, they send also as a present a quantity of artificial gilt flowers, some vermicelli, and bread cakes. The flowers are for distribution among the female members and relatives of the family. These presents are, in the Chinese view, omens of good to the parties most intimately concerned.

The Chinese, in explaining the use of the red thread, refer to a popular story relating to certain events said to have transpired some time during the Tang dynasty. The story runs thus :—

" In the time of the Tang dynasty, Ui-ko was once a guest in the city of Sung. He observed an old man by the light of the moon reading a book, who addressed him thus : ' This is the register of the engagements in marriage for all the places under the heavens.' He also said to him, ' In my pocket I have red cords, with which I tie the feet of those who are to become husband and wife. When this cord has been tied, though the parties are of unfriendly families, or of different nations, it is impossible to change their destiny. Your future wife,' said the old man, ' is the child of the old woman who sells vegetables in yonder shop at the north.' In a few days Ui-ko went to see her, and found the old woman had in her arms a girl about a year old, and exceedingly ugly. He hired a man, who went and (as as he supposed) killed the girl. Fourteen years afterward, in the country of Siong-chiu, was a prefect whose family-name was Mö, surnamed Tai, who gave Ui-ko in marriage a girl who he affirmed was his own daughter. She was very beautiful. On her eyebrow she always wore an artificial flower. Ui-ko constantly asking her why she wore the flower, she at length said, ' I am the daughter of the prefect's brother. My father died in the city of Sung when I was but an infant. My nurse was an old woman who sold vegetables. One day she took me with her out into the streets, when a robber struck me. The scar of the wound is still left on my eyebrow.' "

The red silk thread indicates that the engagement of the parties in marriage is fixed and unalterable, or, in common language, it is said that *their feet have been tied together.* The

Chinese seem to be firm believers in the sentiments that Fate or Heaven decides who are to become husband and wife, and that the act of parents in engaging their children is an exponent of the will of Heaven or the decrees of Fate, corresponding to the Western saying that "Matches are made in heaven."

Some say that these threads are kept professedly for the purpose of tying together the goblets out of which the bride and bridegroom drink wine on the day of their marriage. Sometimes they are actually thus used on that occasion. More frequently, however, a new red cord or string is then used, and the old cords taken and put into the cue of the bridegroom, or worked into the shoes worn by the bride on the day of their marriage, as omens of good. The use of the large needles in betrothing parties is also auspicious. According to some, they serve to *draw the thread along*. It is sagely asked, What is the use of a thread, unless there is a needle with which to use it? When viewed in this light, the use of the needles is very manifest.

The reader would perhaps be wearied did we attempt to give a complete detail of the customs observed between betrothal and the day of marriage. The time which transpires varies from a month or two to eighteen or twenty years, depending much on the age of the parties. From one to three months before the marriage a fortunate day is selected for its celebration. Generally a member of the family of the bridegroom, or a trusty friend, takes the eight horary characters which denote the birth-time for each of the affianced parties, and for each of their parents, if living, to a fortune-teller, who selects lucky days and times for the marriage, for the cutting of the wedding garments, for the placing of the bridal bed in position, for the finishing of the curtains of the bridal bed, for the embroidering of the bridal pillows, and for the entering of the sedan, on the part of the bride, on the day of her marriage. These items are written out on a sheet of red paper, which is sent to the family of the girl by the hands of the go-between. If accepted, the periods specified become the fixed times for the performance of the particulars indicated, and both parties proceed to make the necessary arrangements for the approaching wedding.

Presenting the wedding-cakes and material for bridal dress to the family of the bride by the other party is next in order. This custom is one month before the day fixed for the marriage. The number of these "*cakes of ceremony*," or wedding-cakes, varies from several score to several hundreds; they contain in the middle some sugar, lard, and small pieces of fat pork, mixed together in a kind of batter, and then cooked : they are, in fact, a sort of mince-pies. There is also sent a sum of money, a quantity of red cloth or silk, usually not less than five kinds, for the use of the bride, five kinds of dried fruits, several kinds of small cakes, a cock and a hen, and a gander and a goose. The top one of the various stacks of these wedding-cakes, as they are carried through the streets, has several small doll-like figures, made out of wheat-flour, each a few inches high, and fastened upon slips of bamboo, stuck into it. The family of the girl, on receiving these wedding-cakes, proceed to distribute them among their relatives and intimate friends. The small cakes are also distributed in a similar manner. The money sent is generally spent in outfitting the bride.

Rich families make much more valuable presents than above indicated. These presents are carried through the streets in such a manner that they can be seen by every one. The rich present costly head-dresses, wristlets, and other ornaments worn by ladies. They add two jars of wine, on one of which is a picture of a dragon, and on the other a picture of the phœnix ; also a male and a female goat, ten or more pieces of silk, or satin, or crape, of five different kinds or colours. Presents of money are also sent for one of the bride's maternal uncles, and for one of her paternal uncles, if she has such relatives living. On some of these parcels, tastefully done up in red paper, are written propitious words or sentences. These presents are accompanied by two large red cards, decorated by the likeness of the dragon and the phœnix, the ancestral names, the name of the go-between, and frequently a number of felicitous words and sentences. All this work of mutual presentation and distribution of presents among relatives goes on tedious to describe, consisting of silks and satins designed for the use of the girl, jars of wine, large cakes of ceremony and small cakes, and other things as custom requires ; pairs of large red candles, one having a dragon and the other a phœnix painted on it, a pair of large pewter candlesticks, two packages of white Chinese vermicelli, a pair of satin boots, a red official cap, and material for a kind of dress-coat, and a large quantity of artificial flowers, made out of velvet, or of pith paper, generally known as "rice paper." Every family makes just as expensive presents as it can afford to make, on account of the strong popular desire to be showy and appear liberal.

We cannot dwell on all the most tedious details of betrothal and marriage. A few days before the day fixed for the wedding, the family of the bridegroom again make a present of various

E

articles of food and other things to the family of the bride, as a
cock and a hen, a leg and foot of a pig and of a goat, eight small
cakes of bread, eight torches, three pairs of large red candles, a
quantity of vermicelli, and several bunches of fire-crackers, and
a variety of absurd symbolical foods and fire-crackers, &c.

Also, two or three days before the time fixed for the wedding,
a red card is sent by the family of the bride to that of the
bridegroom, stating what furniture will be furnished as the
bride's dowry, and the number of loads. The person who takes
this card informs the family of the groom what time these things
may be expected. The main object of this notification is said to
be that the family of the bridegroom may prepare and have in
readiness the proper amount of money, duly put in red paper,
or tied around by a red string, for the bearers of the furniture.
It is customary for this family to pay these bearers on arrival in
money thus prepared ; and if not ready for them, confusion
might arise on an occasion when it is desired that everything
should be pleasant and respectable.

On the afternoon or evening before the sending of the outfit,
there is generally an absurd custom observed called " sifting four
eyes," and is regarded as an omen of good. A large round sieve-
like utensil, made out of bamboo splints, in diameter about three
or four feet, is procured ; also a brass vessel, two or three feet in
diameter and about one foot high, which is placed on a pedestal,
raising it a short distance from the floor. After having placed in
this vessel a quantity of burning coals, they take the wedding
garments one by one, or in convenient quantities ; and having
laid them on the sieve, the women hold it, with its contents, for
a moment or two over the vessel, with a slight sifting movement.
They then remove this portion of her clothing from the sieve,
and, taking another portion, they place it on the sieve and go
through the same ceremony, and so on, until all of her outfit—as
regards personal clothing, shoes, and head ornaments—has been
properly sifted. Sometimes a similar ceremony is also performed
with regard to the small articles of the household furniture
which is designed for the bride's use in her future home. Those
who hold the sieve during the sifting are continually uttering
various sentiments, which have come to be considered as peculiarly appropriate to the occasion and propitious, as, "A thousand
eyes, ten thousand eyes, we sift out; gold and silver, wealth and
precious things, we sift in." On the sieve, during this performance, are placed ten chopsticks. The meaning of this is, that
though so much clothing and furniture shall have soon been

given away with the girl, and thus have become the property of another family, still clothing and food will "remain" to her parents.

Why this ceremony is called "sifting four eyes," the Chinese differ greatly among themselves. In some way, evil and unpropitious influences are firmly believed to be expelled or warded off by the process of sifting the clothing of the expectant bride. After the articles have been sifted, contact with them is carefully avoided by the female members of her family. It is supposed that it would be especially unlucky for her and her affianced husband should any pregnant woman, or any person wearing mourning, handle, or in any manner come in contact with any of the articles already sifted before they are carried over to the future home of the girl. Such a contact would be expected to produce death in her husband's family, or a future miscarriage on her part, or quarrels and misunderstandings between him and her, or some undesirable result. Everything sifted is carefully packed away, and great relief is experienced when the furniture and trunks of clothing have started for the residence of the bridegroom.

A ceremony, called "expelling the filth," is sometimes performed not long previous to the marriage day at the house of the bridegroom, with reference to his personal apparel, especially his wedding suit, for the purpose of warding off any pernicious influences.

At the time indicated on the card, the dowry of the bride is carried in procession through the streets with as much parade and show as the amount of the furniture will possibly admit. The number of persons employed in transporting these things sometimes amounts to one hundred, or even more. Those who can afford the expense have some of the articles bound around or fastened to the carrying-poles with pieces of red silk, or red crape, or red cotton cloth. This is considered a great day for the families most especially concerned, and everything connected with the procession is designed for display. Probably there is quite as much vanity and desire for show, in connexion with a bridal outfit, among the Chinese as in Western lands.

This outfit is procured, in most cases, to a great extent by means of the money which has been furnished the family of the bride by the family of the groom for that purpose. In the case of wealthy families, little dependence is actually placed on receiving money for this object, though valuable presents of money are always made to the family of the bride by the other party.

It is customary for friends and relatives of the bride's family, who have received "cakes of ceremony," to make presents of materials for clothing, artificial flowers, or other ornaments for the head, to her family. These presents are designed to constitute a part of the bride's outfit.

Placing the bridal bedstead in the position where it is to stand is an important ceremony. This placing of the bedstead in position is attended with various superstitious acts. Five coins, belonging to the reigns of five different emperors, are usually scattered around on the bottom of the bedstead. Sometimes four other similar sets of coins are placed under the bedstead, one set being put near the foot of each bedpost. Five bunches of boiled rice, each consisting of five bundles, made in shape like a cone, from four to six inches in length, and done up in leaves and bound around with a red cotton string, are hung up from the frame provided for suspending the curtain of the bed. One of these bunches is larger than the others, and is hung up from the middle of the curtain frame, four smaller bunches being suspended at the four corners of it. With a number of other objects of superstition, is a glass lamp containing oil, and two candles, placed one near each of the front corners of the vessel. The lamp and the candles are lighted, and the vessel is left untouched on the bedstead until the candles and the oil have burned out, after which it is removed. Care is taken that these lights are not extinguished by a draught of air or by accident, as such premature extinguishment would be surely regarded as an omen of evil to those who are expected to occupy the bed. The object of the performance of this nonsensical ceremony, as a whole, is to secure prosperity to the couple after their marriage, especially with regard to the bearing of children in their family in successive generations. The five cash of five successive emperors, &c. are good omens of such fruitfulness on the part of the expectant bride, or of general prosperity to the family. The light of the lamp and of the candles, although in broad daylight, is regarded as peculiarly efficacious in keeping away evil spirits.

Usually, the day before the wedding, the bride has her hair done up in the style of married women of her class in society, and tries on the clothes she is to wear in the sedan and for a time after she arrives at her future home on the morrow. This is an occasion of great interest to her family. Her parents invite their female relatives and friends to a feast at their house. She proceeds to light incense before the ancestral tablets belonging to her father's family, and to worship them for the last time before her marriage. She also kneels down before her parents, her grandparents, her uncles and aunts, and worships them in much the same manner as she and her husband will on the morrow worship his parents and grandparents, and the ancestral tablets belonging to his family. On the occasion of the girl's trying on these clothes and worshipping the tablet and her parents, it is considered unpropitious that those of her female relatives and friends who are in mourning should be present.

The bridal chair is selected by the family of the bridegroom, and sent to the residence of the bride generally on the afternoon preceding the wedding-day, attended by a band of music, some men carrying lighted torches, two carrying a pair of large red lanterns, containing candles also lighted, and one having a large red

BRIDAL SEDAN.

umbrella, and one or two friends or other attendants. The bridal chair is always red, and is generally covered with broadcloth, or some rich expensive material. It is borne by four men, who wear caps having red tassels. The musicians, and all the persons employed in the procession, have similar caps. As in other countries, the procession, the music, and the entertainment of the musicians depend upon the wealth of the parents.

Very early on the morning of her marriage the bride or the " new woman" arises, bathes, and dresses. While she is bathing the musicians are required to play. Her breakfast consists theoretically of the fowl, the vermicelli, &c. sent by the family of her affianced husband. In fact, however, she eats and drinks very little of anything on the morning or during the day of her

wedding, according to the very singular, if not superstitious
notions of this people, which it is not proper to detail. Her
imaginary breakfast on these articles is regarded as an omen of
good, and conducive to her long life in harmony with her husband.
The outer garments, including the veil provided by her husband
for the occasion, are richly embroidered with a likeness of the
dragon.   In ancient times a certain empress graciously granted
the privilege of wearing such apparel to brides on the morning
of their marriage, and also permitted them to be borne by four
bearers, as well as to wear temporarily a very gaudy head-dress,
worn generally by the wives of high officers.

When the precise time approaches for taking her seat in her
sedan, usually between five and eight o'clock in the morning,
her toilet is completed by one of her parents taking the thick
veil and placing it over her head, completely covering her features
from view. She is now led out of her room by one of her female
assistants, and takes her seat in the sedan, which has been brought
into the reception-room of the house. The floor from her room
to the sedan is covered for the occasion with a kind of red carpeting, so that her feet may not touch the ground. She takes
her place in the sedan amid the sound of fire-crackers and music
by the band.   The bride, her mother, and the various members
of the family, are required by custom to indulge during this
morning in hearty and protracted crying—oftentimes, no doubt,
sincere and unaffected.

While seated in the sedan, but before she starts for her future
home, her parents, or some members of her family, take a bed-
quilt by its four corners, and, while holding it thus before the
bridal chair, one of the bride's assistants tosses into the air, one
by one, four bread-cakes, in such a manner that they will fall
into the bed-quilt. These bread-cakes were received from the
family of her husband at the same time as the cock and vermicelli
were received.   The woman during this ceremony is constantly
repeating felicitous sentences, which are assented to by some
others of the company.   The quilt containing these cakes is
gathered up and carried immediately to an adjoining room.

All this is supposed to be an omen for good ; and soon after
this the bridal procession starts *en route* for the residence of the
other party, amid explosions of fire-crackers and the music of
the band.

In the front of the procession go two men carrying two large
lighted lanterns, having the ancestral or family name of the
groom cut in a large form out of red paper pasted upon them.

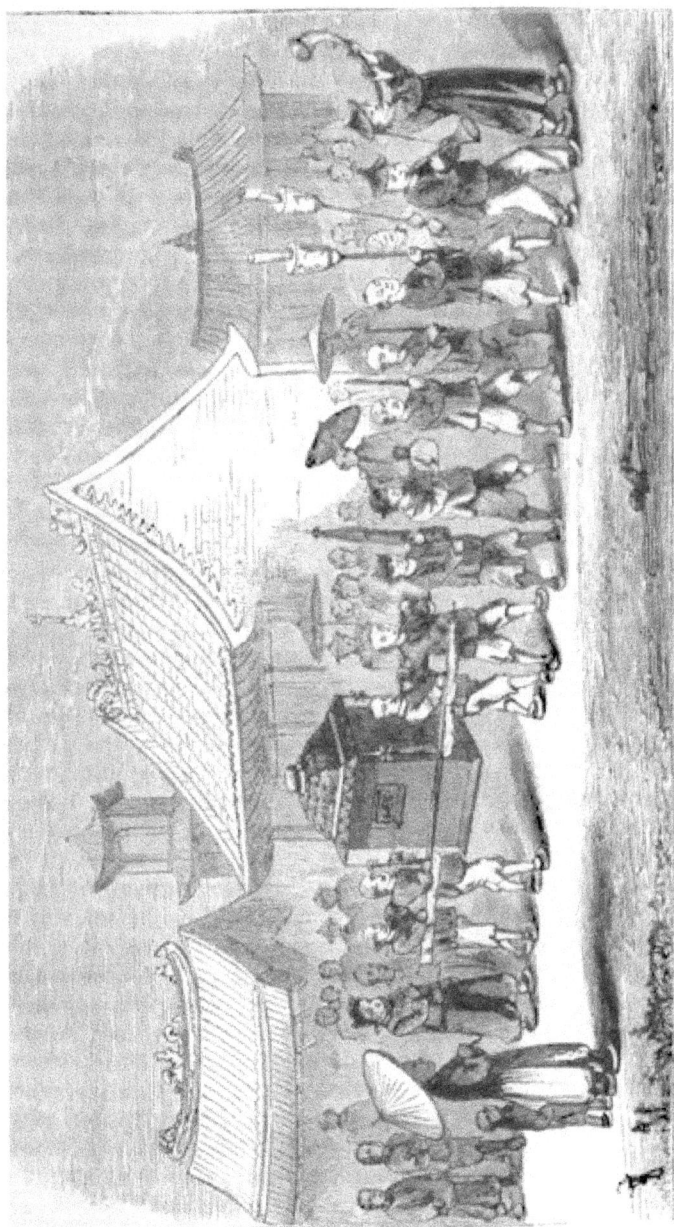

PART OF A BRIDAL PROCESSION EN ROUTE TO THE HOUSE OF THE BRIDEGROOM ON THE WEDDING-DAY.

Then come two men carrying similar lanterns, having the family name of the bride in a similar manner pasted on them. These belong to her family, and accompany her only a part of the way. Then comes a large red umbrella, followed by men carrying lighted torches, and by the band of music. Near the bridal chair are several brothers of the bride or friends of her family, and several friends or brothers of the groom. These latter are despatched from the house of the groom early in the morning, for the purpose of meeting the bridal procession, and escorting the bride to her home. About midway between the homes of the bride and the groom the procession stops in the street, while the important ceremony of *receiving the bride* is formally transacted. The friends of the bride stand near each other, and at a little distance stand the friends of the groom. The former produce a large red card, having the ancestral name of the bride's family written on it ; the latter produce a similar card bearing the ancestral name of the groom. These they exchange, and each, seizing his own hands *à la Chinois*, bows toward the members of the other party. The two men in the front of the procession who carry the lanterns having the ancestral name of the groom now turn about, and, going between the sedan-chair and the two men who carry the lanterns having the ancestral name of the bride, come back to their former position in the procession, having gone around the party which has the lanterns with the bride's ancestral name attached. This latter party, while the other is thus encircling it, turns round in an opposite direction, and starts for the residence of the family of the bride, accompanied by that part of the escort which consisted of her brothers or the friends of her family. The rest of the procession now proceeds on its way to the residence of the bridegroom, the band playing a lively air. At intervals along the street fire-crackers are exploded. It is said that, from the precise time when the two parties carrying lanterns having the ancestral names of the two families attached separate from each other in the street, the name of the bride is changed into the name of her betrothed ; the lanterns having his name attached remaining in the procession, while those which have her (former) name are taken back to the residence of her father's family. From this time during the day she generally is in the midst of entire personal strangers, excepting her female assistants, who accompany the procession, and keep with her wherever she goes.

On arriving at the door of the bridegroom's house, fire-crackers are let off in large quantities, and the band plays very vigorously. The torch-bearers, lantern-bearers, and the musicians stop near the door. The sedan is carried into the reception-room, and a sieve, such as was used in the ceremony of " sifting four eyes," is put on the top of it, over its door. The floor, from the place where the sedan stops to the door of the bride's room, is covered with red carpeting, lest her feet should touch the floor. A woman who has borne both male and female children, or at least male children, and who lives in harmonious subjection to her husband, approaches the door of the sedan, and utters various felicitous sentences. A boy six or eight years old, holding in his hands a brass mirror, with the reflecting surface turned from him and toward the chair, also comes near, and invites the bride to alight. At the same time, the married woman who has uttered propitious words advances, as if to open the door of the sedan, when one of the female assistants of the bride, who accompanied the procession, steps forward and opens it. The married woman referred to, and the boy, are employed by the family of the groom, and receive a small present for their services, which are considered quite important and ominous of good. The mirror held by the lad is expected to ward off all deadly or pernicious influences which may emanate from the sedan.

The bride is now aided by her female assistants to alight from the sedan. While being led toward the door of her room, the sieve which was placed over the door of the bridal chair on its arrival is sometimes held over her head, and sometimes it is placed directly in front of the door of the sedan, so that, on stepping out, she will step into it. During all this time the features of the bride are entirely concealed by the thick covering put over her head by one of her parents at her parental residence.

The groom, on the approach of the bridal procession, disappears from the crowd of friends and relatives who have assembled at his residence on the happy occasion, and takes his position standing by the side of the bedstead, having his face turned toward the bed. When the bride enters the room, guided by her assistants, he turns round, and remains standing with his face turned from the bed. As soon as she has reached his side, both bridegroom and bride simultaneously seat themselves, side by side, on the edge of the bedstead. Oftentimes the groom manages to have a portion of the skirt of her dress come under him as he sits down by her, such a thing being considered as a kind of omen that she will be submissive. Sometimes the bride is very careful, by a proper adjustment of her clothing at the moment of sitting down, not only to prevent the accomplishment of such an intention on his part, but also to sit down, if possible, in such a manner that some of his dress will come under her, thus manifesting her determination to preserve a proper independence, if not to bring him actually to yield obedience to her will. After sitting thus in profound silence together for a few moments, the groom arises and leaves

BRIDE AND BRIDEGROOM WORSHIPPING THE TABLETS OF HIS DECEASED ANCESTORS.

the room. Before going out, the assistants of the bride oftentimes request him to rub the feet of his bride a little, under the impression that, if he should comply, her feet will be prevented by that act from aching in the future!

The groom waits in the reception-room for the reappearance of his bride. The ceremony which they are soon to perform is considered an essential part of the customs observed on the day

of the marriage of heathen Chinese in this part of the empire,
and doubtless all over China.

The ceremony is called " worshipping the tablets." A table
is placed in the front part of the reception-room. The table is
said to be placed " before heaven." Two candlesticks, containing
two large lighted candles, and a censer containing lighted incense,
are put upon this table, the censer between the candlesticks.
Among other things, there are also placed on it two miniature
white cocks, made of sugar, five kinds of dried fruit, a bundle
of chopsticks, a foot measure, a mirror, a pair of shears, and a
case containing money-scales. (Some or all of these are frequently placed on a platter made out of the wood of the willow-
tree.) Two singularly-shaped goblets, sometimes connected
together by a red silk or red cotton cord several feet long, are
also put upon the table. When everything is ready, the bride
is led out of her room, and takes her place by the table on the
right side of the groom. The faces of both parties are turned
toward the table—that is, toward the open light of the heavens.
At certain signals from one of the female assistants of the bride
both parties kneel down four times, each time bowing their
heads once towards the earth in profound silence. They then
rise to their feet and change places, the bride standing on the
left of the bridegroom. They now kneel down four times,
bowing their heads as before. This portion of the ceremony is
called " worshipping heaven and earth." They then turn round,
so that their faces are toward the inner or back side of the
room. The ancestral tablets having been previously placed on
a table in the back side of the room, and candles and incense
having been lighted and arranged near them in the customary
way, the bridegroom and bride now bow down and worship
these tablets eight times, according to the manner after which
they have just " worshipped heaven and earth." They again
resume their original relative positions, differing only in that
they face each other, and do not stand side by side. Separated
from each other by only a few feet, they now kneel down four
times again, and bow their heads once each time toward the
ground. After this they rise to their feet, and remain standing
in silence, while they are helped to the wedding wine. One of
the female assistants takes the two goblets (mentioned above as
tied together by a red cord) from the table, and, having partially filled them with a mixture of wine and honey, she pours
some of their contents from one into the other, back and forth
several times. She then holds one to the mouth of the groom,

and the other to the mouth of the bride, who continue to face
each other, and who then sip a little of the wine.   She then
changes the goblets, and the bride sips out of the one just used
by the groom, and the groom sips out of the one just used
by the bride, the goblets still usually remaining tied together.
Sometimes she uses only one goblet in giving the wine.   She
then places the goblets on the table, and proceeds to break off a

BRIDE AND BRIDEGROOM DRINKING SAMSHU TOGETHER.

bit of the sugar cocks and give to the bridegroom and the bride ;
perhaps also a few of the five kinds of fruit which have been
provided is handed to them.   After this the groom usually takes
the bunch of chopsticks in one hand and the long case which
contains the money-scales in the other, and makes a pretence of
raising up by their means the thick covering which conceals

the head and face of his bride from his view. It is only a pretence, and he returns the chopsticks and the money-scales to the place whence he took them. This usually concludes the ceremony. The lighted candles are taken by the married woman who addressed the bride with propitious language on her arrival, and carried into the bride's room, whither the groom accompanies his bride, but immediately returns to the public room, while she remains attended by her assistants to dress for dinner.

All of the articles of food and of family use placed on the table during the performance of this ceremony are, according to the Chinese standpoint, omens of harmony and of prosperity. Eating from the same sugar cock, and drinking wine from the same goblets, are symbolical of union in sharing their lot in life.

Until this time the bride has worn the heavy embroidered outside garment, head-dress, &c. which she had on when she entered her sedan. These are now removed. She has her hair carefully combed in the style of her class in society, and she is arrayed in her own wedding garments. Sometimes her hair is gorgeously decked out with pearls and gems, true or false, according to the ability of the family to purchase, rent, or borrow.

When her toilet has been completed, and everything has been made ready, the bride and bridegroom sit down in her room to their wedding dinner. He now, oftentimes for the first time in his life, and always for the first time on his marriage day, beholds the features of his wife. He may eat to his fill of the good things provided on the occasion, but she, according to established custom, may not take a particle. She must sit in silence, dignified and composed. The door being left open, the invited guests, and the parents of the groom and his relatives, improve the opportunity to scan the bride and observe her deportment.

Several times during the day, if living conveniently near, the family of the bride send some refreshments for her to eat. These are received with thanks, and the bearer rewarded with a small present. Custom does not allow her to partake of this refreshment from her parents, but demands its being sent and received.

Some time during the afternoon the male guests sit down to their dinner around tables which accommodate eight persons, the seat of each being determined according to the nice rules of Chinese etiquette. A curious custom prevails here, according to which every invited guest is expected to make a present in money to the family of the bridegroom. This should be sent

in to the family the day before the wedding, though sometimes
it is brought by the guest himself when he comes to the feast.
The amount of the present is entirely optional, and varies according to the wealth of the guest and the nearness of relationship.
Even should the formal invitation not be complied with, the
person invited remaining away, the present is nevertheless
expected, and it would be disreputable not to give it.

BRIDE AND BRIDEGROOM TAKING THEIR WEDDING DINNER.

According to another established custom here, except in the
case of marriages in the families of officers and the gentry,
neighbours, uninvited friends, or even perfect strangers to the
parties, if they please, are allowed to come in and see the bride
during the evening of the day of her marriage. This is a very
trying ordeal for her, as she may not refuse to be seen by them,
nor absent herself from the gaze of the public. She is obliged

to stand while a company of spectators observes her appearance and criticises her deportment. They indulge oftentimes in great liberty of remark about her, which she must hear with composure. What at other times would be likely to be regarded as insulting and highly indecent, must be passed over as though she heard it not. Should she allow herself to laugh, or should she forget herself enough to manifest anger, it would be a source of annoyance and of regret. Her husband generally absents himself from the public room during this evening. It not unfrequently occurs that some of his intimate friends or neighbours stay very late, refusing to depart unless he pledges them a considerable sum of money with which to pay the expenses of a feast on the following day.

The large candles which were transferred to the bride's room from the reception-room at the close of the ceremony of " worshipping heaven and earth " are permitted to burn all day, and unto the evening, if they will. As it is eminently desirable that candles should be burned all the night long in the bridal chamber, these are usually, during the evening, exchanged for another pair, which it is calculated will last until the following morning. These are two feet long, more or less, and of a bright red colour. Usually on one is made, in a lively yellow colour, a picture of a dragon, by the use of gold leaf, or of a liquid preparation called " gold oil ; " and on the other the picture of a phœnix, representing respectively the groom and his bride. Sometimes auspicious characters or phrases are written on the candles. These, lighted on the evening of the wedding, and arranged on the table in the bride's room, are desired to burn during the whole night, and as much longer as they will last. It would be considered very unlucky should they be extinguished by accident. Should one or both of them go out during the night, such an event would indicate the premature and untimely death of one or both of the parties. The material of the candles should not melt and trickle down the sides. This is regarded as a bad omen, the trickling down of the material being thought to resemble the flowing of tears down the cheeks, and betokens, on wedding occasions, that there will be much sorrow in the family of the newly-married couple, or that they will not live happily together. If the candles should burn out about the same time, it is supposed that the couple will die about the same period in the future ; and should one burn much longer than the other, it is inferred that one will long survive the other.

CHAPTER III.

THE wedding festivities generally last at least two days. The first day the male friends and relatives of the groom are invited to "shed their light" on the occasion. On the second day the female friends and relatives of the family of the groom are invited to the wedding-feast. This is often called the "women's day."

Not long after the family and guests have breakfasted on the morning of the second day, the newly-married couple, amid the noise of fire-crackers, come out of their room together for the purpose of worshipping the ancestral tablets belonging to the household, the grandparents, and parents of the groom. This custom is known by the name of "coming out of the room." In case of those families who devote only one day to the marriage festivities and ceremonies, this custom is observed on the afternoon of the first day.

The tablets of the family are arranged on a table standing in the back part of the reception-room, or in a niche placed on the table. Incense and candles, arranged near the tablets, having been lighted, the bridegroom and his bride kneel down three or four times before the tablets. They now arise, and two chairs are placed before the table which contains the incense, candles, and tablets. If the paternal grandparents of the groom are living and present, they take their seats in the chairs, the grandmother being on the right hand of the grandfather, with their faces turned away from the table, or toward the front part of the room. In case either has deceased, the tablet which represents that person is placed in the chair which he or she would have occupied if living. The bridegroom and bride advance, and kneel down three or four times before them, bowing their heads toward the ground, as in worshipping the tablets. In case either parent is

F

dead, the ancestral tablet for that person is placed in the chair, as in the supposed case of one of the grandparents having deceased. The paternal and maternal uncles and aunts of the groom, if present, in the order of their rank, now take their turns of being worshipped by the couple. Standing on these occasions is regarded as a mark of humility.

Not long subsequent to the ceremony of "coming out of the room," the couple proceed to the kitchen for the purpose of *worshipping the god and goddess of the kitchen.* This is performed with great decorum, and is regarded as an important and essential part of marriage solemnities! Incense and candles are lighted, and the bridegroom and his bride kneel down, side by side, and bow in worship of the god and goddess of the kitchen. It is believed that they will thus propitiate their good-will, and especially that the bride, in attempting culinary operations, will succeed better in consequence of paying early and respectful attentions to these divinities.

On the third day the parents of the bride send an invitation to their son-in-law and his wife to visit them. With this invitation they send sedans for them. Until this morning, since she left her former home, two days previous, the bride has seen none of her own family, and generally none of her own relatives or acquaintances. She and her husband now receive the congratulations and compliments of her brothers or other relatives, and prepare to visit her parents. The bride enters her sedan first, and proceeds a short distance in front of her husband. They do not start together, nor is it proper that they should arrive at the house of her parents at the same time. The chair provided for the bride on this occasion is a common black sedan in all respects, except that its screen in front has a certain charm painted upon the outside. This charm is the picture of a grim-looking man, sitting on a tiger, with one of his arms raised

CHARM TO WARD OFF EVIL SPIRITS
FROM A BRIDE.

up, holding a sword, as if in the act of striking, representing a certain ruler of elves, hobgoblins, &c. The object of its use on the occasion of a bride's returning to her parents' house, on the third day after her marriage, is to keep off evil and unpropitious influences from her. It is said that, in former times, whenever a new bride in her chair passed by a certain place, evil spirits would invariably approach and injure her, causing her to be sick. The great magician (represented by the individual on the tiger, and brandishing a sword), who is the head of a class of Tauist priests, on being invited to destroy these evil spirits, or counteract their pernicious influences, exerted his great powers, and actually accomplished the object. In commemoration of this signal blessing to brides in particular and to mankind in general, and in order to secure immunity from these depraved spirits to future brides in other parts of the empire, the happy device of making a picture of this magician, and of placing it on the screen of the sedans they occupy on going to see their mothers on the third day after the marriage, was adopted.

On arrival at her paternal home, the bride's sedan is carried into the reception-room, and she alights amid the noise of firecrackers. The sedan which contains the son-in-law stops a few rods from his father-in-law's residence, where he is met by one of his brothers-in-law, or some relative or friend deputed to conduct him into the house. The two parties, standing in the street, respectfully shake their own hands toward each other on meeting. The newly-arrived is now invited to enter the house. He is seated in the reception-room, where he is treated successively to three cups of tea and three pipes of tobacco. Afterward he is invited to go and see his mother-in-law in her room, where he finds his wife. There he sits a while, and visits after a stereotyped manner, being careful to use only good or propitious words, avoiding every subject and phrase which, according to the notions of this people, are unlucky. He is soon invited into the reception-room, where he is joined by his wife. Everything being arranged, the husband and wife proceed to worship the ancestral tablets of her family, her grand parents and her parents, if living and present, very much in the way they worshipped, on the preceding day, the tablets of his family, his grandparents and parents. At the conclusion of this ceremony the bride retires to her mother's apartments, or to some back room, where she and the female relatives present are feasted. Her husband is invited to partake of some refreshments in the reception-room, in doing which he is joined by his bride's brothers, or some others of her family relatives. According to the rules of etiquette, he must eat but very little, however hungry he may be. He soon takes his departure in his sedan, leaving his bride to follow by herself by-and-by, accompanied usually only by a servant or female friend.

It is a common custom, on the morning of the tenth day after her marriage, for the parents of the bride to send an invitation for her to spend the day with them. If accepted, she goes and returns unattended by her husband. At the end of a month, should they again invite her, she usually goes and visits with her parents, and brothers and sisters, for a few consecutive days, spending the night there. Her husband calls upon them during this visit perhaps once or twice in the daytime, but is careful neither to go there with his wife nor return home with her. Husbands are never seen with their wives in public.

At the expiration of a month after marriage, the bride expects to receive a present from her parents, consisting, in part, of the following articles : an image of the Goddess of Mercy, universally worshipped by married women, and a portable niche to put it in ; a censer to contain incense while consuming ; a pair of candlesticks, to hold candles while she is worshipping ; a fan ; two flower vases ; artificial flowers ; and cosmetics.

After the first year of his marriage, the bridegroom is expected every year to make presents of a pig's foot, vermicelli, wine, and large red candles, with, perhaps, some money, to his father and mother-in-law, on the occurrences of their birthdays, at the festivals which take place during the fifth month, the eighth month, and at the winter solstice, and at new year's day. During the first year of his married life, it is customary for his parents-in-law to make *him* more or less presents like the above, at the times of the great festivals, and especially at new year's day.

At various times between the periods of betrothal and of marriage, three incense sticks and a brace of candles are lighted and burned before the ancestral tablets of the families to which the affianced parties belong, for the purpose of informing their ancestors of what is being transacted on earth relating to the betrothment and marriage of their living descendants. Such are some of the sinful and superstitious practices relating to betrothal and marriage among the Chinese.

In addition to those we have described, other practices and sentiments are prevalent, equally strange and opposed to those common in civilized Western nations.

When a girl is born in a poor family, which it feels unable or is unwilling to rear, she is often given away or sold when but a few weeks or months old, or one or two years old, to be the future wife of a son in the family of a friend or relative which has a little son not betrothed in marriage. Generally a small present is proffered by the family to which the boy belongs, as a pair of ducks or of geese, a pair of fowls, and a few pounds of vermicelli, as omens of good. Of the animals, the male is usually received by the girl's parents, and the others returned to the boy's parents. A match-maker is employed, and a formal engagement is made out, as in the case of boys and girls more advanced in age. The girl is called a "little bride," and is taken home, and brought up in the family together with her future husband. When of marriageable age, and the family can afford the little additional expense, she is married on a fortunate day, which has been selected by a fortune-teller. Friends are invited, and a feast is made. No bridal cakes are distributed among her relatives, and no red bridal chair is used, because she is living in the family of her husband.

Occasionally, in the case of families very intimate and friendly, an engagement in marriage between unborn children is entered into by those who expect soon to become mothers, turning only on the circumstance that the children are of different sexes. Generally, before the birth of the children, something valuable, as a head-dress, or rings for the wrists, are exchanged by the families, as proof of the betrothal. After their birth, should the children prove to be a boy and a girl, a go-between is employed, and the betrothal papers are made out and exchanged in the usual way.

Males and females of the same family surname never intermarry in China. Cousins who have not the same ancestral names may intermarry—that is, children of sisters, or of a brother and of a sister, but not children of brothers. The Chinese say that marriages among those of the same ancestral name would "confound the human relations." No matter how remote the relation between parties having the same ancestral name, and no matter if they be from distant provinces, and their ancestors have not known each other for hundreds or even thousands of years, they may not marry. This fact relating to the Chinese might be adduced to aid in giving an answer to the question, "What is in a name?" The same principle carried out with us would result in different families of "Smiths" never intermarrying, however remote their blood relationship might be.

It not unfrequently occurs that a rich family, having only one

daughter and no boys, desires to obtain a son-in-law who shall
be willing to marry the girl and live in the family as son.
Sometimes a notice is seen posted up, stating the desire of a
certain man to find a son-in-law and heir who will come and live
with him, perhaps stating the age and qualifications of an acceptable person. In such a case, the parents of those who have a
son whose qualifications might warrant such an application, and
whom they would be willing to allow to marry on such terms,
are expected to make application by a go-between, when the
matter would be considered by the rich man. He who agrees to
go and live with his father-in-law sometimes agrees also, at the
time of marriage, to take the ancestral name of his father-in-law,
and regard himself as his son. Only a poor family will allow a
talented and literary son to ignore his own family name in this
way. On the day of marriage he is carried in a black sedan,
decked off with some pieces of scarlet silk on the outside, to the
residence of his father-in-law, where he and his bride perform
the worship of "heaven and earth," of the ancestral tablets of
her family, &c. in accordance with the established customs
relating to wedding occasions. While, perhaps, there is not any
disgrace in obtaining a wife in this way, and becoming the heir
of a rich family, at the loss of one's ancestral name, the opportunity is not coveted as much as the opportunity of obtaining a
wife and a valuable present in money from a rich man with the
privilege of retaining one's own ancestral name. Some wealthy
men are glad to bestow one of their daughters, and a valuable
dowry besides, on graduates, for the honour of having a literary
son-in-law who has the prospect of becoming a mandarin.

Widows are obliged by custom to wear a white, black, or blue
skirt, when they wear any skirt at all. They are not allowed to
dress in a red and gaudy skirt, as though they were married and
their husbands were living. Hence the expression, "*marrying
the wearer of a white skirt,*" applied to a man who marries a
widow. Poor families sometimes arrange to marry one of their
sons to a widow, when they feel themselves unable to procure a
girl of good character on account of the necessary expense in-
curred in such a case. The expense attendant on marrying a
widow is comparatively small. It is considered a disgrace to a
family for one of its sons to marry a widow, as well as a disgraceful or shameful step on the part of the widow to consent to
marry again. No rich and fashionable family ever marries a son
to a widow. A widow is not allowed to ride in a red bridal
chair *en route* from her residence to the residence of her intended

husband. She must employ a common black-covered chair, borne by two men. Many families, which have a widow connected with them, are exceedingly unwilling that she should marry again on account of the dishonour which such a procedure would bring upon them, and especially upon the memory of her deceased husband. Generally his relatives, if in good circumstances, prefer to assist in her support, or support her entirely, than that she should marry the second time. Sometimes, however, when they are unkind to her, she tries to marry clandestinely, if she is assured they will not give their consent and assistance in finding her a second husband. A case occurred in this city in the fall of 1861, when a widow, who was not kindly treated by her husband's family, by practising deceit succeeded in engaging herself to a man without their knowledge, by the means of a go-between. It was arranged that she should start from the go-between's house. She was on the point of starting for her intended's house, when her deceased husband's friends, having ascertained the facts, came in time to prevent her second marriage, after a spirited struggle with the friends of the man to whom she had clandestinely engaged herself. This engagement was regarded as improper and unlawful, because the elders of her deceased husband's family were not cognisant of it nor a party to it.

For a person to enter the married state under three years, or, more correctly speaking, under twenty-seven months, subsequent to the death of one of his or her parents, is contrary to the law of the empire. Still, in point of fact, some marry inside of a hundred days after the death of a parent, in case that there is an urgent need of the services of a female in the family. *Custom*, which in China is oftentimes more carefully followed than the letter of the law, now allows in this place such marrying in the case of the common people, although the law, strictly interpreted, forbids it. Such a marriage in an officer's family would not be tolerated.

Oftentimes, when the girl dies before the wedding-day arrives, especially if nearly or quite of marriageable age, a custom called *asking for her shoes* is observed. Her affianced husband goes in person to the residence of her parents, and with weeping approaches the coffin which contains her corpse. He soon after demands a pair of the shoes which she has recently worn. These he carries home, having three lighted sticks of incense in his hands, as he walks or is borne through the streets. At the corners of the streets, *en route* to his residence, should there be

any, he calls out her name, and invites her to follow. On
arriving at his own home he informs her of the fact. The incense
he brought with him he puts in a censer. He arranges a table
in a convenient room, and places behind it a chair. The shoes
of the deceased girl are placed on the chair, or under it. The
censer containing the incense brought from her parents' residence
is placed upon the table, together with a pair of lighted candles.
Here he causes incense to be burned for two years, when a tablet
to her memory is placed in the niche containing the ancestral
tablets of his family. By all this he acknowledges her as
his wife.

When a girl has been betrothed, but her affianced dies before
their marriage, the term *broken thread* is used in speaking of the
matter, just as though the feet of the parties had been tied
together by a thread, which had become broken. Her parents
often endeavour to keep the fact of the death of her betrothed
from coming to her knowledge. They are generally very anxious
to engage her as soon as convenient to another person, concealing
the circumstance of her former betrothal, if possible, from the
family among whose sons they hope to find a husband for her.
Should it become known, many families would decline to engage
one of their boys to her, the death of her betrothed being
regarded as an inauspicious event.

It oftentimes occurs that the parents do not succeed in keeping from their daughter a knowledge of the fact that her affianced
husband has died. Most girls, in such a case, are quite willing
to be engaged in marriage to another person, and therefore
make no opposition or trouble; but some stedfastly oppose any
rebetrothal, and demand to be permitted to go over to the family
of her affianced husband's parents, and live with them as his
widow. If she cannot be persuaded to desist from this plan,
the families concerned are obliged to make the necessary preparations, providing furniture and clothing as though her husband
was living. When everything is ready, the procession of men,
carrying her outfit of furniture, &c. proceeds through the streets
to the residence of the deceased. The furniture, however, must
have white strips of paper pasted on it, or it must be bound
around with pieces of white cloth. The bridal procession is also
different from what it would have been had her affianced been
living. Though she is preceded by a band of music, and by
men bearing lanterns, and though she is dressed in red clothing,
she may not ride in a red bridal chair with four bearers, but in
a common black or blue sedan. On arriving at the house where

the parents of her betrothed reside, she proceeds to worship
heaven and earth, and the ancestral tablets of his family. She
then puts on mourning apparel, and goes to the side of his
coffin, where she weeps and laments. Afterward, for the
customary period, she performs the usual ceremonies connected
with mourning for a deceased husband, and continues to live in
the family, secluding herself from her friends and from the
public, waiting on his parents as their daughter-in-law until her
own death. Such is the theory. Few, it is said, carry it out
now-a-days in all its strictness. For a girl to adopt the resolution
to live as a widow in the family of her affianced husband is not
desired by either family concerned. It is particularly undesirable to the parents of her betrothed, on account of the trouble
it makes them, and also on account of the anxiety they constantly suffer lest she should not continue stedfast in her
purpose. Should she change her mind, and not live up to her
original intention, after having taken the preliminary steps, she
would bring much shame and dishonour on them. Should she,
however, live a life of chastity and of filial obedience to her
parents-in-law, and die at an advanced age with an unsullied
reputation, it would reflect great honour on herself and the
families most intimately concerned. She would be sure of
having an honorary portal erected to her memory, by especial
permission of the Emperor, and in part at his expense, should
her virtue and her filial piety be represented to him by the
proper mandarins.

Marriage after betrothal is sometimes postponed, and then,
when every other resource is exhausted, and the family of the
groom come to the conclusion that the other family have no
good excuse for delaying the marriage, the expedient of stealing
away the affianced girl from her parents' residence, and carrying
her to the residence of the other party, is adopted as an effectual
way of settling the question. It is necessary, in stealing away
the girl, that her betrothed husband should go in person and do
it. He provides a common black sedan, and has it ready near
the house where the girl resides, or is expected to pass along, or
is visiting. He takes along with him a party of relatives or
trusty friends to aid him, if help is needed. Some one of the
company carries along a common bed-blanket. On finding the
girl, she is seized by her betrothed, and the blanket thrown over
her head. She is taken to the sedan in waiting, placed inside,
and carried off directly to his home. *En route* he places himself
directly before the door of the sedan, and his friends follow near

by. No one dares interfere or hinder in any way the affianced
husband and his party in thus kidnapping and carrying off his
betrothed wife, except her parents and brothers. This intended
course on the part of him who has a right to her, if it should
become known to her relatives, oftentimes brings them immediately to terms, and they agree to allow the departure of the
bride in the usual reputable way, seated in a red bridal sedan,
and preceded by a band of music, &c.

When the girl is kidnapped, and carried to her betrothed
husband's home, the ceremonies usual on wedding occasions are
observed there on her arrival, as nearly as the circumstances of
the case admit. Should the kidnapping party make a mistake,
and seize another girl and carry her off, the leader would be
liable to prosecution before the magistrate, and to suffer heavily
for his blunder. Such a mistake does occasionally occur, mainly
owing to the fact that the features of the affianced bride are
unknown to any member of the other party.

A case occurred in this city not long since, when the bridegroom endeavoured to gain possession of his bride by kidnapping
her. But it happened that the girl was not at home when the
kidnapping party arrived, and she could not be found. In this
case, the family to which he had belonged had become very poor
since the betrothment ; when the parties were betrothed, both
families were rich. It seemed very hard to the parents of the
girl that she should marry a poor man, and hence they delayed,
under various pretences, the fixing of a fortunate day for the
wedding, and endeavoured to have the engagement cancelled,
and the betrothal papers belonging to the families exchanged ;
but when they saw by the effort to kidnap and carry her off
that the bridegroom was unwilling to give her up, and that there
was danger of the affair becoming known to the magistrate, they
consented to her marriage in the usual way.

When a marriage contract is broken up by the consent of both
parties, a writing is sometimes given by the affianced husband
to the other family, called a "retirement from the marriage,"
and the original documents relating to betrothal in the possession
of the parties are exchanged. The marriage contract is comparatively seldom cancelled. Generally it is done, if done at all,
on the girl giving what is considered good reason for the step.
Poverty, or illness, or ugliness, are never regarded as good
reasons ; but a reputation for lewd habits, on her part, seems to
justify the giving up of the match by the family of her affianced
husband, although the same character on his part is not con-

sidered a sufficient reason for demanding a release from the marriage contract by the parents of the girl. Immorality on his part is not taken into the account, but her character must be above suspicion. If one party becomes leprous before marriage, or is greatly physically deformed, or is a notorious thief, the other party may demand a release from the engagement. Generally the party which insists, even for good reasons, for such a release, has to pay a comparatively large bonus in order to get it from the other party. The richer the party, the greater the sum demanded. It is considered disgraceful either to give or to receive a written release.

There are seven considerations which will justify a husband in giving a bill of divorcement after marriage and putting away his wife, according to the ancient standards. There does not seem to be any valid ground, according to Chinese views and customs, why a wife, or her friends in her behalf, should demand a separation from him. The power is all in his hands. Should she desire to get a bill of divorcement from him, because he treats her unkindly, or because he is a thief or an adulterer, the attempt would be in vain. There does not appear to be any lawful reason to justify a wife in leaving her husband. The idea of a wife divorcing her husband for adultery, or for any reason whatever, is one which excites a smile, as absurd and preposterous, whenever mentioned to the Chinese. Duty with her is simply and solely to follow her husband, submit to his caprices, and the domination of his parents, until death releases her, or she is sold by him, or divorced for some of the seven reasons which justify a divorcement. These are :—1. Unfilial conduct (towards the parents of her husband) ; 2. Adultery ; 3. Jealousy ; 4. Loquacity ; 5. Theft ; 6. Virulent disease (as leprosy) ; 7. Barrenness. It is said that at the present time the last two reasons are not regarded among educated men as sufficient grounds for a divorce. There are three things, any one of which, except in the most aggravated cases, will prevent, according to theory, a divorce of the wife by her husband. These are, first, if she has lived with him, and served his father and his mother until they are both dead ; second, if he has become rich and honoured with office under the Government since their marriage, at the time of marriage he being poor, and not in the enjoyment of official trust ; third, if she has no home to which she can go, her parents and brothers being dead.

It is not necessary for the husband, in giving a bill of divorcement to his wife, to do it in the presence of an officer of the

Government, as witness, in order to make it legal. He does it on his own authority and in his own name. It is often written in the presence of her parents and in their house. Very few divorces occur in China.

Very poor families are frequently unable to find reputable girls who are willing to marry their sons ; and sometimes they are quite unable to be at the expense of buying a wife, and of marrying her according to the established customs. They therefore sometimes plan to purchase *the wife of a living man*, who may desire, for some reason which, to his mind, is a justification for the act, to sell her. The price paid for such a wife is much less than it would be necessary to pay for a girl, or for a female slave ; and the expense of the marriage festivities would also be much less than in case of marrying a reputable girl. The purchaser of a living man's wife must receive from him a bill of sale, stating that she is sold by him to be the wife of the buyer. The woman must be willing to be thus disposed of. She is conveyed in a common black sedan to her purchaser's residence, where she and he worship heaven and earth, and the ancestral tablets of his family, and each other, in much the usual manner as on other wedding occasions, and his friends and relatives are invited to a feast. The custom of marrying the wife of a living man is not very common. It is done oftener in country places than in cities. What a state of society which will tolerate such a custom !

Rich married men have often one or more concubines living in their families. Doubtless many a man who is childless marries a second or inferior wife, with the consent and approbation of his first or principal wife, and while she is living, who would not have taken such a step in other circumstances. The desire of having male children to perpetuate one's name, and to burn incense before one's tablet after death, has an immense influence over the mind of the Chinese. Generally speaking, only female slaves are willing to become a second or inferior wife in the family of a man whose principal or first wife is living ; respectable families are adverse to allowing their daughters to form such connexions. The inferior wife must submit to the principal wife, and obey her as her mistress, and must kneel down before her, and worship her, on arriving at her future home. She does not worship heaven and earth together with her husband, on the morning of her marriage, as is invariably the custom on the part of the principal wife, but she is required to worship the ancestral tablets of the family.

Some widows, on the death of their husbands, resolve not to survive them, and proceed to take their own lives. *Chinese sutteeism* differs from Indian sutteeism in that it is never performed by burning. The manner of doing it is various. Some take opium, and lie down and die by the side of the corpse of their husband. Others commit suicide by starving themselves to death, or by drowning themselves, or by taking poison. Another method sometimes practised in this place is by hanging themselves in public, near or in their own houses, having given notice to that effect, so that those who desire may be present and behold the act.

The real reasons which induce some widows to practice sutteeism are various. Some, doubless, are moved in a great degree to do it by a devoted attachment to the dead ; others by the extreme poverty of their families, and the difficulty of earning an honest and respectable living ; others by the fact or the prospect of unkind treatment on the part of their husband's relatives. Occasionally, when poor, the brothers of her deceased husband advise or insist that the young widow shall marry again. In one of the cases which occurred here about a year ago, the inciting cause why the young widow decided to kill herself by public hanging was that a brother-in-law insisted that she should marry a second husband. On her refusing to do it, he insinuated that the only way for her to gain a livelihood, in the indigent circumstances of the family, was by her becoming a prostitute. This unkindness maddened her, and she resolved to commit suicide. She appointed a certain time for its accomplishment. On the morning of the day appointed she visited a certain temple, erected to hold the tablets and perpetuate the memory of "virtuous and filial" widows. She was borne to and fro through the streets, seated in a sedan carried by four men, dressed in gaudy clothing, and holding in her hand a bouquet of fresh flowers. After burning incense and candles before the tablets in this temple, accompanied with the usual kneelings and bowings, she returned home, and in the afternoon took her life, in the presence of an immense crowd of spectators. On such occasions it is the practice to have a platform erected in the house of the widow, or in the street before it. At the appointed time she ascends the platform, and sprinkles some water around on the four sides of it. She then scatters several kinds of grain around in the different directions. These are done as omens of plenty and of prosperity in her family. After being seated in a chair on the platform, she is generally approached by her own brothers, and by her husband's brothers who worship her. This is oftentimes accompanied by the offering to her of tea or of wine. When everything is ready, she steps upon a stool, and, taking hold of the rope, which is securely fastened to a high portion of the platform or the roof of the house, adjusts it about her own neck. She then kicks the stool away from under her, and thus becomes her own murderer.

Formerly certain officers of Government, if the current report is trustworthy, used to sanction the self-destruction of widows, not only by their presence on the occasion, but also by their taking a part in the worship. Once, it is related, a woman, after the honours had been paid to her, instead of mounting the stool, and adjusting the rope about neck, and hanging herself, according to the understanding, suddenly recollected that she had forgotten to feed her hogs, and hastened away, promising to be back shortly, which promise she omitted to keep. Since that hoax no mandarin has been present at a suttee at this place. A public suicide by a widow always attracts a large crowd of spectators. Public sentiment encourages the practice enough to make it considered honourable and meritorious, though not to make it a very frequent occurrence. The brothers and near relatives of a widow who thus immolates herself soon after the decease of her husband regard it as an honour to the family, and not unfrequently feel gratified in having themselves referred to as her brothers or relatives.

Sometimes a girl who has been betrothed to a man who dies before the marriage-day resolves to take her own life by public hanging, in view of his death, rather than be engaged again in marriage, or live unmarried. If she cannot be persuaded to take a different course, she is allowed to appoint a day for her suicide, visits the temple referred to above, if not too far distant, mounts the platform provided at the house of her affianced husband, and launches herself into eternity, in much the same manner as do those widows who resolve not to survive the loss of their husbands. The coffin of the girl, in such cases, is interred by the side of the coffin of her betrothed, and at the same time.

The widows and the girls who take their lives as above described may have their names recorded on the large general tablets erected in the temple which they visit before they commit suicide, or they may have a separate tablet, made in the usual shape, but as costly as they please to make it, placed among the other tablets at the temple, on the payment of a sum of money for the current expenses of the institution, or as a present to its keepers or managers. Incense and candles are burned in this temple on the 1st and the 15th of each Chinese month, in honour of these "virtuous and filial" women, by some of the gentry of the city; and it is the official duty of certain mandarins, either in person or by deputy, to offer oblations at this temple in the spring and autumn of each year.

Honorary tablets or portals are sometimes erected to the memory of virtuous widows who have obeyed with filial devo-

HONORARY STONE PORTAL TO THE MEMORY OF VIRTUOUS AND FILIAL WIDOWS.

tion the parents of their husbands. The tablets are made out of fine black stone or of common granite, and are generally erected by the side of a public street. They consist generally of four posts of stone, more or less elaborately carved, fifteen or twenty feet high, with several horizontal cross-pieces, also of stone. Inscriptions are sometimes graven upon the upright and cross-pieces in praise of chastity and filial piety. Near the top of the tablet are always found two Chinese characters, denoting that it is erected by "imperial permission." Such portals cost from a few tens of dollars to several hundred, according to their size, material, and finish. The chaste and filial widow, after arriving at fifty years of age, while living, may have a tablet erected in her honour, provided she has influential and wealthy friends. After making the necessary application to the emperor, through the proper mandarins, and after obtaining his special consent, a small sum of money accompanies the permission of the emperor, paid out of the imperial treasury, to aid in the expense of erecting the tablet. Her friends and relatives are expected to supply what is needed for its erection, over and above the donation from the emperor. When completed, some mandarin of low rank goes to worship it; and, if finished during the lifetime of the widow whose memory and example it is designed to commemorate, it is customary for her to go and worship it. The widows and the chaste unmarried girls who commit sutteeism by suicide on the death of their husbands or their affianced husbands are also entitled, in accordance with the customs of the country, to an honorary tablet, if they have friends or relations who are willing and able to procure the imperial sanction, and to supplement the imperial present with the necessary amount of money to build it. In fact, however, few who are entitled to a tablet do have one erected to their memory.

CHAPTER IV.

MARRIED life in China, unless attended with male children, is seldom happy. The wife is exceedingly anxious to present her husband with sons, who will perpetuate his name and burn incense before his tablet after his death. In case of real or supposed barrenness, various superstitious expedients are often resorted to by her, in order to facilitate the conception of children ; to ascertain the sex of an unborn babe ; and, as the time approaches, to render confinement safe and expeditious.

When the woman has been married for a long time, but remains childless, the following expedient is sometimes adopted. A girl belonging to another family is adopted by the childless woman as her own child. She is brought up in her family, and professedly treated as though she was her own child. The Chinese have the idea that, in some way, this course will aid the woman in the conception of children. The train of thought is explained thus : The woman is represented by a tree in the unseen world. Whether she will have children or not, and what will be their number and sex, is indicated by the condition of the tree which represents her, whether it has flowers or not ; and if it has flowers, what is their number and colour. If the tree has red flowers, she will have girls ; if white flowers, she will have boys. If the flowers be of different colours, some white and some red, she will have boys and girls ; if no flowers at all, the poor woman will not naturally have any children at all. But as, in this world, men graft one tree by a shoot of another tree, and thus have the desired fruit, the Chinese have devised the astute expedient of adopting a child into a childless family, hoping that thus there will in due time be flowers on the flowerless tree in the spirit land, representing the barren

G

wife ; and if so, she will be sure to have children, in consequence of this wonderful art of grafting.

Sometimes the childless married woman hires a sorceress, who pretends to be able to see into the other world, to examine the flower-tree which represents her, and to report to her its condition, whether it is flourishing or whether it is diseased, what flowers it has, and whether the red or white flowers will probably blossom first.

When, after a marriage of several years, no children are born to the wife, or none but girls, or the children die in infancy, the woman, fearing she shall never have any male children, or any that will live to mature age, not unfrequently engages a sorcerer or sorceress to perform the ceremony called "changing the flower-vase." Bearing children is fancied to have great resemblance in some respects to rearing flowers in flower-vases : much depends on the earth used in the vases. If no child is born, or if it dies, it is supposed to be like producing sickly flowers, the earth being bad. The person employed, some explain, is expected to go to the other world, and change the earth in the vase which has the flower-tree which represents the particular wife in question, or, as it is briefly called, "change her flower-vase ;" or she hires some one to make a quantity of artificial paper flowers, which are then placed in two paper flower-vases. The sorceress or sorcerer first performs certain ceremonies over these vases, and then changes their relative positions. Afterward, the paper vases and paper flowers are burned. Changing their relative positions is thought to indicate something like changing the earth in the flower-vases in the unseen world. The object of all this is to obtain male and healthy children.

Every year, between the 11th and the 15th of the first and of the eighth Chinese months, several of the most popular temples devoted to the worship of a goddess of children, commonly called "Mother," are frequented by married but childless women, for the purpose of procuring one of a kind of shoe belonging to her. Those who come for a shoe burn incense and candles before the image of "Mother," and vow to render a thanksgiving if she will aid them in bearing a male child. The shoe is taken home, and placed in the niche or by the niche which holds the family image of the goddess, where it is worshipped in connexion with "Mother," though not separately, on the 1st and 15th of each month, with the burning of incense, candles, and mock-money, and fresh flowers. When the child thus prayed for is born, should such a fortunate event take place, the happy mother causes, according to her vow, two shoes like the one obtained from the temple to be made. These two, and the original one, she returns to the temple with her thank-offering, which consists generally in part of several plates of food.

Some women, instead of asking for a shoe of the goddess, ask for some of the flowers which she usually has in her hands, or in a flower-vase near by. The shoe is *lent*; the flower is *given*. On reaching home, the woman wears the flower thus obtained in the hair of her head, or it is placed in a flower-vase near by the niche which contains the household goddess "Mother." No worship is paid to it. Should the supplicant not become a mother, no thanksgiving would be expected by the goddess whose aid she has invoked.

After she has gone about five months, the husband of the woman frequently returns thanks to the goddess "Mother," or some other divinity whom he pleases to worship on this occasion, and begs in the following manner a continuance of favours. A table is arranged in some convenient place near the open heavens. On it are placed ten plates of meats, fish, fowl, rice, &c., a vase of flowers, five kinds of seeds or dried fruits, a lantern, three sticks of incense, two candles, and ten cups of wine. A priest now begins to recite his formulas. At the customary period of the performance, he remarks, in substance, as if addressing the divinity worshipped, "that such a man has begotten by his wife a child for these five months. He now presents these offerings as an expression of his gratitude, and begs that she may be protected during the rest of her time in good health, and give birth to the child without detriment, on which event taking place he will present another thanksgiving."

Near the end of her time, on a lucky day, a ceremony is performed in many families for the purpose of propitiating the good will, as some explain it, of two female demons, which are believed to be present with an intention to destroy the woman's life at the time of childbirth. Others say that the object of the ceremony is to frighten and drive away these evil spirits, so that they shall not be present and injure the woman. A table is spread with eight or ten plates of food, with incense, candles, flowers, and mock-money. A priest recites the classics appropriate to the occasion. Ten or twenty pieces of a kind of grass cut up about an inch long, and several likenesses of the crab, cut out of common paper, are put into the censer and burned. Or sometimes several live crabs, after being used in the ceremony, are taken and turned out into the street. It is thought that these will greatly aid in frightening these bad spirits or propitiate their good will, so that they will not dare to come into the room at the time of childbirth. The reason why crabs are used is that the name of one of these demons sounds like the name for "crab" in the dialect of this place.

After the conclusion of this ceremony, the meats and other eatables are removed, and another quantity of incense, candles, seeds, wine, and a cup of clear water, are brought and placed on the table, but *no meats*. The ruler of the Bloody Pond in hell, and various evil spirits in the other world, are then invited by the priest to come and receive the worship of the husband of the woman. The priest performs certain ceremonies; the object is to gain the goodwill and protection of the ruler of the Bloody Pond in regard to the approaching case of childbirth. A part of the ashes of the incense used at this time is enveloped in a piece of red paper, and suspended near the censer belonging to the family, where it remains until thirty days after childbirth; it is then taken and put in the censer and burned during a thanksgiving ceremony made in honour of the ruler of the Bloody Pond. Twice every day, previous to the period of childbirth, one stick of incense and one pair of candles are burned before this parcel.

If a woman wishes to know the sex of her unborn babe, the following method of ascertaining the interesting fact is sometimes adopted. She reckons up the number of her age in years, and the number of the month, day, and hour she was born. This sum is added to the number of the day of the month and of the hour of the day when she determines to make the calculation. She then, remembering the sum total, commences to count the images or pictures of the thirty-six female assistants of the goddess called "Mother," until she arrives at the one which corresponds to the sum total of her calculations; if this sum exceeds thirty-six, she keeps on counting the images or pictures of the assistants until she arrives at the number she has in her mind. Now it is supposed that, by observing the sex of the child in the arms of the assistant goddess which corresponds to the sum total of her calculations, she may know the sex of her unborn child! If the assistant should happen to have no child at all in her arms, the woman comes to the conclusion either that the goddess will not inform her, or that her child will be stillborn, or will not live.

In case of very difficult labour, it is thought that a certain evil-disposed spirit prevents the child from coming into the world. A priest is therefore invited to come and perform a ceremony, the object of which is to drive away this bad spirit. Three cups of wine, a plate having five kinds of seeds or fruits, with incense and candles, are arranged on a table, and mock-money of several kinds is provided to be burned at the proper time. After the priest has mumbled over some unintelligible jargon or formula, attended with thumping on the table, for about half an hour, he produces three yellow paper charms, two or three inches wide, and a foot or more long; one of these is to be stuck over the door of the bedroom or on the bed-curtain, one is to be worn on the head of the sick woman, and the ashes of the other, mixed with hot water, is to be given to her to drink.

If the child is not born after waiting a longer time than usual, and much pain is suffered by the woman, and it is feared that her life is endangered, sometimes some of her family or friends obtain a kind of puppet show, among which is a puppet of the goddess "Mother." These puppets are made to play and dance, back and forth, near the door of the sick woman's room several times; they are then taken away. Sometimes the puppet representing "Mother" is placed on the body of the woman, and then made to dance or walk downward three times.

When much pain is suffered, and a delivery is not effected, the following artifice is resorted to by some families: two sheets of a kind of mock-money—one representing gold and the other silver—three sticks of incense, and two candles, are taken and lighted before the image of an assistant god called "Straight Charm," which may be always found standing just before the image of the "Great King" in the neighbouring temple, with its face toward the "Great King." After lighting these tokens of respect, the offerer turns around this image, so that its face will be turned toward the outside or directly away from the "Great King." The object of this is to procure the aid of this assistant god to turn around the infant and cause a speedy birth, it being supposed that the reason why a delivery has not already taken place is because the child is in a wrong position. If the child is born subsequently, the family is under obligations, some time during an interval of thirty days, to present a thank-offering of meats, fish, rice, incense, and candles before and in honour of the idol. The image is turned around to its proper position just as soon as possible after the child has been born into the world.

Sometimes it is believed that the child at the time of its birth is exposed to some very unpropitious influences, which, unless prevented in due time, will certainly cause its death. It will not eat nor cry, and it appears lifeless. Consequently a performance, very similar in most respects to one which has been already described, is transacted in some families, with the following distinguishing difference in regard to the use of the three yellow charms furnished by the priest.

After the conclusion of the ceremony, one of these charms is hung up on the curtain of the bed where the sick woman lies, the second is doubled up into a three-cornered shape, and then put on the cap of the child on the third day after its birth, or it is worn about its body for an indefinite period. The other is burned, and its ashes are put into the water with which the child is washed on the third day after birth, as a kind of purification.

On the third day after the birth of a child, the midwife washes it for the first time. This washing is performed before an image of the Goddess of Children already referred to, called "Mother." This divinity is supposed to have the care and oversight of children of both sexes until they are sixteen years old. About the time of washing the child, an oblation of five or eight plates of meats, fruits, &c. is made to the goddess, arranged on a table before her picture or image, with wine, incense, candles, and fresh flowers. This is regarded as a thank-offering for the aid of "Mother" thus far. The food is subsequently taken away and eaten by the members of the family. On this day friends and relations take occasion to send various kinds of food, as fowls, vermicelli, and cakes, to the family, in token of their congratulations.

Immediately after being washed, the important custom of binding its wrists is observed. In regard to this, there seems to be great diversity of practice. Some families simply bind around each wrist one or more ancient cash of a particular kind by means of a red cotton cord, where the cash remains for eleven days or longer. Others only put around each wrist a loose red string, as though it were a ring.

Other families provide several silver toys, as a miniature seal, a small bell, drum, pestle, and mallet. One or more of each kind of these toys, with an ancient cash, are bound around each wrist. The string used is generally about two feet long, each end being put about the wrists, leaving about one foot of loose string between them. These things are worn till the child is fourteen days old, when some families remove them. Sometimes, however,

a ring of red cord or of red tape, with or without some cash or
toy, is worn for several months, or even for a year. When
soiled, the tape or cord is exchanged for another clean one.

The ancient cash is used as a charm, in order to keep away
evil spirits or influences. The silver toys are designed as omens
of good relating to the future life of the child. The wrists are
thus tied together, in order to prevent the child becoming
naughty and disobedient. It is thought that such a tying of the
wrists will tend to keep the child from being troublesome in
after life, and from meddling with what does not belong to it,
just as though he or she was bound. When boys and girls are
naughty and troublesome, they are often asked if their "mammas
did not bind their wrists?" implying that if their wrists had been
properly bound when an infant, they would have been restrained
from misconduct in subsequent life.

On the third day after the birth of the babe, two Chinese
characters are written on a piece of red paper, which, having
been carefully folded around a parcel inclosing certain articles,
is hung up on a nail or peg on the outside of the door of its
mother's room by means of a red string tied around it. The
design of this paper and contents is to ward off unfavourable
influences from the child; and persons who are not very intimate
with the family, on seeing it, understand it to constitute a
request that they should not enter the room. Some say that
only those persons who were present at the washing of the babe
are allowed to enter the bedroom as long as the red paper is
attached to the door, which is for eleven days.

This parcel contains two of a certain fruit full of seed used in
the manufacture of a material employed somewhat like soap in
washing, some pith of a rush used for wicking, two chopsticks,
one or two onions, two pieces of charcoal, some cat's hair, and
some dog's hair. A pair of the trousers of the child's father are
put upon the frame of the bedstead, in such a way that the waist
shall hang downward, or be lower than the legs. On the trousers
is stuck a piece of red paper, having four words written upon it,
intimating that *all unfavourable influences are to go into the
trousers* instead of afflicting the babe. The hair in the package
on the outside of the bedroom door is to keep the noises which
may be made for eleven days by the dogs and cats in the vicinity
from frightening the babe. The coal is to aid in making it hardy
and vigorous. The onions are to cause it to be quick-witted and
intelligent. The pith is explained as contributing to make it
fortunate or successful in life. The two fruits are to aid it in

being cleanly and neat. It is believed that if persons come into the bed-room for the space of eleven days, while the parcel remains on the door, who ought not to come into it, the child will assuredly have white sores on its gums, and that it will be sickly and difficult to rear.

On the fourteenth day after the child's birth the parcel is taken away from the bedroom door, and the trousers are removed from the frame of the bedstead. Most families have on this occasion a kind of thank-offering to "Mother" for her assistance in protecting and preserving the babe, consisting of meats, fruits, and vegetables, spread before her image, which is kept in the bed-room. Such a thanksgiving, however, is not made to "Mother" in case of the death of the child previous to the fourteenth day.

When it is one month old, mother and child, according to theory, leave the bedroom for the first time after her confinement. On this day occurs another important ceremony, that of shaving the child's head for the first time. Some are careful to have it done before an image of "Mother" if it is a girl, and before the ancestral family tablets if it is a boy, incense and candles being lighted in front of the image and the tablets. A thank-offering is also presented to the goddess on this occasion. Relations and intimate friends are invited to a feast. Those who come must bring with them presents of money or silver rings, vermicelli, or fowls, &c. In case of its being the first-born, Tauist priests are often invited to perform the ceremony, called "passing through the door," for the benefit of the babe. The maternal grandmother of the child is always expected to bring or send presents of clothing or food on this day. Among these articles there are usually about twenty painted duck's eggs, and a quantity of soft sweet cakes. On the upper side of each of these are stamped or painted several pictures of the flower of the apricot, using several colours ; white is not allowed, as that is the symbolical colour of mourn-

SHAVING A CHILD'S HEAD WHEN ONE MONTH OLD.

ing. The pictures on the duck eggs are representations of children, flowers, and animals, in bright gaudy colours. The maternal grandmother is usually invited to a feast on this day. If belonging to the upper class of society, she seldom accepts the invitation, sending her presents by a servant. The day is one of joy and festivity, and among the rich it is observed with considerable show and expense, especially if it celebrates the shaving of the head of the first-born son.

About this time the child's parents return their acknowledgements of the kindness of friends and relatives, who sent presents on the third day after the child's birth and at the end of a month, by sending some presents back to them. These presents consist usually of small round bread-cakes or biscuits, which have been split open, and into which have been put small slices of boiled pork, making, in fact, a kind of sandwich. The number of such cakes presented to a family varies from ten to a hundred, depending much on the pecuniary circumstances of the party making the present, and having some proportion to the quantity or value of the articles previously received.

When the child is four months old, " Mother" is again thanked ; relatives and friends are again invited to a feast, who bring or send presents of food. As at the end of a month, so now the maternal grandmother, or her present, if she does not come in person, occupies a prominent position. If the circumstances of her family allow her to do so, she makes expensive presents of food and clothing, and a kind of chair, sometimes painted red, together with a quantity of molasses candy. The various articles of food are presented as an oblation before " Mother." The happy father, or the paternal grandfather or grandmother, bows down before the goddess, and begs that the child may be good-natured and easy to take care of, that it may

CHILD SITTING ON A CHAIR WHEN FOUR
MONTHS OLD.

grow fast, that it may sleep well at night, that it may be wide awake in the daytime, that it may not be given to crying, and that it may be kept in good health. The edibles are subsequently feasted on by the family and invited guests, having been previously presented before the ancestral table.

It is not usual to allow a child to sit in a chair until the day it is four months old. At a suitable time during this day, the soft molasses candy provided by its maternal grandmother is taken, and put in the seat of the chair on rollers. The child is then put in the chair so as to sit down on this candy, which sticks it to the chair for the time being. This is done in order that it may learn to sit in the chair, and not require to be carried very much in the arms of the nurse or mother. This chair is often prettily painted and gilded, and has various playthings attached to it. Before this day the child has been carefully prevented from tasting animal food. On this occasion such food is given to it.

On the anniversary of the child's birthday another thank-offering is presented to " Mother," and other presents of food and of clothing are received from the maternal grandmother. If it be a boy, among other articles of clothing are a pair of boy's shoes and a cap ; if a girl, besides clothing are wristlets and head ornaments. The provisions for the thank-offering are provided by the maternal grandmother of the child ; should she be unable to furnish all that is needed on the occasion, the balance is procured at the expense of her son-in-law, the father of the child, though everything professes to be provided by the delighted grandmamma.

Before the feast on this occasion, a large bamboo sieve, such as farmers use in winnowing grain, is placed on a table before the ancestral tablets of the family, where incense and candles are already burning. On this are laid a set of money-scales, a pair of shears, a foot-measure, a brass mirror, pencil, ink,

GRASPING PLAYTHINGS WHEN ONE YEAR OLD.

paper, and ink-slab, one or two books, the abacus, a silver or a gold ornament or implement, and fruits, &c. The child, dressed in the new garments just presented, is placed upon the sieve in the midst of the articles upon it. The object now is to see what it will first take hold of and play with. The moment is one of great interest to the parents and assembled friends. It is said that the article or articles the child first takes up indicate its future employment, character, or condition in the world. If the child be a boy, and he takes a book or an implement connected with literature, as pen or ink, it is surmised that he will become a distinguished scholar ; if he seizes the money-scales, or the silver or gold instrument or ornament, that he will become famous for his wealth and for his talents in making money.

In the Sung dynasty, a certain lad, on the day when he was one year old, while seated on the sieve, first seized hold of two miniature military weapons in one hand, and in the other two vessels like those used in sacrificial ceremonies on some state occasions. After a few moments he laid these articles down and took up a seal. After this he paid no attention to the other playthings before him. Now mark the result : this lad became a Chancellor of the Empire

FATHER TEACHING HIS CHILD TO WORSHIP.

On all the occasions when incense and candles are burned before the image of the goddess or before the ancestral tablets with special reference to a child, the child is taken there, if well, and made to worship in a certain manner by moving its hands up and down a few times. The child is taught from its earliest infancy to worship idols and the tablets of its ancestors.

On the birthday of children, every year, until they are sixteen years old, unless the ceremony of "passing through the door" is performed, many parents present offerings of food before the idol of "Mother." This is called "burning paper to Mother," and is designed as a thanksgiving for her past favours. Usually no priests are employed. Some families have the custom of "passing through the door" and of "burning paper to Mother" both observed in their houses on the birthdays of their children, should there be any special occasion for them on account of their health.

It is the custom in many families, when a child is just beginning to walk alone, for a member of the family to take a large knife, often such as is used in the kitchen to cut up vegetables, and, approaching him from behind, as he is toddling along, put it between his legs with the edge downward, and then bring it toward the floor, as if in the act of cutting something. This is called "cutting the cords of his feet." The motion is repeated two or three times. Sometimes it is not put between his legs, but is passed down toward the ground two or three times right behind him, while he is walking along. This is done in order to facilitate his learning to walk. It is supposed to be of great use in keeping the lad from stumbling and falling down.

The ceremony of "passing through the door" sustains a very important relation to the welfare of children, according to the sentiment and practice of many Chinese. Some families have it performed regularly every year; others every second year, as in the first and third; others every third year, as the third and sixth; and so on, until the child is sixteen years old, or the ceremony of "going out of childhood" is observed. Sometimes, when a child is sickly, the door is passed through once or twice per month, or several times in the course of the year, according to the condition of the child and the will and ability of the parents. Probably there are few families here which do not have this ceremony performed more or less frequently between the third day after the birth of a child and the period when it is supposed to pass out of the control of "Mother."

A day is usually spent in "passing through the door" and its attendant ceremonies. Several priests of the Tauist sect (never any of the Buddhist sect) come to the residence of the lad's parents in the morning, and first arrange an altar, made out of tables placed one upon another. On the uppermost of the tables they place censers, candlesticks, and various images of their gods. Behind the altar they suspend three paper-hangings, upon which are painted several tens of goddesses, among whom that of "Mother" occupies a conspicuous position. In a convenient

"PASSING THROUGH THE DOOR."

part of the room is placed a table, having upon it five, eight, or ten plates of meats, vegetables, fruits, and cakes. After everything is properly arranged, one of the priests rings a bell while chanting his formulas, another beats a drum, another strikes his cymbals together, &c. The grand object of this is to invite certain goddesses to be present, which is supposed to be done when their names and places of residence have been repeated in the accustomed manner. The celebrated female divinities who are honoured as midwives or "mothers," and who are believed to be particularly concerned in the rearing of children, or who originally lived in the surrounding country, are invited to be present.

At the proper time, usually in the afternoon, these goddesses are invited to partake of a feast. Besides eight or ten kinds of food, there are also provided a wash-bowl of hot water, and a towel, a fan, and cosmetics and artificial flowers for the especial use of the female divinities in making their toilet before partaking of the feast. The priests ring a bell, beat a drum, and clap their cymbals, reciting their liturgies for an indefinite time, which constitutes an invitation for those goddesses to partake of the collation.

Some time during the afternoon a table is placed in the front part of the room, "before the heavens," as its relative position is called, and on it is put a common rice measure, having various articles in it, and seven little piles of rice are arranged on the table in the position of the seven stars which make up the Dipper in the constellation of the Great Bear. On each of these piles of rice is placed a kind of lamp. Incense, candles, and lamps are all lighted up, and three priests, one standing in front of the table and the other two at its ends, perform the ceremony of "worshipping the measure" in the usual manner.

The "door" is finally passed through in the middle of the afternoon or near sundown. This door is made out of bamboo, covered with red and white paper, and is some seven feet high by two and a half or three feet wide, costing perhaps twelve or fifteen cents. The furniture in the room is so arranged that the priests and the party which passes through this door can go around and around without doubling on their track. Sometimes a table is placed near the centre of the room, and an open space is left on all sides of it. One of the priests—who wears a fancy-coloured skirt, and has on his head a curiously-shaped head-dress—takes in one hand a small bell, or a sword having small bells fastened to the handle, and in the other a horn, and commences reciting formulas or incantations in front of this door, which is often at this time standing near the centre of the room. The priest, thus dressed, personates "Mother" in the act of performing magic spells for the purpose of saving children from evil spirits and unhealthy and malignant influences. The pater-familias calls the children of the family together. He takes the one which cannot walk or which is sick in his arms, and the other children, if any, each take a single stick of lighted incense in their hands. The priest after a while blows his horn, and advances slowly through the door. He is followed by the pater-familias or his representative, and all the children of the family, who thus pass through the door. All the other priests are at this time doing something to aid, as beating the drum and clapping their cymbals. The head priest brandishes the sword in the air, or in its place he sometimes flourishes a whip made in the shape of a snake, as though he was striking an invisible object.

The door is then taken and placed at one of the four corners of the room, and the priest, father, and children again pass through it in a similar manner. It is then successively placed at each of the other corners, and again in the centre, where it is respectively passed through by the priest and his followers. Soon after this the door is hacked in pieces, and its parts set on fire and burned in the open court of the house, or in the street in front of the house where the ceremony is performed.

While performing this ceremony, a small wooden image, a foot high, more or less, is invariably used to represent the child for whose special benefit it is celebrated. When first performed for any child, a new one is obtained to represent it ; and when not used, it is carefully preserved. Oftentimes it is placed by the side of "Mother's" image in the bedroom. The name of the child is usually written on the back of the image. In case the child dies before sixteen years of age, this image is placed in the coffin with its corpse, and buried with it. After the cere-mony of "going out of childhood" has been performed, it is often used as a plaything by the children of the family. In case the child is exceedingly sick, and may not be carried in person through the door, this image, with or without some of the clothing of the child placed on a platter, is taken and carried through the door, instead of the child, which amounts to the same thing as though the child itself was carried through.

The design of all this is to benefit the children, causing them to recover if sick or feeble, continuing them in health if well, and enabling them to arrive at a good old age. The performance is oftentimes quite showy and imposing, at least in the estimation of the Chinese. The expense ranges from two to ten or twelve dollars for each celebration. Usually the priests are entertained with a part of the provisions used on the occasion.

Some families, at the close of this ceremony, have a table spread with food for the hungry spirits in the lower regions, consisting of vegetable soup, rice, two or more plates of biscuit or bread-cakes, large and small, perhaps three plates of meats, mock-money and mock-clothing; incense and candles are also provided, and set on fire at the proper time. A priest is employed to ring his bell and chant his liturgy. Spirits in the lower regions are believed to have an important influence for good or for evil in the affairs of this world, and many parents are quite solicitous to secure their friendship and kind offices in behalf of their children.

Many parents, after the first shaving of the head of a child, when one month old, allow the hair to grow on a part of the top of the head, if a boy, in the shape and of the size of a small peach, until eight or ten years old, or even until sixteen years old; if a girl, a patch of hair is often allowed to grow on one or both sides of the head. Many Chinese seem to be at a loss why the tuft is left. Some explain that which is left on the pate of a boy to be for a defence of the soft part of the skull. They all seem to regard it as an omen of good, or a kind of charm, and conducive to the health or welfare of the child.

Sometimes neither the "peach" nor the cue is allowed to grow until the lad is some six or eight years old, the whole head being regularly shaven. The cause of this delay is sometimes said to be the death of his father or mother when it was decided to let one or both of these grow. Sometimes, in the case of him who is the only son of his parents, and born long after their marriage, they vow to give him up to be the child of some idol or to be a Buddhist priest. They will not then let his hair grow on his pate until six or eight years old. Their object in making this vow, and in treating their dearly beloved son in this way, is to procure good health and longevity to the lad. They apply various sorts of derogatory names or epithets to him, as "Buddhist priest," "beggar," "refuse," "dirt," imagining that he will thus be allowed to live, and that no evil spirit or influence will injure his health. By and by, when he seems to be established in health, they allow his hair to grow like other boys.

A singular custom, which derives its name from the fact that mock-money is burned monthly, is extensively practised at this place in families which have few and sickly children. The Chinese believe that there is a god and goddess of the bedstead, a goddess who rules over the eaves of a house, and a goddess who presides over the bedroom. Many families therefore burn mock-money,

and incense, and candles, to the honour of this god and these
goddesses, regularly on the first and fifteenth of every month.
The children of the family at whose house this is done are made
to kneel down near the places while the mock-money is burning,
and one of the heads of the household call upon the god or the
goddesses referred to to protect their children, and make them
grow fast, easy to nurse and take care of, have a good appetite
for their rice, &c.   It is expected that in this way the god and
goddess of the bedstead will be led to use their influence, and
cause the children to lie down quietly and sleep soundly when
their parents wish, whether by night or by day; that the goddess
of the eaves will keep them from stumbling or falling down on
the stones near or under the eaves of every house; and that the
goddess of the bedroom will make them tractable in nursing,
and good-natured.

The birthday of the goddess "Mother" falls on the fifteenth
day of the first month in the Chinese year.   On that day she
is universally worshipped by married women and by midwives.
Many married women go to some of her temples at that time and
implore her blessing.   It is an established custom at this place
for a midwife to visit the families, if living sufficiently near her
residence, where she has officiated within sixteen years, for
the purpose of collecting contributions from them to aid her in
worshipping "Mother."   She expects a sum of money varying
from a few tens of cash to several hundreds, according to the
wealth and social standing of the family, a couple of candles, a
bundle of incense-sticks, several large sheets of mock-money,
representing silver and gold, and some fresh flowers. Sometimes
she receives only a present of money. The candles, incense, and
mock-money are professedly burnt before the image of "Mother"
in her house, and the money is to be used in meeting the necessary expense of the ceremony of "passing through the door,"
for the especial benefit of the children whom she has helped into
the world. She furnishes each family a kind of schedule, which
is returned to her after having been filled up with the names
and precise ages of the children in the family in which she has
fulfilled the duties of a midwife.   This document is burned at
the proper time, during the performance of "passing through
the door," which is done at her expense, and in her own house,
before the image of "Mother," which she worships. "Mother"
is supposed in this manner to become acquainted with the express
wishes of the midwife, and to be reminded of the importance of
her kind offices in behalf of those children whose names are thus
submitted to her inspection.

H

On the fourteenth or fifteenth day of the eighth month, there is very frequently performed a ceremony called sometimes "worshipping the measure." Although almost universally celebrated in families having weak and sickly children, every year, the Chinese seem to have very often exceedingly indistinct ideas in regard to this custom. The expressions "southern measure" and "northern measure" occur frequently in their efforts to describe it. These two terms are explained as referring to two stars, or collections of stars, one in the northern heavens, and the other in the southern heavens. When worshipped, they are most usually represented by their names being written on paper when any emblem is needed. Pictures or images of them, when made, represent two grave old men. The "north measure" is supposed to be the god of longevity, and to regulate or fix the time of one's death, having the control of the book in which such dates are recorded. The "south measure" is regarded as the god of official emolument, or the god which regulates one's salaries and income during life. In other words, one is the divinity which rules over death, and the other the divinity which rules over life. They are often worshipped on the birthdays of children, and of adults when sick. When worshipped about the middle of the eighth month, it is usually done for the benefit of children of the family sick or well, the object being to secure to them longevity and plenty of money.

The origin of this custom is traced by the Chinese themselves to a certain historical incident, as follows :—

A long while ago, a certain lad, on going into the street one day, met an old man, who proved to be a celebrated fortune-teller named Kuan-lo. He addressed the lad, saying, "You are a fine boy. What a pity that your life is to be so short." The lad at once asked him how long it was to be, and he told him that he was to die at the age of nineteen. This frightened the lad, who was near that age, and he went home crying, and told his mother what he had heard. She, in turn, was made very sad also, but told the lad to go and inquire farther of the fortune-teller. He did so, and was instructed to take a plate of preserved venison and a bottle of wine, and carry them to the top of a certain mountain, where he would find two old men playing chess. He was told to place the venison and the wine down by them without saying a word, and then wait patiently until they had finished the game, when he might advance and make known his requests. The lad proceeded to do as he was instructed, and was surprised to find two men there engaged in a game of chess. After he had silently placed the food and drink by them, they kept on playing until they had finished the game, without noticing the lad. They then seemed hungry, and began to eat of the provisions they saw by their side. After they had done eating and drinking, the lad advanced and told his story, weeping while talking, and besought them to save him from dying at so early an age. They heard the lad, and then took out their records, and found, on examination, that his life was indeed nearly finished, according to the record. They, however, took a pen, and interpolated before the nineteen the Chinese figure for nine, thus making the record read ninety-nine. They then ordered the boy to return home and tell the old man he met in the street that he must not do in like manner again ; that the time appointed by Heaven was not to be divulged to mortals. The lad thanked those old gentlemen, who were no other than the "north measure" and the "south measure," went home, and narrated to his mother what had occurred.

In worshipping the measure, the Chinese, instead of the dried venison, use a few small balls of a kind of Dutch cheese made of the milk of the domesticated buffalo. They also use candy made out of molasses in which hemp-seed has been mixed, some of the root of the lotus, vermicelli, several dishes of meats, fowl, and fish, seven bowls of pea-soup, ten cups of wine, and three cups of tea, arranged on a table. On the table also is placed a rice measure with a flaring top, half filled with rice. On the outside is a Chinese representation of the seven stars which make the Dipper. In it, at each of the four corners, is placed some utensil, viz., a case containing a set of money-scales, a foot-measure, a pair of shears, and a small metallic mirror. Besides these, ten chopsticks are arranged around the sides of the measure in a perpendicular position. It also contains one stick of incense, two candles, an oil-lamp, and a small wooden image, being the representative of the child for whose benefit the ceremony is performed.

A priest of the Tauist sect spends a short time by the side of the table, chanting his formularies adapted to the occasion, and then departs, to go through the same at some other house, as very many families observe the same custom on this day for the welfare of their children.

Some time during the spring, usually in the fourth month, according to established custom, schoolmasters invite their pupils to a feast, where they engage in the worship of Confucius. It is customary for pupils each to make a small present of money to their teachers at this time, which is appropriated, in part at least, toward defraying the expenses of the feast. As there is no image of Confucius for use on such occasions, a slip of red paper, of only a few inches in length, on which has been written in black ink an expression meaning " the Teacher, a pattern for 10,000 ages," is put up on the wall of the schoolroom. In front of this inscription is placed a table, having upon it a censer and a brace of candlesticks. When everything is ready, the teacher, having first lighted and put in the censer three sticks of incense, and in the candlesticks a couple of candles, kneels down before the table, and placing his hands on the floor, bows his head toward the earth slowly and reverently three times. He then arises, and one of his pupils takes his place before the table, and kneels down, making the same number of bowings in the same manner. Another pupil now takes the place, and performs the same ceremony ; and so on, till all have engaged in the worship of the sage. After this, the food which is to be consumed in the feast is placed on the table before the red paper inscription to Confucius, where it remains a short time. It is then removed to another table or tables, around which the teacher and his pupils gather and partake of it. Before the feast, the teacher usually presents to each one of his pupils a white paper fan, on which he sometimes writes a quotation from the classics, or a favourite and popular stanza of poetry. Besides this, he provides a number of toys equal to the number of his pupils, each representing a graduate of the first, second, or third literary degrees, which are distinguishable by the shape and colour of their dresses. It is decided by the throwing of dice in what order the pupils shall choose these toys. These toys are valued as an omen for good, or rather as an index of the success in study which each may hope to attain.

On a Chinese youth entering a school as pupil for the first time in any year, he is expected to bring with him two small candles, a few sticks of incense, and a small quantity of mock-money, which are to be lighted and consumed before a slip of paper having some title of Confucius written upon it, the pupil making the customary prostration, or bowing before it, after these things have been lighted and while they are being consumed. This is called " entering school," or " worshipping the sage." One morning, some six years ago, a lad, dressed in his best clothes, marched into a free school under the charge of a missionary, carrying, besides his books, three sticks of incense, two small candles, and a few sheets of mock-money, designed, in accordance with established usage, as an offering to the Chinese sage. It seemed that the teacher had neglected to inform his parents that in the Mission school those who studied the books of Jesus did not burn incense in honour of Confucius.

The ceremony called "going out of childhood" is performed by many families when each of their children is sixteen years old or thereabouts. It is very nearly like the ceremony called "passing through the door." The theory entertained is, that at sixteen years of age the boy emerges from boyhood into manhood, and the girl from girlhood into womanhood. From the time of the performance of this ceremony, the goddess of children, "Mother," ceases to have the superintendence of the boy or the girl, and the individual comes under the government of the gods in general.

Some families delay the celebration of this custom for a year or two after, or have it performed earlier, than the usual time, in case their children are expecting to marry soon after or before they are sixteen years old, making it come a short time antecedent to the marriage-day. Other families, in consequence of extreme poverty, or because their ancestors have not been in the habit of celebrating the ceremony, or for some other reasons, do not celebrate it at all on the arrival of their children at adult age, as the age of sixteen years may not improperly be styled. The child becomes a man or woman at this time, or becomes of age. He or she, at the age of sixteen years, becomes amenable to punishment if guilty of crime. If guilty and convicted before this period, it is said the culprit must be imprisoned until the proper age is reached, when punishment may be legally inflicted.

Let it not be understood, because one becomes of age or arrives at adult age in China when sixteen years old, that he comes out from the legal control of his parents at this time. While his parents are alive, a son must continue to obey them. Such is the doctrine of the classics, the laws, and the customs of China. No matter how old, how educated, how wealthy—except he has become an officer of the Government, and while he is serving the emperor—he must render prompt and implicit obedience to his father and mother. After he has become an official, and is away from his paternal home in the service of the state, he is subject to the commands of the emperor. His parents cannot then control him in any respect, though he must conform in everything to the established customs of the empire in regard to his parents. The time never arrives when a man in a private station, while his parents are living, may engage in the pursuit he chooses, or may keep his earnings for himself, or

spend them as he pleases, without their free consent and
approval. His wages are given to them, and they can oblige
him to do anything or take any course they please, without
asking his consent or caring for his preferences. Such is said
to be law; but in fact and in practice he is treated with some
consideration, often consulted, and his wishes frequently complied with.

A daughter, after she is married, is not subject to her own
parents, but comes under the control of her husband's parents,
if they are living. To them she is often little different from
a slave. Very frequently she is treated by them with great
cruelty.

After the son has attained his sixteenth year, in case of
the decease of his father, he generally manages the outside
affairs of the family pretty much as he pleases, unless his
mother should happen to be a strong-minded woman. The
classic says the woman has three obeyings: 1st, She must
obey her father (before her marriage); 2d, She must obey her
husband (after marriage); and 3d, she must obey her son
(after her husband's death), i.e. when he shall have arrived
at mature age.

The principle of a woman's obeying her son after the decease
of her husband must not be understood as allowing him to
abuse, or insult, or injure her. Neither would custom tolerate
nor the laws justify such unfilial conduct.

In cases of extreme unfilial conduct, parents sometimes accuse
their children before the magistrate, and demand his official aid
in controlling or punishing them; but such instances are comparatively rare. It is said that, should a parent whip his child
to death for unfilial conduct, notice would seldom or never be
taken of it in the shape of a prosecution of the parent before
the magistrate; only the maternal uncles of the disobedient lad
or man would have a right to interfere in the case. When a
parent brings his incorrigible son before the magistrate for filial
impiety, and demands punishment to be inflicted, the maternal
uncles of the accused have a right to interfere or to be consulted,
especially in case very severe punishment, as death, should be
demanded by the indignant and dishonoured parent. It is
affirmed that no magistrate would dare to whip an unfilial child
to death at the instigation and demand of his parents without
first consulting and obtaining the testimony or consent of his
maternal uncles. They are required to bear witness to the
character and the conduct of their nephew who is under prosecution. The magistrate may exercise his prerogative of advising

the parent in regard to the course to be pursued, as well as of exhorting the refractory son in regard to his duty; but he may not set himself firmly against carrying out the punishment demanded by the offended parent. If the parent requires his son to be publicly whipped by the command of the magistrate, the latter is obliged to order the infliction of the whipping. If the former demands a public exposure of his son in the wooden cangue, with the crime of "not filial" written upon it, then the latter must cause the son to be thus punished for a specified time. If, after punishments, the son remains undutiful and disobedient, and his parents demand it at the hands of the magistrate, the latter must, with the consent of the maternal uncles of the individual, cause him to be taken out to the high wall in front of the yamun, and have him there publicly whipped to death.

If a son should murder his parent, either father or mother, and be convicted of the crime, he would not only be beheaded, but his body would be mutilated by being cut into small pieces; his house would be razed to the ground, and the earth under it would be dug up for several feet deep; his neighbours living on the right and the left would be severely punished; his principal teacher would suffer capital punishment; the district magistrate of the place would be deprived of his office and disgraced; the prefect, the governor of the province, and the viceroy would all be degraded three degrees in rank. All this is done and suffered to mark the enormity of the crime of a parricide.[1]

[1] "A man and his wife had beaten and otherwise severely ill-used the mother of the former. This being reported by the Viceroy to Pekin it was determined to enforce in a singular manner the fundamental principles of the empire. The very place where it occurred was anathematized as it were, and made accursed. The principal offenders were put to death : the mother of the wife was bambooed, branded, and exiled for her daughter's crime ; the scholars of the district, for three years, were not permitted to attend the public examinations, and their promotion thereby stopped ; the magistrates were deprived of their office and banished. The house in which the offenders dwelt was dug up from the foundations. 'Let the Viceroy,' the edict adds, 'make known this proclamation, and let it be dispersed through the whole empire, that the people may all learn it. And if there be any rebellious children who oppose, beat, or degrade their parents, they shall be punished in like manner. If the people, indeed, know the revenerating principle, then fear and obey the imperial will, nor look on this as empty declamation. I instruct the magistrates of every province severally to warn the heads of families, and elders of villages, and on the second and sixteenth of every month to read the sacred instructions, in order to show the importance of the relations of life, that persons may not rebel against their parents, *for I intend to render the empire filial.*'"—Davis's *Chinese.*

CHAPTER V.

WHEN the Chinese are sick they oftentimes have recourse to some god or goddess which they suppose has the control of the particular disease with which they are taken. They burn incense before the image, and implore a speedy recovery. If they should recover, the credit is given to the divinity worshipped, and an offering of meats or vegetables is made.

If the person dies, the divinity worshipped is not regarded as to blame, but the thank-offering which would have been rendered in case of recovery is withheld. The death is simply accounted for by saying it is in accordance with the "reckoning of Heaven." They do not seem to regard recovery from illness to be at all connected with the "reckoning of Heaven." If one dies it is because Heaven wills it, or it is according to the decrees of fate. If one recovers it is because the god or goddess which controls the disease wills recovery. It is all to be credited to his or her power and benevolence.

When the members of a family are sick one after the other, the sickness is very often attributed to the evil agency of a god called the "destroying god," which is believed to cause diseases in families. Some families which are afflicted with repeated and inexplicable sickness, having first made a solemn vow to have a ceremony performed, the object of which is to beg or bribe the god to dissipate or destroy these influences, proceed to have it done as soon as the health of their sick ones will admit. They employ several priests belonging to the Tauist sect. The ceremony lasts, according to the option of the families who employ the priests, from one day and one night to three days and three nights, according to the amount of money they determine to expend on the occasion. They erect a temporary altar out of common tables. On this are arranged various portable images of gods, candlesticks, censers, and implements used in the ceremony. Oftentimes a large amount of meats and vegetables is also offered. The priests chant their liturgy or formularies, ring their bells, and march in concert around the altar. The merit of their performances is all supposed to go to the benefit of the sick, and it is hoped that the "destroying" demon will be prevailed upon to extirpate the baneful influences under his control, letting the sick not only get well, but keep well.

Should any one who has had general good health be suddenly and mysteriously taken with dizziness in his head, pain in his eyes, or with inability to use his hands or feet as usual, his illness is not unfrequently ascribed to the influence emanating from some one of seventy-two malignant spirits or gods. Immediate measures must be taken to counteract or expel this evil influence. A table is placed in the lightest part of the room in which the sick man is. On it are arranged three cups of wine, a platter having on it five kinds of fruit, and a censer, and a pair of candlesticks. A quantity of mock-money is also procured, ready for burning. A Tauist priest is hired to recite the proper formulas, in order to secure the expelling of this malignant influence from the sick man. Sometimes he invokes the aid of a certain headless demon in this important work. The priest provides himself with a small bell, which he rings while he repeats his formulas ; and with a bowl of water which he sprinkles or snaps with his fingers on the articles offered, and on the sick person. He has also a bundle of various kinds of paper charms ready for use when needed, and a small stick of wood, with which he strikes the table at intervals during the recitation of his formulas. The incense and candles are burning all this while, and at the proper time he sets the mock-money on fire. About the close of the performance he produces three paper charms, one of which is to be stuck up over the door of the room, another is to be worn on the person of the sick, if it be a man, or on her head, if it be a woman ; and the third is to be burnt, and its ashes, mingled with hot water, are to be drank by the sick one. Sometimes one of these charms is suspended on the curtain of the bed on which the afflicted person sleeps, according to the directions of the officiating priest. He is supposed to know which of the different methods of using the charms should be practised in any given case. In case the priest is successful in expelling the malignant influence at an early period, medicine is rarely used in restoring the disabled individual to health. When the evil influence is removed, the person will soon regain his usual degree of health, as a matter of course.

When an important member of a family is taken very ill, and the disease does not yield to medicine or nursing, it is often affirmed to be caused by an evil spirit or influence, only subject to the great gods. A member of the family goes with dishevelled hair, and wearing a white garment around the waist or over the shoulders, to the temple of one of the principal idols worshipped in the city, and beats the drum, which notifies to the god that there is an urgent need of his kind offices. Sometimes the individual carries a stick of lighted incense in his hands, weeping and kneeling down in the streets every short distance. This indicates the greatest distress and danger. On reaching the idol's presence, he hastily lights incense and candles before the god, and proceeds to state, in a kneeling position, the circumstances of the family of the sick person, and the importance of his immediate recovery to health, as having several small children, or as having aged parents dependent on him for support. The applicant begs an *arrow-like* utensil, less than two feet long, on which is sometimes written a single word, "command." This arrow is taken home, and placed in an upright position on the centre of a table, or it is suspended over it, or it is put in a frame prepared for its reception, or in the censer used by the family of the sick man. It is then worshipped, and incense and candles are burnt daily before it in its honour, until the sick person recovers or dies. Should he recover, a thank-offering, consisting of meats, &c. is prepared by the family, and presented before the image of the god on the occasion of returning the "arrow" to the temple from which it was obtained.

If the "arrow" is ineffectual, and the sick person dies, it must be returned to the temple where it belongs, accompanied with a simple offering of mock-money, incense, and candles. These are not to be regarded as a *thank*-offering, but only as tokens of respect, without which the divinity would be offended.

This "arrow" is regarded as the warrant or command of the god invoked for the departure of the evil spirit, or the expulsion of the wicked influences which are supposed to infect the sick person, and constitute the main cause of his illness.

The sick person's illness is sometimes attributed to the spirit of his or her former wife or husband (that is, in a previous state of existence), which, after long search, has finally succeeded in finding its partner. The sick person sometimes declares this to be the fact, or rather the mouth of the sick is used by the spirit to make the disclosure. In such a case, some one of the family makes a vow to have performed a certain ceremony, the object of which is to "ferry over" the wandering spirit; or they employ a magician to perform a certain other ceremony for the relief of the sick, by "catching" the spirit which possesses or disturbs him. If such a procedure does not result favourably, a resort is finally had to some popular divinity, by soliciting an arrow, as above described.

Sometimes a person is suddenly attacked with an unaccountable disease. His family attribute it to some god or goddess unknown, which has become offended through some act or word of the person, and which, as a punishment, has sent the disease upon him. After such a conclusion, one of the family takes three sticks of incense in his hand, approaches the individual, and fervently and reverently inquires, in substance, "What god has this man offended that he is thus afflicted? I beg that the divinity will make it known by the mouth of the sick, so that I may readily go and render thanks." If the sick person then should speak the name of any god or goddess, it is taken for granted that such a god or goddess has been the cause of his illness. Offerings of meats and vegetables, together with incense, candles, and mock-money, are, according to custom, prepared and presented before an image of the divinity whose name was mentioned by the afflicted one. The object of all this is to propitiate the goodwill of the divinity, and thus expedite the recovery of the patient.

Sometimes recourse is had to divination, by means of a tortoise-shell and three ancient cash, in order to ascertain what divinity has been offended, and what must be done to propitiate it, and where the ceremony must be performed, &c.

Often the sick person will himself (speaking for the god offended) declare the day, month, and year when he abused or paid manifest disrespect to some idol in a specified place, and that his soul is to be taken to the lower regions to suffer punishment for this sin, which punishment it now becomes the object of the family to prevent, by propitiating the offended divinity through offerings of meats, incense, and mock-money.

It is a very prevalent belief among the common people that those who insult the images of the gods and goddesses worshipped here will be seized with colic, or with some painful disease, as the positive punishment for such conduct.

Sometimes, when one is taken with sudden and severe pains, and becomes quite ill, or when one's business goes wrongly, and he loses money, such a state of things is frequently ascribed to the grudge or enmity of the spirit of some person, now deceased, but who was offended, either in the present or in a former state of being, by the sick man, or the man whose business languishes, or by his ancestors, for whose follies or for whose vices he is held responsible, and for whom he is made to suffer. In view of such suspicions, the family proceed to prepare several suits of paper clothing, a miniature paper umbrella, several pairs of small straw sandals, and a large sheet of paper. They provide also an offering of meats, mock-money, candles, and incense. Several priests belonging to the Tauist religion are then invited to repeat "the formula for dissolving or untying grudges." They perform the ceremony either in the sick man's house or in some temple, burning the paper articles and offering the eatables according to the established custom. The object of this is to propitiate the inimical spirit, or cause it to take its departure.

If one has very painful ulcers, malignant sores, or inflamed eyes, recourse is often had, by some of his family on his behalf, to a god of medicine, in somewhat the following manner : The friend goes to the temple erected in the god's honour and for his worship, but, as the god is quite deaf, he must be aroused and interested in an extraordinary way. Some, therefore, rub or tickle one of his ears, and then present their requests, speaking into his organ of hearing thus excited. Others rub the part of the image which corresponds to the part of the body of the sick man which is affected, in order that the god may know precisely where his services are needed. The suppliant, having burned incense and candles before the image of the "Doctor," returns to the home of his relative, the patient, carrying some of the ashes taken from the censer standing before the god, or from the medicine-box of one of his attendants, whose images stand near by. Now these ashes represent the "Doctor," and must therefore be treated with respect and reverence by the family. They are done up in red paper, and placed in the censer belonging to the household, and incense and candles are daily burned before them, accompanied with kneeling and bowing. If the man's boils or ulcers disappear soon after this, it is attributed to the efficacy of the god of medicine, and the man must make a thank-offering to him in the temple, consisting of five or ten dishes of vegetables (no meats), with the customary burning of candles, incense, and mock-money, returning at the same time the ashes which were previously obtained from the temple. This doctor is a Grahamite.

They get ten men to become " security " for the sick person. When one is sick, and medicine seems to do no good, sometimes his relatives and friends, of ten different families, endeavour to benefit him by becoming a kind of "security" for him. Each family contributes one hundred cash, which is paid into the hands of a member of his family. They purchase a quantity of eatables, as pork, fish, fowl, eggs, fruit, wine, cakes, &c. and provide a feast for these ten friends in a temple. These articles are, however, first presented before the idol worshipped there, as an offering, in order to obtain the aid of the god in restoring the sick man to health. The names of these ten persons, written on a piece of paper, are also burned before the idol, as a fancied security for him. Besides, several priests are employed to recite their formulas, and perform certain other ceremonies for the benefit of the sick man. After the conclusion of these preliminaries, the articles provided are arranged on tables for eating, and the ten friends, the priests, and other guests, sit down to the feast. When the representative of the family returns home, he carries a certain wooden vessel, holding about a peck, being four-sided, and larger at the top than at the bottom, containing some rice, ten chopsticks, which are placed in an upright position around the sides of the measure, also one pair of shears, one foot-measure, one metallic mirror, and one money-balance or scales. These four articles are placed in the centre of the four sides. In the centre of the measure is a burning lamp, in front of which, or on the sides of which, are two candles and three sticks of incense, all lighted ; and, finally, a small wooden stick or image representing the sick individual.

As soon as he reaches home, some of the rice in the measure is immediately taken and made into congee, which is given to the sick man to eat, if possible. The measure, with its contents, is placed in the room where the sick one is. The lamp, the candles, and the incense are allowed to burn as long as they will. They must go out of themselves, and not be extinguished by design, as that would be a very inauspicious omen.

When one is very sick, the following method is adopted to prevent the death of the sick man, and restore him to health. Several priests of the Tauist sect are engaged to repeat their formulas in a temple for his benefit. At the house, or near it, another ceremony is performed ; sometimes, however, that too is performed in the temple. A bamboo, eight or ten feet long, having fresh green leaves at its little end, is provided. Near this end there is often fastened a white cock. One end of a red cord is tied around the centre of a two-foot measure, and the other end is made fast around the bamboo, among the green leaves. A coat belonging to the sick man, and very recently worn, is suspended on this measure, its ends being put into the arm-holes of the garment. A metallic mirror, having a handle to it, is then tied on this measure in such a manner that it will come a few inches above the shoulders of the garment, in the place where the head of an individual would come were the coat to be worn. Some one of the family takes this bamboo pole

BRINGING BACK THE SOUL OF THE SICK INTO HIS CLOTHES ON THE BAMBOO.

and holds it loosely in his grasp in a perpendicular position, standing not far from the house, or in the temple if conveniently near. A priest now begins to call over the name of the sick person, and to ring his bell, and to repeat certain incantations, the object of which is to cause the sick man's spirit to enter the coat. The white cock and the bright mirror are supposed to perform an important part in effecting this desirable object. After a while the pole is sometimes observed to turn round slowly in the hands of its holder, which circumstance is believed to be a sure proof of the presence of the spirit of the sick man in the coat. At the conclusion of the ceremonies the coat is taken from its place on the bamboo pole, and placed as soon as possible on the body of the sick man, or it is spread over him as he lies on his bed, if he is too sick to allow its being put on properly.

It should have been premised that the spirit of the sick man is supposed to have left his body, and yet to be hovering around in the vicinity. It is supposed also that it can be induced by the performance of the ceremonies above described to return to the coat which has been but recently worn by the person to whom the said spirit belongs; and, if it but enters the coat, it can be transferred to the body of the sick man, and perhaps be prevailed upon to remain there.

There is a very singular method of treating unimportant diseases of children, or their common pains, as headache, colic, &c. very frequently resorted to by their parents at this place. A small book, said to have been made a long while ago by one who was then the chief of Tauist priests, contains a list of days, with directions how children should be treated who are taken with certain symptoms on these days. If a parent wishes to follow out the teachings of this book, when his child is sick, he has only to look for the day and the hour when it was taken unwell, and ascertain whether there is any correspondence between the symptoms given therein and the symptoms of his sick child. If there should be a correspondence, he is instructed what to do to remove the disease from his child, and also what evil spirit is the cause of the illness. What he is instructed to do is designed to appease this spirit. Specific directions are given, according to the time, disease, and spirit concerned.

When one is very sick, sometimes a ceremony is performed, the object of which is principally to propitiate the god which, according to them, rules over the current year. The ceremony takes its distinctive name from a rude picture of a human being drawn on or cut out of a piece of paper, representing the sick man. This is pasted on a slip of bamboo. About one hundred pieces of mock-money having been pasted into a certain form, and placed together in a square or round package, the paper image is stuck into it by means of the bamboo slip. This package is then put into an open, shallow bamboo basket, such as farmers use oftentimes for drying grain. A plate containing a small piece of uncooked pork, one duck's egg, a little fowl's blood, and one unbaked cake, is also placed on this shallow basket, with three cups of wine, and some incense and candles. This basket and its contents are then placed under a table, on the ground, or on a low stool. On the top of this table are also placed a pair of candlesticks, and a censer for candles and incense, together with five, or eight, or ten plates of meat, fish, fowls, bread, and vermicelli. After the officiating priest has recited his formulas and incantations, some member of the sick man's family takes the package of mock-money, having the paper image still sticking in it, and, holding it so that the face or front of the image shall be toward the outside of the house, carries it out of doors. The priest follows him after pronouncing one or two sentences, ordering the departure of the disease,

PRIEST ASCENDING A LADDER OF KNIVES.

or whatever troubles the sick man. After both parties are out
of the house, and while standing in the street, the priest spouts
from his mouth some water over the man, and the mock-money,
and the representative image. Afterward the image and the
mock-money are burned, and the whole ceremony is concluded
by the company feasting on the edibles which have been offered
to the presiding and governing deity for the current year. This
representative image is supposed to carry off whatever interferes
with the recovery of the sick man. The bread, the vermicelli, and
the duck's egg are all omens of good, and sustain an important
relation.

Sometimes a company of Tauist priests are engaged by the
family of a sick man to perform their incantations and repeat
their formulas for his benefit, accompanied by *ascending a ladder
of knives.* A ladder is extemporised for the occasion, the rounds
of which consist of swords or long knives, with the edge upward.
At a certain part of the performance, one of the priests, barefooted, ascends this ladder, and, after arriving at the top, he
stands there a while and recites some spells for the relief of the
sick man. It is thought that
the wicked spirits, who take
delight in troubling mankind,
will see the swords, and will be
frightened, not daring to approach the man to do more evil.
The gods, too, it is hoped, will
thus be influenced to take pity
on the afflicted man, and expedite his recovery to accustomed
health.

The Chinese dread the ravages
of the small-pox and of the
measles among their children.
They have goddesses to cure
these diseases. From the time
when it is known that a child
has the small-pox until its recovery, there is more or less worship of some goddess of small-
pox.

GODDESS OF SMALL-POX.

On the third day after the pustules have begun to appear, it
is a universal custom for one of the family to go to a baking
establishment and procure ten small bits of Chinese yeast.

I

These are steamed in the usual vessel for steaming rice belonging to the family. They soon begin to swell, and become several times larger than they were before steaming. These are then removed from the steamer, and placed before the picture of the goddess, or whatever represents her majesty. The design of this operation is to cause her to exert her influence to have the pustules redden, fill up, and swell out, in resemblance to the swelling out of the balls of yeast when steamed. Two days after this, ten more of the yeast bits are procured, steamed, and presented before the goddess, in a similar manner and for the same purpose. After waiting two days more, ten bits of yeast are again treated in the same way. The most important and critical period is said to be these seven days after the pustules first appear.

On the ninth day an offering is generally made to the goddess, designed as an expression of thanks for her goodness in case the pustules have filled well, and the child is getting better. The offering consists of fish, meat, fowl, and vegetables. If the child should not be doing well on the ninth day, the thanksgiving is deferred, or, if the child should have died, no thanksgiving is made.

After the pustules have come out, and before the end of the seventh day, whenever it thunders, some member of the family beats on a drum or gong, placed ready for use when circumstances demand. The noise produced in this way is kept up as long as the thunder lasts. The beater has some one to assist him, telling him when the thunder has ceased, as the beater of the drum or gong is unable to tell when there is no thunder. The object of this is to prevent the pustules of the small-pox from breaking or bursting. As some explain the custom, the ringing of the bell or the beating of the drum, producing very familiar sounds, is designed to keep the lad from being frightened by the noise of the thunder, and from doing anything which would cause the pustules to break. Others say that it is feared that the noise or the reverberations of the thunder will make the pustules sink down and dry up sooner than is desirable, and therefore they use the gong or the drum to counteract such a result.

On the fourteenth day after the lad has been taken down with the small-pox, some one of the family procures a few black beans which have a small green speck upon them, and roast them in the iron vessel used for cooking rice. After roasting these beans until they become brittle, they are placed before the goddess of small-pox. The lad who is the object of solicitude is placed in a sitting posture upon a large winnowing sieve made out of bamboo splints. On the top of his head is then put a small piece of red cloth, and the parched beans are taken from before the goddess and laid upon this red cloth, whence they are allowed to roll off. The scars left by the pustules of this disease are thought to resemble somewhat this bean in their general appearance. The name for the bean, pronounced in the dialect of this place, is identical in sound with the common name for the small-pox.

After it has become known among friends and relatives that the lad has broken out with the small-pox, they oftentimes send to his family presents, such as a few soft sweet cakes, one or two pounds of white sugar or the white date, one or two parcels of arrowroot, or two or three pounds of ham. The design of making these presents is to express their sympathy with the family of the sick lad, and to indicate their hopes that the *scabs of the small-pox may fall off*. The period for making this present, which is named the " scabs of the small-pox falling off," extends from the seventh to the fourteenth day after the pustules begin to make their appearance.

If the child recovers, the family make to those who presented the tokens of their sympathy during his illness a return present, which is regarded as an expression of their gratitude to them for their kindness. The return present consists principally of Chinese sandwiches. The number of these sandwiches sent back varies from fifteen or twenty up to a hundred to each family.

At the end of one month from the appearance of the disease, if the child is well, the family make a thank-offering to the goddess of small-pox for her benevolent and powerful aid in restoring the child to health. The ceremony is oftentimes quite imposing, and the kinds of food presented numerous and of good quality. The poor are frequently able to make but a meagre thank-offering to the goddess, though it is probably as sincere and as kindly received as a thank-offering made of costly and numerous kinds of edibles.

When a child has broken out with the measles, recourse is usually at once had to the goddess of measles for her aid in bringing it to a happy termination. At various times during the progress of the measles, more or less applications are made to her majesty, who is generally represented by a slip of paper on which her name and title have been inscribed. On the recovery of the child, the family offers a thanksgiving in honour of the goddess of measles.

The people believe, or profess to believe, that epidemics in summer, and malignant diseases in general, are under the control of "the five emperors or rulers." This term refers to five idols, or images, much feared by the common people of this place. It is a very usual method of frightening children to

SHORT BLACK DEVIL.

obedience to tell them that the "five emperors will catch them" —that is, will give them the colic.

There are numerous temples dedicated to them. These rulers have several attendants. The representations of two of them are very frequently paraded through the streets, especially in the hot summer months, forming part of an "idol procession." Foreigners usually call them "The Tall White Devil"

TALL WHITE DEVIL.

and "The Short Black Devil," from their general appearance, size, and colour. The former is often eight or ten feet high. Its body consists of a slight bamboo framework, usually covered with light-coloured silk, or bluish or white cotton cloth. It has a head, arms, and hands, but, as it appears in the streets, no feet, and is made to move by a man who gets into it, his own feet being seen below the dress of the image. There is a small hole made in the front part of it, as high from the ground as the head of its carrier comes, so that he can see out, and thus be enabled to walk without the constant danger of falling down, or running against objects. The other image is from four to five feet high, very corpulent and very black, its framework being in like manner made of bamboo. It is also carried by a man or boy inside of it. A hole is made in its hat, so that the person inside can see out. Both of these "devils" are horrid-looking objects, and when seen by the foreigner for the first time, parading in an idol procession, are enough to strike him with dismay, as well as arouse his indignation.

Idol processions, consisting of images of the five emperors borne in pomp in large sedans by eight bearers, and their servants, the white and the black devils, attended by a numerous retinue of living worshippers, as lictors, heralds, &c. had thronged the streets of this city and suburbs in greater numbers and more frequently than in former years for several weeks previous to the appearance of the cholera, which broke out at Fuhchau with great virulence in 1858. These processions marching to and fro, sometimes in the day and sometimes in the evening, through the bye-lanes and narrow streets as well as the main thoroughfares, were accompanied by men and boys furiously beating gongs and drums, and bearing lighted incense before the idols. Each temple dedicated to the worship of the five emperors sent forth its portable images. Sometimes the companies proceeding from different temples, uniting in the streets, would form a long, and, in the estimation of the Chinese, an imposing procession.

The object of this display was to propitiate the goodwill of the five emperors, and to induce them to banish, or to keep away from this city, epidemics and the diseases which usually prevail in hot weather. For this laudable purpose the Chinese were willing to subscribe money to defray the necessary expenses, which, in the aggregate, must have been considerable. It is customary for these processions to appear in the streets in July and August, in order to prevent summer complaints.

These processions were principally brought to an end during the first part of August with the burning, on the banks of the River Min, of several tens of paper boats twenty or thirty feet long. These boats, whose frames were made out of bamboo covered with variously-coloured paper, presented a pretty appearance as they were borne along through the streets to the riverside at night by men with torches. Previous to the carrying forth of each boat from the temple to which it belonged, there was a performance of superstitious ceremonies before it, as it were to consecrate it, consisting, in part, of the burning of incense and candles, the chanting of formulas by priests, with special offerings to the five emperors, attended with the beating of gongs and drums. After arrival at the side of the river, just before burning the boat, all the "black" and "white" devils which happened to be there ran at the top of their speed around the boat, and then reverently kneeled down in a row near by until the flames had consumed it. The object designed to be accomplished by the burning of these boats was to collect and send out to sea the diseases and the unhealthy influences which the five emperors were willing to send away from the place.

But these precautionary sanitary measures proved unavailing. Only a short time after these proceedings were finished, and still while the people were rejoicing in the expected exemption from pestilence in consequence of the conciliation of the gods, and the large amount of good deeds they had performed, the cholera broke out.

The magicians said that the boats were not furnished with funds sufficient to pay the expenses of the ocean voyage; others said that the boats were too small to answer the purpose desired, and of course they were obliged to return to port, in order to part with the diseases they contained. According to the hints or the revelations made by these men, the managers of some of the temples dedicated to the worship of the five emperors again determined to go through the operation of collecting money, sending out the images to parade the streets, and burning boats, in the hope to be more successful in securing for their own particular neighbourhoods exemption from the ravages of the dreaded scourge.

In addition to these processions, which were specially connected with the temples of the five emperors—which to disinterested and unsophisticated foreigners would seem to be sufficient to accomplish the prevention or the expulsion of epidemic diseases, if any sort or amount of idol processions could accomplish it—there was another kind, which became quite general and popular among the Chinese here in view of

the alarming prevalence of the cholera.   It was said that resort
had not been had to this particular kind of idol procession for
thirty or forty years to anything like the extent which it reached
during the August of 1858.

This kind of procession originates with the inhabitants of
different neighbourhoods, who contribute money for its expenses,
and who expect to share its benefits.   The time of performing
it is only during the evening, extending until nearly or quite
midnight.   It consists, in part, of carrying around fancy lanterns,
lighted with tapers, made in a large variety of sizes and shapes
out of several kinds of gaudily-coloured paper.   Some of these
were of the form and dimension of the official red umbrellas of
the mandarins, and, being made to revolve, looked in the evening
very pretty, if regarded only as a toy.   Others took the shape
of the official fans carried before high mandarins when they
appear in the street.   There were also men and boys who carried,
suspended at the end of a bamboo pole, common cheap lanterns,
or who bore nothing but burning torches.   Besides these there
were also some persons who, as they walked along, kept beating
at intervals gongs and drums with all their might, and others
who played on various other kinds of musical instruments ; and
others still who bore with great solemnity some idol seated in a
sedan or or on a kind of throne, having in front, either carried
separately by men or attached to the sedan or throne, incense
and candles burning.   If the image of one of the five emperors
should appear in the procession, then his two servants, the black
devil and the white devil, would be sure to attend him.   If
some other idol should be carried, then men dressed in a manner
which has been chosen to designate or represent his servants
would attend him, besides many other with lamps or lanterns
and torches.   The kind of idol for the occasion being decided
upon by any particular neighbourhood, a certain number of persons would go and prepare to appear in the procession, imitating
the dress, position, and utensils appropriated to the servants of
that idol.

It was one of the privileges of every person who contributed
to pay the expenses of this kind of procession to have it march
in order past his door, if his house was situated upon any street
or alley which allowed of any such passing by of the procession.
This course was believed to insure him and his household immunity from the attacks of the epidemic disease it was designed
to avert.

This sort of procession, besides going through all the alleys

and lanes of its own neighbourhood, frequently united with
similar processions belonging to adjacent neighbourhoods. Then
the din of all the gongs and drums, mingling with the outcries
of the excited multitudes, became almost deafening and dis-
tracting to any one who was nigh, and who did not sympathise
in the performance. It was asserted that by this means the
evil influences and the epidemic diseases which existed in one
neighbourhood or district would surely be driven away to another,
and then from that neighbourhood to another, and so on until
the city and the suburbs became entirely free from their influence
or presence.

All classes of the population seemed to have a personal interest
in these processions, and sanctioned and encouraged them by
their presence and their active assistance.

But these extraordinary measures to cure or remove cholera
signally failed even to protect the performers ; many who took
an active part in the procession themselves fell a prey to the
scourge they hoped in vain to expel. The people, however,
have not grown wiser by their failure. Every year, in the
hottest months, the processions of the five emperors and their
servants parade the streets, that there may be less sickness and
fewer deaths than there otherwise would be.

For two days in the spring and two days in the autumn, the
streets of the city and its southern suburb are paraded by several
thousand men and boys, in connexion with the annual processions of two of the highest gods worshipped in this part of the
empire, in the performance of vows which they have made.

These vows are made either under the open heavens, or before
the images of the god in whose processions they propose to
engage, and relate to their own health, or the health and long
life of their parents, grandparents, and brothers. Most generally
the vows are made in view of the ill-health of parents, or with
a desire to promote their continuance in health and their longevity. The person who makes a vow promises to perform certain
acts for a specified number of years, as for one, two, or ten years,
and in connexion with the annual procession of a certain idol
· through the streets, in case his own health or the health of his
sick relative should be restored.

The performance of this vow, if it relate to benefits believed
to have been already received by himself or his relative, is
regarded in the light of a public thank-offering ; if it relates to
benefits yet in the future, it is regarded in the light of a meritorious act, in view of which it is hoped that the god will bestow

the desired good.   In the case of a vow made in behalf of a sick
person, unless recovery should follow, no token of gratitude is
offered in the public procession.

A few days before the time fixed for the public procession,
those who, in the fulfilment of their vows, expect to take part
in it, go or send a friend to the temple of the god in whose
honour the procession is to be made, and report their names,
and the particular nature of the vow they have made.   These
items are recorded in a book belonging to the temple.   Each
applicant pays the clerk of the temple eight or ten cents, and
receives in return a printed schedule, which is filled out with
his name, and the kind of vow made, and a few other particulars.   This paper is dated and numbered, corresponding to
the order in which application is made.   Two printed slips of
paper are also given to most applicants, which are numbered
in like manner, and are to be used as a kind of seal, as will be
hereafter described.

On the days appointed
for the procession, each of
these classes of performers
of vows appear in the
streets, dressed according
to custom, and having the
appropriate utensils.

Some have a small stool
about one foot long and
four or five inches wide
and high.   On the face of
this stool the two strips
of paper received from the
temple have been pasted
in the form of the letter X.
On one end of the stool
there is a nail, or a piece

WORSHIPPING WITH INCENSE AND STOOL.

of iron, extending upward, having a hole in it, so as to
hold sticks of incense.   These men are all neatly dressed in
short coats, having straw or rush sandals on their feet, and a
yellow charm stuck into the hair of their heads.   Some of
these have also a large wallet suspended from their necks,
coming down to their sides, for the purpose of holding the
incense which they intend to use during the time of parading
the streets.   Thus arrayed, they join the procession very early
in the morning.   After walking along a few paces in the streets

through which the idol they honour is to be carried, at an indefinite distance before it, they turn round, and, facing it, though it may be out of sight, and even several li distant, kneel or squat down, both hands grasping the stool, which is placed on the ground. Usually their knees do not touch the earth, they only making believe, or pretend, to kneel down, balancing themselves on the stools. The end of the stool in which the nail is driven, holding one or three sticks of lighted incense, is turned from the performers and toward the approaching idol. They now rise to an upright position, still grasping the stool with both hands, and reverently raising it about as high as their heads. Then lowering it about as low as their waists, they wheel about, carrying it before them, take a certain number of steps in the street, usually seven or ten steps, when they turn round, and, facing the idol, go through the same ceremony again. They then turn round, go the same distance, wheel about, and pretend to kneel again in a similar manner, and so on until they arrive at the limit of the procession of the idol for that day. On returning home from this place, they do not bow down in the streets, as they did in going to that place. Sometimes a company of four or five persons who have made this vow happen to be together, or very near each other; in such cases they simultaneously turn round toward the idol, place the stool on the ground, pretend to kneel, rise to an upright position, lift up their stool grasped with both hands as high as their heads, wheel about, walk the customary distance, again turn round, and perform the same ceremony.

Another class of persons appear in the procession having a large wooden cangue about their necks, in general shape and appearance like the cangues worn by culprits as a punishment, though not so heavy nor so large. The two slips of printed paper, having the number of the applicants written on it, given at the time of recording their names at the temple, are pasted on the front, or upper side, of the cangues, in imitation of the written inscriptions put by authority of mandarins on the cangues worn by culprits. These have the yellow charm stuck into the hair on their heads, like those who have the stools, and who bow every few paces. They, however, do not kneel down, but walk slowly in the street along which the idol is to be carried. Their number generally is much less than the number of those who carry the stool. Some also wear handcuffs.

Another class of these performers of vows have much smaller

cangues about their necks than the class just described. Sometimes there are two or three thousand of this class in a single procession. Besides wearing the small cangue, which has the two slips of paper pasted on it as on the larger cangues, these persons generally have their hands thrust into a kind of leathern or wooden cuffs. To these cuffs there usually is attached a chain made out of brass wire, which passes over the necks of the wearers. Sometimes those who have cuffs on their hands have no cangue about their necks, but in its place a small chain

WEARING THE CANGUE AS A TOKEN OF GRATITUDE.

which is locked on their neck, the lock coming under their chins. The ends of this chain hang down, or are attached to the cuffs around their wrist.

Sometimes there will be seen in the procession several persons who have on a kind of red coat over their other clothes, and on that will be written a few words denoting in substance that the wearer is to be beheaded. These simply walk slowly along in the crowd.

Another class of persons have neither the cangue for their necks nor cuffs on their hands, nor stools, but carry a single stick of lighted incense. Every few paces these kneel down in the streets, having first turned around so as to face the idol, and still holding the lighted incense in their hands. They then rise up, and, wheeling about, walk along the customary distance, when they turn around and kneel down, and so on, much as those do who carry the stool, as above described.

On returning home from the place where the idol is to turn around and be carried back to its temple, the devotees take off their cuffs, cangue, &c., and carry them in their hands or under their arms, as is most convenient.

Those who dress in red, and who thus profess themselves as willing to suffer capital punishment, are regarded as those who have made the highest or greatest vow possible, in order to promote the recovery of their dear relatives, or to secure their long life. Those who wear cangues on their necks or cuffs on their wrists acknowledge themselves as sinners against the idol in whose honour the procession is made, and voluntarily take the place of culprits.

In the course of a few days subsequent to the public procession, all those who received a schedule on their reporting their names and the vow they have made at the temple a short time before the procession took place, are expected to take this schedule and the two slips of paper torn off their stool or cangue, as the case may be, to the neighbourhood temple near which they live, and burn them before the image of the Great King, accompanied with the burning of incense and candles. At the end of the number of years during which the persons vowed to engage in the procession once annually, as above described, the cangue which they have used is burnt under the open heavens, and an offering of meats and mock-money is presented before the Great King. This Great King is believed, as some affirm, to act the part of a local constable, and report these transactions to his superiors in the other world.

CHAPTER VI.

DEATH, MOURNING, AND BURIAL.

It deserves to be particularly mentioned* that when children or unmarried persons die, many of the customs which will be described are not observed. Generally, it is only when the deceased is an adult and married, and the head of a family, his own parents or grandparents having already deceased, that these customs are observed.

It is very desirable that the members of a family should all be present, if possible, at the moment of the death of its head. Sons, daughters, and the wives of sons, grandchildren, male or female, as well as the brothers and sisters of the dying man, as far as practicable, should gather around his bedside. When the

---

* The character of the Chinese religion is admirably described and summed up by Dr. Gutzlaff as follows:—"Astrology, divination, geomancy, and necromancy, prevail everywhere in China. Though some of these practices are forbidden by the Government, yet the prohibitions are never carried into effect. The Chinese wear amulets, have titular deities, enchanted grounds, &c. all the offspring of China superstition. We lament the deep degradation of human nature in a nation endowed with sound understanding, and nowise destitute of reflecting minds. We, at the same time, cannot help noticing their general apathy towards all religious subjects. They are religious because custom bids them to be so. Forms and ceremonies are the whole which occupy their mind; their hearts scarcely ever participate in any religious worship. That the doctrines of Confucius have greatly contributed to form the national character in this respect is doubtless the fact. With him everything is form, and the outward ceremony is worship. Earthly pursuits fill the whole mind of a Chinese; to gain money, to obtain honour, to see his name propagated in his offspring, are the objects for which he constantly strives. When he has gained his end he relaxes his energy, and calmly enjoys his felicity. He dreads death as the destroyer of all bliss, and frequently builds splendid temples to avert the indignation of the gods on account of his ill-gotten gains. There are few exceptions to this general assertion—that, in religious matters, the Chinese are among the most indifferent people on the earth."

last breath has been drawn, all simultaneously break out into loud lamentation and weeping. Some explain this custom by saying *they thus bid him farewell.* The departure of the dead is attended with doleful outcries and with passionate expressions of grief. The loud lamentation at death is often heard on the death of persons not married, and not the head of a family, nor arrived at adult age.

All beyond death is regarded as dark by the Chinese.. The dead are believed to be unable to see how or where to walk. On this account, *a pair of candles and some common incense are lighted just after the death of a relative,* being generally arranged on a chair by his bedside, or on the bedstead. The incense is put upon a bowl filled with ashes, in a flat position—that is, parallel with the surface of the earth, instead of being placed in an upright position, as usual when burning. The design of the candles is to light the spirit of the dead on its way. The candles are provided by his children or members of his family in the laudable expectation of aiding the dead to find and keep the right path. The proverb says, "One living, is a man, but dead, is a spirit." The spirit is therefore considered able and entitled to receive the odour of incense lighted for its benefit.

After the body has been laid out, a singular custom is observed in many families. Sometimes those families which have no married or betrothed daughters do not practise it on the death of its head. The married daughters, if living within reasonable distance, are expected to return home with their husbands and children.

Several Tauist priests are employed to prepare the "bridge-ladder," and aid in the celebration of the ceremony, at the expense of the son-in-law or sons-in-law of the deceased. A post some seven or eight feet high is placed in a socket or frame standing on the ground, in a perpendicular position. Into holes made in the sides of this post are fastened several tiers of sticks or bamboo, two or three feet long. These sticks project outward and upward a little from the perpendicular post. Sometimes these sticks amount to several tens. The longer ones are placed toward the bottom, and the shorter ones toward the top, the lowest tier being three or four feet from the ground. At the extreme outer end of each is suspended by a wire a kind of glass cup containing oil and wicking, the whole constituting a lamp. On the top of the upright post is placed a candle. Into a hole, about three feet from the ground, made in the upright post, is inserted a pole, projecting at a right angle, some two or three

feet longer than the longest of the sticks having lamps at their end. This "bridge-ladder" is placed in the middle of the room. On one side of the room is placed a table having candles and incense upon it. On the wall or partition of the room by this table are suspended one or two large paper-hangings, relating to the infernal regions. The body of the deceased is lying on one side of the room, or, if there is an adjoining room which can be used, it is placed in it.

When everything is ready, the ceremony is commenced by lighting the lamps and candle on the "bridge-ladder," as well as the candles and incense on the table. The priests chant their liturgy amid the noise of cymbals. The married daughter comes forward, having a white cotton cloth bound about her head, partially concealing her eyes, or she holds to her eyes a white cotton cloth much as one would a handkerchief while crying. The eldest son of the deceased, if there be a living son, now advances, and, taking hold of the end of the long pole, pushes gently against it; the post turning in its socket, the entire "bridge-ladder" moves. The wife of the eldest son, his younger brothers and their wives, the married daughter of the deceased, and her children, &c., now follow slowly the elder brother as he pushes around the "bridge-ladder" for a few times.

In case there is no son, a married or affianced daughter leads the company. During the period that this bridge-ladder is thus made to revolve, all of the party join in loud lamentation and wailing. Their outcry, taken in connexion with the chanting of the priests and the noise of the cymbals, makes a very confused hubbub and tumult of voices and sounds. These, together with the sight of so many lamps and candles burning brightly in broad daylight, produce a very singular spectacle for the foreign beholder, which, once seen, will not be quickly forgotten.

The object of this performance with the bridge-ladder is to lighten and assist the deceased on his way. It is called "bridge-ladder" because it is fancied to resemble a bridge and a ladder. The bridge would aid the dead to pass rivers, and the ladder would help him to climb steep places, should he meet such impediments in his journey.

After the ceremony of "turning around the bridge-ladder" has been concluded, and after the body has been dressed for the coffin according to custom, it is usually placed on the cover of the coffin. The eldest son now approaches and kneels down before the corpse. He then *takes a cup of wine and offers it to the dead* three times. He then takes *some cooked vermicelli,*

K

by means of chopsticks, out of a bowl, and *presents it to the mouth of the dead* for three times.   After this he takes *a bowl of cooked rice*, and makes a presentation in similar manner for three times.   While he is performing these filial acts, all the rest of the family, brothers, sisters, and grandchildren, except the partner of the dead and those higher in rank, kneel down around the corpse and pour out their lamentations.   If the eldest son of the deceased has previously died, his eldest son, if he has one, takes his place.   In case he has no son living, some one who has been adopted as the eldest son performs the ceremony, the second or the third, or any other of their children never performing this ceremony unless adopted as the heir and representative of the eldest son.   Sometimes, in wealthy families, a professor of ceremonies is employed to direct the eldest son in the discharge of his duties on this occasion according to established rules.   The eldest son at this time wears a cap, with his clothing properly arranged, and having shoes upon his feet ; but previously he has appeared with dishevelled hair, clothing disarranged, and in his stocking feet.

The dead man cannot speak.   He is unable to express his approbation or disapprobation of what is done for him by his surviving children.   But this difficulty has been remedied by the Chinese, who fancy *they can tell the wishes or feelings of the dead by the use of cash in a certain manner.*   After the corpse has been clothed, and is about to be put into the coffin, some one takes two common copper cash, and ties them loosely together by a blue or white thread a few inches in length.   These cash are then placed in the sleeve of the dead man.   He is then made, by some one taking hold of his sleeve, to shake them out, so that they shall fall upon the ground.   Their relative positions as they strike are noted and remembered, whether the two obverses come uppermost or the two reverses, or one reverse and one obverse.   These cash are preserved for future use in making inquiries of the dead, previous to his burial, after the table has been arranged before the place of his spirit.   A description of the process of such revelations of the will of the spirit of the deceased, *alias* " spiritual revelations," will be given when speaking of the arranging of the " table before the place of the spirit."

Soon after wine and food have been offered to the dead by the eldest son, and before the corpse is arranged in its grave-clothes, *a small sedan-chair, made of bamboo splints and paper,* and four bamboo and paper diminutive bearers, are arranged on the ground near the house. There are also provided four cups of wine, and four or eight bread-cakes ; one cup, and one or two cakes being put before each bearer. The chair and the bearers, when everything is arranged, are set on fire by some member of the family, attended by one or two priests, who recite their liturgy and clap their cymbals together in approved style. *The chair is provided for the use of the spirit of the dead.* It is charitably supposed that he would enjoy riding, instead of being obliged to walk to the infernal regions. Bearers are also provided for conveying the chair and its occupant, as it seems to be doubtful whether sedan coolies can be readily engaged in the other world. The wine and the cakes are regarded as their wages, though it would appear to be very scant and small considering the length of the journey. The wine they are supposed to imbibe when they feel the need of something exhilarating, and the cakes they use for luncheon *en route.* Though their wages are paid entirely in advance, there seems to be no apprehension lest they should fail in carrying out their contract. Some families provide a fifth man, who is furnished with an umbrella of state, which he is expected to carry in front of the sedan *en route* to the world of shades. He is also thoughtfully provided with his wages in advance. Some affirm that the sedan and bearers are provided for the use of the neighbourhood god, "the Great King," while he is conveying the spirit of the dead down to Tartarus.

The precise time of putting on the *longevity* or *graveclothes* is not fixed. The wealthy families in this place spend a great deal of money in procuring these garments for their dead. Oftentimes many of them are made of silk or crape, and the finest and the most expensive cotton fabrics. It is an established custom that, if three garments are put upon the lower part of the person, five garments must be put upon the upper part. The rule is, that there must be two more upon the upper than upon the lower part of the corpse. Oftentimes there are nine upon the upper and seven upon the lower. Sometimes rich families provide as high as twenty-one pieces for the upper part of the corpse, and nineteen pieces for the lower part. Probably, among the middle classes, about twelve garments are commonly used in dressing a corpse for the coffin. After the grave-clothes have been put on the corpse, it is tightly bound around with several pieces of cloth, usually two of which are white, and one is red. The white cloth comes next to the clothing. Some or all of it is torn up into strips, and, after being wound around the corpse in a certain manner, is tied into a kind of knot, which is considered auspicious or an omen of good. The body is all covered with these auspicious knots. Over the white cloth, or the white silk, if the family can afford it, is put the red cloth, similarly torn into strips, and knotted. The two ends of the red cloth or the red silk are usually cut off, one piece being given to the eldest son, which he divides among his brothers. The other is sometimes given to the sons-in-law of the dead, each having a little piece. This is regarded as an omen of good to those who obtain it.

The children, grandchildren, other relatives, and personal friends gather around to witness the placing of the body in the coffin. Preparatory to this, the corpse, while lying on the cover of the coffin, is turned half way around, so that its head comes where its feet were. The coffin is placed so that its head is toward the front door, or the front of the house. When everything is ready, the corpse is lifted from the coffin cover and placed in the coffin, while the children and grandchildren, &c. break forth into loud lamentation and wailing. The eldest son carries the head of the corpse, and his brothers or other family relatives aid him in placing the body into the receptacle provided. This is made of good wood, quite thick. In consequence of the number of grave-clothes put upon the corpse, the coffin is much larger than otherwise would be necessary to hold the body. On the bottom of the coffin there has been a quantity of ashes spread, and over the ashes some sheets of paper have been placed. Sometimes a large number of small bundles of ashes or lime are placed in the bottom of the coffin and along the sides of the corpse ; or, in place of the ashes, some bundles of the pith out of which artificial flowers are made commonly called rice-paper, are used by some families. Over the corpse a piece of cloth is spread, and the cover is nailed down.

During the performance of all these customs, candles and incense have been kept burning. Subsequently the candles give place to oil lamps in the practice of some families, while incense continues to be incessantly used.

Soon after the lid of the coffin has been nailed down, the children of the deceased produce and arrange in the reception-room of the house a chair, a table, and a bamboo or wooden frame. The frame usually consists of four small posts, about five or six feet high, with cross-pieces or bars, so as to be four or five feet wide, and one or two feet deep. Sometimes this frame is covered over with white paper or white cloth, and the "longevity picture" is hung upon it so that one, on entering the room, can see it readily. The table is placed several feet from the back wall or the partition of the room. Behind it is placed the chair, and immediately behind the chair is placed the frame, having upon it the longevity picture. Near the chair, or under it, is a small foot-stool, on which are placed a pair of shoes. On the chair itself is often placed a coarse-looking rag doll, or, rather, a roll, about one foot high, made out of cotton cloth, which is twisted and knotted, or tied up so as to resemble a human being, especially by the aid of the imagination. This is said to be always used, in case there is no longevity picture, to represent the deceased. This rag doll is made to stand upright, leaning against the back of the chair.

The longevity picture is intended to be a likeness of the person whose death is mourned. It is commonly made about as large as a child six or eight years old; oftentimes the artist is called to paint it after the death of the individual. In represents him in a sitting posture, and dressed in his official robes, with button of rank, if an officer or a graduate ; if not, he is represented as having on a nice suit. The picture is often gaudily painted.

On the table arranged "before the spirit" is placed a bowl having incense in it, which is kept burning for forty-nine days and nights. There are also placed on it a pair of candles or lamps, which are lighted at meal-time, and also whenever anything is transacted before the longevity picture with reference to the dead ; also two chopsticks for the use of the spirit when supposed to be eating. About the centre of the table are arranged a bowl, turned bottom-side upward, professedly to hold rice, and a wine-cup, also bottom-side up, for the purpose of holding wine, at the time of eating or of offering food and wine to the spirit by his children. If the bowl and cup are used, they are, after being washed, placed back on the table, bottom-side upward. These chopsticks, the bowl, and the cup are seldom used at meal-time, but others in their stead, they remaining *in statu quo* on the table. The table, chair, frame, and picture usually remain unmoved until the expiration of forty-nine, or sixty, or a hundred days after the decease of the individual, according as the family decide. Some families keep the whole or a part in position until the expiration of three years.

The two cash which have been mentioned are carefully kept on the table, or are hung on the frame on which the longevity picture is suspended, so as always to be at hand for use when desired. Whenever the family wish to ask anything of the dead, these cash are taken by some one and held in the smoke of the incense kept continually burning on the table, the person at the same time making the inquiry or stating the circumstances in such a way that an affirmative or negative reply, "yes" or "no," can be given. When he has done speaking, the cash are dropped on the table. If their relative positions, as they lie on the table, are the same as when dropped, the reply given by the deceased to the question asked by his children is regarded as affirmative. If different, the reply is regarded as negative. In such a case the inquirer must make some other inquiry, or repeat the same inquiry in substance if he pleases, the form being different, and try the cash again, and so on until an affirmative answer is obtained, as it would not do to desist when the answer is negative, and the dead appears by the reply to be displeased or dissatisfied.

The Chinese believe that in consequence of the dead man's not being able to pick his way safely to the infernal regions, but liable to lose the right path, the king of Hades furnishes a "little devil" to act the part of guide and servant to the dead man. Accordingly, the family make provision for the wants of this servant-imp, who is generally spoken of as the "devil who follows," by placing on a corner of the table before the longevity picture a chopstick and a small bowl for his use while piloting down to the Land of Shades the mortal recently deceased. Surviving relatives are anxious to treat this devil-servant well, so that it will serve respectfully, and guide safely the manes of their departed parent; consequently, whenever they give any rice to him, they are always careful to give a little to the imp; and when they burn mock-money for their deceased relative, they are sure to burn some for the special benefit of the servant, thus keeping him in food and spending-money. The object of all this is to flatter and please the little devil, so that he may perform his duty faithfully and satisfactorily to the dead person. Unless he be treated with proper decorum, it is feared that he will become offended, and harm his master, lead him astray, or refuse to pilot him.

After the various things which have been described have been properly arranged, three bowls or plates of food, as meat, fish, &c. are brought and placed on the table. The eldest son approaches, and, kneeling reverently down before the table, makes three solemn bows towards the ground, crying and wailing. When he arises and retires, sometimes his brothers, if there are any, come and kneel down in similar manner, with tears and lamentations. All this is for the purpose *of comforting the soul of the dead, or one of its three souls, as the Chinese believe.* This soul is believed, after this ceremony, to be or to remain somewhere in close proximity with the table, the chair, or the longevity picture. Some families, who can afford the expense, employ several priests, who recite their liturgy, ring their cymbals or gongs, and perform a variety of ceremonies, having for their object the pacification and repose of the soul of the dead.

The eldest son, and his younger brothers, if he has any, and they are able to bear the exposure, *commence the observance of sleeping by the side of the coffin, as a token of their filial and dutiful spirit.* They keep up the custom until the table, chair, and the picture are removed, or until the coffin is taken away. During the night, as well as during the daytime, a particular kind of incense is used, called "dry incense." It is like a straight, small stick, about three feet long, and nearly as large as one's little finger, designed to last all night. It is considered quite important, as far as the dead is concerned, that the incense should not go out during the night. This incense is used, it is said, because it is straight, not crooked, and is representative of a straight road. A straight road is much less likely to be lost by the spirit of the dead than a crooked road. Hence the "dry incense" is employed, as it were, to lighten the dead man on his way. If it should be allowed to go out, it would be a matter of regret to the family, and especially to the eldest son, on whom the main responsibility rests at this time, as it might be the occasion of the dead man's losing his way to the infernal regions, notwithstanding the aid of his servant-devil. The eldest son must not absent himself from the coffin at night, unless too ill to perform his duties and trim the lights.

For forty-nine, sixty, or a hundred days, as the case may be, the following customs are observed by the children of the deceased, male or female.

They bring hot water in a wash-basin early in the morning to the side of the coffin, as if for the dead man to bathe his hands and face.—This is attended by all the family with loud and violent outbursts of grief. They also offer him refreshments, and burn mock-money for his benefit.

At meal-time, twice per day, they bring to the side of the coffin, before they have eaten themselves, a bowl of cooked rice, and several plates of vegetables and meats. These are first placed on the table, after which they weep and lament, burning mock-money and incense ; afterwards they take the food away, and proceed to eat their own meals.

At bedtime they all come again to the table with weeping and lamenting, and, as usual, inform him of their intentions to "go to bed," as it were "bidding the dead good-night."

The sons sleep by the coffin on straw, without matting or pillows, keeping company with the dead *by night*.

Not long subsequent to the death of the head of a family, the eldest son sends around to near relatives a card informing them of the year, month, day, and hour of the birth of the deceased ; the year, month, day, and hour of his death, and stating the day when the family will go into mourning. Those who receive such a card must provide some money, and put it in an envelope made of yellow or white paper. On the outside of this envelope, if made of white paper, is a strip of blue paper attached, upon which they write a couple of characters denoting the object for which the money is designed and the name of the donor, with three words meaning " I respectfully bow my head," or " my respectful salutations." This is sent to the family, together with a quantity of mock-money. The money sent varies from twenty cents to eight or ten dollars. The two words written on the outside of the envelope indicate that the money is to be employed for buying something to be used in sacrifice.

Friends and relatives sometimes present to the family on this occasion a pair of hangings made of paper, or silk, or broadcloth, on which are inscribed a couple of popular mottoes or sentences. These are hung up in some conspicuous place in the rooms occupied for public purposes during the period of mourning.

They kneel down and worship before the longevity picture.— Friends and relatives, who call to present their condolences to the afflicted family, are expected to kneel down and worship before the picture representing the dead. Whoever thus worships, never worships alone. He expects some of the family, the eldest son, if not otherwise engaged, to kneel down and bow the head simultaneously with him, to keep him company. Some kneel down only once and bow the head three times. During this ceremony, some female member of the family, hid from view behind a white screen made of cotton cloth, or made of sackcloth, which is placed before the coffin in a corner of the room, breaks out it in piteous and violent weeping. After the parties have risen to their feet, and before they retire from before the table, the female weeper comes forth, and thanks the relative for this expression of his sympathy. No friend or relative would be willing to kneel down and bow his respects before the longevity picture unless he was sure that some one was in readiness behind the "filial screen" to weep and lament at the proper time. He would feel very indignant should such a thing occur as paying his respects unaccompanied by the weeping of some one, feeling that they could not afford to weep, though he came to mourn and condole with them. If of higher rank, he is not expected or allowed by the customs of society to kneel as do relatives of lower rank and common friends. He simply stands erect, and pays his respects by moving his hands, clasped together, up and down in the approved manner. Few persons of rank higher than the deceased come to condole with the family; generally only those come who are of equal or lower rank.

Among the majority of the families at this place, on the sixth day after the death of its head there is performed at the house a ceremony, the object of which is said both to be *to inform the kings of the infernal regions of his death, and also to pray for the forgiveness of his sins.* Several Tauist priests are employed to officiate. They suspend three large hangings, two of which represent the ten kings of hell, and one represents the Three Pure Ones,—divinities worshipped by the priests and devotees of the Tauist sect. They also arrange a table "in the presence of heaven," having on it eight or ten plates of meats, vegetables, and wine. The offering of these things to the ten gods is accompanied with the recitation of formulas and the ringing of cymbals. At the conclusion of the ceremony, two of the priests sit down by the side of the coffin and inform the deceased of what has been done for his benefit, saying that his children, married and unmarried, and grandchildren, are present.

They observe a ceremony in honour of the seven kings.—This is done for the first time on the seventh day after the death of the individual, and is generally repeated on every seventh day for seven times in families which are able to bear the expense of the ceremony. It is always performed before sacrifice to the dead on these days. Its special object is to propitiate the good-will of seven divinities, who, it is affirmed, will, in all likelihood, seize and beat the dead, unless this ceremony is performed in their honour. It principally consists in placing a common table " before the heavens," having upon it three cups of wine, three bowls or plates of vegetables, two candles, and mock-money. The candles and the incense are lighted, but the latter is not put upon the table, but on the ground or floor, where it is left for a while. The sons of the dead, wearing hempen clothes as badges of mourning, kneel down, the eldest son taking three cups of wine in succession and pouring out some of the contents on the ground, all making three bows towards the ground. On rising, the mock-money is set on fire and left to consume, together with the incense on the ground. The candles and eatables are taken and placed on the tables before the place of the spirit of the dead, as an offering to him. This is done or concluded usually about eleven o'clock in the morning, when other services or ceremonies may be had, according to the programme settled upon by the family. The coffin is oftentimes painted on each of these days.

Generally, after the preceding ceremony in honour of the seven kings, priests are employed to perform certain ceremonies, beating their cymbals, and chanting their formulas for a short time, having regard to the rulers of the infernal regions. After this the family put on mourning. This is a very formal and important affair. The sons put on garments made of hemp cloth, of the natural colour, over their other clothing. The grandsons put on garments made of hemp cloth, but of a yellowish tinge. Sons, daughters, and grandchildren, according to strict rules, have braided in their cues threads of hemp, or blue or white cotton. No red garment must be worn nor silks nor satins for the nominal period of three years, which is understood to mean twenty-seven months. The dutiful sons of the deceased may not sleep on a bedstead at night, nor may they sit on a chair for the space of forty-nine or sixty days if any guests or friends are present. They must stand or sit on the floor. They wear a white strip of cotton cloth as a belt, and their caps, collars, and shoes are decked in mourning. On every seventh day for seven times the sons wear brown sackloth over their ordinary clothing, and grandsons yellow sackcloth, when engaged in sacrificing to the manes of the dead when guests or friends are present. On other days they may wear white cotton garments. The eldest son, on every seventh day, when going out to meet and escort guests, carries a staff about three or four feet long, on which, commencing at a few inches from the top down to the bottom, at intervals of a few inches, are pasted small slips of white paper.

On the first seventh day those relatives and friends who have been specially invited are expected to be present at the time of offering sacrifice to the manes of the dead.

On the fourteenth day—that is, the second seventh day after

the death of the individual, occurs another ceremony, attended
with the presentation of four plates, consisting of various kinds
of vegetables and wine, arranged on a table placed before the
table in front of the spirit's place. Its particular object is to
implore Buddha to ferry over the soul of the dead. The Chinese
are taught to believe that his soul in this manner becomes comparatively free from guilt.

On the *twenty-first day* the afflicted family generally provides an entertainment for those relatives and friends whom
they see fit or are com-
pelled by the usages of
society to invite. The
guests are expected to
worship the dead in the
way which has been pre-
viously described. The
feast is first offered in
the usual way on a table
in honour of the ten
kings of hell. A professor
of ceremony is employed
to read at the proper
time a kind of sacrificial
ode or prayer, praising
the dead for his virtues
and calling for pity on his
soul. After the guests
are seated at the tables,
the professor of ceremo-
nies calls out the "filial"
sons and grandsons, and
great-grandsons, if any,
of the dead, from an
adjoining room. They
come forward, and, kneel-

ELDEST SON DRESSED IN MOURNING, AND CARRYING
THE FILIAL STAFF.

ing down on the floor, incline their heads towards the floor
three times in front of the guests, which performance is designed
to be an expression of their thanks to these guests for their
generous presents of money to the living, as well as for their
kindness to the dead, as evinced by their coming to condole
with the bereaved family.

On the *twenty-eighth and on the thirty-fifth day*, the family
purchase food and other articles, and present them before th

picture of the deceased, so similar in manner to the ceremonies performed on previous days that it is not necessary to describe them.   The rich continue to have some meritorious performance on these days done by priests, but the poor seldom have anything more than a few dishes of food and a quantity of incense offered or burned at the established place, as a kind of sacrifice to the dead.

The forty-second day is generally regarded as a very important occasion.   If the deceased have married daughters, it is their duty, and doubtless they feel it as a privilege, to be at the expense of ceremonies which are believed to benefit their departed parent.   They are at the expense of a feast to the invited friends and relatives of the dead at the house occupied by his family.

It is the popular belief that the dead arrives on this day at a certain place in the spirit world, whence he looks back on his home and neighbourhood, and becomes for the first time aware of his own decease. Consequently, sad and afflicted in mind, he loses his appetite, and is unable to partake of rice cooked at home.   In consequence of this belief the family are unwilling to use rice cooked at home in these ceremonies.

The forty-ninth day is also regarded as a very important occasion.   Its services consist principally in performing "meritorious acts" of various kinds.   The mourning family again provide a feast for invited relatives and friends.   These first, one by one, kneel down before the table in front of the longevity picture, and bow their heads toward the earth for three times.   After the food, wine, &c. have been offered in sacrifice to the dead, the friends and relatives present proceed to feast upon it.   The sacrifice is, of course, attended with weeping on the part of the sons, daughters, and grandchildren of the dead.   Some families have a particular ceremony performed, which indicates that the "sevens," that is, "the "meritorious" and other mourning services which have been performed on the seventh days from the date of the death of the individual, are now discontinued. This is a very busy and eventful day.

A ceremony is usually performed on the forty-ninth day, called ceasing to offer the rice, but some families defer it to the sixtieth, or even the hundredth day.   The custom is always observed whenever the family decide to discontinue the offering of food to the dead at the regular meal-times.   Some families procure several plates of meats, as pork, flesh of the goat, fowl, some vegetable dishes, bean-curd, wine, rice, tea, tobacco, salt, a kitchen-knife, a wooden block, some wood, oil, water, and some luxuries à la Chinois, and place them on the table. Other families only provide a few small bundles of wood, a little uncooked rice, some salt, and some oil. *This is to indicate to the dead that he must procure and cook his own food after this, as his surviving descendants do not propose to furnish it to him any longer, cooked or uncooked,* at a regular meal-time. It is imagined the dead will understand these gentle hints, and make provision for his wants accordingly. In order to supply him with spending-money, a large quantity of mock-money is prepared and burnt at this time, his filial children readily believing that now, as he must board himself, he will require a larger sum of ready cash than usual. At this time is burnt one stick of incense and one candle; the sons, daughters, and grandchildren kneel down in front of the table, and break out into most piteous weeping, calling on the dead, using the most affectionate and endearing appellations, according to the relation they formerly sustained to him whom they now lament, as wife, son, daughter, &c.

After this ceremony they do not offer the customary articles of food at meal-time to the dead.

When a daughter's husband's father or mother dies, it is customary for the family to which the daughter belonged to send to the afflicted family, on the day they put on mourning, a quantity of common mock-money, and paper representing silk, incense and candles, cash for buying articles to be used in sacrifice, a sacrificial prayer, a "gold" mountain and a "silver" mountain, that is, paper made in shape like mountains, and covered with tinfoil, some of a natural or silvery colour, and some coloured to resemble gold, all to be used in sacrifices to the dead. On the twenty-first day they make another small present for a similar design. On or after the forty-ninth day they send a present of two kinds, as it is termed, designed to be eaten by the daughter, called a present to dry up the tears. The idea is that for the last forty-nine days she has wept a great deal for the dead, and now it is time to dry up the fountain of tears, and partake of suitable food; in other words, it is now high time to stop her crying. The meat is always of some kind which is regarded as particularly palatable and nutritious.

On the sixtieth day they provide a number of plates of food, and incense, &c. But, besides these customary offerings, which are placed on the table, they place on it a wash-bowl full of water. On the water they put the half of the shell of a duck's egg, which is left to float on the surface. A likeness of a duck, made of bamboo splints covered with paper, and painted, is brought forward. A paper image made in imitation of the human figure is placed on the duck, and the duck is caused to stand in the water in the wash-basin. The paper image personates the deceased individual. The egg-shell denotes a boat provided for his use. The duck signifies the means by which he gets over!

It is a general practice at this place, on the occurrence of the *fourteenth and the thirtieth of every month*, after the family have intimated that no more rice will be offered to the manes of the dead at meal-time, to observe the following ceremony :—In the evening the sons and daughters of the family all assemble together, if practicable. They provide a plateful of biscuit, or bread-cakes, a plate of bean-curd, plates of meat, fish, cooked rice, a cup of wine, a stick of incense, and a pair of candles, which are placed on the table before the place of the spirit. They remember to provide a little of something for the special use of the servant-devil. The family simultaneously weep and cry bitterly, and think of the departed. The alleged reason why they observe this custom on the fourteenth and the thirtieth of the month is because it is believed that the spirit of the departed parent or relative returns home on these days, and therefore the family are in duty bound to provide a plentiful repast for it, and to show it proper respect and honour—which surely is a good reason, if the fact be as believed. This custom is kept up on the days specified until the three years of mourning are completed, or until the ancestral tablet representing the deceased is put in the niche or on the shelf where the other family tablets are kept.

At the end of one hundred days, and at the close of one year from the date of the death of the individual, several plates of food, wine, &c. are offered on the table, attended with weeping, much as on the sixtieth day, with this wide difference, there is no paper man, no shell of a duck's egg, no bamboo and paper duck, and no wash-basin with water in it, placed on the table or used on the occasion. At the expiration of one complete year married daughters and grandchildren remove their badges of mourning, while sons and their wives, and the widow of the deceased, if a man, are required still to wear their badges of mourning nominally two years longer.

At the end of three years in theory, in fact at the end of twenty-seven months, the sons, daughters-in-law, and the widow remove their deep mourning, and put on light or half-mourning, to be worn for three months. Before the deep mourning is removed from their garments, caps, and cues, several plates of eatables are offered on the table, and incense and mock-money are burned. All kneel down, bow their faces toward the ground, and weep with accustomed bitterness. The rejected badges of grief are thrown into the censer or furnace where the mock-money is burned. They then place the ancestral tablet in its niche, if ready, and not already placed there, again offering food to the dead, kneeling down as usual. They now remove the table, the chair, and the frame having the longevity picture upon it from the places where they have been for so long a time, if these things have not been previously taken away ; the chopsticks and bowls, which usually were to be found on the table, the chair, and the stool which stood behind it, together with the two cash which have been used so many times in questioning the dead, are never hereafter used in the family.

After the tablet has been placed in the family shrine, the family twice a year must observe a ceremony like the following, in memory of the day of the birth and the day of the death of their honoured dead. Several plates of meat, cooked rice, with cups of wine, incense, candles, and a quantity of mock-money, are provided. They are presented to the spirit of the dead, before his tablet, in the usual manner. Some families only observe this ceremony to the third generation, while most families observe it to the fifth generation. At the end of five generations, some of the Chinese believe the spirits of the souls of the dead may be born again into this world, or become the spirits of birds, beasts, or reptiles, according to their deserts, in obedience to the laws or principles of the doctrine of the transmigration of souls. Hence no tablet of the dead is worshipped after the posterity of the individual it represents have reached the fifth generation.

Of the ceremonies which are almost always performed on the last day, viz. the forty-ninth, four will be described when speaking of four superstitions practised for the benefit of destitute and unfortunate spirits, viz., "mounting the platform," "letting go the water lanterns," "breaking into hell," and "spirits passing over the bridge." It is not necessary to dwell on these ceremonies here, except to say that, as performed in private houses, with special regard to the soul of a single person, and at the expense of a single family, they are on a much smaller scale than when performed in some public place and at public expense, and with reference to the hosts of destitute and unfortunate spirits which are believed to abound in the land of shades or roam about in this upper world.

The ceremony of " informing the ten kings of hell of the death of the individual " is introductory of all these meritorious cere-monies. After its celebration by families which decide to have others performed on the following day, arrangements are made for the notification of the " supreme ruler, the pearly emperor," of the proposed celebrations. This service is performed late in the afternoon or early in the evening, and consists principally of burning two paper horses and two paper riders, and a document in the name of the eldest son, giving information to his " pearly " majesty of the transactions to be performed on the following day. This is done by priests, who burn incense and candles, beat the drum, and recite the usual formulas. This preparatory ceremony is performed only once during all the celebrations. Some explain its object to be to inform the gods generally in regard to the transactions of the succeeding day.

On the same evening, after the issue of the notification, a long bamboo pole is erected in front of the house. On the top of the bamboo is fastened the image of a crane, made principally out of bamboo splints and the fibres of the bark of a palm-tree. Under this image is a covering, oftentimes several feet square, made also out of the fibres of the same material, and so constructed as to ward off the rain, in ordinary storms, from a lantern which is placed underneath. On the outside of this lantern, which is coarsely constructed out of bamboo splints and white paper, are written in black or in red ink the names or titles of seventeen Buddhas or gods. Hence the name of the lantern, the " bright lantern of the seventeen Buddhas." A candle is lighted in the lantern every evening. It is lowered and raised to its place by means of a rope and pulley. Now the grand object of thus erecting the lantern is said to be to let all the Buddhas and the gods know of the performances soon to be transacted, so that they can be present, and partake of the food which will be offered. During the next day the meritorious ceremonies decided on are commenced.

In the afternoon, the priests who are employed to officiate, and the dutiful sons of the deceased, go forth to some hill, if there be one sufficiently near the house. Here the priests light incense and candles, and chant their formulas a short time ; some one then sets on fire a sheet of paper, which has a statement designed for the inspection of the " supreme ruler," informing him of the approaching completion of certain ceremonies. They soon after return to the house. Some families never perform this ceremony on a hill-top, but always at home, and in or by the house.

For convenience' sake, several ceremonies are here grouped together. A paper image, which has been provided, is taken by one of the sons and placed in a small paper sedan-chair, to which wheels have been attached. In front of the sedan and connected with it by means of two pieces of bamboo, which keep it three or four feet from the ground, is a paper image of the crane, just as though the crane was to act the part of a flying pony and drag along the sedan. In front of the crane, and in a row, there are arranged several paper trunks, which contain mock-clothing and mock-money of various kinds, representing, in the fancy of this people, sycee, gold, dollars, and cash. The paper clothing is either paper cut into miniature articles of clothing and pasted together, or paper on which the likeness of coats, caps, and shoes has been printed or stamped, or it is simply rolls of paper of various colours, which are imagined to be silks, satins, or cotton goods.

Sometimes friends and neighbours of the deceased embrace the opportunity of sending to their relatives and friends in the world of spirits boxes or trunks of clothing and money, by the "politeness" of the individual for whose special benefit these ceremonies are principally designed. As the living take advantage often of a neighbour or a relative who intends to travel for health, or pleasure, or business, to send to distant friends parcels of value, so the Chinese have invented the happy expedient of sending to their deceased dear ones, by the care of the dead, money and clothing. It is certainly a cheap, expeditious, and convenient method of making remittances to the other world, if really sure of accomplishing its object. It is believed that the dead man will deliver to its real owner the valuable property intrusted to his care immediately on its reaching its destination. Each trunk intrusted to his care is generally sealed up by two strips of paper, which are pasted upon its top from opposite corners, much like the letter X. These strips or seals are usually furnished by a priest. He also provides a strip of stamped paper having the name of the owners of these trunks who are in the infernal regions. This is called the "proof," and it may be considered a letter to these persons on the subject of the articles sent. At the proper time it is burnt along with the trunks.

When everything is ready, a priest recites a particular formula, the object of which is to procure the services of a guide to conduct the occupant of the sedan on his journey. All the family reverently kneel down on the ground at some little distance from the sedan, weeping and lamenting. The priest now sets on fire those trunks which are most remote from the sedan, and, gradually coming nearer and nearer the sedan, he at last sets it on fire; and the effigy of the deceased, the crane pony, and the paper sedan are shortly turned into ashes, amid the loud, mournful outcries of the bereaved family.

Among the paper trunks filled with clothing and money, burnt at the close of the ceremony just described, there is oftentimes a small paper money-chest of a particular kind, and designed for a particular purpose. The Chinese differ widely among themselves in regard to the special object to be attained by the burning of this trunk.

Some say that the design of these funds is to pay the debts of the deceased whether known or unknown to him. It is intended as a kind of squaring up of his accounts. His surviving relatives do not wish him to be annoyed by demands presented in the other world for the debts of this, and therefore furnish a box of cash for the express purpose of liquidating these liabilities.

Others explain the remittance of the ready money as designed to be for the use of the animal under which the deceased was born. It is designed to aid him in getting the good will of the animal in question, without which he will be obliged to carry the said animal after he arrives in the world of shadows. Now every Chinese is believed to belong to some animal, i.e. he is born in a year which is said to belong to some animal. For example, if born in a certain year, he will belong to the "Rat," the rat being the horary character which, in the Chinese cycle, represents that particular year. If born in a certain year, he will belong to the "Buffalo," for a similar reason. If born in a certain other year, he will belong to the "Rabbit." In some way, the animal to which he belongs, unless he brings a chest of money to propitiate it, is believed to get the possession or the control of the dead man on his arrival in Tartarus, making him carry it. To avoid such a fate for their lamented parent, or relative, the members of his family send along a trunk full of ready cash for the special benefit of the animal. How the latter manages to use the money so kindly or so selfishly furnished, the Chinese do not explain.

Besides the above meritorious services, there are several others which some families have performed when they imagine there seems to be a particular necessity or propriety for them.

On all of these occasions there are several priests employed to officiate. The ceremonies are supposed, as a whole, to constitute prayers "for the diminishing of the calamities and the loosening of the difficulties" which the dead may have to encounter in the spirit world. The principle acted upon is, the more worship and the more ceremony performed by the living, the better will it be for the dead.

The particular design of one ceremony is to free the dead from any calamity which might be sent on him as a punishment *for using in any way too much water* in this world, or for using it in an unworthy manner. Such a course offends the god of water, and he very properly punishes the sin in the other world. A certain classic or formula, relating to this subject, is chanted. The recitation of this particular formula makes the distinction between this and the other ceremonies performed on the death of relatives. If children, on the death of a parent, do not have this ceremony performed, they are liable to be charged with a deficiency of filial regard for the happiness of him who, perhaps, is suffering from the cause above specified.

There is a ceremony when a book said to contain the *names of one thousand Buddhas* is repeated by each Buddhist priest employed. All their voices blend together as they chant it in concert. The object of this ceremony is the general one of engaging the friendly and the powerful offices of the Buddhas whose names are chanted to "ferry" the spirit of the dead across.

A ceremony called *the Bloody Pond ceremony,* as some explain, relates to married women who die, it may be, several years subsequent to their having children ; others assert it refers to those women who, having borne a girl, die within four months, or who, having borne a boy, die within one month. These say that a woman's uncleanness, in the case of having given birth to a boy, extends only to one month, while it extends to four months in the case of having given birth to a girl. The Chinese believe that in the infernal regions there is a pond of blood, into which deceased married women generally, or, as some say, women who have died in childbirth, or within one or four months after confinement, are plunged on their entrance into that world. Virgins, and married women who have never borne children, on their death never have this ceremony performed on their account. The object of the Bloody Pond ceremony is to save the spirit of a deceased mother from the punishment of the Bloody Pond. Sometimes it is performed several times on the death of the mother of a family of children. This is one way by which they manifest their filial love for the deceased.

A ceremony designed to propitiate the good-will of the ten kings who rule over the affairs in the lower world is often performed for the benefit of either parent. It is believed that the punishment of the dead may be alleviated by obtaining favour with the governors of the ten departments of hell, through which they will be obliged to pass, and in which they will be obliged to suffer punishment for the sins of this life. If these kings are willing, they are supposed to have the prerogative, or at least to be in the practice, of punishing the dead but slightly, imposing on him such penalties as are easily borne, or even of passing him along through the different departments without any penalty. Thus do this people fancy they can bribe the rulers of hell !

CHAPTER VII.

DEATH, MOURNING, AND BURIAL—*continued.*

THE very poor are often obliged, in order to save expense, or for other reasons, to bury their dead in the course of a few days after death. This is likened to a mandarin who proceeds to his official trust by the swiftest post, without the usual delays, receptions of honour, &c. *en route.* It is considered disreputable, and a mark of the very lowest poverty, or that the dead is destitute of friends and relatives who take an interest in the honour of the family.

If the body is buried in the course of a few days after death, it is called "blood burial," or a burial of blood. The corpse is believed to have blood in it, or the blood has not yet dried up. "Blood burial" is used as a term of reproach, and refers to hasty burials, preceded by few mourning solemnities.

On the decease of the paternal head of the family, it becomes the duty of the sons to procure a burial-place, unless it has been previously purchased, sufficiently large to contain at least two graves side by side. The coffin of the father must be placed on the left side, leaving the other for the coffin of the mother. If the mother die first, her coffin must be placed on the right side, in like manner leaving room for the father's coffin. It is considered a mark of want of filial respect to separate widely the coffins of one's parents, unless circumstances make it necessary.

If the ground for burial is not ready for any reason, and it is not convenient to have the coffin remain in the house until the burial-ground is ready, a dead-house is built or rented, in which the coffin is placed for the time being. In front of this house, just after the coffin has been deposited in it, three plates of food are placed on the ground, and incense, candles, and mock-money are lighted. These are designed as offerings for the local deity presiding over the ground in that neighbourhood. The coffin while being conveyed to this temporary resting-place is followed by the dutiful sons.

Near the coffin are arranged, as an offering to the dead, a bucket of boiled rice, plates of meats, fish, vegetables, and a kind of cakes called si, and two small lanterns, on one of which are the two characters which mean "hundred children," and on the other are the two characters which mean "thousand grandchildren." While these things are being offered in sacrifice to the manes of the dead, the sons kneel down and bow their heads toward the coffin.

The tablet to represent the dead, and which has been lying on the coffin, is taken by the eldest son, and placed in a sedan, and carried home ; or he sometimes takes it in his arms, and, entering a sedan, carries it carefully to his home, with the lanterns above referred to hung from the poles of his sedan as an omen of good, they being lighted with a candle, though it be in mid-day.

Rich families, and families which have children employed as mandarins, when the time has arrived to bury their dead, often rent a kind of hearse, on which the coffin is placed and carried to the burial-ground. Before the coffin is placed upon it a sacrifice is made unto it or the god which is supposed to control it. This procedure, it is thought, will cause the soul of the departed to be more peaceful *en route* to the grave than it would have been had the sacrifice not been made. It will help the bearers to carry it more easily. It is feared, unless it is done, the god of the hearse will injure the coffin in some way, making it difficult and heavy to bear. Either eight, sixteen, or thirty-two bearers are employed in carrying this hearse and coffin, according to the rank or the wealth of the family. The hearse is trimmed with emblems of mourning, having strips of white cloth, which cross each other at intervals, and are tied in knots, on various parts of it.

The order observed in funeral processions while going to the burying-ground, for the middle classes, is usually much like the following, though there is no general rule :

First come a pair of large white lanterns and a company of musicians, who play at intervals along the road.

Then comes a portable open pavilion, carried by four bearers, and containing the "longevity picture" and the tablet of the deceased, usually having burning incense in it.

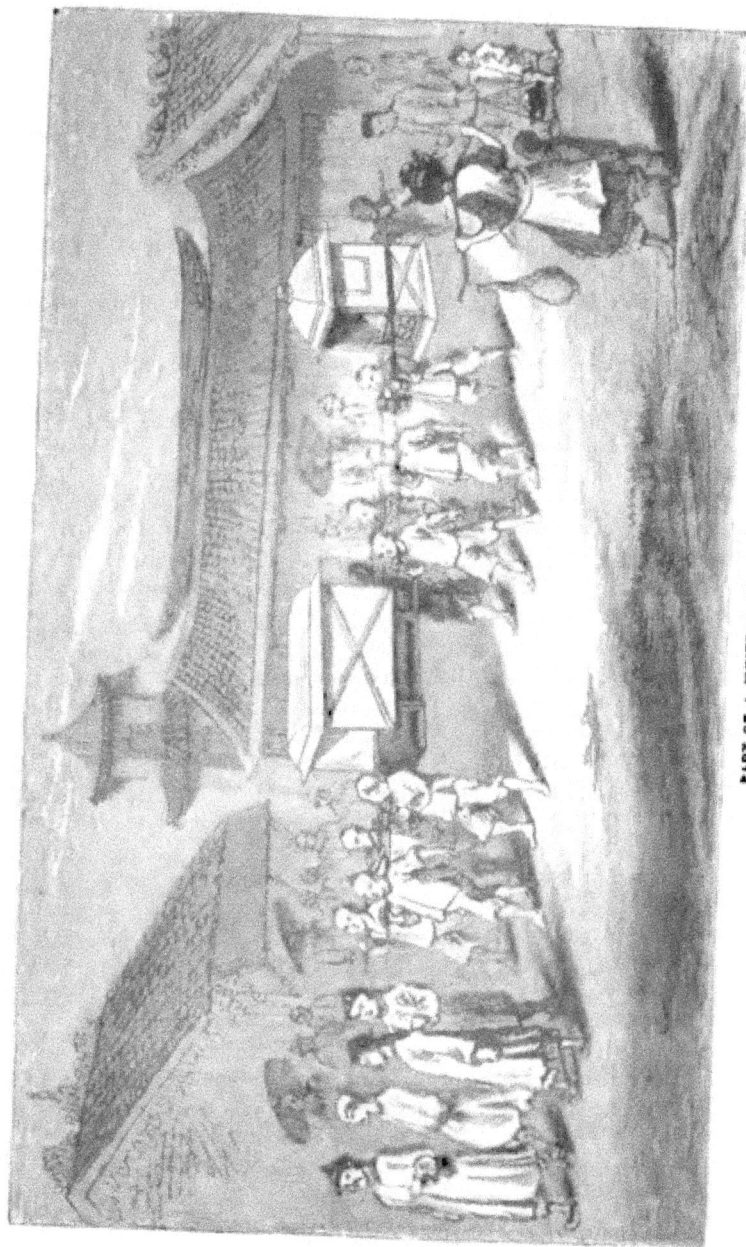

PART OF A FUNERAL PROCESSION.

Afterward appears a man scattering at intervals along the street mock-money of a particular kind.

Relatives and friends of the deceased come next, who are sometimes attended by a band of music.

Then the coffin, with its bearers often wearing white coats, furnished at the expense of the family.

Following the coffin are the sons of the dead, and his grandsons and great grandsons, if any, all dressed in mourning. These are all on foot, if able to walk, and weep and cry as they walk along.

Next come sedans containing the females belonging to the family of the deceased. The occupants of the sedans endeavour to keep up a continuous wailing and weeping along the streets.

Finally come men with rice and food for offerings at the grave, incense, candles, and mock-money. Unless provision has been made for taking the tablet in the front of the procession, it is carried by one of the men who are employed to carry articles for sacrificial use at the burial-place.

As intimated above, near the front part of the funeral procession go one or two men, who scatter along the road pieces of mock-money. These usually are of white and yellow colours, and about two and a half or three inches in diameter, perforated in the centre. This money is designed to propitiate the spirits along the road which may be disposed to make disturbance affecting the coffin or its contents. In this manner the right of way is secured for the remains of the dead. It is literally called "buying the road," and the cash-money employed are variously called the "cash which buy the road," or the "cash which open the road." The unseen spirits allow the coffin to pass without molestation on receiving the cash. Sometimes the mock-money used is not the round kind above described, but pieces of coarse paper in the shape of a parallelogram, some five or six inches long, each sheet being perforated several times. Each sheet represents as many cash as it has holes.

In the front of a funeral procession, when a high mandarin is carried to his burial, sometimes will be seen two immense likenesses of men, one dressed to represent a civil, the other to represent a military officer. These are very light compared with their size, being made out of bamboo splints, covered principally with red paper. Each is borne in a horizontal position by two men. They are from ten to fifteen feet long, and four or five feet in diameter. These are burned in front of the grave. Their design is to open and clear the road over which the dead is about to pass. The spirits which infest the road flee when they perceive these gods opening the road, as they are called. Some explain their use by referring to the practice of great mandarins while living, to have runners or lictors to precede them and clear the way when they go forth into the streets. These objects are never used by the common people while conveying to the last resting-place the remains of their honoured dead.

An imposing ceremony is sometimes performed at the expense of personal friends or relatives in honour of a distinguished man, either a civilian or mandarin, at the house of the dead, and while the coffin is en route to the grave. Its distinctive name is "displaying or arranging a sacrifice." In the summer of 1850 an illustration of this custom occurred at Fuhchau on the occasion of bringing home for burial the corpse of ex-Commissioner Lin, of Canton opium-destroying notoriety, who died while engaged in an expedition against the long-haired insurgents who have since attracted such attention, but who were at that time just beginning to elicit serious action from the Peking Government. A large number of tables were arranged along the sides of the street on the island in the river at this place. As observed at that time, the exhibition of articles offered in sacrifice to the manes of the honoured dead was far more extensive than is generally employed when making a sacrifice on the premises occupied by the family of the deceased.

The ceremony performed at private houses is sometimes as follows :

Several tables are placed in a convenient court, having three sizes of bowls or plates arranged upon them. These hold meats and vegetables. There are also sixteen saucers—four holding the gizzards or livers of fowls, ducks, and pigs' tongues, and preserved duck eggs ; four holding fruits preserved in sugar ; four holding ripe fruits of the season ; and four holding dried water-melon seeds. There are also arranged on the tables either two or three, or all of the following animals, roasted or broiled whole : pig, fowl, duck, goose, or goat, and two or three kinds of mock-money, representing silver and gold. There is also a pail full of boiled rice, five bowls of five different colours of bread balls, each bowl having one colour ; five bowls of five kinds of cakes, each bowl having one cake ; five small bread images of five animals,—tiger, lion, elephant, buffalo, leopard ; also two paper deer and two paper cranes. Sometimes there are five large representatives of animals made of paper and bamboo splints, and placed on the ground. Families which have married with the family of the deceased, on such occasions are expected to furnish also a quantity of mock-money, and some mock material for clothing, and paper imitations of a silver and golden mountain about three feet high and two feet long.

When everything is ready, one of the principal persons who unite in making the sacrifice to the manes of the dead approaches and kneels down before "the place of the spirit," or before the coffin. Some of the articles are brought in and handed to the man on his knees, who presents it toward the dead. These are then put on the table standing before the "longevity picture." He retires, when another person takes his place, kneeling, receiving and presenting some food. The food is afterward removed and placed on the tables whence it was taken when the offerers have departed. The food, or a part of it, after a day or two is eaten by the family.

A part of the sacrifice to the manes of the dead, when arranged on tables by the roadside while the coffin is *en route* to the burying-place, is presented in a manner similar to that just now described by some of those who unitedly make the offering. While the sacrifice is being presented, the procession stops, and the coffin is quite near those who kneel down and present the articles toward it. Such a sacrifice honours the memory and the virtues of the departed in a manner very gratifying to the family of which he was once a member.

At the appointed time, fixed by a fortune-teller, the coffin is lowered into the grave amid the tears of the mourners. Immediately afterward, the sons of the deceased hasten to scatter some earth into the grave. This earth they have previously put into the lap of their sackcloth mourning garments, which they manage to shake out so as to fall upon the coffin if possible. After the grave has been filled up by the gravediggers, the sons place in a perpendicular position their mourning staves on the new-made grave.

Afterwards an offering is made to the buried man in the following manner : a pail full of cooked rice, with several plates of meats, is placed directly in front of the grave, and quite near it. Among the eatables presented are two pails full of small round white cakes, made of the flour of rice. The ceremony takes its name from these cakes, called in this dialect "si."

At the proper time incense and candles are lighted, and a quantity of mock-money is burnt, attended with the usual solemn ceremonies. At the conclusion of the sacrifice to the manes of the dead, the cakes are divided among his children and grandchildren, attending relatives and friends, not forgetting the gravediggers. Each consumes his portion of the sī on the spot. Now the name of these cakes being in the dialect of this place the same in sound as the Chinese word for "time" or "times," the eating of them under such circumstances is regarded as a wish that the eaters may have a good time, or that the times may be propitious and happy to the parties. The rice is always taken home with the other eatables offered in sacrifice at the grave.

It is believed that the hills which are used as burial-places in this vicinity have gods which protect the graves of those who are buried there. The friends and relatives of him who has just been buried must pay proper reverence to these local divinities, or they need not expect the coffin will remain undisturbed, or the spirit of its occupant rest in peace in the lower regions. They therefore, before sacrificing to the dead on the day of burial, as well as on subsequent sacrificial occasions, must offer three plates of meats, wine, incense, candles, and various kinds of mock-money, all placed on the ground for the use of these local divinities.

Usually about this time of the proceedings an offering is also made to the distressed and destitute spirits in the infernal regions, such as the spirits of lepers and beggars. The offerings consist principally of mock-clothing and mock-money of a very inferior kind, incense, and several plates of steamed cakes, of a particular sort, of which these spirits are supposed to be very fond. Seldom is any meat offered to these unhappy creatures, but sometimes a little cooked rice, and a bowl of vegetable soup, bean curd, vermicelli, or a plate of bread-cakes or biscuits. It is a matter of wonder that the immense number of these hungry and naked spirits, which are believed to swarm about on such occasions, can be contented with such scant and poor provisions. But, according to the general supposition, they, on receiving what the friends of the dead are disposed to bestow upon them, allow the sacrifice to the dead to go on without interruption.

These degraded spirits are objects of frequent worship at this place, and in much the same manner as is described above, both on the part of shopkeepers in the streets in front of their shops, and on the part of the common people in front of their residences. In case of a slight illness, as well as oftentimes on planning business affairs, if one fears the matter will not succeed to his satisfaction, at dusk he causes mock-clothing and mock-money to be burnt for the use of these "gentlemen of the lower regions," as they are often called, and also some cakes are presented for their entertainment. These offerings are always placed on the ground. These imps are believed to have great influence in these upper regions, injuring the health of individuals, and causing derangement in business, &c. so that many are led to fear them, and to make them numerous presents in order to propitiate their good offices. Health and success, if they are to be secured by the use of these means, are within the reach of most mortals.

During the performance of sacrificing to the dead described above, the tablet which has been provided to represent the buried dead is placed in front of the headstone, or of the place where that is to stand. The mourners now kneel down before it, while the eldest son, also kneeling, repeats some sentence to the purport, " Let the bones and the flesh return to the earth, and the spirit enter the tablet." Ever afterward this tablet is regarded with great interest, and especial care is taken of it. Sometimes the eldest son of the deceased enters a sedan and carries it home in his arms ; or it is placed in a kind of open pavilion, and carried back to the homestead with pomp. The poor carry it home frequently placed on the pail of cooked rice, which constitutes one end of the load of a servant, as suspended across his shoulders. A man is frequently sent with two small buckets to get water from the hill on which the grave is made, if he can find it, carrying it to the residence of the family. It is called " dragon water." It is regarded as an omen of good, inasmuch as it comes from the Dragon's Hill, the hill where the grave has been made being referred to under this appellation, which is esteemed an auspicious term.

The tablet, on arrival at the home of the deceased, is first " dotted," and then placed in the niche among the ancestral tablets of the family. An acting mandarin, if it be possible to engage the services of such a man for the occasion, is called in ; the higher his rank, the greater or the more auspicious the omen for good to the descendants of the person whose tablet is to be dotted. It must be premised that, to this period, one of the characters which have been written upon its front is deficient in one dot or stroke. The deficient character, meaning " king," by receiving a small dot above the uppermost parallel stroke, becomes " lord," which is what is desired. The mandarin dotter, or the dotter whatever his rank, uses a vermilion pencil. The

eldest son kneels down reverently before the dotter, who dots
the "king" character with the required stroke, making it into
the "lord" character. He then returns it to the kneeling son,
who reverently places it in the niche provided, where it represents the dead for three or five generations.

Some refer the dotting ceremony, when performed by a
mandarin with a vermilion pencil, to the dotting of the eyes
of the dragon's head which has been engraven upon the front of
the upper part of the tablet. Of course but few families are
favoured enough to have mandarins to assist in the ceremony,
whether it refers to the dotting of the eyes of the dragon, or the
dotting of the "king" character as above described ; and oftentimes it is performed with a common pencil, using black ink, by
a member of the family or a friend, without much pomp or
ceremony. After this time the tablet is regarded as a *bonâ fide*
residence of one of the three spirits of the departed. The performance is considered auspicious.

Soon after the performance of the important ceremony of
"dotting the tablet," the relatives who have been invited sit
down to a plentiful repast, and endeavour to assuage their sorrow
of mind by replenishing the wants of their stomachs.

The widow on the death of her husband is required to wear
deep mourning for three years. No red may be worn. After
the expiration of that time, when all the rest of her family cease
wearing mourning, and when they may wear whatever kind of
clothing and of any colour they please, she, if belonging to the
small-footed class, must on no account put on a bright red skirt,
such as women of her class whose husbands are alive always
wear when they appear in public or dress for company ; she may
wear blue, black, or green, but may not wear a red skirt. The
widow of more than three years' standing, if belonging to the
large-footed class, usually has something about her dress or the
ornaments on her head which points her out as a widow. Of
course, when widows marry, every trace or badge of widowhood
is removed. The widow is required to take a prominent part in
the weeping and wailing on receiving the condolences of friends
at the set periods of public mourning. The widower is not
required to put on as deep mourning on the death of his wife as
a widow is required to use on the death of her husband. He
does not wear sackcloth at the stated periods of weeping and
wailing, nor does he weep loud and long, if at all, on these
occasions. At such times he wears a white coat over his other
garments, a cap without red tassels, and a white cotton-cloth

girdle about his waist. At other times he may wear garments made of silk or satin, if not of a gaudy colour. He is required to wear the white girdle for one year. If he should take another wife before the expiration of a year from the death of his first wife, still he must, as some say, wear the white girdle at the time of his marriage and until the end of a year. Others say he may, at the time of his marriage, leave off the girdle, but must resume it in the course of a few days, and wear it until a year is completed. Those who marry before the expiration of a full year are apt to be laughed at by their neighbours and friends, because they do it while in mourning for deceased wives.

If one's father or mother dies, and there is no member of the family living as high in rank as grandparent, it is customary for the family to prepare strips of narrow white cloth, about two feet in length by one in width, measuring by the chopsticks used in the family. These are given to a class of relatives who come to weep with the family for the dead. A bit of red paper is pasted on each piece. A female relative coming to mingle her tears with the bereaved family receives also, in addition to the white cloth, two artificial flowers, as omens of good. These strips of white cloth are called " cloths to cry with," and are designed to be used for wiping away the tears, and for holding up to the face or eyes of the weepers while lamenting, according to established rule. White being an emblem of evil or sorrow, the red paper is auspicious of good or joy to the possessors, indicating that they will, after all their grief, have food and clothing in their family. These strips are always taken away by their owners when they return home.

When two families are living in the same house, having a common hall for receiving company, and a death occurs in one of them, the coffin is usually placed in the hall during the period of mourning, and the established ceremonies are performed there. The afflicted family purchases some artificial flowers and a set of red chopsticks, and presents them to the other family as an omen of good. Rich families buy also a piece of red cloth or red silk and present it, in order to aid in preventing any unlucky consequences to the other family. As death is an inauspicious event, and the presence of the coffin containing the corpse in the common hall is an inauspicious circumstance, the Chinese have endeavoured to dispel or prevent any unhappy results from reaching to the other family by the expedient of presenting red articles. These, under the circumstances, are emblematical of continued good fortune to that family, and are considered a surety that it will certainly have sufficient "food and clothing," the unlucky presence of the coffin, tending to the contrary result, notwithstanding.

There are shops where ready-made grave-clothes can be had. These are patronised principally by the poor, who cannot afford to buy good material and have it made up by tailors. What is strange and singular about these establishments is, that the caps and boots offered for sale, to be worn by the dead, are usually made of paper, or the very poorest silk or satin, and simply pasted together. At a short distance, and unless closely examined, they look quite well. The boots have soles nearly an inch thick, which are made very white by a kind of wash. The coats, pantaloons, skirts, &c. are also sometimes pasted together, or, at the best, are but slightly basted together. Those who purchase such grave-clothes for their honoured dead feel that, to be considered respectable by their neighbours and relatives, they must conform to the absurd custom which requires that the dead should be clothed in several suits of garments when laid in the coffin, although they cannot really afford the expense of procuring respectable materials out of which to construct these garments. Fashion, to save public appearances, grinds the face of the poor in China as hardly as it does the faces of the poor in Western lands. The son who should fail of dressing the dead body of his father with several suits would be regarded as destitute of filial respect; and, instead of being laughed at should he feel himself obliged to use paper boots or paper caps, and garments made of very inferior material, and but basted or pasted together, he is regarded as exhibiting a dutiful and filial spirit provided the suits used were enough in number. Grave-clothes never have metal buttons, but are fastened together, if necessary, by strings.

It is unlawful for one to beget children for three years after the death of his father or mother—that is, during the period of mourning. In case this law is violated by the members of poor and obscure families, as a general rule, no notice would be taken of the circumstance by the officers of the Government. But if it should be transgressed by mandarins, or the gentry, or by literary men who have acquired the privilege of wearing a button in their caps, denoting that they are graduates, during the fixed period of mourning, it is affirmed that they would be fined, or degraded, or punished, unless they should be able to succeed in bribing those who otherwise would prosecute them for their unfilial conduct. The violation of this law is regarded as proof of a want of the respect they should bear the memory of their deceased parent—as proof that they are largely destitute of the sentiments of filial piety.

The coffin is an object of great solicitude and interest in China, as many instances might be adduced to show.

Several years since, a literary person stated to a foreign friend his perplexity of mind concerning the best way of investing a sum of money which he had lately received. One of the ways which had suggested themselves to him was the purchasing of some "longevity boards," as the four heavy pieces of timber out of which coffins principally are constructed are politely called, for the use of his aged adopted mother, when she should have need of such an article. The argument which seemed to weigh upon his mind was that, if he waited till she should die, he might not have sufficient ready money to procure the "longevity boards," and turn them into a suitable coffin; and, besides, such a present from her adopted son would be all the more acceptable to her, as it would be a visible and tangible proof that he was intending to honour her memory in a becoming manner when Providence should furnish the occasion. On the other hand were to be considered the discouragements to purchasing the boards, as want of storeroom, danger from fire, and the expense of transportation in case he should be obliged to move.

Five or six years ago, a poor old widow woman living at Fuhchau came into the possession of fifteen dollars ready money. In order to secure having available funds for purchasing a coffin, and in part for other incidental expenses connected with her burial, in view of the poverty of her family and relatives, she determined to lay out this sum in gold earrings, which she could use during her lifetime, and which could be at once converted into current money on her death. This purpose she carried out, and it proved a good investment; for, on her death, her earrings were sold, and the proceeds used in the manner she designed.

When the head of a family has arrived at the age of seventy or eighty years, if the family are in good circumstances, it is no uncommon occurrence to purchase materials for grave-clothes and for the coffin, and have them all made up in proper order, so as to have them in readiness when death calls away the beloved parent or grandparent. A piece of red silk or cloth is put on the coffin after it is finished, as an omen of good. Some red silk or cloth is also hung over the door on every succeeding birthday of the aged relative until he dies. An intercalary year

M

is often selected ; also a feast is made on the occasion, relatives, intimate friends, and near neighbours of respectability being in-vited. The guests come and congratulate the aged one on having these arrangements completed, the idea being, not " May you die soon," but " May you live a long while." The intercalary year is an omen of good in this connexion, because it has thirteen instead of twelve months. This circumstance interpreted means, " May your precious life be lengthened out and made longer than the lives of ordinary persons, just as this year is longer than usual." A large piece of red paper is pasted on the coffin, on which is written a sentence of four characters, which may be rendered "enduring as the heavens, and lasting as the earth."

The expression " preparing for death," which, as used in Western lands, often means to settle one's worldly affairs, or to leave them in such a state that heirs or executors can easily arrange them, or which often means to repent of sin, leave off all wicked habits, and believe in the Saviour, among the Chinese would rather be understood to indicate the importance of pur-chasing the coffin-boards, and the materials for the grave-clothes, or the gathering together of a sufficient amount of money for these and other necessary expenses connected with mourning and burial, so that it would be immediately available on the death of a parent or grandparent.

The coffin is first made air-tight by the use of a preparation made of Chinese varnish and lime, or varnish and broken crockery pounded fine like sand. This preparation is put into all the cracks and crevices on the inside, together with strips of cloth. This, of itself, makes the coffin very tight. In addition, sometimes it is painted or varnished on the inside, at the expense of the sons-in-law of the deceased.

It is subsequently painted several times with oil, in which pounded crockery, or lime, or some other substance, has been mingled to make the coating hard and firm, always on one of the seventh days after the decease of its occupant. At the last course the coffin is covered with black varnish. The rich usually have the coffin of their honoured dead painted or varnished on every seventh day for seven times. A coffin made of good material, and treated in the way just described, may be left unburied for a long period of years without producing any unpleasant effects.

No coffin with a corpse inclosed is allowed to be carried into the city of Fuhchau, nor are those who die within the city walls allowed to be buried in the city. One ancient grave, said to be the grave of one of the kings or princes who reigned here in olden times, is pointed out in the northern part of the city. But now-a-days the corpses of even the highest officers, and of the oldest and the richest families and proprietors, are all required to be interred outside, though there is considerable unoccupied ground on the hills and elsewhere within the city walls.

When the head of a family which has been in the habit of having servants dies, and it is determined to have meritorious ceremonies performed on an extensive scale, it is also generally decided to provide the dead with a male and a female servant to wait upon him in the other world. For this purpose an effigy is made to represent the dead person, which is placed in the chair between the table for the place of the spirit and the "longevity picture." On one side of the chair, and near one end of the table, is placed a paper and bamboo representation of a male servant, called the "golden lad;" and on the other side of the chair, and near the other end of the table, is placed a corresponding representation of a female servant, called "gemmeous lass." The servant-boy is made to hold in his hands the tobacco-pipe and tobacco-pouch, while the servant-girl is made to hold in her hands a tea-cup and saucer, or some other household utensil. These are designed as slaves or servants to the dead man in the future world. If not provided by his family, he, it is thought, would miss the attendance which he has always been accustomed to have in this world, and would be made so much the more unhappy. At the conclusion of the ceremonies, when the sedan, with its crane attached in front, is burned, these three effigies are also consumed. The effigy of the deceased is put in the sedan, and they take their departure for the world of spirits, the lad and lass keeping up with their master *en route*, or, finding him after arrival, serve him according to the understanding in this world.

A singular custom prevails in this part of China in connexion with transporting to the residence of his family the corpse of one who dies while away from home. When still at a distance, some of the family go forth to meet the coffin, taking with them a living white cock, or an image of a white cock, made as large as life out of bamboo splint and paper, coloured so as to appear quite natural.

The fowl, with feet tied together, is usually made to stand on the coffin, and the procession proceeds homeward, the cock retaining its position, amid the wailing of the mourners. Some-times, as in the case of high officials, the cock is placed in a sedan-chair, and borne home by four or eight bearers, according to the rank of the deceased. Sometimes it is placed on the top of the sedan which contains the wife of the deceased or the nearest of kin present. It is not an unusual sight to see a white cock perched upon the top of a coffin or the top of a hearse, where he rides along with a dignified gravity, as though the procession was designed to do him honour. The live cock retains its proper position, while the image of a cock most usually assumes an unnatural position, being inclined backward or forward, or over to one side, or some of its parts become broken or bent.

WHITE COCK ON A COFFIN LURING HOME ONE OF THE SPIRITS OF THE DEAD.

The Chinese say that one of the three spirits of the dead comes into the cock at the time of meeting the corpse, and that the spirit is thus allured back to the residence of the family. In case the corpse is not brought home to be buried, a letter, or some of the clothing recently worn by the deceased, or his shoes, or part of his baggage, is often sent instead. The white cock and the mourners go forth to meet the letter or relic of the departed, just as they would go to meet the corpse. On meeting the letter or the relic, the spirit passes as readily into the fowl as it would pass into it were the corpse itself met, and the spirit is conducted home just as surely.

Occasionally along the road, and specially at the corners of the streets, the name of the deceased is loudly called by one of the procession. Sometimes two priests are engaged to beat along the road each a brazen instrument, and the spirit is greatly aided in finding its way by following their peculiar sound. At such times the spirit is not believed to have entered the cock, but simply to regard it as a kind of escort.

After having served as a temporary residence or the escort of a spirit of the dead, the fowl is never killed for the table, but is nourished with care until it dies a natural death. The Chinese seldom eat the flesh of a white fowl, and many will not rear such a fowl on their premises. Some explain this fact, and the use of a purely white to the exclusion of any other coloured cock on such occasions, by saying that white is the badge of mourning; others by saying that the white cock is a "divine" or "spiritual" fowl.

The Chinese cannot explain the origin of this custom, or show its reasonableness or even fitness to the end desired by any course of argument. They are remarkably fond of accounting for their established customs by saying that "anciently people did thus and so, and we now-a-days imitate their example." They seem to think that this is a most satisfactory reason why they should do as they are in the habit of doing.

CHAPTER VIII.

ANCESTRAL TABLETS AND ANCESTRAL HALLS.

THERE are at least two traditionary records relating to the origin of the ancestral tablet. According to one account, it originated during the Chau dynasty, B.C. 350. An attendant on the Prince of Tsin cut a piece of flesh from his thigh and had it cooked for his master, who was perishing from hunger. He was unable to continue to travel on account of pain. He was afterward burnt to death in a wood that was set on fire. His prince found his corpse and erected a tablet to his memory, and offered incense before it daily.

The other account is derived from one of twenty-four popular stories relating to filial piety. According to this story,

Some time during the Han dynasty, which ended about A.D. 25, lived Ting Sean, who, having lost his father and his mother when he was young, never was able to obey and support them. While thinking on their toils and troubles on his account, he carved images of them, and served them as though they were alive. His wife would not reverence them. One day she took a needle and in sport pricked their fingers, when blood ran out. Sean afterward, on looking at the wooden images, observed their eyes filled with tears. Inquiring of his wife, he learned the circumstances of the case, and immediately divorced her.

In another edition of the book a different story is given of the treatment which the wooden images received. It is there said that a neighbour's wife one day desired to borrow some article. Sean's wife first inquired of the images in the usual way. They returned for answer that they were unwilling to lend the article, and consequently she did not produce and lend it. On receiving this refusal, and understanding the reason, the neighbour's wife was angry, and, taking a stick, struck the images, whereupon they wept. Sean, seeing them shed tears, inquired the reason. His wife having informed him of the circumstances, he was very much exasperated, and proceeded not only to beat his neighbour's wife, but prosecuted her before the magistrate. The magistrate eulogized him for his filial devotion, and petitioned the emperor to bestow on him an honorary tablet to put up over his door.

According to another tradition, when a little boy, Ting Sean was disobedient to his parents, but finally became very docile and filial. One day, as his mother was taking some refreshment to him, while labouring in the field, she tripped her foot against the root of a fir-tree and fell to the ground. From the effects of this fall she died; whereupon Sean took the root of this tree, and made some images of his parents.

If what Ting Sean did was the origin of the ancestral tablet, he doubtless did what he had no intention of doing. He easily and unwittingly effected what few are able to achieve, though myriads spend their lives in the pursuit—he made his name immortal in history; he inaugurated a custom which has been imitated by untold millions—that of worshipping deceased parents and ancestors under some visible and tangible symbol.

Whatever may have been the original appearance of the ancestral tablet, it now retains no resemblance to a human form.

A minute description of its size and appearance, as found to prevail in one part of the country, will not be applicable to another part of the country.

The ancestral tablet, as used at this place in families, varies from eight or nine inches to about one foot and a half in height, and from two inches to three and a half or four inches in width. The best are made of fragrant wood, parts of which are elaborately carved, costing sometimes several dollars apiece; while the most inferior and the cheapest are made out of common wood, and can be purchased for less than a quarter of a dollar. It consists of three pieces of wood, one of which serves as a pedestal, and the other two as upright pieces. The tablets used in ancestral halls, where the representatives of a family clan meet several times a year to worship their ancestors, and the tablets commemorating ancient sages and worthies placed in temples, are much larger than those used in private houses, and often are made of only two pieces of cheap wood, viz. a pedestal and a perpendicular piece.

A block, varying from about four to seven inches long, and from about one to two and a half inches thick, and from about two to three and a half inches wide, constitutes the pedestal of such tablets as are generally used in private dwellings.

ANCESTRAL TABLET REPRESENTING ONE PERSON.

On the front side of the block which forms the pedestal of the tablet there is usually carved the image of a fabulous animal which is said to flourish only when sages appear. On the front of the projecting knob of the longer of the upright pieces is carved the head of the Chinese dragon, another fabulous animal said to have existed in ancient times. On the right and the left hand sides of the front of the shorter of the upright pieces are often engraved what are regarded as side views of the dragon. It is on the central portion of the same piece in a straight line, beginning at the top and extending down-

ward, that the name of the reigning dynasty, the title (if it has any)
of the deceased whom the tablet is designed to commemorate,
his ancestral and his given name, are engraven, usually in raised
characters ; sometimes, however, the inscription is made with
black ink, the strip on which the characters are written having
been neatly painted or varnished. The name of the son who
erects the tablet is also similarly carved or written, but in
smaller characters, and is placed a little to the left-hand side of
the bottom of the other characters. In the case of a tablet
erected by a son in memory of his mother, the ancestral name
of her father—that is, her maiden surname—as well as that of her
husband are put upon the tablet. The engraved and the lettered
portions of the tablet are generally overlaid with gold leaf. The
other portions are often left of the natural colour of the wood,
though sometimes they are painted. The flat surfaces of the
two upright pieces, where they impinge upon each other, are
always left unpainted. The dates of the birth and the death
of the person, and the place of the grave, are sometimes
recorded in black ink on the inner surface of one of the upright
pieces.

This tablet represents only one deceased individual, either
male or female as the case may be. The tablet for the father
and the tablet for the mother of a family are alike in form
though they may vary in size. The essential difference consists
in the inscription or the engraving on it. Only one tablet of the
above description is allowed to be erected in honour of one's
father or mother. This belongs to the eldest son, and is usually
kept in his house. All the ancestral tablets which belong to
the father and mother of a family descend to the eldest son,
and become his property on their death. When the eldest son
dies, they fall into the hands of his son, if he has any. Almost
invariably, when the eldest son, if of adult age and married,
has no son, he adopts some child of his younger brothers, or
some other relation, in order to keep up the family name and
retain the tablets in his own family line.

Daughters are not allowed a tablet of either parent. After
marriage they worship the tablets belonging to their husband's
family. On their death their tablet is placed among the tablets
which belong to their eldest sons, never among those which are
worshipped in the families of their own brothers.

As long as the sons of a family live together, they worship
the tablet erected by the eldest son. When, however, the family
breaks up and the younger sons, receiving their share of the

patrimony, separate to live each by himself, if married, they may each erect a kind of tablet, quite different in several respects from the tablet already described. The tablet which the younger brothers may provide for their own use consists of a single piece of board from ten to twelve inches square, fitted into a frame a few inches high. It is then painted or varnished either black or reddish. In the middle of the front side, reaching from the top toward the bottom, there is a sentence written or engraved, and frequently gilded, which indicates that the tablet represents or commemorates all the ancestors of a family of a certain surname. The person who erects it also, if he pleases, has recorded on it the names of his male ancestors, beginning with his father, back to three or five generations, on the right of the inscription in the centre, his father's name occupying the place nearest the right edge of the board. In similar manner, he may have recorded on the left of the centre the surnames of his maternal ancestors, beginning with his father, back to three or five generations, commencing with his mother's surname, which is placed nearest the left edge of the tablet. The names of his grandfather and of his grandmother are respectively placed next to the names of their father and mother, and so on; the more remote the ancestor, the nearer his or her name comes to the centre of the board. This kind of tablet, as will be readily understood, is a general tablet for all his ancestors in common, and for his ancestors of three or five generations in particular, as he chooses to inscribe the names for three or five generations. At his death this descends to his eldest son, who has the exclusive right to erect the other kind of tablet to the memory of their father and mother, while his younger sons may each erect the general tablet to the memory of their father and mother, and of their more remote ancestors having the family surname.

The ancestral tablet representing one's father or mother is usually worshipped for only three or five generations. During this period it is preserved with care in a portable niche or shrine made in the general shape of a house, but only a few feet square. If unable to procure such a niche, the tablets are simply arranged on a shelf or table. If the family has a niche, it is usually placed in some of the inner apartments, where easy access can be had to it for the purpose of performing the customary worship before it. The niche is designed to hold all the tablets worshipped by the family and belonging to it, unless they are too numerous. After the third or the fifth generation has passed away, the tablets which represent it are sometimes taken away and buried in or near the graves of the persons they represent, or they may be burned to ashes ; at least they must be removed from the niche, to furnish room for the tablets representing the individuals of a less remote period, every generation furnishing two tablets.

WORSHIPPING THE ANCESTRAL TABLET IN ITS NICHE.

The ancestral tablets of both kinds are worshipped at fixed times or occasions, and according to certain established forms.

On the first and fifteenth of every month, tapers or candles and incense are regularly burned before them. Two tapers and three sticks of incense are lighted in the morning. The incense is permitted to burn up, but the tapers oftentimes are put out when about half consumed. At evening the tapers are relighted, and three more incense sticks are burnt. For use in worshipping the tablets, a censer to hold the incense is placed before them, and a pair of candlesticks is arranged, one on each side of the censer, to hold the candles.

On the recurrence of the anniversary of the birthday of any living member of the family, or on the occasion of preparing cards to be used in negotiating for the engagement in marriage of any of the family, as well as on the evening of the twenty-ninth of the first month of the year, tapers and incense are burned before the tablets. On the birthdays an additional offering of three bowls of a kind of vermicelli is also made. On the evening of the twenty-ninth day of the first month referred to, besides the burning of tapers and incense, there are presented before the tablets several bowls of a black-looking, dirty kind of rice-soup or congee, in which have been boiled together various articles, such as sugar, dates, and pea-nuts. The offering of this soup is believed to indicate the strong filial affection which exists in the heart of the offerer.

On the occurrence of joyous events, or on the anniversary of the death of an ancestor whose tablet is among those worshipped, not only are tapers and incense burned, but offerings to the dead are made of several kinds of meat, as fowl, fish, and pork. On the fourth day of the first month of the Chinese year, and on the last evening of the year, some boiled rice, in addition to meats, tapers, and incense, is presented. On the festival of sweeping the tombs in the second or third month, besides the meats, &c. some greenish cakes, made of rice-flour and coloured with the juice of a certain vegetable, are offered to the ancestral dead.

On the fifteenth of the first month, and at the festival of the Dragon Boats on the fifth day of the fifth month, and at the festival held about the middle of the seventh month, and at the festival of mid-autumn, and at a certain time in the twelfth month, tapers, incense, and meats are presented before them. The ceremony in the seventh month referred to is also attended with the burning of mock-clothing and paper houses, i.e. paper on which the shape of different kinds of clothing, as caps, coats, shoes, &c. has been stamped ; miniature houses and household furniture, all made of paper, are also burned for the use of the departed relative in the spirit world. These are believed to be changed into clothing, houses, and furniture, by the process of burning, owing to the potent agency of a charm which is also burned at the same time.

At certain festivals in the ninth and eleventh months respectively, besides the meats, candles, and incense, there are also offered before the tablets a plate of a certain kind of rice-cake and a quantity of rice-balls, as a token of continued filial regard and remembrance.

Whenever there is an offering of anything besides tapers and incense, it is customary for all the adult male members of the family present to kneel down once before the tablets, and bow their heads toward the earth several times. They also on such occasions burn a quantity of paper prepared in different ways, which is believed to represent gold, silver, and cash. In this easy and cheap method are remittances supposed to be made for the use of deceased relatives.

On the anniversary of the death of an ancestor, his surviving descendant embraces the opportunity to make of him or of her, as the case may be, some friendly and kind inquiries in regard to health or food, by dropping on the floor before the tablet two pieces of wood, each piece having an oval and a flat side. The character of the answer of the dead is supposed to be indicated by the relative positions of the same after reaching the floor. If the first reply is unfavourable, another trial is made, proposing perhaps a different question, and so on, until a satisfactory reply is given, for it would never do to desist inquiring so long as the reply indicated displeasure or dissatisfaction on the part of the deceased.

Few foreign residents in China, who have not made particular inquiries on the subject, have any adequate idea of the amount of ancestral worship in this empire, and of the aggregate expense of such worship. Ancestral halls may be divided into two classes; those in which all the ancestors of families having the same ancestral name and claiming relationship are worshipped, and those in which the ancestors of a particular branch of the families having the same ancestral name and claiming near relationship are worshipped. These latter are called "branch" ancestral halls. A branch hall is usually erected at the expense of a wealthy family only when the families having an interest in a general hall are very numerous.

Many Chinese do not profess to have an interest in any public or common ancestral hall in the vicinity. These are generally the descendants of immigrants from another part of the province or empire.

Ancestral halls differ largely in size, plan, style of finish, and expense. The smallest perhaps are only twenty or thirty feet wide by fifty or sixty feet long, and consist of only two or three apartments. Others are some eight or ten times as large, as regards width and length, having a large number of rooms designed for different uses. The expense, of course, is variable, from a few hundred dollars to several tens of thousands, including the permanent fund.

At the time of erecting an ancestral hall, rules are made by the proprietor in regard to the qualifications of those who may have their tablets placed in it, or the sum of money which must be paid into the general or permanent funds of the hall, by the particular families to which the new tablets belong. These rules are very definite and strict, and are rigidly enforced, else the place devoted to holding or arranging the tablets in the halls would in a few generations become crowded.

In case of the entry of the tablet of a high officer, as of a viceroy or literary chancellor, among the tablets of his ancestors in the hall, it is said that especial permission to do it is usually obtained from the emperor. It is not necessary to obtain such permission, but the family of an officer who holds a very high station takes occasion to obtain it in order to add increased glory to his family and to his ancestors. The procession got up at the time of carrying such a tablet from the residence of the deceased to the ancestral hall is as large and splendid as possible, and is accompanied by bands of music. In this procession a tablet, having two words which give the imperial sanction, holds a prominent place.

The tablets placed in a hall for worship are generally at least two or three times as large as those made for use in private houses. They are oftentimes placed in a niche built expressly for the purpose, with divisions or shelves in it, so that they may not be all on the same level. At other times they are arranged on a platform or shelf at one end of the room devoted to their worship.

At the time of erecting an ancestral hall, a permanent fund is established by the family or the families who unite in erecting it. The profits of this fund are designed to be used in defraying the expenses of the worship and sacrifices made at the appointed or customary times. This fund usually consists of arable land, houses, or stores, the produce or rent of which is appropriated to the support of the hall. Such property is inalienable except by the unanimous consent of the elders of all the families interested in the hall.

The hall belonging to wealthy families usually is kept in order by some one who lives on the premises. It is the duty of this individual, or the keeper for the time being, to keep a record of the days of the death of each person whose tablet is placed in the hall. On the arrival of these days annually, he should carefully remember the fact, and burn incense, and candles, and mock-money before the particular tablet representing the deceased, in the customary manner. Sometimes feasts are made in honour of the deceased on such anniversaries.

Besides the observance of the anniversary of the death of the person to whom a tablet belongs, there are various other times when the dead are worshipped by their surviving descendants. These times are generally specified by the founder of a hall. In such a case, the descendants feel under obligation to follow his will. If the time and the manner of worship are not definitely fixed by the founder, those concerned in a particular hall soon come to agree when and how everything should be done. There are some five or six occasions per annum when worship of the ancestral tablets in the halls at this place is commonly observed.

1. On the "opening of the temple," generally before the third or fourth day of the first month of the new year. This refers to the first burning of incense in the hall after the beginning of a new year.

2. On the fourth or fifth day of the first month, when they worship in a circle. This takes its distinctive name from the circumstance that all the representatives of the families who are present, stand *in a circle* before the tablets in the main room of the hall, with their faces toward the *inside*, and, at a given signal, each having grasped his own hands, make their obeisance once, after Chinese fashion. After this they sit down to a feast before the tablets.

3. From the eleventh to the fifteenth of the first month, in the evening. At these times the halls are brilliantly lighted. Frequently a pair of huge candles for each of the living male descendants is burned before the tablets, each person sometimes furnishing his own candles. The one whose turn it is to superintend the affairs of the hall for the current year usually has his candles placed in the centre. Mock-money is always burnt at these times for the benefit of the dead. During this period, they

feast together in the evening from two to four times after worshipping the tablets. This is called keeping company with the
spirits of the dead by night.

4. A sacrifice is made to the spirits of ancestors, some time
during the second month. This is called a "vernal sacrifice."
This sacrifice consists of meats, vegetables, fruits, &c. and is
attended with considerable show and solemnity.

5. About the middle of the seventh month, another season of
special worship and feasting takes place before the temples in the
halls. In addition to the mock-money consumed on other occasions, mock-clothing must be burnt at this time for the benefit
of the dead, and, among the other articles, there must be provided at the feast at least two ducks and two water-melons.

6. Some time in the eighth month, at the regular day, there
occurs the "autumnal sacrifice" to departed ancestors before
their tablets. In connexion with large and rich ancestral halls,
this sacrifice is also attended with considerable pomp and solemnity, and is terminated by a feast, of which all the representatives of the families who are present partake. It is
customary at some halls to divide the pork sacrificed among the
representatives of the different families, which they may take to
their homes and consume. It is a saying that the meat thus
divided will have a tendency to procure male children. If,
among the descendants of the ancestors worshipped, there are
any who have attained to office, it is usual to give such an extra
pound of this pork, which is said to aid the sons of such a family
in becoming celebrated, and competing successfully at the literary
examinations. At some halls there is also an extra season of
worship at the time of the winter solstice.

These few notes may perhaps serve to give some Western
readers a more adequate and intelligent idea of the importance
attached to ancestral worship, and the expense attending it,
among this people, than they were in the habit of entertaining.
Generally speaking, the customs which relate to the worship of
the ancestral tablet in private houses and in public halls are
more fixed, and are deemed more important, than those customs
which relate to the worship of idols and spirits, especially in
literary families.

What resident in China from Western lands has not visited
many a temple devoted to the worship of idols ? and who has
not read descriptions of such visits ? Heathen temples occupy
most conspicuous positions in this empire, and seem to invite
a visit from the stranger. Ancestral halls are, however, erected

in more retired places than temples, and, being considered private property, are not open to the public. Hence they attract less attention than do temples, and much less is known in relation to them.

On the morning of September 21st I visited one of the largest ancestral halls in this city. The invitation to visit it was given by one of the literati, who had an interest in it, being a member of one of the families descended from its proprietor. He was my *cicerone* during the visit, and was very ready and frank in replying to my inquiries, which were not remarkably few.

The day fixed for the visit was the one for the "autumnal sacrifice." This enabled me to witness some of the preparations for that sacrifice, though it was understood that I was not to remain during the attendant ceremonies.

We arrived at the hall about 11 A.M. The outer doors were opened, and, being accompanied by the gentleman alluded to, there was no opposition made to my entrance. We found the tables and furniture already arranged for the approaching worship, though the articles to be offered in sacrifice to the spirits of the departed had not all been brought in, it being too early in the day.

The premises occupied by the hall and its surroundings were about fifty-eight paces wide, by about three times that distance in length, including a "false hill" and an artificial fish-pond. The latter was about thirty by fifty feet, and its sides were stoned up very substantially. The ground of the open courts between the buildings and in front of them was covered with large smooth slabs of granite. There were numerous halls or apartments. The primary hall, being nearly in the centre of the premises, was the place which contained the principal tablets, and where the sacrifice was to be offered, and the worship performed. A large niche or shrine, the bottom of which was some three or four feet from the floor, and in which the tablets were standing, had in it several shelves or steps somewhat like a flight of stairs. On the back and highest step was placed a large tablet about four or five feet square, which represented all the ancestors of the families who were interested in the worship soon to be performed. In front of this were arranged, on various steps in the niche, nine tablets in all, richly gilded, and about three feet high and seven or eight inches wide, each representing, it was said, two individuals—that is, a man and his principal wife. On one of the lower steps was placed a kind of rack, which contained two small rolls. These were the "credentials" or "letters-patent" given

N

to two deceased members of the families by the emperor when
they were commissioned as officers of Government.   In front of
this shrine was a large table of a particular kind and shape, much
used in worshipping.   On this were placed a pair of high and
large candlesticks, a large censer, and two high flower-vases.
Near each end of this table, which was eight or ten feet long,
were two small tables, designed to be used for holding the pig
and the kid which were to be offered up in sacrifice.   The hair
and the entrails of these animals having been removed, they were
to be placed, uncooked, on the tables prepared—the pig in a
kneeling posture, with its nose resting on an upright peg, and
the kid in a standing posture, resting on a frame.   Two small
pieces of cloth were prepared, ready to be put upon these animals
after they had been arranged on the tables during the sacrificial
worship.   In front of these two tables, along each side of the
room, were three or four tables, each having a pair of candlesticks, but no censer, and also some singularly-shaped and odd-
looking utensils, which were to be used during the approaching
worship.

Directly in front of the shrine, and about forty feet distant
from it, was a small table placed crosswise the room, which held
nothing but a censer.   This was the place where the head man
or chief of the families represented was to stand during the
ceremonies.   The place where the others were to stand and
perform their part was some thirty or forty feet still farther from
the shrine, and behind the master of the ceremonies.   A large
iron censer, to be used for burning mock-money, and the silk to
be offered to the spirit of the ancestors, was directly between the
places allotted to the chief actor in the ceremonies and to the
other company of performers.   On the right and left sides of
this room were suspended on the walls two large pictures of some
of the ancestors of the worshippers.   Higher up, and fastened
near the roof to cross-pieces, were arranged in this and in adjacent apartments fourteen honorary wooden tablets, given to
members of the families concerned in the sacrifice as tokens of
success at literary examinations.   Another tablet contained the
names of fourteen who had become masters of arts.   Some
thirty notifications of the success of the same number of candidates at the lowest order of literary examinations were carefully
pasted up on the walls of an adjoining apartment.   In a part
of the front portion of the premises were arranged, in a conspicuous position, under cover, a set of a certain kind of implements
or portable tablets, oftentimes seen in mandarin or idol pro-

cessions, designed to be used in case of the public carrying of a new tablet to the hall from the residence of the person it represented.

An adjoining apartment, called the "secondary hall," contained a much smaller niche than the one in the "primary hall." This niche was designed to hold the tablets of the inferior wife or concubine of the members of the families connected with the institution, provided she were a woman of especial merit, such as being the mother of a son who became a very learned man or an officer of the Government. There were only five or six small tablets in this hall, each representing a secondary wife or concubine, who in some way had become famous or distinguished in her family.

Another apartment contained one solitary tablet, designed to commemorate a woman whose husband died when she was twenty years old, leaving a son only four months old. She lived, it is said, for a long while, on account of extreme poverty, on one meal a day, and thus was enabled to support and educate her son. He subsequently became a master of arts. She and her husband had a tablet erected to their memory in the primary hall; but she, in consequence of her extraordinary virtues and merits, was adjudged the additional right and honour of a tablet erected in this "chaste and filial hall." Peace to her memory!

In another apartment was an image about one foot high, representing *the local god of wealth*.

Another apartment or hall was devoted to the worship of *the god of literature*. His idol is less than two feet high. In front and on the sides of it were several smaller images, associated with the god of literature, who is worshipped by students as the bestower of success in literary pursuits and honours. Several dishes of food are placed before this image, and incense and candles are burned there in his honour by members of the various families interested in this ancestral hall, when they are successful at the examinations, and also at other times, whenever, according to the sentiments and customs of this people, there seems to be a call for such tokens of thanksgiving, or of supplications. On the first and fifteenth of each Chinese month, incense and candles are regularly burned before the god of literature in this particular hall, and also at the other fixed times for sacrifice or worship before the ancestral tablets, in the hope of obtaining this god's kind offices in promoting the literary pursuits of the members of the families connected with it. Besides the apartments or halls already mentioned, there are rooms designed for the reception and temporary accommodation of mandarins and their retinue, for study, for recreation, and for various other purposes.

This ancestral hall was built about seventy years ago by the great-grandfather of my informant and guide. The cost of the ground, buildings, furniture, walls, &c. including the permanent fund for defraying the regular expenses, he affirmed amounted to 300,000 dollars, which seems a very high sum, though everything about the establishment was evidently made in very good style. The annual expense for the stated sacrifices and worship is about 300 dollars.

In the afternoon after I left, according to my informant's account, there were offered in sacrifice to the spirits of his deceased ancestors in the hall before their tablets, *a pig weighing one hundred pounds,* a kid, five kinds of green vegetables, of each kind two heads or bunches, five kinds of fruit, and five kinds of seeds, as rice, wheat, beans, &c.; also salt, red dregs of wine, a piece of dried beef, bread-cakes made into five different shapes, a piece of raw pork, a *small quantity of pigs' hair and of pigs' blood, ten cups of tea, and ten cups of wine.* The vegetables and meats were all uncooked. Similar offerings are presented at the autumnal sacrifices from year to year. Besides these, there were also ten dishes of food already cooked, consisting of meats, fish, fowl, and vegetables, arranged on a table placed before the tablets.

A professor of ceremonies was present directing the worshippers when to kneel, bow, and rise up. The faces of these worshippers were turned toward the tablets. The head person among them was a lad some six or eight years old, being the eldest son of the eldest son of the eldest son, &c. of the remote male ancestors from whom all of the Chinese having his ancestral name, living in this city, claim to have descended. He was the chief of the clan, according to the Chinese law of primogeniture. This lad, instructed by a professor of ceremonies, took the lead in the worship, all the rest kneeling down when he knelt, bowing their heads towards the ground when he bowed his head, and rising to their feet when he rose. The head man, at the proper time during the ceremony, while on his knees, all the rest of the worshippers being also on their knees, received three cups of wine, which he poured out, one by one, upon some straw placed in the bottom of a certain vessel. These cups were then refilled and replaced on a table before the tablets, whence they had been taken by the professor of ceremonies. Before the wine was poured out, he lifted the cups up reverently in front of him, as though offering them to the spirits supposed to be in the tablets. Three bowls of vegetables were presented, as if to the spirits, in like manner, and then taken away and placed upon a table. The professor of ceremonies, at the proper time, knelt down and read, or rather chanted, a kind of sacrificial prayer to the spirits of the departed ancestors of the company present. They being all the while on their knees, then bowed down their heads toward the ground three times, when several rolls of coarse silk, or something in imitation of silk, were burnt. The great drum was beaten. All rose up at the command of the professor, and left their allotted places. The cooked provisions intended for the feast were soon arranged on tables, in the proper or customary manner at feasts. The representatives of the families interested in the hall took their seats, and partook of the feast provided in the presence, as they believed, of their ancestors. All of them were males, no female being allowed to be present or participate in the festivities or solemnities of such occasions. At the close of the feasting, each representative took home with him some of the flesh of the pig which had been offered whole before the tablets.

During the progress of the worship they all knelt down five times, and while on their knees bowed down their heads simultaneously three times. There was no weeping, no smiling, and no talking, except by the professor of ceremonies. All was orderly, still, solemn, and reverent.

I have only spoken of the manner of performing ancestral worship as practised at one hall on a certain occasion. The practice at other halls doubtless varies largely in various particulars from what has been described. It will readily occur to the reader that a description of only a small part of the ceremonies performed has been attempted.

CHAPTER IX.

PRIESTS OF THE THREE RELIGIONS.

THERE are three classes[*] of native priests in China, understanding the word "priest" to denote a person who officiates in religious worship. The *Buddhist* religion is not native to China. It was imported from India in the early part of the first century of the Christian era. It is usually regarded as more popular than the Tauist religion in this part of the empire. There are several hundred Buddhist priests in this city and its suburbs. The priests live in buildings dedicated to the honour and worship of Buddha, such as are usually called monasteries. Of these there are nearly thirty in all at this place, including those which are located a few miles east and west of the city.

Three of the largest of these monasteries have each an abbot, who has great power and influence over the resident priests. A large and celebrated monastery, situated about six miles east of the city, on Drum Mountain, has between one and two hundred priests connected with it. The abbot is not always an old priest, or one of a venerable and commanding appearance. The abbot of the large monastery above alluded to, a few years ago, was a

---

[*] But Père Huc says, "The religious sentiment has vanished from the national mind; the rival doctrines have lost all authority, and their partisans grow sceptical and impious, have fallen into the abyss of indifferentism, in which they have given each other the kiss of peace. Religious discussions have entirely ceased, and the whole Chinese nation has proclaimed this famous formula, with which everybody is satisfied, 'San-kio-y-koio,'—that is, 'the three religions are but one.' Thus all the Chinese are at the same time partisans of Confucius, Lao-tze, and Buddha, or rather they are nothing at all; they reject all faith, all dogma, to live merely by their more or less depraved and corrupted instincts."—Huc's *Chinese Empire*, vol. ii. pp. 195-198.

Middle Island. Stone Bridge in front of the Methodist Chapel.
(Salt) Granaries.

DISTANT VIEW OF KUNSAN, i.e. DRUM MOUNTAIN.

young man between thirty and forty years of age, of a retiring disposition, and of thoughtful and sedate cast of countenance. The priests who are trained at those monasteries which have an abbot, provided they are furnished with a certain document or certificate of character signed by the abbot, are entitled to claim admittance to any monastery in the empire, and to receive the rites of hospitality for a few days gratis.

Most of the large monasteries own land or other property, from which rent in rice or money is annually received, though usually not sufficient to defray the current expenses of the institution. The deficiency is made up in part by begging from visitors and worshippers, and by voluntary presents made by officers, the literary class, and the common people, either in consequence of some vow, or as a means of increasing their merits.

A company of priests from two or three of the largest monasteries in the vicinity parade the principal streets of the city and suburbs, for the purpose of begging for the support of their respective monasteries, or, in more polite terms, of receiving the voluntary contributions of the people. Sometimes they appear to the number of thirty or forty in one company, each dressed in the peculiar costume of the Buddhist priesthood, with uncovered heads, and carrying in their hands a kind of gong or cymbal, which they beat slowly at regular intervals. With solemn countenances, they walk leisurely along the public streets in single file, not unfrequently in profound silence, though sometimes chanting or reciting together the name of Buddha, or some formulary. The people who happen to be passing along the streets, and the shopkeepers, contribute what they please either in cash, rice, or oil. They are usually followed by men who take and carry along whatever is proffered.

Both the common and the official costume of the Buddhist priests is quite different, as regards colour and fashion, from the costume of the common people. The coat is distinguished by its having a very wide turn-over collar. When they officiate they usually dress in yellow clothing, made of cotton or silk. At other times they commonly wear garments of an ash colour, though sometimes they are white.

They shave off all the hair from their heads two or three times per month, so that their pates are perfectly smooth. From this circumstance arises the expression "bald-headed asses," which sometimes is derisively applied to them. Many of them, perhaps all who are regularly educated at a monastery, have several places or spots on their pates, burnt with coals of fire in such a manner that the hair never grows there again. Only an abbot is entitled to perform this ceremony. It is a kind of badge of their profession, or rather of their standing in it.

They are monkish in their mode of life. They cast off and refuse obedience to their parents; they never marry; they do not acknowledge, much less exhibit, any affection toward their brothers or sisters, or other relatives; they possess no friendships; they reject and disown any common sympathy with the rest of mankind. They profess to ignore the constant relations and duties of life. Hence the common expression Chok-ka, which is applied to them, indicating that they have left or gone out of the house or family. It is asserted that they may not sleep in a dwelling-house with other people. They profess to have wholly given up the world, and its honours, pleasures, and excitements, and to be supremely desirous of being entirely un-influenced by things of sense, as other men are, seeking only to be absorbed into Buddha at death. They are solitary, unsocial, contemplative beings, reminding one of the monks of the Middle Ages. They profess no allegiance to the emperor; still, of course, they yield obedience to him through the civil magistrate. They are professedly under the control of an officer living in the south-eastern quarter of the city, who, according to report, was formerly a priest himself, and who received his title of office directly from Peking for the special purpose of governing them. It is, however, found to be the fact that he has little or no real authority over them, except in unimportant matters, they being more immediately under the superintendence and jurisdiction of the abbots of their respective monasteries.

They spend their time variously; much of it is occupied, when at their monasteries, in chanting their Buddhist classics, or sacred books. Many of these are, substantially, a representa-

BUDDHIST PRIEST.

tion of the sounds of the words of the original books brought from India, by the use of Chinese characters, not a translation of the sense. They attach much merit to the repetitions of their classics, keeping an accurate account of them by means of a string of beads. Many of the priests are engaged more or less in conducting various religious or superstitious ceremonies in the families resident in the city and suburbs, and surrounding villages. When not thus employed, they return to the monastery to which they belong, unless they are appointed to take the charge of temples.

In connexion with the celebrated monastery lying east of the city there is a ponderous bell, which is struck so frequently and so regularly that the sound is said by the priests never to cease day or night from one year to another. In fact, however, the reverberation does sometimes actually cease for a moment or two through inadvertence on the part of the bellman, who is a priest officiating *pro tempore* in rotation. The priests are unwilling to admit that the sound ever ceases. The bell is rung, not by any machinery which would insure regularity, but simply by pulling a rope which causes a suspended stick of wood to strike upon it.

In the monastery on Drum Mountain, morning worship is held before daylight, and the evening worship about four or five o'clock in the afternoon. Length of service is from an hour to an hour and a half. All the resident priests are required to attend and join in the service. It is held in an immense room, where are three colossal images of Buddha side by side. The altar is furnished gaudily and costly. In front of it are low wooden stools and mats for the priests to use when kneeling. The service consists principally of a chant or recitation of passages from the Buddhist classics in Sanskrit, represented by Chinese characters used for their sound, not meaning. The accompaniment is not organs and viols, but bells, large and small, a wooden skull, and an iron urn, which are struck with sticks from time to time. The chant is monotonous, but sometimes musical and impressive. All the priests keep exact time. Part of the ceremonies consists in leaving their places and moving in procession, winding their way, back and forth, between rows of stools, proceeded by a little bell-ringer, all busily and solemnly chanting. Their tone of voice is slow, measured, and reverent. Some occasionally kneel down and bow their heads toward Buddha. At times the music and utterance increases to the very climax of rapidity, and then gradually diminishes. Repetition of Omitu, the name of Buddha, is exceedingly numerous, and believed to be meritorious in a very high degree.

A large monastery has numerous rooms, as a library, reception-room for officers or other distinguished guests, as well as one for the common people, a large room for daily prayer or worship, a study-room, a place where living animals may be kept, &c. The animals referred to are not kept or reared for food, but as a work of merit. At the largest monastery near here there is a fish-pond, which is full of fine fish of various kinds, not one of which will the priests allow to be caught and used for food on any consideration. There is also a part of the establishment appropriated to the keeping of those animals which are supported at the expense of the monastery, or of the people who have placed them there in the fulfilment of a vow. Here may be found cattle, swine, goats, hens and chickens, ducks and geese. At that monastery, a few years ago, there were several tens of cattle feeding on the hill under the care of servants, kept there as a meritorious act. It is required that those who bring animals there to be nourished and kept alive should contribute money or grain, monthly or annually, to support them until they die a natural death. If domestic fowls, thus kept, lay eggs, the eggs are buried in the ground, not used as food. Such, at least, is the theory. When any animal dies, it is buried, and the donor or supporter of it is duly notified of the fact, if it is considered a case of sufficient importance.

The priests and their servants, or the men employed to till the ground by the monastery, and do the heavy work about the establishment, professedly eat nothing but vegetable food. The consumption of meat of any kind, including fish, is believed to be a sinful act. Everything that has had animal life is theoretically refused as an article of food. It is generally believed, however, among the common people, that many of the priests eat animal food when they can do it unobserved. Those connected with the larger monasteries, where there is an abbot, and where the laws or regulations of Buddhism are more generally carried out, it is thought consume comparatively little meat. Most or all of the travelling, or, as the people often call them, "wild" priests, probably indulge in eating meat quite often. The idea that water and vegetables are full of living animalculæ, when advanced to the Buddhist priests as a proof that they cannot live without the destruction and the consumption of animate beings, is rejected by them with indignation, the fact being denied.

Although they are much detested and abused by the Chinese

generally as men whose example in disowning the common and
the constant relations of life it is neither reasonable nor even
possible for all to imitate, they still are much sought after and
employed to officiate at religious and idolatrous ceremonies at all
seasons of the year. They always hold themselves in readiness
to engage in worship in private houses when invited. They
receive a small pittance in money for such services, besides being
boarded at the expense of the family as long as the ceremonies
last. They are employed principally to perform what are considered meritorious ceremonies for the benefit of persons recently
deceased, or for the benefit of destitute and wicked spirits in the
lower regions generally, or for the benefit of sick or feeble persons. The merit of their performances is supposed to accrue to
the family which employs and pays them, or to the particular
individuals on whose behalf the ceremonies are performed.

They keep up their sect, in part, by the buying of boys, who
are trained up for the priesthood. The number of boys thus
bought and educated must be very few, at least in this part of
China. Some persons, who have become sick of the world and
tired of life in consequence of the death of relatives or of adversity
in business, instead of taking their own lives, go and join themselves to the priests in a monastery, who gladly receive them,
shave the hair from their heads, and instruct them in the tenets
and ceremonies of Buddhism. Few leave the priesthood and
engage again in the common pursuits of the world. It is also
said that some who have violated the laws of the empire, in order
to avoid arrest and punishment, run away and become priests,
changing their dress and shaving their heads, and thus escape
detection. Probably only those whose crimes are capital, or the
punishment of whose offences against the laws would be attended
with great disgrace, endeavour to save their lives or escape the
disgrace by becoming priests. The prosecution for crime of those
who thus become Buddhist priests usually ceases when that deed
is accomplished.

There are oftentimes in connexion with the large monasteries,
one or more priests who, for a specified number of years or of
months, have no intercourse with the outward world, spending
their time entirely in their cells, usually in a sitting posture, very
much like that assumed by tailors when at work in Western
lands. Their simple food is brought to them, which they receive
through a small hole in the door or in the side of their cells.
Their thoughts are professedly fixed on Buddha, and their hope
is to attain such a degree of blessedness, by the uninterrupted

contemplation of him for so long a period, as to be absorbed into him or to become Buddhas when they die. Such is the prevalent opinion of the design of their voluntary and self-inflicted banishment from the world. It is regarded very creditable to the monastery to have such devotees connected with it, as well as very meritorious in the individuals themselves.

The corpses of the priests are burned soon after decease, instead of being buried in the manner common among other Chinese. I witnessed, over ten years ago, when visiting the large monastery to the east of the city, the burning of the body of an aged priest. The corpse was placed in the coffin in a sitting posture. The coffin was made of Chinese pine boards, unplaned, being about two feet and a half or three feet square at the bottom, one and a half or two feet square at the top, and three and a half or four feet high. It was carried to the burning-place by two men by means of a common carrying-pole laid across their shoulders, the coffin being suspended between them with ropes. Priests in their yellow robes, chanting some formula, accompanied the corpse to the place of burning, distant a quarter of a mile from the monastery. The coffin was deposited in a small building of brick and earthen walls, evidently erected for the purpose of holding coffins while they were being consumed. A quantity of wood was piled on and around the coffin, and fire applied. The priests, standing a rod or two in front of it, commenced their chanting, and in less than half an hour the ceremony was concluded, and most of the priests retired to their monastery. The ashes were subsequently gathered up, with the unconsumed bones, and placed in an earthen vessel, which was deposited in a building devoted to containing such mementos or relics of deceased priests.

Sang Pö, "*the Three Precious Ones*," is the title by which the three large idols always found in Buddhist monasteries,* arranged

---

* These images are usually colossal, and so thickly gilt as to appear of solid gold; they are sometimes placed in a great solid temple, or huge excavation, but although surrounded by silence and by shadows they do not seem calculated to exercise any considerable influence over the senses and the imagination; they are usually made of clay, and although so thickly gilt, Gutzlaff says, "Though we were in a dark hall, standing before the largest image of Buddha, there was nothing impressive; even our English sailors were disgusted with the scene; several times I raised my voice to invite all to adore God in spirit and in truth, but the minds of the priests seemed callous, and a mere assent is all that this exhortation produced." These huge gilt gods are not sublime works of the imagination, and cannot be contemplated with the same feelings as the gods of ancient Egypt and Greece.

side by side, are generally known. They refer to Buddha Past, Buddha Present, and Buddha Future, according to the adopted explanation, being three different incarnations of Buddha, either already actually accomplished or prospective.

There are three days in every year when it is said celebrations are made in honour of Buddha. The eighth day of the second month is distinguished as the time when he "left the house," or devoted himself to the life of a recluse, eschewing his parents and family friends, and determined to reside away from the abodes of mankind. This was before he became a god. His birthday is said to occur on the eighth day of the fourth month.

THE THREE PRECIOUS ONES.

He "became Buddha," or "attained to perfection and entered Nirvan," on the eighth day of the twelfth month. Buddha is worshipped on those days with greater pomp and parade than on other days. His worship in monasteries is attended with chanting the classics, and with many genuflexions and prostrations, and in marching round and round, or back and forth, &c.

The Tauist sect of religion is much less popular than the Buddhist. There are only four or five temples belonging to the *Rationalists* or *Tauists* in Fuhchau, and connected with them are not more than twelve or fourteen priests, properly so called.

Of them very little is known by foreigners. They seem to shun the acquaintance of the "stranger from afar" much more than do the Buddhist priests. They are very uncommunicative in regard to their opinions and practices. They confine their official labours principally to the temples where they reside, though on great and special occasions they sometimes officiate at other places. In many respects they are very much like the Buddhist priests. They never marry, nor do they confess to the relations of life, as emperor, parents, friends, &c. Their sect is perpetuated in much the same way as is the Buddhist priesthood. They do not confine themselves, even in theory, strictly to a vegetable diet ; they may eat animal food. Their dress is different from that of the common people.

Some of their objects of worship are said by the common people to be the same as those which are worshipped by the Buddhists, but these are probably very few. Many of their customs and ceremonies are quite similar to those practised by Buddhist priests. Buddhist and Tauist priests never officiate together, though they are sometimes employed in different parts of the same premises.

They do not shave off all the hair from their heads, like the Buddhist priests, nor do they braid up what is left in a tress, like the common people, but coil it up on the top of the head, after the costume of the Ming dynasty. They do not trim it and make it short. The Buddhist priests seem to act on the principle that to have any hair on the head is either a sin or a shame ; while the Tauist priests appear to believe that to have long hair on theirs is neither a shame nor a sin. Some Tauist priests do not shave the hair off at all, but let it all grow, while others shave off some on the outer edge or on the sides of the head, nearly as much as do the common people ; all, however, coil up the long hair on the top of the crown in a peculiar fashion, never braiding it into a cue. By the inspection of the hair on the head or the absence of hair there, one can tell whether a certain person is a priest or not ; and, if a priest, to which sect, Buddhist or Tauist, he belongs.

The above remarks relate to the class of priests called in this dialect Tö-ing, and believed to be, strictly speaking, Tauist priests. There is another class of priests called Tö-tai, who also belong to the Tauist sect. These have been frequently referred to as a certain kind of Tauist priest. They are, however, very different in several respects from the former, as well as from the Buddhist priests.

They, except when officiating, usually wear the dress of the common citizen.

They do not live in temples, but in common dwelling-houses, and among the common people.

They marry and raise families, marrying and giving in marriage, after the manner of other men.

They neither shave off all the hair on their heads like the Buddhist priests, nor coil up upon their crowns what they have unshaven like the other class of Tauist priests, but shave, comb, and braid their hair in all respects as do the common people, letting the cue dangle down their backs, except when engaged in officiating at some ceremony. At such times they coil up the cue on the back part of the head, or on the top of the head. It is usually fastened there by a wooden pin until the ceremony is completed.

Their food consists of meat, and vegetables, as they please. There is nothing in their rules to prevent the members of their families from engaging in business. As a general thing, however, fathers train up their children to follow the same calling. Their wives and daughters take in sewing, or engage in any light employment which is profitable, as they please. It would appear that this class of priests become or continue priests in order to obtain a livelihood, just as other persons become doctors, fortune-tellers, musicians, &c.

They derive their living principally from the regular pay they receive for the performance of the ceremonies of their sect. They are always boarded when employed by the people at their houses. The head priest, who has several apprentices or journeymen priests under him, usually has twice as much wages as any other one—that is, he counts as two. If the others receive seventy cash each per day for their services, he receives a hundred and forty.

This class of priests is quite numerous, probably much more numerous than the Buddhist priests. They are also much oftener employed than are the Buddhist priests. Their services are very frequently in requisition, on mourning or funeral occasions, for the performance of so-called meritorious ceremonies. On a multitude of occasions, in all seasons of the year, and relating to almost all subjects, they are invited to perform their singular superstitious or idolatrous ceremonies. Their great harvest is in the seventh Chinese month, when, according to the current adage, "they need not buy any rice," from the fact that they are so constantly employed in the discharge of their official functions that they are not at home during the day. On the birthdays of

o

gods and goddesses, and on established festival days, they are also very busy, oftentimes spending only a few minutes in each family where they have been invited, merely the time absolutely necessary for the customary ringing of cymbals and the chanting of their formulas.

This class of priests is under the control of a head man, who is a priest himself, but who has been appointed to the office he holds by imperial authority, having a title and a button of rank. The mandarins, if they have occasion for the services of these priests in saving the sun or the moon when eclipsed, or in praying for rain in a time of drought, &c. have only to apply to their head man, who has authority to insure the attendance of the requisite number at the time and place appointed. If any violate the laws of the land they come under the control of the civil mandarins, their head man having little authority over them except as regards the exercise of their official functions as priests.

THE THREE PURE ONES.

Sang Ching, the *Three Pure Ones*, is the title of certain three idols found in temples belonging to the Tauist religion and worshipped by the Tauist priests. The images are seated side by side. One of them, as some explain, represents Lö-chü, or the *Old Boy*,* the founder of that religion. Others explain that the

* Or Lao-Tsew, or the Old Child, an appellation bestowed upon him because he was born grey-headed. He was, according to a very judicious writer, a man of profound original genius, who invented or revived a system of philosophy which greatly resembles that of Pythagoras, and in some respects that of Plato.

three images refer to three different incarnations of Lö-chü. There is very little known among the common people about these divinities, and they are seldom worshipped by them. Tauist priests of both classes universally worship the Three Pure Ones. Those priests who dwell among the people, the Tö-tai, use a paper-hanging which has pictures of them when called upon to perform ceremonies in private houses. The other class, the Tö-ing, living in temples, burn incense and candles incessantly before these images in their temples. Some account for the origin of this trio by saying that " Lö-chü in one breath was transformed into the Three Pure Ones."

The priests of Confucianism, or the Sect of the Learned, have been frequently referred to under the appellation of " professors of ceremony," or some equivalent term. They are of two classes —those employed by mandarins, and those employed by the common people.

All the mandarins, from the district magistrate to the viceroy, each have a professor of ceremony, who is paid out of the imperial treasury a small monthly stipend. Their official duty is to conduct the ceremonies which the mandarins, their masters, are required by the emperor to have performed at certain temples or elsewhere, at certain times of the year. When they go to make offerings to heaven and earth in the spring and fall, or to the god of agriculture, to the god of war, to Confucius, &c. the mandarins are accompanied by their teachers of ceremony. It is their part to read or chant the sacrificial or adulatory ode to the object of worship, to tell the mandarins when to kneel down, to knock their heads on the ground, and to arise to their feet. These teachers or professors are entitled to dress like graduates of the lowest degree, and to wear a cap with a gold button. They are always treated with great respect and deference by the mandarins. According to established usage and law, on state occasions, while the mandarins represent the emperor in worshipping objects terrestrial or objects celestial, objects real or objects imaginary, according to imperial rescript, they must obey the instructions or commands of these men. Although the mandarins might know what, according to the rites, should be done, and the precise time of doing it, they must not presume to do anything on their own responsibility. They must abide by the intimations of those who are called "priests of the Confucian religion," or the religion of the learned, from the fact that they are a special class of men, who are appointed by Government and paid out of the imperial coffers to conduct the ceremonies according to the

established rites and laws. These persons profess to understand
what the rites demand on all occasions of state ; hence their
appointment to the office, and their willingness to assume the
responsibilities of it.   Everything must be done according to the
programme the rites establish as proper, or rather as they understand the rites to establish, considering the circumstances of the
case, the rank of the performers, and the object designed. These
men are employed by mandarins when performing the rites of
the state religion.   They themselves are Confucianists, and so
are the mandarins in their private sentiments.

There is another class of these professors of ceremony who are
employed occasionally by
the common people to assist
them when they please to
invite them.   These are not
paid from the imperial treasury.   Their assistance is
rewarded by fees or wages,
which vary according to circumstances.   Besides their
food, they expect a liberal
fee from rich patrons. Those
who can afford the small
additional expense, invite
the attendance of a professor
of ceremony when they put
on mourning for the decease
of a parent, and at different
periods during the mourning
solemnities.   The common
people are not obliged by
law to use these directors
of worship.   Custom makes
their employment reputable and fashionable in wealthy and
literary families.   For instance, when making a sacrifice of food
to the dead, if a teacher of the rites is at hand to instruct one
when to kneel and when to rise up, when to begin doing a
particular act or to cease from doing it, everything is performed
with less confusion than though he were to act according to
his own memory or judgment of what was proper and becoming
under the circumstances.   It is a portion of the duties of the
professor of ceremony to read the sacrificial ode at the proper
time of presenting a sacrifice to the manes of the dead, to instruct

PROFESSOR OF CEREMONY.

the mourning family when and how to make presents in acknowledgment of presents received from sympathizing relatives, &c. He makes himself generally useful and even necessary for those who endeavour to carry out an undertaking according to the rites.

These men, who are employed by the common people, are quite numerous and influential. They, as well as those who are employed by mandarins, are necessarily literary men, of respectable connexions, of polite demeanour, able to assume, when occasion demands, a grave and dignified appearance; self-possessed and authoritative, else they could not discharge to the satisfaction of their patrons the functions of their calling.

The moral character of the priests which have been noticed has very little to do with their acceptability and popularity. Suavity of manners, tact in the management of business, and a clear understanding of the part he is to perform, have much more to do in forming the popular estimation in which any particular individual of either class is held than does purity of morals or integrity of character.

Confucianism consists of the religious, moral, and philosophical tenets and doctrines which are to be found in the Chinese classics, the writings of the sages, and the worthies of antiquity.* It numbers among its adherents and followers all the learned men of the country. Many of them might also be considered Buddhists and Tauists, if regard be had to what they perform as religious acts, or permit to be performed in their families. Confucius admitted that he did not know much about the gods. In his view they were beyond the comprehension of mortals. He does not inculcate obedience to one who has a right to the love and the services of the human races. The obligations of man, according to him, consisted in doing good to his family, his friends, and his country. He exalted filial virtue above all other moral and social virtues. The principle of obedience to superiors extends through all his writings, and forms the grand basis of society and of government as he would have them. A child should obey its parents, a wife her husband, and a subject his prince. This principle of subordination to superiors he elucidated and applied to the most important departments and relations of society. The subjects of his discourses to his followers, as well

* Subsequent inquiries, however, appear to prove that the doctrine of Confucius, like that of Spinoza, is a kind of philosophical pantheism, from which all religion, properly speaking, is necessarily excluded.—See an able article, "Christianity in China," *Foreign Quarterly Review*, 1830.

as the themes discussed in his books, are those which have a
most important and practical bearing in a political and social
point of view, and which the experience of more than twenty
centuries has shown to be singularly adapted to meet the approval
of the Chinese mind, and to satisfy Chinese wants.

In the Chinese classics much is said on benevolence, righteousness, politeness, wisdom, and fidelity, the five cardinal virtues,
which is beautiful in theory, but which the literati most woefully
overlook or forget to put into practice. In general, it may bo
said that, while every one now-a-days applauds the sentiments of
the ancient sages and worthies, there are few, if any, in China
who attempt or profess to practise them. By many the literati
are regarded as essentially and practically atheistic. One of
their most learned and popular philosophers affirmed, in relation
to the existence of gods and spirits, " that sufficient knowledge
was not possessed to say positively that they existed, and he
saw no difficulty in omitting the subject altogether. His system
is also entirely silent respecting the immortality of the soul, as
well as future rewards and punishments. Virtue is rewarded
and vice punished in the individual or his posterity on earth ;
but of a separate state of existence he or his disciples do not
speak."

There are no priestesses of the Tauist religion or of Confucianism in this part of China, nor are there any of the Buddhist
religion tolerated in this city and vicinity at the present time.
Thirty odd years ago there were comparatively a large number
of priestesses or nuns of the Buddhist religion dwelling in
convents or nunneries at this place. But these were summarily
suppressed about twenty-eight or thirty years ago, on account of
the dissolute character of their inmates, by a provincial treasurer.
About the middle of the reign of the grandfather of the present
emperor, as the treasurer was passing by a certain nunnery in
the city during the evening, his attention was arrested by the
numerous lights connected with the establishment, and the
manifest proof that it was improperly visited by men. After
making ample inquiries in regard to the dissolute life of the
nuns, he determined to suppress the nunneries in the city, and
oblige the inmates to marry or leave the section of country.
Very many gladly changed their state of single blessedness for
the state of matrimony, a sufficient number of unmarried men
being found to marry them.

Buddhist nuns with shaven heads are occasionally seen in the
streets while passing through the place to nunneries located in

adjoining prefecturates or townships. The blow dealt thirty years since by the treasurer upon the nunneries situated in the provincial city still is felt. The buildings they occupied, a kind

BUDDHIST NUN WITH CAP AND ROSARY.

of temple, have been used for other purposes than the raising of licentious maids under the garb and name of religious devotees. There has been since that summary act no successful effort made to establish and support Buddhist convents at this place.

CHAPTER X

THE ancient mythology of deities worshipped by the Chinese is yet to be written in English. The present, not ancient, customs and sentiments relating to the most popular objects of worship at Fuhchau and vicinity will be briefly attempted.

Nearly all the gods and goddesses have reputed birthdays. On the occurrence of such days, most of them have special ceremonies performed in their temples in honour of the event. Some of these celebrations of birthdays are very expensive and showy. By command of the emperor, at stated times in the spring and autumn of every year, and on the first and fifteenth of every month, officers of government must go to the temples of some of the principal gods and goddesses, and burn incense in their honour, or make sacrifices unto them.

Siâng Huông, the god called *the Lord of the Province*, is one of the greatest divinities worshipped here. His temple is the largest within the city walls, and is situated near the treasurer's office. It is the same in kind as the one frequently styled by Huc the "municipal palace," and by Dr. Williams "the palladium, or municipal temple." It is also sometimes called "the temple of the city wall and moat." In theory, every provincial, every prefectural, and every district city has a temple devoted to this god. In the temple in this city are three images very like each other. The largest one represents the god which rules over the affairs of the whole province in the world of spirits. The other two images represent the gods which regulate the affairs of the other world, which are connected with the two districts intersecting each other in this city.

In times of great drought, and when it has not rained for three months, an iron chain is put around the neck of one of his portable images. The image is then sometimes carried forth in procession to the temple of the " Pearly Emperor Supreme Ruler," to pray for rain. Some believe he has the general oversight of this world and of Hades as regards life and death, the rewarding of the good and the punishment of the wicked, reporting matters to the " Pearly Emperor," who decides authoritatively and unreservedly in regard to them. This idol is taken out of the temple and carried in procession three times per annum.

At the time of the Festival of the Tombs, in the spring, it is carried to the western altar, outside of the western gate of the city where a ceremony is performed called " letting out the spirits." It is supposed that at this time the spirits are allowed to come out of Hades and visit their old homes.

On the fifteenth day of the seventh month the image is again carried to the western altar, where a ceremony is performed called " counting the spirits." He is expected to have a strict oversight of the ghosts which he has let out of Hades to visit the earth, and he regards it important to call over the roll.

On the first day of the tenth month his image is carried through the principal streets of the city out to the western altar, where a ceremony is performed called "gathering the spirits." The idea is, that he shuts them up on this occasion in Hades, after they have had a long recreation upon the earth.

The idol is then taken within the city walls, where it passes the night in some house, not in the temple, as the work of the god being unfinished he cannot go home to sleep. Next morning it is carried out in the southern suburbs and paraded through all its principal streets, returning home in the evening. The procession on these two days is very long. Several thousands of men take part in it as an act of homage in the fulfilment of a vow. It is very common for people belonging to all classes of society to bow before the image of this god to perform a particular act of penance, or of thanksgiving, in case he grants them the object of their desires, as success in business, the restoration to health of their sick parents, the living of their parents to old age, the attainment of a literary degree, &c.

Ngük Huông Siong Tä, the *Pearly Emperor Supreme Ruler*, is regarded by many as the highest divinity worshipped by the Chinese. Others speak of him as being the chief god of the Tauist Pantheon. He is often referred to as the producer of all things and the governor of all things, seen and unseen, terrestrial and celestial. The common people believe him to receive the reports of the higher class of the gods in regard to the transactions done on the earth, and to examine into the merits and demerits of mortals, rewarding or punishing them according to their just deserts.

His birthday, all agree, comes on the ninth day of the first Chinese month ; but his pedigree is enclouded in mist. While some native scholars affirm him to be a descendant of Tiong Lu, of the Hang dynasty, others stoutly deny it, and declare that it is impossible to state his age, or to ascertain the time when he flourished on the earth. Some even venture to affirm that the being really worshipped under the name and title of "Pearly Emperor Supreme Ruler" is identical with God, the only proper object of religious worship.

In times of drought the high mandarins go also to his temple to burn incense and pray for rain.

The proper manner of worshipping the Supreme Ruler consists in the use of the "three kneelings and nine knockings," or kneeling down on the ground three distinct times, each time bowing the head to or toward the ground thrice.

Tài Sang, the divinity·called *Great* or *Universal Mountain*, whose temple is a mile and a half outside the east gate of the city, is regarded by many as the most influential and important god worshipped in this part of China, unless the "Pearly Emperor Supreme Ruler" be excepted. He is sometimes referred to as the "emperor of the infernal regions." The "Great Mountain" is spoken of as the grandson of the "Supreme Ruler of the Sombre Heavens."

In books which describe the Chinese Hades, the "Great Mountain" is represented as presiding over the seventh of the ten departments of that region. He is regarded as one of the rulers who have to do with the spirits of good and of bad men after death. Sometimes he is spoken of as the one who controls life and death.

The twenty-fourth day of the third month is spent by his devotees in carrying an image of the "Great Mountain," placed in a large sedan chair, and borne by eight stalwart men, in procession through the principal streets of the city. The following day the procession passes out of the southern gate into the southern suburbs, which it visits and inspects in a similar way. A large multitude of well-dressed men engage in honouring the god on these days as a kind of thanksgiving to him for benefits supposed to have been received from him in answer to special requests and vows. The streets are crowded on these days, and the people seem generally much interested and excited.

The birthday of the "Great Mountain," which occurs on the twenty-eighth of the third month, is observed and honoured by many families with great rejoicing. Some use what is called "great offerings," as a whole hog, a whole goat, a whole goose, or duck, or chicken ; others only a hog's head, goat's head, and a goose, and other meats, and various dishes of vegetables, with immense candles, and costly incense, wine, mock silver and gold, &c.

The Manchu Tartars resident in the city, as well as the Chinese, worship the "Great Mountain." It has become a custom for several days before the occurrence of his birthday for Manchu ladies of the first respectability, and of high rank, to go to his temple and wait upon the image which represents his wife. They put one of her images to bed with one of his images, and properly arrange the bed-clothes for several successive nights. In the morning they bring water with which to wash her face, and during the day, from time to time, they bring tea, tobacco, and other refreshments for her to use, just as though they were waiting upon a lady of the highest rank in the capacity of attendants and slaves. During the nights which occur while these birthday festivities are celebrated these Tartar women sleep on the premises in apartments provided for the use of guests.

The temple is very extensive, having many departments, or apartments for the worship of various subordinate divinities. It is kept in excellent repair.

A singular circumstance occurred a few years ago in connexion with the principal image of the "Great Mountain," which caused much talk at the time—his head fell suddenly from his shoulders, just as though his neck had been broken off. On examination, it was found that the principal posts or timbers which supported his head in position had become very much weakened by white ants ; they became too feeble to support the head.

The rest of the image was removed to a back part of the premises, and, together with his head, buried, and a high mound raised over the place where his mortal remains were interred. The occasion of this incident was made use of by the trustees of the temple to solicit the contributions of the deluded devotees of the god which was not able to retain his head upon his body, or to keep insects from committing depredations upon his frame-work, for the purpose of repairing the injury done and burying the old image. A large sum was raised without difficulty. For weeks, if not months, the temple was frequented by visitors in view of the idol's losing his head, even while workmen were employed to build up an image *de novo*.

Hieng Tieng Siong Tä, the "Supreme Ruler of the Sombre Heavens," is much worshipped at this place. He is sometimes called the "Sombre Ruler," or the "North Ruler," and is believed to have special control of regions connected with the north. The people sometimes speak of him as the "Water Ruler," or the governor of water. He is believed to be able to prevent conflagrations, and therefore, though he is not, properly speaking, the god of fire, he is often worshipped in order to secure his good-will and services against the breaking out of a fire in certain localities. There are many images of him, with a representation of a tortoise and of a snake near his feet, and also images of thunder and of lightning, one on each side, erected near the entrance of alleys or of by-streets, under a pavilion or a niche in the wall. The wind and the rain are represented by images, and are regarded as assistants. Being reckoned as an eater of vegetables, no meats are used in making offerings to him.

Huo Sing, *the god of fire*, frequently styled the "Fiery Ruler of the Southern Regions," is much reverenced because much feared.

In very many neighbourhoods, annually, in the fourth month, there is a ceremony performed for the purpose of propitiating the good-will and aid of the god of fire, in preventing conflagrations in the vicinity. The Chinese have, with good reason, a great dread of fires. Their houses easily ignite, and as soon as a conflagration breaks out, fellows of the baser sort, who are not few, rush to the scene for the purpose of robbery and pillage. The family whose house is burning, if it have not friends numerous and promptly on the ground, fares sadly, for the plunderers will take clothing, furniture, and everything worth carrying off.

The owners and renters of unburned buildings which are in the vicinity of a recent conflagration often invite some Tauist priests to go to the temple of the god of fire in their behalf, and perform a certain superstitious ceremony, and make an offering of various things before the divinity. This is designed as a kind of thanksgiving to the god for his having preserved their property from destruction by fire. Or they employ them to perform the ceremony on some part of the space burned over, for the same purpose. Sometimes this ceremony is attended with a display of many kinds of food, wine, and tea. The candles used on this occasion may none of them be red, the usual colour, but all must be white, or yellow, or green ; red, being the colour of fire, would be an inauspicious omen, and, if used, might have a tendency to produce a conflagration, which it is the object of the ceremony to prevent.

Kuang Ing Huk, *the goddess of mercy*, has various titles, which it is not necessary to mention. This goddess is held in very great veneration by this people, especially the married female portion. She is often represented very much as a man, or, as the Chinese say, half man and half female. Her images are sometimes made of fine white porcelain, or of brass, or of coarse clay. Sometimes her name or title is simply written on paper, and used instead of an image, and it is believed answers just as well. She belongs to the Buddhist Pantheon.

Married women, without exception, worship this goddess at their homes. If childless, they often go to some of her numerous temples and petition for a male child. This divinity is regarded as a goddess of midwifery and of children.   ˙

There are three particular days in every year when this goddess is specially worshipped besides the first and fifteenth of every month. These are the nineteenth day of the second month, the nineteenth of the sixth month, and the nineteenth of the ninth month. The first period is represented to be her birthday proper, the second period is regarded as the time when she became Buddha, and the third period as the time when she first put on her neck the string of pearls which she wears as an index of her dignity. Some say that the third period indicates the day of her death. On these days she is feasted and worshipped as though they were each her natal day. The worshippers on these occasions eat vegetables, because she is regarded as a vegetarian, and they present a vegetable offering unto her, arranged before her image, whether in the temple or in private families.

Ma Chu, *the goddess of sailors*, is very extensively worshipped by all heathen families which have business connected with the navigation of rivers or the ocean. Her temples are numerous, and sometimes large and expensively built. Probably the largest and most costly temple in the southern suburbs of this city was built by traders from Ningpo for the worship of the

sailors' goddess.   Traders from other prefectures or other
provinces, who come here and live, usually build large exchanges or assembly-halls, where people from the same section
of country as their builders may meet and transact business.
These always, or with exceedingly few exceptions, have an
image of this goddess put in them as their patron divinity.

MA CHU, THE GODDESS OF SAILORS, AND HER TWO ASSISTANTS.

This goddess, it is taught, is the daughter of a man who,
with his sons, was engaged on the ocean in the pursuit of a
living. He was born during the Sung dynasty, and lived in the
Hing Hua prefecture of this province.   One day, while she was
engaged in the employment of weaving in her mother's house,
she fell asleep through excessive weariness, her head resting
upon her loom.   She dreamed that she saw her father and her
two brothers on their separate junks in a terrific storm.   She
exerted herself to rescue them from danger.   She immediately
seized upon the junk which contained her father with her mouth,
while with her hands she caught a firm hold upon the two junks
which contained her two brothers.   She was dragging them all
toward the shore, when, alas! she heard the voice of her mother

calling to her, and, as she was an obedient girl, forgetting that she held her father's junk by her mouth, she hastily opened it to answer her mother. She awoke in great distress, and, lo! it was a dream, but not all a dream; for in a few days the news arrived that the fleet in which the family junks were had encountered a dreadful storm, and that the one in which her father was had been wrecked, and he had perished, while those in which her brothers were had been signally rescued. The girl knew that she had been the means of the salvation of her brothers, and that opening her mouth to answer her mother's call was the occasion of her failure to rescue her father's vessel.

This girl became, as the result of her dream, one of the most popular objects of worship in the empire. The emperors of China have, at different times since her death, conferred various high-sounding titles upon her, some of which seem blasphemous. She is called " Queen of Heaven," " Her Ladyship the Heavenly Queen," or " the Holy Mother in the Heavens above." One is often reminded by the titles given her, and the worship and honours paid her, of the titles which are given to the mother of Jesus by the authority of the Pope of Rome.

Sailors belonging to junks which go out to sea, and those who work the boats on fresh-water rivers and lakes, often take with them some embers or ashes which they obtain from the censer before some popular image of the goddess. These ashes they carry about their persons in a small red bag, or they suspend them about the junk in some convenient place, or they put them in the censer before the image of the goddess which they worship. When there is a violent storm at sea, and there seems but little hope that the junk will outride it, the sailors all kneel down near the bow with incense in their hands, and call out in doleful and bitter tones upon Ma Chu to send deliverance. In case they reach port without shipwreck, they are bound to offer to her an especial thanksgiving of food, with or without theatrical plays in her honour, according to their vow. It is affirmed by sailors that sometimes, in storms, a manifestation of this goddess becomes visible in the shape of a ball of fire going up or down a mast. If it is seen going up, they regard the circumstance as an omen of evil, as the departure of their goddess, and they look forward to serious disaster. If it seems to come down the mast, they interpret the appearance as an auspicious omen, and feel confident that they shall be preserved. The boatmen on the rivers and inland lakes in this part of China, when a very high wind arises and they are exposed to its violence, constantly keep calling upon Ma Chu to save them, crying out in piteous tones, "Grandmother Ma Chu!" "Grandmother Ma Chu!"

The sailors' goddess has two principal assistants, whose images stand one on each side of her own in her temples. One is called *Favourable-wind-ear*, and is believed to have an ear which can catch the least breath of a favourable breeze. The other is called *Thousand-mile-eye*, and is regarded as having an eye of remarkable acuteness of vision, able to perceive clearly at the distance of a thousand li. The latter assistant has of late years, in this place, become celebrated for his skill in curing the fever and ague, as well as for his abilities as a seaman. A particular temple near the water-gate of the city contains an image of this sailor-doctor, which is frequently visited by those who desire to be cured of the fever and ague. The sick man, after burning some incense before the image, takes away with him some of the incense ashes which he finds in the censer, and, after arrival at his own dwelling, worships it as he would the image itself, if he had one. After he recovers he must make the assistant god a thank-offering. A kind of very thin pancakes must form a principal part. This "thousand-mile-eyed" assistant seems to be remarkably fond of these cakes. Perhaps he does not like the hard fare of sailors.

Ling Chui Nü, a goddess which is generally called simply "Mother" by the people, is believed by some to be the most frequently worshipped of all the gods and goddesses at Fuhchau. She was born in the southern suburbs of this city, and lived in the time of the Tang dynasty.

She seems to be worshipped in part on account of her superior skill as a midwife.

She is also considered as a goddess of children, and is sometimes represented in pictures as standing with a sword in one hand and a horn in the other. With the sword she drives away enemies and evil influences, and with a blast from the horn she can summon to her aid hosts of heavenly assistants. She is also frequently represented in a sitting posture.

It is taught that every kind of meats may be offered to her in sacrifice excepting ducks. It is recorded as a veritable fact that once, while performing some of her arts for the purpose of procuring rain in a time of excessive drought, standing on a piece of matting which was simply placed on the surface of the River Min, opposite this city, and just below where the Big Bridge is situated, she was in great peril from the malicious attempts of some evil-disposed demon in the water, which tried to draw the matting down into the water. A certain tall white devil is charged with this mischievous attempt to undermine the security of her footing. What the sad results would have been to her personally, as well as to married women and children generally, had he succeeded, it is not necessary to attempt to deplore or depict ; for, as her good fate would have it, four ducks came boldly and bravely to her rescue. Each seized hold of one of the four corners of the matting with its bill, and held it firmly in position, so that the imp could not drag it from underneath her. In view of this signal deliverance in her hour of peril, she vowed, as a token of gratitude, never to partake of ducks' meat again—but is believed to have no objection to ducks' eggs. A small island in the river at this place, called "Duck Island," was raised from the bed of the river by the goddess in commemoration of her escape, and named after her deliverers ; so many Chinese soberly and stoutly maintain. This goddess of midwifery and of children is assisted in the discharge of her onerous and numerous duties by a large staff of female assistants ; thirty-six of them constitute one class or rank, and seventy-two another.

Sang Huông, "the three Emperors," are explained to be the heavenly emperor, the earthly emperor, and the human emperor, viz. Fuh Hi, who invented the eight diagrams, and was the first physician whose name has been handed down to modern times ; Shing Nûng, who first practised agriculture, before whom men lived on roots and fruits ; and Huang Ti, who was the first tailor, before whose time people dressed with leaves. Their birthday is unknown. These gods collectively are worshipped by a very large proportion of the common people, especially cap-makers, shoe and boot makers, doctors, masons, stone-cutters, tailors, fortune-tellers, manufacturers and dealers in tin-foil, and various other classes of tradespeople, artisans, and manufacturers. Generally speaking, each class by itself once per annum has theatrical exhibitions and a feast in the temple devoted to the worship of the three Emperors, designed to honour and praise these its patron divinities.

Kuang Tü, *the Chinese god of war*, or the Chinese Mars, was a distinguished military officer, as well as a faithful and honest courtier, who flourished in the time of the after Han dynasty, during the wars which agitated the three states. He has had a number of honorary and pompous titles added to his usual title by emperors of various dynasties. One of his most honourable titles is that of the " Military Sage," a title by which it is indicated that he occupies a position in military affairs corresponding to that of Confucius in literary matters.

He has now come to be spoken of as the patron deity of the present Manchu dynasty. Hien Fung, the grandfather of the present emperor, added to his former appellations of dignity by decreeing him to be the "Joyous Sage."

His image is worshipped by many people in their houses. He is believed to make men courageous and daring in their character, and successful in their undertakings.

Uong Tieng Kung, a divinity, the translation of whose common name is *King Heavenly Prince*, has an immense image in each of the temples devoted to the worship of the "Pearly Emperor Supreme Ruler" located on the hills in the southern part of the city. He is represented with three eyes, one being situated in the middle of his

KUANG TÄ, CHINESE GOD OF WAR.

forehead. His whiskers are long, and of a fiery red colour. He holds up before him in one of his hands a whip, or instrument of punishment. Men from all classes of society, sick and poor, officers and populace, as well as some females, worship this three-eyed and red-whiskered god. The principal objects sought for are protection in times of evil, and success in business and in study. Prayer to him *à la Chinois* is affirmed to be very effectual in cases of sickness.

Ung Chiong Tä Kung, the god of literature, is universally worshipped by literary men. He is spoken of as the giver of ability to write prose and poems of high literary merit, and as the arbiter of success at the literary examinations for the different degrees.

There are two stars which the Chinese profess to have discovered to have the supervision of the affairs of this world relating to literature and the pencil. One of these, Kue Sing, is said to be the fifteenth star of the twenty-eighth constellation, answering to parts of Andromeda and Pisces. The other is commonly called the god of literature. His image is made in the form of a handsome man in the sitting posture. The other star is also represented as a man, but extremely ugly looking, with a head having two long, crooked, horn-like projections. He is made to stand by one foot on the head of a large fish, with the other foot lifted up. In one hand he holds an immense writing-pencil, and in the other a kind of cap, such as is worn by the chief of a class of graduates. His image is always placed directly before the image of the other god of literature, though he is not regarded as his assistant.

There are said to be thirty or forty temples here devoted to the worship of these gods of literature. In large ancestral halls there is usually an apartment devoted to them, where the members of the families interested in the halls may burn incense and candles before them at the regular times of sacrificing with their ancestors, and whenever they please to worship them. In all the governmental colleges or high schools they are worshipped on the first and fifteenth of every month in the usual manner. Besides superintending affairs which relate to literature, this god is believed to take cognisance of the merits and the demerits of men, their virtuous and their vicious actions. Some speak of him as the governor or the ruler of thunder, fire, and the pestilence.

Ngûong Saùi, *a god of play-acting, wrestling, music, &c.* is represented to be the third son of the "Pearly Emperor Supreme Ruler." Play-actors, both apprentices and journeymen, worship him regularly, for the purpose of securing his aid in enabling them to remember their parts, and to perform them in·the established manner, and to the acceptance of their patrons. Those who engage in sham fights, fencing, wrestling, and similar athletic sports for recreation or amusement, or who set

KÛK SÎNG, A GOD OF LITERATURE.

themselves up as teachers of these, also worship this god, depending upon him for protection against making false movements, and against injuring the life or maiming the person of others. By the side of his image in the temples erected to his honour there are usually four assistants—one playing on the harp and one playing on the flute; the other two are in the attitude of fencing or boxing.

He is said to have been distinguished for his success in literary and in military pursuits. Accordingly, he is sometimes represented as a literary individual—that is, his image is plain and simple. At other times he is represented as being half in a military costume and half in a literary costume—that is, one side of his person is made plain, while the other half is arrayed in military apparel, as though it was covered with a coat of mail. From his head or his cap there are usually seen two long, curved feathers, projecting behind.

Tu Te Kung and Chai Sing, the *gods who preside over wealth*, are worshipped generally by traders, store-keepers, bankers, receivers of the customs, play-actors, clerks, and underlings connected with yamuns, and by some people in their houses, in order to propitiate their good-will in granting success to their plans for the acquisition of wealth. Those who have shops or offices burn incense and candles regularly before the paper inscription which represents one of the gods of riches, or the idol which represents the god, always found in their shops or offices. The first-mentioned is a kind of Penates, and is worshipped in households more frequently than the latter.

Lu P'ang, the person who is now worshipped as their patron divinity by all who use the chisel and the saw in their professional employments, as house-builders and carpenters, ship-wrights, umbrella-makers, cabinet-makers, &c., in olden times was a man who lived in the province of Shangtung, then called the kingdom of Lû. His ancestral name was Pang; hence the designation by which he is now held in remembrance. He was celebrated for his skill and dexterity in the use of mechanical tools, some of which he has the credit of inventing. People who use the chisel and the saw, each class or profession by itself, meet once per annum in the temple devoted to the worship of their patron deity, for the purpose of consulting together about the interests of their trades and occupations, and regulating the price of their labour, or of the articles they manufacture, &c. They feast together, and witness the performance of theatrical shows, in honour of the memory of him who invented the chisel and the saw, and to propitiate his good offices on their future efforts to use them with skill.

Tü Kék Sai, *the god of swine*, is represented as a deaf man standing, and holding in one hand a long staff, with which he controls swine. He is dressed in common plain clothing. Various reports are in circulation among the people in regard to the antecedents of this god. Some say he was, a long while ago, a butcher of hogs living in the city ; others affirm that he was simply a successful swine-raiser, who died from vexation because his swine suddenly died. The following story is related about him :—

He had a stand in the city, where he vended pork. One day a poor but talented student, who had already become a graduate of the first degree, went to his stand and bargained for a small piece of pork, which the pork-vendor was to let him have on trust, as he had not the cash in hand. The seller of pork, soon after the departure of the student with the flesh, changed his mind, and concluded not to trust the poor man. He there fore went secretly, and took away the piece of pork out of the pot while it was cooking. This offended the student, who did not forget the circumstance. Afterwards he became a very distinguished scholar, and attained unto the dignity of president of one of the boards at Peking. Coming back to his native place on business, as he was passing in his sedan the stand of the butcher, it happened that the butcher recalled the circum- stances, and began to tell them to the bystanders at the precise moment when the high mandarin was passing. The latter, incidentally looking out of the window of his sedan toward the stand, saw the butcher gesticulating, with his knife (while telling the story) pointed, as he imagined, toward his sedan, as if in the act of threatening. The mandarin, indignant that he should be treated thus in his native town, proceeded at once to his lodgings, and drew up a statement for the inspection of the emperor, telling how he saw a butcher threatening to kill him with his butcher-knife while he was riding along the public thoroughfare in the city, and requested the imperial consent and authority to decapitate him without trial, as a punishment for the insult, and a warning against other evil-disposed men. The emperor granted the request, and the man was summarily beheaded. Soon after his death he became an object of reverence and worship by his countrymen.

This god is worshipped by swine-owners, not so much in order to procure his aid in raising swine as to prevail upon him to grant his assistance, after swine have been lost or stolen, in enabling them to be found. Such go to his image, and, having lighted some incense and candles, rub his ears, he being deaf, and pat him gently on the back, in order to excite and interest his attention. They then tell him what they desire, stating the facts, as nearly as they know them, in regard to the lost swine, and ask him to start off and search for them. If they succeed in finding the lost or stolen hogs, they must make a thank-offering to him in the usual way.

Tu Chiêng Kúi, *a god of gamblers*, represents a certain man who spent his time in gambling, until, having lost his property, he died of want. An image of him was subsequently made, and called a "devil gambling for cash." His body was represented as clothed with ordinary garments, very much dilapidated, with his cue coiled around his head, and with a gambling card stuck into his hair. This god is much worshipped by gamblers, especially when there is a kind of lottery to be drawn. Having lighted incense and candles before him, they cast lots by the use of bamboo-slips, and kneel down and knock their heads on the ground. Some confirmed gamblers have an image of this divinity made for use in their homes, before which they pray for auspicious dreams, as aids in gambling. They prepare for having such dreams by lying down to sleep before the image, having first lighted some candles and incense. When this is done it amounts to a kind of vow. Sometimes tobacco and cakes are offered in the evening.

Sometimes the gambler takes thirty-seven slips of bamboo, each of which has certain characters written upon it, and arranges them before the image, covering each with some kind of shell. Incense and candles are lighted, as before, at bedtime. In the morning these slips are carefully examined to ascertain if any have been moved during the night. If one has been stirred, though but a little, the characters upon it are selected by the gambler upon which to bet with regard to this lottery, under the idea that the god has caused it to be moved as a favour to him, indicating that these characters will be the lucky ones for the day. One of these thirty-seven sets of characters are selected by the lottery-directors to draw the prize for a particular day. The gambling consists in trying to guess the lucky characters for any specified day. Those who guess them make thirtyfold on their venture. Oftentimes the phrase "devil gambling for cash" is used to describe a man who has become a desperate gamester, probably from his haggard and poverty-stricken appearance.

CHAPTER XI.

Noó Hieng Kung.—The birthday of the "god of thieves" falls on the seventeenth of the eighth month. Within ten or fifteen years the number of the worshippers of this divinity has very rapidly increased in this place, and the number is now annually increasing. The main object of worshipping him is to gain wealth. Some sick people, travellers, and traders worship him. Now-a-days many who are not professed or regular thieves worship him on the recurrence of his birthday. He has no temple devoted to him in the city or the suburbs, nor has he any image. He is worshipped under the open heavens.

Sometimes the people use two characters, meaning "midway in the heavens," as a part of his title when speaking of this divinity. These words imply that he dwells in the midst of the heavens. He is believed to be unwilling to come down to earth, and therefore men do not prepare an image of him, and worship it, as they do in regard to most other objects of worship.

Ngú Hieng, it is taught, *was a thief himself*, and was noted not only for his cleverness in stealing, but also for his filial piety. About daybreak one morning, it is told, he came home with a kettle for cooking rice, which he had purloined. His mother, kind-hearted woman that she was, scolded him roundly for stealing such an article, thus depriving people of the means of cooking their food, and finally told him that, if he sold it, and bought rice with the money he got for it, she would not taste a mouthful of it. He asked what should be done with the thing. She advised him to return it to the place whence he took it. But he objected, saying it was already light, and he would certainly be detected in the attempt. His mother replied that, if he would attempt to return it, the heavens undoubtedly would become darkened so that he could do it in safety. He concluded to try, and started off with the kettle, and, behold! just as he reached the house whence he stole it, the heavens all at once became very dark. He embraced the favourable moment and deposited the kettle on the premises, and ran off with all speed to report to his mother the result of his efforts.

OOD OF THIEVES.

Iöh Uong Chú Sü, the god of medicine, is said to have been formerly a distinguished doctor, who, after his decease, was deified. Now he is generally worshipped by the vendors of medicine, and their clerks and assistants.

I Kuang Tāi Uông, the god of surgery, it is taught, was a foreigner, originally from the Loochoo Islands, who came to the middle kingdom and practised surgery. Surgery, in the Chinese sense, relates to the cure of diseases which appear on the surface of the body, as sores, ulcers, cancers. As, while living, he was partially deaf, his devotees imagine this defect remains now that he is dead, though deified, and therefore are careful to make application by speaking into his ear, as well as to offer the customary incense and candles, which appeal more directly to his olfactories and to his eyes.

Uŏk Uông.—The temple which contains the image of an ancient king of the Min country, who reigned during the Han dynasty, is located on the Great Temple Hill, in the suburbs of this city. In a time of drought the temple is visited by rain-prayers in order to burn incense, hoping to procure rain thereby. The premises are extensive and well kept. There is a famous well upon them. In a time of drought, if the bones of a tiger should be let down into this well, called the "dragon's well," and kept there for three days at the most, there will, it is sagely affirmed, most likely be rain soon. The bones must be drawn up as soon as possible after the rain has begun to fall. The common belief is that the dragon and the tiger always fight when they meet, and that, when the tiger's bones are let down, it will stir up or excite the dragon. If he arouses himself and combats the tiger, *alias* his bones, clouds, it is asserted, will certainly ascend to the skies, and rain will shortly begin to pour down.

The image of Uŏk Uông is placed on the right hand of the image of the goddess, his wife—that is to say, the wife is sitting in the seat of honour, according to Chinese notions. The occasion of the husband yielding the seat of honour to his wife, an exceedingly unusual thing in China, is related to have been the following: One day he jestingly, or rather boastingly, told her that, by casting his boot into the dragon's well, he could bring the dragon to the surface of the water. She promptly denied its possibility, and, on the other hand, affirmed that she, by throwing into the well one of her earrings, could induce the dragon to come up and get it. He promised her that, if she could thus draw up the dragon to the surface, while he could not produce the same effect by tossing his boot into it, he would yield the seat of honour to her, and she should henceforth sit on his left hand. She accepted the proposition. He threw his boot into the well, but no dragon came to the surface. She disengaged one of her earrings and tossed it into the well, and the dragon immediately came up for the pearl it contained! The dragon is famed for his extraordinary attachment to pearls, as well as for his intense hatred of the tiger. The wife of the king, after this, always sat on the left of her husband, who was true to his promise, and, after the death of each, when their images were made, her image was placed in the seat of honour, *i.e.* at his left hand.

Ngu Tä, or "the Five Rulers."—The worship paid to the Five Rulers, taken in connexion with the idol processions through the streets in honour of them and the confused and monstrous notions which are prevalent relating to their powers, constitutes an idolatry of the most peculiar and extraordinary character.

The opinions prevalent among the common people are exceedingly confused in regard to the objects or beings these Five Rulers represent or denote. They are explained by some as referring to the five elements of Nature, which, according to the Chinese, are metal, wood, water, fire, and earth. They are also believed to represent the five colours, yellow, green, red, black, and white. They are also thought to denote the five directions, North, East, South, West, and Middle.

The following table was furnished by a priest who is employed more or less constantly in performing ceremonies connected with their worship, and may be as near the popular notions as any which could he prepared. The people differ greatly among themselves in regard to them.

The names of the Five Rulers, and what they are supposed to represent, is as follows :—

Names.	Five Colours.	Five Elements.	Five Directions.
Tióng,	Yellow,	Earth,	Middle,
Chüng,	Green,	Wood,	East,
Láu,	White,	Metal,	West,
Sü,	Red,	Fire,	South,
Tien.	Black.	Water.	North.

The order above given is their order of rank. The chief, *Tióng*, is represented with a pleasant human countenance, and having three eyes, one situated in the middle of his forehead, and with a long red beard. Often his face is made of a golden hue, and, according to theory, the face of each should be of a colour corresponding to the colour which each represents. This, however, is not always carried out in fact. The appearance of all the Five Rulers, except the one first mentioned, is ugly and repulsive. These four have hideous faces, having a snout projecting much like swine, or having extremely large noses, or having eyes and features generally similar to a monkey. Sometimes the mouth is four-cornered, or coming to a point like the mouth of a fowl. The images in different temples are not alike. There seems to be very much licence taken by the architect in regard to shape and colour.

The temples where the Five Rulers are worshipped are professedly dedicated to the god of war. There is a tablet, with his title or name upon it, attached generally to the front or the outside of the numerous temples where they are worshipped. The origin of this custom is said to be this :—Some fifteen or twenty years ago, a high official, whose yamun was in the city, one day met, while riding in his sedan in the street, a procession in honour of the Five Rulers. The procession did not yield him the right of way, but kept on as though it expected the mandarin would retire, or be carried to one side, while the Five-Ruler procession was passing along. This course highly exasperated the mandarin, who ordered his lictors to seize and flog some of the chief actors in the procession on the spot. The procession was speedily broken up, and its members scattered in all directions. On inquiry, the mandarin learned that the worship of this class of idols, "the Five Rulers," was not recognised by imperial rescript, and he determined to prevent all future processions in their honour, and to exterminate the images themselves. As soon as this purpose became known to the devotees of the Rulers, arrangements were made by which the title of the god of war, Kuang Tä, should appear on their temples, and an image of this god was placed in them. This title was used as a shield for the Five Rulers, as it could be said, "These are temples of the god of war." As the god of war was in high favour with the ruling dynasty, no mandarin dare interfere with any temple called after his name or title.

These Five Rulers, notwithstanding their immense popularity, are classed among the "corrupt gods"—that is, they have not been honoured with the approbation or recognition of an emperor —they have not been declared to be gods by some occupant of the dragon throne. The corrupt gods, those unacknowledged by the state, become correct gods by the decree of an emperor. After they have been officially and formally recognised by an emperor, no one, people or mandarin, would have the boldness to interfere with them, or treat them publicly with disrespect, unless they or their human directors and protectors should plainly be to blame, or violate some law of the land.

In the fall of 1859, the Emperor Hien Fung conferred the honorary title of "Heu," or Marquis, upon these Rulers, on the representation of Uông Hi Taik, a viceroy who had finished his term of office here, and was removing to another place.

During the fifth and sixth months, the processions in their honour are the most numerous. Sometimes a procession requires from one to two hours to pass by any given locality. Chinese in common sedans must allow their sedans to be put down on the ground when they meet any one of the principal idols, which are borne by eight men each. If on horseback, they must dismount. The sedan containing the idols carried in procession are so large, and the bearers so insolent, that it is usually impracticable to pass in sedans following from behind, if one wished to go past. The common people observe a most respectful attitude while the larger images, in their sedans, are passing them. It is believed that any insult to them would be speedily followed with colic or dysentery, or some similar painful and dangerous disease. Men of very respectable positions in society frequently engage in these processions, in consequence of some vow, usually made for the benefit of the health of their parents.

There are numerous unions in this place, the particular object of which is to worship and carry in procession the Five Emperors through the streets, in order to expel pestilential diseases and influences from the country. These unions are usually connected with a temple where images of the "Rulers" are kept." Each union every year collects enough money with which to purchase a boat, and, after carrying it in procession, sends it out to sea filled with the pestilential influences which have been collected.

The time of collecting money for the purchase of the boat, and other expenses connected with it, falls in the hot summer months, when there are more or less people sick with the kind of diseases which it is the laudable object to prevent or expel. The collectors go through the principal streets in companies, with drums, gongs, and flags, expecting to receive contributions from every shop. Private dwelling houses in the neighbourhood where the temple is located, or where the members of the union principally reside, are also visited in this manner. The collectors willingly receive incense, candles, or anything worth money—as mock-money, mock-clothing, salt, and rice.

The boat is usually twenty or twenty-five feet long, and made as light as possible, the frame of it being of bamboo, and small and narrow pieces of wood. The frame is covered with paper. Various apartments are formed, professedly to store goods, and for the accommodation of people on board. It is carried by eight, or sixteen, or a larger number of men. In it is put a little of almost every sort of article used in families, as rice, salt, wood, fruits, &c. together with miniature articles of furniture, as tables, chairs, bowls, and plates, made out of paper, or paper and bamboo splints. Miniature paper images of the crew are also put in the boats.

Paper images of the Five Rulers are made at establishments where such work is done, in order to be put into the boats when sent out to sea. When completed, they are usually escorted home to the temple with which the union that bargained for them is connected, with considerable pomp and parade. Each paper image is placed in a sedan carried by eight men, and in the procession there are more or less of the tall white and the short black devil servants. The procession is accompanied with men who beat gongs and drums. All this parade is to take away a few diminutive images made out of paper and bamboo, weighing in the aggregate not nearly what one man could carry

with great ease.   After arrival at the temple where they belong,
they are treated with great reverence.

At a convenient time, the wooden images of the Five Rulers,
which are kept in each temple dedicated to them, are taken out
and carried through the principal streets with a great show of
honour.   Each image is carried by eight men, and is accompanied by a set of servants real and imaginary.   The real
servants are lictors, incense-bearers, and criers, who make every
now and then a most doleful and prolonged noise.   The imaginary servants are immense images (carried by men who get inside
of them), made out of bamboo and cloth, of a variety of shapes

BOAT CARRIED IN PROCESSION ON MEN'S SHOULDERS.

and representing a variety of assistants to the Five Rulers.
This kind of procession usually takes place in the afternoon and
evening.   When over, the portable and substantial images are
carried home to the temples to which they belong, and the
company which composed the procession disperses.

This procession with the boat is sometimes an imposing

spectacle. The boat is carried along in the evening, lighted up with numerous candles or lamps.   Very frequently, when a boat in procession from a large and rich temple is carried along, the sides of the streets are thronged with idle men, women, and children, anxious or curious to see the spectacle.   Usually in every such procession are a large number of portable hideous images, carried by men inside, accompanied by their lictors, and bands of music, and men who join in it, in consequence of some aid supposed to have come from the Rulers benefiting themselves, or their parents or families.   They join in it to express their thanks.

CARRYING THE HAPPY BUCKETS.

In the procession there frequently is a well-dressed man carrying a couple of pails, which contain a little of the blood of swine, the buffalo, and fowls, and some of their hair and feathers. He carries what are called the "Happy Buckets."   Carrying them in the procession is regarded an especial work of merit. Formerly it was performed only by hired beggars ; now-a-days by a volunteer from a respectable family, out of gratitude to the Five Rulers for the recovery of a near relative from sickness, or in the hope of procuring such a result. The contents represent the filth which cause pestilence and epidemic diseases. They are poured out into the river when the boat is burned.

In many large idol processions there is also a man dressed neatly, carrying the instruments of torture and punishments in common use in a ma-gistrate's office, as the cangue, leathern thong for slapping the face, instruments for compressing the ankles and the fingers, &c. It is supposed that some of the utensils for punishing and torturing employed in the other world are similar to the instruments used in this world. These instruments are paraded in procession in order to indicate or intimate to the spectators the punishments which await the wicked in the world of spirits.

CARRYING INSTRUMENTS OF PUNISHMENT AND OF TORTURE.

Usually not far from the front of the boat are the members of a "sailors' society." This society is formed, and its expenses provided, by men who are fond of sport generally. They profess to desire to furnish men who shall row out to sea the boats which are provided for the accommodation of the Five Rulers. The directors select fifteen or twenty lads of ten or twelve years of age, and hire some music-teacher to instruct them in the parts they are expected to perform. They are taught to play, for a month or longer, on various musical instruments, and beat the gong and the drum in unison. When boats are carried in procession, these quasi-sailors precede them on foot. Some of them play on their instruments. Two carry a pewter anchor a foot or two long. One carries a small oar, another a compass, such as is used on junks, &c. The trousers and shirts worn by them are usually made all alike out of black cotton or grass-cloth. They have a red or blue belt around their waist. Their braided cues are twisted up in a knot behind their head—not coiled around it, as usual. They wear a small hat made of bamboo splints and leaves. As they walk along before the boat, they sometimes chant a song praising the Five Rulers, or relating to peace and plenty.

These boys work or play thus without wages. They have their food and clothing found them free of expense while engaged, and they like the prominence or notoriety their position in the processions gives them. The same company of boys usually perform in several processions during the season. They are not found in connexion with any processions but those in honour of the Five Rulers.

On the boat arriving at the river's bank, where it is embarked on the water and sent out to sea, or, in plain language, where it is burned, it is placed in some convenient position. All the images in which men have ensconced themselves run rapidly round the boat, and then kneel down in a circle not far distant from it, with their faces turned toward it. When everything is ready the boat is set on fire and consumed, attended with the beating of gongs and drums, and this is called sending it out to sea.

But a small space can be devoted to a description of the portable images found principally in processions of the Five Rulers, and in those in honour of Tài Sang and of Siàng Huông.

These usually go in pairs, or in a company of four.

1. The *Tall White Devil* and the *Short Black Devil* are very numerous. The former is said to be a policeman in the infernal regions. The image is ten or twelve feet high, as it appears carried in procession. The head, face, and hands are made of pasteboard and paper, and the body of bamboo, usually covered with white or whitish cotton cloth or silk. Its head has upon it a long, square, bent hat, two or three feet tall, with a strip of red cloth often wound around it. In one hand it carries an immense fan, and in the other a kind of wand, on which are words which teach that this assistant of the gods is designed "to reward the good and punish the evil." Around the waist usually a strip of light blue cloth is tied as a belt. The face is long, hair dishevelled, eyes protruding, tongue red, and often extending out of the mouth. The body is slim. The image is carried erect by a strong man, who gets inside. The clothing comes down only to the man's knees, leaving his feet and part of his legs to be seen as he walks along. An orifice is made in the clothing in front, where the head of the man inside comes, so that he can look out and see to walk. It is comfortable with the dignity of this devil servant to walk slowly and with long strides. There are usually two boys beating gongs in front of it. Oftentimes there are several men playing on musical

instruments going before. Preceding the image there are generally two men, each carrying a large lantern upon a pole above their heads, having an inscription which implies that it belongs to some officer in the world of spirits. It is also often accompanied by one or two persons who aid the man inside when he requires to steady it.

The *Short Black Devil* is stubbed and pursy. Its face and dress are very black. It always wears a large black hat. A strip of red cloth is usually tied about it. Its tongue protrudes, and is red, as if covered with blood. It is moved about occasionally by the persons inside by means of a string, producing a very disagreeable appearance. Its gait is very undignified, as it is made to jump or spring suddenly from one side of the street to the other. Sometimes it turns around in the street and gazes back, wagging its head and moving its tongue. This image is carried usually by a strong lad or a very short man, who has a looking-out place made in the forehead or hat of the image, whence he can see where to go. The face and framework generally are made out of pasteboard, paper, and bamboo-splints.

These assistants are represented by heavy stationary images in the temples where such objects are reverenced. Oftentimes their pictures are found on the walls of temples. The same remark is true of the assistants which remain to be described. All of these images are made in a similar way, with particular variations as regards shape, size, and features, to suit the fancy of those who have invented them and who use them.

2. The *Buffalo-headed assistant*, the *Horse-faced assistant*, the *Cock-headed assistant*, and the *Duck-mouthed assistant*, are images eight or ten feet high, and usually go together. There is nothing particularly frightful about their appearance. They, by means of the man inside, pass along slowly and solemnly in the procession. They are mainly distinguished by the peculiar shape of their faces or their heads. The colour of their dress is usually white or bluish. They appear like immense giants, excepting their peculiar heads.

3. Two tall images in human form, which are distinguished from each other principally by the one carrying a cangue, and the other carrying a chain and a lock, are sometimes seen. They appear to be ready to seize and put the cangue or lock the chain on offenders should their majesties the Rulers give the command. Their countenances are grim and severe.

4. The *one-horned* and the *double-horned devils* appear with hideous countenances. One has the top of his head coming to a

blunt peak, and the other has two horn-like projections coming from the right and the left sides of the top of his head, from which circumstances they derive their names. One carries cudgel in one hand bristling with spikes, and something in the other resembling a large leaf. The other carries a smooth, large-headed cudgel in one hand, or a wooden sword, and in the other some chains. These, and the two just described, represent some of the lictors of the Five Rulers.

BUFFALO-HEADED ASSISTANT.   HORSE-FACED ASSISTANT.
(Like their stationary images or pictures seen in temples.)

5. The *accomplishing assistant* and the *transforming assistant* are believed to perform important offices in preventing pestilential diseases. One carries in one hand a gourd-like vessel for the purpose of collecting the poisonous vapours and the unhealthy influences which prevail, and in the other a leaf of the banana, or something to represent such a leaf; the other carries in one hand an immense wooden sword, to drive off, and in the other a large brush, to sweep away all the evil influences and unhealthy odours which may be encountered.

There are two classes of objects—human, because they are men, and inhuman, because their faces are painted to represent devils. These seldom appear in an idol procession.

One class is painted so as to represent, according to Chinese notions, the four seasons—Spring, Summer, Autumn, and Winter. Spring is denoted by a man with a greenish face;

Summer, by a man with a reddish face ; Autumn, by a man with a whitish face ; and Winter, by a man with a blackish face. Another class is painted so as to represent the five demons or spirits which rule over the five directions—North, East, South, West, and the middle. They are by no means pleasant-looking. The stationary images of the five directions, as found in some of the temples, or as they are sometimes painted on paper or on the walls of temples, are horrid and frightful in the extreme. As represented by men who appear in an idol procession, they are much less frightful than when in the temples, but sufficiently horrid and ugly to produce a lasting and unpleasant impression when seen in connexion with the many other unnatural and devilish-looking objects which have been enumerated.

It will require but little imagination on the part of the reader, aided by the above description, to conceive that idol processions constitute a very strange and imposing spectacle as a whole. Few foreigners who have seen one do not retain an abiding impression of its general appearance.

There are probably, at the least calculation, fifteen or twenty "unions" connected with temples which send forth to the ocean one or more boats annually, and which have other public processions previous to those when their boats are carried to the water's edge and burned. There are not many days in the summer months which are not occupied more or less, either in the city or suburbs, with some kind of an idol procession. Not unfrequently there are days when for hours the main streets in places are almost, if not quite, impassable to those who in sedans wish to go in a direction opposite to that which the procession is taking. If going in the same direction, the progress is slow and annoying to a high degree.

Beside the above idols, images and pictures of animals are worshipped, illustrating the nature and the genius of heathenism, as existing and as practised in this city and vicinity by the people who "serve the creature more than the Creator."

The Monkey.—It is represented as a man sitting, the face only being like a monkey. The image is usually made of wood or clay. Sometimes a picture of it is made on paper, or simply the title under which the monkey is worshipped is written on a slip of paper, and used instead of an image. There are several large temples at this place erected for the worship of "*His Excellency the Holy King,*" *one of the titles much used in speaking of the monkey as an object of worship.* Oftentimes the niche

Q 2

holding the image or a written name is placed in a hollow tree, or in the wall at the corners of streets, or at the heads of alleys or lanes.   Such places, in this city and vicinity, where the monkey is worshipped, reckoned together with the small temples or buildings dedicated to it, amount to several scores.   The worship consists principally in the burning of incense and candles, sometimes attended with the presentation of meats, vegetables, and fruits.   The monkey was first worshipped in return for some supposed services rendered the individual who went to India, by special command of an emperor of the Tang dynasty, to obtain the Sacred Books of the Buddhist religion— so some affirm.   This emperor deified the monkey, or at least, he conferred the august title of "the great Sage equal to Heaven" upon that quadruped.   The birthday of His Excellency the Holy King is believed to occur on the twenty-third of the second Chinese month, when his monkey majesty is specially worshipped by men from all classes of society.   The monkey is believed to have the general control of hobgoblins, witches, elves, &c.   It is also supposed to be able to bestow health, protection, and success on mankind, if not directly, indirectly, by keeping away malicious spirits or goblins.   People often imagine that sickness, or want of success in study and trade, is caused by witches and hobgoblins.   Hence the sick or the unsuccessful worship the monkey in order to obtain its kind offices in driving away or preventing the evil influences of various imaginary spirits or powers.

The Fox.—This animal is worshipped by the viceroy, and by other high mandarins at this place.   *The fox is supposed to have the control of the official seals belonging to high offices of government.*   In the viceroy's establishment is a room in the second story of a building which is devoted to the worship of the fox. It has no image, nor is there any picture of the animal worshipped.   The viceroy, on arrival at his official residence after appointment, repairs to his room, kneels down, bows his head toward the ground three times, and offers three cups of wine, three sticks of incense, and two candles, in order to propitiate the good-will of Reynard, the keeper of the seal.   Unless the fox should be worshipped in some way, it is asserted by the common people that it would cause the seal to disappear, and otherwise injure the mandarin, as setting the establishment on fire.   There are very wonderful stories in connexion with the power of the fox in mandarin establishments current in this city.   The fox is believed also to have the power of changing at pleasure into the human form, or of entering the bodies of men and women. Sometimes diseases are attributed to this animal, which is accordingly worshipped by the sick one, or, on his account, by others, in order to induce it not to molest, vex, or injure the sick individual. Its invisible agency in preventing success in business is very much dreaded by the people.

The Tiger.—This animal is worshipped by two different classes of people and for two different objects.

By gamblers.—It is the god of gambling, or one of the gods worshipped by gamblers. Sometimes an image is made of wood or clay, or a picture is delineated on paper or a piece of board, of a *winged* tiger, standing on its hinder feet, and grasping a large cash in its mouth or in its paws. Sometimes merely a title of the animal, "His Excellency the Grasping Cash Tiger," is written on a piece of paper. This is then put under the gaming-table, between two bunches of mock money, which are suspended; or it is placed on a table in the gambling-room, or fastened to the wall behind a table. Incense and candles are often burned before this image or this inscription. On the second and six-teenth days of every Chinese

TIGER GRASPING A LARGE CASH : A GOD OF GAMBLING.

month, offerings of meat, fish, &c. are frequently made before it. Sometimes gambling saloons or dens are recognised from the street by the sign, placed over the outside door, of a tiger painted on a board in the position above mentioned. The tiger is worshipped by the proprietor of a gambling den in order to bring success.

By mothers in behalf of their sick children, not separately and alone, but always in connexion with a goddess of children. This goddess is represented as sitting upon the back of a tiger in a crouching posture. The tiger is supposed to have the power of absorbing or of counteracting the pernicious influences which cause children to become sick. When a child, for example, has the small-pox in a very virulent form, and fears are entertained for the child's life, some one interested in its recovery burns incense and candles before an image of the woman and tiger, or before something which represents them, either in a temple or in a dwelling-house, promising to make certain specified thank-offerings in case the child recovers, as the burning of mock-money, and a fresh and raw pig's tail (of which the tiger is believed to be very fond), meats, fruits, and vegetables. It is estimated that a very large proportion of the mothers in this city—perhaps more than half—worship the tiger in connexion with the goddess as above represented.

GODDESS OF MIDWIFERY AND CHILDREN SITTING ON A TIGER.

The Dog.—An image or representation of this animal is found in connexion with several objects of worship at this place.

It occurs on a painting extensively used by married women as an object of worship in their sleeping apartments. It is called a "heavenly dog," or a "dog in the heavens." The picture represents a certain genius, surrounded by several children. He is in the act of shooting a dog with a bullet by means of a bow, the dog being in the air much above the level of the shooter and the children. This dog in the heavens is believed to eat the children of mortals, and this genius is famed for his skill in shooting this bad dog. A literary man has furnished the following explanation of the use of this painting : Some women are born on days which are represented by the chronological or horary character which means "dog." These women, after marriage, and before they give birth to a child, must procure a picture of the genius shooting the "heavenly dog," and worship it by the burning of incense and candles. The child then may be expected to live. In the picture, the children are represented as gathering around the genius, in order to insure protection from the dog, which would certainly devour them if the shooter did not defend them. Twice every year, on the third day of the second month, and on the twenty-third of the eleventh month, offerings are presented to this genius, such as incense, candles, mock-money, vermicelli, and seven balls made of the flour of rice. These balls represent the balls with which the hunter shoots the dog. At other times during the year, when the household gods are worshipped, only incense and

ONE OF THE NINE GENII SHOOTING A DOG IN THE HEAVENS.

candles are burned before this picture. Others say that this picture is worshipped by mothers in behalf of a child only when the child is declared by a fortune-teller to be under the influences of the "heavenly dog," or exposed to them. In all cases, the genius is resorted to for the purpose of securing the child from the depredations of the dog.

One of the servants of Ngûeng Saùi, a god of music, playacting, and war, is represented as a dog. This god is represented in both a civil and a military dress. When represented, whether by an image or in pictures, in the military costume, one foot is sometimes placed on the back of a dog-headed animal. At other times this animal is represented as having a dog's head, with the body, feet, and hands of a man, holding a flag. Ngûong Saùi, it is said, had a favourite dog, which afterward became one of his assistants when he was deified. Hence the association with him of an animal having a dog's head. This god is much worshipped here by certain classes.

In a celebrated temple located outside of the east gate of the city is an image of a large dog. It is currently reported that if bread-cakes or biscuits made of wheat flour are placed in the mouth of this image of a dog, and afterwards eaten by children, they will prevent or cure the colic.

The Black Monkey and the White Rabbit.—These are represented both by images and by pictures, and are usually regarded as the servants of the god of courtesans. This god is regarded as having power over men and women. He is said to have seized the spirits of the black monkey and white rabbit, and to have made them his assistants. In what manner he accomplished this feat, and how these animals aid him in his evil purposes, the Chinese are not able to explain with clearness. They are represented as having a human body, but the head of a monkey and of a rabbit, the monkey being black and the rabbit white.

The Dragon.—This is regarded as the giver of rain. In times of drought it is worshipped in order to obtain the needed element. A temple located near the eastern gate of the city is devoted to the worship of this fabulous animal. It is among those objects or images which are worshipped, by command of the Emperor, in the spring and fall of each year by certain mandarins.

In a certain temple near the governor's yamun in the city is an image of a white cock, which is worshipped in connexion with a certain goddess. Some say that this goddess is the deified daughter of a governor of the province who lived in the time of Kanghi, and who killed himself during a local tumult or rebellion which he could not quell. She had a white cock, of which she was very fond, and which seemed exceedingly attached to her. On hearing of the death of her father, this girl threw herself into a well and was drowned. This cock, seeing his mistress leap into the well, leaped in also, and perished. She afterwards became, by order of some emperor, an object of worship, and an image of the faithful cock was made, and worshipped in connexion with his mistress. She is reckoned now among those objects which are worshipped twice every year, in accordance with the mandate of the emperor, by the local mandarins. Few of the common people, it is believed, now-a-days actually worship this goddess. When worship is performed before her shrine, incense and candles are always burned in honour of the white cock.

Various popular gods and goddesses, as the " Three Precious Ones," worshipped by Buddhists, and the " Three Pure Ones," worshipped by Tauists, the goddess of small-pox and the goddess of measles, &c., have been already mentioned, and need not be described here. There are many other objects which are more or less commonly worshipped by the people, but which it would be tedious to describe in detail. Objects terrestrial and celestial, objects visible and invisible, and objects real and imaginary, are made the recipient of the homage of the Chinese. It is worthy of remark and remembrance, that among them all there is not one the object of the worship of which is to make the devotee more pure and more sincere, more honest, more virtuous, or more holy. The object whose attainment is desired is always selfish, sensual, or secular.

CHAPTER XII.

In the provinces there are many mandarins representing various functions in the state.

The viceroy has the general superintendence of the provinces. He has the power to execute high offenders, and to degrade or deprive of office the prefect and officers below the prefect.

The governor presides over the province, and is frequently called the " Lord of the Province." The governor and the viceroy act as a kind of spy on each other.

The treasurer is a very important officer. He is accountable for all the money paid into the treasury by the district magistrates in all the province. He pays out the salaries and the lawful allowances of the civil and military officers, and the wages of the soldiers, repairs the city walls, and superintends and pays for all the public works in the province. On the death of the Emperor, or on his birthday, the treasurer takes the precedence of the higher officers in the mournful or the joyful demonstrations made in the Emperor's temple. In the one case he is dressed in white clothes, and weeps as though he had lost his father, being sometimes called the " child of the Emperor ; " in the other case he is dressed in his official robes, and presents his congratulations to his imperial father before the yellow tablet which represents the Emperor in the temple.

The provincial judge presides over the examination and the punishment of ordinary criminals from all parts of the province. The judge can revise and reverse the decisions of the prefect and inferior officers in any part of the province relating to criminals or persons charged with crimes. His is a place of great power, responsibility, and pecuniary profit.

The salt commissioner controls the manufacture and sale of salt in the province. He has the power to oblige rich men to carry on the salt business. Those who are obliged by him to carry on the salt business always become poor. There are so many ways of disposing of salt clandestinely, on account of the deceptive practices of their underlings, that they always lose money in the course of their connexion with the salt business. When any salt contractor does not pay up promptly the monthly revenue dues to the salt commissioner, he is often dealt with very harshly. Sometimes he is thrown into prison. Being

MANDARIN AND HIS WIFE IN ROBES OF STATE.

wealthy, and usually very respectably connected, he always desires to avoid all contention with his superior, and therefore aims with great solicitude at having the necessary sum ready. When he is positively unable to meet his monthly payment, and falls largely in arrears to the government, some other rich man is compelled, by being flogged, or by being made to kneel on chains, or by some other distressing and unjust course, to consent to engage in the salt business, and to take upon himself the payment of the arrearages of his predecessor.

The provision commissioner controls the provision and land-tax departments. He receives and accounts for the taxes, which are paid in grain, from all parts of the province. He provides the rice and provisions for the soldiers of the province.

The prefect rules over a prefecture or county, a division of territory next smaller than a province. He reports to the governor. He takes part in the regular examinations of the undergraduates, both civil and military. He is the head actor in the annual procession in honour of spring. Foreign consuls have to do generally with the prefect.

The marine inspector presides over the marine affairs of this part of the province. Ships from foreign countries come under his supervision. He has some revenue officers connected with ocean commerce under his control. He must report to the Tartar general on matters relating to revenue.

The two district magistrates rule over the common people in their respective districts. Many matters which are to come under the supervision of higher officials must first be brought before one of these magistrates, according to the section of the city or the adjacent territory to which they refer, or in which the parties belong. These officials report to the prefect the important affairs which are brought before them. They preside over the lowest series of examinations of civil and military undergraduates belonging to their respective districts, but have nothing to do with the examination, government, or punishment of graduates.

The literary chancellor is a high officer sent from Peking, whose term of office is of three years' duration, to examine the literary and military undergraduates, and govern the graduates of the first degree of the literary class.

The Tartar general governs the Tartars living in the city, and the affairs which relate to the city wall. He is the city keeper. The keys of the seven gates of the city, after they are closed, are delivered into his possession every night. It is the common saying that if the gates should be opened contrary to law during the night, owing to the neglect of the Tartar general, and it should be reported at Peking, his head would pay the forfeit. In fact people go into the city and out of it nightly in large numbers, by scaling the walls after dark, through the connivance and the assistance of the gate-keepers, whom they bribe.

The lieutenant-general, or the major-general, who is always a Tartar, is professedly but little inferior in rank and power to the Tartar general. He has a voice in the decision of matters relating to the Tartar population. He is believed to be appointed by the emperor to watch the Tartar general. He is usually the poorest of all the imperial officers, but is eligible to the station of the Tartar general, an office of great influence and emolument.

The dignity of the great officers of the state proportions the number of bearers they may command for their sedans. The viceroy, the governor, the Tartar general, and the literary chancellor, may have eight, and four assistants to steady the sedans. The Tartar lieutenant-general, and the Chinese admiral, and the Chinese general, may also use each eight bearers, and four assistants to steady their sedans if they please, though they oftener employ only four bearers and the assistants. The low military officers usually appear in the streets on horseback. If the major-general and the adjutant-general choose to ride in sedans, they have four bearers. Of the civil officers, the treasurer, the judge, and the commissioners of the salt and of the provision departments, have four bearers, and four persons to steady the sedan. The prefect, the marine inspector, and the two district magistrates have four bearers, and no one to steady their sedans. The incumbents of the offices still lower have only two or three bearers. For a low officer, entitled to have only two bearers, to appear in the streets with four bearers, would be an offence for which he would be severely reprimanded, if he did not receive some heavy token of disapproval or disgrace, according to the pleasure of his superior.

The rank of some officers may be ascertained by observing the colour and the number of flounces on the umbrellas which are carried before them, and by the colour of the buttons or balls on their caps. Some are bright red, and have three storeys of flounces; others have two storeys; while others still are of a dark colour, and are plainly made. Some five or six of the highest officers, when they leave their yamuns and when they return home, have three cannon fired off as a salute of honour. When they parade the streets, some eight of the highest mandarins each have one or two men preceding their sedans, with a pole laid across their shoulders, having a gong on one end and a flag on the other. The bearer beats it occasionally three blows in regular succession. When entering a yamun it is beaten quickly and continually for a short period.

When high officers appear in the street, it is accounted a misdemeanour for the common people to mix up in the procession. When it is passing by, a civilian in a sedan must cause his sedan to be put down upon the ground, and people bearing loads or walking must stop, and stand still by the side of the street. People on horseback must dismount and stand in a respectful

LICTOR WITH WHIP IN HAND.

manner. The sign-boards of stores and shops, which sometimes are placed in front of the stores, must be removed from the street when the high mandarins pass by, as a mark of respect on the part of the shopkeepers. Should they be left standing in their usual positions, it would be considered disrespectful to the mandarins, as though civilians should sit in the presence of high officials. When the mandarin is below the fourth official rank, the common people may mix up in the street with his runners and assistants with impunity. In regard to high mandarins, the lictors are sure to see that the established customs are properly observed, beating unceremoniously and unmercifully any one who does not make haste to comply with their orders as they pass swiftly along.

High mandarins have sometimes quite a numerous retinue when they appear in public: there are two men bearing gongs and flags in front; ten or more men or boys carrying red oblong boards, having various inscriptions: some of these denote the officer's rank, command the people to keep silence, and order idlers to get out of the way; two men on horseback; two men, one carrying a large official fan and the other a large umbrella of state. Two men carrying a trunk full of changes of clothing.

Eight men carrying whips, whose business it is to clear the way, call out when passing the yamuns of other officers, and when turning around corners ; four men carrying censers having burning incense ; four men carrying swords ; two men, whose

BEARER OF FAN OF STATE.

business in part is to receive petitions, if presented in the street; four men to steady the sedan of the mandarin ; four men on horseback, holding each a flag having a long handle.

BEARER OF UMBRELLA OF STATE.

Sixteen soldiers following the sedan, carrying swords, spears, flags, hammers, iron chains, &c.

On occasions when he wishes to appear with extraordinary pomp and parade, he employs more men and more soldiers.

When a district magistrate appears in the streets he has two men dragging along two halves of a large bamboo. There are also two who carry leather whips and perform the duty of lictors, and two who carry iron chains in their hands, as if ready to seize and chain any culprit they may happen to find.

LICTOR DRAGGING ALONG THE HALF OF A BAMBOO.

The lictors with leathern whips clear the way, preceding the magistrate in his sedan. Following him, usually on horseback, are a couple of his interpreters. There is almost always a servant on foot carrying pipe and tobacco, and his card-case.

The uniform worn by the attendants of mandarins as they appear in the streets is not according to a cultivated taste. Many appear in dirty and ragged garments. The lictors are generally dressed in long black garments, having either tall black or tall red hats, made out of bamboo splints. High officials usually have eight lictors, half having red and half having black hats. Lower officers have two with red and two with black hats. These all usually have leather whips in their hands, and go in pairs. They are cruel and hard-hearted men. The soldiers have a round piece of white or red cloth upon their back and upon their breast, with black characters upon it, indicating the camp or the company to which they belong. The *executioner* belonging to the viceroy's yamun sometimes appears in his master's procession. He is dressed partly in red clothes made after the fashion of the Ming dynasty, wearing about his loins a kind of petticoat, and carrying a large sword of a peculiar shape. In his hat he wears two feathers of a kind of pheasant. It is the common saying that those who aspire to the position of executioner practise in

EXECUTIONER.

striking at a mark. They take a turnip, and drawing a black streak around it with ink, aim at cleaving it into two parts at a blow, striking precisely on the line. When they can invariably do it on successive trials, they feel qualified to become candidates for the post when there is a vacancy.

The third, thirteenth, twenty-third, eighth, eighteenth, and twenty-eighth days of every month are the appointed days when the civil officers and the expectants of office in the city and suburbs are required to call on the viceroy and the governor. They first go to the yamun* of the viceroy and send in their

* It seems the Yamun must be realized by the reader as inclusive of our ideas of mansion-house, town-hall, and police-station, and local prison. The yamun is a large building, where the courts of justice, prisons, and offices, and houses of the mandarins, and other officials are situated. It consists of four divisions. The outermost contains the gaols, and places of confinement for short periods, as also the dwellings of inferior officers. The second contains a hall of justice, for the formal trial of causes and criminals, as also apartments for public records, treasury, &c. The third includes the office of the mandarin himself, and rooms for the public reception of visitors; while the innermost division comprises the private residence of the mandarin and his family. Attached to each of these

R

cards. If he wishes to see any one he sends word for him to be ushered into his presence. All those who are not requested to remain consider themselves dismissed, and take their departure to call on the governor. When the one who has been invited in to see the great man has been shown out again, he proceeds to call on the governor, as the others have already done.

The same days, those in which three or eight occur, are also the regular periods for the reception, at the different yamuns, of the different complaints. On other days of the month the mandarins do not open their offices for the admission of accusations. When any one wishes to appeal to the law in regard to affairs which do not admit of delay until the next day for receiving complaints, he sometimes bribes a clerk connected with the yamun to which his business properly belongs, to take his written accusation to the mandarin and recommend its acceptance.

There are certain other six days in the month when, early in the morning, all the officers below them in rank, and expectants of office below them, are required to call on the treasurer, the judge, the salt commissioner, and the provision commissioner, to pay their respects and receive instructions. Unless the inferior officers and expectants should wait at the appointed times upon their superiors, they would be apt to incur their displeasure.

establishments are the Shi Ye, the judicial advisers, the private secretaries of the mandarins. The interior of a yamun is said to present a very strange and bustling scene. "The almost unceasing, flail-like sounds" (says Mr. Meadows) "of beating with the bamboo, either as a punishment for ascertained guilt, or to extort confession and evidence—the cries of the sufferers—the voices of the examining mandarins questioning, bullying, and wheedling—the voices of the porters stationed at the doors, between the first and second, and second and third divisions, transmitting in a loud singing tone orders for different officers to repair to certain places where they are wanted—the constant running hither and thither of some of the inmates of the place, and the frequent appearance of criminal and witnesses being escorted to and from the prisons and rooms for examination—are sounds and sights that bewilder and agitate those who have not been accustomed to them, and serve to heighten that dread which all Chinese entertain of entering a yamun." The yamun of a district magistrate thus comprises within itself what may be called the general police-station on a great scale—the county gaol, as it were, for the custody of debtors, and of criminals awaiting trial or execution—the place where quarter sessions and assizes are held—the offices of all the subordinate officers of these courts, and office and residence of the chief mandarin, who is at once judge, sheriff, coroner, and commissioner of taxes. In a populous district such a building is calculated to contain from three hundred to five hundred individuals, and in a less populous place two hundred. The Chinese, however, in their domiciles, contrive to pack into amazingly little room, so that their buildings do not at first view appear so extensive.

The regular routine of attention and respect must be carried out between superiors and inferiors, if the latter would stand well with the former, and expect to be promoted by them. In front of the yamuns of some four or five of the high mandarins is a small eight-sided building, called "the drum-pavilion," designed to be occupied by the band of music attached to the mandarinate, where they play at the usual times for the amusement or in honour of the mandarin. When he rises in the morning, washes his face, and partakes of his luncheon, they must perform on their instruments, the fact of the mandarin being thus engaged having been duly communicated to them by his servants striking a large, hollow wooden fish, or upon certain iron utensils, which are suspended in several of the different halls leading from his apartments to the outer gates. While employed in eating breakfast, dinner, and supper, they also play some airs. His going to bed is also celebrated in a similar way. On various public occasions these musicians are also required to practise their parts. They are paid from the provincial treasury, and the honour of having them is conferred by the emperor as a special privilege, hoping to gladden the hearts of his servants, and induce them to be faithful to him.

There is no scale of fixed fees in China regulating the charges for official work performed by mandarins or by their underlings. The official demands as much as he imagines he can get, considering the circumstances of the case. The mandarins have a regular salary from the imperial treasury. Within a comparatively short period (commenced in the reign of Kien Lun, of the present dynasty) an extra allowance has been made them by the emperor. The design of this was to remove the need of bribery and extortion by furnishing an ample support.

Should a prisoner before the bar, in the judgment of the mandarin, deserve the rod, either as a punishment for acknowledged or proved crime, or in order to elicit confession of violations of law, or for contempt of court, he has only to throw down upon the ground some bamboo slips. Every bamboo counts five strokes. The whipper seizes the man and throws him down on the ground, and proceeds to beat him. He is often bribed not to strike hard, though he pretends to be inflicting very heavy blows.* Sometimes, also, the prisoner has a man provided to

* Of the cruel administration of justice in China, Père Huc gives a vivid description :—"For ourselves, at the first glance we cast into the hall, we felt a cold perspiration come over us, and our limbs tottered under us ; we were ready to faint. The first object that presented itself on

R 2

receive the blows which should fall upon his own person. This individual is usually connected with the establishment. This can be accomplished only by bribing the assistants and underlings. It is done by the company of attachés rushing in between the magistrate, who is sitting on his tribunal, and the prisoner, who is some distance from him. In this way the magistrate is sometimes kept from seeing who actually receives the blows. Such a bribing of the inmates of the yamun requires the expenditure of a considerable sum of money, especially if the one who desires to escape a personal flagellation should be wealthy, and accused of high crimes.

Every document, in order to be considered binding or genuine, issuing from a mandarin's establishment, must have his official stamp upon it, not his signature. The stamp is received when he enters upon office, and must be kept with great care ; for if it should be lost, or stolen, or burnt up, he would assuredly be severely fined, or punished in some way. He would be fortunate if not degraded from office. Mandarins do not sign their proclamations or documents with their names. The stamp makes them official and authentic.

The couriers who take government dispatches from one place to another are commonly called ."horses of a thousand li," on account of their speed. It oftentimes occurs that some especial emergency requires the transmission of a dispatch with the utmost speed. At such times, in the absence of railroads and

entering this Chinese judgment-hall was the accused—the person on his trial. He was suspended in the middle of the hall, like one of those lanterns, of whimsical forms and colossal dimensions, often seen in the great pagodas. Ropes attached to a great beam in the roof held him tied by the wrists and feet, so as to draw the body into the form of a bow. Beneath him stood five or six executioners, armed with rattan-rods and leather lashes, in ferocious attitudes, their clothes and faces spotted with blood—the blood of the unfortunate creature, who was uttering stifled groans, while his flesh was torn almost in tatters. The audience present at this frightful spectacle appeared quite at their ease, and our yellow caps excited much more emotion than the spectacle of torture. Many laughed, indeed, at the horror visible in our faces. The magistrate, to whom our coming had been hastily announced, rose from his seat as soon as he perceived us, and crossed the hall to meet us. As he passed near the executioners, he had to walk on the tips of his toes, and hold up his beautiful silk robes, that they might not be soiled by the pools of half-coagulated blood, with which the floor was covered. He saluted us smilingly, and saying he would suspend the proceedings for a moment, conducted us to a small room behind the judge's seat. We sat down, or rather we fell upon a divan, and were some moments before we could recover our composure."
—Huc's *Chinese Empire*, vol. ii. pp. 245, 246.

telegraphs, the courier is furnished with some hen's feathers, which are usually placed in the top of his lantern, to indicate to all whom it may concern that he carries messages which demand the utmost speed. Such a messenger must be helped on his way with all possible celerity by all those whose business it is to assist in the transportation of government dispatches. It is asserted that in some parts of the empire such messages are sometimes transmitted at the rate of eight hundred li per day, or over two hundred English miles. The dispatch is contained in a parcel which is bound on the shoulders of the courier, who is changed at certain intervals, using boats or horses, or running on foot, as circumstances show will be most speedy.

Generally speaking, cases of murder are never investigated by the mandarin unless a formal complaint is made, on the same principle that he never arrests thieves until a complaint has been made against them. The underlings of the magistrates often lend their help to do justice to innocent parties in circumstances like the following : A dead body is clandestinely placed during the night on the premises of some person, in order to injure him or to extort money, by an enemy or a rogue. For example : The corpse of a beggar found in the street is placed on the premises of a rich man. In the morning the rogue comes along and charges the rich man with having quarrelled with and having killed his brother or cousin, or other relative, and threatens to apply the law to him. The man appears to be dreadfully shocked at finding the body of his dear relative under such circumstances in the street. If the man really only wishes to extort money, he finally agrees to compromise the matter. " His relative being dead, he cannot be restored to life. A public prosecution of his murderer would not bring the dead back to his family and to his friends." In view of such philosophical and practical considerations, he is willing to desist from prosecution for a pecuniary consideration. Should the rich man, feeling that he was innocent of the crime of murder, and understanding the real facts in the case, refuse to silence the other party by giving him money, the latter has only to call to his aid a few of the underlings of some mandarin, and promise them a share in the spoils. They come to the house or store of the rich man and make a great disturbance, as though sent by their master to inquire into the circumstances of the case. The rich man by this time has probably counted the expense in case the other party should really inform against him, and knowing that it

would cost far less to settle the matter at once than to wait until
more harpies should arrive, or a mock prosecution should have
been instituted against him, has concluded to agree to the terms
proposed by the other party, or make some offer which is
accepted, and the matter drops.   There is a large class of men
who are none too good to engage in such an affair, and who are
much feared and hated by the common people.   They are exceedingly bold and violent, and are on good terms with the
lowest class of official underlings.

In every neighbourhood is a local officer, corresponding to a
village constable, who is of great help to his superior, the district magistrate, in keeping the peace.   It is a part of his duty
to prevent quarrels from occurring in his neighbourhood, and
report any disturbance of importance to his superior.   Should
any trouble arise which he cannot quell, it is his duty to send in
a notice of the facts in the case as soon as possible to the district
magistrate in whose limits his neighbourhood is situated.   Should
he delay to do so he is liable to be severely whipped, or put in
a cangue for a month or two, or be degraded from his position.
It is also his business to report in regard to important lawsuits
which relate to his neighbourhood.   He is the organ through
whom the magistrate communicates to the residents of the neighbourhood his will in regard to matters which concern them.   It
is also his business to see that the villagers observe the regulations to promote the public interests which emanate with the
magistrate.   He acts the part of a policeman, permanently
stationed at one place.   His term of office usually continues
during good behaviour.   Oftentimes it descends to his son.

The title-deeds to sales of houses must be reported, in order
to be stamped and taxed, before five years after the sale.   The
treasurer, on application through the district magistrate, attaches
a piece of paper to the deed, stamped in red with his official seal,
and having also a few sentences relating to the deed written
upon it.   An unstamped deed would be worthless five years
after date, as it would justify the seizure by Government of the
property involved.   A sale of land must be reported within three
years, that its deed may be stamped and taxed in a similar
manner.   The rate of taxing is fixed by law, being usually eight
or ten per cent. on the purchase money.   A stamped deed is
called a "red" deed, because it has the impress in red of the
seal of the treasurer.   An unstamped deed is referred to as a
"white" deed.

There is a singular custom or law relating to this place which must be annually observed, or the mandarin whose duty it is to attend to the matter would be severely reprimanded, or perhaps deprived of rank and office. An annual tribute of three kinds of fruit, for the production of which this place has become celebrated, must be sent on to Peking so as to arrive there at a certain time. These presents, as tribute, are the loose-jacket orange, the olive, and a certain kind of very fragrant but inedible fruit called usually "Buddha's hand." The oranges are required to be in Peking on the morning of new year's day at the latest, so as to be used at the worship and sacrifice in honour of Heaven by the emperor. As soon as oranges are in a state fit to be dispatched, a quantity is picked with care and packed in wooden buckets, and started off for Peking, carried by coolies under the charge of two officers, one civil and one military. If they should arrive there with only a large plateful of good ones, the grand object would be duly accomplished. If none should arrive in season for use at the sacrifice to Heaven on the first day of every new year, the officers in charge would be punished for their tardiness, and the high mandarins here, whose business it is to attend to this important matter, would be liable to be fined or otherwise punished. The use of this kind of orange is considered felicitous and lucky on new year's day here as well as at Peking. The olives and the Buddha's hands are sent on in much the same way at the proper season of the year.

One of the most absurd and remarkable official duties of mandarins is to "save the sun and moon when eclipsed."

Prospective eclipses are never noticed in the Imperial Calendar, published originally at Peking, and republished in the provinces. The imperial astronomers at the capital, a considerable time previous to a visible eclipse, inform the Board of Rites of its month, day, and hour. These officers send this intelligence to the viceroys or governors of the eighteen provinces of the empire. These, in turn, communicate the information to all the principal subordinate officers in the provinces of the civil and the military grade. The officers make arrangements to save the moon or the sun at the appointed time. On the day of the eclipse, or on the day preceding it, some of them put up a written notice in or near their yamuns for the information of the public.

The Chinese generally have no rational idea of the cause of eclipses. The common explanation is that the sun or the moon has experienced some disaster. Some even affirm that the object eclipsed is being devoured by an immense ravenous monster. This is the most popular sentiment in Fuhchau in regard to the

procuring cause of eclipses. All look upon the object eclipsed
with wonder. Many are filled with apprehension and terror.
Some of the common people, as well as mandarins generally,
enter upon some course of action, the express object of which is
to save the luminary from its dire calamity, or to rescue it from
the jaws of its greedy enemy.

Mandarins must act officially, and in virtue of their being
officers of government. Neither they nor the people seem to

MANDARIN SAVING THE SUN WHEN ECLIPSED.

regard the immense distance of the celestial object as at all interfering with the success of their efforts.

The high mandarins procure the aid of priests of the Tauist
sect at their yamuns. These place an incense censer and two
large candlesticks, for holding red candles or tapers, on a table

in the principal reception-room of the mandarin, or in the open space in front of it under the open heavens.

At the commencement of the eclipse the tapers are lighted, and soon after the mandarin enters, dressed in his official robes. Taking some sticks of lighted incense in both hands, he makes his obeisance before or facing the table, raising and depressing the incense two or three times, according to the established fashion, before it is placed in the censer. Or sometimes the incense is lighted and put in the censer by one of the priests employed. The officer proceeds to perform the high ceremony of kneeling down three times and knocking his head on the ground nine times. After this he arises from his knees. Large gongs and drums near by are now beaten as loudly as possible. The priests begin to march slowly around the tables, reciting formulas, &c. which marching they keep up, with more or less intermissions, until the eclipse has passed off.

A uniform result always follows these official efforts to save the sun and the moon. They are invariably successful! There is not a single instance recorded in the annals of the empire when the measures prescribed in instructions from the emperor's astronomers at Peking, and correctly carried out in the provinces by the mandarins, have not resulted in a complete rescue of the object eclipsed. Doubtless the vast majority of the common people in China believe that the burning of tapers and incense, the prostration of the mandarins, the beating of the gongs and drums, and the recitations on the part of the priests, are signally efficacious in driving away the voracious monster. They observe that the sun or the moon does not seem to be permanently injured by the attacks of its celestial enemy, although a half or nearly the whole appeared to have been swallowed up. This happy result is doubtless viewed with much complacency by the parties engaged to bring it about.

The lower classes generally leave the saving of the sun or the moon, when eclipsed, to the mandarins, as it is a part of their official business. Some of the people occasionally beat in their houses a winnowing instrument, made of bamboo splints, on the occurrence of an eclipse. Some venture to assert that the din of this instrument penetrates the clouds as high as the very temple of Heaven itself! The sailors connected with junks at this place, on the recurrence of a lunar eclipse, always contribute their aid to rescue the moon by beating their gongs in a most deafening manner.

Without doubt, most of the mandarins understand the real

occasion of eclipses, but they have no optional course in regard
to the matter. They must comply with established custom, and
with the understood will of their superiors. The imperial
astronomers having been taught the principles of astronomy, and
the causes which produce eclipses, by the Roman Catholic missionaries a long while since, of course know that the common
sentiments on the subject are as absurd as the common customs
relating to it are useless. But the emperor and his cabinet cling
to ancient practices, notwithstanding the clearest evidences of
their false and irrational character.

The blunders, or the ignorance, or the superstitions of the
Chinese in regard to eclipses are sometimes made the occasion
of flattering the vanity of the Emperor of China. Davis, in his
" History of China," remarks that during the dynasty of Sung,
which ended about 1260 A.D., an expected eclipse having failed
to take place, " they congratulated the emperor that the heavens
had dispensed with this omen of ill luck in his favour." Williams,
in his " Middle Kingdom," mentions that some clouds, on a certain occasion, having prevented the eclipse being visible, " the
courtiers joyfully repaired to the emperor to felicitate him that
the heavens, touched by his virtues, had spared him the pain
of witnessing the *eating of the sun.*"

It sometimes occurs that a high officer falls into disrepute at
Peking, either because he is really guilty of maladministration,
or because he has some powerful enemy who is poisoning the
minds of those who are in power against him, and he is required
to appear in the capital for trial with chains about his neck, and
in the attitude of a felon. When an officer is commanded to
" arrest and chain " a brother officer, he proceeds to arrest, chain,
and forward him to Peking, if he manifests any unwillingness to
go, and if the exercise of force is necessary. It, however, seldom
happens that positive force or personal violence are employed.
The man usually, as soon as he learns his fate, resigns his office,
and provides himself with a light wooden or paper cangue for
his neck, and with a small chain for his hands, arrests and chains
himself, and starts as fast as possible for the capital of the empire.
He delivers himself into the custody of the proper tribunal there,
and begs of the emperor the favour of a speedy examination and
punishment for his crimes. If he can get the start of the official
order from Peking for his arrest, it is usually reckoned as worth
considerable in his favour. At such times he uses his money
freely in order to secure the friendship and influence of the high
officials at the capital.

The mandarin is sometimes condemned to suffer the penalty of death by strangulation for some flagrant dereliction of official duty, or for some wilful violation of the laws which he did not succeed in concealing, &c. According to strict law, there are many cases where mandarins ought to be deprived of life as a punishment for their crimes. High mandarins oftentimes do not report the truth to the court at Peking because they are bribed. The system of bribing seems to be effective in every department of the administration, and in cases where the facts become known at head-quarters, and the higher culprit should, according to law, lose his life and have his property confiscated to the Government, high officials at Peking are very often bribed to intercede for him before the proper tribunal, but such bribing costs a large sum.

In case of the highest officers, as chancellors of the empire, or presidents of the six boards and viceroys of the provinces, when they have committed deeds for which the emperor wishes to punish them capitally, instead of beheading them, he sometimes, in his clemency, intimates his wishes by sending them a piece of silk or a silk cord. They understand the meaning of the silken present to be "strangle yourselves," which they proceed to do. If they should hesitate too long, or decline altogether to commit suicide at the implied request of their imperial master, they would soon lose their heads by decapitation. Self-strangulation is more honourable than beheading by the executioner, as the body is left whole and unmutilated. Allowing those capitally convicted to take their own lives is considered a mark of especial favour on the part of the emperor, for which they are expected to return their grateful acknowledgments. Officers of low rank are seldom or never allowed the honour or the privilege of strangling themselves with a white cord or girdle of silk presented by the emperor. They are summarily beheaded, unless they commit suicide on their own account and responsibility. Swallowing gold-leaf is a very popular way of committing suicide by mandarins after their condemnation, or when in despair of an honourable acquittal during the progress of their trial, or when some great disaster occurs for which they will be held responsible.

When an officer has fallen largely behind in the amount of revenue which it is expected he will deliver over to the imperial treasury for government use, the high mandarins sometimes decide to search his house, in order to ascertain whether he is able to pay the sum for which he is in arrears, or whether he is really poor; but the house which is searched is not the yamun in which he lives, but his paternal or ancestral home in another province, where his parents, if living, reside, and where it is surmised his property will be found. The search is instituted without his knowledge by men deputed by his superior mandarins. The searching of his paternal home instead of his actual residence is based on the presumption that, if he were wealthy, sufficient evidence would be furnished there. His parents, or the members of the family at home, would be living in luxury, the grounds and buildings would be spacious and kept in good repair. Chinese mandarins are famous for sending their gains of office home, or away from the place where they play the mandarin and acquire it.

It is not a very uncommon occurrence for an officer of high rank to be fined the amount of his salary for one month, or two months, or a year, as a punishment for negligence in the discharge of his duties, or for some maladministration not requiring a heavier punishment. The occasions where the mandarins may be thus fined are numerous; but as their stated allowance from the imperial coffers is but a small portion of their actual receipts, the stoppage of salary for a short time is a matter of little pecuniary consequence; and it is regarded as a thing of import only as it affects their character and prospects of advancement in rank and purse with their superiors.

In cases where maladministration is of a too flagrant character to be punished simply by a fine, sometimes recourse is had to a heavier degree of punishment—that of degrading him from his rank and titles, but obliging him to continue to discharge his official duties. This punishment is generally only temporary. His cap, when worn during this period, must be without its button, and the feather denoting his rank or office must be laid aside until he has cleared up his character, or made for himself a new reputation.*

When one degraded from his rank, but retained in office, is

* "In the course we had witnessed a curious instance of the severity of military discipline in China. A mandarin, whose cap with a gold button was borne before him, was marched about in procession between two executioners blindfolded, with a small flag upon a short bamboo, pierced through each of his ears; before him was a man bearing a placard with this inscription : ' By orders of the General Soo and Sung; for a breach of military discipline his ears are pierced as a warning to the multitude.' After being paraded along the bank he was taken round the different war-junks, and then on board the admiral's vessel. We subsequently heard that his offence was having allowed our boat to pass the fort without reporting it."—*Voyage of Ship Amherst*, p. 82.

unable to clear himself from the charges against him in a reasonable time, to the satisfaction of his superiors, the next grade of punishment is to remove him from the official trust. He returns to the position of a citizen, liable to arrest and further punishment, should the punishment already inflicted not be deemed sufficiently severe. Oftentimes he is commanded to appear as soon as possible at Peking, to be tried by the proper tribunal.

There are occasions when it is made the duty of a mandarin to resign his office for a specified time or for a special reason, expecting to take office again when the time has expired or when the reason no longer exists. For example :—Every civil mandarin, on the occasion of the death of a parent, must immediately resign his office, announce the sorrowful fact to the emperor by a memorial, and ask leave to go and mourn the usual period of three years at his ancestral home. He need not wait until an answer is returned. Such requests are never refused ; and not to resign one's office, and return to the home of the deceased parent, and engage in the established rites, would be a crime not tolerated by Chinese law or Chinese custom. The duties of his vacated office will be cared for by the high officers of the province for the time being, until other arrangements can be made. Military officers of the three highest ranks only are allowed to resign their appointments and return home to mourn three years on the death of a parent. Military officers of some lower ranks are allowed to be absent a shorter period. Such a resignation of office oftentimes produces considerable confusion in the administration of government, but the derangement is regarded as unimportant compared with the sin of violating the ancient custom of resigning office and returning home to mourn, which custom Confucius himself honoured and observed on the death of his mother, when he held office. The expense and fatigue to the filial son are also sometimes very great, but such considerations are of little moment compared with the transcendent importance of showing due regard to the memory of a deceased parent. It will not answer for a high mandarin to fail in the exhibition of filial piety if he wishes to stand well with the imperial government, or with the people whom he governs.

When a mandarin has been a long while absent from his parents, or when he hears that they, or one of them, are very ill, it is very creditable for him to ask permission of the emperor to leave his office and its duties for a year or two, for the purpose of going home and taking care of his parents. Should he be made acquainted with their dangerous illness, and not petition for a release from office to go and visit them, he would be charged with a want of filial love, which is one of the most serious charges that can be made against the character of a man in China.

It sometimes occurs that a mandarin asks permission of the emperor to resign his office and return home, for the purpose of remaining with his aged and infirm parents as long as they live. Before granting such a request, the emperor usually causes inquiries to be made in regard to the circumstances of the parents of the professedly filial mandarin by or through the high officials of the province where they reside. If the facts are as stated by the suppliant, and the emperor's advisers regard him as really desirous of spending his time with his parents as long as they live, because of his filial affection for them—not because he wishes to enjoy or invest the money he has already made—his application is granted, unless there are manifest and urgent considerations of state which make it desirable that he should postpone the gratification of his filial heart to a more remote period. Such applicants are always treated with respect and honour, even if their requests are refused.

Not unfrequently does it occur that a man who is appointed to office is in duty bound to offer his resignation because some member of his family, or some relative or very intimate friend, has an appointment in the same province of inferior rank to his own. For instance, if a son should be appointed to the governor-ship of a province in which his father already held the office of a prefect, or a district magistrate, or any other office lower in rank than that to which he was appointed, it would be the duty of the son to resign his office without delay; or if a younger brother should be appointed to some office in a province where his elder brother had official employment less honourable or less elevated in rank than the one to which the younger brother was appointed, the latter is required to tender his resignation. The general rule is, that the more honourable in family relations may not be in office of a lower rank under one less honourable. A son may not hold office in the same province of higher rank than his father; a younger brother may not be put over his elder brother; a nephew may not be a mandarin of superior rank to his uncle in the same province, &c. On the same general principle of reasoning, à la Chinois, two warm and mutual friends must not hold office in the same province of different ranks. A greater must not worship the less; and equals must not be placed in official positions so that one must worship the other as higher or lower; and friends must not "worship" each other. Such a relation of things would be contrary to the order of nature. This matter is a difficult one to regulate in China.

Sometimes a mandarin asks to be relieved from the cares of official responsibility for a short time in consequence of being wearied out with his previous labours, secretly intending oftentimes never to take office again. Mandarins who have amassed considerable wealth are oftentimes anxious to retire temporarily or permanently from Government service, in order to secure the wealth and the titles and honours they have gained. If they remain in office they are liable to be fined, or degraded, or severely punished for innocent mistakes, and for unsuccessful efforts to do what falls to their duty to do. But their applications are seldom granted, unless they bribe largely the high officials to report favourably, and to use their influence at court in their behalf.

Officers of an advanced age sometimes ask for leave to retire from office on the score of their old age and their increasing infirmities. The emperor is generally anxious to retain in office his long-tried and experienced servants as long as he can, and therefore is always loth to grant permission for them to retire to private life. Unless they can bring the emperor, or his confidential or influential advisers, to believe that they are really becoming more and more infirm, blind, or deaf, &c. it is usually quite difficult to obtain a favourable reply to their requests for a furlough on account of old age. There is considerable danger of urgently pressing the request for respite on this account, if there is not most manifest reason for it. The emperor may become displeased, and deprive the petitioner of his honours and titles, and let him go home as a plain citizen, which is a result not at all desired, and which is regarded as really tantamount to dismissal from office in disgrace.

When sick, mandarins frequently ask leave of absence or permission to resign office, in order to return home and take measures to cure themselves. Sometimes the emperor, in a manifestly urgent case, grants the permission to resign. At other times he permits them to remain nominally in office, but relieved of its cares for a time, thus enabling them to employ medical aid without the necessity of attending to official duties at the same time, expecting them to resume the responsibilities of office as soon as they recover. This is a very common excuse for trying to rid themselves of official duty, and danger, and responsibility, when they are really not very unwell, and when the actual reason for desiring to be allowed to retire is to obtain an opportunity to secure or invest their property in some profitable manner, and to enjoy in private life the honour and rank which they have already attained in Government employ. When this is suspected to be the real cause of preferring a request to be allowed to retire from office "on account of sickness," of course the request is promptly denied. There is a saying here to the effect that those who feign sickness in order to go to their ancestral homes and enjoy their wealth and honours, will be sure to become really ill there, as a punishment for their duplicity and mendacity toward their sovereign.

The Chinese Government seem to act on the adage, "set a thief to catch a thief." There is a class of men connected with civil official establishments, but living more or less among the people, who have the superintendence of matters relating to thieves and thieving. These men enjoy the reputation of having been great thieves themselves before they were recognised as chiefs of this branch of police. It is currently reported among the people that many of these men were detected in stealing, and, instead of being punished, they were pardoned, on their agreeing to catch other thieves, and to aid the magistrates to obtain possession of stolen property. The people affirm that they are head thieves, or chiefs of the local robbers which infest neighbourhoods, and know, in case of any particular theft, who the robbers are, and where the stolen goods are deposited, because they instructed the thieves where to rob and where to carry the property taken, promising to protect them. After the robbery has been committed, the thief-catchers are summoned, and make a great ado, pretending to be sincerely desirous of recovering the property and ascertaining the thieves, and having them arrested and punished. Unless, however, they are bribed largely to recover the property, it is seldom ever seen again by its owner. If the matter, after a while, should die away, they divide the spoils or the profits with the thieves. If, however, the party who was robbed does not give up the affair, but makes repeated applications to the magistrate whose duty it is to attend to the affair, and there seems to be no other way of proceeding, the magistrate insists on the thief-catchers finding out the robbers and restoring the goods. The thief-catchers, in case they perceive their magistrate to be really in earnest, usually produce some one who confesses to the robbery, and perhaps a small part of the goods stolen is restored. The thief is flogged and put in the cangue for a month or two, and the matter is dropped.

Thief-takers have the reputation of being partners, or personally concerned, in the principal places where stolen goods are deposited for a time, and afterwards offered for sale. The places where they are sold generally are an illegal kind of pawn-shops, not authorized or recognised by Government, but simply tolerated.

The men connected with military yamuns, required to act the part of thief catchers, are known by a different name from those belonging to civil yamuns. These are generally common soldiers, who are employed to patrol the street at night. In this way they have opportunity to find out, if they really desire to do so, all who in their section of the city or suburbs are regular or professional thieves. The theory is that they secretly watch any who are out thieving until they have entered a house. They remain outside, and when the thieves come forth with their plunder they seize them, and restore the property to its owners, but deliver the robbers over to their mandarins for punishment. The theory is a very fine one, but the practice does not correspond to it. They divide the spoils with the robbers, and let them go. The lion's share falls to the lot of their official protectors.

It is the current belief among the people that those who have once stolen, and have shared the plunder with the thief-catchers, may never lead honest lives again if they continue to reside in the place, but must rob and plunder, dividing the profits with the official thief-catchers. If the former are afterwards seen by the latter with any valuable property in their possession in the streets they claim a part of it; and, if they have any respectable clothing upon their persons, they strip them of it, on the charge of being robbers. If they do not yield peaceably, the thief-catchers proceed to beat and abuse them, and threaten to take them into custody, and deliver them into the hands of their masters as thieves. It is said that many who would be as honest, and lead as exemplary lives, as the majority of the population are obliged to become thieves and robbers, sharing the profits with the thief-police, in order to gain a living, after they have once been detected in pilfering or stealing.

Common fame affirms that every mandarin receives valuable presents more or less regularly from his subordinates.*

* Mr. Meadows exhibits a table of the Government salaries of the state officials, and the actual incomes which they derive by extortion, and other means, deduced from the best information he could obtain. Thus, a governor-general receives from Government £60 per annum, but he con-

On arriving at the place of his mandarinate, it is customary, in this part of the empire, for clerks and inferior officials connected with his own establishment to make presents to the new mandarin. He expects a present graduated in value according to the comparative lucrativeness of the stations which the officers fill. The amount from each is fixed by custom. Unless they should give it on the arrival of the mandarin, professedly as an expression of their satisfaction and respect, but really in order to ingratiate themselves in his good-will, matters would not go smoothly with them. They would be frequently detected, and required to do their work over again, &c. They give the customary present to the mandarin, as soon as he arrives, as a bribe to treat them well.

All of the officers inferior to the newly-arrived in the district, prefecture, or province, who are under his supervision, are expected to make him a present. The district magistrate expects a present from all who are beneath him, the prefect from all who are beneath him, the governor from the officers under his jurisdiction who report to him, and the viceroy from all the principal officers in the two provinces under his control. Those who do not make the customary token of respect may be sure that they are marked, and that they will suffer the consequence of their violation of custom in the subsequent inattention and ill-will of their superior. Some of these presents, given by a single subordinate to his superior of high rank and in a high office, are said to amount to several hundred dollars, especially if he has a great favour which he hopes to gain from him, or if he desires to be promoted through his influence.

The newly-arrived mandarin is to a large extent under the influence of the subordinates whom he finds connected with his yamun. He is usually accompanied by a number of family relatives and confidential advisers, who aid him. Still, he is necessarily very much under the control or influence of those who are attached to the establishment. The new mandarin is very frequently entirely unacquainted with the customs of the place and with its dialect. He finds sometimes several tens or scores of men belonging to the yamun who are strangers, and whom he cannot understand when they converse with each

trives to make his actual income £8,333. A governor of a province gets nominally £50, and makes it up to £4,333. A judge has £43 of salary, and makes up £2,000. The collectors of taxes from £1,500 to £1,000. Even a subordinate officer, with a nominal salary of £10 or £12, ekes it out, by various means, to £200 and £300.—MEADOWS' *Desultory Notes on China.*

other in their vernacular. The statement that he is to a great
extent under the control or influence of his subordinates connected with his yamun will be evident in the course of the
following observations :

There are a large number of men, called "great sires," always
found in yamuns of the higher rank, with whom the chief
mandarin has constant intercourse.

Some of the great sires act as interpreters to the mandarin.
The mandarin, being generally from another province, requires
an interpreter to explain the dialect spoken by natives of the
place who may have business to do with him, if they cannot
speak the court dialect. In case of a criminal trial where the
culprit is from a distant part of the province, and speaks the
brogue of that section, it would be necessary for an interpreter
to translate the language of the culprit to the mandarin, and the
language of the mandarin to the culprit.

Should the great sire for any reason desire to favour the
person interrogated, it is sometimes an easy matter to put a
plausible colouring upon his statements, especially as he readily
learns, from constant intercourse with his master, the manner in
which he may dupe him ; and, unless he should receive a bonus
from the party interrogated by the mandarin, it is very easy to
misinterpret, or to fail of interpreting the whole truth, and
nothing but the truth, to that party from the mandarin, or from
the mandarin to that party. It is for the interest of the mandarin to gain and keep the good-will of his interpreter, and it is
also for the interest of the other party to stand well with him.
Without the use of much imagination, it is not difficult to
perceive that the mandarin necessarily comes under the influence
of his great sires to a large extent.

Another of these great sires has the charge of the entrance-
door to the yamun. All who desire to see the resident mandarin
must have their cards of introduction, or their visiting cards,
received and passed along by him or his assistants. He levies a
contribution, from those who wish to see his master, called "the
door-parcel." Sometimes he demands an exorbitant sum before
he will receive and pass along the card, and announce the
arrival of a stranger who wishes to see the mandarin on urgent
business. On the arrival of a new incumbent of office at the
yamun whose door-keeper he is, he generally reaps a large
harvest, as a great number of official visitors must call to pay
their respects to their superior. Unless the inferior mandarins
call to see him or send in their cards, the newly-arrived will be

s 2

offended at their want of politeness ; but to succeed in doing this they must come to terms with the chief door-keeper.

Even on occasion of making presents to the mandarin on the recurrence of his birthday, and of the great festivals during the year in accordance with established customs, the door-keeper must be largely bribed by those who would show their respects and intimate their congratulations to his master, else he will not allow their presents and the accompanying card to be taken into the premises. After a successful application for an office in the bestowment of the high mandarin, his door-keeper is usually sure to fleece the applicant when he comes at the appointed time to receive his credentials and return his thanks ; for, unless he calls to receive his credentials at the appointed time, the mandarin would be displeased at his want of punctuality, and might possibly change his mind ; and the other party cannot proceed to the place of his mandarinate until he has obtained the requisite documents. The deeply-interested caller can do no better than come to terms with the door-keeper.

Among the permanent attachés, during good behaviour, to a mandarinate, is a class of men usually called the mandarin's "teacher" or "adviser." Every civil mandarin has at least one whom he regards as his right-hand man and his chief "teacher," who really is indispensable to him. He usually has been a long while connected with that mandarinate, and is acquainted with the recorded decisions of his master's predecessors, and with the laws bearing upon the matters generally investigated and decided at that yamun, and is familiar with local customs, sentiments, and feelings. In regard to these subjects the new occupant of the office is at first ignorant. In fact, he is often quite dependent on his "teacher," who is always a man of talent and experience. In regard to most cases he is consulted, and his opinion obtained. He is always treated with great respect by the mandarin ; eats at the same table with him, and occupies the post of honour, being the mandarin's guest according to Chinese notions of etiquette.

The process which it is customary for a man to adopt at this place when he wishes to engage the services of any particular individual to be his teacher, is like this : he prepares a large sheet of red paper, and on it writes his invitation, stating the business he desires to have him do, and the salary he offers him, and when to be paid, whether monthly or quarterly. In signing this document, the mandarin often styles himself "his stupid younger brother." This paper and his card he sends by some one to the individual, together with a present of ten or fifteen

dollars, more or less. If the man receives the present and the
document, and retains them, it is understood that he accepts the
terms and consents to fill the station. He considers himself engaged for a year. But if he declines to receive the present with the
red paper and card, sending them back, the meaning is that he is
dissatisfied with something, or that it is impossible for him to accept, being engaged or in feeble health. In this case the mandarin
must make another offer if he wishes to secure his services, or he
must look out for another suitable person to act as teacher.

In connexion with mandarin establishments of the first rank
in the provincial city will be found six separate offices or boards,
in imitation of the corresponding six boards at the imperial
capital. The head clerk at each of these offices is a man of
ability, and well acquainted with the history and the condition
of his department. The first relates to offices and vacancies ; the
second relates to revenue, as provisions and moneys received for
taxes ; the third relates to official ceremonies and rites, as sacrificing in spring and autumn ; the fourth relates to war, as the
number of soldiers, their pay and rations ; the fifth relates to
punishment, as regards degree and kind ; the sixth relates to
public works, as building and repairs. These head clerks are
paid out of government funds a regular and handsome salary.
After they have served with credit for six years, they are entitled to the honorary reward of wearing a button on their caps,
denoting the sixth degree of rank, conferred by the emperor. It
is manifest that every new incumbent of the mandarinate is
dependent upon these men to a very great extent in regard
to the details of their departments, as well as in regard to the
proper decision of important questions which concern them.
Their opinions are oftentimes of necessity of more value, and
generally much nearer the requirements of the law, than his
opinions on disputed and delicate points.

These head men sometimes work under the personal supervision of the mandarin their master, and they submit their
reports to Peking, and public notices for the region where
they live, to him for criticism and correction. These are
issued in his name, and have his official seal. They are men
of ready talent, quick in the use of the pencil, and possessed
of much more than an average amount of general intelligence.
When they and the principal teacher agree well with each
other, everything usually works smoothly : but when they are
not on good terms with him, the wheels of government turn
with friction, producing oftentimes actual enmity and ill-will.

CHAPTER XIII.

FEW mandarins are popular,* and have the confidence and esteem of the people over whom they rule. They generally are too desirous to become rich to administer affairs with justice, usually deciding the causes which are brought before their tribunals in favour of those who give them the most money in presents or bribes. But there are exceptions to the above remarks, which are the more honourable and noticeable because they are few. Some mandarins are universally spoken favourably of by the people, because of the general regard to justice which they evince in their decisions, and on account of their evident desire to promote the happiness and the prosperity of their subjects. When they die in office, their death is regarded as a public calamity; and when their term of office expires, and they are transferred to some other station, their departure is regarded as a public loss.

It is sometimes the custom when such a popular officer departs, for the rich people and the gentry to join together and bear the expense of presenting him with one or more umbrellas of state, made in a rich style. From this circumstance they are called " umbrellas from ten thousand of the people." It is presented in the name of the people. It is made generally out of red satin, or of red silk, having three tiers of folds or flounces. Usually the names of the principal donors are put upon the outside of it in golden letters. When he departs from his yamun, *en route* to another place where he is to discharge the duties of office again, this umbrella is carried in procession in connexion with his own proper retinue. Generally, also, a large number of

* " Our mandarins are rogues, but the people are your friends."— *Voyage of Ship Amherst.*

those who live in the place which he is leaving join in the procession for a distance. This umbrella is received with great pleasure by the popular mandarin. It is a source of real joy and satisfaction to him and to his family, as, when spontaneously presented, it is a proof of his having the affections and confidence of the community.

On the same principle, and for the same reason, sometimes a certain kind of outside official garment is made out of rich red satin, at the expense and in the name of the people, and presented to him about the time of his departure. This is called a "garment from ten thousand of the people." The names of the most prominent of the contributors are placed on the outside in golden letters. When presented it is borne on a kind of pavilion, so as to be seen by the public, accompanied by a band of music. This kind of popular testimonial to the character of its recipient is regarded as much more honourable than the umbrella of state, and is much more rarely given. It is a mark of the greatest respect and confidence.

It is contrary to the principles of Chinese filial piety for a son to enjoy a title of high rank and honour without getting a title of higher rank and honour for his paternal ancestor. According to law a dutiful son must ask the emperor to confer upon his father a title of rank one degree higher than his own. If the son is of the third rank, his father should be of the second rank. The mother of the hopeful and dutiful son also receives a proper and corresponding title. Whether living or dead, the parent must be honoured if the son is honoured.

One of the most common and most valued marks of imperial favour and approbation (promotion in rank and office excepted) bestowed upon civil or military officers as a reward for their faithful services, is one of a certain kind of feathers, generally called peacock's feathers. There are various kinds of these feathers, each kind indicating a certain degree of honour, or the comparative value put upon the services which the emperor wishes to reward and to commemorate. One kind is spoken of as the "flower" feather, another as the "green" feather, another as the "one-eyed" feather, another as the "two-eyed" feather, and another as the "three-eyed" feather. These are treasured up as marks of great honour by the recipients, and worn on public occasions. By simply inspecting the feather worn by a mandarin, and regarding its colour, or whether it has one or more "eyes," he who is acquainted with the comparative value set upon these things understands the degree of approbation which the emperor has been pleased to bestow upon the wearer. One of the great incentives to bravery on the part of soldiers is that of expecting to receive the reward of wearing a peacock's feather bestowed by the emperor.

In this country, where the worship of ancestors pervades the entire national sentiment, when a mandarin considers himself under lasting obligations to a family relative (beside his father and mother) for services done him in former times, he sometimes endeavours to reward the person by obtaining some high title from the emperor for himself, and then receiving permission to transfer it to the individual. The title sought for is sometimes of a higher rank than the one enjoyed by the mandarin. The emperor is specially requested to transfer it to the person designated, not so much to bestow a favour upon the petitioner as to reward merit, and to indicate his approbation of the kindness shown to one who afterward rose to high official dignity. For example, the parents of the petitioner may have died while he was very young, and the individual referred to might have received the orphan lad into his family, and educated him with great care and wisdom, resulting in his becoming a high mandarin.

The principle of transferring honours and titles which are of a *lower* rank than those enjoyed by the mandarin himself upon some of his family relatives, in return or as a reward for services formerly rendered, is also recognised by the laws or regulations of the land. The prospect of a talented but destitute lad hereafter becoming a high officer of Government is sometimes a powerful motive with his richer and more fortunate relatives for treating him well, and assisting in his education.

Every yamun has one or more head constables or policemen connected with it, whose principal employment is to arrest those who are charged with crimes. The position of the head man of these constables is often bought or obtained by bribery, and at other times it is bestowed as a reward for faithful services. If there is a large amount of business for them to do, they amass considerable money by their oppressive and extortionate course. They, as a class, are universally detested. Respectable people do not care to be associated with them in any way. They become very hard-hearted and unjust men. They abuse and oppress those who are accused of crime, and those who are convicted of crime, demanding, and often receiving, large sums of money from the wealthy who fall into their clutches. They often enforce the giving of money, or treating with wine or opium, by the families to which the accused or the condemned belong, by destroying or injuring the chairs, or the tables, or the crockery which come in their way.

It frequently occurs, when the constables cannot find the man their master bids them arrest, they seize, imprison, torture, and cross-question some near relative of the missing man, in order to find out the place of his concealment. This is a very unjust and cruel course to pursue, but one which is authorized by custom and practice, if not by the laws. It is done on the supposition that the relative arrested is privy to the place of concealment, and perhaps interested in his escape. When he reveals the place where the suspected man is concealed, and he has been actually arrested and imprisoned, the relative is usually set at liberty on paying the policemen and jailors their fees for their trouble in regard to him. In this land of lawful lawlessness on the part of constables and mandarins in regard to suspected persons, it is impossible for friends and relatives to secrete one long from those who are seeking for him on account of the brutal course pursued toward his family. It usually occurs that the man who gives the constables considerable trouble to arrest and imprison, so as to be on hand when the mandarin desires to examine him, fares the worse after his actual arrest. They often treat him more cruelly, and make more extortionate demands as a compensation for their extra trouble.

It is the custom for shopkeepers located near the scene of any extensive disorder produced by mobs in the street, or a fire, which calls together a rabble, to close their establishments, lest they should be robbed. This is called "white market," and is an unlawful course for the people to pursue, or, rather, it is a course which the mandarins are anxious should not be pursued, lest unhappy consequences should result to themselves. They are held responsible for the preservation of the peace, and for protecting the people in an uninterrupted prosecution of their lawful calling. The existence of such a state of affairs as to oblige the people in self-defence to close their stores in daylight would be interpreted to the disadvantage of the mandarin in charge. He would be liable to degradation in rank, if not from office, if known to his superiors. He comes at once with his followers, not only to arrest those who make the disturbance, but also to persuade the people to open their establishments.

The mandarins are also held responsible if a large conflagration takes place. If public property or buildings are destroyed by fire, they are liable to be degraded or punished in some way. Some twelve or thirteen years ago the Temple of Confucius, located near the south gate and inside the city, took fire just after it had been left one morning by the officers whose business it was to burn incense there. The city officers were greatly alarmed lest the burning of the temple should be made known to the officials at Peking, in which case they expected to be punished. The affair, however, was managed in such a manner that none of them were punished for permitting the conflagration of the temple. Good officers, it is expected, will keep everything in order. When any event occurs which ought not to have occurred, they are, *in theory*, held responsible for permitting its occurrence, and treated as though they were guilty.

In cities which contain yamuns of high mandarins, there is an office where *manuscript daily gazettes* are prepared, giving the public news relating to the important doings of the mandarins, and facts which concern them, such as appointments, advancements in rank, degradations, arrivals and departures of officers. This is prepared for the different high officials, the gentry, and subscribers generally. It corresponds somewhat to a daily gazette, but is not printed and published, and hawked about the streets. This costs for city subscribers several shillings per month. It is uninteresting and valueless except to those who desire to keep posted up with affairs relating to mandarins. Besides this daily, there may be had manuscript copies of the *Peking Gazette* as often as there is an arrival of one from the capital. Generally one copy comes down from Peking to this city, from which copies are made for regular subscribers. It is always very much behind its date. There are no regular dailies or weeklies to which the people have access, containing the news of the day. Almost all of the public information in regard to current events in other parts of the empire is conveyed by family letters, and by travellers, who detail the news as they go from place to place. The means of transporting letters are very dilatory, unsafe, and expensive, so that members of families widely separated, or personal friends remote from each other, seldom correspond, giving the news, unless it relates to their mutual interests.

When it is necessary that the people should be instructed in regard to important affairs, the mandarins cause proclamations to be posted up more or less numerously, in the most frequented streets of the city and in the country villages, containing the information. These proclamations are sometimes printed and sometimes in manuscript. These proclamations, together with handbills and advertisements, and notices issued by store-

keepers, &c. constitute the newspapers of China, and are
found on the posts and walls of houses and shops. They
take the place of dailies and weeklies, and cost the people
nothing.

During the reigns of the last two or three emperors it has
become more and more common, and, at the same time, more and
more unpopular, for the mandarins to "exhort the people to
subscribe money" for the use of the emperor in the administration of the government. Orders are occasionally sent down from
Peking stating the urgent need of more funds, and authorizing
the officials to "exhort" the people to contribute to the imperial
treasury. In obedience with the intimations from Peking, the
mandarins undertake the task of endeavouring to "persuade"
the rich men and the gentry under their jurisdiction to supply
the wants of the emperor. The kind of arguments used are
sometimes very forcible and powerful, as threats, arbitrary arrests,
or personal violence, together with the promise of obtaining an
office or a title, or the privilege of wearing a button or feather
denoting some degree of rank. It is put to their credit if they are
able to report enormous sums paid into the provincial treasury
as contributions from the people, and they expect to be rewarded
in a suitable way for their patriotic efforts.

Bribery is common. Many who are now in office in the Middle
Kingdom have obtained it principally by bribery or by purchase,
or by the union of both bribery and purchase. The two are
so intimately related that perhaps the obtaining of office by the
dexterous and ample use of money, *as if by purchase*, is invariably connected with a greater or less degree of bribery of the
officials who manage the procurement by purchase. It requires
practical tact of a high order to manage the affairs of Government with success. A talented business-man is often dull at his
books and in the use of his pencil, and, unless he has money to
help him in climbing the rounds of official employment and
emolument, he would generally remain at the foot of the ladder,
looking upward, but unable to ascend. A poor scholar without
funds stands ordinarily but a sorry chance to become a mandarin
of high rank, no matter how great his talent for governing and
for transacting business may be.

It frequently occurs that graduates of the first or second
literary degree, by the payment of a sum of money into the imperial treasury, may enter at once on the discharge of official
duty and power. The sum paid by graduates of the low literary
degrees varies with their rank as scholars, and the rank of the

office to which they aspire. The higher their rank as scholars, the less is the sum necessary to pay for the position they seek. Some men, who are rich but not learned, and who desire to play the mandarin without any literary rank already obtained, must pay comparatively very dear for an office—much dearer than a scholar would have to pay. Those who buy any particular office usually enter without delay upon its duties, having the precedence of those whose talents have earned them the station, or who have acquired it by gradual promotion.

A man of talent, having arrived at the rank of doctor of laws by his own ability in the use of the pencil in literary compositions, need not fear that he will be long without official employment, if he desires it. Should he succeed in graduating at the fourth examination before the emperor, he is sure of entering the imperial college at Peking, or of receiving immediate official employment somewhere, without the necessity of using much money in bribing the officials there. Should he fail to graduate at the examination before the emperor, and yet have arrived at a certain rank on the list of graduates of the third degree, he is entitled to enter upon the duties of some magistracy without delay. The particular place in the empire is decided by lot, and the incumbent of the position which falls to the doctor of laws by lot must give way to him, or the higher mandarins there must provide for him immediately on arriving with an office either temporary or permanent. The late incumbent must be supplied without long delay with another office.

Legal tortures and punishments are divided into the Inferior and the Superior.

The *Inferior* class includes—

1. *Wearing the Cangue.*—This is a square collar made of boards, and is locked upon the neck. It is usually three or four feet across, having a hole in the centre for the neck of the culprit. It prevents the wearer from reaching his mouth with his fingers. It is locked on during the daytime, and generally taken off during the night. The crime for which one is punished by wearing this wooden collar, and the time for which he is to wear it, are indicated in writing upon the upper or the front side of it. He is placed in the daytime by the wayside, usually in the vicinity of the spot where he committed his offence. In the evening he is taken away from the public street by the constable of the neighbourhood, who is responsible for his safety. In the morning he is returned to his usual place of exposure in public, where he begs his living, unless his friends supply him with

food. The legal time of wearing the cangue is from one to three months.

2. *Beating.*—This is of two kinds, according to the crime: one consists of beating the cheeks, and the other of beating the posteriors. When the cheeks are beaten, the culprit is usually made to kneel down. The instrument used is about a foot long and two or three inches wide, and is made of leather. The lictor seizes the culprit by the hair of his head with one hand, while with the other he holds the instrument with which he beats the

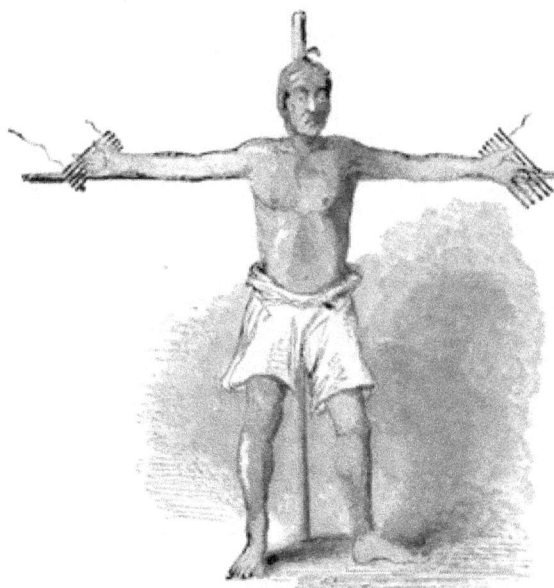

SQUEEZING THE FINGERS.

man the number of blows ordered by the mandarin. The number of blows does not often exceed twenty or thirty.

When the posteriors are beaten, the person is made to lie prostrate on the ground, face downward, and the parts to be beaten are stripped of clothing. The instrument used is made of bamboo, and is of two kinds. One is about five feet long and two inches wide. With this only forty strokes can legally be inflicted. The other is about three feet long and one inch wide An indefinite number of strokes can be inflicted with it, at the direction of the magistrate. In military yamuns, a wooden—not bamboo—ferule or stick is used, without stripping the offender. When a female is whipped with the bamboo in civil offices or courts of justice, she is simply made to kneel, and then the strokes are inflicted upon her thighs or body, only her outer garments having been removed.

Immense suffering is very frequently caused by the cruel use of the leathern scourge and of the bamboo sticks. The lawful number of blows is oftentimes largely exceeded. The severity of the beating, however, is not to be estimated by the number of blows inflicted, but by the amount of strength which the lictor puts forth. If bribed to beat lightly, he lays on accordingly, though he may appear to strike very heavily. This method is oftentimes employed to produce or extort confession, as well as to inflict punishment.

3. *Squeezing the fingers.*—This is a kind of torture used principally to extort confession. The man is usually made to kneel down, and is then tied by his cue to an upright post.

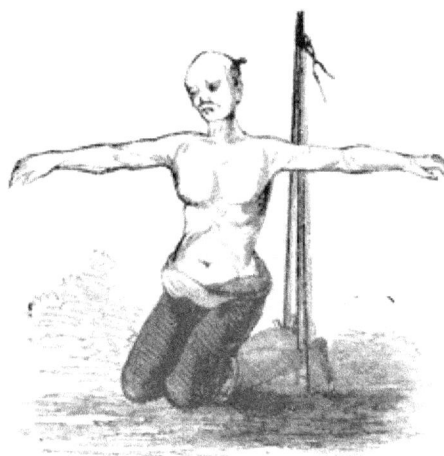

SQUEEZING THE ANKLES.

The fingers of each hand are then put between small rods (a rod coming between two fingers), which are so arranged that by pulling a cord attached to these rods the fingers are squeezed between them. The harder the cord is pulled or twisted, the tighter are the fingers squeezed, and the more painful does the torture become. The victim is finally willing to confess anything which his accuser desires, so dreadful is the pain suffered. He sometimes stands while tortured.

4. *Squeezing the ankles.*—This is also a species of torture. The prisoner is made to kneel on the ground, and his ankles are placed in a frame consisting of three sticks or poles fastened near each other at one end. Each ankle comes between two sticks. By

pulling on the cords fastened to the other end of the sticks, the ankles are squeezed by the sticks as they are made to approach each other.

5. *Imprisonment.*—This kind of punishment, except in the case of those who are rich, or who have rich friends willing to bribe the jailors to treat them well, is awful and revolting beyond description. Insufficient and vile food is given them, and horrible tortures unknown to the laws are inflicted.

The *Superior* class of punishment includes—

1. *Beheading.*—The condemned man is carried forth to the execution-ground in a kind of cage or box made of slats or

CARRYING FORTH TO THE PLACE OF EXECUTION.

bamboo. The crime for which he is to die is written upon a slip of paper, fastened to a piece of bamboo, which is then stuck into his hair. In his cage is a pail for holding his head, which is often suspended on the city wall, or on a pole near the street, as a warning to the public.

Beheading consists of two methods, differing in degree of ignominy. One is that of simply striking off the head of the wretch at a blow, while kneeling, with his hands tied behind him, and while bending down his head. The other is that where the body of the victim is mangled, or cut in several pieces, previous to his head being struck off. This is called " cutting into small pieces." It is described as cutting into the eyebrows or over the eyes, the cheeks, the fleshy parts of the arms, and the breasts, in such a way that the skin or the flesh in these different places will hang down. Then a stab is made with the sword by the executioner into the abdomen, which is followed by cutting off the head. Then, as above stated, the head is put into a kind of cage or pail, and hung up on the wall of the city, or on a pole in some public place, as a warning to the people. The second kind of beheading referred to, that of " cutting into small pieces," is regarded as the most ignominious of all capital punishments. Women who are condemned to die as a punish-

JUST BEFORE DECAPITATION.

ment for committing adultery are oftentimes made to suffer death in this way. A parricide is also thus punished.

2. *Strangulation.*—This is regarded as the least disgraceful of capital punishments, because the body is left unmutilated. The condemned is sometimes made to kneel on a frame, with his hands tied behind him, or stretched out and fastened to a cross-piece. His head is secured to a perpendicular post by his cue, his face being turned outward, or away from it. In the post there is sometimes a hole made about as high from the ground as the neck of the prisoner comes. Through this hole the two ends of a cord, which has been passed around his neck, are put.

Tightening the ends of the rope by pulling or twisting them soon produces strangulation. Oftentimes, when the victim is almost dead, the cord is loosened, and he is allowed to take breath, only to go through the pain of strangulation again.

3. *Banishment beyond the frontiers of the Empire.*—This is a form of punishment state criminals, convicted of peculiarly aggravated offences, when they are not sentenced to death by beheading or strangulation. High officers of government, when they fall under the displeasure of the emperor, or when they have political enemies sufficiently powerful to procure their ruin, are often condemned to be exiled to the vast territories which are tributary to China lying outside of the north-western provinces. They are required to serve the emperor in the army. Oftentimes, by good behaviour in their exile, they acquire such a stock of merit as to cause them to be recalled and reinstated in office. Banishment beyond the frontiers is a happy expedient of temporarily disposing of eminent men who have become too popular or too powerful, or for some reason obnoxious, until the time arrives when they may safely be again intrusted with power, or until their services become necessary in the administration of government, or until their political enemies have become unpopular and are overthrown. This kind of exile is almost always preceded or followed by the confiscation of a part or the whole of the victim's property.

4. *Banishment three thousand li from home.*—This oftentimes is the punishment accorded to murderers of the second or third degree, noted robbers, or culprits whose high crimes are regarded as having some very extenuating circumstances, and who may have money and influence enough to escape the sentence of death. They are sometimes supported by funds derived from the imperial coffers. They are obliged to reside in specified districts, and are under the superintendence of a local officer. Sometimes they are allowed to engage in business and support themselves. They are required to return to their former homes at the expiration of their term of exile, unless they desire to remain where they have been living, and have influence and money sufficient to procure the consent of the Government to remain.

5. *Banishment one thousand li for three years, or to another province.*—This is the lightest form of exile. It is said that under some circumstances those who have been condemned to this punishment can often escape its infliction by the payment of money as a fine. The crimes for which this punishment is

T

usually allotted are gambling, fighting, thieving, and very miti-
gated cases of manslaughter.

There are occasionally to be seen in the streets of this city
exiles from other provinces, wearing the badges of their banishment. These badges consist sometimes of an iron rod several
feet long, or a stone weighing ten or fifteen pounds, attached to
a chain locked around their necks. In such cases the stone or
the iron rod is carried on the shoulder, steadied by the hand.
When not in the public streets they unlock the chain, and lay
aside the badge of their exile. According to law, it is affirmed,
in the case of those who carry the stone on their shoulder, it
ought to be made too heavy to be readily carried about, and the
stone should be placed in the daytime, with the culprit securely
locked to it, in public, near some yamun, as a warning to the
people passing by.

There are occasions when the sentences of criminals throughout
the empire are remitted one grade or more, such as the accession
of a new emperor to the throne, the espousal of an empress, the
birth of a firstborn son to the emperor, or the celebration of an
advanced imperial birthday.

Jailors and magistrates frequently resort to modes of punishment and torture entirely unauthorized and unrecognised by law.
Jailors unlawfully torture the prisoner for the purpose of extorting money, and magistrates unlawfully torture him for the sake

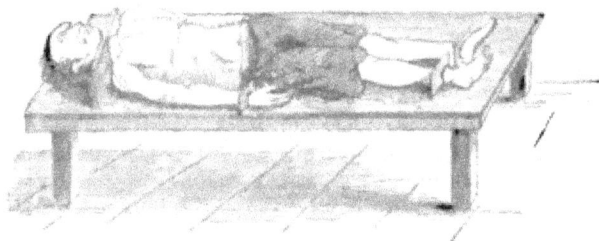

FASTENED ON A BEDSTEAD.

of eliciting confession of guilt or information about his accomplices. The kinds of torture are not few, and the torment
caused is often dreadfully excruciating.*

* Huc refers to this spirit of reckless illegal cruelty even before trial
of prisoners :—" One day when we were passing along the road leading to
Pekin, we met a party of soldiers, with an officer at their head, escorting
a number of carts, in which were literally piled up a crowd of Chinese,

It should not be supposed that all of the methods mentioned are in general use in every part of the empire. They are resorted to, with various modifications, when jailors and magistrates are pleased to use them. In different provinces, probably, there are in use illegal methods of torture different from those described. If a prisoner does not promise money sufficient to satisfy the demands of his keepers, he is liable to be put to bed on a wooden bedstead. He is placed on his back, and his body made nearly immoveable in something like the following manner : Boards with holes are passed up through openings in the bedstead. One is placed over each ankle, and one over each wrist, and another over the neck. They are then pressed down, more or less tightly, on these parts of the body, and fastened under the bedstead in such a way that he cannot change his position. Besides this, sometimes a pole is fastened at right angles to a bar of wood placed across his ankles, the pole extending to his chin and pressing against it, so that his head will be thrown backward or upward. In this position he is made to pass the night, unless the jailors relent or he comes to their terms. No one is willing to sleep the second night on such a bedstead, if he can arrange matters with his keepers. Rich men are often unmercifully tortured by their jailors, in order to extort from them a large sum of money.

The " frame of the flowery eyebrow " is said to be an instrument named after a certain bird, which, being tied to a frame by

who were uttering horrible oaths. As we stopped to allow these cartloads of human beings to pass, we were seized with horror on perceiving that these unfortunate creatures were nailed by the hand to the planks of the cart. A satellite whom we interrogated replied, with frightful coolness : ' We've been routing out a nest of thieves in a neighbouring village. We got a good many of them, and as we hadn't brought chains enough, we were obliged to contrive some way to prevent their escaping, so you see we nailed them by the hand.' ' But do you not think there may be some innocent among them ?' ' Who can tell ? They have not been tried yet. We are taking them to the tribunal, and by and by, if there are any innocent men among them, they will be separated from the thieves.' The fellow seemed to think the thing quite a matter of course, and was even a little proud of the contrivance. Perhaps what was most hideous of all in this dreadful spectacle was the mocking hilarity of the soldiers, who were pointing out to one another, with an air of amusement, the contortions and grimaces of the miserable creatures in their agony of pain. If a people can exhibit such barbarity as this in quiet and peaceable times, it may be imagined of what excesses they are capable under the excitement of revolution and civil war. In the provinces now in insurrection, horrible abominations must be passing."—Huc's *Chinese Empire*, vol. ii. pp. 269, 270.

a short string, is continually hopping about, or flying away to the length of its string, and then returning. If such is the origin of the name, it indicates the intense agony which the wretched man suffers, not allowing a moment's ease. It consists of an upright post, and two cross-pieces firmly fastened to it. The culprit is made to kneel on the lower of the cross-pieces, with his back to the post. His arms are outstretched, and fastened to the other cross-piece, which is placed several feet higher than the lower one. Across the calves of his legs is laid a stick several feet long. To the two ends of this stick are attached cords which pass through holes made in the ends of the cross-piece on which he kneels. By tightening these cords, the pressure on his legs becomes dreadful ; kneeling of itself would soon cause intolerable pain. To this is added the pain caused by pressing down the piece laid on the upper sides of his legs while he is in a kneeling posture. Some say that the wrists or arms are pressed at the same time and in a similar manner between the upper cross-piece and another stick placed on the upper side of the arms. This form of torturing a prisoner is sometimes employed by officers in order to extort confession.

Monkey grasping a peach.—The name of this torture is said to be derived from the fancied resemblance of the victim while enduring it to a monkey grasping something in his paw. It is used by mandarins to compel a prisoner to confess his guilt. It consists in suspending the man by one arm over a horizontal stick several feet from the ground, with the other arm passed down under one or both legs, and the hands then securely tied together by the thumbs under or near the knees. In this way no part of the body is allowed to touch the floor, and the whole weight comes under the arm-pit on one arm passed over the stick or

MONKEY GRASPING A PEACH.
(Culprit suspended by the arm-pit.)

pole. Simply to bind together the thumbs of a person whose hands are brought in contact under the knees would alone produce intolerable agony in a short time, even if the victim were permitted to sit or take any position at pleasure. How dreadful, then, must be the torture when, besides the agony arising from such a cramped position of the body, the whole weight of the prisoner is sustained on a small piece of wood passing under one of his arms!

Standing in a cage.—The cage is made of slabs of wood, and high enough to contain the wretch sentenced to stand in it, his head protruding out of the top of the cage. He is obliged to stand on his tiptoes, and the orifice in the top is only large enough for his neck. In this way the man is made to suffer intense pain. To stand long on tiptoe is impossible. But the victim is obliged to stand partially on tiptoe, or be hung by the neck if he draws up his feet in endeavours to rest himself. Only momentary relief is obtained by drawing up his legs, for that movement brings his whole weight on his neck. It is said that some time during the latter part of the reign of the emperor who died in 1850, a noted robber was compelled to stand in public in such a cage in the suburbs of this city until he died.

Smoking the head in a tube. —A large tube of bamboo, with the natural joint or division in one end still remaining, is put upon the head of the culprit, and extends down a little below the chin. Sometimes a small tub or pail, turned bottom-side upward on the head, is used, the object being to incase the head

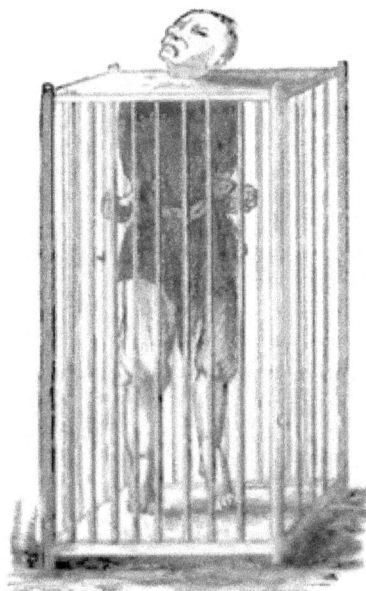

STANDING ON TIPTOE IN A CAGE.

in something air-tight on the top and yet open at the bottom. Some incense is lighted, and placed so that the smoke shall ascend into the tube. As the smoke cannot escape through the top, suffocation ensues unless the instrument is removed, or, to say the least, the victim endures indescribable agony. This torture is not very frequently used.

A shirt made of iron wire.—This kind of torture, it is affirmed, was formerly used in this part of China, and is now occasionally resorted to at Peking. A shirt-like garment, made of very fine iron wire, with interstices something like those of a fishing-net, is put on the prisoner, the clothing from the upper part of his body having been removed. A cord is attached to it in such a way that when pulled the shirt will press down closely on the body, and the skin and flesh will protrude more or less through the interstices. A knife-like instrument is then passed over the wire shirt on the outside, cutting or rasping off the protruding skin and flesh. This operation is repeated at the option of the dispenser of justice !

Hot-water snake.—A coil in form somewhat resembling a snake, and manufactured out of pewter, or some other malleable metal,

HOT-WATER SNAKE.

is arranged in such a way that an arm of the prisoner can be thrust into it. Each arm is put into such a coil, the head of the metal snake being higher than the other parts. Sometimes a similar tube is coiled around the body. A quantity of boiling water is then poured into the mouths of the snakes, and as it passes down the tube burns the flesh, and causes intense pain. It is asserted that this kind of torture is now-a-days seldom resorted to in the south of China, though it is believed to be still occasionally used at the capital on state prisoners. The Chinese place it in the list of illegal tortures.

Whip of hooks.—A large number of very fine hooks are securely fastened to a handful of the fibres of hemp. The whole is then

used as a whip with which to beat
the prisoner, in order to elicit a
confession. When a blow is given
with this whip, many of the hooks
will stick to the body of the
victim, and, unless a satisfactory
confession is forthcoming, the
whip is pulled or jerked back by
main force, and another blow
given. The operation is repeated
according to the dictation of the
presiding officer. This kind of
torture is represented to be seldom
employed in this part of the
empire.

*Kneeling on chains or bits of
crockery.*—The prisoner is made
to kneel down on chains or bits
of crockery, with the arms outstretched at right angles to the
body. If the culprit lowers his
hands, he is mercilessly whipped.
At other times he is made, with
his hands tied behind his back,
to kneel down on these hard and
uneven substances. The pain induced by kneeling on one's bare
knees on a chain or any sharp-
pointed mineral substance, even
without any whipping, and without being obliged to hold out the
arms, is soon absolutely intolerable. Not unfrequently, in the
case of stubborn criminals, are
several hundred blows inflicted
with a ratan thong while in the
position above described—so the
Chinese say.

The accompanying outline sketch
of some of the ways of torture and
of punishment used by jailors
and mandarins, though declared
to be unknown and nnauthorized

THREE KINDS OF TORTURES (taken from
Canton pith-paper pictures).

by the statutes, are perhaps sufficient to intimate the inhumanity
and injustice which accused, as well as convicted persons, are
liable to experience at the hands of the administrators of the law.

As illustrations of the customs which prevail here, touching
the law and its violations, going to make up a correct view of
Chinese society as it is, several practices will be described.

The opening of *gambling dens*, or the assembling of men
for the purpose of gambling, and the manufacture of gambling
utensils, as cards, dice, dominoes, &c. are forbidden by law,
but are openly practised.   There are certain streets or alleys
near the Big Bridge and the south gate of the city where
almost every house is a gambling shop.   In a certain part of
the suburbs is a neighbourhood where probably a majority of
the population is engaged in the manufacture of gambling
cards ; in another part is a public green, where oftentimes, day
after day, may be seen several mats, on which are strings of
cash, with cards, dice, and other kinds of gambling utensils
spread out on the ground, surrounded by a crowd of men
openly engaged in the very act of violating the law.

Lotteries are also prohibited, in consequence of their exceedingly pernicious influence on society.   Mandarins are anxious to
prevent them, and succeed only by the use of the most stringent
measures.   A few years since, the head man of a certain lottery
was arrested and beheaded by order of the viceroy, which decisive
course struck terror into all who were engaged, or who were
desirous of engaging, in the business.   The secret in regard to
this consists in guessing which set, out of certain thirty-seven
sets of names, is the successful one for a particular day.   The
set selected as the successful one for any specified day is, of
course, known only to the managers of the lottery.   Those who
happen to guess it draw thirty cash for every one they stake.
This great per centage of profit induces many to engage in this
kind of lottery.

The opening of gambling shops, and the overt act of gambling,
together with the manufacture of gambling tools, are connived
at by petty local officers, constables, and official employés generally.   The head men who engage in such violation of the law
bribe these local officers, and the spies and servants of the high
mandarins, to silence in regard to their illegal acts.   The high
officials, as some assert, are not aware of the extent of these
unlawful practices ; but it is much more probable that they are
content to have the law violated, if the neighbourhoods particularly concerned permit it, and no one commences a prosecution

of these violators of the law. Without the aid of their under-lings, who are already in the paid interest of these men, magistrates would make but poor progress in ferreting out, arresting, and punishing the guilty. In fact, such is the condition of things here, that it would be next to impossible to prevent gambling or to suppress lotteries without the most extraordinary and determined personal efforts on the part of high officials.

The keeping of brothels is also prohibited by law, but tolerated by custom in certain neighbourhoods. No Chinaman is willing to commence in earnest, and from correct motives, a regular prosecution against them ; and the mandarins do not feel sufficiently interested to interfere and put them down, unless compelled in the execution of the laws, in consequence of legal prosecution, to do so. The local constables and the policemen, and runners connected with official establishments, have the reputation of being bribed to be silent, or represent matters in a favourable light to their superiors, should any prosecution be attempted. The quarter of the suburbs where brothels principally prevail has been burnt over twice during the past six or eight years. At the latest fire, while the buildings were being consumed and the inmates were being scattered in all directions, some of the mandarins, who were present with their body-guard, as is the custom at fires, made no great efforts to put it down. One of them is reported to have said he was willing to have the place burnt over. A certain class of sharpers, who live principally by obtaining money by false pretences—either connected with literary and influential families, or on intimate terms with mandarin employés—sometimes go to the proprietors of these haunts of vice, and threaten them with prosecution before the magistrates. The design and the effect of such threats is the obtainment of money ; for, should they be properly prosecuted before the mandarins, the latter would be obliged to execute the laws, unless they could find some pretext to defer the matter or dismiss the complaint; and in all such cases the defendant would be required to spend comparatively a large sum of money in presents or bribes to mandarin runners. It is much cheaper for the brothel-keepers to make a present to those blacklegs who threaten to prosecute them, than for them to delay to compromise the matter until it gets into the hands of the employés of the magistrate.

Private or unlicensed pawn-shops are illegal. The large and legal pawn-shops have a license from the Government. They are allowed to charge certain rates of interest per month on the money advanced on the estimated value of the articles pawned. This is now said to be three per cent. per month on the smallest sums advanced, and two and four-tenths per cent. on larger sums. The smallest sum charged as monthly interest on a loan is one and six-tenths per cent. The licensed pawn-shops receive, when first licensed, a small sum from Government as a loan, on which they pay annual interest, professedly used as capital in the transaction of their business. Besides these there are unlicensed pawn-shops. Their proprietors charge an exorbitant rate of monthly interest on the sums lent on the security of the property they receive, being often nearly three times as high as that of the licensed pawn-shops. A part of their large gains is spent as bribes to gain the connivance of the mandarin runners and the local constables. The value at which articles are received by the former is estimated at comparatively much higher rates than would be allowed by the latter, should they be willing to receive them. These unlicensed and unlawful pawn-shops are opened only by widows, orphans, exiles, or by persons in their name, and professedly for their benefit.

Clandestine manufacture or sale of salt is unlawful. Salt is a Government monopoly. What is not made or what is not sold through certain agencies is liable to be confiscated to Government. The gains of the illicit trade in it, if undetected, are great, prompting to the invention of various methods of violating the law, and of evading the vigilance of those who are appointed to superintend the manufacture, the transportation, and the sale of this indispensable article. It has been found impossible to prevent the illegal sale of salt and its smuggling, because of the venality of the subordinate officials. They are sometimes principals in the illegal acts, or interested accomplices. When neither principals nor active accomplices, they are often ready to be bribed to wink at the violation of the salt regulations. The official agents not unfrequently steal salt from their superiors, and sell it as opportunity offers. The sale of brine among the common people, in which fish or meat has been preserved, is also illegal. The explanation of this is to be found in the fact that brine contains salt, and after evaporation the salt remains. If the sale of brine should be tolerated, it is feared that the revenue to the Government from salt would soon be greatly diminished, as salt would be converted into brine to avoid the payment of customs dues, and brine could be easily made into salt, if necessary. Brine, if containing a proper amount of something edible, manifestly put in for preservation, is salable according to law. The illegal sale of brine is, however, connived at more or less by the agents of the farmers of the salt business. It may be retained by his owner for his own private use, but may not be publicly or privately sold for use in another place.

Some men have extraordinary abilities at counterfeiting bankbills, which they cultivate, notwithstanding that such counterfeiting is, in theory at least, a capital crime, when proved against one. These men generally become known to the proprietors of banks, and, through them, to the employés of officers of Government. Instead of having them arrested and punished, so as to prevent them from practising their cunning in the future, the principal bankers, it is alleged, make an agreement with them not to counterfeit their bills, and not to teach others to counterfeit them, paying a stipulated sum per month or per quarter, according as they can agree. Subordinate officials of the mandarins, according to established custom, demand and receive money from these counterfeiters, if they become known to them, as the price of not molesting them. It is said that in this way less counterfeiting of bank-bills is really performed than would be performed if the counterfeiters were not hired not to counterfeit. If the mandarins should arrest a counterfeiter of bankbills, he would usually only have to fee largely the petty officials, and undergo the punishment of being bambooed or of wearing the cangue in the streets a month or two, after which he would be again set at liberty and allowed to resume the practice of his art. The bankers protect themselves from being largely harmed by counterfeited bills by making it the interest of a head counterfeiter not to counterfeit their bills, and not to teach his art to others, and not to connive at counterfeiting when done by others, if known to him. A certain man who flourished here some twenty or thirty years ago, is spoken of among the people as exceedingly successful in his efforts at counterfeiting bills. The imitations he made sometimes could not be distinguished from the genuine, even by the bankers themselves. This man became notorious for his illegal but tolerated cleverness, and received many presents from various rich bankers, who were desirous of propitiating his good-will, and of securing his active efforts in their favour by inducing him to discourage counterfeiting on the part of others. For several years he received regular stipends from the proprietors of banks. He was the recognised chief of counterfeiters. By engaging such a man not to counterfeit, and not to instruct or abet others in counterfeiting the bills of their banks, they were comparatively safe from extensive frauds, and they could have his aid in detecting and individualizing other clever imitators. If he still lives, he doubtless receives regular stipends from those who are most deeply interested in his not exercising his gifts. All this is in perfect accordance with the Chinese system of employing a rogue to catch a rogue, and of making an honourable mandarin out of a notorious chief of pirates.

Counterfeiters of cash, and persons engaged in deteriorating silver, comprise a tolerably large class of men, who would be arrested and severely punished by mandarins, if they could ascertain their rendezvous and reach it with faithful followers before the guilty have been warned of the attempt to take them. But policemen in the employment of Government, and the constables living in the neighbourhood where the illegal work is secretly carried on, make it their interest to maintain silence on the subject when not personally called upon to furnish information or aid, and also to screen these men from detection and arrest, whenever possible, by giving them timely warning of the approach of a posse of officers, or by throwing the latter off the track. Holes are made in foreign dollars or lumps of silver, and quicksilver, lead, white copper, or brass, &c. is put into the centre, and the outer edge of the orifice is neatly filled in with pure silver; or sometimes, in running ingots of silver, the baser metal is put into the centre of the mould, and then the pure metal is poured into it. In regard to foreign dollars, the skill exhibited in removing a part of the middle of them—filling up the cavity with some cheaper yet heavy metal, and closing over the orifice—is so great, that detection of the fraud from the external appearance is often very difficult. Silver wristlets, silver ornaments for the hair, and silver ear-rings, are very often served in a similar way. The common copper cash is sometimes counterfeited, the counterfeit being smaller and thinner than the genuine, and made out of adulterated metal.

CHAPTER XIV.

THE STATE RELIGION.

THE Chinese usually speak of only three native religions—Confucianism, Buddhism, and Tauism. There is, however, another religion, using that term in a modified sense, which is properly and distinctively called the Religion of the State, or the State Religion, because it is intimately connected with the administration of the Government according to the established *regimé*. It includes the various superstitious and idolatrous acts which mandarins are obliged to perform in virtue of their being officers of Government.

The high mandarins are required to make sacrifices in the spring and autumn, and to burn incense on the first and fifteenth of every Chinese month, before certain gods or objects of worship.

The most important and imposing of the vernal and autumnal ceremonies are performed in honour of the "Literary and the Military Sages," viz. Confucius, and Kuanti, the Chinese god of war. These take place in the temples devoted to them. The principal officers are required to be present, each performing his respective part. There is much pomp and show on these occasions.

The high officers must also make a sacrifice or burn incense in honour of Heaven and Earth, and in honour of the mountains and the streams of the province in the spring and autumn of every year, at an altar on Black Rock Hill in the city, and at an altar on Great Temple Hill in the suburbs. They are held responsible for the performance of an appointed ceremony twice per annum at the altar of the Wind, Clouds, Thunder, and Rain. About the time of planting or sowing seed in the spring, it is also made the duty of the high mandarins to offer a sacrifice in honour of the gods of the land and grain, in a place not far from the south gate of the city.

The high officials, as the viceroy, the provincial governor, the Tartar general, &c. must themselves officiate in regard to a class of objects which have been referred to as requiring a vernal and an autumnal sacrifice and worship. It is not optional to do it by proxy, if they are in the city and in good health. The objects which the emperor himself at Peking annually or semi-annually worships, and unto which he makes sacrifices, it is the imperative duty of his high officials in the provinces to worship and sacrifice unto in person for him, representing his majesty himself. A failure to perform these official and representative acts with due solemnity and in accordance with the established rites would surely be visited with his displeasure, should it become known to him.

The temples dedicated to the literary and the military sages must be visited regularly early in the morning of the first and the fifteenth of each Chinese month by some high mandarin or his substitute, in order to burn incense and candles before their images or their tablets.

The prefect presides at an annual procession through the streets of the city, composed of mandarins lower in rank than himself and of the gentry, in honour of spring. In the suburbs, the marine inspector is chief of this annual procession. A military officer is chief in a procession in which military utensils are paraded through the streets of the city in the autumn.

Besides the altars and temples which have been specified, there are a number of others where high officials are expected, in person or by proxy, to make a sacrifice twice per annum, or to burn incense twice per month, according to specific directions from Peking. But of these distinct account is given in other portions of this volume.

The expense connected with these official sacrifices is paid out of the provincial treasury in the case of some; in the case of others it is defrayed by the neighbourhoods in which the temples are situated, or by funds belonging to the temples. The actual expense of most of these observances is quite small. Some of the temples have an annual stipend granted by the emperor for the purpose of meeting this expense; others only receive a stipend at the time the divinities worshipped in them are admitted into the number of objects worshipped by officials.

On the recurrence of the birthday of the emperor, or in mourning on account of his death, the high and the low mandarins are required to "rejoice" or to "lament" in the temple devoted to him, or in some other place appointed, using the highest ceremony known in China, viz. the "three kneelings and the nine knockings."

The viceroy, as generalissimo of the Chinese army, whenever he is about to start on a warlike expedition, or whenever he sends away with a detachment of soldiers any high military officer as his deputy to fight the enemy, and, generally, whenever any high military officer is about to proceed into battle, must worship the flag of his division or brigade. The worship is often per-

formed on the public parade-ground in the suburbs near the south gate of the city. The viceroy sometimes chooses to sacrifice to the flag on his own private parade-ground connected with his yamun. The time selected is often about daylight or a little later. Usually, however, the day, hour, and minute are fixed by some fortune-teller. This is often a high civil, military, and religious ceremony. In the centre of the arena is placed a table having upon it two candles, one censer, and several cups of wine. The candles are lighted at the proper time. Some officer, kneeling down,

FLAG BEARER, OR GOD OF THE FLAG
(worshipped by military mandarins and by soldiers).

holds the large flag by means of its staff near the table. The viceroy, or other officer who is to command the expedition, standing before the table and the flag, receives three sticks of lighted incense from a professor of ceremony, which he reverently places in the censer arranged between the candles. He now kneels on the ground, and bows his head down three times. Some of the wine taken from the table is handed to him while on his knees, which he pours out on the ground. Then a cup of wine is dashed upon the flag, the professor of ceremony crying out, " Unfurling the flag, victory is obtained ; the cavalry advancing, merit is perfected." The whole company of officers and soldiers, who had previously knelt down and bowed their heads in the prescribed manner, now simultaneously rise up with a shout, and commence their march at once for the scene of action or their appointed rendezvous.

We have seen how, on an eclipse of the sun or moon, mandarins must engage in certain superstitious ceremonies to save the luminary eclipsed.

The mandarins, on arriving at their official residences from Peking, to or from their previous homes—from the viceroy down to the district magistrate—(as some Chinese assert) are required by custom, if not by law, to perform three superstitious ceremonies. They first worship their seals of office ; they then offer sacrifice to the god of the gate or door ; finally, they worship the fox. After these acts, they may proceed to perform official business with the hope of success.

There is, in connexion with some of the principal civil yamuns, a small two storied building, devoted to the worship of his majesty Master Reynard. There is no image or picture of a fox to be worshipped, but simply an imaginary fox somewhere. Incense, candles, and wine are placed upon a table in the room of the second story of this building, and before this table the mandarin kneels down and bows his head in the customary manner, as an act of reverence to Reynard, the keeper of his seals of office. This sacrifice, it is affirmed, is never performed by deputy. The Chinese believe the official seal of the mandarin, after he has arrived at his yamun, to be in the keeping of the fox. They assert, with great earnestness and apparent sincerity, that if the mandarin did not worship the fox on his arrival at his residence, his seal of office would shortly disappear in some inexplicable way, or some singular and strange calamity would certainly befall him or his yamun.

Probably this *worshipping of the fox, as the keeper of the seals of office*, is nothing more than a custom—possibly a merely local custom, and not required or recognised by the laws of the empire. It has, however, all the power of law in this place—a practice observed by new incumbents of high office as reverently as though it were one of the most important and momentous of duties. Any disrespect or slight of the fox, on the part of the mandarin, is said to be always sure to be remembered and avenged by his invisible majesty in such a manner as to produce repentance and the exhibition of proper respect and fear.

Many of the mandarins are intelligent enough to know that these superstitious acts are quite absurd and useless. Most or all of the officials may indeed sympathize heartily in the worship paid to Confucius; but, in regard to many of the other objects which they are required to worship officially, they would not think of reverencing them in the manner described if they were left to themselves, and if they would not be deprived of their official positions in case they declined or omitted to conform with the established practices. The Chinese people in large numbers, who are much less intelligent than are the mandarins, in theory admit the folly and the uselessness of many of these practices, but assert that the custom and the laws of their country must be obeyed and observed.

It is not difficult to perceive that under existing regulations no sincere Protestant native Christian can be an officer of Government in China.

The manner in which the worship of Confucius is conducted will show the high estimate in which the sage is held, and will illustrate by example what is meant by the term " State religion."

There are three temples dedicated to the Chinese sage at this place. The largest was built ten years ago, and belongs to the prefecture. The two smaller ones belong to the two districts which join or meet in the city.

The old temple, on the site of the present prefectural temple to Confucius, was destroyed at daybreak one morning in the fall of 1851 by a fire, which originated in the temple at the close of the usual autumnal sacrifice to Confucius. In two months a new temple, on the same site, was commenced, built by subscription of funds from the mandarins, gentry, and literati of the city and vicinity. The needed amount was easily raised. It was considered a work of merit to aid in rebuilding the temple of the sage of China. In the summer of 1854 the building was finished, at the cost of 74,000,000 of copper cash, a sum at that time equal to about 53,000 dollars. The mason's bill amounted to a little less than two-tenths of the whole cost; the carpenter's and the painter's bills to more than six-tenths; and the stone-cutter's bill to about two-tenths. The same amount and kind of labour and material would probably have cost in England or America several times the sum reported as the entire cost of the new temple. The well-cut pillars or posts of solid granite, of which there are several scores of various heights and diameters, some of which are very tall and large, would alone have cost a

U

very large sum at the West. The temple inclosure is about three hundred and forty feet long by about one hundred and five feet wide, and consists principally of three parts. One is a large hall or room about seventy-five feet deep, in which the tablet to Confucius is erected, and the sacrifices and worship are performed. This tablet is about one foot wide and six feet high, painted red, and partially gilded. Its inscription, in large gilded characters, denotes that it is erected to "The Most Holy Ancient Teacher Confucius." The room also contains sixteen smaller tablets of Chinese worthies and famous scholars, among which, in the highest place of honour, stands that of the sub-sage Mencius. Near it is the tablet of the great commentator of the Chinese classics, Chufutze. Another part is a large court, to the south of the main hall, and is about one hundred and fifty-four feet long. On the east and the west sides are long buildings, in which are contained about one hundred and thirty-four tablets of the pupils of Confucius and of distinguished scholars; sixty-seven tablets are deposited in each building, arranged in eleven niches or apartments. In each niche is a long table or a stationary altar, made of stone, on which incense and candles, &c. are to be placed when the sage is worshipped in the spring and autumn. The open space between these long rooms is neatly paved with granite, and is kept in good repair. In this court are two gaudy pavilions, six or eight sided, each containing a large stone tablet covered with Chinese characters. Still farther to the south is another court, about one hundred and ten feet deep. On its east and west sides are several small rooms for the reception of officers and for tablets of very distinguished literary men. In one of these rooms are five small images, the origin and design of which have not been ascertained, the keepers of the temple always declining to communicate information about them on the

TRADITIONAL LIKENESS OF CONFUCIUS.

plea of ignorance. These images offer a striking contrast to the tablets in the other parts of the temple, and to the large and numerous images to be found in almost all Chinese temples. Some have thought them to be local deities, which for some reason have obtained a place in the Confucian temple. In the old temple to Confucius, an image made of clay, brought from Shantung, his native province, instead of a tablet, was worshipped.

The established times for offering sacrifices to Confucius usually fall in the second and the eighth Chinese months. The

TRADITIONAL LIKENESS OF MENCIUS.

TRADITIONAL LIKENESS OF CHUFUTZE.

autumnal sacrifice for 1858 came on the 11th September. The vernal sacrifice for 1859 fell on the 10th of March. These sacrifices are performed about four or five o'clock in the morning, by torch and candle light.

It was my good fortune, in company with two other missionaries, to be present at the autumnal sacrifice to Confucius, which occurred on the 11th of September, 1858, in the prefectural temple.

On the afternoon of the 10th, two of us went into the city to witness the preparatory rehearsal, which was attended in a large temple adjoining that of Confucius. A crowd of noisy young-sters, and of dignified and self-complacent literati, had collected there, together with some of the subordinate officials of the city, to look on while the business of rehearsing some of the parts of the ceremony, to come off in grand style on the following morning, was being performed by those who were appointed to help in the ceremony. None of the high officials who were to take a principal part in the worship were present. They received private instructions from their professor of rites and ceremonies in regard to what they were to do. At the close of the rehearsal we called at the Confucian temple.

We found a crowd of idlers loitering about, while some men and boys were busy at work preparing for the approaching sacri-fice. We noticed a large number of vessels, made after strange and unique patterns (said to be like those used in ancient times), of various sizes and shapes, and capable of holding from a quart to several quarts apiece. They were designed to be filled with rice, salt, fruits, uncooked vegetables, &c. and to be put upon the stationary stone altars which stood in front of the tablets of the sage and the worthies. We observed that, instead of honestly filling up the vessels from the bottom, they sometimes pasted a paper around the sides, just below the brim of the vessels designed to hold small articles, leaving the space in the vessels underneath the paper quite empty. On this paper they care-fully laid rice, salt, and other articles comparatively dear. One kind was put on one vessel ; there was quite a large number of vessels having the same kind of article upon them.

On some one of our party asking whether they expected to deceive Confucius, and how they dared to try to deceive him by offering to him vessels containing only a very small quantity of the articles, while the bottom was empty, a young man pertly answered, " Yes, it will answer to deceive Confucius, but it will not answer to deceive Jesus."

While two of us were making our observations on the temple and the preparations for the approaching sacrifice, the other, standing with his back toward the tablet to Confucius, addressed the crowd (which gathered about him as he began to speak in the vernacular of the place) on the folly and the sin of worship-ping deceased men, and the duty of worshipping and serving the only true and living God—perhaps the first Gospel discourse ever delivered in a temple dedicated to the worship of the Chinese sage.

The next morning, about four o'clock, we repaired to the

temple to witness the sacrificial worship rendered to Confucius by the high mandarins. The premises were lighted up with fires built on elevated iron racks and by torches. A large number of idle spectators of the lower class and of literary men had already gathered together, though the high officials had not arrived. We improved the opportunity to notice the arrangement of the articles to be offered as sacrifice.

On a large stone altar, which stood directly in front of the tablet of Confucius, were placed two large tall candles, and four shorter and smaller ones, already lighted, and a quantity of burning incense, a large piece of cooked pork, a piece of venison, and quite a variety of other kinds of food. A few feet in front of this stone altar were one large and two small tables. On the large table, which was placed between the other two, was the carcass of a yearling bullock. On one of the small tables was the carcass of a small hog, and on the other that of a very poor goat. The hair of these animals had been very carefully removed, and the bodies, uncooked, were placed in a kneeling position, with their heads toward the tablet of Confucius, as though they were devoutly contemplating the virtues of the sage. On the large table there were also several dishes of food, two large and two small candles, and a quantity of incense already ignited. Besides the altar before the tablet of Confucius, there were four other similar but smaller altars. Two of these were placed before the eight tablets representing eight worthies on one side of the room, and two placed before other eight tablets on the opposite side of the room. In front of each of these altars were a pig and a goat, arranged on two tables, but no bullock. On these altars were several plates of food, with candles and incense. The various vessels seen on the day previous, containing fruits, grains, vegetables, &c. were partly arranged on the altars in the main building, but the most of them were distributed about on the altars before the tablets in the two long rows of rooms on the sides of the large court in front of the main building. Before the large altar in front of the Confucian tablet, behind the bullock, and at several other places in the main hall, pieces of matting were spread on the pavement at the spots where the high officials were to kneel.

While we were awaiting the arrival of the high mandarins, one of the district magistrates came to us, attended by an interpreter, and very courteously said that he had been sent by the prefect to assign us a place, so that there should be no confusion during the service. Accordingly, a very eligible position was assigned to us, just outside one of the large doors of the main hall, enabling us to observe to a great extent what was going on within and without. We could not have selected a better position.

Soon after, the beating of an immense drum suspended near the most eastern entrance to the main building, and the sound of musical instruments at a distance, betokened the approach of the expected great ones. A herald proclaimed their arrival, and the flare of a multitude of torches and lanterns confirmed the fact. These officers and their attendants halted at the proper places in the large court, while a company of twelve or fifteen players on musical instruments, together with some twenty-four boys, attended by two or three persons who directed their movements, marched up an inclined plane leading to a level arena in front of the main hall. The musicians entered the hall and disposed themselves in several parties. The boys, with their directors, stopped on the open arena in front of the hall, and divided themselves into two companies, arranging themselves along the opposite sides of the large central doors. These urchins wore clad in an embroidered tunic, much the worse looking for service, and they wore on their heads the red official cap used by the Chinese on grand occasions. They were provided with instruments about two feet long, consisting of two parts. One of these parts was hollow. The other was solid, and passed partially through the hollow one. A nail or spike was driven into the upper end of the solid sticks, and, according to the regulations of the ceremony, there ought to have been a feather of the pheasant stuck on this iron point. But on this occasion the feather was wanting, if our observation was correct. Perhaps only very small feathers were used, which could not be seen in the distance.

When everything was ready, at signals given by the drum, some five or six officers, attired in very rich dresses and caps, were seen slowly and solemnly ascending the stone steps on the east and west sides of the arena in front of the main hall, one following another at a short interval. Each mandarin was preceded by one or two "professors of ceremony." The viceroy was not present on this occasion, being absent from the city, on a rebel-quelling expedition in the western part of the province. The highest functionaries who took part in the sacrificial worship, were the provincial governor, treasurer, criminal judge, the two commissioners of the salt and of the provision department. The Tartar general, and other Tartar and military officers, and the prefect, and other subordinate civil officers, not being allowed to participate personally in the main hall, stood below in the court in front, ready to bow down at the proper time.

The officers, having ascended to the elevated arena with great solemnity, entered the hall by the doors on the right and the left of the centre, and proceeded to the places appointed for kneeling in front of the altars and the tables covered with offerings, all under the escort of their professors of ceremony. Here they slowly knelt down, and bowed the head towards the pavement three times, holding with both hands some sticks of burning incense, which, after the bowing was completed, they delivered back to their attendants from whom they had been received. The attendants handed to their officers, still kneeling, a vessel taken from the altar or the table in front of which they were, which, having received very carefully with both hands, they presented with a very reverential air toward the tablet in front, whether of Confucius or of some of the worthies, as though requesting them to partake of the contents. They then returned the dish to the attendants, who replaced it upon the table or altar whence it had been taken. Sometimes the same ceremony was repeated with other articles of food. Some or all of the officers passed from one altar to another, performing similar ceremonies.

The musicians all this while were playing on their instruments, and chanting the words of an adulatory ode to Confucius. The big drum gave forth its sonorous peals occasionally, and the urchins outside of the hall were performing certain evolutions with their sticks, accompanied with kneelings and bowings. These manœuvres, in the estimation of the Chinese, indicated great reverence and majesty. The manipulations of the two sticks seemed to consist principally in moving one up through the other as far as its handle would allow, the movements being slow and deliberate, designed to be in accord with the music.

Soon the high officials, piloted by their professors of ceremony, walked slowly out of the hall and descended into the court, taking the same route by which they ascended. Shortly afterward they and their *cicerones* came up again, went through with similar performances, and retired. The same routine was repeated for the third time, with slight deviations. At a certain period of the performances, while the officers were below in the court, a professor of ceremony entered the hall, and, proceeding to a particular spot, where was placed a small stand by itself, reverently knelt down and chanted, in a shrill and most doleful tone of voice, a sort of sacrificial ode to Confucius.

Shortly after the third and final descent of the worshipping officers into the court, a company of men walked out of the hall through the large central door, and passed directly down the inclined plane into the open area below, each holding with both hands a roll of coarse white silk above his head. These rolls of silk were burned on the pavement of the court as a special offering to the Chinese sage.

A few moments more, and the ceremonies were brought to a conclusion by the retiring of the chief and subordinate mandarins in their sedans.

Only those who had a public and official part to perform seemed solemn and reverential, while many of the spectators laughed, talked, and jested, apparently enjoying the performance. The lictors or subordinates of the officers several times chocked the idlers who happened to be near us, lest their mirth should attract the attention of their superiors.

It is said that, according to the established regulations, the carcases of the animals used in sacrifice on the occasion of the vernal and the autumnal worship of Confucius are subsequently cut up and divided among the principal officials of the city. Some one has estimated that the number of temples dedicated to the Chinese sage, in all parts of the empire, is 1,560, and 27,000 pieces of silk, and 62,606 pigs, rabbits, sheep, and deer, not to specify the quantity of fruits, vegetables, &c. are annually presented upon their altars—an estimate which seems not to include the number of bullocks slaughtered and offered as oblations in his honour.

The Chinese are all required to mourn for the death of the emperor, the empress, and the widow of an emperor, in certain established ways, according to their rank and position in life. I propose to describe the national mourning, as it was observed at this place in the fall of 1861, on the occasion of the death of Hien Fung. It will be remembered that he died at Yehol, in Tartary, on the 22d of August, 1861, whither he had fled in October of the previous year, not long antecedent to the destruction of his summer palace by the allied English and French troops.

The courier, bringing an official dispatch from Peking, with a blue seal on it, announcing his death, arrived here thirty-four days after it occurred. The viceroy immediately issued a proclamation, announcing the fact and date of the emperor's death, and commanding all the civil and military officers, the gentry, and the people to put on mourning, commencing from that day. The mandarins accordingly had the large and hideous figures on the doors of their yamuns painted black, and the neat red inscriptions on their door-posts and the posts of their yamuns covered over with reddish-blue paper. They removed their buttons of

CHINESE GENTLEMAN, OR ONE OF THE GENTRY.

rank from their caps, began to use sedan-chairs covered with plain black cotton cloth, and wore plain black clothes, with a white long coat or tunic on the outside, which extended down to their ankles, and which was fastened round their waist with a girdle or belt of white cotton cloth.

The imperial rescript, giving specific directions in regard to the public mourning, after being waited for quite a number of days, not arriving, the high mandarins decided not to delay longer for it, but to mourn and weep according to the method practised in 1850 on the death of the preceding emperor. Accordingly, on the 17th of October, the viceroy issued a proclamation, ordering the civil and military officers, and the gentry and others who ought to take a part in the public demonstration, to meet twice per day, on the eighteenth, nineteenth, and twentieth days of the said month, in a certain temple adjoining the prefectural temple to Confucius, and there to "lift up their lamentations." The times specified were seven o'clock A.M. and three o'clock P.M.

On the same day he issued another proclamation, notifying the common people that thereafter, reckoning for one hundred days from the day of the death of the emperor, they should not shave their pates as usual, nor should there be any marriages, nor any festivities whatever. On the following day, the governor of the province issued a proclamation to the same general effect, rehearsed the news previously made known by other proclamations, and reiterated the commands of the viceroy for the officials and the gentry to meet together and "weep" at the temple and on the days above specified. On the following morning, the 19th of October, appeared proclamations from the two district magistrates of the city, ordering the people to put the usual badges of national mourning on their sign-boards, if engaged in trade, and on the common red inscriptions found very numerously on the posts of their houses.

The sign-boards of the stores, hongs, banks, &c. which had the names of the firms painted thereon in red characters or gilded, were put in mourning, in obedience to the proclamations of the district magistrates. Sometimes the sides of the sign-boards were first covered over with green paper, and then the name of the firm was written on the paper with black ink. At other times, the paper attached to the sign had two characters written on it in black ink, which indicated that the "nation was in mourning." Sometimes several such pieces of paper, of a square or oblong shape, were pasted on the same sign ; at other times, only one, according to the fancy of the proprietor, or perhaps that of his clerks. Red paper was not used, red being the symbol of joy.

According to law, on the death of an emperor, barbers, play-actors, and players on musical instruments, are deprived of their usual methods of obtaining a living for the space of one hundred days. Barbers may not shave the crowns of their customers, though they are allowed to comb and braid their cues.

Before official news of the emperor's decease arrived, and after reliable intelligence of that event had reached this port, a large number of marriages were celebrated among the people. This was owing, in many cases, to the law, that for one hundred days subsequent to that event, marriage processions through the streets in the customary manner would not be allowed. Some marriages that, according to previous expectations, would have been celebrated during the latter part of the hundred days, were hastened so as to be over with before the prohibitory proclamation should make its appearance. If the parties are willing to have the bride carried through the streets in a plain black sedan, with no show of rejoicing, and without any band of musical performers preceding it, marriages during the period of national mourning could be celebrated, and no notice of them would ordinarily be taken by the mandarins. But few respectable families are willing to have a marriage connected with them celebrated in this private manner.

On the afternoon of the 19th of October, in company with several friends, I went to see the mandarins, gentry, and expectants of office of certain ranks engage in the "lamentations" on account of the decease of Hien Fung. We were rather early, and found a rabble of men and boys assembled round the outer door of the temple where the lamentations were to take place, and desirous of slipping into the premises along with the attendants and retainers of the persons who were entitled to enter. We were at once allowed to enter, but several Chinese friends who tried to follow us were summarily pulled back by the guard stationed at the gate. The company inside was quite select, the majority being attendants and sedan-bearers of their masters, who constituted the minority. The latter were easily recognised by their being all dressed in white cotton tunics, reaching down to their ancles, and having about their waists a sash of white cotton cloth. They all had on black satin or black cotton boots, with very thick white soles. The caps were all plain and conical, coming to a point a few inches above the crowns of their heads, and without the usual button of rank on the apex. Their number was increased by new arrivals every few minutes, until the viceroy himself, in a plain black cloth sedan, carried by eight bearers, arrived, when all who were to take a part in the lamentations proceeded to their appointed positions.

Two coarse unpainted oblong tables had been arranged near the north end of the temple, one a little longer and a little higher than the other, being about five feet long and four or five feet high. The higher was placed behind the other. On its centre was a large censer, containing burning cake-incense, the fumes of which were not altogether pleasant. On the east and west sides of the censer were tall vases, containing fresh white flowers, commonly known as the China-asters. Near the ends of this table were two candlesticks, made of pewter, some three or four feet high, each having a large yellow candle in it. We were told that candles were kept burning night and day during the period devoted to weeping for the emperor. This may be the theory and the intention of the higher officials, but those who had the matter under their charge, we were subsequently informed, extinguished the candles as soon as the officials departed, and charged the cost of candles all the time, putting the money saved into their own pockets. In the centre of the front and smaller table was another censer, having three sticks of burning incense incased in yellow paper, and near its ends were two large yellow candles burning. On the south or front side of each of these tables was a plain coarse screen of yellow cotton cloth, hanging down nearly to the ground.

Some ten feet behind the tables was a small pavilion, about two feet square and seven or eight feet high, covered principally on the sides and along its posts with yellow cloth. There were strips of cloth having two or three other colours, not red, mingled with the yellow, on some parts of the pavilion, knotted or braided together in a certain manner. The reason why yellow cloth was used in various places on this occasion is that yellow is the imperial colour, and refers to or denotes the emperor.

A platform about fifteen feet wide and sixty or eighty feet long, raised about one foot from the ground, and made of un-planed boards, beginning about fifteen feet from the tables, and on a level with the ground on which they stood, stretched down toward the south. At the north end of the platform, in front of the tables, were a few pieces of palm matting. The most of the platform was carpeted with common white cotton cloth. An awning of the same material was arranged over the platform, and large screens of it were placed on the north, east, and west sides of the pavilion and tables.

The mandarins, gentry, &c. who were entitled to take a part in the farce which was to be enacted, advanced slowly and silently to the positions they were to occupy on this platform. The particular place which the various ranks of officers, or expectants of office, were to occupy, was indicated by inscriptions or tablets suspended above the outer edge of the platform. The military mandarins arranged themselves along the west side of the platform, and the civil mandarins along its east side. The highest in rank were on its north end, and immediately in front of the tables.

A professor of ceremony took his position facing the west and near the north end of the platform. When everything was ready, he called out in a commanding tone of voice, using the mandarin dialect (all the rest of the company preserving a most profound silence), "Take your places in proper order!" which meant simply prepare or make ready, as all were already standing where they should stand, with their faces toward the pavilion. He immediately cried out, "Kneel down!" all simultaneously knelt down. He then ordered them to "knock their heads once" on the ground, which they proceeded to do by placing their hands on the ground, and then inclining their heads forward and downward until they touched the platform. All the performers then raised their bodies to an upright position, still remaining on their knees. The professor immediately cried out, "Knock your heads the second time!" and they accordingly bowed their heads down in a similar manner. They then assumed again an upright position, when they were commanded by the professor of ceremony to "knock their heads the third time!" which command they submissively obeyed. He then ordered them to "rise up" on their feet; and when they had succeeded in attaining to a standing position, he immediately ordered them to "kneel," "knock heads," &c. as has just been described. When they had knocked their heads three times on the ground, they were commanded to rise to their feet, after which they were again required to kneel and perform the knocking of their heads for another three times. But, instead of ordering them to stand up at the end of the third time of knocking their heads on the ground as before, the professor, while they were still on their hands and knees, commanded them to "begin their lamentations!" and they all began to moan and weep in a whimpering, subdued tone of voice. This was kept up for a minute or so, when they were ordered to "stop their crying!" "rise up," and "disperse from their places," which they all seemed to be quite willing to do. Thus ended the ceremony of "three bowings and nine knockings." The assembly immediately broke up.

What has been said of the official mourning performed by mandarins and expectants of office will illustrate what is meant by the State Religion.

CHAPTER XV.

COMPETITIVE LITERARY EXAMINATIONS.

THERE are numerous primary schools in China, supported by the people of a neighbourhood who choose to send their children. There are no school-houses, schools being commonly held in a spare hall or room belonging to a private family, or in a part of the village temple. There is no village tax nor any aid from Government received for the support of schools. Each parent must pay the teacher for the instruction of his children. Besides these, there are private or family schools, the pupils being few and select, belonging to rich families. In this city there are no free schools, where the pupils can attend without expense for tuition. In former years there were some such schools, sustained principally at the charge of a very wealthy bank. But this bank failed six or eight years ago, at the time of a general panic among banks, and its suspension of business was the signal for the suspension of the various charitable works which it supported.

Girls are seldom sent to school or taught to read at home. Education is not regarded as fitting them to fill in a better manner the stations they are expected to occupy. Pupils do not study, in school, books on mathematics, geography, and the natural sciences, but the writings of Confucius and Mencius. These they are required to commit to memory, and recite with their backs toward the book. This is called "backing the book." They are not taught in classes, but each studies the book he pleases, taking a longer or shorter lesson according to his ability. They all study out loud, oftentimes screaming at the top of their voices. They first learn the sounds of the characters, so as to recite them *memoriter*. After years of study they acquire an insight into their meaning and use. They

SCHOOL-BOY WITH FAN AND PARCEL OF
BOOKS.

commence to write when they begin going to school, tracing the characters given them as patterns on paper by means of a hair pencil and China ink. It requires an immense amount of practice to write the language correctly and rapidly.

There are three collegiate institutions at this city which are connected with the Government. The studies pursued in them are the same in kind as are pursued by advanced scholars in village or family schools, viz. the "five classics" and the "four books," being a part of the thirteen works which collectively are often called the "Chinese classics." Compositions in prose and verse on themes selected from these books are regularly required. These books are the main subject of thought and research—not that they are recited there, or that the teachers require certain parts to be studied in their presence. The teachers once or twice per month expound certain parts, or

PUPIL "BACKING HIS BOOK," i. e. RECITING HIS LESSON.

deliver lectures on the subjects discussed, or the sentiments
advanced in these books. They pay no attention to any historical, mathematical, or philosophical books or subjects. These
things are considered as not worthy of research at the colleges.
If a student wishes to pursue any literary studies different from
the classics, he must do it at his leisure, without expecting to
receive any particular aid from his teachers. The study of
mathematics and philosophy, or the sciences generally, is regarded as of exceedingly small importance compared with the
study of the classics. The latter are of use in the composition
of essays and poems, required at the regular examination as trial
pieces competitory for the literary degrees, which are so highly
prized by ambitious men in China; but attainments in the
natural sciences afford no special aid in writing these essays
and poems, or of advancing one to a higher rank as a literary
man or as an officer.*

The design of establishing the colleges was to encourage and
stimulate the students to write essays and poems of a high order.
They have not failed of producing the effect designed, judging
from the interest manifested by graduates of the first degree, as
well as undergraduates, to become connected with them. The
small monthly stipend given to a part of the successful candidates
for admission doubtless has some influence in leading scholars
who are not possessed of ample means to desire to enter them.
But probably the benefit to be derived from attendance and the
honour of being connected with them have, in the case of the
majority of the students, a greater influence than the pecuniary
reward in causing such a general interest to become members of
the colleges.

Two of the colleges are under the supervision of the provincial
governor. He appoints the teachers. The salary of the teacher

* "The number of individuals acquainted with letters in China, is
amazingly great. One half of the male population are able to read;
while some 'mount the cloudy ladder' of literary fame, and far exceed
their companions. The general prevalence of learning in China may be
ascribed to the system pursued at the literary examinations; by which
none are admitted to office but those who have passed the ordeal with
success, while each individual is allowed to try his skill in the public hall.
Wealth, patronage, friends, or favour, are of no avail in procuring
advancement; while talent, merit, diligence, and perseverance, even in
the poorest and humblest individual, are almost sure of their appropriate
reward. This is their principle, and their practice does not much vary
from it. They have a proverb that 'while royalty is hereditary, office is
not;' and the plan adopted at the public examinations is an illustration
of it."—MEDHURST's China, its State and Prospects, p. 171.

x

of one is eight hundred taels ; the salary of the teacher of the
other six hundred taels per annum, which is paid out of the
imperial treasury. The customary presents made to them by the
pupils under their care probably amount to at least one or two
thousand dollars more during the course of the year. These
teachers are men of high literary ability, very frequently being
members of the Imperial or Hanlin college at Peking. The high
provincial officers must treat them with great deference when
they meet. The teachers expect to be regarded as guests in the
presence of the high mandarins—that is, the seat of honour is
accorded to them.

Those of the students who choose are permitted to live in the
colleges, but few do live there. Each college has a large number
of rooms, which may be used by the pupils free of rent. The
janitor, however, expects a present from resident students.
Those who reside there make a more valuable present to the
teacher than those who live elsewhere. Those who pay the
most money stand the chance of receiving the most attention.
The resident students are also expected to make presents to
their teacher on the occurrence of his birthday, and that of his
wife, and of his parents, if living, as well as at the time of the
national festivals in the fifth, eighth, and eleventh months, and
at new year's. These presents consist of curiosities, articles of
food, or money.

At the appointed day, early in the morning, usually some
time during the second month, the provincial governor, with a
proper staff of assisting officials, meets those students, whether
graduates or undergraduates, who wish to compete for entrance
to the highest college at the provincial examination hall. He
gives out one set of themes for the undergraduates, and another
set of themes for the graduates of the first degree. The compositions are finished some time during the same day, when they
are handed over to the governor for his inspection. After
making a selection of those which he regards as the best, he
passes them into the hands of the teacher of the college for his
examination. In this way, two hundred and forty students are
selected as pupils out of the thousands who present themselves,
one hundred and twenty of the graduates, and one hundred and
twenty of the undergraduates. Unjust and unlawful methods
are often resorted to by some candidates for membership of the
colleges. Some students are successful by bribing the high
officials, and others by their favour.

On the following day the scholars of the first degree, and of the class of undergraduates who desire to compete for the privilege of entering the other college under the control of the governor, meet him at the same hall, where they write prose and poetical compositions as usual on themes which he announces. He selects two hundred and forty of the compositions which he regards as most worthy, one hundred and twenty whose writers are graduates, and one hundred and twenty whose writers are undergraduates.

Sixty of the accepted graduates for each of these colleges usually receive one and a half taels per month; the remaining sixty only receive one tael. Of the one hundred and twenty undergraduates, only one half receive any stipend at all, which is one tael per month. The remaining sixty undergraduates are kept as a kind of reserve to fill up any deficiencies which may occur during the year in the number of those who receive a monthly allowance. The reserve of sixty are allowed all the privileges of the institution equally with those who are allowed a stipend. The rule is, that should any student who receives an allowance be absent from three successive examinations, his name would be erased from the list, and some one of the sixty undergraduates be put in its place. Usually, however, should a student be prevented from attending at the regular times, he employs some friend to appear in his stead. The monthly stipends paid these students are received from the treasurer of the province. There are three days during the month when themes are given out and compositions prepared at each of these colleges—i. e., the sixth, sixteenth, and twenty-sixth days. The teacher usually presides at two of these competitory examinations. The students who reside at the colleges are entitled to have their compositions criticised by their respective teachers. The teachers discourse on the classics to their resident pupils twice per month.

It is the duty of the viceroy, the governor, the treasurer, the judge, and the commissioners of the salt and provision departments, each to attend in turn at one of the regular monthly examinations of each of the colleges. In this way, according to theory, each of the six officials attends twice during the year. It is the privilege and the duty of each of these mandarins to preside when he is present, giving out the themes and first looking over the compositions, after which he passes them into the hands of the teacher of the college for his inspection, when a list of the comparative merits of the compositions made by the students is in due time posted up in public.

The literary chancellor is expected to attend and preside once
at the competitory examinations held monthly in each of the
colleges. He gives out the themes, and decides himself in regard
to the comparative merit of the compositions, not handing them
over to the teacher as if for his corroborative opinion, as is the
case with the six officials mentioned above. Most of the high
officials who play the mandarin at this city have for many years
had the reputation of being poor scholars, having obtained their
offices by purchase or by bribery. Such great men must often
make ludicrous blunders when they attempt to perpetrate literary
feats on their own responsibility. Hence the manifest propriety
of the custom which requires them to associate with them, as it
were, the accomplished teacher of the college at whose competitive examinations they preside. But the literary chancellor,
being always a man selected for his position on account of his
literary attainments, is competent to decide on the relative
merits of the compositions which are made at the session over
which he presides.

There is another collegiate institution in this city, but inferior
in rank and importance to the two which have been mentioned.
The chief director of this college is the prefect. His associates
are the marine inspector and the two district magistrates, whose
yamuns are located in the city. The examination of the students
who wish to compete for its privileges is held at the prefect's
yamun. He gives out the themes, and selects two hundred and
forty men, half graduates and half undergraduates. The teacher's
salary is only about three hundred taels per annum. He provides his own house, and the students live where they choose,
meeting their teacher at the college at the regular days of examination or lecture. They are expected to make him a present of
more or less value, according to their circumstances, or according
as they desire to obtain his especial aid in criticising their productions.

The directing officials are expected to be present in regular
turn, and preside once a month at the competitive examinations
held at the college. Should one fail in attending, the teacher
presides in his place. The expenses of this institution, viz., the
salary of the teacher and the stipends to a part of the pupils, are
provided by the officials who are its head. This accounts for the
fact that the stipends are not promptly paid. The sum given
professedly every month is only about half as great as the sum
given at the other colleges.

The competitors for admittance to the collegiate institutions under the control of the governor need not necessarily be residents of this prefecture. They may belong to any part of the province. Those who come from a distance must be supplied with the necessary credentials of their literary character from their literary chiefs or their principal teachers, or they would not be allowed to engage in the preparatory competitive examinations before the governor for admittance to the college which they desired to enter.

Those who become members of the third college mentioned, that of which the prefect is chief, may belong to the different districts which compose the prefecture. The establishment of it seems to have been designed to benefit only the graduates and the undergraduates belonging to this prefecture, not those who belong to other prefectures in the province.

To give an intelligible account of the world-renowned[*] competitory examinations of the Chinese, and to detail some of the unlawful expedients which are often resorted to by candidates in order to gain a literary degree, would require several chapters. It seems certain that, where they are impartially and faithfully conducted, the graduates must be scholars of more than ordinary memory and ability, but, as they really are often conducted, the attainment of a degree is no sure proof of the possession of any more than ordinary capacity, and not necessarily even that.

There are four classes who, themselves or their posterity for three generations, according to law, are not permitted to engage in the literary examinations.

1. *The public prostitutes.*—Among the descendants of these

---

[*] "People have talked," says Mr. Meadows, *The Chinese and their Rebellions*, p. 39, "somebody talked first and others keep on talking after him—about the Chinese nation being the same because it has been separated from other nations by barriers of physical geography, by mountains and rivers, while the nations of Europe have been kept different by being separated from each other by similar barriers. Why, China Proper, a Europe in itself, contains in itself rivers to which the Rhine is but a 'burnie,' and has in it, and crossing it, mountain chains that may vie with the Alps and the Pyrenees in impassability : how is it then that the people in China, on opposite banks of these rivers, and on opposite sides of these mountains, are the same in language, manners, and institutions, and are united under one government, while in Europe the mountains and rivers separate people in all these very qualities into quite distinct nations ? The Chinese are one in spite of physical barriers—it is mind, O Western materialistic observers ! which has produced homogenity by overstepping matter, and not matter which has secured homogenity by obstructing mind."

creatures there are sometimes honourable and talented individuals, but, on account of the sins of their ancestors, these are excluded from the greatest privilege of citizenship, that of competition for literary honour.

2. *The public play-actors.*—This includes those who have earned a living as actors, whether chiefs or subordinates—those who have made play-acting their profession.

3. *The executioners, lictors, and the menial servants connected with mandarinates.*—These include those who precede high mandarins when they appear in public, and who are supposed to be ready to do any bloody or cruel act, if commanded by their masters, whether according to law or opposed to it.

4. *The jailors and keepers of the prisons connected with yamuns.*—The first two classes are believed to be entirely destitute of shame, else they would not degrade their persons for vicious or unworthy purposes for the sake of gain. The last two classes are believed to have very hard and depraved hearts, else they would never consent to engage in the business of their respective positions.

The descendants of these classes, if more virtuous, respectable, and humane than their ancestors, and if they are really desirous of changing their professions, and retrieving or rather gaining a good character, usually remove to a distant place, where their lineage and their antecedents are unknown. Their ancestry is a disgrace to them, and constitutes an obstacle in the way of their rising in society.

Some three years since, the report was current at this place that an actor had been admitted to the third literary degree at Peking, when a censor informed the emperor. As the result, he and about thirty high officers suffered the penalty of death for being privy to the fact that he had been an actor, and yet allowing him to compete at the examinations, whereas they ought to have prevented him from doing so. Among these officers of state was one who was at the time, or who had been a chancellor, and the adopted father of the graduate was one of the presiding examiners at the time of his graduation. The report may not have been entirely true in all of the details given.

According to law, any literary man, without regard to age or condition, excepting the four classes which have been mentioned, may compete in the examination at which he is entitled by his attainments to compete, provided it be not within three years after the death of either parent. Should any bachelor of arts, disregarding the law forbidding competition for a literary degree during the period allotted to mourning for the death of father or mother, be allowed to present himself at an examination for the second degree, and it became known to the examining official, he would be degraded from his rank, and the literary chancellor would in all likelihood be degraded or punished heavily by fines, unless he bribed to silence those who were privy to it. If only an undergraduate, his principal security would be degraded or disgraced. Literary competition is deemed incompatible with sincere mourning for a parent. It would be construed into a kind of filial ingratitude, or want of filial love and respect, punishable by process of law.

The Literary Chancellor is the presiding mandarin at the last examination which decides who are the fortunate candidates that attain the lowest literary degree.

The chancellor is usually a member of the Imperial Academy at Peking. His term of office is three years. Only one is appointed for each province. His official residence is at the capital of the province. His duties call him to travel to each of the prefectural cities of the province twice during his term of office, for the purpose of examining the candidates for the first degree and the graduates of the first degree.

LITERARY UNDERGRADUATE, OR STUDENT.

The literary chancellor sends notice to the different prefects in his province of the time when he will examine the literary undergraduates of the prefecture. Each prefect sends a messenger to each of the district magistrates of his prefecture communicating the notice from the literary chancellor. Each district magistrate issues a proclamation giving the undergraduates in his district notice of the time when they will be expected to meet him for examination at his yamun.

In accordance with this notification from the district magistrate, all of the undergraduates in his jurisdiction who wish to

compete before him, preparatory to competition before the prefect, make arrangements in accordance with established and
well-known regulations. At least three days before the time
appointed, each candidate must present himself at the proper
office, and receive from the clerk, on paying eighty or a hundred
cash, a blank schedule. This paper, already stamped with the
district magistrate's seal, he takes away and fills out with the
requisite particulars respecting himself, as the name of his grandfather, his father, his principal teacher, and his neighbours on
the right and left hand. He states also his own name and age,
whether of large or small stature, his complexion, and whether
he has moustaches or not, and the place of his residence. It
states also that he does not desire to go into the examination in
behalf of another man, using another's name ; that he does not
go for the purpose of acting as teacher or aid to another; and
that he does not go into an examination to which he has no
right, really belonging to another district, &c. The candidate
must take the paper thus filled out to those of the graduates of
the first degree who are appointed to act as securities to undergraduates ; and upon payment of about a hundred cash he
obtains two to sign and stamp the document as principal and
secondary security. It is now carried to the chief of the graduates for the district, who stamps it with his red stamp ; for
doing which he also receives a small fee. After having obtained
all these securities, the undergraduate returns the document to
the clerk from whom he received the schedule. He carefully
keeps it for reference should occasion require. He gives in
exchange for it another paper, stating the name of the candidate,
and the number of his application. The latter keeps this for
use on the morning of the commencement of the examination,
presenting the clerk with about a hundred cash. The clerk
now prepares a small roll of ruled paper, consisting of six or
eight sheets, to the outside of which is attached a slip of paper,
stamped with the seal of the district magistrate, and stating
the name of the candidate and the number of his application,
corresponding to the minutes which the candidate took away
with him.

All this is preliminary to the examination before the district
magistrate.

Very early in the morning, usually before daylight of the
appointed day, the competitor presents himself. He enters the
place provided for writing his essays, and seats himself at a table.
After all the candidates have entered the hall, they are shut in,

and the doors are fastened and sealed, allowing no ingress or egress until the compositions are finished, or until a part of them are finished, and the writers wish to return to their homes. The district magistrate, who, with enough of his underlings and literary assistants to keep order, have been also shut in with the candidates, now gives out the themes for two prose essays and one poem, which each competitor is expected to prepare. These themes are taken from the four classics. The candidates now apply themselves to their tasks.

Each prose essay must contain some six or seven hundred characters, and the poem about sixty characters. The writers are not allowed any communication with outside friends, nor are they allowed to refer to any books. Each one is expected to rely upon himself solely. The food of which each partakes is carried in at the time of his entering the arena. Toward night, the essays and poems of some of the candidates are completed, and delivered to the proper officer or clerk, who delivers them over to the district magistrate, and their writers are allowed to go out of the premises. In a short time another company have completed their work, and are ready to depart. The candidates must all complete what they do before dark. It happens at every examination that more or less are unable to complete their tasks in time, or make some blunder in copying upon the ruled paper, or some may be taken sick.

The district magistrate repeats his examination from two to three or four times. The candidates need not procure any security for the second or following examinations before this officer for the current year. The clerk furnishes him a paper containing his number, and prepares another roll of ruled paper as before, on his paying the usual sum for second or succeeding examinations.

Then follows the examination before the prefect at the prefectural city, who examines the candidates by their districts, having the men from two or three districts come in at the same time.

It requires a considerable longer time for the prefect to complete the examinations under his care than for the district magistrate to complete his examinations. He generally examines them all two or three times, each time several districts being represented. Usually at each session of the candidates from the same districts their number becomes less than the former, owing to want of ability to complete their essays and poetry in time, or to sickness. Unless one wishes, he need attend only the first examination before the prefect, but he must attend that, or he will not be allowed to compete before the literary chancellor, unless he be a descendant of some ancient worthy, as will be mentioned hereafter.

Here let it be observed, once for all, that on the coming out of the arena of the first company of competitors before any of the examining officers at any of their competitory sessions, it becomes the duty of the chief clerk belonging to the proper office connected with the examination to send, on a large red sheet of paper, the themes on which the candidates have been exercised, to all the high officers resident in the city where the examinations have been held. It is important that this should be done as soon as possible after the doors of the hall are opened, as then, according to theory, the themes become first known to outsiders. It is believed the high mandarins will take an interest in knowing the themes which have been discussed in the competitory arenas. For the examination of undergraduates before the literary chancellor for the first degree, and also of graduates of the first degree before him, preparatory to competition for the second degree, the rule is that competitors of all classes of society must attend at the examinations before the district magistrate, prefect, and literary chancellor in regular order. The exception is in the case of descendants of certain ancient worthies, as Confucius and Mencius. These constitute a privileged class, and are not obliged to appear before the district magistrate and the prefect. They may commence their literary competition before the chancellor, if they choose to do so.

The preliminaries to enter the examination before the literary chancellor are essentially the same as those before the district magistrate and the prefect. The "principal security" of each candidate must be present on the morning of entering the arena, so as to aver in public that he secures him as his name is called out by the clerk. Unless he should be there and announce that he stands his security, the candidate would not be allowed to enter the hall.

The candidate proceeds to write his essays and poem on themes given out after the doors have been shut and sealed up for the day. Generally the literary chancellor requires the candidates to appear before him to prepare compositions in prose and poetry only twice. The best on the second list of names and seats of candidates are the fortunate ones who are adjudged to be worthy of the first degree in the scale of literary rank, or

bachelors of arts. The number of candidates who can graduate
at every term of examination held by the literary chancellor is
not the same for every district in the prefecture, nor does it
have any proportion to the number of candidates furnished by
the district, nor to the extent of its territory. The original
standard was one graduate for a certain amount of taxes paid
into the imperial treasury. The number who could graduate
became fixed in this way at a certain time, and remained the
same from year to year, unless an extra number should, by the
grace of the emperor, be added on special occasions of state, as
the accession of a new emperor to the throne, the birth of a first
male child to the emperor, &c. Large contributions of money
for the aid of the Government in cases of special need, by men
living in the various districts, are also rewarded and encouraged
by the addition of one or more to the number which is usually
the quota of graduates for these districts.

The number allowed by law to attain the honours of a
bachelor of arts, belonging to each of the districts in the prefecture, having been selected, there remains still a number of
candidates who may attain the degree on account of the prefecture, and are ranked as belonging to the prefecture at large.
The persons who shall constitute this class are also determined
by the literary chancellor. One or more from the various
districts are selected to belong to the class of the prefectural
graduates in the established manner.

The literary chancellor requires those who stand very high
on the list at his second examination to appear before him
at a supplementary examination, not on themes selected from
the classics, but to exercise them on rewriting from memory the
whole of the "Sacred Edict." The "Sacred Edict" is the name
of a treatise which was prepared by the Emperor Khanghi,
of the present dynasty, for the instruction of his subjects on
matters relating to moral and relative duties. The copying of
this treatise with absolute correctness is regarded as an essential
part of the preparatory examination for the first degree. Much
deception is practised, when the rules are not strictly enforced,
by the candidates taking into the arena with them manuscript
or printed copies of the "Sacred Edict," made on very thin
paper and in very small characters—a course which is forbidden
by law, and which is not connived at by the high examining
officers. Should one fail at this exercise, he would certainly
not attain the degree which his own compositions might entitle
him to receive. But, as this is a fixed exercise, students who

are expecting to succeed generally make themselves very familiar with the authorized text of the "Sacred Edict."

The successful competitors for the first degree, as soon as it is determined who they are, must call upon the master of the graduates belonging to their own districts, or upon the master of the graduates belonging to the prefectural class, as the case may be. The object of their calling is to hand in their names to be entered on the list of graduates in the proper place. It is the custom for the graduates to make their chief at this time a present of money, according to their standing in society and their pecuniary ability. The chief sometimes demands a large sum of money before he will enter the names of the new graduate, especially if he is very wealthy, and if he has attained to the rank of a graduate by the use of unfair and unlawful means. The entering of one's name at the office of the chief of the district graduates, or of the prefectural graduates, is called "entering upon learning," or to "become a sewtsai" or a "bachelor of arts," as the phrase may be rendered.*

From this time the successful scholar comes under the jurisdiction of his literary chief. He may not be arrested in the summary manner as undergraduates and the common people are arrested by the civil magistrate if he is charged with any crime. He must be prosecuted before the literary chief of the graduates of his district, or the chief of the prefectural class, if he should belong to the latter. He is allowed to wear a button on his cap, which indicates that he is a graduate. He becomes at once a man of influence and of honour to his own neighbourhood, and especially among his relatives, who are usually proud of numbering as one of their own kindred the man who has distinguished himself among his fellow-competitors by carrying off the prize. He has ready access to the presence of the lower class of magistrates. His literary rank gives him a great opportunity to play the villain among the common people, if he wishes to do so. Such graduates are not few in this part of China, and they soon become hated and feared by shopkeepers

---

* Dr. Medhurst says : " All persons acquire some knowledge of letters ; and learning, such as it is, is more common in China than in any other part of the world. Six poor brethren will frequently agree to labour hard, to support the seventh at his books ; with the hope that should he succeed and acquire office, he may throw a protecting influence over his family, and reward them for their toil. Others persevere, to the decline of life, in the pursuit of literary fame ; and old men of eighty, have been known to die of sheer excitement and exhaustion in the examination halls."—*China, its State and Prospects*, pp. 178, 179.

and the common people generally. Those of the rank of kügin, or master of arts, the second degree, who use their rank and power to oppress the people, are fewer in number perhaps, but more hated and feared. Their higher literary rank gives them greater opportunity to browbeat and injure without redress their victims, unless they comply with the demands of these pests to society. The Chinese speak of this class of graduates of the second degree with abhorrence and anger.

The above description relates to the established manner of competing for literary rank by participating in the regular examination before literary officers. But there is another way of attaining the same rank, much shorter, surer, and less fatiguing, for those who have the necessary means, and are willing to use them to attain the coveted rank. Those who have more money than brains, by a kind artifice of the Government, are permitted to purchase the privilege of wearing a button on their caps, and of being exempted from arrest and punishment by the civil mandarins. Until a few years ago, the sum which would, if paid into the treasurer's office with that design, buy of the emperor the rank and title of sewtsai (bachelor) was one hundred and eighty-three taels. Nowadays, in consequence of the low state of the emperor's funds, it is asserted that twenty-five taels will suffice. The treasurer receives the necessary sum, whatever it is, and reports the name of the applicant to the proper tribunal at Peking, from which, in due time, he receives the certificate which guarantees certain privileges to the individual who has money to spare, but not enough literary ability to enable him to gain the bachelorship. The possession of this diploma entitles him to compete for the second literary degree along with those who have attained the bachelorship by the exercise of their literary qualifications in the regular and honourable manner. Those who buy their degrees are looked down upon by others. Their number is becoming year by year more numerous, on account of the great cheapness at which it is offered to aspiring men, and the extreme facility which attends an attempt to obtain it by those who have the money.

Several of the competitors before the literary chancellor, whose essays and poems would have entitled them to graduation, if the quota of graduates allowed for their districts had been larger, form a class by themselves. These are a kind of half graduates. They are not obliged to enter the examinations before the district magistrate and the prefect on the succeeding year in order to sustain their standing. They may wait until the time for competing before the literary chancellor arrives, enter into the arena under his jurisdiction, and, if their essays and poems are not of a very decidedly inferior character, they are almost sure of becoming bachelors at the next examination for candidates of the first degree.   At the regular vernal and autumnal sacrifices to Confucius in his temple, these half graduates have a certain part allotted them to perform. Poor candidates are not desirous of sustaining the character before the public of undergraduates of this class, on account of the largely increased expense it involves, without any corresponding substantial advantages.

Every twelve years the literary chancellor holds an extra examination at the prefectural city for the benefit of two or three classes of the best scholars of the graduates of the lowest rank.   At this examination, one from each of the districts, and one from the prefectural class of graduates, may be selected to form another order or class, the members of which are only a little below the graduates of the second degree, and may be appointed to the office of a district manager by the emperor should they have influence enough at court to get an appointment.

It is the duty of those who have attained to a bachelorship to attend the regular examinations held by the literary chancellor in their prefecture.   Should any absent himself from these examinations for three successive years without being excused, or without reporting himself to his literary chief, he would become liable to be deprived by the literary chancellor of his rank and its privileges.   Should he become blind, or be enfeebled by old age or by disease so as to be unable to endure the fatigues and excitements of competing at the regular periods with his fellows, he may petition the chancellor, stating his case. If the latter has no reason for believing the applicant to be trying to impose upon him, he may grant him a document allowing him to retain his rank and privileges, without being obliged to present himself at the regular examinations.   Of course, if he remains away hereafter he forfeits all prospect of obtaining the second degree, or of being employed as an officer of Government, unless he should purchase office, which is seldom done by those who voluntarily retire from the literary arena.

On the other hand, should *an undergraduate* be able to attend the examinations regularly till he becomes *eighty years old*, *without attaining the coveted rank of bachelorship*, the emperor, on being informed of the honourable fact by the provincial

governor, confers upon the aged competitor the title and privileges of a graduate. It becomes the duty of the governor to
report such cases, and to ask for them the customary token of
approval on the part of the emperor. On the receipt of the
title, the old man procures the golden button, which he wears as
a badge of imperial respect. The bestowal of the title on the
octogenarian is designed as a testimony of the approbation of
the emperor, who would encourage the pursuit of letters even to
extreme old age.

It is the duty of the literary chancellor, at each visit during
his term of office, after examining the undergraduates at the
capitals of the different prefectures in the province, to proceed
to examine the old bachelors and the new bachelors, that is,
those scholars whom he has just adjudged to be worthy of the
first degree. He usually has only one examination, not several
sessions, at each visit. The object of this examination at the
time of his first visit is principally to exercise them, and to
prepare them for the next competitive examination for the
second degree at the capital of the province. It has no direct
influence upon their prospects of success other than the benefit
which practice produces. All of the graduates are expected to
enter the lists and compete. The roll of ruled paper on which
they must write their essays and poem must be obtained of the
clerk of the proper office of their respective literary chiefs. The
fee demanded for the roll of paper is about a thousand cash.

The examination of the graduates, on his second visit to the
prefectural cities, is an important one. At the close of this
examination, the literary chancellor divides the competitors
into several classes. Those who belong to the first class are
arranged in order of their excellence, by their seats. The
number of their seats is placarded on the wall in front of the
place of examination. The seats of those who constitute the
second and the third class are in like manner made known to
the public. All those who are in the first and second classes,
and the first ten of the third class, are permitted, without any
farther examination, to compete for the second degree at the
proper time.

But all those below the tenth name of the third class of the
graduates in all the prefectures of the province, and all those
who have bought the bachelorship, unless they are in the first
class, all those who were absent from the prefectural examinations on account of sickness, or for any other reason, if they
wish to compete for the second degree, are required to assemble

at the capital of the province several weeks before the set time
for the beginning of examinations for the second degree, and
enter a supplementary examination before the literary chancellor.
There are usually several hundred or a thousand who come up
in order to take part in this supplementary examination.

The first three companies of candidates who come out from
the hall of the literary chancellor, where they have been engaged
the whole day in writing their essays and poem, are specially
honoured as they come out. The large middle doors are opened
by the breaking of the paper seals and by removing the padlock,
and they are saluted by the discharge of three cannon, and by
music. The cannon and the music are designed to honour them
because they have finished their essays and poems so early.
After each of the first three companies have come out, the
doors are shut, sealed, and locked up, as before the first company
appeared. On the appearance of another company one of the
side doors is opened—no cannon or music salutes them. After
this the door is left open, and each candidate for literary fame
comes out singly. About the time when the doors are expected
to be opened, and the imprisoned scholars to appear, the public
arena in front of the yamun of the literary chancellor is crowded
by the friends and servants of the candidates. The friends
come to congratulate the candidates, and the servants to take
the wallet or bag which contained the remnants of the luncheon
they took in, their pipes, tobacco, inkstand, fan, &c. Advantage
is often taken of the crowd of strangers from distant parts of
the province or of the prefecture, by Chinese who have books
or tracts for distribution, to scatter them among the candidates
as they come out, or their friends, who meet and salute them
with their congratulations.

CHAPTER XVI.

THE provincial examination hall, where the graduates of the first degree who desire to compete for the second degree assemble once in every three years, is located in the north-eastern quarter of the city. It is surrounded by a wall, having back doors or gates, and two very large and high doors on the south side. In the centre, running from north to south, is a wide paved passage. On the east and west sides of this passage there are, in the aggregate, nearly ten thousand apartments, or rather cells, for the accommodation of the competitors. These are arranged in rows in a straight line, beginning in the passage and extending back to the walls on the east and west. Each row is covered with a tiled roof, slanting one way. Each cell is a little higher than a man's head, three feet wide, and three and a half feet deep, having no door and no window. An alley about three or four feet wide extends along in front of the row of apartments. The cells on the side of the alley are open from top to bottom, letting in all the light and air that are needed, and more rain and wind in wet and stormy weather than are required by the occupant. The two sides and the back of the cells are made of brick, plastered over with white lime. The furniture of each cell consists simply of three or four pieces of wide boards, which may be fitted into two rows of creases made in the two sides of the cell at the pleasure of the occupant, making a seat and a table, or a platform on which he may curl up and sleep, if he pleases to do so. One or two of the boards slipped into the lower creases, and pushed to the back side, forms the seat. One or two boards, slipped into the front part of the higher creases, forms the table, on which paper, ink, or food may be arranged. The candidate for literary honour usually sits on the lower

Y

boards, with his back against the wall, placing his writing materials in front of him on the higher and outer tier of boards. Each row of these apartments is numbered by one of the characters of which the Thousand Character Classic is composed, and each of the apartments in each row is numbered so that any particular one can be readily found.

Such are the miserable quarters where the educated talent of the province is expected to congregate and spend several days. Small, uncomfortable, and exposed to the weather, they seem to the foreign visitor but poorly qualified to be the residence of those who would court the Muses, or who would attempt elegant and elaborate prose compositions on a variety of impromptu subjects. They suggest to some foreigners the idea of calf-stalls, and probably many a humane farmer would think his cattle but poorly cared for if they had not better protection from the weather than do the cells or apartments above described afford the candidate for literary rank. The most wealthy as well as the poorest sewtsai in the province, the man of seventy and the stripling of twenty years, must occupy one of them while competing for the second degree. There is no choice between them; all are made in the same way, and all of the same size, and all front to the south. The precise seat of each one is fixed before he enters the arena; so, if there were a choice, there would be no way to make the choice available.

Nearly in the centre of the premises where the cells have been prepared for the use of the competitors there is a two-storied building, in which the two examiners, special commissioners, of high rank and distinguished literary ability from Peking, before the work begins, vow most solemnly, and call upon Heaven to hear their vows, that they will deal honestly in the discharge of their official acts and awards. This is called "The Temple of Perfect Justice." Their vowing to deal justly is called, in the graphic language of the people, "washing their hearts."

On the north side of these premises are spacious grounds devoted to the accommodation of the examiners, and the various assistant officers they have, together with their retinue of servants. Here are large and comfortable quarters for all these parties.

Around the premises there are two walls, distant from each other about twenty feet. During the examination of candidates this space is patrolled night and day by a large number of soldiers, in order to prevent any communication between the competitors inside and their friends outside.

Just before the time for the assembling of the candidates and
their examiners, the premises where the former are to be confined,
and where the latter are to live while they discharge the duties
of their mission, are swept, and cleared of the filth and the
rubbish which have accumulated since their last occupation.
Repairs, if any are needed, are made, and everything is prepared
for the approaching examination.

As the time approaches, the city and suburbs present an
unusually animated and busy appearance. Probably twenty or
thirty thousand strangers from all parts of the province seek for
temporary quarters either at the homes of their personal friends
and acquaintances, or at the houses which they can rent. There
are generally from six to eight thousand graduates who assemble
at the hall ; most of them are from abroad, who come with their
sedans, coolies, and servants, and some are accompanied by
friends, who embrace the occasion to visit the provincial city.

The imperial commissioners make arrangements to arrive here
from Peking a few days previous to the commencement of the
examination. They go to some palace outside of the examination hall, provided for their temporary accommodation. The
doors are shut and sealed, so as to prevent their having company.
It is intended that they shall be watched and guarded, so that
they shall not have any opportunity to be bribed, or to make
friends, or even to become acquainted with those who are to
compete at the examinations, or with their representatives.
Everything is conducted seemingly on fair and just principles,
though, if common fame speaks the truth, there is much that
is unfair and unjust done behind the curtain, or secretly. Anything like open bribery and public corruption would not be
tolerated by the customs of the country, or allowed ·by law, in
regard to the approaching examination.

The imperial commissioners generally enter into their yamuns,
located on the premises adjoining the grounds filled up with the
cells for the competitors, some time during the seventh day of
the eighth month. Each goes to his respective yamun, and, as
soon as they have entered, the large double doors are closed and
sealed, to remain shut until the termination of the examination.
The governor of the province also takes possession of the yamun
provided for him on the same day. The general supervision of
the affairs of the premises belongs to him during the time
allotted for the preparation and examination of the essays and
poems required from the competitors. The prefect of the prefecture in which the provincial city is located also enters and

takes possession of the quarters prepared for him. It is his business to wait upon the commissioners, or rather to carry out their wishes, and have the charge of the red gate between the premises occupied by the candidates and the premises occupied by the examining commissioners and assisting bodies of officers.

The competitors are required to go into the hall and find their appointed seats, known by a slip attached to their roll of ruled paper, usually some time during the night of the seventh, at the latest about the third watch of the morning of the eighth. Each one takes in with him whatever he desires, if according to law, to use for two or three days during the first session of the examination. According to law, his box of provisions and his person are searched, in order to discover whether he is trying to smuggle into the premises anything prohibited. Not a single line of printed or written matter is he allowed to carry in, lest it should be used as a help in the preparation of his tasks. In fact, parts of the classics or other works, written in very small letters, are sometimes taken into the premises unknown to the officials. If any such thing is found upon the person of a candidate or among his provisions, he would sometimes be allowed to remain by giving it up, though oftener he would be expelled from the hall, and punished according to the circumstances of the case.

According to law, one measure of rice and half a pound of meat per day are furnished each competitor at the expense of the Government; but, in fact, this rice is often of such a poor quality, and cooked so badly, and the meat furnished is so small in quantity, that the candidates generally prefer not to depend upon the food provided by law, but to carry their own provisions, and a portable furnace and coal. In this way each can have his hot tea and his meals whenever he pleases. Water is brought at public expense to the outside of the hall, where it is turned into troughs, which convey it to different parts of the inside. Six or eight hundred men are provided by the Government to wait upon the competitors, bringing water to them and cooking for them. No one is allowed to bring his own servant into the hall.

It is the custom for candidates for the second degree to receive from friends and relatives, when about to enter the hall, a present of something to eat, or to use inside, the first time they compete for the second degree after they have attained the first. If given the first time, it need not be given the second year. These are understood as expressions of the desires of their givers that their friend or relation may attain the degree for which he proposes to strive.

It is estimated by Chinese that as many as three or four thousand men are required to assist in the management of the affairs of the examination, besides the students themselves. The number of candidates usually is from six to eight thousand, who, with the three or four thousand other men necessarily employed, make up the aggregate of the occupants of the two premises, which are separated only by a wall, to some ten or twelve thousand men, enough to constitute a formidable army or a respectable city. Some estimate them to be much more numerous.

The great outside doors of the premises occupied by the officers, as well as the doors of the premises occupied by the students, are shut, locked, and sealed up in a very formal manner as soon as all who are to take any part in the examination exercises have entered. Both egress and ingress at these doors are equally forbidden.

Early on the morning of the eighth, usually before daylight, the calling of the roll is commenced, or the reading over of the names of all the candidates who are entitled to be present at the examination. Each one present is required to take the cell which is appointed for him. During the morning a side door is occasionally opened to allow the bringing in of vegetables and the entrance of men, should there be any who have been detained until that time. No one is allowed to go out.

When the side-doors have been shut for the last time, and the competitors have found their seats, four themes for the essays and the poem are given out, and the students know for the first time what are the subjects on which they are to try their talent at composition. These are selected from the four volumes of the Chinese classic called the "Four Books," by the joint action of the first and second examiners, three being themes for a prose composition and one for a poem. The eager competitors at once begin to ponder the subjects selected and arrange their thoughts. Each alley or row of cells is under the constant watch of men who profess to be anxious to detect any violation of established rules.

1. As soon as any of the essays are finished, they are taken by the proper officer to a body of talented literary men, whose number is said to amount to several tens, and whose business is to examine each essay or poem as soon as offered, to see if it is composed and written out in accordance with the well-understood rules. If there is any violation of these rules, it is at once stuck

by means of paste upon the wall in a public place. The luckless writer may not enter the arena and compete at either of the succeeding sessions for that year. He may be considered as plucked.

2. The essays and poem which are correctly done, as regards form and appearance, are then delivered over into the hands of a body of copyists, numbering perhaps two or three hundred men, whose duty it is to transcribe them with neatness upon other paper, using red ink. The original manuscripts are kept from the inspection of the examining commissioners, in order to prevent, or avoid as much as possible, all chance of their knowing to whom the composition belongs. The writer might otherwise, by means of blots or marks, or some private sign made on the paper, intimate to the commissioners who was its owner, provided there had been any previous understanding to that effect, as the result of bribery. These copyists are employed by Government.

3. These essays and the poem having been transcribed, both the copy and the original manuscript are delivered to a class of scholars, who number one or two hundred men, and whose duty it is to compare copy and original together, to see that there have been no additions or omissions of characters, and no secret marks made on the copy. They work by twos, one looking at the copy, while the other reads the original, comparing them character by character. The characters of the copy must be the same as in the original manuscript, and must be well written.

4. These, if found to correspond with each other, are delivered to a certain officer, who is aided by several assistants. The original, written in black ink, is delivered over to the governor to be kept, not for his inspection. The copy on paper written with red ink is passed along to a class consisting of twelve men of acknowledged literary talent. Each man reads his share. If he considers it well done, he signifies his approbation by putting upon the top or front part of the roll a small red circle. If he considers its literary ability as decidedly inferior, he lays the roll of essays and poem aside. Those marked with a red circle are put into the possession of the prefect, who beats a drum suspended at his office on the premises. This drum is called the "recommending drum," which indicates that an essay and its accompanying poem are recommended to the examining commissioners for their inspection. It often happens that the writer who does well at the first session does quite poorly, or is sick or absent, on the next two sessions, when his manuscripts, however

well written, must be disregarded in making up the final estimate of the merits of the compositions at the close of the third session. The compositions are supposed to be examined, weighed, and approved or rejected on their merits alone. When their respective merits have been decided upon, the original paper in the hands of the governor is torn open, and the name of the writer becomes for the first time known to the commissioners.

Those whose essays and poem are finished are allowed to come out in companies, commencing about the third watch in the morning of the tenth of the month, having spent two days in the examining hall. The doors are unlocked and the seals are broken under a salute of three cannons, the beating of drums, and the playing of instrumental music, all designed to honour those who come out. The doors are then shut, and locked, and sealed, until about daylight, when another company is ready to come out of the arena, and similar tokens of honour attend their exit. About ten o'clock A.M. another company come forth, saluted in like manner. After this time, when any one is ready, he comes out.

Of all the officers and assistants who have been imprisoned inside, only the governor is permitted to come out on the morning of the tenth, after the students have left. He must return in the afternoon or evening, having visited his yamun and attended to his business. All the rest of the officers and the assistants employed inside remain busily engaged in the discharge of their duty.

All those whose essays have not been posted up in public on the wall during the first session, because of some violation of the rules, may enter the premises again some time during the night of the tenth. The calling of the roll and the seating of the competitors commence about the third watch of the eleventh of the eighth month, less than a whole day being allowed for the recess. Doors are sealed, themes are given out, and everything is carried forward very much as at the first session. There are five subjects given out instead of four. The five are taken from five volumes of the Chinese classics, known as the "Five Classics," not from the "Four Books," four being themes for prose compositions and one for a poem. The competitors come out, as from the first session, in companies, under the regular salutes of guns, drums, and music, commencing before daylight on the morning of the thirteenth, and finishing some time in the forenoon. They return to the hall late in the evening of the same day, or exceedingly early in the morning of the next.

The names of the competitors, who are much less numerous than at the first session, are called over on the morning of the fourteenth, seats taken, the doors being locked and sealed up as usual. There are five themes on miscellaneous subjects, and one theme for poetry. The candidates usually are all done with their tasks and are out of the hall some time during the afternoon of the sixteenth of the eighth month, having commenced to make their last exit some time in the morning.

As has been intimated, the examining commissioners select three rolls of essays and poems, one from each of the sessions, which must all belong to the same scholar. They decide upon the literary abilities of as many sets of three rolls as the law will allow them to decide upon as worthy of procuring their masters the coveted rank of Master of Arts *à la Chinois*. At the proper time a list of the successful candidates is made out, the names and surnames being written in very large characters. This list is posted upon the south side of the Drum Tower in the city, thirty or forty feet high from the ground, where it is left for a certain time for the inspection of the public. It is regarded as a very high honour to head this list, or to be one of the three highest names.

The original compositions of the successful competitors are collected together, and prepared for transmission to Peking, professedly for the personal inspection of the emperor. A copy would not be sent, as the manuscript must have the seal upon it which was there when the unwritten roll was received from the clerk of the treasurer's office. All the tolerable blunders, blots, &c. which did not prevent the success of the manuscript in the provincial hall of examination, would become intolerable when transmitted to Peking for reference and preservation; hence they must be all erased or mended, so that the document will present a fair and neat appearance. The singular nature of Chinese writing-paper, and their practice of writing on one side only, makes this "washing and repairing" possible, and comparatively an easy task, which would be impracticable if the essays and poems were written on foreign paper, even if written on only one side of the paper employed. Sometimes, even on Chinese paper, the writing is blotted so badly or so many mistakes are perpetrated, that it requires an immense amount of skill and patience to repair the manuscript and make it look neat. Unless this repairing and washing is done properly, the imperial commissioners would be liable to be severely reprimanded, and perhaps punished by being degraded from their rank. It will not answer for the essay to be left behind at the provincial city, nor will it do to present one at Peking not having a neat and clean appearance.

It often occurs that during the three sessions some persons are taken suddenly ill, and die before the doors are allowed to be opened. In such a case it is contrary to law and custom for the body of the deceased to be carried out of the arena through the large front gates. It must be taken to the back side, or to one of the east or west sides, and passed over the wall. This is not done to dishonour the memory of the dead, but to prevent the front gates from being defiled by the passage of the corpse. It would be considered a very bad omen for a corpse to be taken out through the front gates. Should any of the mandarins suddenly become ill and die during any of the sessions, the corpse might be carried out, after the session is ended, through a small door on the back side of the premises. The presence of a corpse, or passage of it through certain places, is regarded by the Chinese as defiling, and ominous of evil.

Graduates of the second degree are obliged to go to Peking if they wish to compete for the third literary degree (doctor of laws), or "chin-tsz." The regular examination of masters of arts for the doctorship is held once every three years. The competitors who wish to go to Peking on this errand, on presenting themselves for the first trip at the provincial treasurer's yamun with the proper vouchers, formerly received forty-eight taels for the purpose of defraying in part the expenses of the journey. This is designed to encourage the poor scholar who has not funds enough of his own—a present from the emperor. Of late years only half of the sum is received here before starting; the balance is drawn at some place about half way, or after return home, having attended the examination at Peking.

Great are the rejoicings, festivities, and honours in view of successful competition, and the deficiency in means for giving the news by daily papers in China is obviated, in part, by some enterprising individuals having the names of the highest of the list of candidates, before the district magistrate and the prefect, engraved and published on slips of paper, which are hawked about the streets for sale. The list of the successful competitors at the examination for the second degree is obtained by bribery of the clerk of the treasurer's office some time in advance of the placarding in public of the sheets which contain them—unless published as a speculation by the clerk himself, the sale of which is sometimes very great. When first out, it frequently brings as

high as twenty or thirty cash ; but after the list has been exposed on the Drum Tower, the price falls to one or two cash.

The clerks and underlings make haste to write out the names
and the seats, or the numbers of those who stand toward the
highest on the lists of the respective examinations, each on a
sheet of large red paper. This they carry or send, at as early a
period as possible, if not too distant, to the family to which each
belongs, with their congratulations. This is styled "carrying
the information." It is done for the purpose of obtaining a
present from the family.

In the course of a few days after the names of the successful
competitors have become known, the family to which each
belongs gives a feast to celebrate the event. Two or three days
before the feast, a large card of light red paper, inclosed in a
deep red envelope, is sent round to each one of the family relatives, or intimate friends or respected neighbours, whom his
family have decided to invite to the festive occasion, requesting
them to "shed their light" on the entertainment. In due time
the invited guests make their appearance with their present of
money called "congratulating politeness."

At the appropriate time during the festivities, the successful
competitor must worship heaven and earth, as an indication
of his thanks for the honour put upon his family. Afterwards
he must, for a similar reason, worship the ancestral tablets of his
family, and then he must kneel down before his parents, if both
are living, and bow his head down toward the ground three times.
Should one be deceased, his or her tablet occupies the chair which
he or she would have taken if alive. His mother-in-law, or his
own mother, or, if engaged to be married, the mother of his
affianced bride, proceeds to invest him with the red silk scarf,
in the established manner for graduates of the first or second
degree. This is a long strip of red silk, which is placed over
one shoulder and under the other, crossing twice on his breast
and on his back, in the form of the letter X, if he is graduate of
the second degree, and finally tied round his waist as a belt.
If a graduate of the first degree, the strip does not cross twice
on his breast, but is simply put over one shoulder and under the
opposite arm, and is then tied round his waist, having gone only
once over his breast.

On a day appointed for the graduates of the first degree to
appear before the literary chancellor to pay him their respects,
they all rise very early in the morning, in order to make the
customary sacrifice to heaven and earth. Invested in his red

scarf, he now sets off in his sedan for the yamun of the literary chancellor.

Each of the graduates on this imposing occasion is dressed in an outer long dress of light blue silk. His boots are square-toed, and usually made of satin. His cap is not the little skull-cap usually worn, but the larger cap of ceremony, on two sides of which (those which come by his ears) has been fastened a kind of artificial flower, professedly made of gold leaf, but really of brass foil, fastened to a wire. These project up several inches above the cap perpendicularly.

When the time has arrived, all the graduates of the first degree enter the presence of the literary chancellor, and arrange themselves in order before him. As soon as the master of ceremonies gives the word of command, they kneel simultaneously before him, and proceed to bow their heads down to the ground three times in unison. After this important ceremony, which is intended to express their profound obligations to their venerable teacher, they rise to their feet and disperse. Sometimes the officer before whom this ceremony is performed rises to his feet, and, grasping his own hands, inclines his body forward slightly, moves his hands gently up and down, and, as it were, toward the body of graduates before him, repeatedly utters his thanks in a low tone of voice, while they are on their knees and making their bows before him. Such an act on the part of the literary chancellor is believed to be a mark of his humility, and to indicate his unworthiness to receive such honour.

After they have left the yamun of the literary chancellor, they proceed singly or in small companies, as they please, to call upon the prefect, and pay him their respects in a similar manner, upon their knees. They then make similar calls upon their respective literary officers which are subordinate to the literary chancellor, and upon the district magistrates of their respective districts. In case of those graduates who live out of the district in which the prefectural city is located where they have obtained their degree, they must, of course, return to their own district, in order to pay their respects to their respective district magistrates. They must in like manner pay a visit to their principal teachers—that is, those who have in former years taught them the classics, and how to write prose compositions and poems. After this, they call upon their parents-in-law, their relatives on their father and their mother's side, upon their personal and intimate friends, and their respectable neighbours and acquaintances whom they wish to honour.

The graduates of the second literary degree, instead of first calling upon the literary chancellor, as do the graduates of the first degree, are invited to a feast at the yamun of the governor of the province. They have on their shoulders a thick cape. They have the red scarf, the square-toed boots, and the golden flowers, like those of the first degree. After worshipping heaven and earth on the morning of the feast, they proceed to the yamun, and at the proper moment present themselves before the tables professedly laden with rich provisions, of which they may partake, but which are principally quite unfit to eat. According to the popular representation of this feast, it is a ridiculous farce. The treasurer should furnish money to set the tables

A KUJIN, OR LITERARY GRADUATE OF THE SECOND DEGREE.

with a variety of palatable viands, one table for each graduate. In fact, the food provided is miserable in quality and of few kinds, and small in quantity. A table is professedly spread for each, some of the dishes on it being partly filled with food. The rest are filled with sawdust or something which will fill up, the top being covered with paper. Every table is provided with a small plate, wine-cup, and tea-cup, made out of real silver. Each graduate takes his position before a table. At the proper moment, during the time allotted for the feast, the graduates arrange themselves in order before the provincial governor, who may sit or stand as he pleases. At the command of the master of ceremonies, they must all kneel down and bow their heads three times. After this they disperse, to call upon the literary chancellor and the other officers, their teachers, &c. in regard to whom law or custom makes it their duty to call upon for the

purpose of presenting their respects. After a little time has
elapsed, the master of ceremonies calls upon servants to clear the
tables, and, accordingly, men appear and carry the contents to
the homes of the graduates, or to the place where they are
temporarily living, if not resident at the capital of the province,
for which a present of several hundred cash is expected on
delivery. If these articles reach their homes, they are taken
and placed before the ancestral tablets of their family, to show
the departed how their descendants have been honoured. In
the case of those who live at a great distance, doubtless the
provisions furnished by the bounty of the emperor are not taken
home. The difference between the real cost of the feast and the
sum charged or allotted according to law of course is pocketed
by the high officers and their subordinates, who have the handling
of the money and the getting-up of the feast. It is affirmed by
literary men that every graduate of the second degree costs the
emperor about one thousand taels, but that of this sum the
high mandarins and subordinate officials manage to pocket all
but the few taels which are really spent at various times on
his behalf.

A few days before the newly-made masters of arts go to the
feast at the governor's yamun, they are honoured by the reception
of a black silk outer dress or coat, a cape, *a court cap, and a pair
of square-toed boots*, sent from the treasurer, but in the name of
the emperor, and ostensibly paid for by him, but in reality by
the family of the father-in-law. The provision of these articles
is altogether a fine instance of commissariat jobbery. If Government provide cap and boots, none but the very poorest of the
graduates ever think of wearing them, they are so poor and
worthless, while the emperor is charged for them at the highest
rate.

In calling upon their personal teachers, relatives, friends, and
neighbours, the graduate, whether of the first or the second
literary ranks, goes in as good a sedan as his circumstances will
allow, dressed in his suit of ceremony, with cap, flowers, and
scarf. Two men always precede his sedan, carrying each a
bamboo twelve or fifteen feet in length, having toward the
smallest end several yards of red silk entwined in the green
branches. These banners have been presented by friends or
relations as an expression of their joy. There is also a band of
eight musicians who precede his sedan. Close by his sedan
follows a servant or two, who are provided with a large number
of cards. In many of these joyous processions there will be

seen a red screen, borne along by two men. On the two sides are several lucky characters, made of gilt paper, and of a very large size. This screen is a token that the graduate has a father-in-law or mother-in-law living. It is always furnished by the family to which his wife, if already married, or his affianced wife, if only engaged, belongs.

The main streets of the prefectural city, on the days when graduates pay their visits of ceremony, present an animated appearance. Generally there are three days spent at the provincial city in making these formal calls. These processions may be seen going back and forth in the streets, accompanied with music and waving of banners. The graduates seldom sit down at these calls, but pay their respects, and then depart to find other relatives or friends. Sometimes they do not kneel down, but only make the customary salutation of raising and lowering their clasped hands, while they bend their bodies very low, as if bowing towards their friends. On arrival at the house occupied by his parents-in-law, he is expected to kneel down and bow three times before the ancestral tablets of the family, as well as perform the same marks of respect before the parents of his wife, or the parents of his affianced bride, if not already married.

At some convenient time, the graduate, whether of the first or the second degree, is invited to a feast given in his honour at the house of his parents-in-law and at their expense, provided he is married or engaged. They invite such relatives and friends as they please. The honoured one, immediately after his arrival, is led to the place where the ancestral tablets of their family are to be found, before which he kneels and bows three times. He then performs the same act of homage or respect before the persons of his father-in-law and mother-in-law, who sit side by side. After this he sits down to the feast, and drinks three cups of wine, and pretends to eat a little from dishes containing three kinds of vegetables or three kinds of meats. He then refuses or declines to eat any more, soon rises up, and takes his departure, as though he were in great haste and had no time to spare. All these things are done in accordance with established usage on such occasions. Drinking three cups of wine and partaking of three kinds of food are good omens, and refer to the three grades of literary rank—A.B., A.M., and LL.D., or Sewtsai, Kujin, and Chin-tsz, to all of which the happy and ambitious son-in-law would have his admiring and loving parents-in-law understand he is making haste to attain in regular order and without interruption, as men count one, two, three—one, two, three.

Graduates of the second and the higher literary degrees are entitled to erect an honorary tablet, which is usually suspended over the principal outer door of their residence; another is put in the ancestral hall. The one who heads the list of successful competitors for the second degree has a tablet which contains two characters, which to the initiated intimate that honourable fact. The graduates from the second to the fifth name inclusive on the list have certain characters which indicate the fact to those who understand their application and meaning. Those from the sixth to the twelfth inclusive have other characters to denote their relative standing in the class. All who come below the twelfth are included under certain two characters, which are usually black and highly varnished. Besides these letters, which occupy the central portion of the tablet, there is an inscription in much smaller characters stating the name or title of the emperor, the year of his reign, the surname and title of the literary chancellor, and the number and the name of the scholar on the list of graduates. The near family relatives having the same surname, as paternal uncles, or brothers, &c. are permitted to erect a duplicate of this honorary tablet over their doors. Some houses have several of these tablets, erected in honour of different members of their family relatives, over their front doors.

Those who, at the literary examinations of Peking, are graduated of the third rank of scholarship, have terms applied to them when speaking of them, and put on their honorary tablets, which indicate their relative position on the list of the successful competitors. Besides, there is an inscription which denotes the title of the emperor, date of year, title of viceroy, &c. Family relatives on the father's side are also permitted to make duplicates of the tablets, and suspend them as badges of honour or as ornaments to their home.

When a graduate of the first degree has kept up his regular attendance at the examination for the second until he has arrived at about the age of eighty years without being able to attain the much-coveted literary rank, it becomes the duty of the governor to report his case to the emperor. His majesty presents the aged scholar with the title of Kujin, in honour of his long literary struggles. On the tablet which the old gentleman is authorized to place over the door to his residence he must put two words, which indicate that the honour was conferred by

especial favour of the emperor himself.   After the reception of
this title, he may, if he pleases, and has the strength to endure
the fatigues of the trip and the money to pay its expenses, go up
to the capital and compete for the third degree, which, however,
is very seldom done.

There is a still higher literary degree, obtained after an examination before the emperor of the best scholars, of the doctors
of laws.   But it is not worth while to speak at length of this
and other literary examinations of students at the capital.   It is
enough for our purpose to see them begin to climb the ladder of
honour, wealth, and fame.   The successful competitors on these
occasions are sure of immediate, honourable, and lucrative positions as mandarins in the provinces, as members of the Hanlin
College, or as members of some of the Six Boards.

A feast at the expense of the emperor is given at Peking in
honour of the graduate of the third degree who has lived to the
sixtieth year after he became Chin-tsz, LL.D.   Such a man has
lived through one complete cycle since his graduation.   He may
erect an honorary tablet over his door which shall contain the
four Chinese letters which denote the feast in his honour to
which he has been invited by the emperor.   Such a tablet is but
rarely found, and is a token of great longevity.

In the same manner, a feast is given to the graduates of the
second degree who have lived sixty years after their graduation,
if they have not attained to the third degree.   The literary
graduate has four characters indicating the fact put upon his
tablet, and the military graduate has four other words indicating the same honourable fact.   In these various ways does
the emperor honour those who devote themselves to a literary
life.

CHAPTER XVII.

COMPETITIVE LITERARY EXAMINATIONS—*continued*.

ENOUGH assistants and servants are employed in connexion with these examinations to prevent fraud, provided the principals and the subordinates were to be trusted, and were sincerely desirous of carrying out the laws and regulations. But the fact seems to be that the district magistrate, and the prefect, and the literary chancellor, or the imperial commissioners appointed to preside over examinations of candidates for the second degree, are oftentimes anxious to bestow favours contrary to law and justice, as well as their subordinates to receive bribes for violations of the rules on the part of competing candidates. The officers feel they cannot trust their assistants, and the assistants are on the alert for ways and means to deceive the officers, or to wink at the violation of rules in order to benefit certain scholars, whose personal friends they are, or who have bought their aid or silence.

Allusions have been made to certain well-understood regulations, which it is the duty of the door-keepers, servants, and assistants of the officers to see carried out faithfully. If one of the competitors is found whispering with another, if he is detected in copying from or consulting any printed or manuscript volume or sheet which he has taken into the arena with him, or if any such helps are found on his person or in his possession, or if he is seen passing along to another person any written scroll, or if he is seen to use paper different from that provided by the clerk, or if it becomes manifest that he is writing for another to copy, that he is acting an assumed part, &c. it is the duty of some one of the assistants of the presiding officer to seize a certain stamp, and proceed to impress it upon the roll of ruled paper with which the student competitor was provided on

z

entering the arena. This stamping means that the individual
in question has "violated the rules," and after his roll has
been stamped it will not be read and examined, no matter how
good it may be. Nor will the violator of the regulations be allowed
to enter any subsequent examination for that year. Doubtless
many violations of the regulations are connived at by the clerks
and assistants if done by a personal friend, or by one whom it
will be profitable to allow to cheat, especially if a bonus should
have been previously slipped into the hands of any principal
clerk as a proviso lest something should unfortunately occur. In
such cases the culprit is screened, if possible. Of course, if the
violation is noticed by the presiding officer, the roll of the
violator of the rules must be promptly stamped, to save the
honour and the reputation of the examiner.

Some time after the doors have been sealed and locked up for
the day and the students have taken their seats, the following
device is resorted to in order to prevent a certain kind of deception on the part of competitors. About an hour or two after the
themes have been made known, and the students have had time
to arrange their thoughts and have commenced the copying off
of their essays or poem, a man goes round to each competitor's
seat with a stamp, and stamps the paper at the precise place
where the last character has been written, as at the middle of the
eighth line, or the end of the fifth, as the case may be. If no
beginning has been made on the roll of ruled paper, the scroll is
simply stamped on the outside. After this stamp has been
impressed upon his scroll at the place where he had arrived in
writing off his prose composition or his poem, the presiding
examiner is pretty sure that no deception will be practised upon
him, unless aid be received from some sheet or book which has
been smuggled in and consulted ; for at that stage of the proceedings it is usually too early to receive essays or poems written
by confederates within the arena or without it. And unless a
beginning has been already made, and should the roll be stamped
on the outside, any essay or poem thereafter written out in it
will not receive any attention from the examiner and judge.
Suppose that a beginning has been already made on the first
theme in anticipation of this stamping of the roll, and an essay
which had been composed by an accomplice, who could not know,
of course, how the commenced essay began, should afterward be
received in time to be copied off on the ruled paper, the two
parts would be very unlikely to match each other. The style of
the part which was furnished by a confederate would be apt to

differ very much from the style of the part at the beginning, written by the competitor at his seat in the hall. Unless the parts should be so composed as to match each other very well, the examining officer can readily detect any attempt at deception, so far as regards the splicing on to the part above the stamp enough to complete the essay from a composition made outside of the premises or by an accomplice within. It is barely possible that the competitor may have genius enough so to alter and modify the beginning of an essay prepared by a confederate as to have it properly match, or splice on the few lines he may have been able to compose before the paper was stamped. But it is not often that one who is not able to prepare his own essay so as to have it accepted, has genius enough to modify and change that of another man so as to join it on to a fragment of his own composition, in such a manner that both parts shall seem to the practised eye and judgment of those who are on the look-out for discrepancies to have been composed by one person.

It has been already explained that the candidates before the literary chancellor have their seats fixed upon before they enter his yamun to compete for the first degree. The seats are arranged in rows, the rows being numbered with some character in the Millenary Character Classic in regular order. The seats in each row are numbered regularly one, two, three, &c. A slip of paper attached to his roll of ruled paper has the character indicating the row of seats and the number of his allotted seat in that row written or stamped upon it. He must, according to the regulations, occupy this particular seat during all the time that he is in the hall writing his essays and poem. During the session, at any time, the examining officer may send around one or more clerks or assistants to examine the slip on the roll and the seat occupied by the competitor to whom the roll belongs, or is supposed to belong from the fact of its being in his possession, and from the circumstance of his being engaged in writing upon its pages. If the memoranda on the slip correspond with the row and the seat occupied by the candidate, it is taken for granted that everything is right. Should, however, there be any discrepancy in regard to either row or number compared with the items of the slip at any time during the period allotted to the composition of the essays and the poem, it is taken for proof that there is an attempt at deception being practiced, and the paper of the student is summarily stamped with the stamp indicating that the rules have been violated. Any excuse or explanation which may be attempted is regarded only as a corrobo-.

z 2

rative evidence that the person detected is not honest. Should he say, "I mistook the range of seat," laying the blame upon poor eyesight, or haste, or want of attention, he would be answered, "Are you not a scholar, and are you really as stupid as you pretend? If so, there would be no use in trying to compete." This comparing the slips and seats to see if they correspond is called "examination of the marks." Notwithstanding all the vigilance of the examiner and his assistants, even if these officials are desirous of doing honestly their duties, students sometimes devise means to accomplish their ends by changing their seats without detection, and, of course, without exposure and dishonour.

It sometimes occurs that the literary chancellor orders the clerk at the proper office connected with his yamun to have fifty or sixty of the best scholars, according to the lists recommended by the district magistrate and the prefect, to sit in a certain part of the hall during the sessions of his examinations, near which he himself is to be engaged. The others are distributed over the east and west sides of the hall, some of them at a considerable distance from his tribunal. The principal object of this arrangement, while it is professedly intended to honour these men by having them occupy seats near the person of the literary chancellor, is to have them under his personal supervision. In this way he can the more readily detect any attempt at deception on their part, either by consulting sheets of printed or manuscript papers, or by receiving aid in any form from people connected with the yamun directly or indirectly. When these competitors are thus seated under the immediate and watchful eye of the chief, his servants or his literary assistants find it usually extremely difficult to pass to any of their number a scroll received from persons outside of the arena or composed within the premises. Notwithstanding the honour of being thus seated, even honest students generally prefer to be seated in some other part of the arena, as it affords no advantage, and they feel they are under the constant personal espionage of their literary judge. Of course, students who desire to make use of unfair and unlawful means to attain success dislike extremely to be obliged to take their seats at the upper end of the arena, and within speaking distance of the literary chancellor. As these honoured competitors are few in number, and as they may not at pleasure vacate their seats and ramble over the premises, but must remain at their posts, it is competent for the literary chancellor to prevent their communicating with any of the servants or the assistants more than he is pleased to permit, and he may personally inspect all that is done to them or for them, and prevent, if he is sincerely desirous of preventing, the use of unlawful means.

It is affirmed that very often the literary chancellor and the imperial commissioners are bribed to confer degrees upon certain competitors. Sometimes large sums are given in order to corrupt these officials. It is an easy task to arrange such matters with the literary chancellor, if he is willing to be persuaded, for he dwells at the provincial capital for three years, and respectable men may readily gain access to his person. In regard to the imperial commissioners, it is more difficult to gain access to them after their arrival at the capital of the province, for, as has been remarked, they are shut up inside of sealed doors in their temporary residences before they enter upon the discharge of their official duties in the premises allotted for their use during the preparation and examination of essays at the hall. It is the design of the emperor that they shall have no intercourse with the people of the province, lest they should be tempted to do unlawful things. This practical difficulty is often remedied by those who wish to bribe them, as well as by those who wish to prefer some claim for their favour, by sending on messengers with letters and proposals to meet them while several days' journey distant from the provincial city. The stanza or clause of the poem, or the characters which are to be inserted at specified places in the compositions to be made, are fixed upon, and it only remains to be seen whether the commissioner interested in the individual will succeed in getting possession of these compositions, which cannot always be affirmed with certainty.

Sometimes the district magistrate or the prefect, as a matter of favour to a relative, or for friendship's sake, will consent to place at the head of the lists of the candidates they recommend to the literary chancellor names of certain candidates, and frequently they are induced to make certain individuals head their lists, in view of the sum of money which is secured to them in case these individuals actually came out of the arena before the literary chancellor accepted "bachelors." Sometimes, it is affirmed, they dare even to intimate to the literary chancellor the pleasure it would give them, and the obligations under which they would be laid, if certain persons on their list could be deemed worthy of a degree. In such cases, their intimations are understood by the chancellor, and if he is friendly with them, and cannot

advance his own interests in a better way, these persons are
almost sure to become successful competitors. In like manner,
occasionally the high officers found at the provincial city use
their influence with the literary chancellor privately, but in such
a manner that he cannot misunderstand their meaning. He is
generally believed to have no personal objection to making friends
among high mandarins by doing little favours for them which
come in his line of business, or to replenishing his purse with
the voluntary presents of his affectionate and obliged pupils.

Stories are current relating to literary chancellors who were
very strict, and to others who were very remiss. Of a certain
literary chancellor it is related that he was so strict that he
would allow no one but himself in the hall after the themes
had been given out. He actually turned all his assistants and
servants out of the premises, shutting and fastening the inner
doors with his own hands ; but one of his chief clerks managed
to speak with him during the session, and to fasten upon his
garments a paper which had been prepared on the themes given
out by an accomplice, in accordance with a previous understanding. This paper the literary chancellor unwittingly took back
into the arena, where it was dexterously removed from his
clothing by one of the competitors.

Generally speaking, the examining officers are not averse to
receiving bribes to give the preference to certain individuals,
and sometimes they are themselves desirous to confer favours
upon certain candidates to requite an act of kindness received
on a former occasion, or to oblige a friend or relative.

Should either of the commissioners presiding over the examination of candidates for the second degree wish to confer a
degree upon a certain individual, he has only to give him two
or three characters to insert in a specified part of the essay,
and the essay will then be easily recognised. Should the
composition be posted upon the wall for violation of the rules,
the individual would be rejected, and there would be no resource ; or should it fall into the hands of the other commissioner, the individual might not be successful. It would depend
more on its merits.

Nowadays it has become more customary for the commissioners to give the favoured one a line or two of poetry to use
at the end or the beginning, or the middle of his poem, than
to give certain characters to be used according to a private
understanding. A few years since, a very large proportion of
the graduates of the first degree were very young, and it was

said in explanation, that the literary chancellor who presided at the examination when they graduated loved to graduate young candidates. Others, it is said, sometimes carry out the contrary caprice of graduating old men. In all such cases, it is not probable that the selection of the fortunate ones was made according to the merit of their compositions.

It occurs not unfrequently that the chief clerk in connexion with the yamun of the literary chancellor, or some of the high literary assistants who are employed in connexion with the examination of candidates for the second degree, become interested in the success of certain candidates either because they are relatives or personal friends, or because they have been bribed to forward their interests. In such cases they take occasion to recommend strongly certain manuscripts, which they are able to distinguish from all others by private marks. It the examining judge should seem disposed to pass them by as unworthy, they sometimes presume to recommend again and again with great persistence, yet with the exhibition of great humility and respect, the same manuscripts to the favourable judgment of their respected and venerable teacher. At such times he generally at once suspects that there is some private influence being brought to bear; and, provided the manuscripts are not decidedly inferior, and provided the reception of them into the number of approved manuscripts will not interfere with his own private plans and interests in regard to the list of successful competitors, he often consents to look over the roll of compositions again, and concludes to agree that they are worthy. Sometimes a repeated recommendation of the high merits of certain manuscripts, contrary to the manifest judgment of the chief examiner, on the part of his subordinate, would but decide their fate unfavourably, as he might be indisposed to be a party to the success of any secret intrigue in regard to the probable pecuniary profits of which he was not sure of being a partaker. He might also feel that, for the sake of his reputation, he must at once oppose the success of any competitor who, as he believed, had interested one or more of his assistants in a conspiracy in his favour. He must show himself just and impartial in his judgments.

It is a common practice for a student who resides in a country place, and who has money to spare for the purpose, to hire a good scholar who lives in the city, and who has the reputation of being a quick and accurate composer of literary essays and poems, to go into the proper examinations in his name and in

his behalf.   Country students are not usually as talented and as
skilful in literary compositions as are scholars bred in the city.
By hiring a city man, if of good natural and acquired parts, the
countryman is supposed to stand a better chance of success than
though he trusted to his own abilities.   This course is manifestly unfair and unjust to the other candidates of his district ;
for by as much as this hiring a stranger, who is a better scholar
than himself, increases his prospects of success, by so much does
it diminish the chance of the graduation of some one of the
rest.   They generally resist any such attempts to acquire a
bachelorship by personal violence, if threats do not intimidate
the hired man, or by revealing his true character after assembling
in the examination hall.

Those candidates for the first degree who for any reason are
detained from meeting with the rest of their fellows, and competing before the district magistrate or the prefect, and yet are
in season for competing at the regular examination before the
literary chancellor, when they have money which they are
willing to spend in this way, resort sometimes to the following
expedient in order to be able to enter that examination.   They
go to the proper clerks connected with the yamuns of the district
magistrate and the prefect, and bribe them to supply them with
the necessary sets of rolls of ruled paper, on which they proceed to write essays and poems on the themes which have
already been discussed at the examinations which he missed.
These essays and poems are then handed to the clerks, who take
them and mix them up with the essays and poems prepared by
the other competitors in the usual manner and at the proper
time, but which were not regarded very worthy.   The clerks
are also bribed to annex the names of those absentees on the
list of those who really entered the examinations.   In this way
those real delinquents have their names recorded on the list of
candidates recommended to the literary chancellor, and have
also rolls of essays and poems, which may be referred to by the
literary chancellor, should they, while competing in the examination presided over by him, write essays and poems which
rank high.   It may be deemed desirable by him to compare
the essays which they wrote at the other examinations, as
regards style and handwriting, in order to detect attempts at
deception.

Sometimes, in case an undergraduate knows he cannot be
present for some reason at the lower examinations, he engages
a personal literary friend to go into the arena and compete in

his name, doing as well as he can ; or he hires some scholar to go in and write essays in his behalf. On his arrival, his friend or the hired scholar retires, allowing him to take his proper place, under his own name, at the future examinations. He need not pursue the course described in the preceding paragraph, but simply " exchange rolls "—that is, he bribes the clerk or clerks to furnish him the number of rolls of ruled paper required, and to lend the rolls which contain the essays and poem composed in his behalf by his friend or the hired scholar. He keeps these borrowed rolls of manuscript only long enough to copy off the compositions made by his proxy, which he hands into the possession of the clerk or clerks. The copies are mixed up with the other manuscripts, and the original rolls are destroyed or put out of the way. Should he, at a future examination, write approved essays and poems, and should the literary chancellor like to compare those made at the lower and previous examinations, the copies, which of course are in his own handwriting, would be produced for comparison.

Sometimes two students wish to sit very near each other at the examinations, that one of them may be of service to the other. In such cases, one is hired to aid the other because of his ability to compose with celerity and correctness. It is his object to compose the essays and poem for his employer to copy. The nearer they can sit to each other, the less probability will there be of being detected and exposed in any attempts to pass manuscripts back and forth. For example, A and B wish to sit near each other, but they find that their scrolls of paper indicate widely distant seats. One is marked for the eleventh seat of the first row on the east side of the main passage-way in the centre of the hall, and the other is marked for the fourth seat of the fifteenth row on the west side of the passage-way. A tries to make an arrangement with some one whose seat is near the appointed seat of his friend B, so that he may use that seat instead of his own. At the same time, B tries to make arrangements to sit by his employer or friend A. If either can find any one who will accommodate him for friendship or for money, he exchanges his ticket for the ticket of the other ; for, as it has been observed above, should an "examination of marks" be made, the scroll must be found at the place where it is appointed to be, or it is summarily stamped. The men, in effect, simply change seats, the one using the scroll prepared for the other. It is said that sometimes comparatively a large sum of money is paid for the privilege of occupying some conveniently-located seat. The arrangement must be concluded, and the exchange of tickets corresponding to the rolls of ruled paper must be made, before the names of the candidates are called over, and the men are obliged to take their places on the morning of the examination day. It would not be possible to make an arrangement subsequent to that time, as the competitors are required to take their seats as soon as they receive their rolls of ruled paper in exchange for their tickets.

According to law, a man ought to compete only in the district to which he belongs; but oftentimes, in the case of two very populous districts adjoining each other, as at this city, the eastern part of the city belonging to one district, and the western part belonging to another district, students manage to compete in two districts, all in order to increase the chance of success. If the examinations fall on the same day in both districts, a student cannot, of course, be present at both. The course he takes is to have his patronymic, or family name, recorded in the proper offices of the two districts, but with different given or personal names, one of which is his true, and the other an assumed name. In case the examination falls on the same day in both districts, he makes use of only one of his names, of course, going into the examination which he thinks affords the surest prospect of success, hiring some one to go into the other examination for him, or selling out the opportunity to the highest bidder, or allowing a personal friend to take advantage of the opening for his own benefit.

English Universities have a method for the assistance of dullards called "coaching." The assistant who helps the wearied and hopeless graduate on his way to a degree is called "a coach." A similar help in the Chinese examination is called "a horse."

Sometimes an enterprising man, a little before the time when an examination of candidates for the first degree is to commence, prepares a room or building near the arena, and invites a number of talented men to come there and hire out their services to rich candidates who wish to obtain secret aid. The premises are called a "horse-shed" or a "horse-stable," and the men who come there to write essays for their employment are called "horses." Their employers are said to "ride horses." The "horses" are necessarily men of superior gifts at literary composition, and are often graduates of the first or the second degree, who are needy, and willing to do an unjust and unlawful action for a pecuniary consideration. The head man of the horse-shed employs men to act the part of go-betweens, who go round secretly to the rich candidates and try and find out who are willing to pay liberally for literary help. These candidates are brought to the rendezvous for consultation and decision in regard to price for the aid to be rendered and the particular "horses" they are to ride. The man whose service is engaged then lays his plans, whether to go into the examination in person, or remain outside and prepare the essays and the poem. He sometimes tries to get into the arena by hiring a student to stay out, taking his ticket, and assuming his name for the time being, or by finding out a competitor who has his name recorded in two districts, and purchasing from him the privilege of using his name in one. All this is contrary to law, and the guilty parties are liable to be punished with severity in case of detection. The head man always receives a certain percentage, usually about ten per cent., on the sums agreed upon between the horses and their riders. The horses, if detected, are sometimes put in the cangue for a certain number of days, or, if graduates, they may be degraded from their literary rank.

In accordance with established custom, the one who acted as go-between between the rich candidate and his literary "horse," in case the former should succeed at the examination, will expect to receive a certain percentage on the sum agreed upon as pay for the services which he negotiated, over and above what he received at the time of making the contract, if he received any. This is called " turning-round-the-head-cash," referring to cash which is paid after some understood event has transpired, and which requires one to turn round, go back, and receive it. The custom of paying " turning-round-the-head-cash " extends to many other subjects besides those which relate to literary matters. Sometimes these men who sell their services are called by other names than horses, and their services are frequently engaged for examinations before the district magistrate, prefect, and the literary chancellor. It is always understood that, if successful in obtaining a degree by the aid of another, the competitor must pay the one who was his horse ten times as much as he agreed to pay him whether successful or not. The man gives his note of hand, with the signature of some relative or friend as security, to be paid after the close of the examinations. The sum paid for aid at the first examination before the examiners, as district magistrate and prefect, is oftentimes quite small. The nearer the examination for which aid is purchased is to the last one before the literary chancellor, which is generally the decisive one, the higher the sum demanded and promised. Sometimes a particular sum is fixed upon provided the competitor's name should head the list before the lowest two examining officers at their last session, as such a person is almost sure of attaining the degree, in accordance with the established custom.

In examinations of candidates before the imperial commissioners for the second degree, sometimes aid is only procured for the composition of poetry, or for the third or fourth prose essay, the competitor himself having succeeded in preparing the other essays to his liking. Such help is usually hired of those who happen to occupy adjoining cells or apartments, and who have already finished their own tasks, and have time and strength to spare before the doors open and the session closes. It is reported to be seldom practicable for horses outside of the hall to prepare and send in essays and poems to their riders inside to copy. Strange stories, however, are told of compositions made in very fine characters, and written on very thin paper, being smuggled into the hall by being incased in a coating of wax, and put into the water-buckets, which are turned into the troughs or reservoirs which connect with the inside of the hall. These are picked out of the water by accomplices who act as servants or watchmen inside, and conveyed to the owners, whose names or whose seats are known at once to those who understand the private marks on the surface of the wax balls. Of course, the marks being unintelligible to the uninitiated, if these balls should happen to fall into the hands of those officers or servants who are not in the secret, the circumstance would not implicate any assistant, and could not be used as proof against any particular competitor. He would only lose the benefit he might have derived from the use of the contents of his ball.

It is also related that outside accomplices formerly used to contrive to get manuscript essays and poems conveyed to their friends inside the arena by using underground communications, and by sliding the manuscripts up the hollow legs of tables or hollow posts, which connected with a cellar or tunnel, the cellar or tunnel of course connecting with some adjacent building outside the premises. It was necessary in such cases that some person inside the hall should be on the look-out for the appearance of the manuscript, who would convey it to the competitor for whom it was designed.

It sometimes occurs that the competitor at the first and second examinations before the district magistrate and the prefect manages to slip undetected or unchallenged out of the premises after his name has been called, and after he has obtained his roll of ruled paper in exchange for his ticket obtained from the proper clerk, but before the doors are shut and sealed, usually with the connivance of the door-keeper. In such a case, he goes to a convenient place, and prepares his essays and poem on the themes given out, either alone or with the help of friends, using all the helps he pleases to use. The themes are often made known to accomplices or friends outside by servants or literary assistants connected with the premises, who write them on a piece of tile, or on a piece of paper tied to a stone, which is then thrown over the outside wall at a particular place, or the paper is thrust through a crevice in an outside door or a hole in the wall. By preconcerted arrangement, the themes are taken by a confederate and distributed to those who have bribed the clerks to procure them.

Frequent allusion has been made to the assistants, clerks, and servants, who allow themselves to be bribed to aid the competitors by carrying in to them, to copy, sheets of manuscripts received from outside accomplices, or scrolls already written out, on the appointed roll of ruled paper, or by communicating information in regard to the themes given out by the examiner. There is so much of this kind of deception done that there is a regular scale of charges for services in ordinary cases rendered to competitors by these men. For example, the regular bribe for carrying in a paper containing essays and poems written outside for a candidate within, at the first examination before the district magistrate, is said to be four hundred cash ; at the second examination, eight hundred cash; at the third, one thousand six hundred cash ; and at the fifth, six thousand four hundred, doubling the rate at each higher session. Sometimes the magistrate suspects that deception is being carried on in regard to certain persons or a certain class of competitors. He therefore requires them to sit in a more retired part of the premises, or nearer him. In such cases the difficulty of conveying secret dispatches to them is greatly increased. The assistant or clerk who conveys manuscripts to such students expects to receive at least twice as much as though they occupied the seats that would naturally fall to their lot. When the standard of the amount of the bribe for the first examination before any examiner becomes fixed or settled upon for any given year, the charge for any subsequent examination can be readily figured up by doubling that sum for each intervening examination until the number in question is reached. Of course, extraordinary services are paid for at extraordinary prices, such as are agreed upon.

It must be evident that the lists of successful candidates at examinations for the first and the second literary degree furnish no positive proof that the individuals concerned succeeded by their own merit.

There are regular competitory examinations of candidates for military honours in China, conducted much after the same

MILITARY CANDIDATES COMPETING WITH THE BOW AND ARROW.

manner as the examinations for literary rank are conducted. Competitors for the first military degree, a military bachelorship, are examined by the same officials as are literary competitors, but candidates for the second military degree are examined by the provincial governor instead of special commissioners from Peking.

It seems strange to those who are accustomed to Western ideas that common civil officers, who know nothing about the practice of arms, should be deemed entirely competent in China to superintend military examinations, and decide in regard to the relative merits and attainments of the competitors. It seems also very strange that in a land where the use of gunpowder has been known for centuries, no skill in the employment of guns and cannons should be required in candidates for military rank. Skill in archery and great physical strength are deemed of more importance than any other attainment relating to war.

Those who desire to compete for the first military degree are required to present themselves before the district magistrate of the district where they properly belong at the time he appoints. The preliminaries are very similar to those already described for other graduates, but at the first examination before the district magistrate they are exercised in the practice of archery, standing : they are examined in regard to their proficiency in shooting at a mark, each one shooting three arrows. At the second examination before this official they are exercised in the practice of archery on horseback. In like manner they are required to shoot three arrows at a mark, but while the horse is running. At the third examination they are all exercised with large swords, and with heavy stones, and with stiff bows. There are three kinds of swords which they are required to brandish ; one, it is said, weighs 100 pounds, the second 120 pounds, and the other 180 pounds. The stones are also of three different sizes ; one weighs 100 pounds, another 120 pounds, and the other 160 pounds. These they are required to handle according to a certain rule. The bows they are exercised in bending are also of three different degrees of stiffness. It requires the expenditure of 100 pounds of strength to bend the smallest, 120 pounds of strength to bend the second size, and 160 pounds of strength to bend the third size. It is probable that, in fact, the strength necessary to bend the bows, to handle the stones, and to brandish the swords, is considerably less than is indicated by the above figures, illustrating the difference between theory and practice, or between law and custom. No archery is exacted at the third session, but simply bending the bows, and manœuvring and practising with the swords and stones, each man by himself, and each man for himself.

The names of the competitors who do not fail entirely, or come below the lowest standard of merit allowable, or violate some of the well-understood rules of the examination, are paraded in public on large sheets of paper, according to their relative attainments and worth, soon after the close of each session. The one who heads the list at the end of the third examination it is customary for the literary chancellor to graduate. A list of competitors is made out by the district magistrate at the close of his sessions for the literary chancellor to examine.

At the proper time, these military champions pass through three sessions of examinations before the prefect in much the same order, and with the same kind of weapons or instruments, as they have already passed through before their respective district magistrates. In like manner, the prefect causes a list to be made out of the candidates which have been examined before him, which he sends up to the literary chancellor. The head man on the list at the third examination before the prefect is also sure of gradation provided he does only tolerably well before the chancellor.

The literary chancellor has also three sessions before him, which are usually held at his yamun, or he may have them appointed on the parade-ground south of the city, as he pleases. The mode he employs to ascertain the merit of the candidates is similar to the course pursued by the two lower examiners. At the close of the third session, a list of those who are regarded as the most proficient and dextrous, and therefore the most worthy, is prepared. These competitors are required to come into the yamun for a fourth exercise of a literary kind. They are required to copy from memory a certain short military treatise. The literary chancellor can graduate as many men of the first military degree for each prefecture as he can graduate of the first literary degree. The military bachelors, with artificial flowers in their caps and with silk scarves round their shoulders, parade the streets, with banners and with a band of music, in very much the same manner as do the literary bachelors after their gradation. A noticeable difference in the dress of the two classes is that the former always have round-toed boots, while the latter have square-toed boots. They are permitted to wear the button denoting their rank on their caps, but they have no pay and no employment as soldiers unless they enter the ranks of the soldiers. In such a case they have rations, and have the advantage over the common soldier of being able to compete for military employment as officers. Few of the graduates, however, enter the ranks as common soldiers.

The examination for the second degree, or master of arts, of the military bachelors of all the province, takes place at the provincial capital, under the supervision of the provincial governor as chief. He usually has four sessions. The first consists of shooting at a target with three arrows while standing on the ground. The second consists of shooting at a target with the same number of arrows from horseback while the horse is running. The third consists of archery on horseback. The target is three-sided, placed on the ground, and is called "the earth," or the "earthly ball." It is made out of leather, and measures about a foot across each of its sides. The fourth consists of an exercise with the three large swords, the three large stones, and the three large bows, much as in the lower examinations before they attained their bachelorships.

The number of successful competitors for the second military degree for all the province is only about sixty. These men engage with great show and pomp, having banners and music, in the custom of calling upon their friends, to honour them or to receive their congratulations, after they have paid their respects to the higher mandarins, whom law or custom makes it their duty to call upon soon after they have obtained their degree.

There is doubtless considerable bribery employed by the richer class of these military candidates in order to secure a degree, and considerable favour shown at times by the examiners, but not nearly as much as in the case of literary competitors. The trials are more openly conducted than are the trials for literary degrees, and success depends very much on personal skill and physical strength, which are tangible and visible in their developments at the examinations. There is not much room for successful bribery unless there be also a tolerable degree of attainment in the use of the weapons employed.

Those in the different provinces who have attained to the second military degree must go to Peking in order to compete for the third degree. The successful competitors there are always sure of finding immediate employment in the army or navy somewhere in the empire. The unsuccessful competitors, on their return to their own provinces, may, if they please, connect themselves with the body-guard of the provincial governor, and become a kind of personal attendants upon him. They have no regular salary while in this position. After following the governor for three years, they are entitled, according to law, to employment by the Government as military officers of the rank and title of a chiliarch or colonel. In fact, however, it is affirmed, generally only those who are special favourites of the governor, or who have money to spend in the shape of presents, *alias* bribes, succeed, even after the expiration of three years' attendance upon

him, in becoming colonels. Those who use money enough in
the proper, or rather improper, way, need not wait three years
before they are appointed to a command.*

* Mr. Doolittle does not appear to give any account of the competition
for the highest degree of all, and the entrance into the Court of the Forest
of Pencils. Dr. Medhurst says : "The fourth degree follows a very close
examination in the presence of the emperor.   The three newly-made
doctors are summoned in the imperial palace, where they all compose
essays on given themes.   A small number of these are chosen to enter the
Han-lin-yuen, the Court of the Forest of Pencils, or National Institute :
where they reside, most liberally supported and patronized by the emperor,
to prepare public documents, draw up national papers, and deliberate on
all questions regarding politics and literature.   The members of this court
are considered the cream of the country, and are frequently appointed to
the highest offices in the state.   The three principal candidates at this
fourth examination are forthwith mounted on horseback and paraded for
three days round the capital, signifying that 'thus it shall be done to the
man whom the king delighteth to honour.'   The chief of the first three is
one of a million, occupying the most enviable post in the nation, and yet
a post to which all are eligible, and to which all aspire."—*China, its State
and Prospects*, p. 176.

CHAPTER XVIII.

CHINESE ANECDOTES.

EVERY nation delights in recording the wise sayings and the remarkable deeds of its *precocious youth*. The Chinese form no exception. They have wonderful stories to relate about children in olden times, who were wise and gifted above their years. A few of these stories are subjoined. Perhaps it should be first stated that it is sometimes impossible, and very often exceedingly difficult, to render from the Chinese into English a smart saying in such a manner as to do it justice, on account of the play on the sound or the meaning of the words in the original. Some one has said, in substance, that "a pun can no more be translated than it can be engraved."

During the Northern Sung dynasty, which began about 421 and ended 479 A.D. there lived a little boy whose name was Noo. At an early age he was noted for the versatility of his talents and the tenacity of his memory. In studying a book, it is said he needed only to read it over once and then he could repeat it. One day, when he was four years old, a guest remarked in the hearing of the lad that "Confucius had no elder brother." Noo instantly replied, in the language of the Classic, "He took his elder brother's daughter and gave her away in marriage," thus proving that Confucius had an elder brother. The whole company greatly wondered at this extraordinary reply.

In the same dynasty lived a little boy whose name was Kuang. One day, while playing with a company of children, one of them happened to fall into a large earthen jar full of water. All of the other boys except Kuang were too much frightened to render any assistance, and ran away. He, taking a stone, broke the jar, and saved his playmate's life by letting the water escape.

A A 2

Every one who heard the circumstances admired the boy's uncommon wisdom and presence of mind.

In the same dynasty there lived another bright lad, whose name was Yenfoh. While quite small, he was once playing ball with some juvenile companions. The ball lodging in the deep cavity of a post, all gave it up as lost except Yenfoh. He took water, and pouring it into the hole in the post, the ball floated to the surface.

During the after Han dynasty, between 221 and 265 A.D. at the age of seven years, the boy Pa perfectly understood "Spring and Autumn," one of the profound text-books studied by the Chinese, being one of the " Five Classics." On proceeding to study the remaining classics, his father and mother endeavoured to dissuade him, saying, " You are only a little boy; you are not able to study them." He answered, " Yes, I can study them, and have leisure too." He had such extraordinary abilities that he was often called Tsang-taze, after one of the most renowned of the seventy-two disciples of Confucius.

In the time of the same dynasty lived a man named Wan, who at an early age was distinguished for his ready wit. When he was only seven years old, his grandfather was prefect in the country of Wei. An eclipse of the sun occurring the prefect informed the emperor of the fact. The queen dowager inquired how much of the sun was eclipsed. The prefect did not know what to answer, when his little grandson, standing by his side, suggested to him, " Why not say the part of the sun not eclipsed is as large as the moon in the first of the month ?" The old man returned the indefinite reply thus suggested, greatly surprised, and wondering at the quick understanding and ready expression of his little grandson.

In the kingdom of Wei, during the third century, lived two intimate friends, whose ancestral names were Yang and Kung. Kung is the first character of the expression in the Chinese language for *peacock*, and Yang is the first of the two characters which denote the fruit *arbutus*. One day Mr. Kung called to see Mr. Yang, but not finding him at home, called his little boy Sew, a very bright and intelligent lad of nine years, to come and talk with him. In the room were some of the first *arbutus* of the season, provided for the entertainment of company. Mr. Kung, wishing to jest with the boy on his name, pointing to the arbutus, playfully remarked, " I suppose this is a family fruit, a relative of yours ?" Sew immediately rejoined, " I never before heard that the *peacock* was a member of your family !"

In the same country lived a little boy whose name was Lin. One day a friend of his father came to the door of his house, and inquired of Lin, "Is Pehtsin (mentioning the given name of his father) at home?" The lad did not answer, nor did he make the customary bow of respect. The man, surprised, said, "Why do you not make a bow to me?" Lin replied, "I ought, indeed, to make a bow to you; but if you speak to me about my father, using his given name, for what reason should I be polite to you?" According to the rules of Chinese etiquette, using the given name of one's father in addressing his son indicates a lack of good breeding. He should be referred to as the Distinguished Great Man, or the Venerable Gentleman, &c. The little boy meant, "If you are not polite to me in speaking of my father, why should I be polite in speaking to you or in recognising you? You are yourself impolite, why insist on my being polite?"

During the Ming dynasty, which began 1368 and ended 1643 A.D. lived the lad Tapin, who was a youth of uncommon intelligence and propriety. Having studied the Four Books and the Five Classics only once, it is affirmed, he did not forget them. When eight years old, he called on a literary man of high rank, and conducted himself with the self-possession and propriety of an elderly gentleman. His host, pointing to a chair as the subject of an impromptu verse, in Chinese style, giving out the first line, said, "With a cushion made of tiger's skin to cover the student's chair." Tapin, being expected to pronounce the second line, all the words of which were to have certain correspondence to the words found in the first line, immediately answered, "With a pencil made of rabbits' hair to write the graduate's tablet." The gentleman struck the table before him in delight, and rewarded the boy. At the age of thirteen he graduated Master of Arts the second in the list. At an examination in the capital for Doctor of Laws, during the reign of Ching-tik, his name was second among the successful competitors. In a trial before the emperor the same year, he came out number third, and became a member of the Han Lin, the imperial college, at a very early age.

During the southern Sung dynasty (960—1280 A.D.), the famous commentator on the Chinese Classics, Chufutze, when only eight years old, was master of the doctrines of the treatise on Filial Piety. He wrote on the cover, using eight characters, "He who does not comply with this is not a perfect man." While engaged with other boys in juvenile plays, he was accustomed to take sand, and, having arranged it in lines on the ground, like the eight diagrams invented by Fuh Hi and now commonly used in divination, he would then sit down and gaze at them in perfect silence, as though absorbed in study.

In the time of the northern Sung dynasty lived Wang Yooching, who at the age of seven years could compose literary essays with correctness. A certain assistant prefect, who afterwards became prime minister, hearing that the lad's father was a miller, and desirous of trying his genius, one day asked him to pronounce an impromptu verse about the mill. He pronounced without hesitation four lines, which not only were admirable specimens of Chinese poetry, but also indicated the lad's high ambition. The assistant prefect was so delighted that he took the boy home, and allowed him to study with his own children. On a certain day the prefect invited his assistant to dinner. While at dinner he gave out, as the first line of an impromptu stanza, the sentence, "The parrot, though it talks, cannot compare with the phœnix." None of the guests were able properly to match it with a line. On returning home the assistant prefect inscribed it on a flower-vase. Yooching, happening to see it, immediately wrote underneath, "The spider, though skilful, cannot compare with the silkworm." The assistant prefect was greatly delighted, and caused the lad to dress himself in clothing made after the fashion worn by adults, and afterwards addressed him as his "little friend."

The following anecdotes are perhaps as fair specimens as any which can be selected from the history of this people, to show what examples are held up for the imitation and encouragement of the student in his endeavours to pursue study under unpropitious circumstances. It is worthy of notice that the heroes of these stories almost always succeeded in their efforts to acquire literary fame and official employment.

He fastened his hair by a cord to the top of the house when he studied.—In the feudal state of Tsu, during the Chau dynasty, several hundred years before Christ, Sun King was in the habit of shutting himself up in his house when he studied, in order to prevent his mind from being diverted from his books. For the purpose of keeping awake when he was drowsy, he tied one end of a cord to the hair of his head, and fastened the other end to a beam in the top of his house. Whenever he appeared in the streets, the people were accustomed to call out as with one accord, "The teacher who shuts himself up (to study) is coming."

He traced the characters on the sand with a reed.—During

the southern Sung dynasty, Ngan Yangsui, when only four years old, lost his father. His mother, vowing never to marry again, taught her son how to read ; but the family were so poor as to be unable to procure paper and pencils, and she therefore wrote the characters on the sand with a reed, and thus instructed him. The lad was quicker at learning than lads usually are. By reading anything only once he could immediately repeat it. After he arrived at manhood he obtained the third degree. In three examinations at the capital he came off with the very highest honours, and became a member of the Han Lin College.

He studied by the light reflected from snow.—During the Sung dynasty, Sung Kang's family was poor and destitute of oil. In the winter evenings he was accustomed to study by the light reflected from snow. When young, he was regarded as of correct principles, and would not associate with men of unworthy habits. Afterwards he became an officer of the high rank of imperial censor.

He studied by the light of a bag full of glow-worms.—In the dynasty of Tsin, which began about 265 and ended 419 A.D. Che Yin, while only a boy, was very sedate and courteous, as well as a diligent student. In consequence of the poverty of his family he was not able always to obtain oil ; so, during the summer months, he collected a large number of glow-worms in a white gauze bag, and by their light was able to pursue his studies in the evening, as it were lengthening out the day. He afterwards became an officer of a very high rank, and had the title of president of one of the six boards.

He did not open his family letters.—In the Sung dynasty, Hu Yuen, before he had obtained the first degree at the literary examinations, in company with two friends, went to the celebrated mountain of Tai to pursue his studies. He applied himself with great diligence, and ate very poor food. It is said he did not sleep during the night, nor for ten years did he return home. As soon as he saw the two words "peace and health," which were written on the outside of his letters from home, he would throw them aside. He did not open and read them, lest his attention should be diverted from his books.

She cut the web of cloth in order to incite him to study.—During the Chau dynasty (B.C. 1122—255), Mencius, at the age of three years, lost his father. His mother, whose name was Siu, was a woman of distinguished worth and virtue. Mencius went to school, but soon threw aside his books and returned home. His mother was very much incensed at this course, and taking a knife, cut the web of cloth she was weaving, saying, "My son, your desisting from your studies is like my cutting this web." Mencius, trembling with apprehension, returned to school, and studied with diligence; nor did he intermit his literary pursuits until he became a worthy, next in rank to the sage Confucius.

She was grinding the pestle down to make a needle.—In the time of the Tang dynasty (620—906 A.D.), Lei Peh, while yet young, and before he had completed his studies, left school and started for home. On the road he saw an old woman engaged in grinding away an iron pestle. Peh inquired why she was thus grinding the pestle? She answered, "I want to make a needle." He was surprised at her words, and, influenced by them, returned to school, and studied with most assiduous application. He finally became a member of the Imperial College at the capital.

He concealed fire to light his lamp.—Probably between 479— 501 A.D. lived T'su Yung, who, when he was only eight years old, was so fond of study that his parents were afraid he would impair his eyes by his diligence. They therefore forbade him the use of books, but he would not obey them. Constantly he hid fire until his parents had retired to rest, when he would light his lamp and study. He took his clothes and the coverlet of his bed, and hung them up over the window of his room, lest the light, escaping through it, should be seen by some one of the family. In this way his name became very widely celebrated as a scholar. At home and abroad the people called him the "little sage." At the age of twelve he became a high officer of Government, and was afterwards promoted to the Superintendency of the Offering of Wine.

His curtains retained the traces of the smoke of his lamp.—In the Sung dynasty, Fan Shun Jin day and night was diligent in study. He was in the habit of placing his lamp within the curtains of his bed, and thus study until past midnight. Afterward he became a very distinguished officer. His wife preserved the curtain, which at the top was sooted over as black as ink. Occasionally she would bring it forth, and show it to her children and grandchildren, saying, "Your father and grandfather, when he was a boy, was very studious. Here are the marks of the smoke of his lamp."

He used a round stick of wood as a pillow to prevent deep sleep.—During the Sung dynasty, Sie Ma Wan, when a boy, whether he was moving about or at rest, in all his conduct was dignified and decorous, like a perfect old gentleman. At seven years of age he heard an explanation of the volume called "Spring and Autumn." He was very much pleased, and, having returned home, conversed with the members of his family in such a manner as to show that he understood its principles. He was accustomed to use a round block of wood for a pillow. When he became sleepy and fell into a doze, this pillow would roll a little and awaken him. Once awakened, he would apply himself to his studies again with vigour. He finally became an object of worship, his tablet being placed in the temple of Confucius.

He was stimulated by the pomp of a magistrate to make the study of books his calling.—In the time of the Sung dynasty lived Chang Yih. It so happened that when he was young his parents were poor, and he was not even taught to read. He was obliged to hire himself out to work for others. One day he suddenly heard the heralds of the district magistrate proclaiming his approach, and clearing the road for him to pass. His mind was greatly excited and interested, and he asked, "How did this man arrive at such a place of dignity and honour?" "By the study of books," was the answer. From this time he put forth all his energies in the acquisition of knowledge. He afterward received instruction from the famous commentator Ching. He became his disciple, and subsequently taught and handed down the deep and abstruse doctrines of his master. Ching used to speak to others in this manner: "In my old age I have begotten two children"—referring to his disciple Yih and his own son I-Teen.

He lived on vegetables, and on gruel made of coarse rice.—In the same dynasty, Fan Chung Yen, when a young man, lodged with a friend in a Buddhistic monastery, situated on the Long White Mountains. They pursued their studies together. They made congee, or a thick kind of gruel, out of two measures of coarse rice or millet, or (as some explain the original) out of unshelled rice, by boiling it in water, afterwards pouring it into a vessel, where they let it stand over night. By morning it had congealed. They then cut it with a knife into four pieces. Morning and night they ate two pieces. They took ten or more of a certain vegetable, resembling onions or chives, and, having cooked them, ate them. They lived in this way for three years. Afterwards Chung Yen became a graduate of the third degree at the examinations, and was promoted to the rank of President of the Board of War. After death he had an honorary title conferred on him.

He chiselled a hole in the partition to get the light through.—In

the Han dynasty, which began about 205 B.C. and ended about
25 A.D. lived Kwang Hung, who was very indigent. Though
very fond of books, he was destitute of the means of purchasing
oil. His neighbour in the adjoining house had candles, but the
light could not penetrate through the wall. Hung therefore
made a hole in it, in order to procure rays of light by which he
could prosecute his studies. In the city a wealthy man, whose
surname was Great, had a large number of books. Hung was
anxious to work for him, though not for the purpose of receiving
wages ; he only desired the privilege of reading the rich man's
books as his pay. Mr. Great was so much interested in the
proposal and in the man that he gave him some of his books
as his wages. Hung became a very learned man, and finally
obtained the office of prime minister.

He cast an iron ink-slab as an index of his resolution.—
During the Sung dynasty lived a literary man named Sang Wi
Hang, who was very ugly-looking, being deformed. His body
was remarkably short, and his face very long. He would often
look in a mirror, and, wondering at his odd appearance, say,
" A man seven feet high would not have a face a foot long."
His essays were frequently selected as worthy of procuring him
the third degree at the examinations ; but when the judges
knew his name they erased it from the list because the character
for it, which meant " mulberry," was of the same sound as the
character for " funeral." Some friends of Wi Hang advised him
to turn his attention to some other pursuit, but he caused an ink-
slab to be made of iron, and, showing it to them, said, " When
by grinding my ink I have made a hole through this ink-slab,
then I will change my calling." He afterwards graduated at the
head of the class which obtained the third degree, or Doctor
of Laws.

The Chinese have a favourite proverb that " of the hundred
virtues, filial duty is the chief." There is, perhaps, no maxim
more early and more carefully instilled into the minds of the
youth of both sexes among this people than that of implicit
obedience to parental authority. To illustrate the nature and to
inculcate the importance of this virtue or duty, as well as to
indicate the rewards which attend its performance, seems to be
the object of a small book called " Twenty-four Examples of
Filial Piety." It is published with coarse wood-cuts, twenty-
four in number, each story being illustrated by a picture of its
hero engaged in the act commemorated. Some editions, besides
the pictures, have a piece of poetry relating to the incident,

giving other particulars, and making what the Chinese deem suitable reflections. The incidents related in this little volume have probably influenced in no small degree the minds of the Chinese youth. Teaching by historical example is always interesting and impressive, and this book illustrates, by examples drawn from ancient Chinese history, the meaning of the popular maxim above quoted; for, incredible as it may appear, the Chinese generally regard the examples given in this book as real facts, as actual occurrences. They are loth to admit that there may have been an exaggeration or misunderstanding of the truth. Are not the incidents related to be found in the history of China? and, if recorded in the history of the nation, they must be true!

A translation of some of these notable examples of filial devotion will be given, with occasional remarks or explanations. Different editions, while agreeing in the main, have various discrepancies in the narration of particulars about these ancient worthies. Where such variations occur, the edition which seemed to give the best story has been followed.

The filial devotion which moved heaven.—Yu Shun, the son of Ku Lau, had a very filial disposition. His father was stupid, his mother depraved, and his younger brother proud. Shun cultivated the Leih hills. He had elephants to plough for him, and birds to weed for him. In such a manner did his filial devotion influence heaven! The Emperor Yaou heard of him, and sent nine of his sons to serve him, and gave him two of his daughters in marriage, and finally resigned the throne to him.

These events, according to Chinese chronology, transpired more than 2,200 years before Christ. It is elsewhere stated more fully that Shun suffered much from the enmity of his younger brother, and from the harshness of his parents. His father commanded him once to go down into a well, and then his brother threw large stones down. At another time a granary was set on fire when he was in it. But he escaped without injury from his many perils. He laboured with all his ability either on the farm, or in fishing, or in burning earthenware. He continued to reverence and obey his parents, though they did not love him. At length, assured of the rectitude of his conduct, he invoked heaven with tears. Heaven was moved by his sincerity. The elephants and the birds volunteered their services, the former in rooting up the ground with their probosces, and the latter in exterminating the weeds with their bills. The emperor having learned his ability to govern his household by

means of two daughters sent to be his wives, as well as by the
concurring testimony of nine sons sent to be his servants, hence
inferred his ability to govern the nation. Accordingly, he
resigned the empire to him rather than to any of his own
children. The example of Shun in obeying his parents is
declared "worthy of being handed down to posterity through
myriads of ages."

She bit her finger, and it pained his heart.—During the Chau
dynasty, Tsang Tsan served his mother very obediently. He
often went to the hills to get wood. Once, when thus absent,
some guests came to his house, and his mother knew not what to
do. She was expecting Tsan; but he not arriving, she bit her
finger. Suddenly his heart was pained, and, taking the wood
on his back, he returned home. Kneeling down before his
mother, he inquired the reason of her perplexity. She answered,
"Suddenly some guests came, and I bit my finger to arouse
you."

According to Chinese etiquette, it is improper for a female to
receive male guests, and wait upon them herself. In this case
the son, whose place it was to meet and entertain company, was
absent, and his mother induced him to return home by gnawing
her finger. The idea is, that he was so filial, and loved his
mother with such tender devotion, that he sympathized with her
grief of mind, the pain in her finger being felt in his heart. The
hearts of mother and son are mutually affected, one influencing
the other in the same manner as the amber draws the small
strands, and the loadstone attracts the slender needle. From
the remotest period sages have been able to control their dispo-
sitions, and in the deepest silence have revolved their actions as
in a breath. The moving influence that such minds have on
each other, the generality of men cannot understand. The de-
votedness with which they serve their parents, and the respect
with which they cherish them, who can comprehend? Behold
how perfect a medium between mother and child is filial piety.
This youth afterwards became one of the most illustrious of the
disciples of Confucius, and author of one of the "Four Books"
studied by Chinese pupils.

He furnished his parents with deer's milk.—During the Chau
dynasty there was a man named Yen, whose disposition was
very filial. His father and mother were old, and troubled with
sore eyes. They desired to obtain some deer's milk to use. Yen
clothed himself in the skin of a deer, and, going far away into
the mountains, entered into the herd of deer and obtained some

milk, which he gave his parents. The hunters saw him in disguise, and desired to shoot him with their arrows ; but Yen explained the circumstances of the case, and thus escaped.

This narrative is accompanied by a cut representing Yen with a fawn's skin on his back, in the act of disclosing his character and explaining his object to a couple of hunters. It would seem that he endeavoured to imitate on all-fours the appearance of a fawn. How fortunate that the hunters did not shoot the supposed deer with their deadly arrows, for, had that mournful event occurred, his aged parents would not only have failed to obtain the milk with which they hoped to cure their sore eyes, but posterity would also have been deprived of the wholesome influence of this impressive example of filial affection. It is to be deeply regretted that no account is given in the records of history of the effect of deer's milk in this case of sore eyes. Still, this omission ought not to detract from the praise due to Yen, for he performed his part most devotedly and most successfully. Though over two thousand years have elapsed since these events occurred, one with a lively fancy can imagine how the faint echo of the fawn-like cry, " Yew, yew," reverberated in the deep forest, for it is affirmed that the hero closely imitated the cry of the fawns while searching for the tracks of the deer.

He put the oranges in his bosom to give his mother.—In the time of the after Han dynasty, Luh Tseih, when he was six years old, went to Kew Keang to see Yuen Shuh. Shuh brought out some oranges and gave him. Tseih hid two of them in his bosom. When about to return home, while he was bowing and taking leave of his host, the oranges fell to the ground. Shuh said to him, " Do you, sir, while my guest, conceal oranges in your bosom?" Tseih, kneeling down before him, answered, " My mother loves oranges very much. desired to give them to my mother." Shuh greatly wondered at this reply.

Shuh and the father of Tseih were officers of high rank. This incident occurred during a visit of the boy in the family of his father's friend. Its interest consists in the filial desire cherished by a son only six years old to contribute to the enjoyment of his mother.

He fed the musquitoes to satiety on his blood.—During the Tsin dynasty, Wu Mang, when only eight years old, served his parents very dutifully. The family were so poor that they had no musquito curtains to their beds. Every summer, at night, the musquitoes were very numerous, piercing the soft flesh. Mang allowed them to feed without restraint on his blood till they were satisfied. Although exceedingly numerous, he did not drive them off, fearing that, leaving him, they would go to his parents and bite them.

Maug is represented as lying on a bed, a passive victim for the bloodthirsty musquitoes. What a *feeling* instance of filial duty! How profoundly must he have been affected by the restlessness of his parents, as they, stung by the musquitoes, tossed from side to side. How courageous must have been his little heart to invite and sustain the attacks of so many enemies; for, it is said, he went early to bed, hoping that the musquitoes would become satisfied before his parents should retire. A Chinese poet represents him to have discoursed thus when he felt their bills: "I have no dread of you, nor have you any reason to fear me. Although I have a fan, I will not use it, nor will I strike you with my hand. I will lie very quietly, and let you gorge to the full." History does not state what effect his filial devotion had on the minds of the musquitoes.

He slept on the ice to obtain the carp. — During the Tsin dynasty, Wang Liang, at an early age, mourned the death of his mother. His stepmother, Chu, did not like him. In the presence of his father she was repeatedly finding fault with him, and consequently she lost the affection of his father. She was fond of eating fresh fish, but in the cold winter time the rivers were covered with ice. Liang took off his clothes, and went to sleep on the ice to procure the fish. Suddenly the ice opened of itself, and a couple of carp sprang forth. He seized them, and, returning home, gave them to his mother. His neighbours wondered at the fact, and admired him. His filial affection had caused what had taken place.

This remarkable instance of filial devotion is represented by the picture of a lad apparently asleep on the ice, and of a brace of fish with their heads just protruding above it. It is a little surprising that, if his body was so warm as to melt the ice at a distance from it, so as to allow the fish to jump out, it should not also thaw the ice under him, thus endangering his precious life, or, at least, giving him a cold bath by falling into the water. But an answer entirely satisfactory to the sincere disciples of Confucius is ready to all sceptical objections or curious questions: Heaven, moved by his filial love, preserved him, and enabled the fish to come forth. A poet has beautifully said, "A thousand ages cannot efface the remembrance of the crack in the ice, nor obliterate the fragrant traces of so worthy an action."

On account of his mother he buried his child.—During the Han dynasty, Ko Keu, whose family were very poor, had a child three years old. Keu's mother usually took some of her food and gave to the child. One day he spoke to his wife about it, saying, "We are so poor that we cannot even support mother. Moreover, the little one shares mother's food. Why not bury this child? We may have another; but, if mother should die, we cannot obtain her again." His wife did not dare to oppose. Keu, when he had dug a hole more than two feet deep, suddenly saw a vase of gold. On the top of the vase was an inscription, saying, "Heaven bestows this gold on Ko Keu, the dutiful son. The officers shall not seize it, nor shall the people take it."

In the picture, the wife, holding the little one in her arms, stands looking on, while the father digs what he intends to be the grave of his living child. It seems strange that the Chinese should so plainly teach that heaven rewards one who, ignoring the affection of a father for his child, and mindful only of his duty as a son, deliberately plans murder, and proceeds to commit it, till supernaturally prevented. "The end justifies the means," say some. This example illustrates, perhaps as forcibly as any of the twenty-four, the exceedingly eminent position which affection for one's parents sustains among the virtues cherished by this people.

He fanned the pillow and warmed the coverlet.—During the Han dynasty, Hwang Hiang at nine years of age lost his mother. His mind was so constantly and so intensely occupied in thinking of her that the neighbours praised him as very filial. Employing himself in assiduous and fatiguing work, he served his father with perfect obedience. In summer, when the weather was hot, with his fan he cooled his father's pillow and bed. In winter, when the weather was cold, with his own body he warmed his father's coverlet and mat. The prefect Tein presented him with a banner as a token of distinction.

A piece of poetry referring to this example of filial piety has been translated in prose in the following manner : "When the heat of summer made it difficult to sleep quietly, the lad knew what would be for the comfort of his venerated parent. Taking a fan, he slowly moved it about the silken curtains, and the cool air, expanding, enveloped and filled the pillow and the bed. In winter, when the snow threatened to crush in the roofs, and the fierce winds shook the fences, and the cold penetrated to the bodies, making it hazardous to unloose the girdle, then Hiang warmed his father's bed, that he might not fear, because of the cold, to enter the place of dreams."

The bubbling fountain and the leaping carp.—In the Han
dynasty, Kiaug She served his mother very dutifully. His wife
Pang obeyed her with even greater assiduity than he. Their
mother loved to drink the water of a river distant from the
house six or seven li. Pang was in the habit of going after it
to give to the old lady. She was also exceedingly fond of
minced fish, and, moreover, did not like to eat it alone. Husband and wife managed, though with great expense of strength,
to provide her with the fish, and she always invited in a neighbour to eat with her. By the side of the house suddenly there
bubbled forth a spring, the water of which tasted like the river
water, and every day a brace of carp leaped out, which they took
and gave their mother.

The cut represents two ladies seated at a table enjoying the
fish, while the son and the daughter-in-law stand by in the most
respectful manner, ready to wait upon their dear mother and her
guest. It would seem that they never tasted of the fish. Filial
piety among the Chinese requires compliance, without displeasure
or the exhibition of reluctance, with the wishes or commands of
the parents. On account of serving their mother thus dutifully,
though she was unmindful of their comfort and appetites to a
very unreasonable degree, Heaven rewarded She and Pang with
" the gushing fountain and the leaping carp." This and several
other of these examples of filial duty, however, appear to be
calculated to teach that Heaven approved the conduct of the
parents as much as of the children.

With sports and gaily-coloured garments he diverted his parents.
—In the Chau dynasty, the venerable Lae obeyed his parents
very dutifully. He provided them with the sweetest and most
delicate food. When he had arrived at the age of seventy years,
still he did not call himself old. He was accustomed to dress
himself in clothing variegated with five different colours, and
would act like a little child, playing by the side of his parents.
He would also take a pail of water, and, while going up into
the house with it would pretend to slip, and, falling down to the
ground, would cry like a child. He did these things in order
to amuse his parents.

According to Chinese notions of politeness, one must not
represent himself as old in the presence of his parents, or even
while they are living, lest the remark should excite in them
unpleasant reflections, thinking, " If our son is old, how much
more are we !" It is said that Lae's parents were peevish and
fretful ; consequently, in order to please them, though he was

seventy years old, and had lost almost all his teeth, he called himself their little boy, dressed in garments which, both in regard to fashion and gaudy colours, were worn only by children, adopted boyish manners, and indulged in childish sports.

Hearing the thunder, he wept at her grave.—In the country of Wei, Wang Shwai served his parents very dutifully. His mother, while living, was exceedingly frightened whenever it thundered, and, having died, she was buried in the hilly forest. Afterward, when there happened wind and rain, and he heard the noise of Hoheang rumbling and thundering along, he immediately ran to the grave, and, reverently kneeling down, wept, saying, " Shwai is here, dear mother, do not fear."

Hoheang is the name of the female demon or goddess who manages the chariot of thunder. Shwai refused to take office because it would interfere with his frequently visiting the tomb of his mother in the forest. When he came to the passage in the Book of Odes, " Alas ! alas ! my parents have borne and nourished me with much trouble and care," he always read it three times, each reading being accompanied with a gush of tears. His pupils often took the precaution to tear out this passage from the book, in order to prevent their teacher from being so deeply affected.

He wept by the bamboos, and they produced sprouts.—In the Tsin dynasty, Mang Tsung, when young, mourned the death of his father. His mother, when aged, was taken very sick. During the winter season she wanted some bamboo shoots made up into soup to eat, but Tsung had no means to obtain any. Finally, he went into the bamboo forest, and, grasping a bamboo with his hands, burst into tears. Such filial devotion moved Heaven and earth, and in a little while the earth opened and shot forth several bamboo sprouts. These he took, and, returning home, made soup, which he gave his mother. As soon as she had finished eating it she became perfectly well.

It is said that, previous to this filial conduct of Mang Tsung, the bamboos did not put forth their sprouts till spring, but that, having begun to do it for the benefit of his mother in the winter time, they have kept up the laudable practice until the present time. It should be remarked that they continue to grow as late in the spring as they did formerly, notwithstanding they sprout so much earlier in the season than they did before his day. Taking this view of the subject, it is but just that the Chinese should celebrate the praises of Tsung, who thus not only cured his venerable parent with his soup made of bamboo sprouts, but influenced Heaven and earth to cause that vegetable to shoot forth some months every year sooner than it was in the habit of doing. Behold the power of a single act of sincere filial piety !

CHAPTER XIX.

ESTABLISHED ANNUAL CUSTOMS AND FESTIVALS.

BEFORE describing the principal annual customs and festivals observed at this place and vicinity, a few preliminary observations will be made relating to the yearly periods which among the Chinese are regarded of very great importance. The customs noticed are performed at the same time every year on the recurrence of the period or term used to denote certain epochs in the season, or on fixed days of the month.

A Chinese year contains thirteen or twelve months. In five successive years there are seven intercalary months. There is no distinct name for each month. A month has always twenty-nine or thirty days. Every year has four seasons, each season being divided into six periods, named *chăik* and *khé*. The word *chăik* signifies a joint, and the word *khé* breath. The seasons are divided in the following manner :—

Spring.— 1st chăik, called "commencement of spring."
　　　　1st khé, 　,, 　"rain water."
　　　　2d khé, 　,, 　"excited worms."
　　　　2d chăik, 　,, 　"vernal equinox."
　　　　3d khé, 　,, 　"pure and clear."
　　　　4th khé, 　,, 　"grain rain."

Summer.—1st chăik, called "commencement of summer."
　　　　1st khé, 　,, 　"small fall."
　　　　2d khé, 　,, 　"bearded grain."
　　　　2d chăik, 　,, 　"summer solstice."
　　　　3d khé, 　,, 　"small heat."
　　　　4th khé, ·,, 　"great heat."

Autumn.—1st chäik, called "commencement of autumn."
   1st khé, ,, "gathering heat."
   2d khé, ,, "white dew."
   2d chäik, ,, "autumnal equinox."
   3d khé, ,, "cold dew."
   4th khé, ,, "descending of frost."

Winter.—1st chäik, called "commencement of winter."
   1st khé, ,, "small snow."
   2d khé, ,, "great snow."
   2d chäik, ,, "winter solstice."
   3d khé, ,, "small cold."
   4th khé, ,, "great cold."

In the course of fifteen or sixteen days after "great cold" comes the beginning of spring, which "joint" has been mentioned.

It is said that one of the rules observed by the imperial calendar-makers is never to allow the joint of the winter solstice to occur either in the tenth or the twelfth month. When it falls very near the last day of the eleventh month, then the next year must be an intercalary year.

The Chinese seem very proud of their system of "twenty-four solar terms," as some one has dignified the chäik and the khé; they often ask whether, "on the other side," foreigners have any "joints and breaths," as the Chinese have "on this side?" When told that the system adopted in Western lands is not similar to the system in use in China to denote the months and the changes of the seasons, &c., they appear to pity the Western barbarians for coming so far behind the inhabitants of the "Middle Kingdom" as to be destitute of the "twenty-four joints and breaths."

Nature, according to the Chinese astronomers or philosophers, must have been organized by the application of a singularly strict rule if once in every fifteen or sixteen days there is a definite and regular change of weather, which can be defined and described from year to year, and from dynasty to dynasty. Western observers of the operations of Nature have come to the conclusion that, on or about the two equinoxes and the two solstices, great and sudden changes of weather may be looked for. The Chinese have not only settled on these four periods concurrently with foreigners, as four of the principal "joints" of Nature, but have discovered four others, and sixteen subordinate "breaths" of Nature, which, they affirm, are influenced more or less by the action of the eight joints. Are not the

Eastern philosophers wiser and more profound than the Western philosophers in their observations and conclusions? They manifestly think they are more wise and profound as far as the "twenty-four joints and breaths" are concerned.

Some of the Chinese profess to believe that they can distinguish the days on which these "joints" and "breaths" fall by the evidence of their own personal feelings, without a reference to the calendar. It is customary for wealthy old people, and, in fact, for some persons of all ages and classes, when they can afford the extra expense, to eat some particularly refreshing and invigorating food on the recurrence of these twenty-four solar periods, as chicken-broth, or some tonic, as the liquor of ginseng steeped in hot water, or some other strengthening or stimulating medicine or food. It has passed into a kind of adage that "on the occurrence of the chăik and khé one must eat something strengthening." Many seem to imagine that the occurrence of any of these "joints and breaths" is really a very trying time for people in poor health. The design of eating "something strengthening" at such a period is to fortify the system against any unfavourable and unhealthy influences which may proceed from changes in the weather at these times.

On the day preceding the solar term called "the commencement of spring" occurs a public procession in honour of spring. On some years it falls in the latter part of the twelfth month; on other years it occurs some time in the first part of the first Chinese month. For that day the prefect takes precedence of all the higher officers in the city, although there are some six or eight mandarins of higher rank. In accordance with the customs relating to that single day, should either the viceroy, or governor, or Tartar general, or the literary chancellor happen to meet the prefect in this vernal procession, he would be obliged to yield the place of honour to the latter. Such is the theory; but such a yielding on the part of a high mandarin to a lower one seldom or never takes place, from the simple reason that the higher officials on that day keep at home, not daring to venture abroad, lest they should meet the prefect! It would not be seemly, in the estimation of the Chinese, for the greater in rank to stand on one side or stop respectfully by the side of the street while the less rides by in the centre of the highway, the observed and the honoured of all.

The prefect on this day is attended by the marine inspector and the two district magistrates, and by a large number of well-dressed citizens. The officials proceed in open sedans, and their attendants go on foot in pairs, carrying each a large bouquet of artificial flowers. The officers are dressed in their official robes, and have a band of music preceding them, with a retinue of servants bearing tablets. If they have any umbrellas of state, or garments which have been received as presents from "ten thousand of the people," as tokens of their confidence and love, they are sometimes brought forth and carried in this procession.

In the procession, a paper image of a domesticated buffalo, as large as life, is carried. The paper, which is pasted on a frame-work, consists usually of five colours—red, black, white, green, and yellow, representing the five elements of nature—metal, wood, water, fire, and earth. Besides this paper buffalo, which is carried by several men, a live buffalo is led along in the procession for a part of the distance. There are also several very small images, made out of clay, of a buffalo, which are carried in the procession.

This procession of officers, &c., after passing round through the principal streets of the city, marches out of the east gate to a certain temple or pavilion, where the prefect worships the approaching spring, or, according to the expression often used relating to this official act, "receives the spring." In-cense, and candles, and wine are placed on the altar of spring in the temple, before which he kneels down thrice and knocks his head nine times. The paper image is here destroyed or burned up, and the clay images are broken to pieces. The procession in due time re-enters the city. The living buffalo is butchered, and divided among the officials resident here, the head always falling to the viceroy.

The marine inspector toward evening comes out of the south gate with his attendants, all well-dressed, walking two by two, each having a bunch of flowers, and preceded by an umbrella of state, and passes along the main street leading to the river. In this procession, in the southern suburbs, there is no image and no buffalo. The marine inspector sits, as the Chinese say, "like an idol," in an open sedan—that is, motionless, grave, and dignified The procession passes along at a quick pace, and is not an unpleasing exhibition. It is much unlike a common official retinue, or an idle procession, which always has a large proportion of dirty and ragged men or boys. Here every one is dressed in dark-coloured silk or broadcloth garments, or in fur, with an official or red-tasseled cap.

Many families of this place perform a ceremony in their

homes, which is called "receiving the spring," on the same day that the prefect presides in the public procession.

The celebration of New Year's commences very early on the morning of the first day of the new year. Preparations relating to these festivities have all been made previously, a description of which will be found where the annual customs relating to the latter part of the twelfth month are described.

The festivities connected with New Year's, as observed generally in every respectable family, divide themselves into five parts—1. The sacrifice to heaven and earth; 2. The worship of the gods and idols belonging to the family; 3. The worship of deceased ancestors; 4. Prostration before living parents and grandparents, &c.; and 5. The making of New Year's calls.

The sacrifice presented to heaven and earth, usually called "presentation of rice on New Year's," is the first thing done on New Year's morning, commencing oftentimes as early as four or five o'clock. The adults of many families do not retire to rest on the last night of the old year. The table spread with offerings to heaven and earth is usually placed in the front part of the principal reception hall. On it are put a bucket of boiled rice and five or ten bowls of different kinds of vegetables, ten cups of tea, ten cups of wine, two large red candles, and three sticks of common incense or one large stick of a fragrant kind. In the wooden vessel containing the rice are stuck two small branches of cedar or some flowers, and ten pairs of chopsticks here and there around on the surface. On the chopsticks are placed two large sheets of certain kinds of mock-money, one representing gold and one representing silver, only used on New Year's rice, and on the top of this is placed mock-money of another kind. On one of the chopsticks is suspended, by a red string, a copy of an almanac for the current year. A few of each of five kinds of dried fruit are scattered around under the mock-money on the surface of the rice. Near the centre of the table is always placed a plate or bowl full of the loose-skinned orange. When everything is arranged, fire-crackers are exploded not far distant, often in the street in front of the house or at the door.

The head man of the family now comes forward and kneels down in front of the table, and bows his head toward the ground three times, holding one or three sticks of lighted incense in his hands. On rising to his feet, he places the incense in the censer on the table. This ceremony is designed to express the obligations of the family to heaven and earth, and their dependence

upon them for protection, life, and success. At the conclusion
fire-crackers are exploded, and the common kinds of mock-money
are burned. The plate of oranges and the bucket of boiled rice
are usually left undisturbed for a day or two.

By this time it is nearly or quite daybreak, and preparations
are made to worship the family gods and goddesses. Several
bowls of rice and plates of vegetables, vermicelli, and fruits, with
three cups of tea and three cups of wine, are placed before them
on a table: incense and candles are also lighted. Some families
do not use the vegetables and the rice, while others do not employ
tea or wine at this service. The head of the family kneels down
before the images, and performs in very much the same manner
as he did before "heaven and earth." At the proper time the
mock-money is set on fire and consumed.

It now becomes the duty of the family to pay the customary
tokens of respect and remembrance to its deceased ancestors,
represented by the ancestral tablets. A quantity of things very
much like those which have been paraded before the gods is put
before the tablets. These are worshipped by kneeling, &c. in a
similar manner.

MEN SALUTING EACH OTHER AT NEW YEAR'S.

The performance of another important ceremony now takes
place. The surviving heads of the household, if present, must
be worshipped by their descendants, the junior members of the
family. The parties worshipped, or before whom prostrations
are made, sit side by side in chairs, if husband and wife. No

incense is used. Married sons and their wives, as well as unmarried children, kneel down before their seniors, bowing only thrice, and expressing their congratulations. Uncles and aunts almost always prefer to stand rather than sit while receiving the customary tokens of respect.

The adult male members of the family start forth to see their male friends or relatives, making New Year's calls, on this day, or they may delay such calls for one or two days, if they choose. Friends of equal rank and standing in society, on meeting, must bow to each other, shaking their own hands, each mutually congratulating the other. Relatives of lower social rank bow one knee on meeting their superiors. The higher never kneel to the lower. The husband must call on his wife's parents, if living within a reasonable distance, worshipping them and their ancestral tablets. Husband and wife do not mutually worship each other, being of the same social rank. Concubines living in the house must worship the husband and the wife by kneeling before them, and presenting their congratulations on the return of a new year.

The same Chinese term, "Pai," is applied to worshipping deceased ancestors and living parents; but there is this essential difference between the two ceremonies: in regard to the dead, incense, and candles, and mock-money, and sometimes offerings of food, are made; while in regard to the living, neither incense, nor candles, nor mock-money, nor offerings of food are ever made.

It is customary for all the hongs, stores, and groceries to close during New Year's day, and for at least one or two subsequent days.

There seems to be a superstitious dread of spending money for the first three days, except for candies, sweetmeats, pea-nuts, and similar kinds of refreshments, buying and selling, as matters of business, being regarded as an inauspicious commencement of the year.

The first day of the new year is a day of great festivity and rejoicing among all classes. No unnecessary work is performed. Should it be necessary to hire a coolie or a workman to perform labour, he would expect two or three times as much pay as usual. Much gambling is performed in the streets, in gambling dens, and in private houses, on the first few days of every new year. Gambling, which, according to law, is forbidden to be practised at all, by the universal consent and connivance of mandarins and their underlings is permitted at New Year. Almost every adult

Chinese knows how to gamble in various ways. Custom requires that every boy who calls on his neighbours or his relatives on New Year's day—or any time before the fifteenth of the month, as some assert—should receive a couple of loose-skinned oranges, or the lad would consider himself slighted, and treated shamefully and niggardly. The reason why this kind of orange is so popular at New Year is, that the colloquial name for it, *kĕk*, is precisely the same as the term for "fortunate," "lucky," "auspicious." The presentation of these oranges is equivalent to the wish of an auspicious and lucky year; it is an omen of good. When a man recently married calls on the parents of his bride, or on any of his own family relatives or intimate friends, he must have two or four oranges of this species given to him, and a handful of water-melon seeds, put up in a red paper, for him to carry home when he departs. Adults, when calling at New Year's, must invariably be treated with hot tea to drink, good tobacco to smoke, and water-melon seeds to eat. As the local saying is, " During the first part of the first month no one has an empty mouth."

From the first day to the fourth it is customary for the common boat-women and their children to go round from house to house, presenting their congratulations to the members of respectable families, and begging a present of cakes or food of any kind. They call out at the street door or knock on it, singing songs, until they receive the cakes sought or until they become wearied. Many families make it a point to give to these boat-women. They do not seek out the poor on the occasion, but the poor seek out those who are willing to contribute a cake or two. They carry the cakes home, and eat them at their leisure.

It is estimated that probably ninety out of a hundred families do not eat any meat on New Year's day : this is on account of their reverence for heaven and earth. The custom is sometimes called "eating vegetables in honour of heaven and earth," and is regarded as an act of merit.

The New Year's festivities among the respectable classes of citizens last from the first to the fifteenth of the first month, and among the officers of Government from the first to the twentieth, or rather from the twentieth of the twelfth month of the old year to the twentieth day of the first month of the new year. This month, among the mandarins, is given up to recreation and dissipation.

Between the first and the fifteenth it is common for bands of music to call on respectable and wealthy families in the daytime, and, if their services are not promptly declined, commence playing. After playing three tunes they stop, and expect to receive a present of money. These players come professedly to present their congratulations to the families they visit on the arrival of another new year. Sometimes wealthy householders specially invite a band of players to come to their houses and perform for the amusement of the females connected with their families. Their remuneration is much greater when formally invited than it is when they invite themselves.

During the first half of the month the festivities are frequently diversified and enlivened by fireworks in the evening. These are called "flowers." The occasions when exhibitions of flowers in the evening are made are not few ; for instance, sometimes, when offering thanksgiving before the images of gods and goddesses in their temples, in view of a happy event, or in the performance of a vow, or when a large family worship the ancestral tablets in their ancestral halls or in their private residences, or when the clerks and other underlings in mandarin offices have theatricals performed for the purpose of propitiating the god of riches, or when distinguished guests are invited to a feast in a wealthy family, the "letting off of flowers" is oftentimes attended with great show and expense. Some married women take occasion to visit some celebrated temple, dedicated to the goddess called "Mother," on the evening of the fifteenth of the first month, and have "flowers" let off at their expense in her honour, hoping that this goddess will aid them to have male children, in consequence of their thus worshipping her on her natal day.

From the eleventh to the fifteenth it is customary for bands of play-actors or idle people to go round to the different mandarin establishments, the residences of the gentry and the rich, and places of public rendezvous, and "manœuvre the dragon." The performers expect to be rewarded by those who permit them to play for their amusement on their premises or before their houses. If they happen to go where they are not wanted, a present much smaller than would be expected, were they permitted to play, will send them away in peace. Officers and rich people often give several dollars to a band, after having witnessed the "dragon play" for a part of an evening.

A ceremony performed in every heathen family at this place on the morning of the fourth day is called "offering rice for receiving the gods." It is the belief that the gods who ascended to heaven on the twenty-third or twenty-fourth of the twelfth month of the year just closed, to report to the " Pearly Emperor Supreme Ruler " in regard to the affairs under their supervision, all descend to earth again on the fourth day of the first month. The people prepare an entertainment for them as a kind of welcome, and in order to propitiate their good-will during the year just commenced. This is called " receiving the gods." The kitchen god, the god of wealth, the god of joy, and other household gods, are supposed on this day to come down from heaven to begin their duties on the earth. Some say the spirits of deceased ancestors are also present this day in their former homes. A bucket of boiled rice, with various things arranged upon it, very much like the offering to heaven and earth on New Year's day, ten plates of vegetables, three cups of tea, three cups of wine, with incense and candles, are placed upon a table in the front part of the public room of the house. The head of the family kneels down on the floor, and bows three times before the table, which is understood to be an act of homage rendered to the gods who have already arrived on the premises, or who are momentarily expected. At the conclusion of the genuflexions, mock-money is burned for their use. After waiting a short time, a plate having five kinds of fruit upon it is placed before each image worshipped in the family, with two candles and three sticks of incense, and also before the niche holding the ancestral tablets of the family. Some utter a kind of prayer before the idols while bowed before them on this occasion, asking for wealth, male children, health, success in business or literary employ-ments, &c. There is a proverb in common use to the effect that " when the rice used to receive the gods back again is eaten, then all kinds of work should be commenced."

The custom of keeping company with the gods whose images are found in the neighbouring temples is generally observed for several nights previous to the fifteenth. It consists in making offerings and in feasting before them, under the direction of the trustees of the temple for the current year. Oftentimes the village god, his excellency the Great King, is carried in public procession. The members of the procession are citizens of the neighbourhood or village whose Great King is thus honoured. The procession parades backwards and forwards through the principal streets belonging to the neighbourhood for the avowed object of procuring " peace and tranquillity," which means free-dom from sickness and pestilence during the year which has but recently commenced. In the rural districts in this vicinity, it is the practice of the people in one village to invite their friends and relatives living in a neighbouring village to be present at the time of this procession of the Great King, and to partake of the festivities on the occasion, the guests returning the compliment by inviting their hosts when a similar procession is had in their own village.

A very singular custom prevails, observed by many families which have had a daughter married since the fifteenth day of the first month of the previous year, in case she has not given birth to a male child. A present of several articles is sent to her by her own parents, or by her brothers if her parents are deceased, on a lucky day between the fifth and the fourteenth of the first month. The articles sent are like these : a paper lantern, sometimes representing the goddess of mercy with a child in her arms, and having an inscription upon it, oysters in an earthern vessel, confectionery made from a kind of rice parched and prepared with molasses, ten oranges of the loose-skinned species, wood, and rice, and vegetables of a particular name. Now all these, singly and collectively, signify to the daughter, "We wish you may soon give birth to a son." The oranges, when interpreted, mean in the connexion "speedily," because the colloquial name for this kind of orange is precisely like a Chinese character which means "speedily." The oysters in the earthern vessel mean, "may a younger brother come," the colloquial term for "oysters" being of the same sound as the term for "younger brother," and the common name for the vessel sent being the same as the word for "come" or "has come." The name for the confectionery is the same in sound as one of the common appellations for "elder brother," meaning, "may you have more than one child," so that one shall be an "elder brother." The vegetables indicate the desire that her posterity may be numerous, because their name has nearly the same sound as a term which means "grandchildren and children." The inscription on the lantern means, "may the goddess of mercy present you with a son." This lantern must be preserved by the married daughter with care, to be used during the celebration which will next be described ; then it must be suspended in the bride's bedroom and lighted up brilliantly.

Some time usually before the fifteenth day of the first month, rich families fix upon some evening for the observance of a kind of joyous or lucky festival. The time selected is regarded as fortunate and auspicious. Candles and incense are burnt before the gods and goddesses worshipped in the house, but no edible offerings are presented before their images. Before the ancestral tablets are arranged, on a table, several bowls of meats, a kind of sweet cake, vermicelli, oysters, sugar-cane, and loose-skinned oranges. When everything is ready, the head of the family lights the candles and incense, kneels down, and bows toward the ground three times, facing the tablets. After this performance is completed, mock-money of several kinds is burnt for the use of the dear departed ancestors. About this time various paper lanterns, which have been purchased by the elders of the family for the use of the juvenile members as playthings, are lighted up. Sometimes a bonfire of pine wood is made, the wood having been split quite fine, and piled up in a square form in the manner in which a rail pen is often made. The foundation consists of four sticks, and the pile is made eighteen or twenty inches high. A quantity of fire-crackers is exploded. At the end of the sport the head man of the family again kneels down and bows before the tablets. After this the food is taken away and consumed, the spirits of the dead being supposed to have already partaken of the immaterial and impalpable essence of the viands as much as they chose. The living always seem to regard the coarse and the material substance which is left after the feast of the spirits as amply satisfactory and sufficient for their wants. The grand object of this joyous festival before the tablets is usually explained to be to secure the bestowment of numerous children and more remote descendants in the direct line of the family. Most of the articles used, except the meats, are symbolical of posterity and prosperity. The vermicelli is emblematical of longevity ; the sugar-cane is emblematical of "elder sister ;" the use of "oranges" and "oysters" in a representative sense has been already explained.

The keeper of the neighbourhood temple, on the first and the fifteenth of each month, often distributes a quantity of a kind of cakes, distinctively called "brilliant cakes," among the families living in the neighbourhood. He gives to each family two such cakes. These he has previously presented as an offering to the Great King, the neighbourhood god, with the burning of incense and candles. They from this circumstance take the name of "incense cakes." The keeper receives a present of a few cash from each family which accepts them. It is a common saying that if children eat this kind of cake after having been presented before the village god, they will be kept free from the colic thereby. Some say that these cakes will add to the intelligence of the children who eat them, and that they will more easily become proficient in their studies. The object really attained is that of giving the temple-keeper a small present twice per month, in a way that will not possibly hurt his feelings.

This incident might be adduced as an illustration of the fact that Chinese children are brought up in the belief of the efficaciousness of worshipping the gods. By simply eating certain cakes which have been placed before an idol for a short time in the village temple, they are taught to believe that they will be supernaturally benefited.

The sale of fancy paper lanterns, preceding the Feast of Lanterns, commences usually about the tenth or eleventh, and reaches its culmination on the evening of the fourteenth or the fifteenth. During the daytime there is more or less sale of these toys, but the evening is the time when the largest quantity is exhibited to tempt purchasers, and when the streets are more densely crowded with spectators and with buyers. Sometimes it is almost impossible to make one's way along in the street. Many shops seem to do but very little business except the sale of these toys for several days before the fifteenth.

Some of the lanterns are cubical, others round like a ball, or circular, square, flat and thin, or oblong, or in the shape of various animals, quadruped and biped. Some are so constructed as to roll on the ground as a fire-ball, the light burning inside in the meanwhile; others, as cocks and horses, are made to go on wheels; still others, when lighted up by a candle or oil, have a rotatory or revolving motion of some of their fixtures within, the heated air, rising upward, being the motive power. Some of these, containing wheels and images, and made to revolve by heated air, are ingeniously and neatly made. Some are constructed principally of red paper, on which small holes are made in lines, so as to form a Chinese character of auspicious import, as happiness, longevity, gladness. These, when lighted up, show the form of the character very plainly. Other lanterns are made in a human shape, and intended to represent children, or some object of worship, as the Goddess of Mercy, with a child in her arms. Some are made to be carried in the hand by means of a handle, others to be placed on a wall or the side of a room. They are often gaudily painted with black, red, and yellow colours, the red usually predominating, as that is a symbol of joy and festivity. The most expensive and the prettiest are covered with white gauze or thin white silk, on which historical scenes, or individual characters or objects,

O O

dignified or ludicrous, have been elaborately and neatly painted in various colours.

The Feast of Lanterns, so called at this place, is celebrated in the evening of the fifteenth. Nearly every respectable family celebrates it in some way, with greater or less expense and display. It is an occasion of great hilarity and gladness. The houses are lighted up as brilliantly as possible. There is probably more of revelry and abandonment on this evening than usual at common festivals ; more drinking of wine, and more gambling and playing at cards. As usual, at the end of the worshipping, the family feasts on the food presented. Some place before the idols a plate of the *taro*. The use of this vegetable on the occasion in some way is almost universal in the families of this place. There used to be an invariable custom of " eating taro under the lanterns." Those who observe it prepare a quantity of small taros, and have them boiled soft, the skin remaining upon them. Very late in the evening, or about midnight, all the members of the family, old and young, male and female, assemble beneath one of the most brilliant lights suspended on high, and then proceed to eat the taros provided. Some say that their eyesight will become more confirmed in distinctness, or that they will become bright-eyed and clear-sighted, in consequence of partaking of boiled taros under a bright light. Others say that this custom is annually observed under the impression that transmigration of souls will be avoided by this means. What connexion there is between either result and the eating of boiled taros under a bright light on the midnight of the fifteenth day of the first month of a new year does not seem very manifest.

There appears to be more licence granted by custom to respectable married females on the evening of the fifteenth than on other evenings. They usually are secluded very strictly at home during an evening ; but many go out on the evening of the fifteenth to see the display of lanterns in the street. When conveniently near, they also embrace the opportunity to call at some popular temple devoted to a goddess called " Mother," and offer their thanksgiving and make their supplication, hoping thus to obtain her favour. Married childless women this day or evening sometimes solicit a shoe or a flower from " Mother," which they take home, and worship by the burning of incense and candles regularly, expecting or desiring, as a consequence of such devotional acts to " Mother," to have male offspring.

It sometimes occurs that, after a marriage of several years, and no child has been born to a couple, an intimation is given to the

Great King of the temple in the neighbourhood in which they reside that a present of a set of lanterns of a particular kind would be acceptable. Accordingly, the Great King, by the agency of the trustees of his temple for the current year, causes a set of four paper lanterns to be made, each in the form of a boy. There is a set of four characters, which are to be seen in probably every temple, written, or engraved, or painted, or gilded upon a tablet, which is put up in a conspicuous place, teaching the sentiment that "those who pray in earnest will receive an answer."

These four boy-lanterns are made ready by the evening of the fifteenth, when they are taken to the residence of the childless couple and presented in the name of the Great King, and with his compliments and best wishes. The lantern selected, or the whole four lanterns sent by the Great King, are accepted with thanks, and regarded as auspicious.

There is an innocent amusement of a literary kind, which is practised frequently on the evening of the fifteenth, as well as on other evenings in the first part of the first month, and on the evening of the great festival, which usually is celebrated in the eighth month. This consists in writing various puzzles or riddles on slips of paper, which are then slightly pasted at one end on a four-sided lantern, suspended in front of the house occupied by those who make or publish them. Those who can guess correctly what the answer is are rewarded on the spot. The present which will be given to the guesser of each particular riddle is intimated by a word or two written on the same slip of paper which contains the riddle. Sometimes several literary men combine in this amusement. They compose the riddles, or write out some old ones which they think are not generally known, agreeing upon the reward which shall be given on discovery of the answer. Oftentimes a clue is given to the general subject of the puzzle, when it is regarded as obscure and difficult to be guessed, simply stating the subject or the kind of objects referred to. It is not an uncommon thing, on a pleasant night in the first month, to see a knot of literary men gazing at the riddles attached to some lantern in the streets, talking about them, in the eager desire to solve them and obtain the promised reward, for the sport afforded and not for the value of the article proffered.

On the twentieth of every first Chinese month occurs the "opening of the seals" of all the different officials, civil and military, in this city and suburbs, and probably through the empire. The seals were deposited in a small box, and sealed up on the twentieth of the twelfth month of the previous year.

"The opening of the seals" of office is an event of great interest and importance to the mandarins themselves, the clerks, and other subordinates connected with their official establishments, and that portion of the citizens who have complaints to make, and causes which are waiting to be decided.

The lowest civil and the lowest military mandarins in the city begin the opening of the seals of their respective yamuns about three or four o'clock in the morning of the twentieth. When their own seals have been opened, and the attendant ceremonies are properly performed, they hurry forth to their next superiors in rank, whether civil or military, to be present when their seals are opened, and join in the congratulations and excitements of the occasion. They then all immediately start off for the yamuns of their next superior officers, civil or military, as the case may be, the lower civil officials waiting on the superior civil mandarins, and the lower military officials waiting on the superior military mandarins. Each party, after witnessing the opening of the seal of their superior, and joining with his clerks and underlings in their congratulations, &c., is joined by said superior, and off they proceed, without any delay, to their superior officer's yamun. In this way the company of mandarins, at each successive opening of a seal of office, becomes more numerous, until the governor and the viceroy are reached among the civil mandarins, and the Tartar general among the military.

The ceremony of "opening the seal" at all the official establishments is substantially the same. The paper seal of the box which incloses the seal is broken, and the box is unlocked in the presence of the mandarin who presides over the yamun, and in the presence of his inferior officers, and his clerks and assistants of various names and grades. The box containing the seal is placed on a table in the tribunal of justice, where candles and incense are already burning. The hall is at this time lighted up as brilliantly as the lanterns and lamps in it will admit. The mandarin now presents himself before the box lying on the table, and, under the direction of a "professor of ceremony," kneels down thrice, and bows nine times, according to the established regulations. A head clerk takes the box reverently in both hands, and, holding it up on high, bows down, and expresses his wishes for the promotion of his master, and the prosperity of the yamun during the year. Then the seal is taken out of the box and laid on the table, when it is again worshipped by the mandarin with "three kneelings and nine knockings." The seal is then taken up and immediately used to stamp a piece of red paper in four places, on which, if the seal belongs to an officer of inferior rank, certain four characters have been written. This paper is then taken and pasted upon the main door of the tribunal. The words signify in general that the opening of the seal is an omen of great good fortune. If the officer belongs to the higher grade, other certain four characters are written on the red paper, which in like manner is stamped four times, and is similarly used as an omen of good, the characters expressing the general idea of prosperity and preferment to higher rank.

The opening of the seal is in all cases accompanied with the explosion of fire-crackers and cannon. The twentieth is devoted to hilarity and amusement among the clerks and underlings connected with the yamun. Theatrical exhibitions often take place in the latter part of the day and evening. The festivities are not unfrequently accompanied in the evening by sending up rockets.

The annual respite of one month from the cares and responsibilities of office, except in cases of very great emergency, has now closed, and the mandarins commence the discharge of their official duties for another eleven months.

CHAPTER XX.

A SINGULAR custom is annually observed at this place on the morning of the twenty-ninth day of the first month, often called "the eating of filial porridge." In the morning, instead of cooking the common kind of rice in the usual manner for breakfast, they mix in with it some very glutinous rice. They put in also a variety of edible things, and boil them into a thick porridge. Instead of the rice looking clean and white, as on other days, these ingredients make the porridge very dirty-looking. Shopkeepers who have clerks, and those families which have hired men, as well as rich people generally, prepare, in addition to the "filial porridge," the usual kind of food for breakfast, so that, should any not choose to partake of the black-looking soup, there will be other food ready. In such families the "filial porridge" is taken by those who please as a morning lunch. Probably every heathen family, without exception, at this place annually prepares this kind of porridge on the specified morning. The children and younger members of the families look forward to the eating of the "porridge of filial piety" with considerable interest as the time fixed upon by custom draws near.

After the porridge has been cooked, part of it is dipped into small bowls or cups. Several of these bowlfuls are then placed before the ancestral tablets of the family, together with several pairs of chopsticks. Several bowls of it are also placed before the household idols. There are burned a few sticks of incense and two candles before the tablets, and also before the idols. They do not kneel down and worship these things on this occasion. After allowing these bowlfuls of the mixture to stand before the tablets and the images of the gods a short while, they take them away and eat the contents themselves, fathers, and mothers, and their children living at home, all partaking. Sometimes they set some of the bowls on a table, placed in the front part of their reception-room, as an offering to heaven. This is also attended with the burning of incense and candles in the usual manner. They are always careful to present some of this porridge before the god of the kitchen.

It is customary for a married woman to send to her paternal home a bowl or two of this porridge, which she has prepared at her own home, as a token of her continued love for her father and mother. It is accompanied by a cooked fowl and some other kinds of food. Sometimes they send her in return some of the porridge which they have prepared. The married son, if living away from the homestead, also invariably sends to his parents—if the distance is not too great—some of this porridge which he has prepared, for them to partake of at their homes.

In some families, during the evening, the children or their elders make a particular kind of a bonfire. It consists of common wood split into quite small sticks about a foot long, which are piled up in a hollow square to the height of two or three feet, by laying the sticks on each other after the manner of making a pen out of rails. The lighting of the bonfire is attended with the letting off of fire-crackers and other manifestations of joy among the juvenile members of the household, such as the wearing of hideous paper masks, the sprinkling of salt on the fire to make it crackle, and the burning of a variety of paper playthings. Oftentimes, before the pile is entirely consumed, some of the burning sticks are taken and put into the kitchen furnace for the purpose of procuring good luck to the family for the current year.

The circumstances which led to the establishment of this festival are said to have taken place in very ancient times. Anciently, as the fable states, there lived a certain woman who, on the death of her husband, vowed to live on vegetables the rest of her life, in token of her sorrow at her loss, but who afterwards violated her vow, and ate meats as well as vegetables. This was regarded as a great sin, and after her death she was believed to have been shut up in hell, in very unhappy circumstances, on account of her violation of her solemn vow. She had a very filial son who survived her on the earth, and who was very much distressed at the unhappy circumstances of his mother, and desired to testify his filial affection by carrying her something to eat; but every time when he was going to the place where his mother was imprisoned, carrying rice cooked in the usual way, the hungry devils and the assistant evil spirits in hell availed themselves of the opportunity to get some good food, and impishly stole the rice and ate it, thus depriving the old lady of the provisions which her filial son had provided for her. After being repeatedly foiled in his attempts to furnish his maternal ancestor with nourishing, palatable food, he finally hit upon a device by which he succeeded. He boiled up with the rice various things which imparted to it a black, dirty appearance. The devils, on seeing him carry along this repulsive-looking porridge, condemned it at once, without tasting it, as unfit to be eaten, and so let him pass on unmolested to his mother. The Chinese here who undertake to explain the origin of the festival say that it had its origin in this man's love for his mother, and that the annual observance of the festival now-a-days is designed to commemorate and celebrate this love, as well as to instil into the minds of children the importance and the merit of filial affection for one's father and mother, and the duty of endeavouring to afford happiness to one's parents, even under very discouraging circumstances.

Usually in the latter part of the second month (or the first part of the third month, or early in April) occurs Tsing Ming, the celebrated "Festival of the Tombs," when the Chinese visit the graves of their ancestors and present offerings before them.

The time for it is always one hundred and six days after the winter solstice. It is not only annual, but national, and the day is always specified in the Imperial Calendar. While it is celebrated in all parts of China at the same time, there probably are widely-marked differences in various parts of the empire in the particular method of its observance. The following statements relate to the way in which this festival is observed at Fuhchau.

While the festival is nominally fixed for a certain day, still, in practice, the worship of the dead at their tombs is sometimes performed a few days before or a few days after the time appointed in the calendar, according to the convenience or the necessities of living relations. Often, a few days previous to the worship of the dead, especially in the case of the wealthy, and if residing not far from the family burial-ground, some one goes and sweeps the graves, removes the rubbish, and pulls up the tall grass and woods which may be found growing on them. From this process, this festival is often referred to as "Sweeping the Tombs." At this time the hills present an animated and busy appearance; for the Chinese here select such spots for the resting-place of the dead instead of the dwelling-place of the living.

When the day has arrived and everything is prepared, the persons who are to engage in the worship proceed to the hill where the family tombs are located. Directly in front of the tomb-stone there is usually, if the tomb be large and of the "horse-shoe" pattern, a kind of stationary altar of stone or cement. The ceremony is often commenced by placing a candle on the right and left sides of the altar, or simply on the ground, in these relative positions. There is then placed a quantity of incense-sticks in a censer put on the central portion of the altar, immediately in front of the tomb-stone. After the candles and incense are lighted, the offerings are arranged on the altar or before the tomb-stone. They consist of different kinds of food, several cups of wine and tea. The chief manager kneels down, and bows his head near the ground three times. He then resumes standing, and the others, one by one, go through the same ceremony. A quantity of mock-money is then burned, and fire-crackers are exploded. The contents of one of the wine-cups are poured out on this paper as it is burning, or on the hot ashes just after the paper has been consumed. The cup is then refilled with wine, and placed in its former position. The head man now kneels again, and makes the triple bow; and after him, in turn, one by one, from the highest in rank down to the lowest, all repeat the same ceremony of kneeling and bowing.

About this stage of the proceedings an offering is made to the local deity, or the god which is believed to preside over the hill where the grave is located. It is composed usually of three dishes of food, three cups of wine, two candles, three incense-sticks, and three sets of a particular kind of mock-money. These are all placed on the ground, not far from the tomb-stone. The candles and the sticks of incense are lighted, and the mock-money burned amid the sound of fire-crackers.

Then an offering is made to the spirits of beggars and lepers, and others in the lower regions, as we have already described in the chapter on "Mourning Customs."

Strips of perforated paper, from eight to fifteen inches long, usually of its original colour, though sometimes a part is coloured yellow, are put on different parts of the tomb-stone and the tomb, and held in place by a handful of earth or a small stone.

Wine is poured out on the tomb-stone. The eatables are re-moved from the platform, and are either consumed by the hungry worshippers in the neighbourhood of the grave or at

MODEL-GRAVE, OR OMEGA GRAVE.

home. About the time of starting homeward another quantity of fire-crackers is exploded. A branch or two of the fir or other green tree, or a handful of green wheat-stalks, is taken to the house, and either put in a flower-vase before the tablets of the ancestors of the family, or laid before them on a table. Candles and sticks of incense are lighted, and, with a quantity of cooked rice, and more or less of a meat and vegetable offering, are placed on the table before the tablets by most families.

On the day of this festival, usually, every house in this city and suburbs has a branch of the willow introduced under the tiling of the roof, and hanging down from or near the eaves and over the front outside door, so arranged as to be readily seen from the street by the passer-by. At several different places inside the premises, oftentimes, is another branch of the willow suspended.

The sweeping of the grave, and the placing of paper on the outside of the tomb and on the tomb-stone, indicate that the dead has descendants yet living—that his family is not extinct. The Chinese here say that if a grave is not thus swept and cared for at this time, some one, perhaps the original owner of the ground or his descendants, would be likely to disturb the tomb-stone more or less, or commit some depredations on the grave. If in the following year it should not be swept and repaired, and paper deposited on it, other more serious encroachments would doubtless be made ; and in a very few years, unless a claimant should appear and annually attend upon the grave, in accordance with established customs, all traces of it would be gone, and the ground would be cultivated, or sold to another for a burial-place of the dead.

It has been inquired, What is the use of the green willow-branch hanging down from beneath the roofs of all the houses, so as to be easily seen by the passer-by? The Chinese differ widely among themselves in regard to the interpretation of this emblem. The general idea respecting it probably is, that it is an omen of good to the family. Some say that during the Tang dynasty, which ended more than nine hundred and fifty years ago, Wang Chau selected the willow as the badge of his followers in a rebellion which he planned against the reigning emperor. He secretly ordered those who were favourable to him to stick up a branch of the willow, so as to be under the roofs of their houses and over their front outside door. His soldiers were instructed not to molest these houses. His rebellion is said to have commenced on the day fixed by custom for the observance of this festival. Some affirm that the willow-branch is now annually used as above described in celebration or remembrance of the security it gained to those who used it in this manner on the occasion referred to, and indicates the peace and safety prevailing within the house, whatsoever may be taking place without. Others say that the willow is designed to ward off wicked spirits and evil influences from the household. It is affirmed, and apparently believed by these, that a certain god in the lower world, who is of the same comparative rank as the governor of a province in the upper, opens the gates of Hades, and allows the imprisoned spirits to revisit the earth on the day appointed for this festival. It is but natural to suppose that the spirits malevolently inclined would gladly embrace the opportunity to intrude their society where they were not welcome, and commit depredations congenial to their depraved natures. Now it is taught that, if these spirits see the willow on the roofs of the houses where they desire to enter on a malicious errand, they are immediately taken with fright, and abscond with haste. According to this view, how fortunate are the Chinese in having discovered so potent a charm against the evil influence of imps which so numerously infest the earth on the day of this festival, though invisible to mortal eyes—if, indeed, the gates of the infernal regions are on that day thrown open, and the spirits therein permitted to ramble away to this world. But there are others who attribute to the green branch of the willow another wonderful property,—namely, that of attracting to the houses of their surviving relatives those spirits that are temporarily let loose from the punishment of Hades. It is affirmed that they at once recognise the homes of their living descendants on beholding the willow suspended from under the roof. According to one theory, it has the invaluable virtue of repelling those whom it should repel, and who have no business to visit certain houses. According to the other theory, it has the equally invaluable property or power of attracting those whom it should attract, and who have blood relatives dwelling in certain houses. The spirits that belong, so to speak, to the premises, immediately enter when they see the verdant signal over the outer door, and partake of the grateful odour of the burning incense and of the ethereal portions of the food provided for them.

Some time in the second or the third months, the high officials attend the important ceremony of "ploughing the field" and of "exhorting the farmers." This is done by command of the emperor and in imitation of his own example. If the emperor is sufficiently interested in the success of agricultural pursuits to lead him in person to plough the ground and perform the most laborious duties of the husbandman, the mandarins ought to be willing to imitate his laudable example, in the hope of inciting among the farming community a praiseworthy emulation among themselves, and a proper attention to the culture of the ground. Surely the common peasantry ought not to be above working in the fields, if the emperor and the mandarins, "the fathers and mothers of the people," can personally engage in such humble employments. Such is the noble theory. How ridiculous is the real practice !

On the day appointed, four of the principal mandarins go forth to certain places outside of the four principal gates,—north, east, south, and west,—where, in the presence of the elders of the vicinity, and in the presence of various subordinate officials, they proceed to set an example for the imitation of the farmers of the locality. Although they are dressed in their richest robes of state, the fear of soiling their apparel does not prevent them from the discharge of the duties of their station as representatives of the emperor. They tuck up one of the lower corners of the skirt of their long garments, and proceed to caress the ox, which is already yoked to the plough. They then take hold of the plough-handle, and, with the whip in one hand, start the quadruped to his task of ploughing, guiding the plough a short distance, and giving the beast a few strokes with the goad. The plough, during this impressive ceremony, often has a piece of red silk entwined around its handle. They then resign the arduous work, and, taking a hoe or a similar farming utensil, proceed to illustrate the practical nature of farming by digging up a few weeds or by hoeing the ground for a short distance—all this for the purpose of showing the villagers how farming work should be done, and of setting an example for them to imitate. Doubtless the spectators feel duly benefited by this exhibition of industry, skill, and humility.

The ceremony of *exhorting the farmers* to diligence in their calling is perhaps equally impressive. Generally, a small platform, ornamented and trimmed with festoons or knots of silk, has been erected in the vicinity of the field which has been ploughed. The high mandarins mount this platform, and, calling around them the principal aged farmers of the vicinity, proceed to exhort them to the proper discharge of their duties as husbandmen. They should be diligent in cultivating the ground ; they should sow at the proper season of the year ; they should keep the weeds and grass in a proper state of subjection ; the ground should always be properly prepared for the seed ; harvesting should be done at the proper time, &c. At the close of this agricultural address.they present to each of the farmers who have been selected to receive them certain articles in the name of the emperor, in order to encourage and stimulate them to diligence in their calling. These articles consist of a very coarse fan, a common large leaf hat to keep off the summer heat, and sometimes a silver medal.

At this time, in connexion with these ceremonies, performed

GOD OF THE FIVE GRAINS.

near the south gate, the officials are required to burn incense and offer *sacrifice in honour of the god of the five grains.* The temple to this god is in a very dilapidated state. The burning of incense and candles, and the offering of wine and a plate of fruits of five kinds, &c., before the god of the land and grain, is accompanied with the performance of three kneelings and nine knockings.

On the morning of the third day of the third month it is the universal practice for householders at this place to nail up on each door-post of their family residences, about six or seven feet above the ground, on the side facing outside, a small bunch of a common weed much resembling chickweed. Many windows and doors of shops and hongs have also bunches of this weed nailed upon them, one on each side, corresponding to each other in height and general appearance.

The common people, while they invariably follow the custom, are not able to explain its origin or its significance. The only reason or explanation that they can give is that their ancestors did thus, and they follow their example.

On the eighth day of the fourth month occurs the festival called *Buddha washing vegetables.* Few of the common people observe this festival. Those who do observe it pursue the following course : they prepare congee or porridge made out of glutinous rice in which several kinds of dried fruit and the kernels of several kinds of nuts have been boiled together, much after the manner of preparing the "porridge of filial piety." This porridge is salted ; that was sweetened. Several bowls of it are then offered before the ancestral tablets and the household gods.

On the same day, in the principal Buddhist monasteries, there is placed before the images of the "Three Precious Ones" a brass wash-bowl, and in it is put a small brass image of Buddha in a sitting posture. A small quantity of water is poured into the vessel. Worshippers of Buddha who come to the monasteries are expected to take each a handful of cash and put them on the head of the image, letting them roll down into the water. They then take a brass spoon, and dip up some of the water, and pour it on the head of the god, repeating the operation several times. Generally the offerer kneels down in front of the image, and bows three times before he performs these acts. Many Tartars, as well as Chinese, visit the large monasteries on this day to worship Buddha. The cash deposited on his pate is a donation to the monastery, and is usually spent in buying incense and candles to be burnt in honour of the divinity who is believed to wash his own vegetables on this day.

This is a great day in the largest two monasteries near Fuh-chau, for the reason that on this day the ceremony of burning the heads of candidates for the Buddhistic priesthood is performed. The ceremony is accompanied by the burning of incense before all the idols in the establishments. Small balls of the dried leaves of the artemisia are put upon the head of the candidate, equal in number to the number of spots which he desires, or which it is decided shall be burned upon it. The number ranges from one to nine. These balls are ignited, and the fire burns down into the skin, and sometimes the grease fries out and trickles down the face of the priest. After the conclusion of the ceremony the abbot of the monastery presents the newly-made priest with a document, written on cloth, sealed with the seal of the monastery, and signed by himself, which constitutes the certificate of the owner having attained the Buddhistic priesthood, and acts the part of a passport or introduction to the hospitality of any monastery of the Buddhist religion in any part of the eighteen provinces of China. This is Buddhistic ordination.

The arrival of summer is celebrated by many families about the time specified in the calendar for its commencement. They purchase or prepare some cakes made of rice-flour, salted or sweetened, as they prefer, and steamed, not baked. These cakes, with meats and vegetables, they present before the ancestral tablets, and often before the gods of their households, attended with the usual ceremonies. With some it is the custom to eat a part of the cakes while sitting on the door-sill, or on the rice-mill belonging to them, as an act of good omen. The custom of giving pork to beggars and lepers is confined to this one day in the year.

The first five days of the fifth month are observed with extra-ordinary hilarity and festivity by the people of this place. The time of the year often corresponds to the first part of June. The festival, called the Festival of the Dragon Boats, properly speaking falls on the fifth day of the fifth month, but the preceding four days are regarded as connected with it.

Early on the morning of the first day of the fifth month it is the practice for every householder to nail up to the posts of the doors and the windows of his house a few leaves of the artemisia and a few leaves of the sweet-flag, tied together in a bundle, at the height of about six or eight feet from the ground. The common explanation for this custom is that the artemisia is fragrant, and that the leaves of the sweet-flag will expel noxious influences and bad odours.

These five days are often spoken of as the "children's festival." The great source of amusement for old and young is the racing of dragon boats on the river and the lake.

These boats are made very long and slender in proportion to the width. The length is usually forty or fifty feet, more or less. Each boat is capable of carrying from fifteen to thirty men. It is made, in some respects, in imitation of the fancied shape of the dragon, having an elevated bow, resembling the dragon's head with open mouth. The body and stern of the boat are gaudily painted, so as to represent a dragon according to Chinese ideas. The helmsman stands on the stern. Near the centre of the boat are two men who make a continuous loud noise, one by beating a large gong, the other by beating a large drum. One man sits on the dragon's head, with his face turned toward the stern of the boat, holding in both hands a flag, by which he regulates the motion of the rowers. These men are furnished with stout short paddles, which they handle with a swift or a slow motion, according to the swiftness or the slowness with which the flag-holder waves his flag from side to side.

Large crowds of children and of adults assemble to behold the sport of the racing. Sometimes fans, or cakes, or handkerchiefs are offered by spectators as rewards for the swiftest racer. These rewards often give rise to quarrellings and fightings among men belonging to different boats, who contend, not for the value of the prize, but for the honour of winning it. Sometimes it occurs that two boats run against each other, or other boats, or the stone

RACING WITH DRAGON BOATS ON THE FIRST FIVE DAYS OF THE FIFTH MONTH.

D D

butments of the bridge over the river. The boats are made so long and so narrow that they easily break in the middle ; or, in case of a collision, many of the men on board of each are usually pitched into the water.

The prevalent story among scholars who profess to know regarding the origin of this racing with dragon boats is substantially the following. Kiuh Yuen, a high minister, in the time of the Chau dynasty, in the state of Tsu, about two thousand three hundred years ago, proposed certain salutary reforms to his prince, who was his relative. The prince refused compliance. He proposed them again, but was repulsed the second time. Nothing discouraged, he remonstrated the third time, when the prince not only declined to make the reforms, but dismissed the faithful courtier from serving about his person. Kiuh Yuen, not being able to survive the ruin of his country, which he foresaw was impending, plunged into a river and was drowned. His countrymen, among whom he was very popular, on learning the circumstances of his death, immediately traversed the river in all directions in small boats, filled with men, who worked with all their might, as if in the hope of recovering his corpse. His death is believed to have occurred on the fifth day of the fifth month ; it was celebrated by a similar demonstration on every recurring anniversary.

The festival reaches its period of greatest interest about the middle of the fifth day, when various superstitions and idolatrous performances take place in every family, according to established usage. Charms, consisting of yellow paper of various sizes, on which are painted images of idols, or of animals, or Chinese characters, are pasted upon the doors and door-posts of houses, in order to expel evil spirits. A certain kind of fire-cracker, which is almost noiseless, being filled principally with a substance something like sulphur, but of a more reddish hue, having a very small quantity of powder mixed with it, is let off. The smoke of it is yellow, and has a disagreeable smell. This is believed to be very efficacious in driving away the worms, bugs, and insects which often infest houses. After being ignited, some one, holding it in his hand, writes some characters or draws a charm on the doors of the house, the smoke issuing forth tracing the desired shape on the doors in yellow. Pairs of slips of red paper, on each of which is printed or written in black ink a line of Chinese poetry, are pasted, one on each door-post. Two slips are also put up near the place where the household gods are stationed or worshipped, and two are also pasted on the front side of the niche which contains the ancestral tablets. Various kinds of yellow charms are pasted on other portions of the house inside and outside. Before the idols and the tablets incense and candles are lighted and left to burn. Some *samshu*, or Chinese spirits, in which the kind of reddish mineral substance is mingled, is also often placed before them. A part of this mixture, after having remained some time before the tablets and the gods, is generally daubed on the ears, noses, and heads of children, to keep away bugs and insects ; the rest is drunk by the members of the household. Before the ancestral tablets are arranged eight or ten dishes of meats, vegetables, fruits, &c. Incense and candles are lighted before them, and mock-money is burned. After a while the eatables are taken away from before the tablets and consumed by the family.

In the afternoon of the fifth the shops and stores are all closed. The male members of the families, the clerks and workmen, after feasting at noon, spend the rest of the day in seeing the racing of the dragon boats, or in gambling, &c.

It is customary for shopkeepers to make out their bills for unpaid articles sold since New Year, and present them to their customers for settlement during the time of this holiday. During the fourth and the forenoon of the fifth day, men with a handful of slips of paper are seen hurrying through the streets, seeking out their debtors and requesting payment. The debtor is expected to make a payment of at least one half of the amount of his bill.

Many of the respectable families here observe a festival which occurs on the seventh of the seventh month. Two stars are believed to meet each other on the evening of this day at the "Silver River," or the Milky Way, and, passing to opposite sides, turn around in their orbits and recross the "river" in some other part of the year. One of the stars is or represents a male, and usually is to be seen, according to the Chinese, in the eastern part of the heavens ; and the other star is or represents a female, and generally is to be seen in the western part of the heavens. People take a water-melon, and a quantity of other vegetables and fruits of the season, cakes, flowers, incense, and candles, and place them upon a table arranged in the lightest part of the reception-room, as offerings to these male and female stars. The presentation is generally accompanied with kneelings and bowings in the usual way. It is done principally by or in behalf of married women and unmarried girls, seldom by or in behalf of men or unmarried boys. The principal object which is desired as the result of thus worshipping and honouring these stars is the obtaining of skill and cunning by females in the performance of their appropriate duties, as needlework, making flowers, as well as the bringing up of children. Females, on the evening of the seventh day of the seventh month, often take a needle and try to thread it, without the aid of a light, in some dark place, as under a table and before a stick of lighted incense, maintaining a kind of squatting posture while making this attempt. If successful, they regard the circumstance as an omen of good in the future in the use of the needle. Some of the articles offered are generally given away in presents to members of other families as an emblem of friendship, women giving to women. When men engage in making the offerings, they sometimes divide a part of the articles presented among their male friends.

Some time during the seventh month, generally before or about the fifteenth day, occurs the celebration of a remarkable custom, having a principal reference to the happiness and comfort of the dead. It is generally referred to as the "burning of paper clothing in the middle of the seventh month." Its professed object is to furnish clothing and money for the deceased ancestors. In order to obtain this result, comparatively large quantities of mock-money and mock-clothing are provided, and burned in a large furnace or censer before the tablets of the ancestors, lighted incense and candles having been previously arranged in front of the tablets.

There are two singular customs, in which a married daughter has an important part, connected with this festival, in case one or both of her parents are dead, and if she has borne a son.

In addition to some mock-money and mock-clothing in the usual form, she is expected to "present a gauze trunk" to her surviving parent, if only one has deceased, and to her brothers, if both have deceased. The "trunk" is made in the shape of a wardrobe, some five or six feet high and three or four feet wide, with shelves in it. It is made out of bamboo rods, covered with paper on the back side and the two ends, the front side being left open. On the shelves is placed a variety of miniature household utensils, made out of bamboo splints and paper, as bedsteads, chairs, lanterns, plates and bowls, and paper images of servants, besides miniature clothing of various sorts cut out of paper. This wardrobe and contents are to be duly burned on the premises where her parents lived, and for the benefit of the deceased.

She is also required by custom to make a present of food to

the family, among which must be a duck. A part of the articles she presents her surviving parent, if one is yet alive, or the family of her eldest brother, if her parents are both deceased, including one-half of the duck, is always returned to her. This custom is called "dividing the duck." The duck is presented by the married daughter only once after she has borne a son ; but a present of the mock-money and mock-clothing is expected annually. In this manner is the married daughter required to give yearly proof of her filial affection for her deceased parents. In case neither of her parents has deceased, she may make to them none of these presents. Being designed for the benefit of those who are already dead, it would be very unbecoming to present them to those who are yet alive, and, if proffered, would be regarded as a very unfilial act, and as intimating her wish that they were already deceased.

CHAPTER XXI.

ONE of the great peculiar festivals of the Chinese comes in the eighth month, and is usually called the "Autumnal Festival." It lasts from the eleventh to the fifteenth. It occurs very near the middle of autumn, according to the Chinese reckoning. The moon is a prominent object of attention and congratulation at this time. At Canton, it is said, offerings are made to the moon on the fifteenth. On the following day, young people amuse themselves by playing what is called "pursuing" or "congratulating" the moon. At this city, in the observance of this festival, the expression "rewarding the moon" is more frequently used than "congratulating the moon."

It is a common saying that there is "a white rabbit in the moon pounding out rice." The dark and the white spots on the moon's face suggest the idea of that animal engaged in the useful employment of shelling rice. The notion is prevalent that the moon is inhabited by a multitude of beautiful females, who are called by the name of an ancient beauty who once visited that planet; but how they live, and what they do, is not a matter of knowledge or of common fame. To the question "Is the moon inhabited?" discussed by some Western philosophers, the Chinese would answer in the affirmative. Several species of trees and flowers are supposed to flourish in the moon. Some say that, one night in ancient times, one of the three souls of the originator of theatrical plays rambled away to the moon and paid a visit to the Lunar Palace. He found it filled with Lunarians engaged in theatrical performances. He is said to have remembered the manner of conducting fashionable theatres in the moon, and to have imitated them after his return to this earth.

About the time of the festival of the middle of autumn the bake-shops provide an immense amount and variety of cakes; many of them are circular, in imitation of the shape of the moon at that time, and are from six to twelve inches in diameter. Some are in the form of a pagoda, or of a horse and rider, or of a fish, or other animals which please, and cause the cake to be readily sold. Some of these "moon-cakes" have a white rabbit, engaged with his pounder, painted on one side, together with a lunar beauty, and some trees or shrubs; on others are painted gods or goddesses, animals, flowers, or persons, according to fancy.

B Y WORSHIPPING A PAGODA.

The toy-shops at this time are abundantly supplied with a variety of playthings. And it is customary to illuminate the two large pagodas in the city for several nights previous to the sixteenth of the eighth month, provided the necessary amount of money is subscribed, and the nights are not too windy. The plan sometimes is to hang a lantern at each corner of the pagodas for several stories, commencing at the top.

After midnight of the evening of the fourteenth, if the weather is fine, multitudes of Chinese visit the tops of the three highest hills in the place, two of which are located inside and one outside of the city walls, for the purpose of burning incense to "heaven and earth." On two of these hills are built altars, which are made use of by some; on the other hill there is a temple erected in honour of the divinity often simply called the "Pearly Emperor," to which some of the worshippers resort to burn incense. Homage is professedly paid to "heaven and earth," the supreme divinities, the father and the mother of all things. This adoration by the burning of incense on the hills is performed by the light of the moon, or, at least, by torchlight, and before daybreak.

Great numbers of wooden images, painted so as to resemble the features of a small child, are exposed for sale in shops for several days previous to this festival. Those for boys and girls are alike, except in the shape and painting of the top of the head. Sometimes little pieces of wood, without being painted, but with black marks on them for the eyes, nose, and mouth, are used in place of the costlier and more pretty images. Parents who have had a child born to them since the festival in the eighth month of the preceding year purchase one of these images to represent this child. The child's name is written on the back of the image, and it is used to represent the child in superstitious and idolatrous ceremonies performed on the day or evening of the fifteenth, and on many other occasions.

Many families, on this day, are at the expense of presenting before the image of a popular goddess of children, usually called "Mother," worshipped in their dwelling-houses, various offerings of food in her honour. Many females go on this day and burn incense in some of her temples, and pray for male offspring. At these times, all of the images representing children belonging to the family are brought together and used in the ceremony performed at home. These images are preserved with care until the children are sixteen years old, when the persons become men or women, having passed out of childhood according to Chinese law. After this period no particular notice is taken of the image. But if the child should die before sixteen years of age, it is customary to bury the image which represents the child in his grave, or, rather, in the same coffin with the corpse.

Another female divinity is also worshipped by many families on this day, called *Seven-star Mother*. Some use the expression *Mother of the Measure* when speaking of this goddess. Many families take occasion, in the afternoon or evening of the fifteenth, to pay homage to the "Seven-star Mother," who seems to dwell among the seven stars which form the Dipper in the constellation of the Great Bear. Some, who worship this Mother, simply place a table in the front part of their reception-room, or in an open court, and arrange on it various plates of meats, vegetables, fruits, &c. Other families have a far more extensive ceremony. They use three cups of a kind of buffalo's milk cheese, three cups of tea, and three cups of wine, and light seven candles and place them on the table. They also provide seven bowls of bean soup and seven bowls of fruit soup. A common four-sided rice measure, having a small quantity of rice put in the bottom, is placed in the centre of the table. In this measure are stuck ten pairs of chopsticks. The wooden images representing the children of the family under sixteen years of age, are also put on it. A glass lamp and two candles are placed on the rice, and incense and mock-money are provided. Generally a Tauist priest is employed to officiate. His principal business consists in reciting a short formula and in ringing his bell. The few sentences he repeats are in praise of the " Mother of the Measure." At the proper time of the performance, the head of the family, and the children belonging to it, kneel down and worship in the established manner before the table. The object of all this is to procure the favour of the goddess in preserving the children of the family to old age. The rice deposited in the bottom of the measure used, if made into *congee* and eaten by the children, is thought to be very conducive to their longevity.

On the afternoon or the evening of the last day of this feast there is a general worship of the ancestral tablets and the household gods belonging to the family.

According to established custom, merchants and grocerymen make out their bills and begin to present them to their debtors about the time the festival commences. From the eleventh to the fifteenth days of the eighth month their clerks and assistants are seen hurrying through the streets seeking debtors, busy and anxious to collect their dues before the fifteenth shall have passed away. Creditors are required to pay a part of the charges against them, if they cannot the whole. They would be regarded as very doubtful customers in the future if they positively declined to pay any proportion, and did not give any satisfactory reason for non-payment. It belongs to the creditor to present his bill ; the debtor need not trouble himself to go and demand his account. If he pays only half of the amount, he will be allowed to let the rest lie over to the latter part of the twelfth month.

The holiday of kite-flying on the highest hills in the city and suburbs is observed regularly on the ninth day of the ninth month at this place.

The Chinese explain that, in ancient times, a certain man was informed, by one who pretended to know the future, that on a specified day some calamity would befall his house or his property; so he took all his family on the morning of that day and went to the hills, spending the time as best he could. On returning home at nightfall, he found his domestic animals all dead. That day was the ninth of the ninth month. They also say that, in imitation of his example, they go to the hills on the ninth day of the ninth month, and thus avoid any domestic calamity which might have befallen them at home; and, to while away the time pleasantly, they take along their kites and fly them. This is called "ascending on high," and indicates the flying of kites on the particular day mentioned.

The interest of the sport centres on the day specified. Then, if the weather is fine, the air is full of kites, of all sizes and of a large variety of shapes. Some are in the shape of spectacles; others represent a kind of fish; others are like an eel, or some similar-looking animal, being from ten to thirty feet long, and of proportionate size; others are like various kinds of birds, or bugs, or butterflies, or quadrupeds. Some resemble men sailing through the air; others are eight-sided, in imitation of the eight diagrams, invented by one of the earliest Chinese emperors. Most or all of those which represent animals are gaudily painted.

Every year there is an especial proclamation issued by a city officer with reference to this kite-flying, warning against tumult on the ninth day of the ninth month on the Black Rock Hill. A petty mandarin, with a large staff of policemen or constables, is annually stationed on the hill, on the arrival of the day, for the purpose of keeping the peace and quelling the disturbance, should any arise. Probably *thirty or forty thousand people visit that hill to fly their kites*, especially if the weather is fine on that day.

On the ninth day of the ninth month a festival is celebrated by a few people. These, on the arrival of this period, have, as a part of the articles offered before the family tablets of ancestors, and afterward consumed, a plate of nine large cakes, made very thin out of rice-flour paste, and steamed, not baked or fried. The flesh of goats, pork, fish, and wine, are also offered. This feast and attendant worship are altogether distinct from the custom of flying kites, though occurring on the same day.

In the latter part of the autumn, occurring often in the ninth month, is a procession of military officers on the day of the solar term called "descending of frost." This procession, as some explain it, seems to be in honour of the approach of cold weather; as others assert, it is in honour of the military implements used by the Chinese in war. The procession starts from the southern parade-ground, not far distant from the south gate. The military officials who are required to take a part in it with their attendants meet on the parade-ground, where they first offer sacrifice to the standard-bearer, the god of the flag. The one who presides at the sacrifice, and in the subsequent procession, is an officer of the rank of the Chinese major-general, under the direction of the viceroy. The bow and arrows, the shield, the flag, the sword, the spear, helmet, coat of mail, and some other implements of warfare, are placed on a pavilion, and carried in the procession of the military mandarins present, their attendants, and a few soldiers, through the south gate into the city, and through some of the principal streets of the city.

The shortest day in the year, the twenty-first or twenty-second of December, or the winter solstice, is the fixed time for one of the great annual festivals observed in China. The high mandarins and the common people celebrate the return of the season with great show and *éclat*.

Before daybreak, the viceroy and the other high military and civil mandarins for several degrees in ranks, dressed in their official robes, go to a large building in the city, near the west gate, called the Emperor's Temple. Near the back part of the temple there is the Emperor's Tablet. It has an inscription in gilt letters, implying a wish that the emperor may live ten thousand years, ten thousand years, ten thousand times ten thousand years.

At a signal given by the master of ceremonies, these high mandarins, in perfect silence and in the most respectful manner, all kneel down on both knees in the places allotted to their rank and office, and knock their heads on or bow them near the stone pavement once, twice, thrice. Then they all simultaneously rise to their feet at a certain signal, and in like manner kneel down, and knock or bow their heads three times again. They now repeat the operation of rising and kneeling, &c. After this they return to their respective yamuns, and spend the day in feasting. While their masters and superiors are performing this ceremony, called "three kneelings and nine knockings," their servants and the inferior officers present stand respectfully looking on.

The object of all this is to congratulate the Son of Heaven, the Emperor of China, on the arrival of the winter solstice. High mandarins at the capital perform a similar ceremony before the emperor himself, or before a yellow screen which personates the emperor.

The common people observe this festival in something like the following manner. They purchase various kinds of meat, and other articles of food, together with wine, incense-sticks, candles, and quantities of mock-money. After being properly cooked, the food is arranged before the ancestral tablets belonging to the family. The incense and the candles are lighted and placed before the tablets; the mock-money paper is now burned. The elder members of the family, or all the members of the family present, according to circumstances, one after the other kneel down on the floor and bow the head several times to or very near to the floor before these tablets. After this ceremony

FAMILY MAKING BALLS OF RICE-FLOUR ON THE EVENING BEFORE THE WINTER SOLSTICE.

has been duly performed, the members of the family give their ancestors, one of whose three spirits is supposed to reside in the tablets already worshipped, an opportunity to consume the subtle and the ethereal part of the viands provided, when they proceed to gorge themselves on the coarse and material portion left.

Besides this feasting, a very singular custom prevails universally among the Chinese at this city.

On the evening before the winter solstice, a quantity of flour, made of a certain kind of rice, is mixed with water, and kneaded before the god of the kitchen until it becomes thick dough. If a son in the family has been married since the last similar festival, and brought his bride home, it falls to her lot, having on a red skirt, to knead the dough. This is considered an event

of good omen to her, being said to insure her plenty to eat and
plenty to wear during her life. After the dough is made, the
whole family gather around the vessel containing it, placed
before the tablet of ancestors, and each one, taking a little of it,
works it into a round ball about the size of a filbert. A sufficient quantity having been prepared, they are set aside until
morning. The first thing done in the morning is the cooking
of these balls by boiling them in water. Having put some of
them into common eating-bowls, they arrange them before the
ancestral tablets as well as before the household gods. This is
attended with the burning of incense and candles, but with no
actual worship. In this respect it differs widely from the ceremonies observed in regard to the meats offered before them, as
above described. Afterwards some of these balls are taken and
eaten by each member of the family.

A few of the balls are reserved for another purpose. They
stick them on the outside of the posts of the outer doors and
windows both of the dwelling-house and of the store or hong,
if any such belongs to the family.

The custom of preparing these balls, eating some, and disposing
of the rest by attaching them to posts in the manner described,
has a strong hold upon the Chinese of this place, else it would
not be so universally and joyfully practised. The roundness of
the cakes is supposed to have some reference or resemblance to
the approaching close of the year. As a whole, the custom is
believed by the people to teach, by insinuation or by inference,
the importance of the whole surviving family all living together
in the reciprocal exercise of parental, filial, and fraternal duties.

The families which are in mourning in consequence of having
lost one of their heads during the past year, are not permitted to
prepare the rice-flour out of which the balls are made, but friends
and relatives may make presents to them of the flour. The
idea seems to be that if they were to buy the rice, and pound it
into flour, and sift it, &c., the process from beginning to end
would not be anything like mourning for the death of a parent.

Some time in the twelfth month, usually before the twentieth
day, it is customary for the Chinese to make a thank-offering to
the gods and goddesses for the blessings of the year soon to close.
A few feel obliged, by poverty or business engagements, to delay
it till the last day of the year. The term used to denote this
thanksgiving literally means "divide year," or "dividing yearly,"
and the custom is thus designated because a "division" of the
good things provided is made among the different objects wor-

shipped every year. A separate offering is made before each of the various household gods, or before the several classes of household gods.

When everything is arranged, "thanksgiving" is commenced by lighting incense and candles on the various tables. The pater-familias, if present, or his wife if he is absent, or some adult member of the family, kneels down before each image or each class of images, and bows the head three times toward the ground. Mock-money of several kinds are set on fire before each divinity or class of divinities thanked. The individual who performs the kneeling and bowing sometimes expresses the "thanks" of the family in a low tone of voice before rising to his feet; if he utters nothing, his gratitude is supposed to be implied.

A table of meats is also set before the ancestral tablets of the family, and a similar act is performed before them, for their favours vouchsafed during the year coming to an end. The wine offered to them is offered hot, as an omen of good to their posterity; while, if any is presented to the gods and goddesses, it is cold.

The rich oftentimes make an offering of a hog's head, a goose, and a large fish, with other meats, to heaven and earth—the highest divinities worshipped in China—as an especial thanks-giving.

On some fortunate day, it is the practice of most families, except those in mourning for the loss of parents, to "sweep the house," as an omen of good luck. The instrument employed is not the common limber broom, but a broom made out of the branches of the bamboo. Not only is the floor of the house thoroughly swept, but the sides of the rooms, and the posts, &c. This operation seems to be regarded as an act of festive and joyous import, for it is interdicted to those who are in deep mourning.

The preparation of rice-flour to make into a certain kind of sweet cake is also among the restrictions laid upon those in mourning for the loss of a parent.

Mourners for the death of a parent who has deceased during the year may not even make this sweet cake, even if the flour prepared by others is presented to them, though they may accept, when presented, the cake already made. The cake is steamed, not baked or boiled. It is prepared in immense quantities during the twelfth month, for use during the festivities connected with the close of the current and the commencement of a new year. It is universally regarded as an expression of good-will to receive and give presents of this kind of cake. The common name for it—"year-cake"—by a play on the sound of the word for cake, is used as a lucky or propitious term, and indicates the wish of the giver that the recipient may yearly increase in happiness and wealth, every year becoming higher and higher. This kind of sweet cake is not made at any other season of the year.

Many shopkeepers or grocery-men, toward the end of the twelfth month, make a present to their rich customers who have generally patronised them for the year.

On the twentieth day of the twelfth month there occurs a very important event in every mandarin's yamun, viz. the sealing up of his seal of office for one month. The officers of Government having been engaged, day after day, for eleven months, without any cessation or relaxation, are regarded as worn out with the fatigues and cares of office, and are allowed a respite of one month, except in cases of unusual importance and emergency, not permitting of delay until after the opening of the seals on the twentieth day of the following month. Before the seal is sealed up, several blank or white sheets of paper are stamped with the official seal for use, if necessary, during the month when the seal may not, on any consideration, be actually employed for stamping proclamations or warrants. Very little business is done in the yamuns during this interval. The time is principally devoted to feastings, giving and receiving dinners, and attending theatrical exhibitions. It is a season of general dissipation and abandonment among officials, high and low, civil and military.

The rule is that the highest officials should begin the process or ceremony of sealing up their seals of office, and that the lowest should end it. The subordinate officials must all be present at the yamuns of their superiors and witness the transaction. When the highest officer, civil or military—each of these classes by itself—has concluded the sealing up of his seal in the regular manner, all of his subordinates, except those connected with his own establishment, go to the mandarin next lower in rank and office, witness the sealing up of his seal in a similar way, and so on to the mandarin lowest in rank and office, who performs the ceremony only in the presence of the clerks.

The ceremony commences at the viceroy's about three or four o'clock on the morning of the twentieth. The seal is put upon a table in his tribunal of justice. The mandarin presents himself, clothed in his official robes, before it, where he kneels down three times, and bows his head on the ground, or toward it, nine times, under the direction of a master of ceremony. The seal is then taken by one of the principal clerks or the master of ceremony, who kneels down reverently before the mandarin, and, holding it up with both hands, expresses his wishes for the promotion of his master to a station of higher rank. He then stamps two strips of red paper with the seal three times each. After this is done he puts the seal in the casket or box provided to contain it. The box is shut and locked, the two pieces of red paper are pasted upon it in the shape of the letter X, answering the purpose of seals to the box, having the name of the office and the date of the sealing written upon them. A fine piece of yellow silk is then carefully wrapped round the box, and the whole is put away, not to be opened until the early morning of the twentieth of the first month of the following year.

At the proper time of the ceremony, the officials of inferior rank who are present express their congratulations to the mandarin in view of the arrival of the time of sealing up the seal, and their wishes for his promotion and success. The clerks and underlings connected with his yamun also make the same congratulations and professions, each seeming to vie with the other in joy at this return of the season.

As soon as the ceremony is over, all the official spectators, except those who belong to the yamun, depart to call upon the mandarin next inferior. The crowd becomes smaller and smaller after visiting each successive yamun, as no one goes from his own yamun to one of lower rank. At each yamun the ceremony commences just as soon as the crowd of officials arrive from witnessing the sealing at the yamun next higher in rank. The last seal is usually sealed up after day has dawned.

Each yamun is illuminated as brilliantly as is possible with lanterns, torches, and candles on this occasion. Incense and candles are burned on the table on which the seal is placed while the mandarin is worshipping it. While being sealed up, fire-crackers are let off and cannons are fired in honour of the event. Manifestations of joy are to be seen on every side. Congratulations on account of the arrival of the annual period of relaxation and festivity are mutual and sincere. A month is to be spent free from the common routine of business and responsibility, but filled up with joyous and festive celebrations and employments.

There are two objects of worship, as the Chinese aver, to be found in every family, viz. the ancestral tablet and the kitchen god.—The practice of worshipping the latter is as universal as that of wor-

E E

shipping the former.   Incense and candles are regularly burned
before the god of the kitchen on the first and the fifteenth of
every month, morning and evening. Some families burn incense
and candles before this god daily.   On the occurrence of the
great festivals in the fifth month, in the middle of the eighth
month, and at the winter solstice in the eleventh, and the New
Year, besides incense and candles, offerings of food are presented
before this divinity in most families, accompanied with the burning of mock-money.   *The kitchen god is one of the peculiar
institutions of China.*

To represent this household divinity, some families use simply
a piece of red paper, with a sentence written upon it, referring
to the kitchen god as the ruler of the lives of the members of
the family. Generally, however, a sheet of white paper—on
which the likenesses of an old man and an old woman have been
stamped, together with pictures of various kinds of animals, as
fowls, dogs, buffaloes, &c. and tables, relating to various subjects
—is used instead of the slip of red paper, with a title of the god
written upon it. The two pictures represent the kitchen god
and goddess. In mandarin establishments, the god of the kitchen
furnace is worshipped, in accordance with an ancient custom, as
the Superintendent or Inspector of Good and Evil.

On the evening of the twenty-third of the twelfth month
occurs the annual " sacrifice of meats before the god of the

GOD OF THE KITCHEN.

kitchen." According to estimation, this
is made by some six-tenths of the
families at this place and vicinity.
Those who make it use no rice.
Chicken-meat, duck, goat, pork, fish,
clams, crabs, sweet cake, sugar-cane,
loose-skinned oranges, vermicelli, &c.
with wine, tea, large candles, incense,
and several kinds of mock-money, constitute sometimes the meat sacrifice, in
distinction from a vegetable sacrifice.
These things are arranged on a table
before the old kitchen god. At the
proper time, the head of the family
kneels down before the god and bows
his head three times, in token of his
thanks for the favours of the god during
the past year, while the younger mem-
bers explode fire-crackers.   Usually, at the close of the sacrifice,

the paper having the pictures of the god and the goddess is torn down and burned up with the mock-money presented.

The Chinese believe that the old kitchen god ascends to heaven, and reports to the "Pearly Emperor Supreme Ruler" the conduct of the members of the family during the current year. Some, therefore, prepare a sumptuous feast of meats for him on the

OFFERING SACRIFICE TO THE GOD OF THE KITCHEN.
(The sacrifice is put upon the kitchen furnace before a slip of paper representing the kitchen god.)

evening of his ascension, or the evening before it (some seeming to believe that he does not quit the earth until the evening of the twenty-fourth). They hope thus to bribe him to present a favourable report, passing over the evil deeds of the family relating to the past year. Some interpret this feast also to indicate the wishes of the family for the god of the kitchen to intercede with the "Supreme Ruler" for his protection and blessing during

the year soon to commence. The kitchen god is regarded as an
influential personage, and it is believed to redound to the welfare
of the divinity to treat him with respect, especially at the close
of the year, when he is about to return into the immediate
presence of his master, the Supreme Ruler, to make his annual
report. The family seem anxious to have him leave with favourable impressions of their hospitality and generosity. He appears
to be regarded as a kind of spy on the behaviour of the family,
though he professedly only presides over the domain of the
kitchen.

Some families, at the time when they imagine the kitchen god
is about taking his departure from their premises, take some
handfuls of peas or beans, and a quantity of balls made of straw,
and throw them upon the roof of the building containing the
kitchen furnace. The sound of these falling upon the roof, they
imagine, resembles the noise of the footsteps of the departing
god, or of the horse which he may ride. This is a kind of parting
salute. Some families burn the balls of straw and the peas as
omens of good luck for horses or cattle, typifying that they will
have straw and peas to eat.

On the evening of the twenty-fourth is the appointed time for
those who wish to "make a vegetable sacrifice to the god of the
kitchen." No meats are used. Vegetables and fruits of various
kinds only are employed, with incense and candles, and mock-
money, arranged in due form. No rice is presented. The presentation is attended with kneeling and bowing, as usual on such
occasions.

Before the offering and the worship are made, the picture of
the new god and goddess of the kitchen is pasted up in the place
selected, just after the old picture is torn down and burned.
The object of presenting this vegetable sacrifice is generally
explained to be the honouring of the kitchen divinity for the
New Year.

Early on the morning of the last day of the year, or the day
before the last, there occurs in most families what is regarded as
a very important ceremony. It is commonly called the "offering of the yearly rice." It corresponds very nearly, in some
respects, to the offering which has been described as having
been presented on the morning of the New Year to heaven
and earth.

The rich, and all the families which can find leisure, usually
have the two ceremonies, one on the last morning of the current,
and one on the first morning of the following year. Those who

have both use different vegetables on the two occasions. The new almanac, and certain kinds of mock-paper, and the flowers put on the rice which is offered on the morning of the last day of the year, may be used on the following morning. The other articles are generally changed. It is regarded as absolutely necessary to have, on these two occasions, a certain kind of celery and the loose-skinned oranges, as omens of good. The former is typical of a "red mouth," or of a cheerful, ruddy, and healthy countenance, and the latter of a fortunate or auspicious year.

The last evening in the year is the last period of grace to those who have run up bills at groceries and stores. According to custom, every one is expected to pay his outstanding accounts at this time. It is universally regarded as a great disgrace not to be able to pay one's debts on the last day of a year. Instances occur when debtors, in despair of being able to pay their debts at the close of the year, and being too proud to bear the disgrace and other consequences of a failure to do so, commit suicide.

It falls to the business of the creditor to make out his account and present it to his debtor. The debtor would not be trusted during the following year unless he paid up his debts in the present. He would be known as a man who did not pay his accounts at the end of a year.

It sometimes occurs that a debtor eludes the vigilance of his creditor all the last day and night of the year. After daylight on the morning of the New Year, the former occasionally may be seen going about the streets in search of the latter, with a lighted lantern in one hand and his account in the other. He does not recognise or admit the fact that it is daylight. With him it is still dark, and in proof of this he carries his lantern, with which to see his way while in pursuit of his delinquent customer. According to custom, he may still pursue his debtor if he carries a lighted lantern, as he would be obliged to carry one were it indeed night; but, without such a lantern, the seeking out of debtors and the collecting of unpaid bills would not be tolerated on the morning of the New Year, after daylight.

Some time after dark, and before midnight, on the last day of the year, always called the "thirtieth night," even if the twelfth month has only twenty-nine days in it, the last festival of the year is observed. This is styled literally "rounding the year." All of the members of the family are present who can possibly arrange their business to be at home. A presentation of meats,

vegetables, and fruits is made before the ancestral tablets of the
family.   Incense, candles, and mock-money are burned before
them, and before the household gods.   The father of the family
presents himself before the tablets with kneelings and bowings ;
if absent, the wife or the eldest of the children takes his place in
worshipping.   A bonfire of pine-wood is made before the tablets.
Fire-crackers are exploded by the younger members of the family
while the bonfire is burning.   Salt is thrown upon the flames,
and the crackling which it occasions is looked upon as an omen
of good fortune for the coming year.   After a while, the food is
taken away and consumed by the members of the household.
It is a general time of rejoicing.

After the feast of "rounding the year" is over, near midnight,
in some households, every one changes the clothing previously
worn, putting on new or clean garments.   Now-a-days, few
families provide new suits throughout to be worn on the New Year.
After this the head of the family proceeds to make presents of
money to servants, children, nephews, and nieces, if any are
present.   Making this present is an omen of good for the coming
year ; it provides against beginning the year with an empty
purse.   Sometimes several dollars, in silver or in bills, are put
into the purse of the paterfamilias, as a good omen.   The money
presented around among the members of the household, if in
copper cash, should be strung upon a red string, as a symbol
of joy.   It would not well comport with the festivity of
the occasion to have it strung on a white string, as white
is a badge of sorrow.   The money presented is usually spent
in purchasing candies or sweetmeats soon after the New Year
commences.

In many families, presents to servants are made on New Year's
morning.   They come forward, dressed in their best clothing,
and bow down before their masters or superiors, and present
their congratulations on the arrival of a new year.   On rising to
their feet they expect to receive a present in money, for which
they return their thanks.   Those families who do not make the
usual presents to servants and inferiors, if able to make it, are
stigmatised as "hard" or "tough"—that is, stingy.

The distribution of presents in money on the last night of the
year corresponds to the fabulous visits of St. Nicholas, or Santa
Claus, which gladden the hearts of children on Christmas evening in Western lands.   His stealthy visits occasion much merriment and joy among Western youngsters, while the present of
money from their parent, or master, or superior, on the night

before the New Year, or on New Year's morning, seems equally acceptable by juveniles, or servants, or inferiors in this land.

Not long subsequent to the change of garments and the distribution of presents commences the arrangement of the sacrifice to heaven and earth, to be offered on the early morning of New Year's day, an account of which has already been given.

CHAPTER XXII.

SINGULAR AND POPULAR SUPERSTITIONS.

THE Chinese seem to cherish kind and charitable feelings towards the unhappy spirits in the Land of Shades. They have therefore invented many ingenious methods by which they fancy they contribute to their comfort. They imagine them to be in want of food, clothing, and spending-money, and they contrive, as they think, to forward these necessary articles to them.[*]

The Chinese believe that the spirits in the other world exercise a great influence over the affairs of this world; they therefore desire to obtain their friendly aid in the pursuit of health, wealth, or honour. Oftentimes ceremonies are performed as especial acts of thanksgiving to the spirits. Such ceremonies are regarded also as meritorious.

There are four popular customs, called "thanksgiving by the use of cakes," "presentation of food," "mounting the platform," and "the universal rescue." A day or two subsequent to the performance of the third and fourth, there is always another ceremony, called "a supplementary offering."

---

[*] "The world of spirits," says Dr. Medhurst, "according to the Chinese, is like the world of men: and as, in this life, it is impossible to live without eating, or to obtain comforts without money, so, in the life to come, the same state of things prevails. Hence, those who wish to benefit the departed must not only feed them once in the year, but supply them with cash for unavoidable expenses. In order to remit money into the invisible world, they procure small pieces of paper, about four inches square, in the middle of which are affixed patches of tinfoil, or gold leaf, which represent gold and silver money; these they set fire to, and believe that they are thus transformed into real bullion; passing through the smoke into the invisible world. Large quantities of this material are provided, and sacrificial paper constitutes a great article of trade and manufacture, affording employment to many myriads of people."—*China, its State and Prospects*, p. 213.

It is considered eminently desirable to have these ceremonies performed during the evening, commencing about seven or eight o'clock, and not lasting later than twelve o'clock. The daytime belongs to the male principle of nature, whose influence is more vigorous and powerful than the influence which prevails in the night, belonging to the female principle of nature. The spirits being subject to the female principle, if the ceremonies designed to benefit them should be performed in the daytime, it is feared they would not be able to be present. They perhaps would be unable to overcome the influences which prevail during the day. For the same reason, the performances should close by midnight, because the male influences begin then to abound, or be more powerful.

These ceremonies may be performed at any time during the year ; but, as a general thing, they are observed most numerously during the latter part of the year, commencing with the seventh Chinese month, especially the last three ceremonies. There is a proverb current at this place, which says, "from the commencement of the seventh month the Tauist priests need not buy any rice," implying that they are so constantly employed in the performance of their official functions that they need not be at any expense for food, they being boarded whenever employed. In fact, however, they are not so constantly engaged by the people as the proverb intimates.

The *thanksgiving by the use of cakes* takes its name, in part, from a kind of steamed cakes which are used, made out of wheat-flour and rice. The whole thank-offering of food very often consists of only the following articles : a plate of these steamed cakes, numbering one hundred and forty-four, a few pieces of bean-curd, a little white vermicelli, a bowl of rice, a few baked bread-cakes, a bowl of vegetable soup, and three cups of wine. These are arranged sometimes on the ground before the house or shop of the offerer ; sometimes they are placed on a flat, open bamboo vessel, several feet in diameter, which is put on the ground. The offerer usually kneels while he bows his head three times towards these articles, holding lighted incense in his hands, audibly expressing his thanks to the spirits for their past goodness to him, and begging a continuance of their favours. If the thanksgiving is tendered to the destitute spirits in the lower regions on behalf of a child of the offerer, the child is usually made to kneel down three times, and bow towards the things presented. The mock-money and the mock-clothing which had been provided are now set on fire and consumed. The offerer takes a few kernels of the rice, or a cake or two, and puts them into the vegetable soup, which is then poured out on the ground;

PRESENTING A THANK-OFFERING OF CAKES.

or some of the cakes are thrown around on the ground, and a little of the wine is poured on the embers of the mock-money and mock-clothing. He again bows or kneels down three times before the articles, after which everything except what was thrown down or turned out on the ground is gathered up and taken into the house, where it is consumed by the offerer and his family.

Presentation of Food.—This ceremony is more imposing and expensive than the former. The offerer employs two or three Buddhist or Tauist priests to aid him. Offerings are arranged on a table, never on the ground. From three to seven plates of the small steamed cakes are provided; also several plates of a larger kind, each plate having thirty-six cakes, several plates of fruits, a bucket of boiled rice, a quantity of bean-curd, vermicelli, vegetable soup, several bowls of two or three kinds of cakes, some paste and clean water, and a sheet of paper placed under the table, three cups of tea if the priests are Buddhists, or three cups of wine if they are Tauists, candles, incense, mock-money, and mock-clothing. One of the priests beats a drum; another, standing near the table, rings a bell and recites formulas. The offerer kneels down, dressed in his best clothing, and bows three times, muttering his requests to the spirits, who are supposed to have arrived.

Mounting the Platform.—This ceremony takes its name from the circumstance that the priests perform their parts while mounted on a platform. Six or more priests, either Tauists or Buddhists, are employed, the head priests and the drummer getting double wages.

The platform or altar is prepared in the following manner:— Sometimes a low platform of boards is first constructed, and on this two or three ranges or tiers of tables are placed. Behind the highest table, and behind some other tables of the platform, small stools are placed, which are occupied by the priests during the ceremony. The head priest occupies the highest seat of all. The number of tables used is graduated by the number of priests who are engaged to assist in the performance.

The ceremony is commenced by burning several charms. These charms, when burned, are believed, in some way, speedily to

PRESENTING FOOD TO THE SPIRITS OF THE DEAD.

inform the Pearly Emperor Supreme Ruler, or Buddha, according as the priests employed are Tauists or Buddhists, of what is being transacted on the earth. They take their positions on their stools, placed behind the tiers of tables, and, having thus mounted the platform, they ring their bells, recite their liturgies, beat the drum, &c.

The food offered to the unfortunate spirits is arranged on a table. Among these edibles are several dishes of meats, vegetables, fruits, steamed cakes, boiled rice, vermicelli, and a vessel containing gruel or salted paste. On the vessel containing gruel are paper or earthen spoons. Under one of the tables there is a half pail of water, covered by a sheet or two of paper. A paper image of a certain divinity is placed on the table, whose business is to control the hungry spirits which come to the feast, and keep them from fighting and quarrelling for the food provided for their entertainment. Some call this god the "King of the Spirits." He has ten plates of vegetables placed before him for his eating, if the priests invited to officiate are Buddhist ; but if the priests employed are Tauist, the food provided is principally meats and fruits.

On the upper table of the tiers of the platform there are various idols or images. While the priests are performing their part, the proprietor of the ceremony attends to the candles and incense, or kneels down, bowing toward the ground at the bidding of the priests. At the customary times the mock-money and the mock-clothing are burnt.

Some time during the evening a certain formula is repeated, and a kind of charm is burnt. A certain kind of lighted incense-stick is also put in the food designed for the hungry spirits, and in the ground in front of the house. This formula, and these sheets, and the incense thus arranged, all are supposed to attract the spirits to the place. At the proper time, a few of the cakes, a little of the rice, and some of the vegetable soup are thrown on the ground, designed as a kind of special offering to the spirits. At the close of the performance, some of the food presented to the spirits is prepared for the feast which follows, and the rest of it is often distributed, on the following day, among the neighbours and friends.

It is the custom, on the evening devoted to the celebration of mounting the platform, to have a table covered with various offerings of food placed before the ancestral tablets belonging to the family in whose house the ceremony is performed. Incense, candles, and mock-money are also burnt before these tablets on the occasion.

The water is for the use of the spirits who come to the entertainment. It is sagely surmised that they may desire to refresh themselves by a bath at the end of their journey, and so water is thoughtfully provided. The paper is supposed to answer the purpose of a towel. The paste provided is to supply the peculiar wants of the headless spirits which may find their way to the place. It is believed that there are many spirits which have been unfortunate enough to lose their heads, and as they have no mouth or teeth, they cannot eat as other spirits ; spoons are therefore kindly furnished, by which they may put the paste or gruel into their throats.

On the evening succeeding, a supplementary offering is provided for the spirits which failed to arrive in season to enjoy the entertainment of mounting the platform. It is feared that, out of the immense number of spirits in the Land of Shades which might desire to be present, there are some whose arrival may be delayed.

The Universal Rescue.—The "universal rescue" is the most expensive of the four ; it is also the least commonly observed. It lasts either three, or five, or seven days and nights in succession. In September 1859, one was held in the city, near the viceroy's yamun, which lasted seven days and seven nights. Twenty-seven altars were erected in connexion with it. Over one hundred priests in all, both Buddhists and Tauists, were employed. The aggregate expense was over eight thousand dollars, which were contributed by the people.

Some fifteen or twenty days before the time fixed upon for the beginning of the " rescue," a roughly-built house, called the spirits' house, is erected near the place. This house is sometimes six or eight feet high, five or six feet deep, and twenty or twenty-five feet long. It is usually divided into five apartments. The middle apartment is devoted to the occupancy of a large paper image of a certain god, made in a sitting posture on a bamboo frame.

Adjoining the middle room, on one side, is a room for the accommodation of gentlemen spirits who may attend the celebration, and on the other side is a room for the use of lady spirits, which facts are made known by notices pasted in front. The two apartments at the ends of the house are devoted to the important use of bathing-rooms for male and for female spirits. The ladies' bathing-room of course adjoins the ladies' parlour, and the gentlemen's bathing-room adjoins the gentlemen's sitting-room, which is made known to the spirits by appropriate notices. It is very desirable that there should be no scandalous intermingling between the different sexes. In front of the bathing-rooms are usually suspended bamboo screens.

On the "spirits' house," in some convenient place, is put up what pretends to be a proclamation from the god occupying the central apartment, giving notice to the hungry and destitute spirits of the month and day a " universal rescue " will be commenced, and that an entertainment will be provided for their benefit in the vicinity, and inviting the "good gentlemen" and the "faithful ladies" in the spirit world to be present. They are invited also to take lodgings in the house provided, and are exhorted to behave themselves with propriety.

As the time appointed draws nigh, two or more altars are built up in the form of terraces, of three, or four, or five steps or tiers. One or more of these altars are under the management of Buddhist priests, who arrange on them idols belonging to their religion. One or more are appropriated by Tauist priests, who arrange on them images belonging to their sect. Each altar has several censers and pairs of candlesticks. The number of altars

SECOND DEPARTMENT OF THE BUDDHISTIC HELL.

erected depends on the amount of money to be expended and the time to be occupied in the performance of the "universal rescue." The altars are decked out with embroidered coverings, valuable articles of *vertù*, and rare and elegant curiosities.

When the "universal rescue" is performed on a large scale, in connexion with it is a place where the punishments inflicted on wicked spirits in the ten departments of hell, according to Buddhistic notions, are represented by small images. The images and the machinery representing the scenes and the sufferings of hell are made to move when necessary by strings attached, which are pulled by somebody unseen. For example, a spirit is represented as in the act of enduring a flagellation with the bamboo ; another as being fried in a kettle of oil ; another as being pounded in a large mortar ; another as being sawed asunder ; some are undergoing an examination before the judge or ruler of a department ; others are laid on a board full of sharp nails, or thrown on a hill of knives ; while others may be seen in the very act of transmigration, *i.e.* part of the object is like some animal, and the rest of it is like the human body.

By the side of the street near by there is generally found a miniature exhibition of thirty-six shops. During the evenings of the celebration these shops are lighted up by means of small red lanterns, on which usually is found an expression intimating that it is done at public expense.

The various public streets leading to the place where the altars have been erected are all lighted up in the evenings of the celebration with much more than ordinary brilliancy. Some of the lanterns employed are made of bright red paper pasted on a light bamboo splint frame, being some eighteen or twenty inches long and eight or nine inches in diameter, and having the name of the neighbourhood or the temple where the performance is enacted inscribed on them. Besides these round lanterns there are sets of thirty-six others, of a square or flat form, fastened at intervals upon the sides of the streets, not suspended. On the front side of each, which is made of white paper or of white gauze, and is about two feet long by one foot or more wide, there are painted, sometimes quite neatly, some animal or animals, domestic or wild, quadruped or biped, birds and insects, or classes of persons, as a king, officer, traveller, merchant, courtesan, opium-eater, gambler, or robber ; specimens or illustrations of the different ways of dying, as by hanging, decapitation, drowning, and suicide, together with various gods and spirits, good and bad.

These sets are called "lanterns of the thirty-six classes." There are also found arranged along the sides of the streets at this time other sets of , lanterns, ten in a set, which represent the different orders of created existences, included under ten classes. The Buddhistic idea of transmigration of souls is also depicted on some of these lanterns, as insects becoming men, or *vice versâ.*

When the time has arrived, and everything is ready for the beginning of the ceremony, the Tauist priests engaged burn a certain yellow paper document before one of the altars where they expect to officiate. This document is a statement designed for the information of the principal god of their sect in regard to what is to be transacted at the place where it is burnt. A paper image of a man, seated on a paper horse, is consumed at the same time, who is supposed to convey the document safely and speedily to the Pearly Emperor. The Buddhist priests at the same time are engaged in conveying information to Buddha of what is to be transacted on earth, using the method which is customary on such occasions for their order.

The ceremony does not require much time, and constitutes the principal performance for the first evening.

Early the next morning they first light incense and candles in the principal or most important places in connexion with the various altars, and then sprinkle some water over the altars, idols, and furniture. This is done for the laudable purpose of purifying the various articles. They then take their proper places before or upon the altars, and commence the recitation of their classics and formulas. After a time some one of their number calls upon the head man, or the director of the "universal rescue," to worship, by kneeling down and bowing three times before the principal altar.

For breakfast, before each of the principal idols some slight refreshments are arranged. The inferior idols are also provided with refreshments, but less in quantity and inferior in quality than what is furnished for the entertainment of the superior and principal ones.

In the evening the altars are brilliantly illuminated by the burning of large candles. The various sets of lanterns in the streets near the place are all lighted. Oftentimes a band of music is employed to entertain the spectators. The evening is spent in chanting their formulas. Generally a ceremony like " mounting the platform " is performed at least every other evening, and sometimes every evening during the continuance of the "universal rescue," except the first and the last evenings.

The interest culminates on the last evening. Very often the half of this night is occupied in performing various extra ceremonies, designed to benefit, in several ways, the spirits which may attend, or which may desire to attend.

Frequently a large number of small and cheap earthen vessels, shaped somewhat like bowls, is provided, or sometimes a piece of a board is used. A preparation of pitch and some other inflammable material is put in each. Around the top of the outside of each are fastened paper imitations of lotus flowers, or other pretty flowers. Early in the evening, these vessels are carried in a procession of priests from the place where the principal ceremonies are performed to the edge of the nearest running water, where, the pitch or oil having been lighted, the vessels are placed carefully on the water and allowed to float away. The object of this is explained to be, to afford lights for the spirits that come or go by water. This ceremony is called "letting go the water-lamps."

A farce called "breaking into hell" is enacted in something like the following manner, the object being to rescue the spirits confined there. Five common earthen tiles are placed on the ground a few feet from each other, one being put in the centre

FLOATING OFF THE WATER-LAMPS.

of a square and four at its corners. In the midst are also placed one or more small paper images of persons, also several sheets of mock-money. These tiles represent hell, and the images a part of its occupants. A priest then takes a kind of staff in his hand, and walks slowly and solemnly around these tiles, repeating formulas. After a while he sets fire to the mock-money. When this is consumed he strikes each of the tiles a blow with his staff, which breaks them to pieces. He then seizes hold of the miniature images and carries them off.

Another performance is that of "spirits passing over a bridge." A kind of mock bridge is made out of boards placed on stools or

tables, with a railing on each side, constructed with bamboo and
paper or cloth, to keep the spirits from falling over the sides of
the bridge. Sometimes a kind of arch or covering is put over it.
When everything is ready, the priests begin their chanting,
blowing of horns, and beating of gongs or cymbals. At a signal,
several persons, with their faces painted, dressed as the Chinese
imagine spirits to dress, make their appearance ; and, having
received from a priest standing not far from one end of the bridge
a paper document, pass on over the bridge. After passing the
bridge, the spirits deliver the paper they received before they
went upon it to a priest. These papers are burnt before the
customary image. The spirits come back to the starting-point
by another route, not going back over the bridge. They now
go over the bridge again, and, returning to the front side, pass
over, and so on the requisite number of times, each time carrying a paper document. This bridge is said to represent a certain
bridge in the infernal regions. Only those who are good are
supposed to be able to pass over it safely ; the wicked are believed
to fall over its sides into the water beneath it, where they
perish. The performance of the universal rescue is supposed
to render the passage of the bridge more feasible and safe for
spirits.

Sometimes those living in the neighbourhood desire to send
money and clothing to their deceased relatives, and they take
occasion to contribute trunks of these necessary articles for
them, to be burnt on the last evening of this ceremony. The
dead are supposed to receive the presents of money and of rai-
ment from their surviving friends or relatives on the earth.

Bountiful provisions are made on the last evening for the
hungry spirits. Several stacks of the steamed cakes, two or three
feet high, are arranged on the tables or on the ground. Many
dishes of vegetables, meats, fruits, &c. are also provided.

On the evening following the last night a supplementary
offering is prepared for those spirits who arrived too late to
participate in the feast of the preceding evening.

The Chinese have invented several *ways by which they pretend
to find out the pleasure of their gods.* The objects in regard to
which they are accustomed to make inquiries are various, such
as recovery from sickness, birth of male children, success in
trade, literary pursuits, and the attainment of fame or office.
They profess to believe that the gods will indicate the condition
of things in regard to the future, or their will in relation to the
present, to those who employ certain methods ; and the answer

given is considered a good and sufficient reason for shaping one's conduct and business, in a great degree, accordingly.

The minutiæ of the ceremonies performed in endeavouring to ascertain the will of the gods are considerably modified by the circumstances of the occasion or the caprices of the principal actor.

While making use of any one of these methods of consulting the gods, the burning of one or three sticks of incense and a brace of candles before the idol worshipped is an invariable accompaniment.

By the Use of the Kà-pue.—This is the name given to a utensil, generally made of wood if to be used in private families, and of

OFFERING INCENSE.

the root of a bamboo-tree if to be used in temples. It is usually from two to five inches in diameter at the largest end, and from three to eight inches long. One end is considerably smaller than the other, sometimes tapering to a point. After it is made of the desired size and shape, it is split lengthwise through the middle. Each piece will thus have, of course, a flat and a round side.

The person who wishes to make inquiries of any particular god or goddess kneels down before the image, or whatever represents

it, and bows his head reverently toward the ground several times
while on his knees.   He then proceeds to state his circumstances
or his plans, presenting his request, and begging an intimation of
the will of the divinity, or the condition of things in the future
in regard to his case.   He then rises to his feet, and, taking the
kà-pue, with its plane surfaces placed together, passes it through
the smoke of the burning incense, with a circular motion, a few
times.   He then throws it up reverently before the idol, so that
it shall fall to the ground between him and the idol.   The nature
of the answer is supposed to be determined by the relative
position of the pieces as they lie on the ground.   If the flat sur-

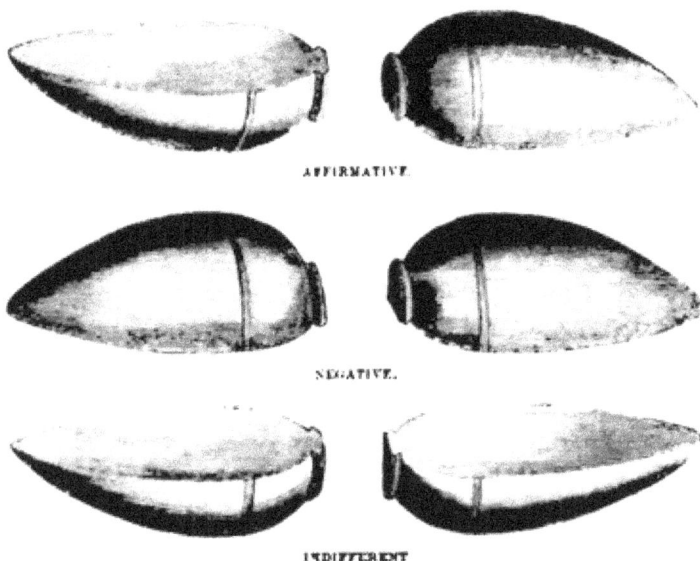

AFFIRMATIVE.

NEGATIVE.

INDIFFERENT

face of one falls upward, and the flat surface of the other falls
downward, the answer is regarded as affirmative, or favourable.
If both oval surfaces fall upward, the answer is negative, or unfavourable.   If they both fall downward, the answer is indifferent,
neither very good nor very bad.

By casting Lots.—Every large temple has belonging to it from
fifty to one hundred stanzas of poetry, relating to a variety of
subjects.   Each stanza is numbered, and is printed on a separate
slip of paper.   Each temple has a quantity of lots corresponding
to the number of stanzas, and referring to them by number. .   ·

These lots are drawn before some idol in a public temple; never, it is affirmed, in a private dwelling-house. The individual who wishes to make application to the god presents himself before his image on his knees, and, after bowing several times, states his name and residence, the object of his inquiries, and whether on his own or another's account. He then takes a bamboo tube containing the lots, and shakes it gently before the idol, until a slip falls to the ground. He now rises from his knees and picks up this slip, which he places on the censer containing lighted incense, being careful to put the side or end having the number of the lot written on it toward the god, so that he can see it. After this, he takes the kà-pue and uses it as

CASTING LOTS.

above described, in order to ascertain whether the god approves the lot. If the god expresses approval of the lot, the stanza of poetry corresponding to its number is consulted, to discover the sentiments or decision of the divinity in regard to the subject submitted to him. If the kà-pue indicates disapproval of this lot, it is put back into the bamboo tube, and the operation of shaking another out is again performed by the person in a similar manner as before.

By the Use of a Medium.—This is a very singular method of consulting some god, and is employed either in a temple, or, more commonly, in a private house, *in some respects analogous to spirit-rapping as practised in the United States and Great Britain.* It is usually performed in the evening, generally more as a matter of friendship and of favour to some one than as a way of earning money on the part of the operators. A present is often given them by the person who invites their assistance.

Two performers are required besides the one who desires to inquire of the god. One of these two takes his seat on a chair before the table on which incense and candles are burning, in front of the idol. The other man seizes a pencil and draws a charm on a piece of yellow paper. He then sets it on fire by one of the candles, and, while it is burning, moves it gently up and down in front of the person seated. The object of this is to expel

CONSULTING THE GOD THROUGH A MALE MEDIUM.

all defiling influences from him, and prepare his body to become a temporary residence of the god invoked. He now rises from his seat, with his eyes closed, and receives from his companion one stick of lighted incense, which he clasps in both hands, and holds calmly before his breast, while he continues to stand with closed eyes and his back turned toward the table. The other person now begins to entwine the fingers of both his hands together in a certain manner believed to be peculiarly pleasing to the deity invoked. He soon approaches the other one who is standing, and, with a sudden motion, throws his hands, with fingers thus interlocked, out toward his face, very much as though he intended to strike him. This motion separates the fingers, which he again interlaces, and which he again throws out toward him. This operation is repeated several times, being regarded as very efficacious in procuring a visit from the god. The person whose eyes are shut during all this time soon gives what is believed to be unmistakeable evidence of being possessed by some supernatural and invisible power. His body sways back and forward ; the stick of incense falls from his grasp, and he begins to step about with the peculiar stride, and assumes the peculiar attitude and appearance, considered as belonging to that god. This is regarded as an infallible proof of the actual presence of the divinity in the body of the medium.

If the individual on whose account the presence of the god is invoked insists on having the principal divinity come to the consultation, the medium, after a short interval, usually assumes the distinctive manners belonging to that god, as a token that he has arrived.

The supplicant now advances, and with three lighted sticks of incense in his hands, bows down on his knees before the medium and begs him to be seated. After he has seated himself, the supplicant states the object in regard to which he has sought an audience with the god. A conversation often ensues between the two parties on the subject, the one professing to give the information desired, and the other receiving it with humility, gratitude, and reverence. Sometimes, however, the god, using the mouth of the medium, gives the supplicant a sound scolding for invoking his aid to attain unlawful or unworthy ends, and sometimes he positively declines to communicate the coveted information. At the close of the interview the medium apparently falls asleep for a few seconds. On awaking, some tea is given him to drink, and he soon becomes himself again.

By the Use of a Pen writing on Sand.—The pen consists in all of two pieces of wood. The larger piece, which usually is between two and three feet long, is often made of mulberry, willow, or peach wood. Its shape is very much like a farmer's harrow, or the capital letter V, being cut out of a very crooked branch, or a branch taken in connexion with the trunk of the tree. The front end of this drag-like stick is usually carved in imitation of the head of the Chinese dragon. A small piece of one of the three kinds of wood above specified, about five or six inches long, is inserted under the front point, and at right angles

to it, giving the whole utensil the general appearance of a very
small drag, with only one front tooth.

When one wishes to consult a god by this means, he makes
his wish known to a person belonging to a society or company
established for facilitating such consultations. A table is placed
before the image of the god consulted, or his representative
emblem.   On this table, besides the candles and incense, are
arranged fresh flowers, and tea or mock-mony is also provided.
In front of this table, and farther from the idol, is placed another
table, having upon it a wooden platter about three or four feet
long by two wide, and several inches deep ; the platter is nearly
filled with dry sand.   After the incense and candles have been

WRITING WITH A FORKED PEN AN ORACLE ON SAND.

lighted, the supplicant kneels down and 'mentions his desires,
with the usual ceremonies.   Having risen from his knees, paper
charms are set on fire, and, while burning, they are brandished
over the pen, the sand, and the two persons who are to hold the
pen, for the purpose of purifying them all.   These two men,
standing with the table which has the platter of sand upon it
between them, and with their backs to the idol, silently and
reverently take hold of the drag-like utensil, one at each side,
in such a manner that the end of the tooth under its front point
shall rest in the sand.

A peculiar kind of charm is now lighted, and placed in the censer standing on the table before the image for the purpose of purification. Another is burnt in some place near by, open or exposed to the direct light of the heavens. This is designed to cause the god to descend, enter the pen, and deliver its oracle in writing. If he does not soon indicate his presence, another charm is burnt. His presence is manifested by a slow movement of the point of the pen, tracing characters in the sand. After writing a line or two on the sand, the pen ceases to move, and the characters are transferred to paper. After this, if the response is unfinished, another line is written, and so on until the pen entirely ceases its motion, which signifies that the spirit of the divinity has taken its departure from the pen. All that now remains to be done is to ascertain the meaning of the oracle, which not unfrequently is found to be a difficult task.

Women frequently employ Female Mediums.—The object of their doing so is to ascertain the news from a deceased relative or friend, or the kind of medicine a certain sick person should use in order to recover from illness, &c. There are two classes of these female mediums.

One class profess to obtain and transmit the news required by means of a very diminutive image, made of the wood of the willow-tree. The image is first exposed to the dew for forty-nine nights, when, after the performance of a superstitious ceremony relating to it, it is believed to have the power of speaking. The image is laid upon the stomach of the woman to whom it belongs. She, by means of it, pretends to be the medium of communication between the living and the dead. She sometimes professes to send the image into the world of spirits to find the person about whom intelligence is sought. It then changes into an elf or sprite, and departs on its errand. The spirit of the person enters the image, and gives the information sought after by the surviving relative. The woman is supposed not to utter a word, the message seeming to proceed from the image. The questions are addressed to the medium; the replies appear to come from her stomach. This is called "finding or seeking for the thread." There is probably a kind of ventriloquism employed. The fact that the voice proceeds professedly from the stomach of the medium doubtless helps to delude. The medium makes use of no incense or candles in the performance of this method.

Another class of women who pretend to be able to obtain information from or about the dead proceed in a very different manner. The medium sits by a table. Having inquired in

regard to the name and surname of the deceased, and the precise
time of death, she bows her head and rests it upon the table, her
face being concealed from view.   On the table are three sticks of
lighted incense placed upright, sometimes in a censer, as usual ;
sometimes they are put in a horizontal position upon a vessel
containing a small quantity of boiled rice.   Two lighted candles
are also placed upon the table.   The woman who seeks information draws near in profound silence.   After a short time, the
medium raises her head from the table with her eyes closed, and
begins to address the applicant.   She is now supposed to be
possessed by the spirit of the dead individual in regard to whom
information is desired ; in other words, the dead has come into

FEMALE MEDIUM BETWEEN THE LIVING AND THE DEAD.

her body, using her organs of speech to communicate with the
living.   A conversation ensues between the living and the dead,
mutually giving and receiving information.   At the close of the
interview the medium places her head down on the table, and
after a few minutes she oftentimes begins to retch or vomit.
After drinking some tea she soon becomes herself again, the
spirit of the dead having retired.

The time of the year when excessive drought usually occurs
is in the sixth or seventh Chinese month, nearly corresponding
to July and August.

There are several methods in use for praying for rain by the people, any one of which is selected.

Sometimes they make an image, which they call "the Dragon King." The head and face are made to imitate the head and face of the dragon ; the body and hands are like the body and hands of a man. No feet are attached to it. Being very light, it is carried in procession by a man, or boy. The head of the image is from seven to ten feet from the ground. In its hands, carried in front of its breast, is a kind of wand, in imitation of the utensil which courtiers in the Ming dynasty were required to hold before them when in the presence of the emperor.

In the procession also are several men carrying gongs, drums, and four flags of cloth, one of each of the different colours, yellow, green, black, and white. The yellow and the white flags symbolize, respectively, wind and water, while the green and black ones represent clouds. On each is an inscription of several characters, to the import that "prayer is offered for rain," or that it is "for the salvation and relief of the people." The men or boys who carry these flags in the procession wave them from side to side as they walk along, crying out "The rain is coming," or " Let it rain," while those who carry the gongs and drums beat them continuously.

One man carries a load of water in two buckets suspended from a pole laid across his shoulder. He holds in one hand a green branch of a shrub or bamboo with leaves, which he occasionally dips in the water, and then sprinkles the water dripping from the leaves around on the ground, crying out, as he does so, "The rain comes, the rain comes."

The people engaged in the procession wear white conical caps without tassels, and are usually dressed in white clothing. Several men carry each a stick of lighted incense reverently before them as they walk along.

Sometimes, in place of the Dragon-King, an image of the Goddess of Mercy, or of a Goddess of Children, taken from some celebrated or popular monastery or temple, is carried in the procession.

Sometimes the image carried in procession while praying for rain represents a deified monkey, an object which is much worshipped by some classes of the people at this place.

Occasionally, in seasons of extreme drought, the wooden images of what are considered the most powerful and most efficacious divinities worshipped in this city are taken out of their temples and paraded through the streets with great pomp and show, under the immediate patronage and superintendence of the gentry and the literary class.

Very many shopkeepers, during the days or the weeks when the people are largely occupied with rain-praying processions in the streets, have on the counters of their shops a kind of paper tablet, on which is an inscription to the "Dragon King of the Five Lakes and the Four.Seas, the Giver of Rain." This is surrounded by several miniature flags of various colours. Three sticks of incense are burnt before it, and the candles used are made of white wax or of white vegetable tallow, being of the natural colour.

The desire for rain sometimes develops itself by an unwillingness among the people engaged to allow the use of umbrellas, or of light summer hats worn usually during hot weather.

Praying for Rain by the Mandarins.—The manner in which they pray for rain differs considerably from the ways adopted and practised by the people. Some of them, in ordinary cases, go twice per day, and usually on foot, carrying a stick of lighted incense before them, to a famous temple on one of the hills in the city, and there burn incense before the idol representing the Pearly Emperor Supreme Ruler (the chief divinity of the Tauist religion). This burning of incense is accompanied with three kneelings and nine knockings. At the same time, a company of Tauist priests are employed to repeat formulas and perform worship according to their custom on such occasions, the grand object of which is to procure rain. These mandarins also proceed to burn incense before the image of the Goddess of Mercy belonging to a temple located on the same hill. A company of Buddhist priests are engaged at the same time in reciting their classics and in worshipping, according to their customs, for the purpose of facilitating the arrival of the needed rain.

In times of excessive drought, the mandarins occasionally issue proclamations forbidding the butchering of swine for three days. Generally, at these times, pork can be had, but somewhat dearer than usual. It is not exposed for sale as publicly as at other times, nor are swine killed and prepared for market as openly as usual. It is always unlawful to butcher cattle for beef.

Sometimes, though rarely, they close during the daytime one or more of the city gates. When done, this is a mark of great distress, and indicates the earnest desire of the mandarins and people for rain.

Almost every year, when the officers engage in praying for rain, they send a deputation to a celebrated Buddhist monastery, distant six or seven miles from the city, and borrow a famous image of the Goddess of Mercy belonging to that establishment. Last summer the prefect and one of the district magistrates in the city went on this important errand. The idol is borne by eight men, and the accompanying officers precede it on foot from the east gate of the city to the temple dedicated to the divinity, located on the hill in the city before referred to, with considerable solemnity and parade. Here incense is burnt before it twice per day by the high officers, and a company of priests employed to perform periodically rain-praying ceremonies until rain has fallen plenteously. Soon after this event has occurred, they render thanks to the goddess for her aid in procuring the highly-desired result.

It came to pass that the *Temple of the Nine Happinesses*, located in the suburbs near the south gate, and devoted to the worship of the "Five Rulers," was in want of money. Its trustees or managers agreed to recommend the practice of a superstition relating to a certain use of loaves of bread or biscuit, hoping thus to replenish its coffers, in which object they were in a few years very successful.

The committee accordingly gave out that, at a specified time, the Five Rulers would have in readiness, to bestow upon those of their worshippers who might ask for them, certain loaves of wheat bread, on the understanding that they were to return the following year as a thank-offering twice the number received. The manner of asking was this : the worshippers presented themselves before the images of the Five Rulers with a brace of candles and three incense-sticks, and having placed them respectively in the candlesticks and the censers belonging to the temple, they knelt down and bowed three times before the images, at the same time making particular requests. On arising from their knees, they received *some of the loaves which had been placed before the idols*, one, or two, or more, as they wished. Their names, the name of the neighbourhood in which they lived, and *the number of loaves given them*, were entered in a book by the clerk or registrar. The worshipper was understood, under the circumstances of the case, to come under the special protection of their majesties. They shared with him some of their food at his particular entreaty, and less could not reasonably be expected than that they should exert themselves to enable him to attain the object of his heart's desire ! Having received these loaves of bread, the man (for women are not permitted to engage in devotional acts in the temples of the Five Rulers) returned home to divide them among the members of his household, all mutually enjoying the favour of these gods, and mutually anticipating the blessing prayed for.

The succeeding year, on days indicated by a public notice from the temple committee, those who had received loaves of bread the previous year were expected to bring to the temple their thanksgivings.

In answer to inquiries why the people should so soon have adopted this use of bread-loaves in such numbers, it is asserted that, not long after its recommendation by the temple of the Nine Happinesses, some individuals did actually succeed in attaining the object for which they specially prayed before the Five Rulers! which success they attributed, under the circumstances, to the favour of these gods. This was noised abroad, and excited others to try the same means. It is reported that a certain person once solicited bread-loaves in the usual manner at the temple of the Nine Happinesses, and afterward went over to the island of Formosa without returning thanks in person, and without having made an arrangement for its being done by another in his name. On his return to this place after several years' absence, having amassed considerable money, but still neglecting to make the usual thank-offering according to rule, it is reported, these gods went themselves, or sent one of their assistant images, to his house one night, and demanded the usual offering. His delinquencies having thus been vividly recalled to mind, he decided to make the thanksgiving of mock-money and of loaves, or the value of the loaves, reckoned according to geometrical progression, the ratio being two, and the terms being equal to the number of years during which he neglected to give the thank-offering. He also had some theatrical shows enacted in their honour and at his expense. Such a story, once afloat in this city, produced a prodigious effect on the superstitious and credulous minds of the Chinese, leading many, who never previously engaged in the custom, to begin it.

The annual aggregate of the profits of the bread-loaf superstition to the temples, though comparatively small in itself, is enormous when considered with reference to the amount of capital invested, being nominally 100 per cent. on the value of the loaves conferred on worshippers each year.

Among miscellaneous superstitious practices, they invite the god to take some tea. When a procession in honour of a popular idol is about to pass along, the residents of a neighbourhood sometimes club together and bear the expense of honouring the divinity in the following manner : They arrange several tables by the wayside, each having a censer with lighted incense, two pairs of candlesticks, each with a large candle ; a flower-vase, with fresh flowers ; a plate of the best fruits of the season, with three cups of tea—in other words, they present him some tea. As the sedan having the god in it comes along opposite the table, some one takes a slip of bamboo having the two words "tea lot" written upon it, and presents it as if for the inspection of the occupant of the sedan. The bearers stop, and the man kneels down on the ground and reverently offers the three cups of tea, one by one, to the god in the sedan to drink. When this farce is completed, the bearers proceed on their way. The object of doing this is to procure the favour of the god in causing the neighbourhood to be healthy, and its residents prosperous in business or in literary pursuits.

They make a Feast for the Idol.—This differs from the presentation of tea principally in the circumstance that it is very much more expensive. A large number of tables are arranged by the side of the street, which are filled with the most expensive edibles used by the Chinese, as bêche de mer, sinews of the deer and the buffalo, fish-fins, &c., together with a hog's head, a goat's head, a whole goose, a whole fowl, a whole duck, besides incense, candles, and mock-money. A large display is made of plates covered with choice fruits, cakes, and preserves. The neighbours who are interested often stand near the tables holding a stick of lighted incense in their hands. When the god comes opposite to the principal table, the bearers stand still, and a priest of the Tauist sect, employed for the occasion, takes, one by one, several of the plates, and holds them toward the idol. He does the same thing with the tea, wine, &c. These are all returned to the tables. He finally reads a paper containing the names of those who furnished the feast, who thereby express their prayers for protection in health, or recovery from sickness, or success in study and business.

They obtain some Incense Ashes.—When an individual is about to start on some dangerous journey, he frequently goes to the temple devoted to the worship of the divinity he prefers to acknowledge as his protector, and burns incense, candles, and mock-money before the image, accompanied with the customary prostrations. He then takes some of the incense from the censer before the image and puts it in a small red bag or paper. Or, in case of sickness in one's family, or for whatever reason it is desirable to worship in the house a particular divinity, the image of which he does not possess, some incense ashes from the censer before the image of that divinity standing in his temple are obtained in the manner just described. The red paper or bag of incense ashes, representing the divinity, is then carried home with great solemnity. The bearer carries it in one hand, held in front of him, in connexion with a lighted stick of incense, and carrying over his head, in his other hand, an open umbrella, if he is on foot. If he does not carry an umbrella, he rides in a sedan, carrying the incense and the incense ashes in a similar way. It is considered necessary to shield the ashes, *en route* from the temple to his home, from the rain, if raining, or from the sun's rays, if the sun is shining. On arriving at his home, the incense is suspended in a convenient place, or put in the censer and worshipped regularly, just as the image of the divinity would be worshipped if possessed.

BRINGING HOME REPRESENTATIVE INCENSE ASHES.

If the man is to go on a journey, he takes the bag of incense along with him, suspended from his neck or from his button-hole. When he stops for the night, he takes it off and burns incense and candles before it, to insure protection from the god it represents. If he returns successful from his journey, and in health, the credit is given to the god he worshipped while absent, and oftentimes expensive offerings, as a token of his gratitude, are made before the idol whence he originally obtained the ashes, and the ashes he took with him are returned to the censer whence he obtained them.

In houses where the ashes are no longer worshipped, the sick having recovered, they are returned to the censer whence they were taken, with the presentation of a thanksgiving. In case the sick one did not recover, or success in regard to the object sought did not result, sometimes they are thrown away, as of no "efficaciousness," and sometimes they are returned to the censer whence they were taken, lest the divinity should be offended, but without a thanksgiving. Occasionally they are put into the midst of mock-money, which is burnt up. This is regarded as a respectful method of disposing of the incense ashes originally obtained.

They pray for a Dream.—Many people, in case they find great difficulty in deciding what course to take in regard to an important subject under consideration, visit some popular temple, and, having burned incense and candles, beg the divinity worshipped to favour them with a dream shedding light on the subject of their perplexity, which they briefly state. They frequently sleep before the idol, burning incense and candles. Should they have a dream, they rise and ask by means of the kà-pue whether the dream was sent by the god to shed light on their course, in answer to their prayer. If an affirmative answer is received, they proceed to study the character of the dream, and endeavour to decide from its teachings what they should do in regard to the subject under consideration, and whether they will be successful.

They burn a Lamp before the Gods.—It is a frequent practice for people to make specific vows in regard to burning a lamp before some particular god or goddess, in the temple dedicated to the divinity, for a month or a year, for the night-time only, or both day and night, during the period specified. They usually employ the temple-keeper to buy the oil and trim the lamp.

They burn a Lantern before the Heavens.—Sometimes people prefer to vow to burn a lantern before the heavens. The lantern is usually suspended in front of the dwelling-house of the vower. In such a case, it is trimmed by himself or some member of his family.

Many also make vows to the "twenty-four gods of heaven," or to the "Mother of the Measure," writing the appropriate title upon the lantern they devote to carrying out their vows. On the occurrence of the birthday of the god or the goddess, the family generally presents an offering of meats, fish, and vegetables. On the first and fifteenth of each month they also regularly burn incense in honour of the divinity whose title is on their lantern, before the heavens. The objects sought are various, as male children, recovery from disease, or success in trade.

G G

They tranquillize the Earth and the Gods.—When one has built a new house, it is the custom not to occupy it until a superstitious performance has been acted, in order to tranquillize the earth. The Chinese imagine that there are local deities, or "wild spirits or ghosts," which would disturb and annoy the inhabitants of a new house unless they are first pacified and propitiated ; hence some priest is employed to come to the premises and recite his incantations which relate to the subject.

In case of building a new temple or making a new idol, a similar ceremony must be performed in order to tranquillize the gods or the local deities.

They present a Sacrifice to the Great Year.—The general appellation of a class of gods is "Great Year." Each has, however, a surname and given name distinguishing him from all the rest. They number sixty, one for each year of the Chinese cycle. When all have been successively worshipped, the first on the list again becomes the real object of worship, ruling over the current year. The god for any current year is very often worshipped by people during that particular year, in order to secure to them exemption from disease or death, or recovery from sickness during the year. On the celebration of birthdays, the Great Year is often worshipped at the residence of the person for whose benefit the ceremony is performed, usually under the open heavens.

Some of the offerings are placed upon the table which holds the incense and the candles. A part is put under the table, on a sieve made of bamboo splints. Some mock-money is placed there, with a small image cut out of paper, representing the man in whose behalf the aid of the god is implored. Some fowl's blood, a raw egg, and sometimes a piece of raw meat, three plates of cooked meats, and three cups of wine, are also put on the tray. When everything is ready, the priest who conducts the service lights the candles and incense, commences the ringing of his bell and the chanting of his formulas, by which he invites the Great Year to protect the individual from death, or restore him to health, according to circumstances. At the proper period the paper image under the table and the mock-money are taken outside and burnt up. This is supposed to denote that the individual's request will be granted.

They see in the dark.—In case things are stolen or lost, or in case of the sickness of a friend or child, people sometimes have resort to a class of persons who profess to be able to "see in the dark" in regard to stolen goods, or to tell what has been done by some devil or imp causing sickness.

CHAPTER XXIII.

BUSINESS CUSTOMS.

The System of Go-betweens or Middle-men in the Transaction of important Business.—The employment of go-betweens or middle persons between the two principals in the transaction of many kinds of business is one of the " peculiar institutions" of society as existing here, and probably all over the empire. The native importer of goods from another port does not personally negotiate with the retail or the wholesale buyer. The owner of house or farm, in market for sale or for rent, may not be called upon by those who wish to purchase or rent for themselves. A sort of professional persons are employed, who are the acknowledged go-betweens betwixt the owners and the buyers. The system does not extend to business between ordinary retailers and their customers, but to importers, wholesale dealers, and owners of houses and lands. Generally, the same person does not negotiate the sale and purchase of more than one class of merchandise or property.

The pay of these go-betweens is usually five per cent. on the sum of money given by the buyer to the seller. Of this percentage, the buyer pays three and the seller pays two parts. It amounts to the same thing as clearing five per cent. commission, all the expense of porterage and transfer being defrayed by the buyer, and the middle-man being at no expense for a clerk, office, or store.

The go-between acts the part of an advertising medium, a living perambulating newspaper, the use of which costs the owner of property and the prospective buyer of it nothing, unless an actual transfer is effected. He spends his time principally in traversing the streets, calling on the wholesale dealers and the retailers, extracting and giving information relating to his particular branch of business. The work of ascertaining where different kinds of merchandise and landed property for sale or rent are to be found, is virtually entrusted by retailers and buyers or renters to middle-men.

The facility for deception in regard to price, quality, and condition of property bought and sold is undoubtedly one of the worst features of this system of go-betweens in business as transacted among the Chinese.

The go-betweens who devote themselves to the effecting of sales of the same general description of property, if quite numerous, often form themselves into a kind of union or club. The members of each of these associations meet in some temple once or twice annually, for the purpose of worshipping and rendering thanks unto the god it has adopted as patron. Wholesale dealers, importers, retailers, and manufacturers must conform to the rules which the go-betweens make, or they would find it impracticable to dispose of their goods on profitable terms, and with dispatch.

There is another class of go-betweens who correspond more nearly to commission merchants at the West than the class above described, having extensive warehouses or go-downs, where the owner may deposit his goods for inspection and sale. The buyer in these cases oftentimes employs a go-between of the class first spoken of to make his purchases. He is obliged to pay the employés or hired men in the establishment a small per-centage on the value paid for the goods, and sometimes is required to reckon a certain per cent. on his purchase, which goes to the commission merchant as part of his commission, the balance being deducted from the sum received for the goods sold. This class of middle-men or commission merchants is quite numerous; many of the most extensive warehouses or stores among the Chinese belong to it.

Females are extensively employed as go-betweens in the transaction of some kinds of business, as in the sale of female slaves, in the hiring of nurses in wealthy families, in contracting marriages, in buying female ornaments and attire, when the nature of the case requires access to the ladies in the private apartments. For their services they receive compensation regulated by the circumstances of the case, or by the peculiar customs of society relating to the subject.

Banking, Bank-bills, and Cash.—The native banks of this place are quite numerous, and are not under Government inspection or control. Any individual who has the capital, or a company

of individuals who can furnish the necessary funds, may establish
a bank and issue bills, without getting a charter or any kind of
permission from the Government.

A few years ago the mandarins at Fuhchau issued bank-bills
in behalf of the Imperial Government, in consequence of the
extreme scarcity of the common copper cash. The Government also issued iron cash, which at first were received as of
equal value with the copper cash. But the iron coin soon was
counterfeited in great quantities. It also became rusty. The

Obverse. Reverse.

FAC-SIMILE OF CASH COINED BY THE LAST EMPEROR, HIEN-FUNG,
Who reigned from 1851—1861, representing ten common cash.

Government bills, being payable in iron coin at par with copper,
became very unpopular and greatly depreciated. The value of a
dollar in Government bills or iron cash was at one time, in 1858,
eighteen or twenty thousand cash. The Government finally
bought up the iron cash and withdrew its bills from circulation, leaving the private banks to supply the paper currency as
before.*

* The invention and priority in the use of paper money by the Chinese
is now generally admitted. Klaproth, Chaudoir, and others have given
details to some extent regarding the history of this currency. From
native records we learn that it was first used by the Imperial Government
in the ninth century, and was continued with intervals till near the close of
the fifteenth; from which, down to recent times, no attempt has been
made to revive the practice. The extensive use of promissory notes, however, in various parts of the empire, and the exhausted state of the
imperial treasury, has suggested the desirability of another attempt, by
this means, to relieve the state from the financial pressure, and, after a

Some of the banks are of long standing, and, as their proprietors are known to be very wealthy and sufficiently honest, their bills are in general use in the transaction of business. Their bills are of various denominations, as representing cash, dollars, or silver. Experience proves that there is little comparative risk from counterfeiters. The real risk in the use of bills arises from the liability of the bank to fail suddenly.

The outline of the bill, with various devices to make counterfeiting difficult, is engraved neatly on a solid block of brass in the case of wealthy banks; poor proprietors of banks use hard wood instead of brass. The right-hand margin is made an inch or more wider than the left-hand margin of the block of brass or wood. The value of the bill and the day of issue are filled in with the pen, and one or more words to facilitate the detection of a counterfeit. Various stamps, some of which are very curiously and elaborately engraved, are impressed on different parts of the bill, using red or blue ink. These add very much to the neat and pretty appearance of the note, and are believed usually to have some secret or private mark, and are very difficult to imitate with precision and exactness by counterfeiters.

But perhaps the use which is made of the wide right-hand margin furnishes the greatest security against counterfeiting. On this margin are stamped or written various words, phrases, or sentences, before the bill is put into circulation. When everything is ready, these stamped or written sentences or phrases are cut through by a sharp knife, leaving the right-hand margin of the bill about the same width as the left hand, though it presents a very different appearance. Of course the edge of the right-hand margin of the bill, and the edge of the paper which was cut off from it, will precisely match each other; but, as the sentences have been cut into two parts, part of the words and stamps will be on the bill and part on the slip of paper cut off. These slips are all carefully kept in a book form ready for reference, each slip containing the value, date, and private marks of the bill corresponding to it.

When a new bank is opened, custom demands that the proprietors, the head directors, or clerks of the principal neighbour-

cessation of four hundred years, Government banks have again been opened in the large cities for the issue of a new paper currency. The success that has attended the experiment is now such as to promise a long continuation of this expedient."—See *Coins of the Ta-Tsing, or present Dynasty of China*, by A. Wylie, Esq., laid before the Shanghai Branch of the Oriental Society, Nov. 17th, 1857.

ing banks, and the principal money go-betweens who are connected with them, shall be invited to a feast at the expense of the proprietors of the new bank. Generally, after this feast, these neighbouring bankers, unless they have especial reason to distrust or be dissatisfied with the new banker, are willing to recognise the new bank, and use its bills, according to custom. The bank go-betweens also consider the new bank as now established, and do business with it on the usual terms, as with old banks in good and regular standing.

The bills are all made payable on demand. If the holder of bills against a particular bank presents them for payment, he may be paid in cash, or the current bills of other banks, or in

Obverse.   Reverse.

FAC-SIMILE OF CASH ISSUED BY THE LATE LONG-HAIRED REBEL EMPEROR,
Who had his capital at Nanking, called Cash of the "Great Tranquillity Celestial State."

silver or gold according to the current rate of exchange. It is not entirely at the option of the bill-holder what shall be the equivalent given him, but more at the option of the banker, especially in case of an emergency. Cash bills are usually paid in cash.

It is an established custom in this place, that if a bank is not able to discharge its obligation immediately on the presentation of bills by redeeming them in some way, the holder of the bills may seize hold of anything in the bank and take it off, to the full amount of his demands, if he pleases to do so, and there would be no liability for prosecution for theft or misdemeanour. Instances have occurred when some rascals and their accomplices have tried to find, or rather make, occasion for rifling banks, by calling in a body, and simultaneously presenting their bills with loud outcries and insulting remarks, and by their improper conduct have caused what seemed to be a temporary suspension of payment. Occasionally, at such times, a seeming pretext has been given, through fear of actual robbery on the part of the bankers, and their assistants and clerks, for the crowd of rascals to pretend that the ready money in the bank was short, and that they were in danger of not getting their bills cashed, all which has resulted in their beginning to plunder the bank. And when an excited and interested crowd has begun such a work, it is exceedingly difficult to prevent the completion of the undertaking. There are plenty of beggars and idlers or vagabonds in the streets who are only too happy to assist in such an exciting and profitable sport as robbing a bank. Intances are not very rare when banks have been completely riddled of every portable thing worth carrying off, even to the sleepers and the rafters.

In the year 1855 there was an unusual panic among billholders. Several banks had just failed, that is, had been unable to redeem their bills on presentation, and had been robbed of everything in their offices by bill-holders and by the lower class of the populace, who joined them in plundering. The viceroy determined to make an example of a few, in order to avert impending anarchy and universal distrust. Early on a certain morning bills were presented for payment by many persons at a respectable bank located in the south street in the city. A large crowd assembled, and soon a robbery of the bank commenced by a multitude of persons. Several of these rioters who had no bills against the bank were arrested by the police, among whom were a poor chair coolie and a respectable neighbour of the bank, a dealer in rice. The viceroy, as soon as he heard of the circumstances, and of the arrest of these men, who manifestly had no plea but robbery for engaging in the "gutting" of the bank, determined that they should be beheaded, without trial, at once, and in the street where the robbery was committed. His subordinate officers endeavoured to dissuade him from the sanguinary measure, fearing that the populace would rise *en masse*, and murder the mandarins, and inaugurate a revolution; but the viceroy was firm, arguing that it was the best, if not the only means of preventing universal anarchy. He issued his warrant for their execution, and the wretches were immediately taken out into the public street in front of the bank, and decapitated. All this occurred, and the report had spread all over the city and suburbs, before nine o'clock in the morning. The viceroy was correct in regard to the effect he said it would produce. The summary act at once quelled the disorderly rabble, and no such disposition to rob a bank contrary to custom was manifested in this city or suburbs for a considerable time.

In ancient times, some emperors coined cash in the shape of a knife and other fanciful shapes. These are now highly prized as curiosities, and are not in general circulation as coins. Coins of modern times are round, with a small square hole in the centre.

In 1850, a dollar was worth in bills or cash at this place 1,400 cash. In 1854 it was worth 1,750. It is now (August, 1863) worth 1,050. The large importation of silver, or its equivalent in value, to pay for the teas purchased at this port, has kept down the price of dollars, and, consequently, in most branches of native trade there is very little business, because silver, brought hither by Chinamen to purchase native products, exchanges for so small an amount in cash or bills,

Obverse.　　　　Reverse.

FAC-SIMILE OF ANCIENT CASH, COINED DURING
THE HAN DYNASTY, ABOUT A. D. 9.

in which the price of articles is usually reckoned here, that they cannot afford to change their silver into cash and purchase what they desire to take away. They are sure of doing a losing business. When dollars or sycee command a high price at the banks, native business is brisk. A dollar or a tael then purchases much more of native products than when the price of a dollar or of a tael is low. The price of native commodities does not fluctuate nearly as much as does the price of silver.

In 1864, a copper mille, a copper cent, and a silver ten-cent piece came into circulation at Hong Kong (an island less than one hundred miles from Canton, belonging to England), and were made a legal tender there. They were coined in England, but were designed for use in Hong Kong. Each coin contains

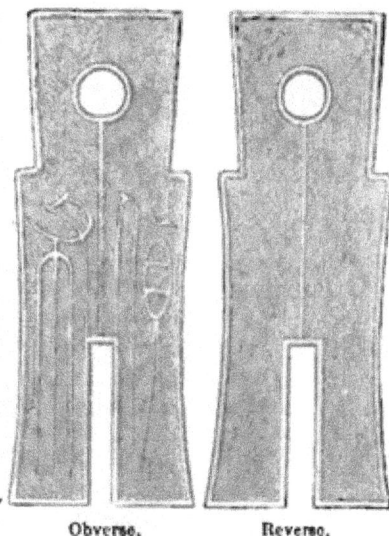

Chinese and English characters denoting its value.   Silver dollars, having Chinese and English characters, were in process of coinage in England, and a mint was to be erected at Hong Kong.   The mille, or cash, which was equal to one cent—fixing the value of a dollar at one thousand mille—was very popular among the Chinese.   They took them into the adjacent Chinese territory, where they were often sold at the rate of seven or eight hundred for a dollar.   The mille is much smaller and lighter

Obverse.   Reverse.

FAC-SIMILE OF A HONG KONG MILLE.

Obverse.   Reverse.

FAC-SIMILE OF A HONG KONG DIME.

Obverse.   Reverse.

FAC-SIMILE OF A HONG KONG CENT.

than a Chinese cash, and has a round instead of a square hole in its centre.   The cent is about the size of an American cent, and the dime corresponds very nearly in size to an American dime. A more convenient currency than the common copper cash is greatly needed in China.

Money-lending Clubs without Interest.—It often occurs that an individual desires to have a certain sum of ready money to use, but which he finds himself unable to command.   Instead of borrowing the sum and paying the exorbitant interest demanded by money-lenders, and instead of trying to raise the sum among his friends, he endeavours to induce them to form one of several kinds of clubs, the immediate object of which is to furnish him with the desired amount, but the future effects of which will be to supply the same sum to each one of its members, without the usual heavy interest.

He induces a trusty friend to become second or assistant, he being its head or principal. Having prepared a number of red envelopes, each containing a small sum of money, he calls upon his relatives and friends who are able to engage in the club, and who, he desires, should enter it, explains to them his plans, states the amount he wishes to raise, each member's share, and all needed particulars. Those who are willing to engage in the club receive one of these envelopes as a kind of bargain-money, and after that they may not withdraw without his consent, or

Obverse.   Reverse.

OMEN OF GOOD USED BY THE MAN WHO THROWS THE DICE.

unless he fails to secure the required number of names. They are regarded by the customs of society as bound or pledged to perform their part in the contemplated union. In case of not succeeding in obtaining the requisite number of responsible names, the undertaking falls through.

The Shaking Club.—This club is thus named from the frequent tossing of dice by its members. The number of members is not fixed, varying from five to twenty or more. Suppose the sum to be raised is 100,000 cash, and the number of members is ten, each man's share will be 10,000 cash. Suppose the time for the payment of the shares is quarterly, there being ten payments, it will require two years and a half before the business of the club will be perfected.

The business is all managed by the head man and his assistant, and the meetings of the club are held at the house of the former, or at the place he appoints. He is at the expense of a feast for the members of the club the first time they meet, it being the time when he receives the sum of 100,000 cash, including the sum which he is supposed also to pay in, though really he does not provide it, but only receives 90,000 from the other members. At this first meeting no dice are thrown, it being well understood that the sum is to be taken by the head man.

At the next meeting each member brings his 10,000 cash, which is given to the one who, on casting the dice, gets the highest number of spots, the head man and his assistant not engaging in the casting of dice, the latter, according to the rules generally adopted, taking his 100,000 cash at the third meeting of the club without any appeal to the dice.

At the fourth and every subsequent meeting, those who have not drawn the sum throw the dice according to the rules of the club, to decide who shall take the 100,000 cash. All who have previously drawn the sum, excepting the head man and his assistant, at any meeting of the club are expected to contribute a small sum for the incidental expenses, as paper and refreshments. If anything is left unexpended at the close of the tenth meeting, it is considered as belonging to the man who has waited until this time when he receives his 100,000 cash.

The Snake-casting-its-skin Club.—This union or club is so called from the circumstance that the head man, the one for whose benefit the money is subscribed, pays it back to the members by regular instalments, as may be agreed on when formed, just as, it is said, the snake sheds or casts its skin gradually, or at regulated intervals. There is no need of an assistant in the working of this club. The members subscribe and pay money but once. There is no division of this money among them; the head man takes it all for his own use when it is paid in, which is done at its first and only meeting. At this time he prepares a feast for its members.

The Dragon-headed Club.—This club is named " dragon-headed" because the first payments made by its members are much larger than subsequent payments, resembling, it is said, the Chinese dragon, in the circumstance that its head is much larger than its body.

There is little of free competition in this land in regard to

the price of goods, cost of labour, &c. Those engaged in the
manufacture of the same kind of articles often combine together
in fixing the price at wholesale. Those who sell by retail similar
descriptions of goods combine together to fix the retail prices.
The main and professed design of this is for mutual protection.
Unless there should be such concert some would undersell the
rest, who, to secure a portion of the trade in the article, would be
obliged to lower their price. Soon there would be, say the
Chinese, ruinous competition and great fluctuations in the price
of the raw material and of the manufactured article. The fact
that a certain shopkeeper is among those who have combined
together in regard to the price of the commodities offered for sale
in his shop is indicated to the public by two characters printed
in a large form on red paper, and posted up in a conspicuous part
of the establishment. According to theory, those who have
agreed to sell at certain prices dare not openly sell at lower rates ;
for, if the fact should be known to other shopkeepers engaged
in the same business, the offender would be obliged to pay a fine
in money sufficient to defray the expense of a theatrical exhibition, or of a certain number of tables at a feast of those engaged
in the sale of the same article.

All engaged in some kinds of business are obliged, not by law,
but by custom, to enter into the union, and abide by the rules
and pay the fines.

Journeymen in the different professions or trades, as carpenters,
tailors, &c., also combine among themselves, each class or trade
by itself, in regard to price of labour and other things which
interest them particularly. Their employers, at the appointed
time, must conform to the new rate of wages adopted. Employers
of journeymen and shopkeepers are thus often obliged to raise
the price of labour and of goods.

In many kinds of shops the prices of articles settled upon at
the meetings of the unions or by the head men are sometimes
written out or printed, and pasted up for public reference in the
shops concerned.

Some shops profess to sell goods at the true price—less than
first demanded, they affirm, they will not take. These go by the
general name of "shops which have not two prices." They pretend
to offer genuine or perfect goods at the real price, and to make no
distinction between their customers, whether man or woman, old
or young, a city gentleman or a country rustic. These shops
used formerly to be more honest, and were much more to be
depended upon, than at the present time. Now they will deviate

from their pretensions—at least, many of them—if a good opportunity to cheat or overreach presents itself. Very many shops
make no pretence of selling genuine goods, and at the proper
price. These, of course, defraud and shave their customers in
every possible method. The only-one-price stores or shops are
much more trustworthy.

Usually about the third or fourth Chinese month, the shopkeepers, journeymen, and master workmen who have entered
into unions regulating their business, meet together in some
temple to feast, behold theatrical shows, amend their rules as
deemed best, and consult about their affairs in common. Offerings are made, and incense and candles burnt, on such occasions,
before the divinity worshipped there, as an important part of

Obverse.   Reverse.

OMEN OF GOOD LUCK PUT BY SHOPKEEPERS IN THE BOTTOM OF THEIR MONEY-BOX,
THE REVERSE MEANING "WITH A PRINCIPAL OF ONE TO MAKE TEN THOUSAND."

the programme of proceedings, in the hope that his or her aid
will be secured in this manner to enable them to conduct their
business wisely and profitably. The time selected is generally a
lucky one, ascertained by referring to the Imperial Calendar.

The commission merchants dealing in fish, wood, fruits, &c.
on the second and the sixteenth of every month make a feast in
their hongs, attended with the burning of incense, candles, and
mock-money before the god of wealth and the tutelary deity of
the district. The design of this feast and the worship of these
imaginary beings is professedly to honour them, hoping to lead
them to bless the proprietors of the establishment with success
in trade. Sometimes these feasts are attended with considerable

expense in providing provisions of extra good quality and kind, as fowls, fish, pork, goat's flesh, crabs, vermicelli, and wine. After having been presented before the gods worshipped as offerings, these eatables are taken away and prepared for immediate consumption, when they are feasted on by the proprietor, his clerks, and workmen. While eating, the proprietor or his proxy takes the wine pitcher and pours out for the others, expressing his warm thanks for their assistance in carrying on his business.

The owner or the captain of the junks and smaller boats engaged in carrying produce and passengers to a distance, before reaching their destination, most generally has a similar feasting on good things, offered first to the sailor's goddess. The food is then given to the boatmen.

Every heathen shopkeeper, banker, and merchant, whether living in the city or suburbs, has a place in his establishment devoted to the worshipping of the god of wealth and the tutelary divinity of the district. The words "god of wealth" are usually only written or printed on a piece of red paper, and pasted up on the wall or partition, in front of which incense and candles are burnt. Seldom is there an image of this god. When an image is used, it resembles an old man having a white face, but black whiskers. The local deity referred to is most commonly represented by an image of wood or of clay, resembling an old man in a sitting posture, having a red countenance, but white whiskers, and having two assistants, one standing on each hand. When no image is used, he is often represented by four characters, meaning "the god of happiness, virtue, and uprightness," which are written or printed on red paper, and pasted up behind the table or shelf which holds the censer and the candlesticks used in burning incense and candles. Sometimes, however, a square or oblong piece of board is neatly varnished, and the four characters are engraved on it and gilded. Not unfrequently is a portable niche, made somewhat in shape like a house, provided by the shopkeeper or banker to hold the images or the tablet. In case there is no niche used, they are placed on a shelf or table in a convenient part of the establishment. Morning and evening are three sticks of incense and two small candles regularly lighted before these gods, in the hope of thereby engaging their protection and assistance in the management of business, so as to increase in wealth. Besides this daily worship, on the birthdays of these divinities there is made unto them special and sometimes expensive offerings of food, which, as usual, is

afterwards taken away and eaten by those connected with the
establishment.   These idols are also generally worshipped by
men connected with Chinese yamuus on the first and the fifteenth of every month by the burning of incense and candles,
and on the recurrence of their birthdays by meat offerings and
by theatrical plays.

On the evening of the second and sixteenth of every Chinese
month, in the street in front of many shops, stores, banks, &c.
and before some dwelling-houses, a quantity of black coarse
incense (but no candles) and mock-money and mock-clothing
are burnt.   These things are designed for the benefit of the
wandering spirits of beggars, lepers, &c. in the lower regions.

When a Chinaman is engaged to make anything to order, he
invariably demands bargain-money. By this expression is meant
a certain sum, which will be reckoned on the completion of the
article as so much on its price. This is often spoken o as
money with which to buy the raw material or to pay the workmen.   But the real reason is to make the contract binding on
both parties, according to Chinese custom.   It is not customary
to consider any simple verbal contract binding without the giving
and reception of a sum of money, however small.   After a man
has received the bargain-money, he may not refuse to fulfil his
part of the contract unless he brings and offers to the other
party twice as much as he received as bargain-money ; and the
latter cannot afterwards compel the maker or the seller to perform the contract, whether he receives or declines the money
offered.   On the other hand, the one who bargained for the
manufacture or the purchase of certain articles, and who sealed
the bargain by paying bargain-money, cannot be obliged, according to custom, to take the articles and pay the balance due, if he
is willing to lose the sum advanced.   If he declines to carry out
his part of the contract, the other party has no other recourse
but to submit, keeping the sum received as bargain-money.   He
cannot be compelled to restore it unless the article ordered is not
finished according to contract.   This custom is in full force
between Chinamen.

It is almost universally true that the family which binds out
a son to be an apprentice of any of the common handicrafts is
obliged to furnish all his clothing for the whole period of his
apprenticeship, and his food for one, two, or three years, or until
his services become remunerative to his master.

An apprentice to a banker, or to a pawn-shop, or any similar
lucrative profession or employment, as jeweller or clockmaker,

usually furnishes his own food and clothing for the whole time. It is on account of the poverty of their parents that there are so many unemployed lads in China. They cannot afford the comparatively great expense of clothing and providing food for their children during the whole or a large part of their apprenticeship.

It sometimes occurs that an apprentice, while living on the premises of his master, or that a recently married wife, dies suddenly or commits suicide. In such case the father and brothers, as well as other near relatives, of the lad or of the wife often go to the shop of the master or the house of the husband and demand an explanation, believing, or pretending to believe, that the death was caused by poisoning, or the suicide was brought about by a series of ill treatment and abuse. Sometimes the exasperated relatives of the dead demand the payment of a large sum of money before they will return home and consider the grievance settled. If not satisfied or pacified by money, or the solemn promise of it, they often proceed to beat the family of the master or of the husband, destroying furniture, as tables, chairs, or crockery, and injuring everything that they can find belonging to the offending party. The officers, in such cases of revenge, do not interfere, unless their assistance has been invoked by one of the parties. Instead of thus " beating man's life," as the proceeding is called, the aggrieved party sometimes, in the failure of threats to extort pecuniary satisfaction, and concluding not to beat and destroy, as above described, endeavour to prosecute the other party before the mandarins for murder or some related crime. A few years since a large and flourishing paper store in this city was sacked on the occasion of one of the apprentices having committed suicide. His relatives and personal friends came in such numbers, and were so exasperated,.that the owners of the store were glad to escape with their lives, and the paper and the moveable furniture that was not stolen were destroyed or thrown into the street. Nothing was left but the heavy and immoveable kinds of furniture, and the bare walls, to mark the spot of the once flourishing paper store.

Money is often loaned by bankers and by private individuals in China, as in other lands, by giving adequate or satisfactory security. There is a singular custom here of obtaining money for use by depositing silver for security, which is sometimes resorted to by wealthy men. An amount of silver more than equal in value to the sum borrowed is deposited in the bank as security. The bank, however, may not use this particular security-silver on any account. To prevent its use, and at the same time to have it accepted as security by the bank, the owner of it employs men to act as witnesses, and in their presence it is examined and sealed up in the bank, where it must be carefully kept with unbroken seal. Its owner now receives from the bank the amount he desires in bills or cash for the use he purposes. On the payment of the sum borrowed from the bank, with the stipulated interest, he is allowed to take away the silver he left in the bank as security. He goes without the use of the silver deposited, on which he gets no interest, while he at the same time borrows nearly the same amount of bills or cash, on which he agrees to pay monthly interest. The true explanation of this singular course is sometimes found in the very variable price of silver from time to time. Sometimes deeds of lands or houses are put in the bank as security.

Men who do business as wholesale merchants or agents for wholesale dealers do not give long credit to their retail customers. It has become a fixed custom for retail storekeepers to pay in ready money, or to promise to pay in ready money in one or two months, on certain specified days. These days are the second and the sixteenth of every month. The clerks and hired men are furnished with bills, to collect the sums due on these days from the retail customers of their employers. The clerks and servants go round to the creditors. If these pay promptly, they would be again trusted, should they desire ; if they delayed payment, and gave no reasonable or satisfactory explanation, the wholesale dealer or his agent would be slow to trust them another time.

As an available means of raising small sums of ready money, frequent recourse is had to the numerous pawn-shops at this place. To carry on these establishments with success a large capital is required. The articles pawned are kept, unless redeemed, for three years nominally, but, in fact, only twenty-seven months, when they are liable to be sold for the benefit of the establishment. The legal rate of interest required on sums loaned on the security of property received varies according to the amount advanced at one time. For sums under two taels, three per cent. per month, or thirty cash for every thousand, is the present rate. For sums between two and ten taels, it is two and four-tenths per cent. per month, or twenty-four cash for a thousand. For sums over ten taels, two per cent. per month is the established rate. These rates are higher than used formerly to be the legal rates.

The surplus funds belonging to the temples devoted to the "Five Emperors," and to some other gods at this place, are sometimes put out at the enormous rate of sixty per cent. per month. This money is under the control of a committee of the temple, who always demand good security when they lend the money. It is loaned in small sums, as in bills of five hundred cash each. One can borrow several bills if he produces satisfactory security. The interest on each bill is ten cash, to be paid daily.

Chinese landlords oftentimes experience much trouble in regard to the collection of the rent for houses or land leased to tenants. The latter seem frequently to act on the principle that possession is nine points in law, and, after a few regular payments of rent-money according to contract, begin to offer less than the sum agreed upon. If this sum is received, the amount tendered is often lessened the next time, or the day of payment is delayed. Unkind words follow; and as litigation is proverbially dubious in regard to the justness and the promptness of the magistrate, very much depending on the amount of bribe-money presented to his honour and his satellites, landlords usually shrink from invoking the law, and resort to the established custom of ordering the obnoxious or dilatory incumbent away, giving him the privilege of remaining three months without rent from the date of the notification. Landlords who serve this notice are content to have the premises vacated at the time intimated, not demanding the arrearage of rent, however great it may be.

When a Chinaman wishes to borrow a certain sum of money, but does not wish to pay interest, and yet has landed property, as houses, or a rice-farm, which he is not willing to sell in order to raise the required sums, he often resorts to the following method of mortgaging his property : He seeks for a man who is willing to let him have the needed amount of ready money, taking a kind of mortgage on the piece of property, as house or farm. A certain number of years is fixed upon, during which time it is impossible to redeem the property, the one party using it without rent, and the other party using the money without interest. After the expiration of the specified time the premises may be redeemed by the payment of the sum borrowed, provided the real owner has the money to spare and desires to redeem it. If he should not wish to redeem the premises by returning the money which he borrowed, the lender of it cannot compel him to redeem it; the borrower continues to use the money without interest, and the lender to use the property without rent.

CHAPTER XXIV.

MERITORIOUS OR CHARITABLE PRACTICES.

Distribution of Moral and Religious Books and Tracts.—One of the methods invented by this people by which they fancy they perform acts of merit is that of engraving and distributing books and tracts admonishing the age.[*] A vast amount of this work is done every year, principally by literary men and candidates for promotion in literary rank, or by men connected with the administration of the affairs of large temples. Oftentimes the distribution of such books is done in the performance of a vow, either as a thanksgiving for favours supposed to have been received from the gods, or in order to procure particular benefits from them in the future. In connexion with the literary examinations of candidates for degrees there is much of this distribution performed. The design of the distributors, or those who are at the expense of the books and tracts given away at these times, is to acquire by so doing a fund of merit which will aid them to succeed at some of the regular literary contests. The object in view is a selfish and personal one, terminating in the donor and his family—not a benevolent one, prompted by the desire to do good to others.

[*] "The Chinese," says Dr. Medhurst, "furnish books to each other, for next to nothing. The works of Confucius, with the Commentary of Choo-foo-tsze, comprising six volumes, and amounting to four hundred leaves, octavo, can be purchased for ninepence ; and the historical novel of the Three Kingdoms, amounting to 1500 leaves, in twenty volumes, may be had for half-a-crown. Of course, all these prices are what the natives charge to each other ; for all which Europeans must expect to pay double. Thus, books are multiplied, at a cheap rate, to an almost indefinite extent ; and every peasant and pedlar has the common depositories of knowledge within his reach. It would not be hazarding too much to say, that in China there are more books, and more people to read them, than in any other country of the world."—*China, its State and Prospects*, p. 106.

These books relate to a variety of subjects, such as the slaughtering of cattle, the eating of beef, reverence for printed or written characters, the eating of vegetables, filial piety, the drowning of female children, the repairing of roads and bridges, &c. The subjects are treated in the peculiar manner of the Chinese, either exhorting to do or to refrain from doing, and enforcing compliance with the sentiments inculcated by the use of arguments and considerations peculiarly Chinese. They generally hold up some temporal good as the reward of compliance, and sometimes refer to calamities, misfortunes, and distresses endured by particular individuals at certain times as being the punishment inflicted by heaven or by the gods for non-compliance. Most of the larger books state where they may be had by those who wish to engage in their distribution, and contain the names and residences of some of those who have already printed and distributed them, as well as the number of copies they have given away. The sentiments inculcated, oftentimes even in the same book, belong more or less to the various popular religions, as Confucianism, Buddhism, and Tauism, being designed to suit all sects of religionists, and to meet the approval of all classes of the people.

Some time since, a priest, aged nearly seventy years, of the Buddhist sect, employed as the keeper of a rich and splendid temple dedicated to the honour of the goddess of sailors, presented to some who called to see the temple a volume of the above general description, saying that it "was a most excellent work." The book purports to have been written by a certain "doer of good works," a native of Suchau. It has been engraved and re-published in this part of China, to accommodate those who wish to embark in the meritorious employment of distributing it. Among its contents are " twelve sentences of good words." Each sentence is followed by a few lines of comment on its meaning and of exhortation to its practice, and by a verse of poetry of twenty-eight characters of similar import. As a sample of the sentiments of these moral books, designed to admonish the age, a literal translation of these good words is given :—

" *Twelve Sentences of Good Words.*

1. You should not disobey your parents.
2. You should not quarrel with your brothers.
3. You should not indulge in depraved and bad acts.
4. You should not utter injurious words.
5. You should not drown female infants.
6. You should not wound the conscience.

7. You should not obtain money by false pretences.
8. You should not beat down articles below the proper price.
9. You should not destroy animal life.
10. You should not be remiss in doing good (*i.e.* meritorious) works.
11. You should not throw down on the ground kernels of rice or any lettered paper.
12. You should not eat the flesh of the dog, nor beef."

Immediately following these " twelve sentences of good words" are fifteen supplementary ones, also designed to exhort the age. They are each followed by explanatory and hortatory remarks, but by no poetry. They are as follow :—

" You should not commit fornication.
You should not commit murder.
You should not impose upon the orphan or the widow.
You should not curse and swear.
You should not open a gambling-shop.
You should not smoke opium.
You should not be the go-between in regard to the marriage of a widow.
You should not instigate men to engage in quarrels or assaults.
You should not plan how to deceive people.
You should not act, or hire others to act, an obscene theatrical play.
You should not oppress the poor.
You should not forget benefits received from others.
You should not charge an exorbitant interest.
You should not neglect the family graves.
You should not burn the coffins of the dead."

These are given as examples of the doctrines and the commandments of men taught by this people, and popular among them.

Among the national characteristics of this people is the respect shown to paper on which Chinese characters have been written, printed, or stamped. This respect is carried to an extraordinary and absurd extent in this part of the empire. Four characters on small slips of paper, usually about five or six inches long, calling upon the people to " reverence lettered paper," are posted up on walls and houses in a great multitude of places in this city and its suburb. Small baskets, holding about a peck, and having this slip pasted on the outside, are found everywhere, hung up by the wayside, on houses and shops, designed to hold any lettered waste paper which the people in the vicinity happen to have. Furnaces, holding from half a bushel to several barrels, are quite frequent, in shape like a house or a pagoda, built by the side of the most frequented streets as well as more retired alleys. These have an inscription like that on the baskets, and are designed to contain waste paper while it is being reduced to ashes. The smaller furnaces are usually attached to buildings, while the larger ones are built up from the ground with brick, and oftentimes are stained with various gaudy colours.

Chinese characters are often styled "the eyes of the sage," and sometimes "the tracks or marks which the sages have left behind." It is said, "If one protects or respects the eyes of the sages (*i.e.* Chinese characters), it is just the same as protecting his own eyes from becoming blind." Those who do not, in their conduct, evince a respectful regard for lettered paper, are likened to a "blind buffalo." It has become a proverb that those who do not reverence the character in this life will be likely to be born blind when they come into the world the next time. Such persons, it is taught, "will receive the very heaviest punishment of hell."

A society, called "Lettered - paper Society," having from eight or ten to a hundred or more members, exists quite numerously here, the object of which is to secure the Chinese character from irreverent use. Generally, each society erects a furnace in which to burn to ashes the waste paper its agents may collect. Each employs men, whose business is to go around the streets and alleys, collecting every scrap of

MAN WITH BASKETS GATHERING LETTERED PAPER.

lettered paper which may have fallen to the ground, or which may be found adhering loosely to the walls of houses or shops. Some men gather together refuse lettered paper, old account-books, advertisements, &c. which they sell to the head man or agent of these societies, often getting only half a cent. per pound, or even a less sum. These societies purchase large numbers of small baskets, which are labelled with the name of the society to which they belong, and then distribute them among shopkeepers and householders. Paper deposited in these baskets is taken away by the agents of the societies. The members of these societies each contribute monthly a sum of money to defray the expenses of gathering and buying the waste paper.

The ashes of this paper are carefully put into earthen vessels, and kept until a large quantity is collected. They are then transferred to baskets, and carried in procession, attended by the members of the society in their best apparel, through the principal streets of the city or its suburbs, to the bank of the river, where they are either poured out into the water, and allowed to float down into the ocean, or placed in a boat and taken several miles down the river, or, as some say, near its mouth, before they are emptied into the stream. A band of musicians is hired to accompany the procession. The members of the society carry each a large stick of incense, already lighted, held reverently in one hand before them as they pass along.

Sometimes a society is connected with a large temple ; or the prosecution of the object for which the society is formed is entrusted to the trustees or the committee who have charge of the temple. In a certain large temple, erected a few years ago, thirty or forty earthen vessels were once seen, holding more than half a barrel a-piece, devoted to containing the ashes of lettered paper until carried forth and emptied into the river. In the fall of 1859 I happened to meet a procession, consisting, in part, of about a hundred men, each carrying two large baskets of ashes, which had been collected by a society connected with the largest and the richest temple within the city. It was passing, with much pomp and show, along the main street in the southern suburbs, *en route* to the banks of the Min, attended by a large number of well-dressed gentlemen and a band of music.

The tracts and books given away by those disposed to engage in meritorious acts relating to "reverencing lettered paper" are very explicit in discriminating between different degrees of merit and of demerit, which depend entirely on the manner and the extent of treating respectfully or disrespectfully the character. The merit or the demerit, it is taught, will affect favourably or unfavourably the fortunes of each individual person, and of his posterity, more or less, for several generations. For the sake of illustrating the subject, a few out of a large number of specifications found in the books referred to will be given :—

"He who goes about and collects, washes, and burns lettered paper, has five thousand merits, adds twelve years to his life, will become honoured and wealthy, and his children and grandchildren will be virtuous and filial.

"He who engraves tracts on reverencing lettered paper, and distributes them to people, has five hundred merits, will be for ever without blame, and will beget many honoured children.

"He who forbids another to wipe anything dirty with lettered paper has fifteen merits, and will become prosperous and intelligent.

"He who uses lettered paper to kindle a fire has ten demerits, and he will have itching sores.

"He who in anger throws down on the ground any lettered paper has five demerits, and he will lose his intelligence.

"He who tosses lettered paper into dirty water, or burns it in a filthy place, has twenty demerits, and he will frequently have sore eyes, or become blind."

It is the learned, the talented, and the influential who are principals in these societies, and who engage in the preparation and distribution of these books. All classes, however, are united in cherishing these sentiments, and engaged in practising these customs relating to the reverencing of lettered paper.

Many professedly think that, by reverencing the character as above denoted, they only evince a proper respect for the ancient sages who invented them and who taught their use. In these ways, they aver they exhibit nothing but a due appreciation of the value of letters in the transaction of governmental, commercial, literary, and social affairs generally.

In this city there is a native foundling asylum, where young children who have been cast away by their parents are supported for several years, or until provided for in some manner.

At present it is under the control of eight or ten of the literati and of the gentry, who, as trustees, take turns in the superintendence of its affairs. They employ to aid them two assistants, two doorkeepers, and wet-nurses according to the number of foundlings. A physician is engaged to visit the asylum at least once every five days. It is a part of the duty of the assistants to prepare a written report of matters connected with the asylum every ten days, for the inspection of the acting superintendent, and a list of expenses every month.

A record is kept of the year, month, day, and hour of the birth of every child received. These items, and the ancestral names of its parents, and a few other particulars, are usually written out on a piece of paper found with the child. When not thus furnished, the time of its reception into the asylum only is recorded. The one who brings a babe to the asylum deposits it in a certain place, beats a drum suspended near by, and departs. The drum announces the arrival of another foundling.

The monthly pay of each wet-nurse is one thousand eight hundred and sixty cash. If she can spare nourishment for another child, and there is one for her to take care of, she receives the additional sum of one thousand cash per month. If, at the end of a month, the child under the charge of a certain nurse is doing well, she having been careful and attentive to her duties, she receives a present of from two to five hundred cash. At the end of every three months, the child being still alive, she receives another present of from four to six hundred cash. When a foundling has the small-pox or the measles, and at the end of one month from the attack is in good condition of health, its nurse is presented with five hundred cash extra for her care.

The girls may not be taken out to be courtesans nor to be slaves, but only for wives—not for concubines, nor for inferior wives. When one makes application for a girl, the te-paou, or local constable of the district, must make strict inquiries about the man, his object and circumstances, lest deception should be practised.

Very often the parents of a foundling make application for their child after she has been in the asylum for a few months or years. In case she is alive, and the records of the institution are properly kept, this is easily done, by mentioning its family or ancestral name, and the precise time of its birth. Should they have furnished these items at the time of its deposit at the asylum, the child can be identified, and would be delivered up to those who sought for it.

Only girls are left at the asylum. In case, however, boys should be left there, they would be cared for, if they lived, for several years, and then bound out, as apprentices, to a useful trade, unless demanded by their parents. The rules of the institution would admit of bringing up boys as well as girls, but, in point of fact, boys are not thus deserted by their parents.

The expenses of the asylum, comparatively speaking, must be large. The funds are obtained from the rent of buildings and landed property, and from contributions from rich men, the gentry, and mandarins, and any one who is disposed to take part in this good or meritorious work of saving alive, and of bringing up those children who would otherwise be destroyed by their parents.

The foundlings are almost always betrothed and taken away long before they arrive at womanhood. Should, however, one be left unengaged on arriving at a marriageable age, and should an acceptable applicant for a wife present himself, she is led out to him, with her face and head closely veiled.

There are societies for the relief of indigent and virtuous widows. These societies are not numerous, nor are they very vigorously supported.

Such a society is connected with a temple of the god of Literature, located in East Street, in the city. The money which it dispenses quarterly is derived from the interest or profit of the original sums contributed by the rich and the mandarins, invested in houses or farming lands, or lent to pawn-shops. The sum now given to each widow receiving its aid is only three or four hundred cash per month ; it formerly was five hundred cash. In case she has a son, this sum is continued until he becomes sixteen years old—if she has no male children, and she remains unmarried, and retains a good character, until her death. When her son marries, he receives four or five thousand cash to assist him in paying expenses. Should she die while receiving help from this society, five thousand cash are paid to her family to aid in burying her corpse. Should she marry again, her allowance stops at once. Those who are accepted out of the applicants for this charity are furnished with a paper by the officers of the society, which is posted up on the front door of their houses, stating their names, and that they are aided by the society, &c.

Another society is connected with the municipal temple of the city, and is conducted in a different manner from the one just mentioned. Its members are usually rich men or gentry, who agree to furnish money monthly to aid a definite number of respectable widows, who must comply with the regulations of the society, each member specifying the number of persons he pledges himself to aid, whether one or more.

A blank book, designed to be presented on the reception of money, and in which the payment of money received is to be recorded, is given to the successful applicant, in which the name of her deceased husband and the date of his death, her maiden name, her present age, and various other particulars, are mentioned. In the front part of this receipt-book is entered the name of the individual who furnishes the money to the widow, her own maiden name, and the name of her deceased husband, as a kind of preface. At the close of this written statement is another sentence, intimating that the persons concerned, according to their ability in the service of Siang Huong, the municipal god, with united hearts put forth their strength, reverently fearing the gods which are above, and guarding against the criticisms of beings which are below.

In order to determine which one of the applicants shall be received to fill a vacancy, on a propitious day a list of their names is made out on a piece of paper, and burnt before the idol, to inform the god of the business to be transacted. Then lots are cast before it, and the widow whose name is on the lot drawn is the accepted one.

A certain paper is given her, which she is to post up on the outside of the front door of her residence. This enables her residence to be easily recognised, and informs her neighbours of the circumstance of her receiving aid. Should she have a son, on his arrival at the age of twenty years she must report the fact, and deliver back to the society her receipt-book, when she will receive as a finality four thousand cash. He is now supposed to be old enough to support his mother and her family.

When the widow dies, on her friends returning her receipt-book back to the society, and reporting the fact, they can receive three thousand cash toward defraying her funeral expenses.

In case she is very poor, and on her decease her friends find it exceedingly difficult to procure means to buy a coffin, on representing the fact to the society a coffin is granted for her remains; but instead of the three thousand cash given by the society when no coffin is provided, they receive only one thousand cash to aid in defraying the expenses of her funeral.

The Chinese are especially noted for their desire to have marriages and funerals in a showy or popular manner.

It not unfrequently occurs that the sum of money required to celebrate the funeral of one's parents, or the marriage of one's son, cannot be raised on account of poverty. At such times a kind of "society" (to use the Chinese expression) is formed for the purpose of collecting the sum needed to bury the parent or to marry the son in a respectable manner. Both of these objects are regarded with favour by all classes of society, and to aid one who is very poor in accomplishing either is looked upon not only as a benevolent, but also as a kind of meritorious act. Neighbours, relations, and personal friends of one who wishes to marry a wife, or to bury a parent, but who is very poor, and unable to do it in a style which shall be creditable to the family, are very frequently willing to subscribe money to help to defray the expenses. The money thus subscribed is given, not lent, to the family or person needing it.

There is also a kind of voluntary society formed by the poor people of a neighbourhood for the purpose of having ready money for use when their parents shall die. The members of this society are adult children of living parents. They meet, and appoint or select some responsible or wealthy man in the vicinity as treasurer and director. They agree to pay into his hands, monthly or bi-monthly, as on the first, or on the first and the fifteenth days of the Chinese months, a small specified sum. This he receives and lets out on interest for short periods, or he uses it in his own business as capital, agreeing to refund the sum received, with a stipulated interest, on demand, or on very short notice, in case of the decease of the contributor's father or mother. The sum which the members of such unions or societies desire to accumulate in this manner is usually from twenty to forty thousand cash. In case one's father or mother should die before the stipulated sum should have been accumulated, he is allowed to draw the amount required by giving good security that the balance over and above what he has paid in shall be promptly handed over to the treasurer in the specified instalments. In case the contributor fails to pay in the sums at the proper times, his security must do it.

Some eight or ten years ago there lived a very rich banker in this city, who was famed for his willingness to aid the poor by receiving small sums of money on deposit, to be paid back with interest when death invaded the family of the depositor, and removed a father or mother. Usually, however, the business is managed by a responsible neighbour, or a kindly and benevolently disposed rich man living in the vicinity of those who constitute the society.

In connexion with the various divisions or companies of the Chinese army at this place there is an institution similar in its object to the one just described. A small part of the monthly wages of each soldier is kept in reserve by the paymaster, so as to be ready for use when a parent of any of the soldiers concerned dies. There are, it is said, very few, if indeed any, of the common soldiers who do not engage in this method of securing some ready money with which to bury their parents, or who do not agree among themselves to help each other to money in case of the death of a parent.

There is a kind of benevolent company or society at this place, the design of which is to aid the exceedingly poor people to bury their dead, or to provide funds for the purchase of coffins to contain the bodies of respectable strangers who die here. These coffins are kept uninterred, in hopes that they will be claimed and taken away by the friends of the deceased. Should no claimant appear and remove them, or the coffins become much decayed, the company pay the expenses of burial. Sometimes a man is hired to collect the bones out of the decayed coffins and inter them, having first carefully put them in small coarse earthen vessels, each vessel containing only the bones from one coffin. The vessels are called golden vessels.

CHAPTER XXV

THERE are vows relating to the lives of animals ; and these may be divided into two classes : one relates to not taking the life of a specified animal ; the other relates to the supporting of the animal in view as long as it may live. Both kinds of vow are believed by the Chinese to be meritorious, and to be sure, other things being equal, to bring upon those who make and keep them the favour of heaven or the blessing of the gods.

Some vow under the open heavens, or in the presence of an idol, not to kill a certain kind of domestic animal for a specified time. Usually, after this vow, such persons will not allow such animals to be killed on their premises. Sometimes they will eat of animal food at another's house, as at a feast, or if killed and prepared by others. Generally speaking, however, they profess to abstain, with scrupulous care, from the eating of the meat of such animals as they have vowed not to kill. Both sexes make this kind of vow whenever they please, though the number of women who do it is much greater than that of men. It is asserted that those who make this vow usually keep it, lest some calamity should befall them as a punishment sent by the gods for their insincerity and faithlessness.

Some vow, not specifically that they will not kill certain animals, but that they will "let them live." This vow includes the idea of providing the means of their support until they die of old age or by accident, should the case admit of making such a provision. This vow is made in regard to various kinds of domestic animals, as well as some kinds of birds and fish. In order to prevent their being stolen, and subsequently being used as food, some persons place the animals they wish to have kept alive in a monastery, under the superintendence and care of the resident priests. In such cases they furnish food for them, or pay monthly a certain sum for their board. In a celebrated large monastery belonging to the Buddhist sect, visited in the September of 1860, there were twenty horned cattle, including calves, sixteen goats and kids, ten geese, ten ducks, and scores of hens and chickens. Near the foot of the hill on which the monastery is located there was a herd of twenty or more horned cattle, of which about half were domesticated buffaloes. These were all supported by people who had devoted them to be kept alive, and had transferred the care and responsibilty in regard to them to this monastery. Near the monastery is a fish-pond which abounds in large fish of various kinds, not one of which will the priests allow, on any consideration, to be caught and eaten. These fish were originally placed there in the performance of vows.

Besides common fish, eels and turtles are "let live" as a work of merit. A kind of club or society connected with a large temple in this city annually "let live" a lot of eels which require a large number of men to carry. They are taken through the main street in the suburb to the river, into which they are put, and thus allowed to live. They are brought up for the express purpose of being thus turned into the water ! A large quantity of mock-money and incense are usually consumed in connexion with the "letting" of these eels alive.

Generally speaking, only small wild birds are made the subject of the vow under consideration. The person who wishes to make it takes the bird in his hand before some idol, or under the open canopy of heaven, and, after expressing his heart's desire, lets the bird fly where it will.

The making of these vows is frequently accompanied by the burning of incense and vegetable candles, with much apparent solemnity.

It is always considered as an index of a "good heart" to let animals live, but not in the sense of a tender heart, or a heart easily affected by the pain endured by animals when dying. Both vowing to refrain from destroying animal life, and vowing to support certain animals as long as they live, are referred to by this people as an evidence of a good and virtuous heart, and as meriting future good fortune from the gods.

The feeling that the eating of flesh is sensual and sinful, or quite incompatible with the highest degree of sincerity and purity, is a very popular one among the Chinese of all classes. It may be owing to the prevalence of the Buddhist religion. The leading of a religious life seems oftentimes to be intimately connected with the eating of a vegetable diet.

The Chinese divide all eatables into meats and vegetables. They have a saying that "among the vegetables are three kinds of meats," and "among the meats are three kinds of vegetables." It means that those who wish and profess to live only on vegetables may nevertheless not eat all kinds of vegetables. There are three species which they are not allowed to eat as vegetarians; these are garlics, onions, and scallions, which are reckoned, on account of their strong taste, as being substantially meats, though they are really nothing but vegetables. On the other hand, though they profess to eschew all animal food, yet there are three kinds which they are allowed to eat. These are obtained from salt water, and are believed to be themselves marine animals, or to be the production of marine animals. On account of an insipid or indifferent taste, these are reckoned as vegetables.

The eating of vegetable food principally, or occasionally, is considered meritorious, and avowed in order to attain certain definite objects from the gods in general, or from the particular god or goddess in whose honour or before whose image the vow is made.

Unmarried females who vow to live on vegetables are called "vegetable virgins," and married women who live according to a similar vow are known as "vegetable dames." These are supposed to belong to the Buddhist religion, or to have imbibed the notions of that sect so sincerely and profoundly as to lead them to desire to live according to the Buddhistic tenets as far as this subject is concerned. They dress their persons, and comb and arrange their hair, according to the customs of the class of society to which they belong. They seem to think they can attain the reward of the Buddhistic heaven by the use of a vegetable diet. The term "vegetable Buddhas" is sometimes applied to males, to indicate that they have vowed to abstain from animal food and subsist on vegetables.

Vegetable eaters divide themselves into two classes—those who vow never to eat animal food while they live, and those who vow exclusively to eat vegetables at specified times, or on specified occasions, until they see fit to cancel the vow.

Vowers of the first class are much less numerous than the second class. It is comprised of poor and rich, ignorant and learned.

The second class of vegetarians form a numerous body, and is composed of people from all ranks and conditions of society.

I I

The end sought by this class is the same as the end sought by the other, as longevity, prosperity in business, or recovery from sickness, &c.

There are over a dozen kinds of vow of this class, some of which will be specified, showing how this people "teach for doctrine the commandments of men."

Some promise not to eat meat for breakfast for a whole year. Those who make and carry out this vow are considered to have less merit than those who vow never to eat meat during the rest of their lives.

Some honour the goddess called "The Mother of the Dipper," one of the goddesses of children quite popular at this port. On the seventh, seventeenth, and twenty-seventh of every month during the year, and during the whole seventh month of every year, the females who make this vow are not allowed by it to partake of animal food.

Some honour the goddess of mercy by abstaining from meats during the third, sixth, and ninth months.

Some vow to honour the "heavens and the earth" by eating only vegetables on the first and the fifteenth of every month.

Some, if eating meat when it thunders, immediately stop eating, and go without meat all the rest of the day. If it thunders in the morning, they go without eating animal food for the whole day. The anger of the god of thunder is much dreaded here.

Some, in honour of the god of the kitchen, on the third day of each month refrain from the consumption of animal food. Others select the ninth and the twenty-fourth, or the eighth and the twenty-third of each month, as the days on which they will eat vegetables in order to gain the favour of the kitchen god.

Some people vow to the gods, in order to obtain certain ends, to eat nothing but rice for a specified time. Some vow to eat nothing but clear rice on certain days of every month, praying heaven and earth, or the gods, to grant the favour desired. After the making of the vow, on the days specified, the person, taking a lighted stick of incense in his hands, kneels down and eats the clear boiled rice.

There are other vows which are designed to honour the Moon, the Three Rulers, &c. Very important are the popular sentiments relating to killing the buffalo and eating its flesh. The term "buffalo" includes the two classes of quadrupeds belonging to the *bos genus* found in China, and the word "beef" refers to the flesh of these animals without distinction.

The slaughter of buffaloes for food is unlawful, according to the assertions of the people, and the abstaining from the eating of beef is regarded as very meritorious.

The domesticated buffalo, on account of its aid in ploughing, is considered as deserving of great praise, and as having great merits; and, therefore, men who enjoy the benefit of its toil should not consume its flesh. The law, it is said, permits the killing of the buffalo to be used in sacrifice to Heaven and Earth by the emperor, and in sacrifice to Confucius and a few other deified men in the spring and autumn by the high mandarins, but forbids its slaughter for purposes of food.

Although the law forbids, custom allows the killing and selling of beef, on the butchers paying a percentage to the runners and policemen in the employment of mandarins. The law has become long since a dead letter, so far as this matter is concerned. It is said that, should any mandarin make inquiry in regard to the beef exposed in the streets for sale, the answer given would be that it was the flesh of a buffalo which had died, or which had been killed by accident.

Unless the percentage is paid regularly, the mandarin runners would seize the beef, wherever found, belonging to the butchers who endeavour to defraud them of their accustomed profits. They also would seize it even if already in the hands of the retailer, should the one who killed the animal not have fulfilled his agreement with them. Oftentimes retailers of beef are called upon for presents to the *employés* and mandarins on account of their calling.

A few years ago a sheet of yellow paper, having on it a rough outline sketch of the buffalo in a standing posture, was numerously placarded on the walls by the side of the principal streets in this city and suburbs. All the inside of this outline, including the space occupied by the legs, was taken up with Chinese characters, admonishing the age against killing the buffalo, and against eating its flesh, and depicting in vivid language the sad and laborious life of that animal spent in ploughing and grinding, and the unthankful fate it often meets at the hands of those whom it has served. The outside of the outline figure was taken up with an exhortation to the public against the practice of female infanticide.

In a certain volume of over two hundred leaves, having many of the moral maxims and admonitory precepts of the Chinese, are several pages devoted to *exhorting the people against the use of beef*. In one article, the spirit of a buffalo whose flesh had been

cooked and eaten, and whose hide had been made into drum-
heads, and whose bones had been manufactured into headgear
for women, and this all after a life of drudgery in toiling for
man, is represented as appearing before one of the rulers of the
Chinese hell, and, with lamentation, making its complaints.
The ruler, deeply commiserating the circumstances of its case,
answers, " The deceased killers of buffaloes are enduring punishment for their sins in hell.   Some are tossed upon the tree of
knives ; others are thrown upon the hill of swords.   Some háve
molten brass turned down their throats ; others are bound upon
red-hot iron posts.   Through eternal ages they shall not be
born into the world again, or, if they are born again, they shall
become buffaloes."   It is added, apparently by the author of the
volume, " The consumer of beef who angrily refuses to listen to
admonition on this subject, and who derides the notion that the
buffalo is a meritorious animal, insisting that beef is highly
nutritious, shall be overwhelmed with calamity, his happiness
shall be destroyed, his children and grandchildren shall be poor,
and his family or posterity shall be exterminated."   Let beef-
eaters henceforth know what a miserable experience is to be that
of their descendants !

    In another passage the buffalo is represented as apostrophising
the butcher, the retailer, and the eater of beef, and depicting
in heart-affecting language its laboriously useful life : " While
my lot in the spring and autumn is tolerable, the heats of summer are dreadful.   I have no hands with which to rub off the
mosquitoes when they bite.   When winter comes, the cold wind
pierces to my very joints and marrow.   If the men of the world
would neither sell me for the beef, nor kill, nor eat me, they
would become Omida Buddhas ; if the magistrates will forbid
the killing and the eating of me, they shall be promoted in office
till they become of the highest rank.   Upon those who seek for
male children, if they will not eat my flesh, Heaven will bestow
a son to be their heir.   Those who are seeking for fame, if they
will abstain from beef, shall in early life succeed at the literary
examinations.   Those who are striving for wealth, if they will not
eat my flesh, shall prosper in their business and become rich.   On
the farms where I am not eaten the five grains shall abound, and
the houses shall be filled with plenty.   The junks whose inmates
shall not consume my flesh shall make profitable voyages.   The
soldiers who do not eat my flesh shall soon achieve distinction
and be promoted.   The mandarin attendants who do not eat beef
shall wait on the great man with profit, yea, with great profit."

In the introduction to a Chinese tract on the "Awards for Killing the Buffalo," butchers are declared to have "hearts of stone or of iron." "Beef-eaters have a nature like wolves or tigers." "Those who raise buffaloes in order to sell them for beef, have hearts more wicked and fierce than the wolf and the tiger."

The tract is full of incidents about butchers, beef-eaters, and persons who neither eat beef nor slaughter the buffalo. A story is related of a man who was informed in a dream by the imps who control the complaints which prevail in the summer season, that the reason why he was free from such attacks of disease was because he did not eat beef. Several instances are recorded of individuals who succeeded at the literary examinations because their families carefully abstained from eating the flesh of the buffalo. It is asserted that a certain butcher one day bought three buffaloes, one of which he killed. One night he began suddenly to bellow like cattle, and for a whole day remained insensible. His family, in alarm, called a doctor, who prescribed medicine to revive him. His family, on his recovering his senses, inquired what was the occasion of his acting thus. He answered that he saw in his dream the two buffaloes not yet killed suddenly begin to speak like men. One of them said, "I am your father;" and the other said, "I am your grandfather." In a short time they became in appearance like men, and, on looking carefully at them, said he, "I saw that they were really my father and my grandfather." The butcher was so painfully affected by these circumstances that he sent the two cattle away to the country, and changed his calling.

A butcher once had a buffalo tied up to a post ready to kill, when a drunken neighbour, who was exceedingly fond of beef, came along, and told him to make haste and kill the animal, as he wanted some of its flesh to eat. The beast suddenly shook its head at him, and, with an angry eye, looked upon the man who thus urged on the butcher. Pulling with all its strength on the rope which held it to the post, it broke, and the animal rushed upon the man, and, having gored him, ran off with him on its horns for forty li without stopping. Over a hundred men pursued the beast, and found the beef-eater dead.

In the Sung dynasty lived a man named Li, who was of a savage disposition, and very much noted for his love of beef. Whenever he was employed by other people, he always insisted on having beef and wine furnished him. He died suddenly in the fourth year of the reign of Chun Hi. Now his family had a cow, which, soon after the death of her master, brought forth a calf. On its belly, in white hair, were found four characters, which were the same as the four characters that denoted the name and nickname of the deceased. Many people came to see this wonder, and among them came his widow and children. These began to weep, when suddenly a tiger rushed in and devoured the calf, even its bones as well as flesh! This was believed to be a punishment sent upon the dead man on account of his inordinate love of beef, for his soul was thought to have entered the calf, or, in other words, *he became a calf*, of which fact the four characters found on its belly in white hairs were the abundant and most manifest proof. What could have been plainer? How evident and impressive the lesson to be drawn from this historical fact! Let beef-eaters read and tremble!

Sometimes, in the hot summer season, there may be found by the side of the streets two large earthen vessels, one holding common hot tea, and the other a kind of warm medicated tea. These frequently are placed on a platform a foot or two from the ground, having a frame for holding over the vessels a piece of matting or a strip of cloth, in order to protect the contents from the direct rays of the sun. If sun-heated, the taste is not only unpleasant, but the tea is regarded as unhealthy. There is often a notice posted up on these vessels, or near them, to the effect that they are "presented." The idea is, to furnish gratuitously to the passer-by a draught of tea or of medicated beverage, to prevent any ill effects of the sun.

We have seen it is another "good deed" to furnish coffins to poor families in case of need. It is said the dead who have been aided to a coffin for their remains remember the virtuous act. Societies are occasionally formed which contribute coffins to the destitute and worthy poor.

Though the climate is not very cold in this latitude (there very seldom being ice or snow), in the winter there is a great deal of suffering among the poor. The rich sometimes buy up quantities of wadded second-hand clothing, which they cause to be distributed among the most destitute. The donors get the reputation of being benevolent, and of doing what is apt to be regarded by themselves and by others as "meritorious deeds." Some officers, at the approach of winter, make to the most needy of their prisoners a present of wadded garments, lest they should die from numbness or cold.

Some people *hang out a lantern in the street at night*, under the idea that it is a good and a meritorious deed. Such lanterns are usually made of bamboo or wooden slats about a foot or more square, covered with thin and coarse white gauze or with white paper. Lighting the streets is not done at the expense of Government, but done, if done at all, by shop-keepers, and those particularly interested in their immediate vicinity. Now, besides these lights suspended by the sides of the streets and in front of shops for the purposes of business, there are many others suspended in a dark place or at the corner of an alley, &c. really oftentimes in consequence of vows made in order to procure longevity or recovery from sickness, &c. but professedly to aid the night-traveller in finding his way.

Another form of charitable or good deeds is that of *repairing bridges and roads*. Sometimes, when a bridge becomes nearly impassable, or when a road or street needs great repairs for any reason, a single rich man or a few rich men undertake to be at the necessary repairs. At other times the required amount is obtained by public subscription from the poor and the rich, those in office and those who desire to get office. The willingness to contribute money toward the performance of these works of acknowledged utility is generally considered among the Chinese as a mark of a good heart, and is not unfrequently referred to as very meritorious. Sometimes people who have a tolerably hard lot in this life engage in the repair of bridges and roads to some extent, in the expectation that they will thus insure future prosperity to their descendants in regard to wealth or fame ; and many engage in such repairs in consequence of a vow made before an idol, or as a thank-offering to one of the popular divinities for a favour supposed to have been conferred by it.

In times of unusual scarcity, or of exceeding dearness of provisions, the gentry and rich men sometimes open certain granaries near the north-east gate of the city under their control, and sell the rice on hand at a reduced price to the poor, often one-fourth or one-third less, compared with the prevailing market price. This grain is usually bought up when it is cheap, and stored till dear. In case no especial dearness or scarcity prevails, it is sold out for what it is worth when it begins to be injured through age. The village constables are required, soon before these granaries are to be opened, to take an account of the people in their respective districts who, according to the regulations in regard to this matter, are entitled to purchase the rice at the reduced price, as poor orphans, poor widows, and the poor blind. A paper is given by the managers of this rice-selling company to each family entitled to purchase, stating how many children and adults can apply for the rice, and at what place and on what days.

Sometimes, in similar circumstances of dearness or famine, the rich, the gentry, and the mandarins contribute money to buy rice for those orphans and widows, &c. who are not only destitute of regular employment, but who have no friends able and willing to help in their support. This is given to them, or sold as above.

CHAPTER XXVI.

THE distinction between the shape and size of the feet of women constitutes the caste of China, if there be anything which constitutes caste in this empire. The common people neither know nor care anything about the origin of the custom of compressing the feet of small girls. Few of the literary class seem to have any clear opinion in regard to its origin. Some say that an empress by the name of Tak-ki, during the Shang dynasty, originated the custom. She had club-feet, and prevailed upon her husband, in order to conceal the deformity, to cause all the ladies of his court to compress or bandage their feet. In this way they were made to appear like hers. Others say that the practice began in the time of the Tang dynasty, which flourished about one thousand years ago. Puang-hi, a favourite concubine of Ting-haiu-chio, according to these, inaugurated the practice by first binding her own feet. By degrees the people imitated her example, until the custom prevailed in all the provinces of the empire.

The dominant race in the empire, the Manchu Tartars, do not allow their women to bind or cramp their feet. It unfits a beauty for entrance into the Imperial harem. The penalty is instant death should any small-footed female enter the Imperial palace at Peking—at least, such is the common saying.

The feet of girls, usually when about five or six years of age, are compressed by bandaging, to prevent their farther growth, and to reduce them to the form and appearance so much admired by the rich and literary people of China. For this purpose the foot is extended at the ankle, the fleshy part of the heel is pressed downward and forward, and the entire foot is carefully wound with a long bandage from the ankle to the extremity of the toes and back again. It will be readily understood that this process checks the circulation of the blood, and retards or entirely prevents the further growth of the foot. The smaller toes are naturally, or rather unnaturally, crowded together, and somewhat bent under the foot. The foot is prevented from spreading out as when the weight of the body is thrown upon it in a state of freedom. It becomes very narrow, and tapering to a point at the end of the great toe. The instep becomes unnaturally prominent, and the *os calcis*, or bone which forms the bottom and posterior part of the heel, is somewhat turned downward. The foot, thus compressed, is placed in a short, narrow shoe, tapering to a point; and sometimes a block of wood is used, so supporting the heel that the body seems to stand on tiptoe, the heel being from one to two inches higher than the toes. The heel also extends backward and upward beyond the heel of the shoe, so that a foot really four or five inches long will stand easily in and upon a shoe only three or three and a half inches in length. The ankle remaining nearly of the natural size, and the instep being very prominent, the organs of locomotion present to Western observers a very uncouth appearance.

Usually it requires two or three years, if properly attended to, for the feet to be cramped into the genteel shape. There is no iron or wooden shoe used for compressing the feet. The instruments employed are strips of cloth like narrow bandages. The foot gradually shrinks and shrivels up. When the bandages are removed for the sake of washing the foot or of bandaging tighter, the small toes, after months or years of compression, are unable to resume their natural appearance and position, but remain cramped up and almost without sensation.

When the process is begun at the proper age, and the bandaging is properly attended to, the heel sometimes comes down to the ground, or rather to the level of the end of the large toe. The heel seems under the process of bandaging to elongate; but when the foot is large, and almost full-grown before the compressing of it begins, the heel oftentimes cannot be brought down to a level with the end of the toe. Then a block is put in the shoe under the heel, so that the bottom of the block and the end of the toe shall be nearly on the same level when the individual is standing. Really she walks on her tiptoes and heels. The ankle or instep bulges outward in front.

The genteel shoe for the bandaged foot is about three inches on the sole. Sometimes the shoes are even shorter than three English inches. The toes and the heel are thrust as much as possible into the shoe, and the shoe is then fastened upon the rest of the foot, leaving the bottom portion of the shoe visible. The upper part of the foot is always much larger than the shoe, and, being bandaged about with cloth, the whole has the appearance of a club-foot. The toes and the part of the foot in the shoe have more or less cloth, or strips of cloth, wrapped around them. It is manifest that no stockings can be worn by the ladies who sport such small feet as have been described.

The operation of bandaging is necessarily very painful. The flesh or skin often breaks or cracks in consequence of binding the toes underneath. Unless proper care is taken, sores are formed on the foot which it is difficult to heal, because it is desirable that the parts should be constantly and tightly bandaged. If undue haste is endeavoured to be made by bandaging more tightly than is proper, in order to have the foot quickly become small, the pain becomes proportionably greater. If the girl is twelve or fifteen years old before bandaging her feet is attempted, it is found very difficult to cause them to assume the required shape, and efforts to do so are accompanied with excessive pain. The bones have by this time become hardened, and almost as large as they ever would grow. Usually, however, in the case of girls of an advanced age, the toes are compressed, while the rest of the foot retains its acquired shape, to a very great extent. The end of the foot is thrust into the shoe, the heel is supported by a block, and the rest of the foot is bandaged in much the usual way.

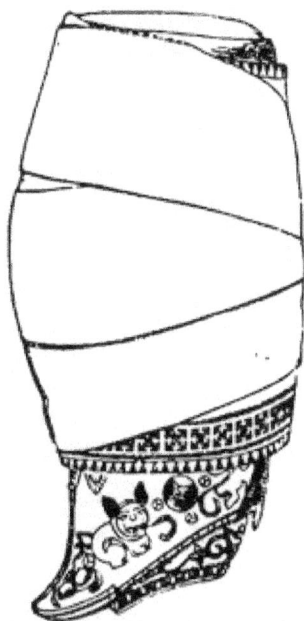

APPEARANCE OF A SMALL SHOE ON THE FOOT.

Instances have been known of females with bandaged feet, when hired out as servants, leaving off the bandages, and discarding, of course, the small shoe, wearing a larger kind, much like those worn by the large-footed class, at least as far as size is concerned. Such persons' feet are more or less deformed, and doubtless they began to wear bandages when considerably advanced in girlhood. There is a good deal of counterfeiting small feet practised at. this place. Stage actors, who are males, sometimes have their feet bandaged when they represent females.

In consequence of thus wearing shoes into which the toes are thrust, this class of females are apparently very tall. As has been explained, they walk and stand, to a great extent, on their tiptoes, and this fact makes them look taller than they would otherwise look. The small-footed class cannot walk firmly. Their gait is mincing and tottering, their steps being short and taken quickly. They are seldom seen to stride along. While they are often quite strong physically, they are generally unable to carry heavy loads, and to manage themselves with ease and adroitness while performing labour which requires moving from place to place. Coarse, heavy work in households, when the women have small feet, is usually performed by males, or by female servants who have large or natural feet.

LARGE OR NATURAL-FOOTED WOMAN AT FUHCHAU.

Small feet are a mark, not of wealth, for the poorest families sometimes have their daughters' feet bandaged—it is rather an index of gentility. It is the fashionable form. Small feet, as they appear bandaged, are considered by most of the Chinese "beautiful." The words "good-looking" are very frequently heard, as indicative of the estimation in which they are held. It is but just to some Chinese to say that they denounce the custom, and view it as crippling the energies of the female sex, and as productive of a great deal of suffering, and as entirely useless.

In some parts of China all the females have bandaged feet, but it is not thus here. There is a large proportion of the inhabitants of the country, and also about six or seventh tenths of the population of the suburbs of this city, according to the estimate of some, whose females have feet of the natural size. It is said that probably more than nine-tenths of the females who are brought up in the city have bandaged feet. It is thought that, were it not for the poverty of the people, all the females would in a generation or two have small feet.

Many poor families prefer to struggle along for a precarious living, bringing up their daughters with small feet, rather than allow them to grow as large as they would grow, and oblige them to carry burdens and do heavy work, in order to obtain a more competent support. As has been said, small feet are not an index of wealth, but of gentility. Families whose daughters have small feet are enabled to marry them into more respectable and more literary families than though their feet were of the natural size. Concubines or inferior wives, hired servants, and female slaves, generally have large feet.

The laws of the empire are silent on the subject of bandaging the feet of female children. Bandaging the feet is simply a custom; but it is a custom of prodigious power and popularity, as may be easily inferred from what has been said.

The Rev. Mr. Abeel, American missionary, made inquiries into the prevalence of infanticide in the vicinity of Amoy eighteen or twenty years ago, and some astounding facts furnished by him were published in America as the result of his personal investigations. Barrow, Bowring, and other writers on China have also remarked on the frequency of female infanticide in specified localities. Some writers have given a flat denial to the statements of others on this subject, principally because instances did not come under their personal observation, or the crime did not prevail in the sections through which they travelled or where they resided, or because it did not seem reasonable and natural. No doubt infanticide is more common in some localities and provinces than in others. But the circumstance that it does not prevail in some places, or that it did not come within the observation of a certain writer, or that it is inhuman and unnatural, by no means proves that it is not common in other parts of the empire. There are most indubitable reasons for believing that it is extensively practised at this place and in the neighbouring districts, and also that it is tolerated by the Government, and that the subject is treated with indifference and with shocking levity by the mass. The following are some of these reasons.

There is a native foundling asylum located within the walls of the city. This is supported by contributions from wealthy Chinese, the gentry, and resident officers of Government.

A large asylum connected with the Roman Catholic church, and designed for girls deserted by their parents, was erected five or six years ago near the south gate of the city, in the suburbs. A native Roman Catholic has stated that at one time it had about four hundred girls under its care.

The Methodist Episcopal Mission has established a foundling asylum at this place on a small scale. It came into operation about six years ago. There are some twenty-five or thirty girls supported by it.

The distribution of sheets and books against the drowning of female infants is very common at the time of the literary examinations. This fact shows conclusively that infanticide is prevalent here, else the distribution of such works would not be tolerated, nor would it have any inciting or procuring cause.

In conversation with the Chinese, they readily admit the prevalence of female infanticide here, and very frequently inquire whether it is practised in Western countries. No one pretends to deny or conceal the monstrous fact that girls in this part of the empire are often put to death very soon after birth.

In the spring of 1861, a female servant employed in a missionary's family confessed that her husband destroyed one of her two little girls at birth. A servant in another family was herself doomed to death by her father soon after birth, but escaped that fate in consequence of his meeting with an accident which the neighbours interpreted to be an omen against killing her. Another servant, in another family, has a relative who destroyed seven girls out of a family of eight children; the remaining one, being a boy, was permitted to live. A woman employed as nurse in an American missionary's family has repeatedly said, in answer to inquiries, that, out of eleven girls born to her mother, her father allowed only four to survive.

In the farming districts in the neighbouring country, the family which has several girls born to it destroys all after one or two, unless some of their acquaintances desire them to bring up as future wives of their boys. In this city the custom of killing girls at birth is probably not so universal as in the country. Some intelligent Chinese estimate that the probable proportion of city families which destroy one or more of their female children, in case they have several, and do not have good opportunities of giving them away to be the wives of the boys of their friends, as about half. Officers of Government seldom or never destroy their female children, as they are able to support them, and, when marriageable, find respectable or wealthy husbands for them.

Some families, after supporting their girls for a few years, feel themselves impelled by poverty to sell them for slaves or for wives. The established price for such children, if sold to be in the future the wives of the boys of friends, is at the rate of about two dollars per year of their lives. A girl one year old usually brings two dollars; two years old, four dollars. After the girl is old enough to work, the price is considerably dearer.

Sometimes, instead of being killed or given away soon after birth, the unfortunates are exposed alive by the side of the street or under some shelter.

The principal methods of depriving the unfortunates of life are three: by drowning in a tub of water, by throwing into some running stream, or by burying alive. The latter method is affirmed to be selected by a few families in the country under the belief that their next child will, in consequence, be a boy. The most common way is the first mentioned. The person who usually performs the murderous act is the father of the child. Midwives and personal friends generally decline it as being none of their business, and as affording an occasion for blame or unpleasant reflection in future years. Generally the mother prefers the child should be given away to being destroyed. Sometimes, however, the parents agree to destroy rather than give away their infant daughter, in order to keep it from a life of poverty or shame.

The professed reason for the destruction of female infants by poor people is their poverty. For an indigent labouring man to support a family of girls, and to marry them off according to custom, is regarded as an impossibility. With a family of sons the case is far different. They, when grown up, can earn money when and where girls cannot. A son is their staff and support in old age and in sickness. He keeps up and perpetuates the family name, and, what is of paramount importance, he will burn incense before their tablets, and will sweep their graves and offer sacrifice to their manes when they are dead.

The rich here usually destroy the girls born to them after they have the number they wish to keep and rear. Boys, on the other hand, are always considered a valuable addition to the family. The proportion of instances of infanticide is probably considerably smaller among the wealthy than among the indigent Chinese, for they are not compelled (to adopt the language of this people) to destroy their female offspring by the want of means of subsistence. This circumstance makes their crime the more aggravated and inexcusable, for it is perpetrated in cold blood and with determination, without any reason or excuse, except that they do not wish to rear them !

Some foreigners in other places entertain the sentiment that the children that are destroyed or exposed by the wayside at birth are principally illegitimates. It is a very great error. If illegitimates, they would not invariably be of one sex, and that the female. The Chinese here emphatically deny that male children are ever destroyed at birth ; and they affirm that girls are drowned, exposed, or given away, not because they are illegitimate, but because their parents are too poor to bring them up, or because, if they are able to bring them up, they determine not to do so. There are some places in the country where female children are seldom kept alive, and where the male children consequently greatly preponderate. A certain village, some twelve or fifteen miles distant, now occupied as a missionary out-station, is noted, even among the Chinese themselves, for the destruction of the girls at birth. The manifest preponderance of boys there is accounted for by its inhabitants by the custom of killing off their female children as soon as born. Owing to the peculiar customs of Chinese social life, there are doubtless far fewer illegitimate births here than in some civilized lands. The girls destroyed are, it is believed, with few exceptions, born in wedlock.

Parents can sell their children to be slaves, or to be the adopted children of the buyer. Husbands can sell their wives to be the wives of other men, not to be their slaves. Those who have bought children of their parents can sell them to others. Children are not unfrequently stolen from their parents, taken to some other part of the province or empire, and sold for slaves.

The Chinese use the same terms to indicate the sale and the purchase of children and wives that they use when speaking of the sale and purchase of land or cattle, or any description of property.

In case of a parent selling his child, a document is given to the buyer, stating the name of the child and the price for which it is sold, whether sold to be the slave or the child of the buyer, &c. This is signed by both parents, if living, and by the writer of the document, the person who is security, and by the go-between. Children thus sold are usually from three to ten years of age.

If the husband sells his wife to be the wife of another man, she must be willing to be thus sold. A document is given the purchaser, stating the fact of sale for such a purpose. This must be signed with the names of husband and wife, and stamped with one of the hands or feet of these parties, smeared with black ink.

The documents relating to the sale of one's children or wife are seldom or never drawn up and signed in a dwelling-house, but in a street or in the fields. The reason alleged for this is that it would be inauspicious to have the papers executed in a house.

When parents sell their children to become the adopted children of others, they may not be used as slaves. Sometimes boys are "sold" by their parents to be play-actors for a certain number of years, during which period their parents have no control over them, but at its expiration they revert to their parents. To be a slave is regarded by some as better than to be a play-actor, as the children of the latter may not compete at the literary examinations for three generations.

The female slave, not many years subsequently to her becoming marriageable, must be provided with a husband by her owner; that is, she must be sold or given away in marriage to a man. Her owner may not retain her in his employment beyond a reasonable time. After her marriage he has no more control over her, nor of the children she may have. She is not then a slave, but the wife of her buyer, her husband, of equal rank and dignity.

The following statements in regard to the marriage of a male slave, and of his owner's control over the slave's descendants, have been furnished by a literary gentleman, in whose family clan there is such a slave. Male slaves are very scarce in this section, even in the richest families.

The owner of a male slave, after he has arrived at about thirty years of age at the latest, should procure a wife for him. Some delay doing this until a considerably longer period, but such delay subjects the owner to reproach, and the slave becomes more and more dissatisfied and unfaithful. His male children and grandchildren "belong," so to speak, to his owner, and must do according to his bidding, though he may not, or at least usually does not, sell them for money. He may apprentice

K K

them to trades, or he may hire them out to work for others, and
take their wages. After they have learned trades, if he pleases
he may claim their wages as journeymen, though this is seldom
done. The fourth generation of males are free, and of course
come out from all control of their ancestor's owner, or from the
control of their ancestor's posterity. A male slave's female
children are not subject to the control of their father's master.
Their father manages them on his own responsibility. Their
betrothal is in the hands of their parents, though usually the
master is consulted on such an important occasion.

The male children or male grandchildren of a slave, if they
are talented and put to school, are sometimes successful at the
literary examinations. They may eventually become rich, or
become officers of Government, when, as is natural, they desire
to redeem their parents or grandparents who are in bonds. It
is said that their owner, in such cases, seldom or never dares to
refuse the redemption-money offered, even if it were no greater
than the price given for the father or grandfather when sold into
bondage. Instances where the descendant of a slave becomes
an officer or a rich man, and redeems his living ancestors, are
rare.

The sole reason in this part of China considered sufficient to
justify the sale of a child to be the slave of another, or of a wife
to be the wife of some other man, is the excessive poverty of
parents or husband, without friends able and willing to aid.
The price varies according to the age, sex, appearance of the
child, the character and age of the wife, the dearness of provisions, &c. from a few dollars to several tens, or a hundred or
two. In the year 1858 a man at Fuhchau sold his wife for
about twenty dollars. Another man, about the same time,
offered his only son, a bright lad of five or six years, for sale for
sixteen dollars. He was offered ten dollars by a man who
wished to adopt him as his son, which offer he refused. Several
years since, a lad who had been attending a missionary free-school
in this place was sold by his mother to be a play-actor. A friend
saw a girl of about sixteen or seventeen years old, not a year ago,
offered for sale for one hundred dollars by her parents, who had
brought her from her native place, some eighty or a hundred
miles to the south of this. A bright girl of about twelve years
old was sold by her parents not long ago for about forty thousand cash.

As has been already intimated, male slaves are comparatively
very few. Female slaves are quite numerous among rich fami-

lies and the families of mandarins. It is said that occasionally very wealthy families have several tens, which are distributed around among the children as they are married off. This large number is not common ; while, generally speaking, all the families which can afford the expense, and require such help, procure one or more. It is regarded as less expensive to buy a female slave than to hire female help to aid in the care of children and in the management of the affairs of the household. Though bought with money, female slaves are treated by their owners very much as women hired to work as servants are treated in Western lands, except that no wages are given them, and that they are at no expense for their food and clothing. They are regarded as a tolerably safe investment of money, for they are readily disposed of as wives or as slaves by their masters in case they become poor. They are regarded as having a better lot than male slaves ; for, when marriageable, or not long subsequently, they are provided with husbands, when they become as free as other wives. The male slave of the first generation has little prospect of gaining his freedom, except in case his parents become wealthy and are willing to redeem him, his owner giving his consent, and delivering back to them the original bill of sale. The male slave is treated as an inferior only by his master, and in his master's family, or among his master's relatives ; by other people he is treated as a free man.

Courtesans are often bought and sold, their price being two or three times as high as the same persons would bring simply as female slaves.

Literary Clubs.—It is very common for students, graduates, and undergraduates, to band together into a kind of club for the purpose of benefiting each other in literary composition. The number who meet together in one club is small, not often exceeding eight or ten. The club is usually composed of friends or mutual acquaintances, not open to any one who is willing to comply with the bye-laws. Undergraduates meet with undergraduates, and graduates with graduates. It generally assembles once in ten days, or oftener, meeting at the houses of its members in rotation. The one whose turn it is to have the club at his house suggests or selects the subjects of the essay and of the poetry, furnishes the paper, pens, and ink used by his comrades, and the tobacco, tea, luncheon, and lights, if held in the evening. It is also his business to collect into a manuscript volume the productions of his comrades, and then take it to some distinguished scholar for his criticism and corrections, and after-

ward to send it round to the members of the club for their
inspection.

One essay in prose and a piece of poetry are composed by each
member at a session of the club. Sometimes they, by mutual
agreement, limit the time of composition to the burning up of a
stick of incense, or from one and a half to two hours. Should
any one fail to complete his essay and his poem by the expiration
of the time fixed upon, he is fined a trifling sum, which is usually
spent in refreshments for the club. The object of limiting the
time of composition is to accustom themselves to rapid writing,
so that, when the examination for degrees comes, they may be
trained to accomplish the work assigned them by their judge at
the appointed time. Sometimes the fines are kept until a member
of the club succeeds at the literary examinations, when the
amount is expended to pay for a feast on the occasion.

Recreating Clubs.—During the sixth and seventh months, rich
men of middle age, and the young gentlemen connected with rich
families, oftentimes form voluntary societies or clubs for recreation and amusement. Several of similar tastes and pursuits band
together and agree to take the direction of matters in turn, the
one who has the management for the day or the trip to pay the
expenses of the occasion. They meet once in three, five, or ten
days, as they please. The best of food and wine is provided,
and they go to a retired and cool retreat among the hills, or to a
temple or monastery, where they amuse themselves by eating,
drinking, playing cards or chess, &c. These picnic excursions
or gatherings for recreation are composed, of course, entirely
of males, respectable females being shut out by the terms
of inexorable custom from participating in such parties for
amusement.

Wine Clubs.—Rich young men often form clubs for the purpose of having social feasts together at each other's houses, or at
such places as may be selected, the expenses being defrayed by
the members in rotation. These jovial unions consist usually of
from five to ten members, who have similar pursuits and congenial tastes. They meet in the morning, two or three times per
month, according to their leisure and inclination, take breakfast
and dinner together, spending the day in feasting, wine-drinking,
and card-playing, in making impromptu verses of poetry, singing
songs, or playing on musical instruments, as suits their fancy, or
as is suggested by the host or head man for the day.

Old Men's Clubs.—Old gentlemen of leisure and of wealth sometimes form a kind of union for the purpose of whiling away their

time and of spending their money in a manner agreeable to themselves. The reason given for the formation of old men's clubs seems to be, that the members delight more in the society and conversation of men of their own age than in the company of young men, or in a club composed of men of promiscuous ages and tastes. This kind of club is said to fulfil the saying of an ancient worthy, "The old man becomes a boy, and delights in sports and pleasure."

Musical Clubs.—It not unfrequently occurs that ten or twelve young men of leisure and of means, who are not of a literary turn of mind, form a society for the purpose of learning to play on musical instruments and to sing songs. They engage a popular teacher, and contribute to pay his wages. During this period incense and candles are regularly lighted before the image of one of the gods of music ; tea, tobacco, and luncheon are furnished on the evening when they meet, at the expense of the members in turn.

CHAPTER XXVII.

SOCIAL CUSTOMS—*continued.*

The celebration of birthdays is one of the peculiar institutions in China—peculiar not in kind, for birthdays are celebrated in other lands, but peculiar in the extent to which the festivities are carried, and in the fixed and stereotyped nature of those festivities. Usually birthdays are not celebrated with any large degree of *éclat* until after one reaches the age of fifty. After that, on the return of the anniversary of every birthday, there is generally at least a small feast, to which some relatives and friends are invited. But it is on the occurrence of every tenth birthday after reaching fifty years of age that there is often a great deal of pomp and expense, especially in families which are able to afford the expense, or which are connected with the Government.

Birthday celebrations of the emperor are called " ten thousand longevities." Those of the empress and of the queen-dowager are called "one thousand autumns." On these days the high mandarins in all the provinces are not allowed to prosecute any criminal investigation, or to inflict any criminal punishment, unless in very extraordinary emergencies. Very early in the morning of those days they are required to proceed to the Imperial Temple, and there prostrate themselves simultaneously, each in his allotted place, before a yellow tablet which represents his majesty, the Son of Heaven, or his mother, as the case may be. On this tablet is a sentence which means "ten thousand years, ten thousand years, ten thousand times ten thousand years," referring to the emperor. For three days previous and for three days subsequent to the birthday celebrated, the mandarins devote themselves to honouring the occasion by feastings, by having theatrical shows performed at their yamuns, and by dressing in their finest robes.

Mandarins, after arriving at the age of fifty, oftentimes have extraordinary celebrations of that and every tenth returning birthday. Sometimes, if not always, on these occasions permission is first obtained from the emperor, or the appropriate board at Peking, to observe and celebrate the anniversary. Several years ago the viceroy at this place had a magnificent celebration of his sixtieth birthday, having first obtained especial permission from Peking, according to common fame, for doing so. Nearly a month was devoted to feasting and seeing play-acting performed at his yamun. According to custom on such occasions, he received a great many valuable presents, or proffers of valuable presents, from the subordinate mandarins. A circumstance which occurred in connexion with the proffering of presents according to Chinese custom at that time created a great deal of talk and diversion, and will be long remembered by friends of the parties most intimately concerned.

The Hai Huong, a civil mandarin next below the prefect, wishing to make a dashing lot of presents to the viceroy, partly for the show they would make and partly in order to gain his favour (which he knew he did not possess), prepared several kinds of articles, part of which he expected would be declined with thanks according to custom. He succeeded in borrowing from a rich retired mandarin, one of his personal friends, a very costly string of pearls, upon which he put a very high estimate, from the fact that they had been presented to him by a certain emperor. These the petty mandarin put among the proffered presents to the viceroy, believing that they would be certainly included among the articles which would be refused or declined when proffered. The viceroy examined the presents, which were brought in and paraded with great show, expressed himself very much pleased with them, and concluded to keep the string of court beads, with some other things, the rest being returned with thanks. It would be difficult to conceive the dismay of the petty mandarin and of the owner of the court beads at this result. The owner demanded of the mandarin the return of the pearls, as they were only borrowed, and he would not set any price upon them. If he had set the proper value upon them, the mandarin would have been ruined, as he could not have raised the sum. The latter dared not go and tell the circumstances to the viceroy, and how the matter would end he could not foresee. Ruin seemed to stare him in the face, do what he could. He thought the latter would know that the pearls were far too costly to be intended as real presents, and were designed only as " horses to look at." After several days of intense suspense and anxiety, he heard that they were exposed at a certain shop in Curiosity Street, to be redeemed at a certain price. It is supposed that he was only too happy to recover them at any price, so as to restore them to their owner.

When the head of a family has arrived at the age of fifty, sixty, or seventy years, &c. the celebration of such a birthday is distinguished from other birthday celebrations by the term of "making ten." A feast is prepared, cards of invitation to relatives and friends are given out, who make in return such presents as they are able and are pleased to make. Sons-in-law are expected to make a valuable present besides the longevity hanging. The pupils of the person honoured, or of his son, if a schoolmaster or a literary man, often join together and make a handsome present on the occasion. It is customary for the host to refuse a part of the presents proffered. Many of the articles proffered are borrowed, on the understanding that, if accepted, they will be paid for, and, if not accepted, they will be duly returned to their owners. Much is done for effect and for show. It is not unusual for rich families to hire a band of theatrical performers to enact plays on the celebration of the birthday of one of its aged and honoured heads.

It is an occasion of great joy. None but what are regarded as good or felicitous words are allowed. Every one tries to be happy himself and to make others happy. It is customary for the guests to salute the head of the family, wishing long life. The guests and the members of the family partake together of as palatable a feast as can be afforded.

If the person whose birthday is celebrated should be sick, and even if well, should the family be pleased so to decide, a ceremony called "worshipping the dipper," or "prolonging the longevity measure," is performed. Its object is to prolong the longevity of the individual. A certain four-sided rice measure, with a flaring top, is arranged on a table in a room. Various things in common use are put into the measure, having been first nearly filled with rice. In front of the measure seven candles are arranged on the table, and seven sticks of incense. Four priests of the Tauist sect are usually employed; sometimes they walk slowly round the table, stopping occasionally at each side to bow toward it. They repeat their formulas, jingle their bells, and blow their horns.

The making of birthday presents is exceedingly common, especially to the aged. A fowl, or a little money, or some

vermicelli, or some common article of food, is invariably presented by friends and relatives, or neighbours, who have been
invited to a feast on the occasion. However poor the family,
it would be considered a grievous insult, or a slight of no
ordinary moment, not to accept the invitation, or acknowledge
its receipt by sending a present.

It is also very customary for one, on the occurrence of his
birthday, to eat a couple of duck's eggs which have been boiled,
or preserved in a certain
red mixture. This is
done as an omen of good.
The duck's eggs are po-
litely called "universal
peace," *Tai ping*, the
same characters being
used which the long-
haired insurgents apply
to themselves. · That
kind of an egg being
regarded as peculiarly
round, the Chinese seem
to think that in some
way it will cause un-
lucky times to be pro-
pitious, or to revolve or
roll along like an egg,
until their fates or their
, fortunes become lucky.
They often refer to the
"revolution of times,"
a term denoting the
changes of fate or des-
tiny, and seem to believe

WOMAN CARRYING A PRESENT.

that the eating of duck's eggs on their birthday has some
intimate connexion with an auspicious change of fortune.
They also eat a bowl of vermicelli as an omen of their desire for
long life.

In large and wealthy families, it is customary for the children,
the sons-in-law, and the grandchildren to unite together in a
kind of preparatory ceremony, in view of the approaching birthday of one of their parents, parents-in-law, or grandparents. In
many families this ceremony is done every year. As an essential
part of the articles used, they procure some "longevity vermi-

celli," a pair of "longevity candles," and a plate full of "longevity peaches."

While the Chinese are born free, they are not all born with
equal rights, privileges, and duties. There are a few privileged
families among the Chinese by hereditary right; but in every
family which has sons born to it, one has special rights and
privileges, if not established by law, established at least by
general consent and common custom.

The first son of his father by his lawful wife has various
peculiar privileges and duties accorded to him in view of his
primogeniture, though he may have numerous brothers, some or
all of whom are more talented and more intelligent than he.

On the death of his parents, the furnace or cooking-range and
cooking utensils which they used invariably fall to him. His
brothers, on no account, may obtain and use them as their own.

In the division of his father's property among the sons, the
eldest son has more than any one of the others. The married
daughters are generally left out of account in the division of the
property, as they are no longer reckoned members of their
father's family. They have already received their dowry at the
time of their marriage. The unmarried girls, whether betrothed
or not, have usually a small sum of money, or a part of the
property, allotted for their dowry when married, or designed to
help defray the expenses of their marriage festivities.

The general rule for dividing the balance of the patrimony,
after deducting the outfit or dowry of unmarried daughters, is
said to be to count the portion of the eldest son as two, and the
portion of each of his brothers as one. If there are four sons,
the property is divided into five shares of equal value, of which
each of his younger brothers has one share, while he takes two.
It falls to his lot to support his mother, if she survives the
division of the family property, and to burn incense, candles,
and mock-money at the established times, and to make the customary offerings before the ancestral tablets of the family. The
homestead falls to his portion of the inherited property, if there
be a homestead.

The division of the family property is oftentimes made while
the parents are still living, especially if of considerable amount.
If the division is deferred until after the death of the father,
experience shows that it is almost invariably accompanied with
much hard feeling and quarrelling, and sometimes more or less
fighting among the children, or between them and their paternal
uncles, who, by custom or by law, are a kind of executors or

administrators of the estate. Usually the living father has so
much authority over his sons that they submit to his decisions,
if made known and carried out during his lifetime, relating to
the division and the disposal of the property to be inherited by
them.

If the number of children is small, and there is but little
property to inherit, it very frequently occurs that there is no
such formal division of the property, either before or after the
decease of their father, and the families continue to live together
for several generations. In large families this is seldom practicable or desirable, especially if the patrimony is extensive and
valuable, provided those concerned are able to agree in regard to
its division—especially if living in a large city. In the country,
where the property consists principally of land, farming utensils,
and cattle, there are very numerous instances where whole
villages are composed of relatives, all having the same ancestral
surname. In many cases, for a long period of time no division
of inherited property is made in rural districts, the descendants
of a common ancestor living or working together, enjoying and
sharing the profits of their labours under the general direction
and supervision of the head of the clan and the head of the
family branches. The Chinese have been distinguished for
immemorial ages for the harmony which prevails among
brothers, cousins, and more remote relatives from generation to
generation, which have common interests and a common surname. Each family generally cooks its food and eats it separately, and has its own private apartments, no matter how many
families live in the same compound or under the same roof.

In case of the death of the eldest son, his eldest son on representative occasions must represent the family. When cards of
invitation are issued, they are issued in the name of the eldest
son of his father, no matter how young the former is, nor how
momentous and important the interests involved, even when
relating to the families of his paternal uncles, or the cousins on
his father's side, &c. It is an invariable principle of usage and
law that the rights, duties, and privileges of primogeniture are
to be confined to the family of the eldest son and his descendants from generation to generation.

In case of the eldest son dying before marriage, or after marriage without male children, it is the custom to adopt some
person as his child and heir, who shall assume his rights and
privileges, and act as his representative. The children of the
adopted heir sustain the same relation to the brothers, uncles,

and nephews of their adopted father as though they were the lineal descendants of the childless man. It is regarded as indispensable that there should be some one to burn incense to the manes of the dead from the eldest son down to posterity in the direct line of the eldest son, either by an own child or an adopted child.

The person who is adopted as the heir of the eldest son is most usually a relative, as his nephew or his cousin. At the time of adoption a feast is prepared, to which the eldest son, if living, invites his relatives of higher rank than himself, his younger brothers, and, in general, the heads of the various branches of the family. If the eldest son has already deceased, the business is taken in hand by the one whose duty it is to see an heir provided to inherit the name and to discharge the duties of the dead. The contract of adoption is usually made out on the occasion of the feast, and signed by the representative parties, who attend as witnesses. The document states the name of the person adopted and the name of the adoptor, who agrees to adopt and regard the former as his legal son and heir, whether he in future answers his expectations and conforms to his wishes or not, &c. The principal parties to this contract burn incense before the ancestral tablets of the family, and worship them. The adopted son worships them as representing his ancestors, and calls himself thereafter their descendant. The ancestors are supposed to be present as partakers of the homage paid, and as witnesses of the transaction of the occasion.

There may be only one head of the clan. Under him there are several heads of families. The latter are the eldest sons of the different branches of the same clan. Their number corresponds to the number of the different branches. The head of the clan has control of all the heads of families in case of quarrels or criminal acts. If the latter, who may be styled patriarchs, are not able to settle the quarrels or knotty questions which arise among those subject directly to them, they are entitled to call upon the arch-patriarch, as the chief of the clan may be styled, for his advice and decision, and the exercise of his influence, which is very great. Magistrates often call upon the heads of families for information about those under them in criminal cases. They and the arch-patriarch are held, in a Chinese sense, responsible for the good behaviour of those whose interests they represent, because connected with them by the ties of consanguinity, and because they are, by the laws of the empire and the usages of society, their chiefs and heads.

It is a very common practice for those who are intimately acquainted, and who cordially love and respect one another, to adopt each other as brothers. Oftentimes women who dearly love one another adopt each other as sisters. Men who adopt each other as brothers sometimes do it by kneeling down and worshipping heaven and earth simultaneously, or by burning incense, with kneeling, before an image of the god of war, or of some other popular idol. Others swear, under the open heavens, to be faithful brothers to each other, imprecating awful curses in case they should become unfriendly, and not fulfil the duties of brothers to each other. Those who adopt each other as brothers promise to sympathise in the sorrows and reverses of one another, and to enjoy the successes and the joys of life together, vowing for themselves and their children to be and behave toward each other on fraternal terms. They are bound, after the ceremony of adoption, in case of the occurrence of festive or of mournful occasions in each other's families, to treat one another very much as real brothers are expected to treat each other on such occasions. In view of such mutual vows, they sometimes help each other in money to a considerable extent, and protect and aid one another as circumstances seem to render fitting, whether as mandarins, should either or both arrive at the dignity of the mandarinate, or as literary men, or traders, &c. The vows of adoption are considered binding as long as one of the original parties survive, no matter whether the relative position in society remain unchanged or not, whether one becomes rich and honoured, and the other becomes a bankrupt or a felon.

A singular custom prevails at this place to a considerable extent. A child, whose parents are living, for a superstitious reason is sometimes professedly adopted by another family which is not wanting in children. Such a lad is usually the only son, or is sickly and puny. The idea of thus having him adopted into another family is that such an adoption will be likely to add to his chances for long life and good health, and will tend to procure good luck for him. He does not become entitled to any share of the property of his adopted family. His real parents imagine that the gods will let him live if his parents think so little of him as to allow him to be adopted into another family, on the principle that he must be a worthless or an indifferent lad. Some believe that certain gods or evil spirits are desirous of ruining the health of bright children, or children of particular promise. Now the parents of the beloved lad, or the only son, though they really almost idolize him, hope to be able to cheat and delude such gods into the belief that their child is of no particular consequence, by having him adopted into the family of some friend. They, in fact, desire he should live to grow up, as one of the greatest boons they can possibly hope for in this world. Influenced by the same secret reasons, parents also sometimes shave off, for the space of several years, all the hair from the head of their only son, just as a priest of the Buddhist sect has the hair all shaved from his head ; they call him "little priest," and pretend to treat him as a worthless child, and of no more consequence in the affairs of the world than is a despised priest. For the same reason, they designate him by very derogative names or epithets, hoping to delude the maliciously-disposed gods into the idea that they care little or nothing about the lad's health or life.

In case the lad has, for the reason indicated, been, as it were, falsely adopted into the family of a friend, it is customary for that family to send several times each year—until he has arrived at the age of sixteen, when he becomes a man—some rice and one or two kinds of condiments through the public streets to the adopted one for his eating.

Ardent spirits in use among this people, made by themselves, among foreigners is known generally under the name of samshu, or Chinese wine. It is most usually, at least in this part of the empire, made from white rice, or a mixture of red and of white rice. When made from red rice, or from a mixture of red and of white rice, it is of a reddish colour. When distilled from white rice, it has a whitish colour. It is sometimes distilled from potatoes, beans, or sugar-cane. The Chinese never make wine from the juice of the grape. Chinese wine is always a distilled liquor, a kind of whisky.

The red wine, as used here on festive occasions, is always drunk hot. When the meal is nearly finished the host proposes wine, and fills all the cups of the table where he is sitting ; then, lifting his cup of steaming wine to his lips, he invites the company to drink with him. They all simultaneously drain their cups, which it is not a difficult task to do, so far as the quantity of their contents is concerned. They then eat a little longer, when they drink another round of wine, and so on *ad libitum*. Many drink only a part of the contents of their cups at a round. Sometimes, and even frequently in the case of the wealthy, and of those who are fond of the cup, from twenty to thirty, or even forty rounds are drunk. Those who cannot drink wine so freely without becoming drunk let their cups stand filled in front of them on the table, excusing themselves from drinking, offering some apology to the company; or they take their cups and raise them to their lips, with or without tasting, as they please, while the others drink. The host urges the company to take wine, and drinking it freely and frequently is understood to be a mark of respect for him.

Females drink wine on festive occasions as universally as men, but they do not imbibe as much. The hostess takes the initiative in pouring out the wine and in inviting her guests to drink. Females at feasts always sit by themselves, and males by themselves, the sexes being in different rooms, if possible.

A noisy game is oftentimes played by two persons on a festive and joyful occasion, the design of which seems to be to see which of them can make the other drink the most wine before drunkenness ensues, or before one withdraws from the contest. This is called " blowing the fist," and consists in both parties simultaneously throwing out toward the other one of their fists, and sticking out one or more of the fingers on these fists. While in the very act of doing this, each pronounces some numeral, which the speakers guess will be the aggregate number of the fingers thus stuck out from both fists. Should the number pronounced by either be the precise number of these fingers, he who pronounced it is reckoned the winner, the other the loser. The loser drinks as the forfeit a cup of wine, and the game proceeds. Should neither guess the right number, the game proceeds without either drinking. If both happen to guess right, each drinks a cup of wine, or both refrain from drinking, as they are pleased to agree, and proceed with the game.

There is another play or game in which scholars or literary men are accustomed to engage on festive occasions, much more intellectual, and less noisy and boisterous, than the one just described. It consists in some one out of those seated around the table, near the conclusion of the feast, pronouncing a line of poetry, which must be matched by another line by all the rest, or, in case of default, a cup of wine must be drunk. Usually the host or the chief guest begins the play by repeating the poetry, which is not original. The reply of the company must be also in selected poetry, and made in the order of their seats. Those who cannot remember and pronounce correctly a line corresponding to the line proposed by the one who commenced the round (*i.e.* corresponding in regard to number of characters, or to the principal word or subject), according to the established rules of the play, is reckoned as beaten, and must drink a cup of wine, unless excused by the company.

In regard to giving and receiving presents, very many instances occur where "there is a mouth, but no heart," or where "there are words, but not the deed," as the Chinese say—that is, where there is a certain meaning on the face of an act, but another and very different meaning intended ; where there is one thing professed, but something else desired. Many things are offered as presents for show, and to obtain a reputable name among neighbours, relatives, and friends.

As we have already said, goods are often only borrowed or rented to be offered as presents, on an understanding with the owner that, should they be accepted, they will be paid for by the borrower or renter, and if rejected they will be duly returned. As it cannot be accurately known beforehand which kinds offered will be actually accepted, and if bought and not accepted the buyer would have no use for the articles, they are simply borrowed or rented for use on the occasion, to be paid for if not returned. Again, oftentimes, instead of really borrowing the articles themselves, the would-be donor gets an order or due-bill for certain articles, as for so many pounds of vermicelli, or a pair of candles, or a ham, and sends it to his friend. If the latter accepts the bill or order, he sends to the shop, obtains the articles specified, and his friend the giver pays for the same. When anything offered is refused or declined, the thanks of the person to whom it was offered are sent to the offerer. The things proffered to a friend as presents are called "horses to look at,"—that is, articles proffered for show, and not designed, as a whole, to be actually received.

The occasions when it is customary to offer and to receive presents are very numerous. Only a few of them will be described.

When one is about to start on a journey, to engage in business, or to act the mandarin in another prefecture or province, it is common for his relatives and personal friends to present him with some "vegetables for the road," as some dates, tea, a ham, or arrowroot.

It is an established custom for one, on his return from a distant place, where he has been trading, acting the mandarin, competing for a literary degree, &c. to make presents to those relatives and friends who presented him with "vegetables for the road" on his starting from home. He comes back with curiosities, or productions of the section of the empire where he has been—

silks, satins, cloth, &c. if wealthy, to divide among his friends and relatives, having due regard to the comparative value and quantity of presents proffered him as "vegetables for the road" when he left home. Unless one should thus remember his relatives and friends on his return, he would be regarded as destitute or ignorant of politeness.

Those friends who receive presents from one recently returned from a distant place, under circumstances just described, are obliged, according to custom, to send back a present in acknowledgment. This is called a "present to pull off the boots." The design of his friends is to feast the far-travelled man, and to con-

TWO MEN CARRYING A PRESENT OF A LARGE JAR OF SPIRITS.

tribute toward recruiting his energies, so well-nigh spent by the fatigues of travel. Now he has leisure to take off his boots and rest a while. Those friends or relatives who do not receive a present from him are not expected to make him any on his return ; or, if they make it, it is not called a present to "pull off his boots."

It is very common for one to make a "present of ceremony" to another on his birthday, or whenever any particular occasion seems to demand especial attention. This is done in two ways— by giving money, and letting the receiver use it for the purchase of whatever pleases him,—this course is taken sometimes when the giver has delayed for any reason to make a present so long that he feels ashamed of himself; or by buying or preparing suitable presents, and proffering them to the individual whom it is designed to honour or please, as broad-cloth, silks, satins antiques, pearls or gems, ginseng from Corea, or birds'-nests.

On joyful occasions, as the celebration of weddings, birthdays, &c. in wealthy families, or those which can afford the expense, it is customary for the lady of the house to invite some female friends to come to dinner, or spend a day or two with her, when they play cards, eat and drink, and make themselves merry in Chinese style. On the return of these female guests to their homes, their hostess is expected by them, and required by custom, to make to each a present of sponge cake and various kinds of sweet cakes bought at the baker's—two, four, or eight boxes, according as she wishes to honour her guests, or according to the circumstances of the families they represent. Unless such presents should be made, or at least proffered, the hostess would be pronounced by her guests as deficient in good breeding, except, perhaps, in the case of near neighbours, or those who come often to dinner. On the first visit of a female guest this present should always be made by the hostess, if she would be considered respectable. On the first visit of a lad to the family of a relative, when he is about to start on his return, it is also customary to make him a similar present.

On the occurrence of joyous events in one's family, as the birth of a first-born son, the friends and relatives will not unfrequently demand of the family a present of money with which to celebrate the event. They usually hire a band of actors, who perform a play, after which the friends, relatives, and actors present feast together. This is not done at the house of the happy family, though at its expense. The sum given varies largely, according to the circumstances of the case.

CHAPTER XXVIII.

SOCIAL CUSTOMS—*continued.*

The tonsure of the common people and mandarins, in distinction from the tonsure of the members of the Tauist and of the Buddhist priesthood, consists in shaving the whole head with a razor once in ten or fifteen days, excepting a circular portion on the crown four or five inches in diameter. The hair on this part is allowed to grow as long as it will grow, and is braided into a neat tress of three strands.

CHINESE RAZOR.

It naturally falls down the back. The lower extremity of the cue is securely fastened with coarse silk so that it will not unbraid. The ends of the silk are left dangling. When the cue or braid of hair is not of itself long enough to suit the fancy of its owner, it is lengthened by braiding in it some hair which has been combed out of other people's heads, and arranged with great care in bunches for this use. The ambition of some is not satisfied until it is made to reach down within a few inches of the ground. When at work, and at other times when the cue would be troublesome, it is coiled about the head, or thrown around the neck ; but to appear in the presence of their superiors or their employers with the hair thus coiled indicates a want of good manners.

Shaving the head, as above described, is practised by all classes except females, Tauist priests, Buddhist nuns, and Buddhist priests, and rebels against the present Government. Females, unless they are Buddhist nuns, are permitted by custom and by law to wear their hair without braiding it into a cue. If they become

such nuns, they must shave off all the hair from their heads
every ten or fifteen days.   Tauist priests either shave their hair
like the common people, or they do not shave at all.   The hair,
left long, they never braid like the common people, nor is it left
to dangle down the back, but it is coiled around on the top of
the head in a manner peculiar to their sect.   Priests of the
Buddhist religion shave off all their hair as smoothly as possible
two or three times per month.   The reason why the Buddhist

BARBER SHAVING THE HEAD OF A CUSTOMER.

priesthood shave their heads in this manner is explained by
some to be an indication of their desire to put away from them
everything of this world ; they do not claim as their own even
their own hair.
    The tonsure of the common people is not a religious habit,
nor is it originally a Chinese fashion.   The first emperor of the
present dynasty, who began to reign in 1644, having usurped
the Dragon Throne, determined to make the tonsure of Manchuria, his native country, the index and proof of the submission

of the Chinese to his authority. He therefore ordered them to shave all the head excepting the crown, and, allowing the hair on that part to grow long, to dress it according to the custom of Manchuria. The Chinese had been accustomed, under native emperors, to wear long hair over the whole head, and to arrange it in a tuft or coil on the head. As might be expected, the arbitrary command to change from the national costume to the shaven pate and the dangling cue was quite unwelcome. The change was gradual, but finally prevailed throughout the empire —so gradual that at the commencement of the reign of Kanghi, the second Tartar emperor, very few at Fuhchau had adopted the custom of their conquerors. At first, those who shaved their heads and conformed to the laws received, it is said, the present of a tael of silver; after a while, only half a tael, and then only a tenth of a tael, and afterward only an egg. Finally, even an egg was not allowed. The law requiring the people to shave the head and braid the cue was not often rigidly enforced by the penalty of immediate death, but it became very manifest that those who did not conform to the wishes of the dominant dynasty would never become successful in a lawsuit against those who did conform, nor would they succeed at the literary examinations. Government favour, as regards lawsuits and literary examinations, was shown to those who conformed to the regulations of the Government. Some of the proud literati and gentry absolutely refused to conform to the degrading and foreign custom, and the result was they lost not only their long hair, but their heads. It has been facetiously remarked by somebody in regard to this matter, that there was more than one example of a man "strangled by a hair." At the end even of the long reign of Kanghi the change was not completed; but during the reign of his successor, the coil of long hair, according to the fashion of the Ming dynasty, completely gave place, in this part of the empire, to the shaven pate and the braided cue, such as are worn by the chiefs of the Manchu dynasty. Ever since, in sections of the empire loyal to the reigning family, the present fashion of the tonsure and the cue has been accepted by the Chinese as the badge of servitude to the Tartars.

These facts serve to explain why the leaders of the rebellion in the centre of China require their adherents, and those whom they conquer, to let all the hair grow, and to coil it in a tuft on the head. They professedly adopt the national costume of wearing the hair which prevailed under the Ming dynasty, that immediately preceding the present one. Long hair on the whole head is the index of rebellion against the Tartar Government at Peking. Indeed, the common name for the rebels, on the part of the Imperialists, is the "long-haired robbers." The shaven pate and crown advertise that the person is a devotee of Buddha, while the unbraided coil on the head, with or without some of the hair around the head shaven off, proclaim the man to be a priest of Rationalism. An inspection of the head of a Chinaman will indicate to the beholder the political status or the religious office or profession of the man.

No Chinaman would dare to appear in the streets of this city, or in any other part of China subject to the Peking Government, with his head dressed in the national costume of the last native dynasty, nor would a Chinaman persist in following the Tartar custom of the shaven head and the braided tress in any of the districts where the power of the rebels prevails. The political condition or the religious profession of a Chinese is indicated by the cut of his hair and the dressing of it.

Notwithstanding the foreign origin of the fashion, the Chinese in Southern and Northern China, where the Tartar power prevails, *seem* to be much attached to the present manner of shaving the head and wearing the cue. They take great pains to keep the cue neat and good-looking, just as though it was an honourable instead of a disgraceful and degrading badge. For two centuries, nearly every male in China, except rebels or priests, has shaven the pate and braided the hair growing on the crown. Now, whatever fashion every one adopts, no matter what may be its origin, design, or means of introduction, eventually becomes reputable and fashionable.

Every neighbourhood has a temple of a particular kind connected with it. This is called the neighbourhood temple, and is under the control of the people living in the neighbourhood. Besides this temple there frequently are several other temples devoted to the worship of particular deities, as the goddess of sailors, the god of war, &c. located in the same neighbourhood.

The neighbourhood temple has the image of a divinity which is believed to have a special care over the interests of the neighbourhood. This god is titled the "Great King," and generally has a wife, who is represented by an image sitting by his side, sharing the honours which are paid to him. In some parts of this temple there is always a place where a very popular female divinity, called "Mother," is worshipped by the married women of the neighbourhood. "Mother" has several attendants. The "Great King" also is surrounded by various servants. Pictures of attendants are often made on the walls of the temples, and images or pictures of various subordinate gods and goddesses are usually found in various parts of the premises. These temples are provided with an elevated platform, where play-actors stand or walk about while performing theatrical plays.

The Great King is not a divinity of high rank in the invisible world. It is a common saying that he corresponds to a village constable in this, the visible world. Oftentimes the neighbourhood committee collect money in the first Chinese month, or early in the spring, and invite several priests to perform super-

TEMPLE AND PAGODA ON A SMALL ISLAND EIGHT OR NINE MILES ABOVE FUHCHAU.

stitious ceremonies in the temple before the idol of the Great King, or outside in some convenient place. The object of this service is to implore the god of fire to protect every man in the neighbourhood from trouble and sickness, and insure prosperity to him in the prosecution of his business throughout the year just commenced. In the last month of the year, some committees have a ceremony performed before the village idol to thank him for his goodness during the year about to close.

It is expected that every family, some time during the twelfth month, will make an offering to the Great King, designed as a thanksgiving for the mercies of the year.

At Tientsin, on the birthdays of some popular divinities, and on other special occasions, a company of men walk on stilts through the streets in procession. Some of them represent women, and all are gaudily and fantastically dressed. Each holds in his hand some utensil. They go usually in single file, singing or chanting. Occasionally one performs some strange act, as kicking out one foot, or jumping up, or whirling round, &c. They train themselves to walk along slowly or fast with perfect ease and self-possession. The performers oftentimes are themselves members of some club or union, or are hired to perform their part in public by a club or union connected with the worship of idols or the practice of superstition. Frequently immense crowds gather to witness their performances in procession.

Besides these celebrations, there are feasts given and shows performed at the expense of the neighbourhood, usually at the regular great annual festivals in the fifth, eighth, and eleventh months, and at any other time or on any other occasion which the neighbourhood may see fit to observe. Many religious ceremonies, attended with theatricals, are also held during the year, at the expense of individual members of the community, either in the discharge of a vow, or in order to express their joy for some event which they are pleased to attribute to the friendly agency of the divinities worshipped in the neighbourhood temple. Small cannon are often fired off, and gongs and drums are beaten with great power and persistence, accompanied with the yells of the spectators, doubtless designed as cheers, during the progress of the theatrical performance.

The committee of trustees of the neighbourhood are elected annually, and serve for one year. They usually are from the most respectable families of the community. The head man or chairman of this committee is distinguished by the appellation of "happy head." It is the business of this committee to look after the religious ceremonies performed in the temple, and to decide the part of the expenses which each family must pay toward providing the various feasts and theatricals which the committee decide upon having. Should the committee not be able to collect from their assessments, or from subscriptions, enough money to defray the current expenses of the temple, it is expected that they will supply the balance, or that the happy head will do it. The happy head is generally one of the most wealthy men of the neighbourhood, and therefore able to make up a deficiency of funds should it be necessary.

WALKING ON STILTS IN A PUBLIC PROCESSION AT TIENTSIN.

It has become an established custom that every flourishing neighbourhood shall have, during the fore part of four nights preceding the fifteenth of the first month, the neighbourhood temple lighted up, and presentations of food made before the idols, which is afterward eaten in the temple, accompanied with the drinking of wine, the burning of incense, candles, and mock-money, under the superintendence of the trustees.

The committee apportion to the families which have had special occasions for rejoicing the amount of money and the kind and quantity of other things they will be required to present, notifying each family by causing a piece of red paper, with the particulars written upon it, to be pasted upon the door of the house it occupies a few days previous to the time of these festivities. Families in a flourishing business generally find little difficulty in meeting the assessment for "joyous gold;" but the families which live on the receipts for daily labour, while their joy may be as sincere, and their willingness to indicate it may be as genuine, as their more wealthy neighbours, find it extremely difficult to pay the "joyful gold," unless the committee make due allowance for their pecuniary condition.

The neighbourhood committee oftentimes endeavour to exert their influence for the good of their village by making various bye-laws or temporary regulations. Sometimes they forbid the practice of gambling on the streets for a certain time, or they forbid the placing of common sedans, when waiting for customers, in certain parts of the village, &c. These regulations usually have all the force of law for the time being, as very few persons would think of persisting in doing anything which was forbidden by his neighbours, and for which he would be sure of receiving their earnest and united remonstrances. It sometimes happens that they seem to be oppressive and restrictive to an injurious degree.

In this notice of matters concerning neighbourhoods, the elders of the community deserve some mention. These are persons who have arrived at the age of some seventy or eighty years. They form, in large and wealthy neighbourhoods, a class by themselves, and are entitled, by the usages of society, to certain well-understood privileges. They are exempted, in ordinary cases, from a forcible arrest by the underlings of the magistrate. If he has any complaint against "the elders of the village," he must respectfully invite their attendance upon him. He must treat them with deference. They have much influence over their fellow-citizens of the same community. In 1850 the villagers took the ground that certain premises in the suburbs of this city should not be rented and occupied by foreigners. The district magistrate having issued a proclamation to the effect that it was in accordance with the treaty for the premises to be rented on just terms, and that there must be no further disturbance, the proclamation was torn down by the neighbourhood rowdies. The magistrate invited the elders of the community to visit him at his yamun, and when they appeared he sternly inquired if they intended to rebel against the will of the emperor. They were nonplussed, and at once answered in the negative. He immediately replied that there must be no more trouble about the occupation of these premises by foreigners, and that no proclamations were to be interfered with. He then dismissed them, remarking that they would be held responsible for the peace and good order of their neighbourhood. From that time there was no more active opposition made by the villagers.

Being unable to labour, and time often dragging heavily, especially if of active habits and good health, these aged gentlemen usually interest themselves in the affairs of their neighbourhood, and crowd themselves into other people's society much oftener than is agreeable. They are not allowed to be treated by any with insult or with positive neglect.

Customs relating to Lepers.—There are two large asylums, or places of refuge and of residence, at this place, for the wretches who are taken with leprosy, located on the outside of the city, near the east and west gates. Two or three hundred lepers live at each of these asylums. A certain number at each asylum has a small stipend allotted them regularly from the Government. When one of those who receive the Government aid dies, his place on the list is supplied by the name of another. It is reported that each leper at the west asylum only receives from one thousand to one thousand five hundred cash per quarter from the Imperial benefaction.

Each asylum is under the control of a head man, who must reside at the institution, and who is nominally or really one of the lepers. It is the duty of this head man to report at stated times to the district magistrate the number of deaths, accessions, &c. and to manage the general affairs of the asylum. Matters which he cannot settle must be promptly reported to the proper magistrate. He has great power over the unfortunates connected with his establishment. The rules are very rigid, and it is said that if one of the inmates should manifest a decidedly insubordinate disposition, and repeatedly and wilfully violate them, and the head man should beat him so severely as to result in death, no notice would be taken of it by the authorities. These head men have the reputation of being rich, and of having money at interest.

Different sections of the asylum are allotted to the different sexes. Husbands and wives are, however, allowed to live together. In case of their husbands being taken with the leprosy, and required to live in the asylum, some wives prefer to accompany them rather than live at their own houses. These asylums present the appearance of a walled village, having streets, a few small shops, and a school. A wealthy leper can hire a respectable house within the compound, and live well by paying extra for what he enjoys. Lepers at the asylums may marry and raise families. It is a popular saying that if either a man or his wife has this disease, the other party will not take it ; and that a male leper cannot impart the leprosy to a woman, while a female leper can give the leprosy to a man who is not her husband.

There are two kinds of leprosy, called respectively the " wet " and the " dry," from the appearance and condition of the body. The " dry " is that form or degree of the disease when the skin is dry and there is no running sore. It is called the " wet " when the skin is moist, and the body, or some part of the body, is covered with maturated or running sores. The two classes are kept separate from each other, so far as eating and sleeping are concerned, living in different quarters of the asylums. By a careful diet and proper medical treatment the " wet " leprosy becomes the " dry " in some cases. Those who have the " wet " leprosy frequently present a most filthy, loathsome, and offensive appearance. A poor " wet " leper, with no friends able and willing to aid him, has a most wretched lot.

When one breaks out with the leprosy, no matter what his social standing or his wealth, established custom requires that he should be conveyed to one of these asylums, have his name entered upon the list of inmates, and remain there for a longer or shorter time. His neighbours, if they know it, will not allow a person taken with the leprosy to remain at his home. On entering an asylum, the leper must give to its head man a sum of ready money, regulated somewhat by the wealth of the individual. In case of a poor man becoming leprous, his neighbours are glad to help him in raising the sum demanded by the head man, in order to facilitate his departure. The sum demanded by the head man as an entrance fee is said to vary from a few to thirty or forty dollars.

Sometimes rich and influential families endeavour to prevent a knowledge of the circumstances becoming public in case a relative is taken with the leprosy by confining him at home, and keeping away from him those who they think would communicate the news to the street lepers or their head man. Should the neighbours become aware of the fact, they generally would inform the street lepers, who would report to the chief; and the neighbours themselves would insist on the observance of the established custom. When the fact becomes known, the matter is sometimes, though very rarely, compromised with the head leper by giving him a large bribe. Some twenty years ago a very rich man, living in the suburbs of this city, having been attacked with this disease, secretly bribed the head man, by a present of one thousand taels of silver, to allow him to remain in his own house. In this instance the family was so influential and respected that the neighbours did not insist on his entering the asylum, as a poor man would have been obliged to do. He remained at home, and subsequently died of the leprosy.

LEPER.

The poor leper leads an unhappy and hopeless life. Obliged to beg in the streets in order to supplement the insufficiency of the Imperial benefaction, in health his lot is a most unenviable one, and sickness would seem to render his misery complete. A physician is connected with each of the asylums, residing without the compound. But money is requisite to secure the attention and the medicines which a sick leper needs. At death the corpse is burned, not buried. Fire is believed to destroy the insects which are supposed to cause the leprosy, and which, unless the corpse was burned, might naturally be expected to infest the neighbourhood and affect travellers.

In the fall of 1859, on a visit to the asylum outside of the east gate, the wretched lepers gathered around, presenting a very unamiable appearance, which it is impossible to describe or to forget. We were told that out of four hundred inmates of the asylum one-fourth were females. We saw thirty or forty children of both sexes who were affirmed to have been born there; a number of the larger boys and girls were out begging. We were informed, in reply to our inquiries, that sometimes the leprosy did not make its appearance on the children of leprous parents in early life, and that the relatives of the children living outside the asylum sometimes took home to bring up those who seemed to be unaffected with the disease. One old man said he was only eighteen years old when taken there, and had been an inmate of the asylum fifty-four years!

Native beggars are very numerous in this city. They are of all ages and of both sexes, blind, lame, maimed, and leprous. Some are enfeebled by vice or by sickness, others are in good bodily condition. Some doubtless follow begging as a profession, partly because they are too indolent to labour, and partly because they can make more money by begging than they could by working. The blind beggars sometimes pass through the streets, to and from the place where they sleep, in single file, by companies, led by one who can see.

Sometimes the beggars visit the stores or shops in companies, with loud entreaties for pity, pounding on the floor or the counter, or making a deafening noise with gongs, in order to expedite the giving of a cash. A single lusty beggar with his lungs and staff, or gong, will make such a noise as to interrupt business entirely by drowning conversation, so that the shop-keeper, in a kind of self-defence, tosses him the cash he demands, when he goes away to vex and annoy another shopkeeper in a similar manner. Some beggars carry a tame snake with them coiled about their persons, or held in their hands, or fastened on a stick. Others have a heavy brick or large stone, with which they pound their bodies, either standing or after having laid themselves down on their backs in the street before the shop whence they expect the pittance. Some have a monkey which they have taught to perform amusing tricks; others, on presenting themselves in or before a shop, commence a song in the Mandarin or in the local dialect, keeping time with bamboo clappers held in one hand. The clothing they wear is generally both scant and exceedingly filthy. Some have on little or nothing more than an old piece of matting thrown over their

shoulders or tied about their persons. Many carry a bowl in
their hands, or have an old bag or pocket suspended from their
necks, for the purpose of holding what they may pick up or
what may be given them.

The beggars, both in the city and in the suburbs, are governed,
so far as they are governed at all in the pursuit of their calling,
by head men. There are several head men, whose names are
entered in the office of the dis-
trict magistrate in the city.
All the beggars residing or
staying for the time within
certain understood boundaries
are under the control of a
certain head man. This man
is not appointed or selected by
the beggars, his subjects. In
the first instances, it is said,
these head men were appointed
by the mandarins a long while
ago, in order to relieve themselves from trouble relating to
beggars, and originally beggars
were appointed to the office or
position of the chief of beggars. This headship has now
become hereditary in certain
families, which are, nominally
at least, beggar families. These
men are not now practical and
acting beggars, but live on the
perquisites and spoils of office. Some of them are said to be
rich, and to live in comparatively good style. They may be
styled " Kings of the Beggars."

A head man of the beggars may make an agreement with the
shopkeepers, merchants, and bankers within his district, that
beggars shall not visit their shops, warehouses, and banks for
money for a stipulated time, and the beggars are obliged to
conform to the agreement, if native beggars. Religious mendi-
cants, or refugees, exiles, &c. from other provinces, who take to
begging for a living, do not come under these regulations. The
head man receives from each of the principal business firms
with which he can come to an agreement a sum of money, as
the price of exemption from the importunities of beggars ; and

BEGGAR WITH A PIECE OF OLD MATTING
THROWN OVER HIS SHOULDERS.

in proof of this agreement he gives a strip of red paper, on which is printed or written a sentence to the effect that "the brethren must not come here to disturb and annoy." This paper is pasted up in a conspicuous part of the store or bank, and the money is taken away and professedly distributed among the beggars concerned, though it is sagely surmised that he appropriates the lion's share to his own use. After a business man has made this agreement with the head man of the beggars, should any native beggar apply for the usual pittance, it is only necessary to point to the red slip of paper and bid him begone. If he will not depart at once, he may be beaten with impunity by the master of the establishment, which beating the latter would not dare to give unless he had the proof of an agreement at hand ; and it is affirmed that the head man might, if the beggar repeatedly violated the agreement, flog or beat the culprit to death, and no notice would be taken of the matter by the higher authorities.

The shopkeepers, bankers, &c. who do not make such agreement with the head men are liable to be called upon by beggars at their places of business, not at their private residences, day after day, and at any time from morning until night, for the contribution of cash. The beggars, while before or in a shop, are oftentimes scolded and abused most shamefully by words, but never by blows, nor are they ever expelled forcibly from a shop unless they attempt to steal, or violate some well-understood custom. If a beggar should be treated contrary to custom by a shopkeeper, the former would at once proceed to annoy and disturb the latter most offensively until what he deemed an adequate compensation or satisfaction should be rendered him. In such cases the beggar always comes off the better of the two parties, as he has no reputation or pecuniary interest to lose, and what he acquires in the shape of money for the abuse or injury is so much clear gain.

When burials connected with wealthy families take place on the hills, or the regular annual sacrifices to the dead are about to be performed in the spring at their graves, beggars often interfere for the purpose of getting food or money, unless forbidden to do so by their head men in consequence of an especial agreement.

CHAPTER XXIX.

The Dragon holds a remarkable position in the history and government of China. It also enjoys an ominous eminence in the affections of the Chinese people. It is frequently represented as the greatest benefactor of mankind. It is the dragon which causes the clouds to form and the rain to fall. The Chinese delight in praising its wonderful properties and powers. It is the venerated symbol of good.

The Five-clawed Dragon is an emblem of Imperial power. The people may not use or make a representation of it except by special permission of the emperor. Some reason that, as the emperor personates the empire, and as the five-clawed dragon personates the emperor, the dragon may with propriety be considered as the Chinese national coat of arms. Others style it the patron god—the protecting deity of the empire.

The emperor appropriates to himself the use of the true dragon, the one which has five claws on each of its four feet. On his dress of state is embroidered a likeness of the dragon. His throne is styled the " dragon's seat." His bedstead is the " dragon's bedstead." His countenance is the " dragon's face." His eyes are the " dragon's eyes." His beard is the " dragon's beard." The pencil with which he writes is called the "dragon's pencil." His body is the "dragon's body." Williams, in his " Middle Kingdom," quaintly remarks, " The old dragon, it might be almost said, has coiled himself around the Emperor of China, one of the greatest upholders of his power in the world, and contrived to get himself worshipped through him by one-third of the human race."

The true dragon, it is affirmed, never renders itself visible to mortal vision wholly at once. If its head is seen, its tail is obscured or hidden. If it exposes its tail to the eyes of man, it is careful to keep its head out of sight. It is always accompanied by, or partially enshrouded in, clouds when it becomes visible in any of its parts. Water-spouts are believed by some Chinese to be occasioned by the ascent and descent of the dragon. Fishermen and residents on the borders of the ocean are reported to catch occasional glimpses of the dragon ascending from the water and descending to it.

It is represented as having scales, and without ears. From its forehead two horns project upward. Its organ of hearing seems to be located in these horns, for it is asserted that it hears through them. It is regarded as the king of fishes.

In times of drought the bestower of rain, the dragon, is oftentimes the object of prayer, both on the part of the emperor and the people, for a supply of the needed element. The Chinese say that in Peking there is a large temple dedicated to the worship of the dragon, and within the precincts of the temple grounds there is a certain well. On the mouth of this well is laid a large flat stone, having the image of the dragon engraved on its under side. This stone, as the story goes, has been removed only once for a long period, for fear that the anger of the dragon will be excited, and result in dire calamity to the people of the surrounding country. In the beginning of the reign of the great-grandfather of the present emperor occurred a severe and protracted drought at Peking. The emperor made many supplications to the dragon for rain, but in vain; the rain-monarch did not deign to answer the humble petitions of the Son of Heaven. At length the emperor, in anger, dared to lift the stone from the mouth of the well, when water immediately fell in torrents from the heavens. At the end of three days the emperor returned thanks for the rain, and requested its cessation; but it continued to pour down. On the sixth day he again expressed his gratitude, yet it continued to rain in torrents without intermission. On the ninth day, the emperor, becoming alarmed at the consequences of the daring act, confessed humbly to the dragon his sin in opening the well. This appeased the anger of the rain-king, his majesty the five-clawed dragon, and the rain instantly ceased.

While the emperor appropriates the five-clawed to his own use, the officials and the people may, and do under some circumstances, use a representation of the four-clawed dragon. One of the doors of the examination hall where candidates for the

second literary degree meet to compete together, is called the
"dragon's door;" and the successful candidates or competitors
for this degree are said to "leap" or ascend the "dragon's door."
Directly in front of the entrance to the main hall in the great
Confucian temple of this place is a very large inclined stone of
superior quality, on which is engraved an image of the dragon's
face and head. A certain kind of boats which, having been
paraded through the streets of this city in idol processions at
times during the summer months, are burnt by the side of the
Min, have their bows made with a hideous likeness of the
dragon's head with a gaping mouth. The boats used at the celebration of the dragon festival in the fifth Chinese month have
similar bows. During the first Chinese month a cloth image of
the dragon is exhibited at theatres in the night-time, and paraded
in the public streets, being moved and worked by men. It is
represented as pursuing a large pearl or ball, which is carried
a little in advance of it, the whole being lighted with candles.
This is a popular sport, and is called "playing with a dragon
lantern." Some paper charms have pictures of the dragon.

While the emperor is represented by the dragon, the empress
is represented by the phœnix. Some say that this bird has
entered China only twice, and these visits were made during the
lives of eminent men who flourished more than three thousand
years ago. The common people dare not use its supposed likeness to promote their private purposes except on certain occasions and under certain circumstances, in accordance with established customs. But should any one have the presumption to
use the likeness of either dragon or phœnix in a manner not in
accordance with established custom to promote his private ends,
he would soon, doubtless, have abundant occasion to regret the
attempt. An incident occurred at this place several years ago
illustrating this remark. A certain banker adopted as his device
on the margin of the bank-notes the image of the phœnix. As
soon as these notes were issued, the servants or runners of some
of the mandarins demanded of him a sum of money, which he
refused to give them, deeming it exorbitant. On the matter
coming to the knowledge of the mandarins, they took or coun-
tenanced measures which resulted in extorting a large sum of
money from the banker, and finally in his ruin. His crime or
fault was simply that of using on the border of his bills the
likeness of the phœnix, which was regarded as a trespass on the
prerogative of the empress.

The language spoken by the common people abounds in proverbs, some of the words of which have no characters to represent them in writing. The language spoken by learned men abounds in terse expressions, oftentimes derived from the Classics, pronounced according to the proper sound of the characters which compose it. The latter may be called "book phrases." The dividing line between proverbs and book-phrases is not very definite, as the latter may be classed among the former when they become so commonly used as to be readily understood by uneducated persons.*

* "Mr. Doolittle," says the *Eclectic Review*, "does not seem to be largely acquainted with the literature of China itself; we should have been glad to see some account of the poetry, their odes and popular songs, perhaps even of their novels, which, we are told, often abound in smart wit and satire. Voltaire borrowed one of his best stories from these sources, in his Zadig, or the Book of Fate, giving to it a more sentimental and European tint of colouring; the story illustrates certainly the power and disposition of the Chinese to work up their fancies into rather a severe form of satire. We perhaps may not displease our readers by quoting the Chinese version from a very able paper on the Chinese from the *Quarterly Review*, vol. lvi. 1836 :—

"'A disciple of the sect of *Taou-tse*, or "Doctors of Reason," while meditating among the tombs, observed a young lady seated by one of them, eagerly employed in fanning the structure. On approaching the spot, and seeing her in tears, he ventured to ask whose tomb it might be, and why she took such pains in fanning it. The lady, with great simplicity, replied, "You see a widow at the tomb of her husband : he was most dear to me, and he loved me in return with equal tenderness. Afflicted with the idea of parting with me, even in death, his last words were these :— 'My dearest wife, should you ever think of marrying again, I conjure you to wait, at least, until the plaster of my tomb be entirely dry ; after which you have my sanction to take another husband.' Now," said she, "as the materials are still damp, and not likely soon to dry, I thought I would just fan it a little to assist in dissipating this moisture." "This woman," thought the philosopher, "is in a monstrous hurry ;" and having recently taken to himself a beautiful wife, he hastened home to apprise her of the adventure. "Oh, the wretch!" she exclaimed, "what an unfeeling monster! How can a virtuous woman ever think of a second husband ! If, for my misfortune, I should ever lose you, be assured I should remain single for the rest of my life."

"'"Fair promises," thought the philosopher, "are easily made, but we shall see." He suddenly became dangerously ill ; a tender scene occurred ; the lady vowed eternal remembrance, and repeated her resolution to remain a widow to her dying day. "Enough," said the philosopher, "my eyes are now closing for ever ;" and, so saying, the breath departed from his body. The desponding widow, with loud lamentations, embraced the lifeless body, and held it locked in her arms. Among the mourners who assembled on the melancholy occasion was a youth of fair exterior, who said he had come from a distance to place himself as a pupil under the deceased sage. With great difficulty he procured a sight of the widow ; she was struck with his appearance ;—saw him again on the following day ; they dined together, supped together, and exchanged tender looks

Should the reader suppose that the Chinese live, or endeavour to live, according to the moral sentiment of the best of these set phrases, he would be sadly mistaken. They love to discuss the reason of things, and the propriety of acting according to reason, while they have not the most distant idea of doing so, unless they conclude it will be for their interest.

To feel after a pin on the bottom of the ocean—[to try to do an absurd or impossible thing].

A cat leading a rat to view the feast of lanterns—[one bad man deceiving another with specious pretensions].

A tiger eating a fly—[disproportion].

A wooden tiger—[an unsuccessful plan to frighten people].

A tiger carrying a cangue—[awkwardness].

To be bold enough to stroke the tiger's beard—[great courage and daring].

If one will not enter a tiger's lair, how can he obtain her whelps ?—[proper means must be taken to obtain a desired object].

and expressions. The youth was half smitten, the lady wholly so; a marriage was speedily agreed upon : the youth, however, previously demanded three conditions, one of which may suffice for our notice : it was that the widow should forthwith turn out of the house the unsightly coffin that contained the remains of her late husband. The lady readily consented ; the coffin was sent into an old shed at the bottom of the garden.

"'Preparations were now made for the marriage feast, but the bridegroom was suddenly seized with convulsions and fell on the floor. The bride was desired by his domestic not to be alarmed, for that these fits were not unusual, and that there was a cure for them—the only and certain cure,—the brain of a man taken in warm wine. "Oh!" said the lady, "my late husband has been dead only a few days ; get me a hatchet, and I will go myself and open the coffin, and take out the remedy." Thus fortified, she posted away to the bottom of the garden, and striking a blow with all her might—behold! the lid flew open, a groan was heard, and, to her great horror, the dead man, rising up, very coolly said, "My dear wife, lend me your hand to get out." The unhappy inamorata, finding all her intrigues'discovered, and unable to survive her shame, hung herself to one of the beams. The philosopher found her, and, having satisfied himself that she was quite dead, cut her down very coolly ; and having repaired his own coffin, laid her in it, fully determined never to take another wife.

"'The Chinese author goes circumstantially through all the details of the story, but Voltaire has taken only the pith of this bitter satire on the ladies, substituting the labour of turning a brook from the side of the tomb, for that of drying it with a fan ; and the readiness of one fair dame *pour couper le nez à Zadig*, for the other's zeal in fracturing the husband's skull to get at his brains.'"

An ox with a ring in his nose—[a man with his passions under control].

A calf without a ring in his nose—[an ungovernable child].

A calf does not know a tiger—[simplicity and innocence].

An old man is like a candle placed in the wind—[disease quickly carries off the aged, as a draught of wind speedily extinguishes a candle placed in it].

After the pig has been killed to speak of the price—[to take an improper advantage of circumstances].

Where there is musk there will, of course, be perfume; it will not be necessary to stand in the wind—[talent and worth will manifest themselves without resorting to trickery].

The heart of a man, the stomach of an ox—[excessive covetousness].

A rat and a cat to sleep together—[bad people to profess to agree together].

The dog lords it over the cat's rice—[interference in other people's affairs].

A thief's mouth uttering imperial language—[a bad man can talk speciously and honestly].

To mistake a village squire for the emperor—[not to perceive essential differences in persons or things].

To turn a somersault in an oyster-shell—[to suppose or to plan an impossibility].

To stand on two ships at once—[impossible to do the same thing at the same time in two different places].

A basket of grain producing only a pound of chicken-meat—[indicates a money-losing business].

An oily mouth and a heart like a razor—[one who makes pleasant and specious promises, but who has evil intentions].

The carpenter makes the cangue which he himself may be doomed to wear—[men often unwittingly do what eventually harms themselves].

A blind fowl picking at random after worms—[working without skill].

A toad in a well cannot behold the whole heavens: to look at the heavens from the bottom of a well—[contracted ideas].

Climbing a tree to hunt for fish—[to look for things where they can by no probability be found].

To eat one's rice looking toward the heavens—[a quiet and approving conscience].

The mouth of Buddha, but the heart of a serpent—[a man of pleasant exterior, but wicked heart].

In a melon-patch, do not stoop down to arrange your shoes; under a plum-tree, do not lift your hand to adjust your cap—[avoid appearances of evil].

To covet another man's horse, and lose one's own ox—[to lose what property one has already in efforts to acquire more].

To carry an olive on the pate of a Buddhist priest—[to attempt what cannot readily be done].

If one has a mind to beat the stone, the stone will have a hole in it—[persevering industry overcomes obstacles].

To grind down an iron pestle to make a needle of—[indomitable perseverance in efforts to accomplish a desired object].

The kettle of him who has a wicked heart is full of rice; the kettle of him whose heart coincides with the doctrines of heaven has none—[prosperity in business is not a sign or proof of the rectitude of one's principles. That the wicked have plenty to eat is no indication of the approval of heaven].

None will carry on a money-losing business, but some will engage in a head-losing occupation—[men will try to make money by any means, however unlawful, which may even result in their own decapitation, while they will not sell goods at less than cost, or engage in an employment which affords no profit].

Don't tell a man with a full stomach that you are hungry—[one just after a plentiful repast does not readily sympathise with the feelings of a hungry man].

To nourish a rat to eat a hole in one's bags—[to support for a time a man in one's family who requites favours received by robbing or in some other way injuring his benefactor].

A house on fire is a fine sight, but it inflicts great damage on the owner—[appearances at a distance are often deceptive; things are not to be decided about simply by their appearance].

In passing over the day in the usual way there are four ounces of sin—[every man is a sinner].

Money in the hands of a poor man, rice in the basket of a beggar—[indicates the loss of money or property without hope of recovery, just as the poor man spends the money he has received, and the beggar eats up the rice he has begged, having nothing left].

When you converse in the road, (remember) there are men in the grass.

The neighbouring walls have ears—[much like the Western proverb, "The wall has ears"].

He that has wealth and wine has many friends.

If one has plenty of money, but no child, he cannot be

reckoned rich ; if one has children, but no money, he cannot be considered poor.

A poor man, though living in the crowded mart, no one will notice ; a rich man, though dwelling amid the remote hills, his distant relative will visit.

An upright heart does not fear demons.

Correct one's self, then correct others.

Seeing an opportunity to make money, one should think of righteousness.

A covetous heart is never satisfied.

To have a bad child is not as well as to have none.

He who does according to heaven will be preserved; he who opposes heaven will perish.

According to heaven and according to fate, not according to man.

Calamity comes from heaven.

All things are according to heaven.

The doctrines of heaven confer happiness on the good and misery on the evil.

A rich man regards a thousand mouths (in his family) as too few ; the poor man thinks his one too many.

If men have good desires, heaven will assuredly grant them.

If one does good, heaven will bestow on him a hundred blessings.

If one does not good, heaven will send upon him a hundred evils.

To die or to live is according to fate.

To be wealthy or to be honoured with office is according to heaven.

Great goodness and great wickedness, sooner or later, are sure to be rewarded.

The doctrines of heaven are not selfish.

True doctrine cannot injure the true scholar.

Of ten thousand evils, lewdness is the head.

Of one hundred virtues, filial piety is the first.

The Chinese have a large vocabulary of curses, oaths, and imprecations. On the most trivial occasions, they almost without exception are in the habit of imprecating upon those who have excited their anger the most direful vengeance, or expressing their feelings in the most filthy language. Their common language, when offended or insulted, is usually of the most vile description, abounding with indelicate and obscene allusions. They seem to strive with themselves, as though a wager were at stake, who shall excel in the use of filthy, loathsome, and vindictive terms.

The Chinese here have a saying that their "mouths are exceedingly filthy," and no one who has acquired their dialect can have the least doubt of its truth. They have another saying that the "heart of woman is superlatively poisonous," meaning that the language uttered by females, when cursing others, is more virulent and filthy than that used by men. All classes of society, whether Confucianists, Buddhists, or Rationalists, without distinction of sect or profession in life, indulge with spirit in cursing those who have aroused their angry passions.

" May the Five Emperors catch you !
  May the Five Emperors arrest you at your door ! "

[The five "emperors" or "rulers" are certain five gods, much worshipped at this place, who are believed to govern the cholera, pestilence, and epidemic diseases generally. The idea, in such curses as the above, is, May you die by the cholera! May you perish by the pestilence !]

" When you die, may you go to Hades, and have your bowels ripped open !
  May you be fried in the caldron of oil !
  May your tongue be cut off !
  May you be thrown on the mountain of knives !"

[These refer to different kinds of punishment supposed to prevail in the lower world.]

" May you have none left to open the door and to trim the lamp !
  May your children and your husband perish ! (said to a married woman.)
  May the pestilence deprive you of posterity !
  May you not live to adult age !
  May you die before marriage !
  May your incense-furnace be turned bottom side up on the wall !
  May your posterity be cut off !"

[These all indicate the worst calamity that can befall one, in the estimation of the Chinese.]

" May fish devour you !
  May fish be your coffin, and water be your grave ! "

[May you die by drowning, and your body never be found by friends.]

" May the crows pick out your eyes !
  May your body be in one place and your head in another !
  When you die may your corpse be unburied !
  May your corpse be eaten by dogs !"

[These all imply sudden and violent death, with the corpse left unburied.]

" May you die in prison !
May your corpse be dragged out of the hole in the wall ! "

[To die in prison is considered very ignominious, because the corpse is not allowed to be carried out through the door, but is pulled out of the prison through an aperture made in the wall on the back side of the premises.]

" May the village constable attend to your remains ! "

[May you be buried at the public expense as a pauper.]

" After death may you never be born again ! "

[Let your punishment in Hades be eternal.]

" May five horses pull you to pieces ! "

[May your death be caused by five horses attached to your body—one to the head, two to the arms, and two to the legs.]

" May the hour when you die be unknown ! "

[The Chinese regard it as a great calamity not to know and record the exact time of one's death.]

" On the mountains may you meet with tigers, and on the plains with serpents ! "

[May you everywhere be surrounded with peril.]

" May your corpse be carried to its burial in a white coffin ! "

[i.e. unstained or unpainted. This imprecates death in extreme poverty, and without friends able and willing to procure a decent coffin for one's burial.]

" May you die by the roadside !
May you perish by the corner of the street !
May you die in the middle of the road !
May you die before you get half-way home !
May the border of the paddy-field be your pillow !
May your whole family be jammed into one coffin !
May the five thunders strike you dead !
Let the fire of heaven consume you !
May you be born again as a dog or a hog !
May you be hacked into ten thousand pieces !
May your bowels rot inch by inch !
May your hands and feet rot off !
May demons carry you off ! "

Women usually perform the work of running into small moulds the tin used in preparing mock-money, making each piece of unbeaten tin about one inch wide by two inches long, and quite thin. An apprentice or unskilful workman takes a sufficient number of these pieces between the thumb and forefinger of his left hand to amount to an inch in thickness, and lays one end of the lot on the surface of a large smooth stone, by which he sits, and with the other hand, holding a heavy hammer, beats the tin laid on the stone blow after blow. After a while he takes hold of the other end, beating in the same way the end which he previously held between his thumb and forefinger. He continues this process until the pieces become several times as large as at first. They are then given over to a better workman, who lays the whole down on the stone, where he steadies one end with his left hand, while he beats the other end with the hammer held in his right hand. The hammer must be brought down with skill, touching the tin evenly, else the upper sheets would be badly torn or the whole injured. During the process of beating, before it has acquired the desired thinness, it is steamed two or three times, and a kind of powder sprinkled between the sheets, so that they will not adhere together and become a solid mass, owing to the constant and heavy pounding. The nearer it is to being finished the greater the skill of the workman, the tin passing generally through the hands of four or five different workmen. When it is sufficiently thin, the two by one inch piece has become two feet, more or less, in length, by one foot or one and a half feet wide. For some time before it is completed a large piece of very thick pasteboard is put over the upper sheet when pounded, in order to prevent the sheets from being as badly torn and damaged as they otherwise would be. When pounded sufficiently thin, the edges of the mass of tin-foil are trimmed, and the foil is sent to market, where it brings from fifty cents to one dollar per pound, according to the quality of the article.

The manufacturer of mock-money cuts the tinfoil into different sizes and shapes.

The labour of pasting the tinfoil upon paper is almost exclusively done by women and girls belonging to poor families. Their wages are graduated by the amount of labour performed. If they work skilfully, fast workers may earn from one hundred to one hundred and fifty cash per day. Young girls and the unskilful women often make only from fifty to one hundred cash per day, or from five to ten cents, they boarding themselves. If unskilful, they are apt to spoil the sheets of tinfoil. The least strength used unskilfully injures the foil so that it becomes worthless until re-melted and re-made. In the suburbs of this city there are doubtless several thousand poor families, the females of which perform comparatively little work during their whole lives other than pasting the tinfoil upon paper, to be used in superstitious and idolatrous ceremonies.

There is a large amount of capital invested in the preparation of mock-money paper at this place. There are more than thirty large establishments where it is kept for sale, of different sizes and shapes. A certain kind, made in sheets twelve or fifteen inches square, is exported largely to Tientsin, in Pechile, and to ports in Shantung province. Another kind, consisting of small sheets, is exported extensively to southern and to northern ports.

When the foil remains of its natural colour the paper money is believed to represent silver, and, when burnt, to be obtained by the dead or the gods for whom it is designed. When the tin-foil is coloured yellow by passing over it a brush which has been dipped in a decoction of the flowers of a certain kind of cassia, it represents gold, which in like manner is remitted to invisible parties by the agency of fire.

A kind of mock-money, called foreign cash, is made out of a round piece of pasteboard of the size of a dollar. Tinfoil is then pasted on both sides. Rude impressions of the obverse and the reverse sides of a Spanish dollar are then made upon the opposite sides of the pasteboard.

Another kind of mock-money, representing copper cash, consists simply of oblong pieces of coarse paper, each piece having eight or ten holes, and each hole representing one cash.

After burning a quantity of mock-money in one place, the ashes are carefully treasured up for the small particles of tin which they contain. These ashes are sold by weight to men who go around from house to house for the purpose of buying them. By the process of heating, the particles of tin are collected together and separated from the paper ashes. This tin is again sold to those who are engaged in the manufacture of tinfoil by beating, who prepare it for pasting upon paper in a manner similar to that which has been described. The paper with the foil upon it is burnt, the ashes again gathered up, the particles of tin re-melted, re-pounded, re-pasted upon paper, &c. An immense amount of it is consumed yearly in this part of the empire. No family is too poor to procure mock-money when occasion demands; and no heathen family is so intelligent, or so free from the trammels of custom, as not to be in the habit of buying and burning it.

CHAPTER XXX.

In this city there are not a few men who make their living by performing wonderful tricks for the amusement of others.

JUGGLER SPINNING A PLATE ROUND.

Some very common jugglers' tricks are such as these : Lying down on the back and causing a large earthen water-vessel to revolve round and round on the soles of the feet, which are turned up toward the sky. Another is to cause a candle-stick, in which is a lighted candle, to stand erect on the top of one's head while he sings some ditty to the sound of clap-traps which he swings or works in his hands. Another is to balance a common plate on the upper point of a short perpendicular stick, which is placed for support by its lower point on another stick held in the mouth of the performer, the plate spinning round with very great velocity. The wonder of this truly wonderful performance is the ease with which the plate is made to spin round so fast. Sometimes one passing along the streets will see a man playing with three or five rings, some six or eight inches in diameter, in a manner which never fails to draw a crowd round him. He throws the rings up into the air separately, catching them in his hand when they seem joined together, or linked into each other like a chain. The performer throws the rings into a variety of shapes without the slightest hesitation or mistake. Another man will be seen throwing up three sticks, one after the other, keeping two of them in the air. With each, as he catches it on falling, he gives a rap on a drum placed before him. Sometimes three kitchen-knives are thrown up in the same manner, and caught as they fall, one by one, and tossed up again. When knives are used, no drum is struck.

At other times the street may be rendered impassable for the time being by any but daring foot-passengers by the exploits of a man who has taken possession of it, and is playing with a ball of iron or lead, weighing several pounds, attached to the end of a strong but small rope, some twenty or thirty feet long. He is engaged in forcing the ball forward and drawing it back by the cord attached, which he holds in one hand, in a line parallel with the ground, and about as high as his neck. The ball passes and repasses by him very swiftly, nearly as quick as he can stretch out and draw in the hand which has hold of the string. It proceeds both sides from him to the extent of twelve or fifteen feet. The wonder of the performance consists in the apparent ease with which the difficult feat is done, the speed of the ball, and the precision with which it flies backward and forward, he all the time not touching the ball. If he were to whirl the ball round his head at the distance of the end of the string, there would be in that operation nothing wonderful; but he forces it back and forth, in a parallel line with the ground, with nearly the same speed and certainty of motion that he could attain by giving it a circular motion round his head. If the ball should hit against his own head while performing thus, it would crush it or dash his brains out, in all probability; or if it should impinge against the head of any of the people in the street, the result would be similar. Every one, however, gives a wide berth to the ball.

What among the Chinese is regarded as particularly wonderful is a performance described as follows: The juggler pretends to kill his son, and plants a melon-seed. The spectators behold him, apparently kill his boy with blows from a sword, cutting off his legs and arms. He then covers up the mutilated parts under a blanket placed on the ground. In a short time the corpse is gone, and is nowhere to be found, having

seemingly vanished from the place. Having planted the melon-
seed in a flower-pot filled with earth, after a while, on lifting up
the blanket, there is seen a large melon on the ground. If a
spectator expresses a wish that the melon should vanish also,
the blanket is thrown over it. After waiting a little while, on
again lifting the covering the melon is nowhere in sight. Yet
after a short time spent in waiting, and on removing the blanket,
there will be seen the lad who had apparently been killed and
mutilated but a little while previously, living and well, without
any mark of having been injured.

Sometimes the spectator sees him cut out a diminutive door
and child with a pair of scissors out of common paper, and place
them under the blanket. In a short time these things have
disappeared, and a bowl of vegetables appears under the blanket
in their stead. A spectator hands the performer an empty
bottle, and requests him to fill it with spirits. It is put under
the blanket, and in a short time, on taking it out, behold, it is
filled with spirits of the best quality !

The following feats are sometimes performed :—A man, having
only a pair of trousers on his loins, with a boy to assist him,
clears a space in a crowd.

From time to time he puts into his mouth several common
sewing needles, and some thread separately. By and by he pulls
out of his mouth several threads, each having strung upon them
a number of needles.

He pretends to swallow several metal balls, one at a time,
each nearly an inch in diameter, and then points out the places
where they will appear just under the skin, or on his neck, or
about the middle of his stomach. And, sure enough, they seem
to be just where he points out, their appearance being indicated
by a rising of the skin about as high and as large as would be
the case if one of the balls had really been there.

He snatches from time to time from the ground a handful of
slips of paper, which he crams in his mouth until his cheeks
protrude, and he is unable to articulate distinctly. He now
places his hands on his hips, and pretends to be causing his
breath to pass through the mass of papers in his mouth. In a
few moments a small stream of smoke proceeds from his mouth,
just as though the paper was on fire, which is really the case.
He continues to force his breath out through the paper, and the
smoke becomes more dense, until it pours forth from his mouth
in a constant stream to the distance of two or three feet. The
spectators in front of him can see the fire in the centre of the

mass of paper in his mouth. As he continues to fan the fire with his breath, a larger and larger quantity of paper is ignited, until apparently half of the mass is ignited, and smoke and sparks issue from his mouth continually, and the man acts as though he felt the heat very sensibly. Considerable merriment prevails among the spectators as they look upon the man whose mouth is full of fire. His grimaces and contortions are irresistible.

After a short time, occupied principally by collecting cash from his wondering and amused spectators, he commences to pull out of his mouth a paper ribbon, being about an inch and a quarter wide. As he passes along round the outside of the cleared circle, he drops the paper ribbon on the ground, until he has passed two or three times round it, where it lies for the time being, while he proceeds to perform some other feat.

He takes a pair of Chinese brass swords, about twenty inches long exclusive of the hilt. The blades are about an inch and a half wide, and are flat, and the edges are not sharp. He places these flatwise, one upon the other, and then puts them into his mouth, point first, and both at a time. He throws his head back, so that his face is about at an angle of forty-five degrees with the ground, and forces the two swords downward. He continues to press down upon the hilts until all but the hilts, and three or four inches of the part of the blades, have disappeared. While the swords are in this position, he walks slowly round the arena, facing the spectators, some of whom are within three or four feet of him. There is evidently no deception in regard to the swords being in his mouth, and extending downward. After a while the swords are drawn out of his mouth and handed to those of the spectators who manifest a desire to handle and scrutinise them.

The Chinese are noted gamblers, and have invented a great many methods of playing for amusement or for money. The shops opened for gamblers are very numerous in some streets and in some localities. Into these dens it is not an unfrequent occurrence that several practised sharpers combine to lead some unsophisticated country greenhorn, who, they ascertain, has ready money which he carries about him. The one who introduces him pretends to be his true friend, and is showing him round the city to see the notable sights. When in the shop he is prevailed to try his hand at a small stake, which he is suffered to win. The gamesters, who are in league with his professed friend, applaud his skill and luck, and some of them offer to play with him. They lead him on in this way, until he is fleeced of his ready money, which probably may not be all his own, but intrusted to him by neighbours and friends with which to purchase goods for them to use or sell in the country. The man's character is ruined, and his money is gone. How can he see his friends and neighbours? How can he survive the disgrace and the shame he has brought upon himself by his false confidence in his city friend? Probably, in many cases, the result is that he becomes a vagabond, in process of time a beggar or a thief, and finally ends his course a suicide.

There are several kinds of street gambling, on a small scale, for money or for sweetmeats, candies, &c. which it is impossible to avoid noticing while passing along, which has, however, not more cleverness than one of our ordinary drawing-room packs of puzzle-cards for an evening's entertainment. One of these is a kind of literary or "poetical" gambling.

One method of gambling is this: the head gambler provides himself with three slender slips of bamboo or wood, eight or ten inches long, and a stool, and seats himself by the street-side, to accommodate those who wish to try their fortunes by an appeal to the three lots. He holds the three lots in one hand by grasping them at one end, the other end projecting outward, and usually separated from each other, so that those who engage in gambling can easily slip cash on any one of them which he selects. There is hanging down from his hand a red tassel or string, professedly attached to one of the three lots at the end which is held in the hand of the operator. He holds the three ends in such a way that a spectator cannot tell which of them it is that has the red thread attached to it. The person who ventures to stake cash, places the amount he pleases on the lot which he bets is the one which has the red string attached to it. If the lot selected is not the one which has a string attached, he simply loses his venture. If it should prove to be the one, the head gambler must restore him the cash, and twice as many more as he ventured. It is very seldom that the head gambler forfeits any money. He usually manages the matter so as almost always to gain, not to lose.

Another common instrument of street-gambling consists in part of a round board some fifteen or eighteen inches in diameter, the circumference of which is divided into eight or sixteen equal parts. From the centre to each of the dividing points is drawn a straight line. A standard or post eight or ten inches high is erected in the centre, coming to a point small enough to allow of cash being put upon it. A slender stick of wood is provided, nearly as long as the diameter of the board, having a smooth hole in the centre of it sufficiently large to allow it to fit loosely upon the perpendicular standard, two or three inches from the top of it. This is designed to be put upon the standard, and to turn round easily, and with as little friction as possible, upon this standard, in a line parallel with the surface of the board. Near one end of this horizontal piece is tied one end of a string, so that its other end will come down nearly to the surface of the board. This horizontal piece of wood, being turned round by a sudden movement of the hand, will continue to revolve some time after the hand has been taken away, and, of course, it is quite uncertain over what part of the face of the board the thread attached to it will finally stop. The gambling consists in guessing where the string will point after the horizontal piece to which it is attached having been made to revolve, stops. The one who wishes to stake some cash upon a certain spot, places the amount of his wager on the top of the perpendicular standard, and specifies the particular

GAMBLING WITH A REVOLVING POINTER.

division he bets upon, or he puts the cash upon that particular division, and then gives the horizontal piece a whirl round with greater or less velocity, as he pleases. If the thread stops, pointing down to the particular division he selected, he has won, and the head gambler must pay him eight or sixteen times as much as he ventured, according as the face of the board is divided into eight or sixteen parts. If the thread stops over any other space than the one he bet upon, he loses his wager.

Many boys spend the most of their time in hawking about the streets various kinds of sweetmeats or preserved fruits, not so much for the purpose of selling them for money as for allowing them to be gambled for.

The Chinese are very fond of farces. A popular farce is that of a Buddhist priest leading a blind man to see the show of lanterns. The thing which seems to be amusing is the main idea of the farce. The priest has professedly abjured the world, with all of its amusements and its diversions, and therefore ought not to be fond of seeing such joyful spectacles as the show of lanterns, and the blind man is wholly incapable of beholding the lanterns. As painted sometimes, the priest appears

BUDDHIST PRIEST LEADING A BLIND MAN TO SEE THE SHOW OF LANTERNS.

to be hurrying on as fast as possible his blind companion whom he is leading, each with joyful and animated countenances as they approach the spectacle.

Another farce represents a tinker engaged in mending a cracked water-jar for a pretty woman. While working at his task and chatting away with the woman, he manages to break it badly on purpose. The painting of the old man, with the jar held between his knees while mending it, represents the woman sitting near by, smoking her pipe and joking with him.

Another farce relates to a Buddhist priest carrying on his back or shoulders a Buddhist nun. Some say they were brother and sister; she became a nun, and he devoted himself to the life of a priest. Afterward he found her in a nunnery on a mountain, from which he rescued her. A picture of a part of this farce represents a priest, with a nun upon his shoulders, descending a hill. Others state that they were not brother and sister; but, happening to see each other, mutually fell in love, and, in violation of their vows, concluded to abscond and live together, which could only be effected by his carrying her off on his back from her nunnery.

A favourite historical play, often enacted, represents the changing fortunes of one of the sovereigns of the Ming dynasty, the grandson of Hung-u, the founder of that dynasty. During the course of the performance the hero appears on the stage, a prisoner, and confined in a kind of carriage, which is drawn along by a man. It seems he had been conquered by an uncle in battle, and dethroned. He ran away from his capital, became a priest, and was subsequently identified and arrested by the agents of his uncle. While he was in a carriage as a captive, and was being conveyed back to the capital for trial, he was met by one of his former courtiers, a faithful and brave man, who drove off the men in attendance, and released his former master, and convoyed him away in safety.

Another historical farce represents a sour-looking officer sitting in a chair, while a person who is described to be a crazy and unmanageable priest, with a broom under his arm, is addressing him with earnest gesticulation. The officer denotes a very unjust and unpopular courtier of the Sung dynasty, and the priest is explained to be one of the kings of the infernal regions, who assumed a human form, and pretended to be a crazy priest of the Buddhist sect, for the purpose mainly of reprimanding the wicked mandarin. He went about with a broom, sweeping now and then, and in this way wandered into the palace of the wicked courtier. As he appeared to be perfectly harmless, he was allowed to go pretty much where he pleased. Finally, he came into the presence of the man whom he sought, and began to upbraid him with his crimes. The angry and surprised courtier endeavoured to have him arrested, but he vanished.

Boys in China have no such games of ball as are common and popular in the West. But among adults, in the Chinese January, and occasionally at other times of the year, there are one or two kinds of amusement practised which perhaps deserve mention in this connexion.

One of these represents a lion pursuing a ball. A figure of an immense lion is made out of bamboo splints and pasteboard, covered with cloth coloured to represent the popular notions in regard to this animal. It is carried by two men or boys, who put their head and shoulders into the body of the animal. Their legs and part of their bodies appear below, about where the fore legs and the hinder legs should come. The parts of the bodies and the lower limbs of the actors, whose heads are concealed in the body of the lion, are sometimes covered with clothing, coloured or painted in a manner which fits them, as the Chinese believe, to represent the four legs of the beast itself. The lion has an immense head, and is made with open jaws, so that one or both of those who personate its legs and feet can see out pretty clearly through its mouth. The front one, at least, can see well where to step, and the other must do as well as he can while in pursuit of the ball. A ball, in imitation of an immense pearl, is carried by some one who runs in front of the beast, or darts across its path, showing it for the purpose of attracting its attention and exciting its pursuit. The lion is believed to be

MANŒUVRING THE DRAGON.

exceedingly fond of playing with the ball. They imagine that when it sees a ball it tries to obtain possession of it, after which it plays with it much as a kitten plays with a ball. It is on account of this prevalent impression that they provide a man or boy to carry a ball in front of the artificial king of the beasts. The royal quadruped follows in the play wherever the ball-bearer leads. Everything about the amusement is coarsely executed, and yet the performance excites considerable interest and produces considerable merriment.

The other sport alluded to is that of manœuvring with an image representing the dragon. This image, as regards its frame-

work, is made out of bamboo splints, some of them tied so as to be nearly circular. This framework of hoops is covered with cloth, and is so arranged that it can be lighted up in the inside. To the under part of the whole, when completed, several short poles are affixed in such a manner that it can be elevated several feet above the heads of the men who carry it. It is sometimes several tens of feet long, and can be turned and twisted into various shapes, on account of the nature of its framework not being stiff and straight, but consisting of hoop-like preparations of bamboo, covered with a flexible material, as cloth. Manœuvring or playing with the dragon is quite common in the festivities connected with celebrations in the first Chinese month.

One of the gods or patron deities worshipped by play-actors was an emperor of the Tang dynasty, which flourished between 620—906 A.D. He is often referred to as the original composer of theatrical ballads. He is usually represented by a small wooden image, which is worshipped by the actors at their homes, where they burn incense and candles to its honour. When they go away from their homes for the purpose of performing a play, they carry this image along in the box containing their dresses and instruments. Being clothed in some fancy-coloured garments, it is used to represent a child, should a child be needed in the representation of a play.

BOY DRESSED LIKE A FEMALE IN ACTING A THEATRICAL PLAY.

There are a large number of theatrical bands in this city. A band or company consists of from about ten to nearly one hundred persons. Some are composed mostly of boys, others of full-grown adults. The boys, while learning to play their parts, are oftentimes treated very hardly, and even cruelly, by their masters. It is represented that, if any one thus engaged or bound out to learn to be an actor should be beaten to death for disobedience, or should die as a result of the infliction of punishment for inaptitude or want of application, no notice would be taken of the circumstance by the authorities.

If a female character is necessary to be personated in the acting

of a play, one of the boys, or one of the adults connected with
the company, dresses in female clothing and carries on the part.
An old man is represented by a person wearing a false beard,
and an old woman by a man who has a shrill voice, or who tries
to speak with a shrill voice.

There is no building erected expressly and solely for theatrical
purposes. Every temple, with few exceptions, has a stage set up
in a convenient part, devoted to the performance of theatrical
representations. There are several hundreds of such temples in
this city and suburbs. Platforms are also oftentimes extemporized
in the street during an evening—seldom during the day—for the
performance of plays.

There is no admittance fee to the theatrical plays. When acted
in temples and in the open streets, they are free to all who please
to attend, and are able to come within a hearing or seeing
distance. Sometimes, when acted in the residences of the wealthy,
and of mandarins, the performances are private, and intended for
the amusement of the females of the establishment and of a select
company of female friends. There is seldom any mingling of the
sexes at theatrical entertainments in private residences. Invited
guests at the plays performed in mandarin establishments, or at
the houses of the rich or the gentry, often reward the actors at
the conclusion of an act, and sometimes of every act, if they are
pleased with the performance. At such times the host is expected,
according to established custom, to reward the actors as much
and as often as his guests. Actors frequently get several times
as much in the form of rewards as their stipulated hire.

The actors do not know what they will be required to perform
until after a large portion of the audience has assembled. The
head man of the party which has invited the band usually calls
upon one of the especially invited guests to select, out of the
plays which it is known the band is capable of acting, some particular one. The actors immediately dress according to the
character of the play selected, and begin its performance.

Besides the historical plays alluded to, which are often acted
out with a great deal of gesticulation, there are two kinds of
puppet-shows frequently seen in the streets, and exhibited in
temples and in private houses—in the latter often for the especial
gratification of females. These are much cheaper than the former,
requiring a much less number of actors, and a much smaller
amount and variety of dresses and other kinds of accompaniments.
One kind of these puppet-shows consists of small images, which
are worked by strings managed by a person concealed behind a

screen, accompanied by singing or instrumental music. The other consists of small images with moveable heads, which, in order to represent various persons, are changed from time to time by the performer, who holds the bodies of the images in his hands.

It is customary in China to perpetuate the names and celebrate the virtues of persons who have attained to extraordinary reputation in regard to several subjects by erecting an honorary portal, by special permission of the emperor. There is one portal in honour of a man distinguished for his filial piety, a Manchu Tartar, and one of two brothers who were exceedingly attached to each other, and who conducted toward each other in the relation of elder and younger brothers, according to Chinese views of the subject; and one of a person who attained to the age of one hundred years. The friends or family relatives of the one who is believed to have merited an honorary portal may report the facts to the district magistrate, who reports them to the prefect or the treasurer. The emperor, in due time, is memorialized on the subject. The memorial, if the Board of Works approve, is submitted to the emperor; and if he should likewise approve of the erection of an honorary portal, he signifies his will by the use of the vermilion pencil. The permission is communicated to the treasurer of the province where the individual lives or lived, who, through his subordinates, communicates the happy tidings to those concerned. In theory, a small sum of money is allotted the family of the distinguished person, to aid in erecting a suitable memorial; but, in fact, money is seldom received. It requires considerable influence to obtain the imperial assent. Bribes *alias* presents are singularly efficacious in expediting and securing the result. Those who are interested in obtaining it are usually willing and able to furnish the necessary funds for erecting the portal.

About two-thirds of the way from the river to the city, at Tating, is a tea station, where there is a fine specimen of the honorary portal, beneath which all who enter or leave the city from the south pass. Including the foundations, it probably cost several hundred dollars. It was erected in the reign of Kien Lung, of the present dynasty, in honour of a native of this place by the name of *Kong*, who was distinguished for his charities to the poor. Though by no means wealthy, he was continually seeking out very poor and destitute persons, to whom he gave money and rendered assistance in various ways. He seemed to delight in doing good in an unobtrusive manner, so different from the Chinese generally. He became so distinguished for his charities, and especially .for his benevolent disposition, that the fact was communicated in a memorial to the emperor, Kien Lung, who signified his will that a portal should be at once erected to his honour, having certain four characters upon it, indicating that "he delighted to do good and loved to bestow in charity," besides the two which imported that it was erected by Imperial will. It was accordingly erected, but became the cause of the death of the man whom it was designed to honour. He "died of fear." He was fearful lest his means would not be adequate to meet the increased calls upon his charity, now that his name and character became everywhere known. He was so apprehensive of the disgrace which would follow in case he should fail to respond to the demands for charity, that he sickened and died, a victim to the misjudged kindness of friends. He died, however, before his means failed, and he was spared the disgrace which he feared. His death occurred the morning after the portal was erected, as some state.

The Chinese have most strange and singular ideas in regard to *thunder and lightning. Both are worshipped.* There is a temple dedicated to the thunder god near the east gate. Sometimes thunder is represented as being in shape and appearance much like a cock, having four claws to each foot, and two hands proceeding from under the wings. In one hand he holds a chisel, and in the other a mallet. Lightning is represented as a woman, having one or two mirrors in her hands. She, in pictures, is sometimes made to hold a round mirror over her head, steadied by both hands. Images of thunder and lightning are found in some temples. On the back of thunder there is said to be "a golden thread." The mirror reflects the lightning.

THUNDER.

Western barbarians speak of people being "struck dead by lightning," whereas the philosophers of the Middle Kingdom never make mention of people killed by lightning, but always "killed by thunder." Good and virtuous people are never killed by thunder, according to the Chinese, but only the unfilial, or those who do not use with proper respect the "five grains," as rice and wheat, or those who, in a previous state of existence, were guilty of murder, or filial impiety, or some other wickedness for which they have not been already sufficiently punished, or those who do not reverence the written or printed (Chinese) characters. They imagine also that thunder kills certain insects or reptiles, which, unless thus destroyed in season, would in process of time become human beings in form, or hobgoblins or elves, but with the powers and desires of evil spirits.

When any one has been struck dead by thunder, that fact is regarded as the best possible evidence that he was really a bad person—bad in a Chinese sense, either in the present life or in some past state of being, no matter what his reputation or his manner of living in this life may have been. His death, by such an instrumentality, is viewed as irrefragable proof that he ought not to have lived any longer, and that he was in heart a very wicked and corrupt man, whom heaven would not permit to live on the earth. News-slips, consisting often of only one or two pages, are frequently offered for sale in the streets for two or three cash, relating to some person recently struck dead by thunder, and giving an account of his wicked acts, viewed from a Chinese point of view, which led the god of thunder to deprive him of life as a warning to others. Exhortations are sometimes added, persuading the reader from the commission of similar wickedness, lest a like sudden and disgraceful death should be his fate.

Frequently after one has been struck dead by lightning, surviving family friends invite a priest to perform a certain superstitious ceremony near the body, reciting his formulas adapted to the occasion and ringing his bells, with the burning of incense and candles, all in order to cause the god of thunder to leave the body of his victim and ascend to heaven. It is believed that the performance of the thunder charm especially facilitates the departure of the god, and his ascension from earth to heaven, whence he came to kill the man. It is a common saying, that by the use of a mirror in a particular way, on examining the back of a person struck dead by thunder, there may often be found characters traced there stating the crime or sin of which he was guilty, and for which he was "thunder-struck."

A singular method of honouring a friend who has started on a distant journey, sometimes resorted to, is to prepare a feast for him on the roadside, while actually *en route*, though not far

from home. An essential part of the ceremony is to accompany
him a part of the way. While pursuing his journey, in company
with his intimate friends as a kind of escort, they arrive at the
place where a table is spread with provisions of various kinds,
wine, and fruit, ordered beforehand by them. He professes to
eat and to drink a little, and then, with thanks to them for
their honour, and with their wishes for his health and prosperity while absent, he proceeds on his way, they accompanying
him a short distance.

At the present time, it is more common for officers to honour
a brother officer on his departing from this, to be employed in
some other part of the empire, than for private citizens to
honour a private citizen in this way.

One table, or several tables, according as the civil or the
military officers who engage in the matter agree to have, are
arranged outside the city walls, at the distance of three or four
li, in a convenient place. A table has oftentimes spread upon
it ten or twelve different sorts of vegetables and meats and
fruits, each in a separate vessel, with one goblet of wine and
two chopsticks. In case of officers, there must be invariably a
kind of sweetmeats, called in this dialect by the same name as
the auspicious character used to denote "promotion," and three
loose-skinned oranges, if this fruit is to be had; if not, three
biscuits or bread-cakes, made somewhat of the shape and the
size of the orange, and painted so as to appear like one. These
are usually strung on a red string.

When the departing mandarin comes along, those who wish
to honour him with a feast get in his way and stop him, each
causing his card to be presented to him. The honoured man
understands all this to mean that they have prepared a feast for
him, if he did not know it before. He alights from his sedan,
and, with the usual ceremonies, drinks three cups of wine, and
receives the sweetmeats and the three oranges, or the three
orange-like biscuits. All these mean symbolically, "May you
speedily be promoted three degrees." He goes through the form
of drinking wine with the proprietors of the different tables,
should there be more than one, and afterward departs on his
way, accompanied by the mandarins a short distance farther.
The escorting mandarins return to their yamuns. The biscuit-
oranges, if used in place of real oranges, are not to be eaten, but
only provided as types of the promotion in official rank and
dignity which is desired by the mandarin for the departing
one. The large amount and variety of edibles provided, in like

manner, are not to be consumed on the spot, but arranged only to be seen and admired.

Those who wish to get access to the premises of rich families, and desire to obtain their favour or their patronage, generally make presents to the doorkeeper and the principal servants of the household. This is called the " presenting of a private ceremony," and generally has the effect of a bribe upon the parties who receive it.

Those who bring round curiosities, or articles of *vertû* and of value, to sell at private houses, must give a percentage on the amount received by the seller, if a sale is effected. Oftentimes a bargain is made between the seller and the doorkeeper what percentage of his receipts will be given the latter before he will introduce the pedlar or vendor of curiosities. In relation to the majority of foreign hongs this custom prevails, and instances are not few where the doorkeeper, in case he does not receive anything, or as much as he expected, stops the seller of curiosities in the street after a sale has been effected to his foreign employer, and takes by force something from the other party, or gives him a sound drubbing, or refuses to admit him on the next occasion of his coming.

It is a universal custom among the people, if one introduces or recommends another to a place where regular monthly wages are received, to claim the wages for the first month, or a certain proportion of them for every month while employed.

Among the Chinese the practice prevails extensively of giving, on the part of the man who rents a building or a shop, &c. a certain percentage on the sum agreed upon as rent, to the servants of the person of whom the premises are rented at the time of paying the first year's rent. This is quite voluntary, or rather it is done in accordance with custom. It is often paid openly. The following actual occurrence will illustrate this phase of the custom under consideration. An Englishman at Fuhchau rented certain premises to a Chinaman for eighty dollars per annum, payable in advance. When the Chinaman had paid the eighty dollars, he inquired of the Englishman whether he had any objection to his paying his servants twenty dollars, in accordance with the native custom. On his replying, in much surprise— as he was not aware of such a custom—that he had no objection, the Chinaman delivered over in his presence to the servants of the household the money mentioned, which he had brought for the purpose. Such a percentage is usually paid servants only the first year of occupation.

CHAPTER XXXI.

CHARMS AND OMENS.

The Chinese profess to stand in great fear of evil spirits and unpropitious influences. For the purpose of preserving themselves from such spirits and influences they have devised numerous spells and charms, which they believe very efficacious.

As a general remark, RED THINGS are believed to be serviceable in keeping away evil spirits. To mark the stops or pauses in the Chinese Classics with red ink, it is thought, will keep away such spirits from the one who is using the book; so can red cloth or red strings aid in protecting one from them. Parents oftentimes put a piece of red cloth upon or in the pockets of

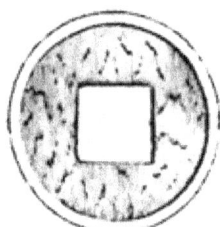 

Obverse.   Reverse.

FAC-SIMILE OF ANCIENT CASH, COINED A.D. 25, BELONGING TO THE EASTERN HAN DYNASTY, AND WORN ON THE ABDOMEN TO PREVENT COLIC.

their little boys, in order to prevent mutilation by evil spirits. They often have red silk braided in the cues of their children, in order to secure them from being cut off by the spirits.

Charms on yellow paper are very numerous. Sometimes a picture of an idol is printed or written upon this paper, or some Chinese characters, or various scrolls, are drawn on the paper with red or black ink. It is then pasted up over a door or on a bed-curtain, or it is worn in the hair, or put into a red bag and suspended from a button-hole, or it is burnt, and the ashes are mingled with tea or hot water, and drunk as a specific against bad influences or spirits.

Ancient coins are in frequent use as charms, suspended by a red string, and worn about the body, or hung up on the outside of a bed-curtain.

A part of the iron point of an old ploughshare is sometimes suspended on the outside of clothing. At other times it is encased in a silver covering, having only a small part of the iron point projecting, or it is folded up neatly in a paper, and, having been put into a small red cloth bag, it is worn about the person.

A knife that has been used in killing a person is highly valued as a charm. It is hung up from the front of the frame of the bed-curtain.· Wicked spirits are supposed to be afraid of such a utensil.

Iron nails which have been used in sealing up a coffin are considered quite efficacious in keeping away evil influences. They are carried in the pocket, or braided in the cue. Sometimes such a nail is beaten out into a long rod or wire, and encased in silver. A large ring is then made of it, to be worn on the ankles or the wrists of a boy until he is sixteen years old. Such a ring is often prepared for the use of a boy, if he is an only son. Daughters wear such wristlets or anklets only a few years, or for even a shorter time.

Some of the Chinese Classics, as the Book of Changes, or the Great Instructor, are regarded as able to keep off evil spirits when put under the pillow of a sleeper, or kept near by in the library. He who is able to repeat *memoriter* passages from these books when walking alone need not fear the spirits.

Connected with the building of houses, various methods have been devised to prevent accidents and keep away malicious spirits. Among these may be mentioned the following :—A large piece of red paper, on which four characters have been written in black ink, is generally pasted on the ridge-pole. These characters refer to a certain star, and indicate its presence. This charm dispels fear of evil influences among the workmen. A small yellow paper, having other four characters upon it, meaning that the charm protects the house and expels pernicious influences, is also often put upon the ridge-pole and other high parts of the house. Two small conical-shaped bags, from four to six inches long, made of red silk or red cotton cloth, are often suspended upon the ridge-pole while the house is being built, or are hung under the front eaves for a while after the house is finished. Into these bags are put sometimes five kinds of grain, sometimes five kinds of copper coins, one for each five consecutive emperors, or five iron nails, each of different lengths. Sometimes five such coins are put under the door-sill, and other five are also placed under the kitchen furnace when built. The object of all this is to secure good luck to the builder or the family inhabiting the house.

The following charms are very frequently seen put up over the door, or somewhere on the front of shops and houses, under the eaves. They are most commonly painted on pieces of board:—A representation of the eight diagrams, invented by Fuh-hi, having the great extreme or the male and female principles of nature painted on the centre of the board, or sometimes the centre of the board is occupied by a concave metal mirror; a flying tiger, or a tiger represented with wings, and grasping with his front paws the eight diagrams, and standing on his hind legs; the picture of a tiger's head, rudely painted on a square piece of board, or on tortoiseshell, the latter being some six or eight inches in diameter,—

EIGHT DIAGRAMS, WITH REPRESENTATION OF THE MALE AND FEMALE PRINCIPLES OF NATURE IN THE CENTRE.

this is quite common, and believed to be very efficacious, as the spirits are thought to fear the tiger; a coarsely-executed representation of a mountain and the ocean, or sometimes the three characters which indicate this charm, written on paper, which is pasted up on a door; a lion grasping a naked sword in his mouth, and playing with a globe or ball with his fore feet; two lions, as though coming down two hills toward each other; on one of the upper corners of an oblong piece of board, a picture of the sun, and on the other a picture of the moon; between these, along the upper part of the board, are arranged seven stars, which refer to the "northern measure," or the Dipper.

On the roofs of houses may be often found some such charms as the following:—An image of a cat, made out of lime and clay burnt, placed near the centre of one side of the roof, in a sitting posture, and looking off, as at something in the distance; a representation of the eight diagrams, carved on a board or block of wood, placed in a perpendicular position on the centre of the highest part of the roof; three arrows placed in an earthen tube, and laid on the side of a roof, the tube pointing toward some distant object — the arrows being fastened in their place by clay; an earthen image of a lion, made in a sitting posture. A representation of a lad sitting on a three-legged nondescript animal, with a bow in his hands, as if in the act of shooting an arrow.

When placed on the side of the roof of a house, the above must be always in a line with the rows of tiles, not crosswise, the design being to counteract some supposed unpropitious, or destructive,

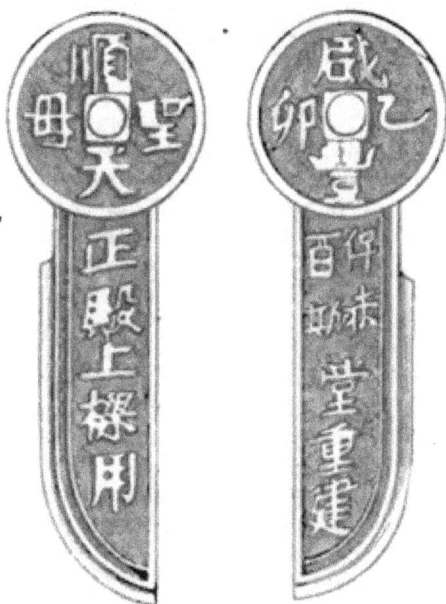

Obverse.   Reverse.

FAC-SIMILE OF A KNIFE-LIKE CHARM USED AT THE TIME OF ERECTING A TEMPLE TO THE SAILORS' GODDESS AT FUHCHAU, DURING THE REIGN OF HIEN FUNG.

or deadly influences existing not far distant, and which tend to render the house unhealthy or unprofitable as a residence.

On the erection of some large temples to the honour of popular objects of worship, as the goddess of sailors, or Confucius, &c. it is customary to have some brass charms cast, to be used while the ridge-pole is being put up and fastened in its place.

A stone slab or pillar is very often erected directly opposite
the entrance of an alley which comes out into the main street
near by one's house or store, in order to ward off the bad or
deadly influences which are believed to emerge from the alley.

Not unfrequently is a concave mirror, made of brass and partially encased in wood, hung up on a house in such a position
(having its polished surface outward) as to counteract or reflect
the bad influences which come from a projecting point in a
neighbouring house or temple. The end of the ridge-pole, or
corner of the roof of a neighbour's house pointing towards another
house, is believed to be unpropitious. The owner or resident of
the house affected must contrive to counteract and avert the
untoward influences, or be the loser in health or wealth. The
Chinese believe such concave mirrors, if properly arranged on
their houses, will counteract all the unfavourable influences
which proceed from neighbouring buildings.

Old fish-nets are often cut up into strips and sold, to be worn
by children around the waist as girdles, as a preventive against
evil spirits and pernicious influences. Sometimes a garment is
made out of such nets, and worn by children for a similar purpose. Oftentimes, when pregnant women, who are nervous and
easily excited, ride out in the sedan, a part of an old net is hung
up inside and over the door, as a preventive against her seeing
evil spirits, or against her being influenced or agitated by them.

What is commonly called a Cash-sword is considered very
efficacious in keeping away evil spirits. It is often hung up on
the front and the outside of the bridal bed-curtain, in a position
parallel to the horizon. About the time of a woman's confinement, a cash-sword is sometimes taken and hung inside of the
curtain. This sword is usually about two feet long, and is constructed out of three kinds of things, each of which is regarded
as a preventive of evil spirits : 1st. Two iron rods, about two
feet long, constitute the foundation of the sword   2d. About
one hundred cash, either ancient or modern (if ancient, or if all
of the same emperor's reign, so much the better), are ingeniously
fastened on these rods, concealing them from view. The rods
are placed in the centre, and the coins are tied on the outside in
two rows. 3d. Red cords or wires are used in tying on the
cash. These three kinds, joined together in the shape of a
sword, make a really formidable weapon, of which the maliciously-disposed spirits are exceedingly afraid !

A silver lock, called a "hundred-families'-cash-lock," is often
used to ward off evil spirits from an only son. The lock derives

its name from the manner in which the money to procure it is obtained. The man who wishes to procure the lock for the benefit of his boy collects a few cash from one hundred different families. The money thus obtained is paid out for silver, which is manufactured into a padlock about two inches long, or perhaps less. A silver chain, or a large silver ring, is also usually purchased, and the lock is used to fasten this ring or chain on the lad's neck. Such a lock will contribute to the boy's longevity, for the evil spirits will fear or reverence it!

Parents who have an only son frequently provide a small silver chain, which they place over his neck as a charm against evil influences, or as an omen of good. It is often used as a kind of suspender for the boy's pocket. Each end is furnished with a flat hook. On the flat surface of the back of each of these hooks oftentimes may be found a felicitous phrase, as the "three manies" on one, and the "nine likes" on the other. The first phrase means "Great happiness," "Long life," and "Numerous male children." The latter phrase refers to nine comparisons found in the Book of Odes: "Like the longevity of the southern mountains," "Like the luxuriance of the fir-tree," "Like the ascending of the sun," "Like the regularity of the moon," &c. These phrases imply the wish on the part of the parents of the wearer that he may attain unto the happy state indicated by the "three manies" and the "nine likes."

On the morning of the first day of the fifth Chinese month, every heathen family nails up on each side of the front doors and windows of its house a few leaves of the sweet flag (*Acorus gramineus*) and of the artemisia. The leaves of the sweet-flag are long and slender, tapering to a

CASH SWORD CHARM.

point, resembling the general shape of the sword. When used as above, they represent swords. It is said that evil spirits, on coming near the house and seeing these leaves nailed up, will take them for swords, and run off as fast as they can!

The gourd-shell, or a painting of the gourd on wood or paper, or a small wooden gourd, or a paper cut in shape like a perpendicular section of the gourd, or a paper lantern made in shape of a gourd, is in frequent use in this place as a charm to dissipate or ward off pernicious influences.

Many believe that the tiger, a species of lizard, the centipede, a certain fabulous animal having three feet, and the snake—which five things, taken together, are called the "five poisons"—have the power to counteract pernicious influences. Sometimes images of these things are procured, and worshipped by families which have an only son. Pictures of them are often made with black silk on new red cloth pockets, worn by children for the first time on one of the first five days of the fifth month. It is believed that such a charm will tend to keep the children from having the colic, and from pernicious influences generally. They are often found represented on one side of certain round brass castings, about two inches in diameter, used as charms against evil spirits.

A small brass mirror, either flat or concave, but always round, is very frequently hung up on the outside of a bed-curtain, or suspended somewhere near by. Its principal use is to counteract, prevent, or dissipate devilish or unpropitious influences. It is supposed that evil spirits, on approaching to do harm, will be apt to see themselves reflected in the mirror, and, becoming frightened, will betake themselves away without delay.

A representation of a certain star, regarded as a god of literature, is frequently used by students as a kind of charm against unlucky influences, or the influences which retard or prevent their success in study and at the regular examinations for the various literary degrees. An image is sometimes made of clay or wood, or frequently nothing but a picture is made, or the characters denoting it are written on paper, and worshipped with the burning of incense and candles. Sometimes a kind of charm is made by so writing on paper four couplets of Chinese characters that they will have, as a whole, when done, a resemblance to the figure of this god of literature. These four couplets mean, "rectify the heart," "regulate the body," "subdue oneself," and "be courteous." Sometimes only four characters are used to make this likeness, meaning, "rectify the heart" and "without selfishness." It is then worshipped with incense and candles.

A kind of charm, usually round, and about two inches in diameter, though sometimes six-sided or oblong, or some other shape, and made out of brass or iron, usually called "warding-off-evil-cash," is in great use among children, being suspended from their necks or from button-holes. Usually both sides have an inscription upon them of characters, or scrolls, or images of persons or things. The characters, of course, are propitious, as "happiness," "wealth and office," or they refer directly to expelling the evil spirits, or warding off bad influences. Sometimes the twelve animals which denote certain horary characters used in reckoning time among the Chinese occupy one side, or the "eight diagrams," or the "five poisons."

It is believed by some of this people that pieces of yellow paper, having stamped upon them the head of a dog and the head of a buffalo, or one of these heads, if used in a certain way, are very efficacious in causing one to become sick, stupid, or obedient to the will of another, and even to die. In consequence of this belief, these charms are sometimes resorted to by a person who has a deadly hate to another, in order to cause his death or to bring on sickness, or by one who desires to gain possession of another man's property, but who fears that his plans to cheat or circumvent him will not of themselves be successful.

In the fall of 1859, I took considerable pains to satisfy myself if these charms, in regard to which I had been somewhat sceptical, were really in use at this place. In company with a native Christian, I went to a certain temple, celebrated for the efficiency of its charms of the above description. We were shown some eight or ten bunches of yellow paper, each bunch consisting of twenty-two sheets about seven or eight inches long, and two and a half inches wide. On the outside sheets was a rough representation of a dog's head and of a buffalo's head, said to have been struck off from iron plates. The temple-keeper showed them to us, and conversed at first quite freely on the subject, under the impression that we wished to purchase and use them.

When one wishes to obtain these charms, he goes to one of the few temples where they can be procured, and proceeds to offer mock-money, incense, and candles before certain idols. Having lighted these offerings, he bows down before the idols, mentions the particular object which he desires to accomplish, and vows, if he is successful, that he will make to them a thank-offering of meats, fish, vegetables, &c. He takes away with him a small quantity of the ashes of the incense from the censer before the idols. He buys of the temple-keeper, at an exorbitant sum, a bundle or two of the charms.

These paper charms are reduced to ashes in his own house, or in some temple, or at a particular place under the Big Bridge across the river at this place. These ashes, added to the ashes of incense brought from the temple where he obtained the charms, he endeavours to bring in contact with the individual whom he desires to injure, as by mingling a little with tea and giving him to drink, or by causing some to be put into his food, or by besmearing his head or his clothing with them. Sometimes, however, only the ashes of the charms, or the ashes obtained from the censor in the temple, are used in the way described. The intended victim should not be aware that he is eating or drinking charmed ashes, or that any has been daubed on his person or his clothing. If he is aware of it, the ashes are believed to be powerless to affect his health, his soundness of mind, or his life, as he will immediately take measures to counteract any evil effect.

When one is led by any circumstances attending failure of health, unfavourable and inexplicable change in his business affairs, &c. to suspect that he is under the evil influence of charms used by another through covetousness or hatred, he usually loses no time in putting forth efforts to counteract or dissipate such influences.

Sometimes, it is asserted, the charm recoils from the intended victim upon the individual who uses it, and inflicts upon him that misfortune which he planned for another. The result is attributed not so much to his being a bad man and the other a good man, as to the fortune or the fates of the individuals concerned.

The Chinese language, both spoken and written, abounds in words and phrases which are considered ominous of good luck. The use of such is very common, especially on occasions joyous and complimentary.

The *Chinese unicorn* is in popular use as an omen of good. This fabulous animal is described as having only one horn, with a body all covered with scales. For several thousands of years it has eluded the vision of mortals, excepting once, when it is stated to have been seen by Confucius in his old age. He regarded it as ominous of his approaching death. They say that Confucius was "the elf of the unicorn." Hence, perhaps, the

origin of the saying that an extraordinarily bright boy is the
" son of the unicorn," or the "gift of the unicorn."

The character for longevity is regarded as very felicitous,
and is used in a great variety of ways.

The character for happiness is considered to be very felicitous,
and is much used at this place as a symbol of good. Oftentimes
it is written with black ink on
red paper several inches square, or
on white paper with red ink, and
then pasted up on the doors of
houses. This is done quite generally about the Chinese New Year.
Sometimes it is engraved on wood
in raised lettering. After being
gilded, it is suspended or nailed
up over a door, inside or outside
the house, or on a cross-beam or
post. Not unfrequently it is seen
written very prettily in a large

HAPPINESS.

form, from two to six or eight feet across, in red ink, on the wall
opposite the front or main door of a house. This custom is
explained by saying that happiness will in this manner be
always near by.

The Chinese here are singularly fond of wearing ornaments
made of gems or precious stones, either genuine or imitated.
The material is first ground or worked down to the desired size
or shape, and then some happy characters or felicitous sentences

HAPPINESS LIKE THE EASTERN
OCEAN.

LONGEVITY LIKE THE SOUTHERN
MOUNTAINS.

are engraved on it, such as "Happiness like the Eastern Ocean,"
meaning abundance, or "Longevity like the Southern Mountains," meaning durability and permanence, or " Long life,

wealth, and office," or "Gold and gems filling the house," or
simply the word "happiness." These badges or ornaments are
of various shapes—circular, square, oblong, or fanciful. Some
are made in the form of certain flowers. They are worn as
finger-rings, or on the caps of men and boys, or as ornaments
for the heads of females, or they are suspended from various
parts of the dress. The design in many cases is not only to add
to the respectability of the wearer, but also to indicate his wish
to obtain or enjoy the thing expressed by the character or
characters.

The expression "a hundred children and a thousand grandchildren," is a very popular and felicitous phrase, consisting of
four Chinese characters. A lantern, covered with white gauze,
and having on one side the characters for "hundred children,"
and on the opposite side those for "thousand grandchildren,"
cut out of bright red paper and fastened on the gauze, is in very
common use here. At burials, weddings, and on removals, this
lantern is used, and is regarded as an omen of good. On ordinary occasions, if used at all, only one is used.

Pictures of two children mutually embracing, or locked in
each other's arms, standing side by side, are often seen exposed
for sale. They are an index of peace and harmony, representing
two persons mutually agreeing and constant companions. Some
families procure this picture and hang it up in their houses as a
symbol of their desire to have all in the household live in peace
and love with each other. On the same picture sometimes is
depicted the likeness of two bats. Such a picture, considered as
a whole, symbolizes the desire for happiness as well as harmony
—the character for bat having the same local sound as the
character for happiness. In some temples there are images of
youths embracing each other as large as lads six or eight years
old. These are worshipped for the purpose of procuring peace
and harmony among those who once were friendly to each other,
or between husband and wife, brothers, or partners in business,
&c. in case of enmity or bad feeling existing between them.
Some of the relatives or friends of the estranged parties go
without their knowledge to the temples where these images are,
and take some of the ashes out of the censer standing before the
images, after lighting candles and incense. Having mixed these
ashes secretly in tea or wine, the potion is given to those whose
reconciliation is sought, to drink. It is believed that in due
time they will become friendly and at peace with each other.
If, however, they are aware of the mingling of the ashes in the

drink, it is asserted that these means for their mutual reconciliation will prove inefficacious.

The character for "joy," written twice side by side, as though the whole constituted only one word or letter, is regarded as a very auspicious combination. It may mean double joy, or joy repeated, and indicates, when used in the manner mentioned below, a desire that occasions for joy may be repeated or numerous.

Concerning omens, the magpie is regarded as a bird of good omen. If one, while meditating on a plan about to be adopted, or while engaged in a pursuit which enlists his interest and attention, suddenly hears the voice of this bird, he is prone to consider it as felicitous, its voice being sprightly and joyous, imparting encouragement to the hearer. There is a proverb which says of this bird that "its voice is good, but its heart is bad," meaning that it is given to flattery.

The Chinese crow, sometimes called the white-winged raven, on the other hand, is an omen of evil. Its cry is harsh and unpleasant. Its voice is regarded as unlucky—perhaps, as some suggest, because it sounds much like *ka*, the common Chinese word for bite. While prosecuting any business or planning any affair, if the person unexpectedly hears the crow crying out *ka*, *ka*, *ka*, "bite, bite, bite," he is often impressed thereby with the idea that he shall not be successful. The proverb says this bird's "voice is bad, but its heart is good."

The coming of a dog indicates future prosperity. Many people believe that if a strange dog comes and remains with one it is an omen of good to his family, indicating that he will become more wealthy.

The coming of a cat to a household is an omen of approaching poverty. The coming of a strange cat, and its staying in a house, are believed to foreshadow an unfavourable change in the pecuniary condition of the family. It is supposed that a cat can foresee where it will find plenty of rats and mice in consequence of the approaching dilapidation of a house, following the ruin or poverty of its inhabitants.

The crowing of a hen is considered ominous of something unusual about to happen in the family to which it belongs. In order to ascertain whether this event is propitious or unpropitious, the relative position of the fowl, while crowing, is to be observed. If the hen crows while her head is towards the outside, or the front of the premises, it is an unpropitious prognostication, foreshadowing poverty or ill-luck of some kind; whereas, if her head is pointing toward the rear of the premises while crowing, it is an omen of good, indicating a more prosperous state of the family.

The coming of swallows, and their making their nests in a new place, whether dwelling-house or store, are hailed as an omen of approaching success, or a prosperous change in the affairs of the owner or occupier of the premises.

The voice of the owl is universally heard with dread, being regarded as the harbinger of death in the neighbourhood. Some say that its voice resembles the voice of a spirit or demon calling out to its fellow. Perhaps it is on account of this notion that they so often assert having heard the voice of a spirit, when they may have heard only the indistinct hooting of a distant owl. Sometimes, the Chinese say, its voice sounds much like an expression for "digging" the grave. Hence, probably, the origin of a common saying, that when one is about to die, in the neighbourhood will be heard the voice of the owl, calling out, "Dig, dig." It is frequently spoken of as the bird which calls for the soul, or which catches or takes away the soul.

The Chinese also speak of omens derived from the sudden changes which occur sometimes in the appearance of certain flowers. A certain species of flower (gynandrus), if it is in very full blossom, and has very green leaves, betokens unusual prosperity in the family of the owner. Few who have such a flower in their possession are willing to part with it, except for an exorbitant sum. If, for any reason, such a flower should suddenly die, or if its blossoms fade, or its leaves become of an unpleasant hue, it is believed to be a sure token of poverty or ill luck. A certain Chinaman at this place dates heavy pecuniary losses in his father's family, over thirty years ago, and subsequent poverty, to the sudden destruction of such a flower, caused, as it was afterwards ascertained, by an offended neighbour, who one evening poured a little salted water into the pot which contained the flower.

The peony is also regarded as an omen of good fortune if it becomes full of beautiful flowers and green leaves. On the other hand, if its leaves should all at once dry up, and its flowers suddenly fade or become of an unpleasant colour, such a change foreshadows poverty, or some overwhelming disaster, in the family of its owner.

A singular way of obtaining an omen, practised by some, is this: If a man has entered upon an undertaking, or is deliberating in regard to a plan, of the future success of which undertaking or plan he stands in doubt, he sometimes adopts the following method of settling his mind : he takes a stick of incense, and, having lighted it, bows down before the god of the kitchen. Holding the incense in his hands, he informs the kitchen god of his plans or his undertaking, and the state of his mind about the same. Placing the incense in the censer before the god, he goes out to the street door and listens to the language of those who are passing by. The first sentence he can distinguish, whatever it may be, he eagerly fixes in his memory, and, having meditated upon it, draws conclusions from its general tenor in regard to the subject of his doubts, whether auspicious or inauspicious, good or evil. Sometimes, before he takes the sentence heard at the street door as the subject of meditation, he first inquires of the god of the kitchen whether the sentence heard is a proper one for his purpose and use. At other times, before going to the street door, and after consulting the god of the kitchen, he puts a small quantity of water in the vessel in which he boils his rice, and on this water he puts a wooden rice-ladle. He then covers it up, and after waiting a while, removes the cover, and carefully observes the direction in which the handle of the ladle lies on the water. He now goes out of the house, and walks in the direction indicated by the handle of the ladle until he hears an intelligible sentence or phrase. This he remembers, and draws an omen from it in regard to the success or failure of his plans. At other times he leaves his meal unfinished, and, taking his chopsticks in his sleeves, goes into the street for the purpose of hearing something which he can use as an omen.

CHAPTER XXXII.

FORTUNE-TELLING.

Six different methods of telling fortunes are found in use among the Chinese.

1. By using the eight horary characters which denote the year, month, day, and hour of one's birth.—This is perhaps the most common and the most popular kind of fortune-telling in this part of the empire. There is a constant reference to the " five elements " and certain " twelve animals."

Of this kind of fortune-tellers there are two classes, blind men and men who are not blind. The blind fortune-tellers are usually led about the streets by a lad. Some of them have a kind of harp, which they play occasionally as they slowly walk along the street. Sometimes they carry a rattle, which consists of two small pieces of wood. These are held in one hand, and, when struck or clapped together in a particular manner, produce a sound much like *kok kok*, or, when struck together in another manner, produce the sound *pok pok*. This sound, when heard, indicates the approach or presence of a blind fortune-teller. These are said to " reckon fortunes."

BLIND FORTUNE-TELLER.

The fortune-tellers whose eyesight is good, are said to " see the fortunes " of their patrons. They seldom or never go about the streets seeking patronage, but generally open a shop in some frequented street, where they await those who wish to consult them.

The rules of the art are the same for both classes. There are books which teach how to prognosticate by a reference to the precise time of one's birth, compared with the five elements, deducing a conclusion propitious or unpropitious. The blind fortune-teller labours under the great disadvantage of having to calculate the fortunes of his patrons without making constant reference to books.

2. By an inspection of the physiognomy.—This kind of fortune-tellers usually select a convenient place in the street, where they can display a chart, to which they make frequent reference. They inspect the eyes and eyebrows, nose, mouth, ears, cheek-bones and temples, the lips, teeth, and the beard or whiskers of the customer, if a man. They compare the " five governors " together (ears, eyes, nose, mouth, and eyebrows) to determine whether they agree or are fitting, and whether the expression or countenance is proper and correct, and whether it is honourable or mean. They observe the manner of one's walking or sitting, and draw inferences in regard to the future fortunes of the individual, whether he will be rich or poor, an officer or a beggar. They dilate on the revelations of the physiognomy as relating to the past good or bad fortunes of the dupe, or to his future good or bad fortunes.

They also carefully examine his fingers, one by one, in regard to length, and the palms of his hands as to thickness, and the lines or natural marks on his palms, whether few or many, and whether the palm is divided into two main parts by lines across it, and whether it is red.

These peripatetic physiognomists carry about with them a kind of cloth satchel, on which are written characters which indicate their profession.

3. By means of a bird and slips of paper.—This fortune-teller, like the preceding, traverses the streets in pursuit of employment. He carries in one hand a piece of the little end of a cow's horn, and a small bamboo stick. These two are tied together loosely at one end, and he manages to strike or clap them together so as to make a peculiar sound. This is his rattle, or the signal of his approach or proximity. In the other hand, or suspended from a front button on his coat, he carries a small bird-cage, containing a little bird of a certain species. He always carries with him on these professional excursions sixty-four small sheets of paper, on each of which is

sketched a figure of a god, or bird, or beast, or person ; on each sheet is also written a short verse of poetry, usually four lines, each of seven characters. These sheets are folded up in such a manner that the picture and the poetry shall be unseen.

When the fortune-teller is invited to tell the fortunes of some applicant, he arranges the sixty-four pieces of paper on a table or on the ground, and places the bird-cage near them. He now opens the door of it ; the bird comes out, and picks up one of the sheets with its bill, which he takes, opens, and explains.

4. By the dissection of written characters.—This class of fortune-tellers seldom or never open a shop ; but when engaged professionally, they select a convenient spot by the side of a frequented street, and, having spread some oiled paper or cloth on the ground, and having arranged writing implements near by, look out for customers. They generally carry with them a small box, which contains a quantity of small sheets of paper folded up. On the outside of each is written one Chinese character. The customer is requested to select or take at random two of these sheets. These are taken by the fortune-teller, opened, and the characters written upon them are noticed. He then proceeds to dissect each by writing out separately the distinct parts of which each is composed. Afterward he discourses on the subject about which inquiries have been made, making frequent reference to the meaning of the separate parts of the characters, and finally decides about it, usually in a knowing and authoritative manner ; at other times he gives comprehensive hints and directions to the customer, so that he may not err in his future course, at least so far as this subject under consideration is concerned. Oftentimes, before the conclusion is reached, he adds strokes by an adroit use 'of his

FORTUNE-TELLING BY MEANS OF A BIRD
AND SLIPS OF PAPER.

writing pencil, to some or all of these component parts under inspection, thereby making new words out of them, from whose meaning he draws sagacious and wonderful inferences in regard to the good or bad fortune of the individual who is consulting him.

FORTUNE-TELLING BY DISSECTING A CHINESE CHARACTER.

5. By the use of the tortoise-shell and three ancient cash.— Those who practise divination in this manner, have shops or offices where they may be consulted by those who prefer this method of ascertaining their fortunes. The cash commonly used are a certain kind coined during the Tang dynasty. They first light incense and candles, placing them before the picture of an old man whom they worship as the deity who presides over this kind of divination. They then take the cash and put them into a tortoise-shell, which they shake once or twice before the picture, invoking the aid and presence of the god. They then empty the cash out, and, taking them in one hand, they strike the shell gently three times with them, still repeating

The spot selected should be quite dry, and the most propitious colour for the soil is a kind of golden yellow.

The cheapest of these six methods of fortune-telling is by means of a bird and slips of paper, the charge usually being only four or six cash. The dearest and the most tedious is the last described—by geomancy. Oftentimes, in the case of rich families, several score of dollars are paid to the geomancer for selecting a propitious site for a grave. The poorer families who employ such a helper in fixing the site for a grave sometimes only pay a few thousand, or even a few hundred cash, for his services. The sum paid a fortune-teller for divining one's fortune by dissecting a Chinese character is small—usually eight or twelve cash; for divining by the use of the tortoise-shell, about a hundred cash, more or less. Of the class first mentioned, the blind man who takes to the streets and lanes in search of employment receives generally about twenty cash; and the man who has the use of his eyes, and who also divines by means of the eight characters which denote the precise time of the birth of the applicant, receives about forty cash for his services. Sometimes the same person is able to tell fortunes in two of the ways above mentioned, to accommodate the preference of his customers. He always endeavours to please and gratify his "guests."

The terms most commonly used by men who practise telling fortunes will now be explained. The object of doing this is to show, more plainly than could be shown without such an explanation, how fortune-telling is performed by a reference to the precise time of one's birth and to the five elements of nature, or to the twelve animals.

The precise time of one's birth in China is denoted by four sets of characters, each set consisting of two characters, collectively and technically called the "eight characters of one's age." In speaking of this subject, it will be necessary to describe briefly the Chinese chronological cycle of sixty years. The invention of this cycle is attributed to the Emperor Huang-Ti, who lived several hundred years before the commencement of the Hia dynasty. It is dated from the sixty-first year of his reign, or from the year 2637 before Christ.

It is formed by the combination of two sets of characters in a particular way, and was originally designed and used only for chronological purposes. One set has ten characters, which are called "the heavenly stems;" the other set has twelve characters, which are styled "the earthly branches." The first of

these " stems " is written on the right hand of the first of these
" branches," and the two characters denote the first year, or
month, or day, or hour of a cycle of years, months, days, or
hours, as the case may be. The second of the " stems " and the
second of the " branches " are joined together in a similar way
to denote the second year, and so on through all the terms.
After all the stems have been thus used once, the first one is
then joined to the eleventh of the branches, the second of the
stems to the twelfth of the branches, the third of the stems to
the first of the branches, the fourth of the stems to the second
of the branches, and so on until the stems shall have been used
six times and the branches five times. The tenth of the stems
and the twelfth of the branches will then come together in
combination. The whole number of different combinations in
this way is sixty, one complete cycle. In a precisely similar
manner is another formed. Since the commencement of thus
reckoning time by this invention of Huang-Ti, there have passed
over seventy-six complete cycles of years.

According to this method, each year in the Chinese calendar
is represented by two characters, each month by two characters,
each day by two characters, and each hour by two characters—a
Chinese hour being just two hours as time is reckoned at the
West. One of each pair of characters is one of the ten heavenly
stems, and the other is one of the twelve earthly branches.
These four pairs, taken together, constitute the ",eight characters " which denote the precise time of one's birth, to which
constant reference is made in some kinds of fortune-telling, and
in the selection of propitious days for the transaction of business, &c.

Each one of these twenty-two characters is believed to " belong " to some one of the " five elements of nature." The terms
" belong " and " five elements of nature " are used in a purely
Chinese sense in this connexion.

The five elements are metal, wood, water, fire, and earth.
There are two formulas in constant use while comparing the
terms which denotes one's age with the five elements. One of
these is this : Metal produces water, water produces wood, wood
produces fire, fire produces earth, and earth produces metal.
The other is this: Metal destroys wood, wood destroys earth,
earth destroys water, water destroys fire, and fire destroys
metal.

These formulas seem to be used to calculate what influence
these elements have over each other in the circumstances and

relations, as indicated by the eight characters of one's birth, with reference to some other time or event; whether to "produce" or to "destroy."

While the twelve earthly branches are frequently spoken of as "belonging" to the five elements, each is also regarded as denoting one of twelve animals. The twelve animals, mentioned in the order of the horary characters to which they refer, are these : Rat, cow, tiger, rabbit, dragon, snake, horse, sheep, monkey, cock, dog, and boar. As some one of the twelve earthly branches, as above explained, forms a part of the phrase or term which denotes the year, and as each one of these characters refers to some animal, every Chinaman is said to be born under a certain animal, or to "belong" to a certain animal. The Chinese usually express this idea by saying "his animal is the rat," or "his animal is the monkey," as the case may be. The phraseology simply means that he was born during the year when the character corresponding to the "rat" or to the "monkey" enters into the term which denotes that year, according to the chronological cycle of sixty.

Now these twelve animals play an important part in fortune-telling as practised by some at the present day. The result often reached by the fortune-teller, after carefully comparing the eight characters which fix the precise hour, day, month, and year of the applicant's birth with the five elements—with particular reference to the time proposed or selected for some specified event—is, that a certain animal is to be feared and avoided at the time that event is to take place. This means simply that those persons who were born during the year denoting the specified animal should not be present when the event referred to is to transpire, as a house-raising, or the putting of a corpse into the coffin, or the celebration of a certain marriage, &c. They should absent themselves, lest some dangerous and deadly influence should be suddenly and mysteriously exerted upon them, resulting in their sickness, injury, or death.

In prognosticating one's fortune by the use of the eight characters, those two which denote his birthday are taken to be what is called the rules, with which the other six (those which denote the year, month, and hour) are to be compared in a certain way, according to the laws of the art, and all are to be referred to the immutable and wonderful properties and principles of the five elements. For example, as some say, if the two characters for one's birthday should "belong" to metal, and the other six characters for the year, month, and hour should "belong" to water, the case would be regarded as unfavourable and unpropitious, for the formulary reads metal produces water, and consequently there would be danger of there being too much water produced. But should some of these six terms "belong" to fire, and some to wood, or some to earth, the result would be modified, according to the rules applicable to such cases. The formularies above mentioned, relating to the five elements producing or destroying each other, are constantly appealed to by the fortune-tellers to ascertain whether, in regard to the particular case in hand, the applicant may expect success or ill luck. It should be stated in this connexion that, while coming to his conclusions, the fortune-teller refers also to something which, for want of a better term, may be called the course or revolution of nature in regard to the individual who has handed him his eight characters, which course or revolution of nature is known from an inspection of the eight characters.

Of the twelve earthly branches, four of them "belong" to earth, and the remaining eight are equally distributed among metal, water, wood, and fire. Of the ten heavenly stems, two "belong" to each of the five elements. While the doctrine of the five elements is very ancient, it is undoubtedly a perversion from the original design of Huang-Ti to take the terms he selected for chronological purposes, and, by referring them to the "elements of nature," to deduce the fortunes of those who keep the time of their birth by the use of these terms.

Selection of fortunate or lucky days for the transaction of important business is done by fortune-tellers. It relates particularly and exclusively to the precise time of doing something for the benefit of the applicant. Those who select lucky days for others open shops, where they can be consulted by the people; and generally the men who do this work are able to tell fortunes by the use of the "eight characters" and the "five elements." They will tell fortunes, or they will select propitious days and hours, according as their employers desire.

The selector of lucky days must know at least the year when, or the animal under which, the applicant was born. He should also be informed in regard to the proximate time when the applicant desires to transact the work or business about which he consults him. It then becomes the duty of the latter to ascertain whether the day specified will be fortunate, and, if fortunate, what particular hour of it should be devoted to the performance of it; if unfortunate, to find out a day as near as possible to the desired day which will be fortunate.

In regard to marriages, whether certain parties may or may not be engaged in marriage is always submitted to some fortune-teller.

In like manner, and for a similar reason, the aid of the selector of propitious days is invoked by the builder and proprietor of houses and hongs, and by the head men in the erection of temples, &c. In the case of temples, the ages of the neighbourhood elders and head men are made known to one who is able to divine what month, day, and hour will be lucky for the performance of several kinds of labour connected with the erection of the proposed temple. In the case of building a house or hong, only the age of the owner and proprietor is reported to the selector of lucky days. He applies the rules of his art to decide on a favourable time as regards month, day, and hour; for beginning to move the earth for laying the foundations of the building; for raising the bents (if the building is made of wood); for putting up the ridge-pole in its place; for hanging the great or main door of honour; for the digging of the well, and for the making of the furnace or fireplace in the kitchen. In theory, times must be selected for the doing of these things which will not conflict with the animal under which the proprietor was born,—that is, which will be propitious for him according to the doctrine of the "five elements."

In order to the selection of propitious times for the doing of several things connected with burials, the ages of the deceased and of his or her eldest son, as well as of his or her eldest grandson, if there be one—that is, the son of the eldest son, not the son of the eldest daughter of the deceased—must be made known to the selector of fortunate days. Sometimes the ages of the second, third, and other sons are also made known to him. The ages of the eldest son and of his eldest son, as representing the family, and as being the chief mourners according to custom, it is regarded as very important to have handed to the one who selects the times necessary to be selected, in order not to endanger the future fortunes of the family, as well as the present health and happiness of all concerned.

CHAPTER XXXIII.

OPIUM AND OPIUM-SMOKING.

Opium is reduced from a solid to a liquid form by boiling it with water before it is consumed by the Chinese. This process for the retail market requires considerable skill and care. When prepared for smoking, it looks very much like thick, dark-coloured molasses. It is often sold in very small quantities—as small as one-hundredth of an ounce. An ounce of this prepared opium is worth about eleven hundred cash. A hundredth part of an ounce is sufficient for a beginner, who can smoke but a few whiffs. After being accustomed to it, the smoker can use from one-twentieth to one-third of an ounce daily.

The smoker of opium invariably lies down, and gives his whole attention to the process while inhaling its fumes.

The inveterate opium-smoker seldom emits the smoke from his mouth—generally through his nostrils, after "swallowing" it, as the Chinese say—after inhaling it into his lungs. Beginners emit more or less of the fumes from the mouth. Some inveterate smokers, it is affirmed, by practice acquire the power of retaining or absorbing in the system a considerable portion of the fumes, emitting the rest through the nose.

Tobacco can be lighted by contact with a coal of fire, or with anything already ignited, but the opium-smoker always uses the steady, constant flame of a small oil-lamp. The opium is introduced into the bowl of the pipe through a small orifice in the projecting point of the bowl. He holds this point steadily in the flame of the lamp until the opium within is ignited and partially volatilized. During this lighting process the smoker gently inhales the fumes which arise from the burning opium, the suction of his mouth always causing some of the flame of the lamp to enter the orifice of the bowl.

If one smokes opium at stated intervals, as every morning or every evening, or once regularly in two days, he acquires in a short time the habit, so that he must smoke it at just such a time, or suffer the disagreeable consequences of not smoking. This condition causes an incessant thinking about it, and a longing or hankering after it, which in a great degree incapacitates the victim for effort, intellectual or. physical, unless he has recourse to the drug again. The habit becomes fixed in a period of time varying from ten or fifteen days to one or two months, according to the constitution of the person and the circumstances of the case. It is not determined so much by the quantity he consumes as by the regularity of his resorts to the pipe. If he smokes at irregular periods, as once in a week, and then once in a day, and then goes for a longer or shorter period before he smokes again, he will not feel this ardent and intolerable longing. He does not become addicted to the vice ; he is still his own master.

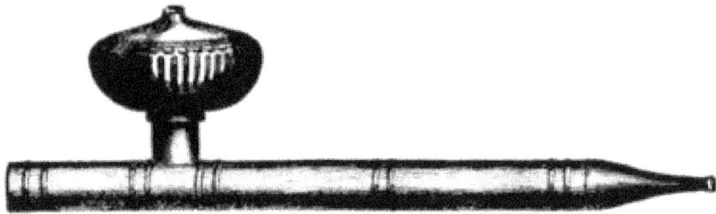

OPIUM PIPE.

Some originally resort to the drug in order to cure the toothache, or headache, or dyspepsia, under the advice of friends. The pain is usually relieved for the time being, but at the expense of acquiring the habit of smoking opium. When this habit has fastened itself on the victim, the usual quantity will not long assuage the pain as at the beginning, and, in order to relieve it, larger and still larger quantities must be used from time to time.

Opium-shops are always provided with platforms, which the buyers of the prepared drug may occupy while consuming the quantity purchased. Here two friends often meet, and, reclining on these platforms, facing each other, with the burning lamp and apparatus between them, and their heads resting on pillows, treat each other, usually each preparing for the other to smoke the pipe which is furnished for their common use. Most

of the poorer and many of the middle classes prefer, for convenience' sake, to consume the opium at the shop where it is
purchased.   In the case of some of the middle class, and of
most of the wealthy and the higher classes of Chinese, the
opium is bought at the retail shops already prepared in a liquid
form for smoking, and taken home to be consumed.   Sometimes, however, they procure the drug in the solid form, and
prepare it by boiling in their own houses.   Perhaps one-half or
more of the quantity imported and used here is thus consumed
at the homes of its buyers.   Many officers, merchants, literary
men, the wealthy, and generally all those who have their time

OPIUM-SMOKERS.

at their leisurely disposal, buy the drug by the ball or in smaller
quantity, and prepare it at their residences, where they smoke
it whenever they please.

Extensive native mercantile firms sometimes keep it on hand
for their large customers or their personal friends who may call.
The best Chinese physicians oftentimes depend upon being
invited to a smoke at the houses of their patients, and take it
unkindly if not "treated." The official *employés* connected
with mandarin establishments, such as policemen and constables, of which class there is a large number, delay or decline
to proceed to the transaction of their business unless first treated
with opium when called to one's house, even on the most urgent

and important affairs. Many wealthy private families keep the opium-pipe and fixtures in readiness for the demands of fashion.

It is comparatively a very costly vice, the expense being graduated by the circumstances of each case, ranging from a dollar or two to ten or fifteen dollars per month, even in regard to persons not of the highest and the most wealthy classes. The lowest mentioned rate, taking into consideration the low price of labour among this people compared with the price of labour in Western countries, is relatively larger and burdensome. With all smokers, however, the effect of this vice on their pecuniary standing is by no means to be estimated by the actual outlay in money for the drug. Its seductive influence leads its victims to neglect their business, and consequently, sooner or later, loss or ruin ensues. As the habit grows, so does inattention to business increase. Instances are not rare where the rich have been reduced to poverty and beggary as one of the consequences of their attachment to the opium-pipe. The poor addicted to this vice are oftentimes led to dispose of everything saleable in the hovel where they live. Sometimes, even, men sell their own children and their wives in order to procure the drug, and finally end their career by becoming beggars or thieves.

In the second place, the smoking of opium injures one's health and bodily constitution. Unless taken promptly at the regular time and in the necessary quantity, the victim becomes unable to control himself and to attend to his business. He sneezes. He gapes. Mucus runs from his nose and his eyes. Griping pains seize him in his bowels. His whole appearance indicates restlessness and misery. If not indulged in smoking and left undisturbed, he usually falls asleep, but his sleep does not refresh and invigorate him. On being aroused, he is himself again, provided he can have his opium; if not, his troubles and pains multiply. He has no appetite for ordinary food; no strength or disposition to labour. Diarrhœa sets in of a dreadful and most painful description, peculiar to opium-smokers; and if still unable to procure opium, the unhappy victim not unfrequently dies in most excruciating agonies. Few, comparatively, recover after the diarrhœa has become virulent, unless they have access to opium, and not always then.

The Chinese, in describing the effects of opium-smoking on the individual, dwell with peculiar emphasis on the weakness and indolence which it induces. The victim is described as unwilling, and usually physically unable, to perform anything requiring muscular strength or mental application, except under the excitement of opium. His habits of sleep are changed, it being impossible oftentimes, owing to the overwrought mental excitement induced by the drug, for him to fall asleep in the early part of the night, as others do. Frequently it is nearly or quite morning before he is able to compose himself to rest, waking only late in the forenoon or early in the afternoon. The Chinese have a common saying that the smoker of opium "makes the day night, and the night day," alluding to his unnatural hours of waking and of sleeping. His features almost always become strikingly changed, being of an unhealthy, pallid, death-like cast. His shoulders not unfrequently become permanently elevated above their natural level, much as when one shrugs them up, at the same time drawing down his head. Such an opium-smoker is expressively described as "having three heads," from the high and unnatural appearance of his shoulders. His eyes become glaring and without expression. Most inveterate smokers become spare and thin, owing in part to the direct effects of opium on the human system, and in part to the fact that nutritious food is taken in less quantities and at more irregular intervals, through loss of appetite, than is usual in the case of persons not addicted to this habit. They are styled "opium devils."

The vice of opium-smoking has long since become a gigantic obstacle to the welfare and the prosperity of this people. The consumption of opium is rapidly on the increase in this city as in other parts of the empire, and its ravages are becoming more and more common. Its unhappy victims are becoming more manifest and more awful. Shops where the drug is offered for sale are becoming more and more numerous. The nation is becoming poorer and poorer.

One of the most common inquiries made by confirmed smokers, as well as by young beginners, of those foreigners who express a hatred of the vice, and who urge them to break away from it, is, "Have you medicine which will cure it?" The Chinese entertain the opinion that, since the drug comes from a foreign land, foreigners must know some infallible remedy which will counteract its bad effects, or destroy an acquired taste for it. Accordingly, the Chinese have opium medicines in abundance, professedly of foreign origin.

There seems to be a bewitching influence connected with opium-smoking which renders it almost impracticable to break away from the habit when once formed. The peculiar pains and sensations which accompany attempts to desist from smoking it also have, doubtless, a great influence in discouraging such attempts.

A strange infatuation impels annually many of the Chinese who have never smoked this drug to begin its use, and, after they have been bound fast in the fetters of the habit they have induced, they seemingly arouse themselves to the fact of their thraldom. They know perfectly well that, if they smoke regularly the bewitching pipe, they will certainly soon come within its power; and yet many yearly voluntarily become its fresh victims. With their eyes open to the inevitable consequences of indulgence, they blindly do what will enslave them for life.

How noble and well worthy of being held in lasting remembrance are the sentiments of the aged heathen emperor Tau Kuang, uttered in 1842, relating to the proposition to legalize the trade in opium, made by Sir Henry Pottinger, the minister of " her most gracious and religious majesty," Queen Victoria : " It is true, I cannot prevent the introduction of the flowing poison ; gain-seeking and corrupt men will, for profit and sensuality, defeat my wishes ; but nothing will induce me to derive a revenue from the vice and misery of my people." But his degenerate son, Hien Fung, who is said to have been himself a smoker of opium before he came to the throne in 1851, gave way in the fall of 1858 to the overwhelming pressure from the ministers of England, France, and America, strongly seconded, doubtless, by the want of an adequate revenue for the support of his tottering throne. He legalized, by his commissioners, the nefarious traffic, fixing the import duty at thirty taels of silver per chest of opium. How much credit and glory should be awarded to the representatives of those Christian and civilized governments for the influence they exerted, directly and indirectly, officially and unofficially, toward bringing about this result, is a question not clearly understood by those who are uninitiated in state secrets. In a moral, benevolent, and Christian point of view, their sentiments and their actions certainly fall far below the views and the conduct of the heathen and the idolater, Tau Kuang.

But, in the expressive language of another, " Opium is as much legalized now as the Gospel." Those who import opium are no longer to be included under the epithet smugglers, provided they pay the duty leviable according to the stipulations of the treaty. In the eye of the law, they are engaged in as honourable and respectable a business as those who import rice or cotton goods. The opium importer and the opium seller are now placed

on the same legal platform as the Gospel messenger and the
Bible distributor. The receiving-ships for opium are often
moored by the side of tea-ships. The tares grow along with
the wheat.

What will be the full practical effect of the legalization of
opium on the Chinese is as yet, to a great extent, an unsolved
problem, involving most momentous interests. Will the Chinese
engage in the cultivation of the poppy more extensively than in
previous years? Will they consume more opium than they
would were it to continue prohibited? Will it be imported in
larger quantities, and will it become cheaper than before, thus
coming within the means of more people? These, and other
questions relating to the cultivation, importation, and consumption of opium, are often the subjects of reflection and discussion
on the part of foreign residents. Some discuss the probabilities
in the case, so that they may, according to the maxims of trade,
invest or refrain from investing their capital in the drug, in order
to make the greatest possible percentage on their money. Others
discuss these questions because the religious interests and the
social and the national welfare of the Chinese people are most
intimately concerned in the practical results, present and prospective, of the legalization of the opium trade.

CHAPTER XXXIV.

MISSIONARY TOPICS.

IN the Chinese religious systems there are two negative features which are worthy of special notice and remembrance,* viz. they do not recognise nor require human sacrifices, nor do they generally worship deifications of vice. These features strikingly distinguish the Chinese religions from the religions of many other heathen nations, ancient and modern.† And so

---

* "The condition of the Chinese would alone go far to prove the necessity of a Divine Revelation for the guidance of man. We see in their creed and practice the standpoint to which intellect can lead us, unaided by the light of the Bible. They are a melancholy specimen of the civilization produced by mere letters and arts unillumined by the ruth that there is one God, our Creator and Judge. Industrious and fond of letters, the Chinaman is at the same time conceited, sensual, and devoid of truth and generosity. His education has only taught him a morality of the lips, not of the heart, and he has a stolid indifference to all real religious feeling. He has no faith here, and no hope hereafter. We have much to impart to this singular race, little to learn from them. The problem of how the change is to be effected is now in course of solution ; and China, we fear, will be no exception to the general law that disorganization must precede reconstruction."—*From an able article in the* "*Quarterly Review,*" 1860, p. 88.

† The Rev. George Smith, Church Missionary for many years in China, says : " Facts of daily occurrence, brought to the knowledge of the missionaries, and frequently gained through the medium of the missionary hospital, revealed the prevalence of the most fearful immoralities among the people, and furnished a melancholy insight into the desolating horrors of Paganism. Female infanticide, openly confessed, legalized by custom, and divested of disgrace by its frequency—the scarcity of females, leading as a consequence to a variety of crimes habitually staining the domestic hearth—the dreadful prevalence of all the vices charged by the apostle Paul upon the ancient heathen world—the alarming extent of opium indulgence, destroying the productiveness and natural resources of the people—the universal practice of lying, and suspicion of dishonesty between man and

far as the knowledge of foreigners extends in relation to the history and the usages of the Chinese, no such custom can be discovered to have existed in former ages, or to exist at present as a necessary or an actual part of their religious belief and practice.

The other peculiar trait, the absence of deified sensuality to any great extent, is, if possible, more remarkable than the absence of human sacrifices in religious worship. In the religious rites of the ancient Greeks and Romans much occurred that was disgusting and obscene; but in Chinese religions there is no goddess corresponding to the Venus of the ancients, nor is Chinese mythology full of the revolting amours of their gods and goddesses—a feature much unlike the mythology of the Greeks, Hindoos, and many other Pagan nations. In the language of another, "Though they are a licentious people in word and deed, the Chinese have not endeavoured to sanctify vice, and lead the votaries of pleasure, falsely so called, farther down the road to ruin by making their pathway lie through a temple and under the protection of a goddess."

There is, however, much to lament in the religious customs and notions of the Chinese, as will be evident after a brief examination of their views relating to several fundamental doctrines and principles of the true religion, and much to show how great is their need of the pure and elevating truths of Christianity. The sages and the worthies of China have never been able to treat with distinctness the doctrine of the Creation; the Governorship of the World; the proper Manner of worshipping the Creator and Governor of all Things; the Origin and Universality of Sin; the Atonement, or Means by which one's Sins can be forgiven; the Agency or Influence which aids Men to do Right and desist from Evil; the Rewards and the Punishments of Men after Death; the Value of the Soul, and the Resurrection of the Dead.

The Chinese, with all their boasted wisdom and knowledge, have most absurd and conflicting notions about the creation of the world. Some of their books speak of the heavens and earth

man—the unblushing lewdness of old and young—the full unchecked torrent of human depravity borne along in its tempestuous channel, and inundating the social system with the overflowing of ungodliness, prove the existence of a kind and degree of moral degradation among a people, of which an excessive statement can scarcely be made, and of which an adequate conception can rarely be formed."—*Narrative of an Exploratory Visit to the Consular Cities of China.*

being formed by kbè, or vapour. The pure kbè, ascending, formed the heavens ; the impure kbè, descending, formed the earth. But no explanation is given of the creation of the khè. Some say a person called Puang-Ku opened or separated the heavens and the earth, they previously being pressed down close together. But they are silent in regard to the origin of Puang-Ku, and of the elements which constituted the heavens and the earth while they were in close proximity to each other. Others explain the origin of all things by ascribing it to the action of the male and female principles of nature—and this, perhaps, is the most popular theory ; but the creation of these important and omnipotent principles is not explained and developed, nor are they able to define with clearness what these principles are. Many Chinese seem to believe that matter is self-existent or eternal. The common people at Fuhchau have a saying, said to have been derived from an ancient book, in regard to the origin of mankind, which is not much less ridiculous and unsatisfactory than any of the preceding, viz. that in very ancient times the heavens sent down a couple of brooms, one of which became a man and the other a woman, from whom the human race has descended.

The Chinese have very indistinct and imperfect notions about the rulership of the world. Many speak of Heaven as the Ruler and Lord of the Universe. They are at a loss to explain and define what they mean by Heaven in such a connexion. Oftentimes, after they have heard the doctrine of the Bible on this subject, they say that Heaven is the same as the God made known in the Bible—the God preached by missionaries. Another term, "Supreme Ruler," which is employed by some missionaries for God, is found in one of the ancient Chinese books, and is used by some of the people of the present day in the sense of Heaven, as already explained.

The proper Manner of worshipping Heaven, or the Ruler of the Universe.—The Chinese abound in religious acts or acts of worship ; but the homage they render the gods and goddesses believed to be concerned in the management of the affairs of this world is exceedingly formal, mechanical, and heartless. There seems to be no special importance attached to purity of heart, nor is their worship adapted to excite solemn and spitual emotions in the worshippers or spectators. According to theory, Heaven is too high and too august to be worshipped to advantage by common mortals. The duty or the privilege of worshipping Heaven devolves, therefore, on the emperor and his highest officers.

The Origin and Universality of Sin.—The Chinese do not pretend to know anything about the origin of sin, and they deride the scriptural account of its entrance into the world. They do not regard it as a very unworthy and exceedingly wicked thing, nor do they admit the reasonableness or the truth of the Bible doctrine of the innate and universal depravity of human nature. They generally profess to believe in the native purity and goodness of the heart, and that it is only by contact with wicked men, or by submitting to temptation to do evil, that one becomes impure, wicked, and depraved. In the first line of the Trimetrical Classic, one of the books first studied by schoolboys in China, it is distinctly asserted that "man's heart is originally good." This good nature becomes evil, or bad and corrupt, by or through the power of habit or education, or the influence of wicked companions or examples. Sin or crime, or fault or error, is a very indefinite and comparatively an unimportant and trivial thing in the Chinese mind.

The Atonement.—The doctrine of good works or of meritorious deeds prevails very extensively among the Chinese as an offset against one's sins. They have no doctrine like that of atonement for sin by vicarious suffering. The merit of a good or of a benevolent deed is sure to be enjoyed by the posterity of him who performs it, if he himself does not enjoy it.

The Chinese do not admit the absolute need of any such agency or influence as the Holy Spirit to lead them to be good and to do good. They acknowledge no other power as necessary to aid them to live virtuously, and desist from evil thoughts, words, and deeds, than the power of their own personal wills.

The strict Confucianists, or those who profess to follow the teachings of the Chinese Classics, pretend often to disbelieve in a future state of rewards and punishments. If one is virtuous, and is faithful in the discharge of the relative and the constant duties of life, the appropriate reward is sure to be experienced in his family or by his posterity in this world. The rewards of such a life—in which the Confucianist believes—are fame, wealth, office, longevity, numerous posterity, and the various forms of worldly prosperity. They do not aspire to be pure-minded or pure-spoken in this life, and holy and happy in such a place after death as the Heaven revealed in the Bible. In like manner, the proper punishment for sin is believed by this class of men to take place in this life. A bad reputation, poverty and its usual attendant hardships, sickness, short life, to be without male posterity, without official employment, without literary fame and rank, &c. are not unfrequently regarded as punishments for unfilial or sinful deeds.

The followers of Buddha profess to believe in a future state of rewards and punishments, which are exceedingly unlike those which the Bible discloses will be awarded to the good and the wicked respectively. The punishments in the Buddhistic hell reserved for the wicked, in their sense of the term, are supposed to correspond, in a great measure, to the punishments for crime in this world as inflicted by officers of government in China! Pictures of these various forms of punishment in hell are quite common. In some temples, and connected with the celebration of certain religious ceremonies, there are representations of these punishments acted out. The images used, having been made from wood or clay, are exhibited in public for the gaze of all who desire to contemplate them. Each human being, after having endured the proper kind and degree of punishment for sins committed during life on earth in each of the ten principal departments into which the Buddhistic hell is divided, is doomed to be born again into the world as a man or a woman, or an insect, bird, or beast, all in strict accordance with perfect justice; unless, during life on earth, the individual should have arrived at a certain degree of perfection in a Buddhistic sense. In such a case he "ascends the western heavens," where perhaps he will become a god or a Buddha; or perhaps, after an indefinite period of duration, measured by ages or kalpas of five hundred years each, he will be born again into this world in some appropriate sphere or condition of being. The punishments and the rewards in the future world, as described in their books, or detailed in the common conversation of the people, seem eminently nonsensical, inadequate, and unimportant, not to say unscriptural.

The doctrine of the Metempsychosis, or transmigration of souls, seems to be firmly believed by all classes of the Chinese.

The views of the Tauists in regard to rewards and punishments in a future state are even more vague and undefined than are the views of the Buddhists, and need not here be particularly mentioned.

The Chinese Classics, and the most popular books in the Chinese language on moral and religious subjects, by heathen writers, are singularly deficient in regard to the nature, powers, and immortality of the human soul. The value of the soul in comparison with the body is almost wholly ignored among the Chinese.

No doctrine of the Bible is listened to with a greater degree of apparent interest, yet with a greater amount of real incredulity and contempt, than the doctrine of the resurrection of the body. Being purely a doctrine of revealed religion, it, of course, was unknown in China previous to the introduction of the Bible and Christian books by missionaries. Considering the extent and the kind of the literature of the Chinese, it is not strange that they should regard the doctrine of the resurrection with undisguised unbelief, and with open ridicule and contempt.

Some of the literary class and the common people frequently use the vilest of epithets relating to several of the above, and other distinctive doctrines and truths of the Bible. When told that people of all nations may, by repentance and belief in Jesus, enter heaven, and when they are exhorted to try and live so that they shall be happy, not wretched, after death, some deride, and say that " if all men should enter heaven, that place would be too crowded for comfort, and, besides, there would be danger of its bottom falling out." They never seem to have thought that, on their principles, if all men should enter hell, it would become too full and crowded ; nor do they ever intimate any fear that its bottom will fall out.

Within a few years much has been said in disparagement* of the vigorous prosecution of the missionary work in heathen lands by the instrumentality of religious schools under the superin-

---

* The most important of all agency for obtaining an entrance into China seems to be the medical missionary; this is illustrated in *The Medical Missionary in China*, by William Lockhart, F.R.C.S., F.R.G.S., and the same interesting and hopeful expectations occur in reading the *Memorials of James Henderson, M.D.*, medical missionary in China. Dr. Henderson says : "Although China has reached what some are pleased to call the highest degree of civilization of which a nation is capable without the Gospel, it presents, I believe, more physical suffering for want of medical knowledge than any other nation on the face of the earth. The multitudes of sick, and lame, and blind which crowd the streets of this and other cities, are ample evidence of her deplorable condition in this respect. In an institution like this a good surgeon may almost every day of his life make the blind receive their sight, the lame walk, the deaf hear, and the paralytic whole ; besides bringing hundreds together, under the most favourable circumstances, to have the Gospel preached to them." The same missionary, speaking of the work of the hospital, in the year 1861, says: " Four hundred and thirty-two persons have been admitted into the wards ; 38,069 have been treated as out-patients. It cannot be doubted that facts like these must tell on the character of Christianity as a remedial institution. Surely, if Jesuitism obtained an entrance into China by the knowledge of the mysteries of the heavenly bodies, we may hope for Protestantism a greater success, as it ministers to afflicted and diseased frames."

tendence of missionaries. It is not proposed to discuss the general subject of schools for the education of the heathen, but simply to declare the favourable conclusion to which I have come with regard to the establishment at every principal or central mission station in China of schools of three kinds—a conclusion which has been reached after some experience, and considerable reflection and observation. These are day-schools, specially for the education of the children of native Christians ; boarding-schools, for the education of the most promising male and female children of such parents ; and training-schools, where pious young men, whether children of native Christians or not, may be properly taught so as to fit them for the position of native helpers in the missionary work, under the direction of foreign missionaries. The great object of these three kinds of schools should be an adequate supply of native teachers, native colporteurs, and native preachers. The text-books should be exclusively in the Chinese language, and relate to a large variety of subjects, and adapted to interest as well as instruct and benefit. Experience has shown that, with very rare exceptions, the Chinese youth who have been taught English by missionaries have soon gone out of their control, and have become servants and compradores in non-Chinese-speaking families, or have become Government interpreters, or agents of foreign merchants. If English had not been taught to them, most could doubtless have been retained under missionary influences, if desirable, after they left their schools. If any wish to learn English, let them not be instructed in it at the expense of missionary societies.[*]

China is so immense and so populous, its distance from America and from England, the present centres of interest in the

---

[*] "*Native Missionary Labourers* (in China).—Their instruction has been conducted in their own language, not in English. Thus the temptation of their being drawn off to engage in secular business has been diminished, and the danger averted of their being alienated from the simple habits of life of their own people, while the expense of their support by the mission is less, and the prospect of their being eventually supported suitably by the native Churches is better than if their education had been conducted through the medium of the English language. Whatever may be true in other missionary countries, it is evident that these Chinese missionary labourers can be well trained through the medium of their own language. . . . . The boarding-schools are still conducted with special reference to the supply of native missionary labourers. Besides these, measures for training such of the converts and scholars as are considered likely to be useful are pursued with a good degree of system and success." —*From the Twenty-eighth Annual Report of the Board of Foreign Missions of the Presbyterian Church, presented to the General Assembly in May* 1865.

foreign missionary enterprise, so great, and the necessary expense connected with foreign missionaries so large and so constant, that it seems idle to expect the evangelization of that empire mainly by the labour of foreigners. The Church, at least in the present state of her zeal in missions, has neither the money she is willing to expend, nor the number of men she is willing to devote, for the prosecution of the work there in a manner at all proportionate to the largeness and the populousness of the empire. The wants of the field must be supplied, and China must be converted to God by the Divine blessing resting principally on the labours of her own Christianized sons and daughters. Able and well-trained native helpers are, under God, her main hope.

Wherever the missionary goes, there is always a great deal of unprofitable excitement and idle curiosity on the part of those with whom he mingles. The native helper can move noiselessly among his countrymen, without attracting notoriety or exciting curiosity. He dresses as they dress ; he eats as they eat ; and there is nothing in his external appearance to prejudice them against him, or arouse their cupidity.

The necessary expenses of the native helper are much less than those of the foreign missionary. The monthly stipend of the former varies from eight to twelve or fifteen dollars, which includes house-rent, his own board and clothing, and the support of a small family. On itinerant excursions into the country his expenses are also comparatively small, while his efficiency and usefulness are great.

The missionary must spend much of his time in learning the language, spoken and written, and, at the best, even after many years of study, has an imperfect, not to say an inadequate, knowledge of it. The native helper speaks his mother tongue.

A well-educated native ministry is peculiarly necessary in China in order to meet on vantage-ground the literary and educated mind of that country. An uneducated native helper is the laughing-stock of the talented and educated Chinaman with whom he comes in contact.

In view of these principal considerations, it is highly important that the three kinds of schools already mentioned should be established and vigorously sustained at all the central mission stations in China. One of the peculiar results of such schools, by the blessing of Providence, in due time would be, wherever established and properly sustained, an annual increase of able, educated native preachers and assistants, qualified to aid largely in the prosecution of the cause of missions in that empire.

Foreign missionaries can have personal access to only a very small part of the immense population of that immense country; but, by means of tracts and books written in the general language, through the agency of a sufficient body of native helpers, the extent of their influence will be limited only by the amount of funds placed at their disposal.

The most successful missions in China, judging by the number of their credible converts from heathenism, are at Amoy and Ningpo. At the former port and vicinity there are eight or nine hundred, and at the latter port and vicinity there are five or six hundred native Church members in connexion with the American and the English missions. There has been especial care taken in some of the missions established at those places to instruct and train the native helpers and the young men who have the native ministry in view. The result is, that at the present time there are men at these consular ports who are competent to carry on the glorious work in an effective manner, and so as to give great satisfaction and comfort to the foreign missionaries under whose care they are.

As an illustration of the manner and the matter of the addresses of native helpers in China, a few notes are here introduced relating to an ordinary religious service held one evening in September 1860, in the Church of the Saviour, situated in the southern suburbs of Fuhchau. Three young men who had belonged to the boarding-school which had been connected with the mission of the American Board (1853–1858) addressed their countrymen on themes they had selected.

The first speaker, aged twenty, had a very bashful appearance. His delivery was rather monotonous, and without gestures. His remarks, however, indicated that he was a sober and earnest thinker. He took as his subject the closing part of the fifth chapter of Matthew, and explained at considerable length the manner according to which Jesus taught His disciples they should treat their slanderers, their persecutors, and their enemies. The way in which he handled his subject, as well as the subject itself, interested and conciliated his auditors. He alluded to several popular customs of his country, and quoted several Chinese maxims relating to the treatment of enemies in China, and exhibited in marked and impressive contrast the principles which the Saviour laid down as rules for the guidance of His followers in regard to those who "cursed," who "hated," and who "despitefully used and persecuted" them. I could not but be thankful for such plain and earnest remarks on this subject, so different from anything which exists in theory or practice among the heathen Chinese.

The second speaker, aged twenty-five, as far as concerned his manner of delivery, was much more pleasing and oratorical than the first. He announced as his theme John xv. 25, "They hated me without cause," and proceeded to show the unreasonableness of the common objections made by the Chinese against Jesus. He declared that his text was fulfilled in Fuhchau in that Jesus was hated without a cause. While he exposed in a masterly manner the sophistry of the popular excuses and objections against the Christian religion, he did not fail to notice the real reasons why the Chinese did not believe in Christ. His words were simple, yet pointed, and his meaning unmistakeable. His appeals were bold and searching. I felt grateful, when he closed, that the truth had been spoken so earnestly, and at the same time so kindly.

The third speaker, aged twenty, discoursed from Matt. ꭓ. 28. His voice was sharp and quick, yet quite distinct. He explained and enforced in a pleasing and direct manner the duty of every one to fear God rather than man. He spoke of the nature, the value, and the immortality of the soul in a way which riveted the attention of the congregation. He denied the sentiment which seems to be entertained, in theory at least, by not a few learned Chinese, that the soul perishes when the body dies. The audience listened with a kind of wonderful interest while he urged them in a bold and spirited manner to fear and obey that Being "who is able to destroy both soul and body in hell," and not fear men, who can only kill the body, but cannot kill or destroy the soul.

What has been said, as well as what has been left unsaid, in regard to the services of that evening, illustrate two interesting and encouraging facts, which are believed to be eminently true not only of native helpers at Fuhchau, but elsewhere in China.

The first fact is that they select very practical and important subjects on which to address their countrymen. They do not love to dwell on abstruse, metaphysical, or far-fetched, or fanciful themes, nor are they fond of presenting doctrinal points and principles, except they have an obvious and useful bearing on the heart and the life. There is not much science, or philosophy, or history embodied in their public addresses, but there is a great amount of most important truth, relating to most practical subjects, propounded, explained, and enforced by them in an earnest and kind manner.

The second fact is that the native helpers are not afraid or ashamed to speak out boldly for the Saviour. They literally and emphatically "stand up for Jesus" in their public discourses.

There are several peculiar kinds of reproach against which native helpers in China must constantly contend in their efforts to do good to their unconverted countrymen. When one considers the nature of Chinese society, and the ingredients which constitute Chinese character, he must perceive that these peculiar reproaches alluded to are exceedingly difficult to bear.

And native helpers are under strong temptation to be unduly influenced by the love of money rather than the love of souls. It is a common remark among heathen Chinese that those who are employed as Christian school-teachers, or colporteurs, or preachers, only perform such work for the sake of the gain which it brings them, very much as they charge the native Church members indiscriminately with the profession of Christianity solely on account of the money they are believed to receive, or the pecuniary advantage they are asserted to enjoy in some way, in return for having abjured the religion of their ancestors and having embraced the Gospel. Native helpers are frequently explicitly told that they worship Jesus and speak favourably of His doctrines because they are paid for it. They are often addressed substantially thus : " You are supported by those who worship Jesus, and of course you profess attachment to the doctrines they preach. You eat Jesus's rice, and you speak Jesus's words. (Nü siah Iasu kî puŏng ; nü kong Iasu kî uā.)" As Satan plainly intimated to the Lord concerning Job in ancient times, so their heathen countrymen slanderously report concerning the native Church members that they do not "fear God for nought."

There is nothing in all this but an imputation to the convert from heathenism of a principle of action universally professed and practised among the Chinese. An incident will illustrate the idea to be conveyed. Several years ago a young man engaged in a clothing-store applied to me for employment, with the statement that he only asked twenty thousand cash besides his board per annum. To the reply that he was not trustworthy, and that he was not a truth-telling man, he replied in a very confidential tone, " If I was employed by you, I would speak in a manner agreeable to your interests. If I work here, I of course must say what is for the interest of the storekeeper. I would lie for you as I now lie for him ! "

Mr. Hung, a young literary man of ability, who died in 1858 in the triumphs of faith, exclaiming, " Heavenly temple, heavenly Father ! "—one of the four who constituted the first native church connected with the American Board at Fuhchau—was once engaged as a native helper in addressing a company of his countrymen. Another of the literary class having listened until the address was finished, and suspecting, from the unequivocal language and earnest manner of Mr. Hung, that he was really a believer in the doctrines he presented, approached him, and inquired whether he actually was a believer, or whether he only exhorted as a means of obtaining a living, intimating that if he did not believe what he preached his course was allowable, but if he did believe it his conduct could not be tolerated ; for, said he, in a very resolute and significant manner, " We Chinese must be disciples of Confucius."

CHAPTER XXXV

CHRISTIANITY makes but slow progress in China. The heavy mass of stereotyped superstition and idolatry there does not give way readily and rapidly to its purifying and elevating truths. Facts show this most conclusively, and, were it not for the promises of the Bible, most discouragingly.

The baptism of the first Chinese convert occurred seven years, and the organization of the first Christian Church in China occurred twenty-eight years, after the arrival of Rev. Dr. Morrison, the pioneer of Protestant missionaries, at Canton, in 1807. At Fuhchau over nine years elapsed between the commencement of Protestant missions and the baptism of the first Chinaman there in 1856. The present number of living and credible converts in China—less than three thousand—is small when compared with the number in some other mission-fields, where the amount of labour and the length of time expended have been not as large.

For many years it has seemed to me that there are several obstacles, peculiar in their nature and extraordinary in their power, which retard the progress of the Gospel among the Chinese.

1. Among the most prominent of these obstacles may be placed the Chinese language. The absence of an alphabet; the large number of its arbitrary characters; the peculiar tones and inflections, and aspirated and guttural modulations, necessary to be carefully observed; the peculiarities in regard to number, case, declension, and conjugation, when compared with most other languages; and the difference between the spoken and the written language as regards both idiom and pronunciation, in the same as well as in different parts of the empire,—all

combine to render the acquisition of the Chinese language very difficult for an adult foreigner.

After the missionary has acquired a tolerable acquaintance with the spoken language, and sufficient for general use in regard to other subjects, he experiences great difficulty in communicating evangelical and spiritual truths through its medium, from the fact that its words and phrases are to a great extent not well adapted to convey such sentiments. He not unfrequently finds it impossible to find suitable terms to teach clearly the distinctive and peculiar truths of the Bible. The invention of the Chinese language has been ascribed to the devil, who endeavoured by it to prevent the prevalence of Christianity in a country where he has so many zealous and able subjects.

2. Another obstacle to the spread of the Gospel among the Chinese is their national vanity. This is one of their most prominent characteristics as a people, and exerts a most powerful influence over them in regard to all that relates to foreign lands. It is manifested in their treatment of foreigners, and in the epithets they apply to them. In some parts of the empire they frequently speak of foreigners as "foreign devils," or "white foreign devils," and in all sections insulting or derogatory expressions are commonly applied to them.

A short extract from one of their most popular essayists (taken from a translation made by another) will illustrate the extraordinary feature of their national character now under consideration better than any mere description can do :—

" I felicitate myself that I was born in China, and constantly think how very different it would have been with me if I had been born beyond the seas in some remote part of the earth, where the people, far removed from the converting maxims of the ancient kings, and ignorant of the domestic relations, are clothed with the leaves of plants, eat wood, dwell in the wilderness, and live in the holes of the earth ; though born in the world, in such a condition I should not have been different from the beasts of the field. But now, happily, I have been born in the Middle Kingdom. I have a house to live in ; have food, and drink, and elegant furniture ; have clothing, and caps, and infinite blessings. Truly the highest felicity is mine."

3. Another obstacle to the adoption of the sentiments of the Bible (nearly related to the preceding, but so different as to justify a separate notice) is the posthumous influence of Confucius and Mencius, and other worthies of antiquity.

Doubtless no man has ever exerted a greater and more lasting

influence than Confucius, if the number of centuries and the
hundreds of millions of men that have been affected and directed
by his writings are considered. The laws of the Middle Kingdom for nearly, if not quite, a score of centuries have been professedly interpreted, if not actually modelled, according to the
principles he inculcated. Many of the present peculiar usages
and opinions of the people, if not originally derived from his
writings, are justified and explained in accordance with the
meaning of his sayings. This one man, more than any other,
has made the Chinese mind, and the Chinese literature, and the
Chinese government essentially what they are at the present
day. His maxims are regarded as perfect in their adaptation to
the wants of society and of government as found in China, and
therefore to be preferred to any which men from an "outside"
country can furnish for the inhabitants of the "Inner Land."

Perhaps somewhat of an adequate idea of the regard with
which the Chinese cherish the memory of the sage may be
gathered from a stanza found in the Sacrificial Ritual, translated
by Dr. Williams in his "Middle Kingdom," as follows :—

> "Confucius! Confucius! How great is Confucius!
> Before Confucius there never was a Confucius!
> Since Confucius there never has been a Confucius!
> Confucius! Confucius! How great is Confucius!"

An incident which occurred in 1835 strikingly illustrates the
powerful influence of Confucius over the minds of his countrymen of the present century. Some missionaries, on entering a
village in Shantung, the native province of this philosopher, met
two aged men, who declined to receive some religious tracts
which were proffered with the remark, "We have seen your
books, and neither desire nor approve them. In the instructions of our sage we have sufficient, and they are far superior to
any foreign doctrines you can bring." How often this feeling
has been exhibited in the conduct of literary Chinese, even
though not expressed in words, many a missionary can testify,
when he has proffered them portions of the sacred Scriptures or
religious tracts. How often has he been told, perhaps in the
very language, that "they knew Confucius, but did not know
Jesus," or that "they understood how to read the words of
Confucius, but did not understand how to read the words of
Jesus."

Next to the influence of Confucius comes, in importance and
extent, that of Mencius. His writings, as well as those of

Confucius, are memorized by Chinese students, and made the subject-matter of the literary essays which they prepare for the regular triennial examinations for the successive degrees of bachelor and master of arts, and doctor of laws *à la Chinois*.

4. But perhaps the greatest of the peculiar obstacles to the rapid evangelization of the Chinese is to be found in the worship of their deceased ancestors.

Habituated as the Chinese are from early childhood to reverence the family tablets and the family tombs, these practices are associated with all that is dear and sacred relating to the honoured dead. Add to this feeling that arising from the reflection that their own graves will not be forgotten nor neglected, and that their own tablets will not be left unworshipped when they are dead, and it will not be difficult to form some idea of the unwillingness of the unconverted Chinese to desist from these ceremonies and denounce them. They have been sanctioned by universal usage from almost immemorial ages, by the bias of education, and by the promptings of a perverted filial affection. A refusal to practise the customary rites is liable to be regarded as a sufficient cause for prosecution before the civil magistrate on the charge of a want of filial piety. He who declines, from conscientious and religious scruples, to conform with the established and popular customs of paying divine honours before the ancestral tablet and the ancestral tomb, is pronounced an ingrate, destitute of filial love, and worse than a brute. He is sure to receive insult, reproach, and persecution from family relatives and hitherto personal friends. He always suffers in his reputation, and in his business and property.

5. Another great obstacle to the speedy conversion of the Chinese is their systematized, superstitious, and idolatrous education. The child and the youth are trained successively and successfully to the practice of idolatrous customs and ceremonies. They are taught to believe in the constant presence and powerful influence of numberless gods and goddesses for good or evil.

6. The difficulty of influencing large and intelligent masses against their prejudices and their convictions makes the progress of the Gospel in China slow and gradual. If the Chinese were ignorant savages or barbarians, and numbered only a few thousands or hundreds of thousands, like the Sandwich Islanders fifty years ago, it might perhaps be expected that they would be influenced to embrace Christianity with comparative ease and speed. But they are a civilized, or at least a semi-civilized, people. They are a literary nation, and their literature is one,

unique, and voluminous. They are exceedingly numerous—
400,000,000 of souls—reading the same written language, ruled
over by one man, and governed by one code of laws, and
attached to the same general national customs and opinions.
They are perfectly satisfied with their own systems of morals
and religions, and remarkably prejudiced against changes and
reform, loving to do as they have been taught to do, and as
they are accustomed to do.

It is possible that more than one-third of my life spent in
China, in daily contact with its people, and its superstitions
and its idolatries, has given me a disproportionate interest in
that land as a field of missionary labour ;* but I cannot avoid
feeling that the Christian world, and especially the American
and the British Churches, are greatly at fault in not putting
forth more interest, more sympathy, more prayer, and more
effort in behalf of its perishing millions, who are hastening to
idolatrous graves at the rate of thirty-two thousand every day.

*China is, all things considered, the Gibraltar, the Sevastopol of
heathenism of the globe.*—Against its bigotry, its superstitions,
and its idolatries the most mighty and persistent attacks should
be made by Christendom. It is neither consistent with the

---

* "We notice that a 'Directory of Protestant Missionaries in China' has
been issued from the press of the American Methodist Episcopal Mission
at Fuhchau. From the figures given in the Directory, it would appear
that there were actually in the field, on the 20th of March last, no less
than 187 missionaries, including ladies, while other 15 were either absent
on leave or on their way out to join the mission. They were distributed
over the various stations, as follow :—Canton, 30 ; Hong Kong, 22 ;
Swatow, 7 ; Amoy, 14 ; Fuhchau, 20 ; Ningpo, 21 ; Shanghai, 25 ; Han-
kow, 5 ; Chefoo, 9 ; T'ungchau, 7 ; Tientsin, 11 ; and Pekin, 16. Of
these, 92 are American, 78 are English, and 18 are German. The religious
body which sends out the largest number is the American Presbyterian
Church, 34 being ranked under this head ; the next is the London Missionary Society, which employs 24 ; and the third in rank is again claimed
by our American friends, whose Board of Commissioners for Foreign
Missions muster 21. These figures, however, it ought to be mentioned,
are equally divided between male and female missionaries. It will be
observed with satisfaction that the American societies, in spite of the
great and increasing difficulties of their position, continue to support as
many labourers as England and Germany put together. The glimpse
which these figures give us of mission work in the empire of China is of a
most gratifying character, viz.: that of nearly two hundred earnest men
and women, of every shade of opinion on matters of doctrine and government, uniting as one, though thinly spread over an area of thousands of
miles, in the common object of imparting to the Chinese the blessings of
an enlightened civilization and Christianity which has made their own
countries what they now are."—*From Supplement to the "Overland China
Mail," Hong Kong, May 13th, 1865.*

dictates of reason, nor the principles of the Bible, nor the developments of Divine Providence in lately opening the empire so largely to the labours of missionaries, that the work of its evangelization should continue to be prosecuted in the leisurely and convenient manner and degree of past years. The more arduous and difficult the strife of quelling the rebellion against God in that empire, the more earnest and vigorous should be the efforts to conquer in that strife; the more numerous and the more mighty the opposing influences and obstacles, the more imperative is the reason, and the more urgent the necessity, for greater boldness and zeal in counteracting these influences and overcoming these obstacles.

The best men in the Church are needed in the prosecution of Protestant missions in China. The Chinese cling most fondly to the sentiments of Confucius and Mencius, and most tenaciously to the dogmas of Tauism and Buddhism. The finest, most acute, and best educated talent of Christendom is required to show them the absurdity, the insufficiency, and the sinfulness of these sentiments and these dogmas, and to teach them a more excellent and a perfect way. Such talent is also needed in preparing in the Chinese language a Christian literature for the Chinese. The importance of preparing such a literature, in view of the following thoughts, can hardly be over-estimated :—

The language is understood by several hundreds of millions of people, more than understand any other language in the world.

The present native literature is secular and heathenish, though extensive. Little true science is taught. Correct morality is not inculcated.

The Chinese are a reading people. While most of the poor are left without instruction to any great extent, the middle and the higher classes are generally able to read ; and their scholars are proud of their present literature, false, unimportant, and unreasonable as much of it is.

Chinese Christians especially require it, to contribute to their proper intellectual and spiritual growth, as much as Christians in Western lands need such a literature.

Native helpers in China stand in great and urgent need of books adapted to assist them in understanding and in explaining the Bible to their countrymen. Able commentaries on the most important and practical portions of the Old and the New Testaments are now urgently needed. An able and well-digested commentary on the whole Bible in the Chinese language would be an invaluable boon to China.

The existing versions of the Scriptures in the general language—the Classical style—require revision. The Bible needs to be translated into the various local dialects for the use of the illiterate and the poor in the Church—those who have neither time to spare nor money to spend in learning the general language. Portions of the Scriptures have already been translated into several of these dialects, and have proved of eminent service in instructing the native Christians. A translation of the Bible is also greatly needed in the Mandarin or court dialect. This is the language spoken by high mandarins throughout the country. It is also the vernacular of probably nearly one-half of the population of the empire—dwelling in the central, western, northern, and north-western provinces. To do this work, men are required not only of ardent piety, but also of eminent ability and scholarship.

And nearly three thousand converted Chinese are scattered over seven or eight provinces, shedding their light in the thick darkness around them to the glory of God. Probably over two hundred of them are regularly engaged in preaching the Gospel to their heathen countrymen, or teaching it in schools to the rising generation. Facilities for acquiring the general language and several local dialects are constantly increasing. A growing acquaintance with Western nations is fast humbling the characteristic vanity of the people and of the government. Christendom has over fourscore of her sons in the field proclaiming the tidings of salvation. She probably annually spends an increasingly large amount of the gold of Sheba in the support of her foreign and her native agencies in that land, and it is hoped that she offers up to the throne of grace in the aggregate, year after year, more fervent, more frequent, and more effectual prayer on behalf of the Chinese.

The glorious results of Christian Missions in China is no more doubtful than in other heathen lands. For "the heathen" are to be "given" unto the "Son" for His "inheritance," and "the uttermost parts of the earth" for His "possession." "He shall have dominion also from sea to sea, and from the river unto the ends of the earth." "Behold, these shall come from far : and, lo, these from the north and from the west ; and these from the land of Sinim."*

* Scholars in general identify the land of Sinim (Isaiah xlix. 12) with China.

CHAPTER XXXVI.

INTERIOR VIEW OF PEKING.

I STARTED from Tientsin for Peking, distant seventy-two English miles, on the morning of March 2nd, 1863, with feelings of deep interest and curiosity. My mode of conveyance was a cart drawn by two mules, one in front of the other. The front mule was attached to the cart by two long ropes connecting his collar with the heavy off-shaft of the vehicle. He had neither halter, bridle, nor rein, being managed entirely by the whip and the voice of the driver. This personage ran along by the hinder mule on the near side, or rode in front of the covered portion of the cart, sitting on the left-hand shaft, his feet dangling down on the near side. He would spring up on his seat while the cart was in motion, or he would occasionally leap down and run along by the side of the animals, talking to them much as though they understood him. Whenever we met a cart we always turned out to the left instead of the right hand. I noticed also that whenever he met a teamster whom he knew, he would generally alight, and walk or run along for a few rods while passing him, instead of simply speaking with him while retaining his seat on the cart: this he did as an act of politeness.

The driver, cart, and the two mules were hired for the sum of 3 dols. 10c. to take myself, Chinese teacher, and our luggage to the capital, the driver being at his own expense *en route*. Those who travel in carts are expected to provide their own bedding. No seat is provided; but the passengers arrange their small articles of luggage and bedding so as to answer for a seat or cushion, disposing their effects as they judge will be most conducive for comfort. The covered portion of the cart being only about two and a half feet wide and three and a half feet long, and not much more than four feet high, it will be readily perceived that there is not much spare room.

The country, for the first day's ride, presented a very uninteresting appearance—no fences, no barns, and but few comfortable-looking dwelling-houses. The fields, so early in the spring, were as barren in appearance as though they had just been ploughed. The trees were scarce, stunted, and destitute of foliage. Everything indicated that the people were active and industrious, though poor. The dwelling-houses, for the first fifteen or twenty miles, except those found in villages, were mostly built of bricks dried in the sun.

During the trip to and from Peking, we saw in use almost all the varieties of transportation and methods of travelling common in Northern China. We saw carts drawn by two mules, or by a mule and an ass, or by a mule and two asses; men riding on horseback, on mule-back, and on donkey-back; and wheelbarrows made for the accommodation of passengers, and for the conveyance of merchandise, grain, &c. We saw a large wheelbarrow so heavily laden that, while it required only one man to guide and manage it from behind, two men were employed, one on each side, to steady and force it along, while a fourth man was engaged in driving two mules and one ass which were fastened abreast to the front part of the vehicle in order to assist in its progress.

I once saw a wheelbarrow, when travelling between T'ungchau and Chefoo, in the native province of Confucius, propelled by a man from behind it, while to the front part of it was attached, by a rope thirty or forty feet long, a solitary black ass for the purpose of aiding in its locomotion. On the wheelbarrow were two Chinese passengers and their luggage—one a well-dressed and fine-looking portly gentleman of some fifty years, deliberately whiffing the smoke from a long pipe as they were wheeled along at the rate of about three and a half miles per hour.

The wheelbarrow and the cart are extensively used in Northern China for the conveyance of passengers and of merchandise. Some of them are very large and strong. Near Peking we saw, the day we left it, a large number of open carts so heavily laden with grain and other productions of the country that each required nine mules to drag it along. Each of the mules, except the one placed between the shafts in front of the vehicle to guide it, was attached, separately, by a couple of ropes to the cart itself. They were driven three abreast.

The second night we spent at T'ungchau, distant some twelve or fourteen miles from the capital. At different places along the road I had distributed copies of a tract on the evils of opium-smoking, which were greedily received by those to whom they were offered. I had abundant reasons for concluding that the victims of the vice of opium-smoking are very numerous in that remote part of the empire, and that their number is rapidly increasing—two deplorable and solemn facts.

Instead of using a bedstead at night during my journey, I slept on a kang. This is a kind of heated platform, and is always to be found in Chinese inns in Northern China, and probably also in every private Chinese dwelling-place in that part of the empire, but never in the southern part. This platform is built of brick, and is as large as two or more common bedsteads, so as to accommodate several persons, if necessary. It is about two feet high, covered over on the top, usually, with large and thin red bricks, so as to present a smooth and neat-appearing surface. Instead of being solid, the interior of the platform is permeated by a tunnel or flue, beginning at one side or end, and passing back and forth in its interior, and finally ending in a chimney on an opposite side or end. A short time before this platform is to be used as a bedstead, or sleeping-place, a small quantity of dry fuel is set on fire in the accessible part of the outer extremity of the flue. The flame, hot smoke, and heated air pass along, back and forth, in the flue in the interior of the platform, and finally goes forth in the chimney. The kang is warmed in this way. The traveller places his mattress and the bedding or blanket he has brought with him on this hard and slightly-heated platform, and retires to rest at his convenience.

Our muleteer had been employed by the English to drive a cart filled with luggage or provisions some years previous to the time of my making my visit to Peking, during the march of the allied English and French forces on the capital. He enlivened the tedium of our way by occasionally referring to the events which took place along the route, and by describing the consternation and discomfiture of the Tartar cavalry when charged by the troops or attacked by the cannon and shell of the allies. As we passed along near the battle-field in the vicinity of the village Chang-Kia-Wang, he pointed out the different positions of the combatants as well as he was able to do. He informed us that he was not far distant with his cart at the time of the engagement, but felt no personal fear. Notwithstanding the great disparity between the numbers engaged, the Chinese and the Tartar troops being vastly more numerous than the forces of the allies, they quickly became panic-struck and demoralized, and fled in dismay from the field.

Although I had spent nearly one-third of my life in China, and had visited the principal cities on the sea-board accessible to foreigners, I expected to find an improved style of civilization at the capital. It was therefore with feelings of considerable interest that I approached within sight of the walls of Peking, from an easterly direction, about nine o'clock on the morning of the 4th of March. Among the first objects which attracted my attention, as we came near the gate through which we entered the city, were a number of camels lying down, and quietly chewing the end, while awaiting the reception of their burdens. None of these animals are to be found in the southern portions of the

PART OF THE WALL OF PEKING.

empire; but, during my visit at the capital, I doubtless saw several thousands engaged in transporting coal to the city from the mines lying on the west of it, or carrying goods into the country situated on the north and the west.

Peking has been called by some one a "city of magnificent distances." Everything seems to have been planned on a large and liberal scale. The streets are wide, the main ones being several times wider than the main streets in large cities in Southern China. Peking is divided into two parts, usually called the Tartar and the Chinese cities. The former is also referred to as the "northern," the latter the "southern" city. The wall which separates them forms the wall on the southern

side of the Tartar, but only a part of the wall on the northern
side of the Chinese city, the Chinese being broader than the
Tartar city. The dividing wall is quite high and broad, having
in it three large gates, which are open from early dawn to dark.
These gates lead into, or rather open upon, the three principal
streets in both the northern and southern cities. Several of the
large and principal streets in both cities run east and west, and
others run north and south, crossing each other at right angles.
The city walls are about thirty feet high, more or less, and are
kept in good repair, which cannot be truly said of most large
Chinese cities at the present day. The residences of the better
class of citizens are ample, well built, in a Chinese sense, and

CART OR CAB DRAWN BY A MULE OR PONY.

have spacious courtyards—from the street generally presenting
but a very indifferent and even shabby appearance. Usually
the best houses are concealed from the view of the traveller in
the public street by a high wall.

Few sedans borne on the shoulders of men are seen at Peking ;
but one-horse carts, some of which are quite neat-looking, are
very numerous, and not expensive. Large numbers of these
Chinese cabs are to be found standing at various unoccupied
places in all sections of the cities, and at all hours of the day,
awaiting employment. They constitute the best way of travelling

from one part of the city to another, and are almost a necessity to residents, as well as to strangers or visitors. They can be hired per day for the small sum of sixty or seventy cents, including the wages of the driver.

The Pekinese do not seem as excitable, curious, and inquisitive as are the Chinese in the southern portions of the empire. They generally appear to be occupied each with his own affairs, and to pay but little attention to foreign visitors, and to care but very little for them in any sense except they may be able to make them a means of pecuniary profit. This fact may be partially accounted for by the circumstance that the inhabitants of Peking have been accustomed for centuries to see strangers from various foreign countries, who visit the capital, bringing tribute, or for purposes of trade or religion. One may see in the streets of Peking Thibetans from the distant West, and Coreans from the distant East; Mongolians from the vast deserts lying on the west and north-west of China Proper, and Manchurians from the country to the north of the empire, the original home of the Manchu family now on the DRAGON THRONE—all wearing their national costumes, and all speaking their native tongues. Roman Catholic missionaries have resided at Peking, in greater or less numbers, for over two hundred and fifty years, and the Russians have had a political embassy there for a considerable period. A foreigner, conducting himself with propriety, may perambulate the streets without being annoyed by crowds of idlers following wherever he goes, or running by his side. The citizens seem much less saucy and impertinent or insulting in their demeanour and remarks towards visitors from foreign countries than are the Chinese in any other large city which I have visited.

The Pekinese, as well as the Chinese generally, residing in the northern part of China, are much more hardy and robust than are the Chinese living in the southern portions of the empire. This is doubtless owing, in a great degree, to the colder and more bracing climate in which they live. Their food is more hearty and nourishing than the food of the people in the south, less rice and less fish, and more wheat, corn, millet, as well as more beef and mutton, being used. Whatever be the natural causes, they undoubtedly are superior to their fellow-countrymen at the south as regards stature, strength of body, and general appearance.

As respects the extent of the capital, let it suffice to say that the wall around the northern city, as I was informed,

measures fourteen miles, and that the wall around the southern
city measures ten miles. If the wall which is common to both
the northern and the southern cities be three miles in length,
the outside wall around the capital would be twenty-one miles
in extent. Some of the suburbs are extensive.

The population of Peking, Chinese and Tartars, is usually
estimated to amount to at least two millions. The capital ranks
for populousness, as every intelligent schoolboy knows, as one
of the three largest cities in the world, viz. London, Peking,
and Jeddo.

THE IMPERIAL WINTER PALACE AT PEKING.

The foreign legations of the United States, Great Britain,
France, and Russia, are located in the southern part of the
Tartar city, and near each other. They are all probably less
than half a mile from the wall which surrounds the Sacred
City, containing the Imperial palace and grounds devoted to
the use of the Imperial family. The hospital, under the charge
of a physician connected with the London Missionary Society,
is on the premises belonging to the British Legation. Most
of the Protestant missionaries, English and American, have
been glad to secure locations not very remote from the same
part of the northern city.

The experience of the foreign residents goes to show that the climate of Peking is healthy and invigorating. The vicinity of the partition-wall between the Chinese and the Tartar cities to the foreign legations makes recreation by walking practicable even for ladies and children, though they live in the midst of two millions of people; for they, as well as other foreign residents, have ready access to the top of the wall, where they may take the air and promenade as often and as long as they please. Large numbers of trees' are scattered over the city in all directions, and these give in the summer season a rural

PRINCE KUNG.

aspect to the scenery as viewed from the central wall, and add much to the pleasure of a promenade. From this wall several imperial palaces can be seen; some of them look finely in the distance. Walking in the streets for recreation and exercise is almost impracticable on account of the absence of sidewalks, and on account of the dust and the crowds of people, and the multitude of carts which are encountered there at all hours of the day, except in rainy weather, and except very early in the morning.

The Hon. A. Burlingame and Sir Frederick Bruce, respectively American and British ministers to China, and the ministers of France and Russia, were in friendly relations with the Chinese government. Their presence at the capital did not seem to disturb the equilibrium of the empire, and occasion any special annoyance, as many predicted and feared. The party in power at Peking was favourable to foreigners. The head of this party was Prince Kung, a near relative of the youthful emperor. He is also one of the regents who have in charge the affairs of state during the minority of the "Son of Heaven." He is a man of acknowledged ability and strength of character. As long as his counsels are followed in the administration of the government relating to foreign countries and foreign interests, there doubtless will be no serious misunderstanding or difficulty.

Among the objects of interest which I visited during my visit at Peking are the Astronomical Observatory, the old Portuguese Burying-ground, the Russian Cemetery, and the Temple of the Great Bell.

This observatory was erected nearly two hundred years ago, in the first part of the period during which the present family has occupied the Imperial throne. It is situated near the south-eastern corner of the northern city, and is built partly on the wall. I was struck with surprise on beholding the excellent workmanship and the remarkable skill displayed in the construction of the globe of the heavens. It was made of copper, and is about seven feet in diameter, and is mounted on a fine standard or framework of copper. Many of the principal stars and constellations are represented in a very neat manner by copper figures fastened to its surface, the figures being of various sizes denoting stars of various magnitudes. In all there were eight pieces of machinery for estimating the distances, the movements, the sizes, &c. of the heavenly bodies. One of them, as I was afterwards informed, came from France. One of these was about fifteen feet high, and made of copper like the rest. They were all exposed to the open heavens, on the top of a level and substantial platform, and all exhibited great skill in their construction, considering the time, place, and other circumstances of their manufacture by Verbiest and his associates, the Roman Catholic missionaries, chiefly in the reign of Kang-hi, the second emperor of the present dynasty. The platform was surrounded by a heavy iron railing.

The Jesuit Burying-ground, often called the old Portuguese Burying-ground, is situated a short distance outside of one of

the western gates of the Tartar city. It was with a deep and
sincere interest that I looked upon the large white marble
tombstones of the Roman Catholic missionaries who exerted
such a great influence at Peking during tho latter part of the
Ming dynasty, and the former part of the present Tartar
dynasty. There were some eighty or ninety tombstones in all.
Some had inscriptions in Latin, Chinese, and Manchu. I
remember to have seen the old, weather-beaten marble tombstones erected to mark the resting-place of the mortal remains
of Ricci, Schall, Verbiest, De Sousa, and others noted for their
part in the missionary and scientific labours which were performed at Peking two centuries ago.* I also noticed two fine

* The mention, by Mr. Doolittle, of the names of these extraordinary
men, whose remains repose in the burial-ground of Peking, calls to mind a
comparatively unknown chapter in the history of European intercourse with
China, and the attempts made to propagate Romanism there in the seventeenth century. To most readers the names of Schall, Ricci, and Verbiest,
are probably unknown ; they were not less truly astonishing men than
their labours were truly astonishing. We fear the most catholic and
dispassionate inquiry would break down in the attempt to pronounce a
favourable verdict upon the means they employed ; they were among the
first emissaries of Jesuitism, and they seem to have obtained an almost
miraculous entrance into Peking, and influence over the Imperial court and
people, partly by working upon the fears of the people through their knowledge of scientific machinery, and partly by a most literal "becoming all
things to all men," in an almost entire assimilation with all the popular
superstitions. Ricci and, perhaps, Schall were not, however, devoid of
virtue any more than ability, although their virtue was a loose suit cut out
after the pattern of the Jesuits. When Ricci died, in the year 1610, so great
was the respect in which he was held, that the chief people of the Empire,
or the capital, which in China would be the same thing, followed in the long
funeral procession, while the crucifix was borne aloft in the sight of all
the great pagan multitude. Schall succeeded Ricci. He was a German
Jesuit, born at Cologne ; his life was a wonderful succession of labours.
He established himself and his fame in the capital by most important
rectifications of astronomical observations; he established, to aid the
Emperor, a foundry for cannon, and introduced a number of mechanical
arts. Beneath the influence of his wonderful labours, it is said, a hundred
thousand Chinese were converted to Christianity, but the services and
the temples were so arranged that the ideas of heathenism were not out-
raged. So far from interfering with the worshipping of the tablet, these
men seem to have set up and worshipped their own, or the tablets of the
eminent men of their order. Adam Schall rose through all the nine orders
of the mandarins till he reached the first, and became prime minister of
the Emperor of China. He was not only ennobled, but his grandfather
and grandmother were ennobled also. By and by a change came, his
patron died, he was loaded with chains, and deprived of his dignities, and
sentenced to be hacked in pieces. From this fearful fate, however, he was
saved, but only to die in prison at the age of seventy-five. Verbiest was
another of these eminent men, who edged his way by scientific and mathe-

large monuments of white marble sacred to the memory of
Xavier, the Jesuit apostle of the East, and of Joseph, the
husband of Mary. Joseph is the patron of Roman Catholic
missions in China. These stand, the one on the right hand and
the other on the left hand of the front gate to the cemetery as
it is entered from the street.

The Russian Burying-ground, situated a short distance outside
of the most eastern gate, on the northern side of the northern
city, possesses a melancholy interest to foreign visitors at the
present time, for it contains the small and plain monument,
"Sacred to the memory" of Captain Brabason, Lieutenant
Anderson, and eleven others, who, with a number of soldiers,
were treacherously taken prisoners by the Chinese while under
the protection of a flag of truce, on the 18th day of September,
1860. These subsequently sank under the cruel tortures to
which they were subjected by the native authorities into whose
hands they fell. In front of the monument are five small
mounds, which indicate the graves of those whose bodies were
recovered after the surrender of Peking to the allied English and
French forces. Peace to the dust of these brave and unfortunate men !

The Temple of the Great Bell is located about three miles to
the north of the western gate, on the north side of the northern
city. The road to it was exceedingly dusty the day I visited it,
and I nearly regretted the attempt to find the temple before I
reached it. But after I had seen and examined the bell I felt
most amply repaid for all the dust and fatigue I had encountered. It is really a great wonder of art, and decidedly the
greatest monument of genius and skill I have seen in China.
The lower rim is about one foot thick. Its diameter is about
fifteen feet, and its height about twenty feet. The apparatus
attached to it for the purpose of suspending it measures about
eight feet in height, consisting of eight immense staple-like
pieces of brass or copper, one foot in diameter, four of which are
said to be welded on the top of the bell. An attendant priest
informed me that the bell weighed 84,000 catties, which would
make it equal to 112,000 pounds. It is covered, both within

matical knowledge to Imperial favour, and acquired sufficient influence to
attain funeral honours for Adam Schall, by way of reparation to his
memory ; and the Emperor sent a chief mandarin to represent him on the
occasion. It is a wonderful story, the history of Jesuitism in China.
The reader will find all about it in *Letteres Vedifantius Missions de la Chine*,
also in Steinmetz's *History of the Jesuits*, and an able paper on "Christianity
in China," *Foreign Quarterly Review*, 1830.

and without, with perfectly-formed Chinese characters. The fixtures by which it is suspended, and the lower rim, have characters (Chinese and Manchu) cast upon them. The priest told me that the contents of eighty-seven sections of the sacred books of the religion of his order constituted the characters found upon this immense bell. The wonder is how the body of this instrument, weighing undoubtedly nearly, if not quite, 100,000 pounds, and so completely covered, both on its inside and on its outside, with perfectly-formed Chinese characters, could have been cast at once, as it must have been. This wonderful bell was made in the reign of Yungloh, one of the emperors of the Ming dynasty, which ended in 1643. The temple was thronged by idle boys and men, who ascended a staircase by which they reached the second storey, whence they could look down on the bell, and whence they endeavoured to throw the copper coin in use at Peking through a small hole in the top of it. A large number of the coin were lying about on the ground under the bell. It was considered as belonging to the temple, to be spent in buying incense and candles for use in it. It was a saying that those who succeeded in throwing their coins through the orifice would certainly succeed in their pursuits in life.

The Christian visitor at Peking cannot fail to be profoundly impressed with the superstitious and idolatrous character of the government of the present dynasty. He will see numerous temples, altars, monasteries, &c., which indicate, by the yellow colour of their tiling, and of the bricks used in their construction, and of the painting of the wood-work connected with them, that they belong to the Imperial family, or are under the patronage and support of the Imperial government.

Not to give a complete list, there is an altar to Heaven, an altar to Agriculture, an altar to Earth, an altar to the Sun, and an altar to the Moon. All of these altars, and the premises connected with them, are on a grand and magnificent scale. I am quite unable to give a description of the altars visited which is adequate to them and satisfactory in itself, nor shall I attempt more than a meagre outline.

The altar to Heaven is situated in the south-eastern part of the southern city, and is surrounded by a wall fifteen or twenty feet high, and about three miles in extent. Along the southern portion of the premises, and running from east to west, there is a broad straight avenue or carriage-road, nearly or quite one mile in length, the sides of which are shaded by large trees kept in good repair. The whole inclosure in many respects

resembles an extensive park, and has large shade-trees planted
in rows at regular intervals.   It contains several large and magnificent buildings—magnificent in a Chinese sense—devoted
to various purposes, and used only on state occasions by the
Emperor himself, or by members of the Imperial family.

The pavilion to Heaven, or the lofty dome in imitation of the
Vault of heaven, as some explain and describe it, is really a
fine-looking object.   It is circular, and, as the keeper of the
grounds informed me, was ninety-nine feet high, consisting of
three storeys.   It is erected on the centre of a magnificent platform, constructed of white marble, twenty-five or thirty feet

DOME IN IMITATION OF THE VAULT OF HEAVEN.

high.   The top of the platform is reached by ascending three
flights of marble steps from any one of four sides, corresponding
to the four cardinal points.   At the head of the first and of the
second flight of steps is a fine flat terrace running round the
platform, each terrace being some twenty feet wide, and protected by a white marble balustrade, in some places elaborately,
if not elegantly, carved.   The outside of the pavilion, and the
tiling on its top, are of a deep blue colour, in imitation of
the azure vault of heaven.   It is the finest and most imposing

structure, especially when beheld from a short distance, which I have seen in China.

The interior of this pavilion is devoted to the worship of the chief god of the Tauist religion, " the Pearly Emperor Supreme Ruler," by the Chinese emperor himself, as I was distinctly informed by the keepers of the premises. Their statement is corroborated by the inscription in Chinese to be found upon the tablet which is used on the occasion of the Emperor's worshipping. Some foreigners, however, seem to believe that the worship is designed to be given to " the Supreme Ruler of the Imperial Heavens," or, as the Chinese expression is rendered by others, " the Ruler on High of the Imperial Heavens,"—that is, as they understand the subject, Heaven, or the true God. Few, however, believe that the Chinese emperor worships the true God. A small tablet, having the usual title of the chief divinity of Chinese Rationalism, Yuh Hwang Shang-Ti (according to the spelling of the Mandarin pronunciation), inscribed upon it in large gilt characters, is placed in a chair standing on the throne erected in the northern part of the interior. On the right and on the left hand sides of the room are placed seven or eight large and elegantly-carved chairs, which are used to hold tablets representing the deceased emperors of the dominant dynasty during the time occupied by the living emperor in burning incense before the tablet of the Supreme Ruler, the Pearly Emperor, and in performing the prescribed acts of worship. The spirits of the deceased emperors are supposed to be present as worshippers, not as objects of worship, during the ceremonies of the occasion. I was told by the men who belonged to the premises, whether correctly or incorrectly I cannot affirm, that sacrifices are offered three times yearly to the Pearly Emperor, Yuh Hwang Shang-Ti, consisting in part of eleven bullocks, twelve rams, three swine, two deer, and twelve hares. Near by is an immense furnace, in which the carcase of a bullock is consumed as a kind of burnt-offering while the others are being offered whole as sacrifices. I noticed ten immense iron openwork censers or furnaces, each large enough to hold several barrels, where mock-money was burnt in large quantities at the proper time during the ceremonies.

The altar to Heaven is located some distance to the south of the blue dome, representing the vault of heaven, just partially described. It is also circular, having two terraces, each reached by flights of nine marble steps, and surrounded by white marble balustrades, &c. similar in some respects to the terraces and balustrades belonging to the dome to Heaven. There is, however, no pavilion or building on its top. It is level, and entirely open to the heavens. The platform which constitutes the altar to Heaven is considerably smaller than the level surface on which the pavilion and dome to Heaven is built, being only about twenty-eight paces across. Near it is an immense furnace for consuming a whole bullock, and twelve large, coarsely-made open-work iron censers or furnaces for holding mock-money while burning. There are also several magnificent large copper censers, used for containing incense. The altar is surrounded by four walls; the innermost one is circular, and the others are square or right-angled. Each of the two innermost walls has three openings on each of the four sides, north, east, south, and west. In each of these openings is erected a splendid lofty arch or portal of white marble, elaborately carved or chiselled, making twenty-four arches in all. The bricks used about the altar and the walls are glazed and coloured; the yellow colour predominates. White marble is lavishly used in constructing several palaces and outbuildings; the walls, altars, &c. giving, in connexion with the glazed bricks and tiling, a neat, costly, and elegant appearance to the immense inclosure.

The altar to Agriculture is situated to the west of the altar to Heaven, in the south-western part of the southern city. The premises are somewhat smaller than those connected with the altar to Heaven, but, like the latter, abound in large trees, set out in regular order. The altar itself is square, and only one storey high. On it and near by are eight immense brazen censers, of most excellent workmanship. I visited the building which contained the tablets to the gods of mountains, the god of the ocean, the god of the wind, the god of thunder, the god of rain, and the god of the green grass and the green stalks of grain. The butchery—where six bullocks, six swine, and five sheep are slaughtered twice a year, as I was told, to be offered up in sacrifice to these gods—was pointed out by the keepers of the premises as an object worth notice. As another object of special interest, they showed me the building in which were deposited, when not in actual use, the implements of husbandry used by the Emperor and by the princes of the empire, in the spring of each year, while setting an example to the agricultural class of the people by personally engaging in ploughing, sowing, &c. The imperial plough, seed-planter, rake, bucket, &c.—that is, those implements actually devoted to the exclusive use of the Emperor himself—were of a bright yellow colour, while those used by the princes of the empire on the same occasion were of a bright red colour. The two plots of ground where the Emperor and his princes engage in the rural employments of ploughing, planting, sowing, &c. in the presence of the grandees of the empire, are situated near the altar to Agriculture, where sacrifices are offered. I went into one of the palaces devoted to the use of the Emperor during his visit to these premises. The ceiling of the roof, which could be seen from below, was covered with numerous gilded paintings or pictures representing the five-clawed dragon, the special emblem of imperial power. These premises, considered as a whole, were much inferior to those which contained the altar and the dome to Heaven.

The altar to Earth is located not far from one of the gates of the northern wall of the northern city, and outside of it. The premises are spacious, and kept in good order. Many large trees are planted in regular rows. The altar consists of two terraces —that is, one built upon the other. The topmost one is reached by two flights of steps, each flight about six feet high. The terraces are faced on the sides with yellow glazed brick. The upper surface of the altar is covered with square, smooth, slate-coloured brick, each about two and a half feet square. The altar is surrounded by a deep, narrow, dry moat, bricked up neatly on the sides, and also by walls. The two innermost ones are yellow. Sacrifices to Earth are made once a year by the Emperor or by his proxy, using, as I was informed by the keepers of the premises, one deer, two hares, nine bullocks, six sheep, and six swine. This altar, and the buildings, &c. connected with the premises, rank next in beauty and magnificence to the altar to Heaven and its surroundings—speaking only of the comparative appearance of the altars which I visited. When too late to visit it, I was told of the existence of a splendid altar to light, located in the sacred or inner city. I saw a photograph of it, and judged it to be only inferior to the altar to Heaven. As our company was leaving the premises devoted to the altar to Earth, we saw a wild fox roaming about, stopping occasionally to gaze at us. The keepers considered the presence of the fox an omen of good, and on no account would consent to have it hunted and killed.

The altar to the Sun is situated some distance to the east of the Tartar city, and outside of one of the large gates on that side of it. I had a good view of it from the wall of the city. The altar to the Moon is located outside of the west wall of the Tartar city, corresponding nearly to the situation of the altar to the Sun on the east. It is approached by a magnificent broad avenue of about a quarter of a mile in length. There was nothing which I saw in the premises which deserves a special notice, as compared with the premises of the other altars visited.

There are two immense Lama temples, or monasteries, at Peking, one a short distance to the north and the other a short distance to the south of the northern wall of the Tartar city— that is, one inside and one outside of it. They abound with yellow-coloured tiling, bricks, &c. showing that they are connected with the reigning family or with the Imperial government, yellow being the imperial badge or colour. It is reported in Peking that the members of the reigning family, as private individuals, are worshippers of the Living Buddha, the head or principal of the Lama religion. The priests in these establishments also worship the Living Buddha, whose residence is in Lha-Ssa, the capital of Thibet.

The premises of the Lama temple outside the city contain a colossal monument made out of white marble. It must have cost an immense sum of money and an immense amount of labour. It is covered with images of Buddha, and a large variety of other beings, real or imaginary. At its four corners are four white marble pagodas, one pagoda at each corner, four or five storeys high, having also carved upon them numerous images of Buddha. I was subsequently informed that, in some way, the carvings and engravings upon the marble monument were designed to be an historical and pictorial representation of the birth, life, and death of Buddha, the founder of Buddhism. It is, indeed, a beautiful work of art. We observed a sorrowful, melancholy-looking devotee, said to have come from outside the western boundaries of China Proper, engaged in performing his devotions towards the monument. He prostrated himself flat on the ground, and while in that posture struck the ground with his forehead, muttering half aloud some formulas, and removing at the termination of each prostration and repetition one of the beads which he wore around his neck along the cord upon which they were strung, thus keeping an account of the number of his so-regarded meritorious prostrations and repetitions.

The Lama monastery inside the city, I was told, was large enough to accommodate three thousand persons. The premises are indeed very spacious, and the buildings large and numerous. As a general remark, the temples, or the buildings devoted to idols, and where more or less numerous and imposing ceremonies of worship are performed, connected with these premises, resemble very much the common Buddhistic temples to be found everywhere in the south of China. There is an immense image of Buddha in one of these buildings, about sixty feet high, said to be the largest idol in China, perhaps in the world. I failed to get a sight of it, through the evasion or mendacity practised by the priest who kept the keys of the building. He engaged to bring the keys on my promising him a reward, and went off professedly for them, but did not return. The priests had just finished their afternoon worship, and were dispersing to their rooms, when I arrived there. They wore very ample breeches of a deep red colour, and, instead of a coat, had something like a red blanket thrown over their shoulders. Some of them were

Obverse.　　　　　　　　　　　　　　　　Reverse.

FAC-SIMILE OF THE LARGE PEKING CASH (worth about 400 to a dollar).

engaged in gambling with the large Peking cash. Some of the Mongol priests had on ash-coloured clothing, and others had yellow cotton or silk garments. It is currently believed that these Lama establishments are principally supported by moneys received from Government. There seemed to be no indication of poverty, everything being kept in good repair.

The facts which have just been mentioned relating to the various altars and the sacrifices made upon them, and relating to the Lama monasteries, go to prove that the present Tartar government is very superstitious and idolatrous, and also that the annual expenses connected with this official or governmental superstition and idolatry are immense.

While at Peking I was much interested in my visit to the temple erected for the worship of Confucius. This temple is situated near the large Lama monastery which has been referred to, in the north-eastern part of the Tartar city. A tablet representing the sage, but no image, is used. The temple proper is not very large, but the abundance of gilding, yellow tiling, yellow painting, and yellow bricks, connected with it and the outbuildings and pavilions, combine to give the premises devoted to the worship and honour of Confucius a splendid and magnificent appearance. In one of the outbuildings there are shown to the inquisitive stranger ten stone drums—that is, ten stones cut out in the shape of drums. These are affirmed to have been made about three thousand years ago. They indeed exhibit marks of great antiquity, but it it is doubtful if they are as old as it is claimed. On the outside of them there are engraved, though not very distinctly, a large number of Chinese characters, in one of the forms or styles of writing used in very ancient times.

Near the Confucian temple is a building which I shall designate as the Imperial pavilion. This pavilion and its immediate surroundings constitute some of the most interesting objects to the foreign visitor. In this pavilion, which is two storeys high, is a throne from which the Emperor is accustomed to confer certain honours upon certain competitors who have successfully striven for literary rank and fame. The table before the throne was covered with dust nearly one-eighth of an inch thick at the time of my visit. Still, the elaborate carving on its legs was visible through the dust. The ceiling overhead was richly or gaudily painted with representations of the five-clawed dragon. Near by the pavilion was the large hall where the candidates who have competed successfully for the third literary degree, meet together to compete at another examination in the presence of the Emperor himself. To come out first best from this literary arena, and to be honoured by special personal attention on the part of the Emperor, is the realization of the highest literary honour attainable in China.

On two sides of the Imperial pavilion, under two long and low corridors, are arranged about two hundred immense granite tablets, each seven or eight feet high, and of proportionate width and thickness. On these are engraved the entire contents of the thirteen books which constitute the Chinese classics. The characters are neatly cut on the two sides of the tablets. On these extensive premises, besides the two hundred tablets, there is an immense amount of white marble used for honorary tablets, posts and pillars, balustrades, &c.; which, in connexion with the numerous buildings, contribute to give to the place a neat and attractive appearance.

There is a large Mosque located on Ox Street, in the western part of the southern city. It had recently been repaired, and seemed new. It was originally built and presented to the resident Mohammedans by an Emperor of China who reigned nearly two hundred years ago. The recent repairs, it was affirmed by some priests belonging to the establishment, cost the large sum of 30,000 dollars. The main room consisted of over forty apartments, as the Chinese reckon, and was very long, wide and low. Some of the Arabic inscriptions found over the principal doors were read off at my request by these priests, showing that the language in which the Koran was originally written is understood by a few, at least, of the many followers of the false prophet in China. This mosque is the largest and the most wealthy of the several mosques in the capital.

The Roman Catholic missions are strong and flourishing at Peking. They seem to be under the special protection of the French minister. They have a large and well-conducted school, where the most promising Chinese converts are trained for the Romish priesthood, taught Latin, &c. I did not succeed, as some Protestant missionaries have succeeded, in gaining access to this school, or to the interior of the largest Roman Catholic church and monastery in Peking; I only saw the exterior of the church, and heard those inside of it chanting in concert. It appears that the magnificent church erected within the precincts of the Sacred or the Yellow city during the reign of Kanghi, in part by moneys given by himself, and described by Huc in the third volume of his "Christianity in China," had long ago been confiscated by the Chinese government, and demolished, after the Jesuits came into dishonour at court. On the premises several smaller buildings had been erected. These extensive and valuable premises had been reclaimed in accordance with the provisions of the recent French treaty, and possession of them had been given to the Roman Catholic missionaries at present in Peking. I was politely shown over a part of the premises by two French priests who were dressed in Chinese costume. They took me to a small chapel, on the walls of which were suspended eighteen or twenty pictures of saints, &c., and where an altar had been built for worship. I was informed that it was the intention to commence the erection of a large and splendid church on these premises without long delay. As I could not speak French, and as these priests could not speak English, we had recourse to the Mandarin dialect, which we all happened to know. One of these gentlemen had but recently arrived at Peking, having come from one of the remote provinces in the south-western part of the empire to represent the facts relating to the murder of a Roman Catholic priest there by the officers of Government, and to obtain redress therefore at the capital. He intended to return before many months to his distant field of labour. Previous to my visit at Peking, and while I was at Tientsin, I was informed by a man who said he was a Roman Catholic, and dwelt at the capital, that there were thirty foreign priests there, and that the number of native converts there was very large. It is not probable that there are quite thirty foreign priests stationed at the capital, though there may be that number in the province of Pechili, in which Peking is situated. Besides the priests at Peking, there are six or eight foreign Sisters of Mercy, who arrived at Tientsin in the fall of 1862—destined for the capital of the empire.

The importance of sustaining Protestant missions at Peking must be manifest, in view of the various facts which have been advanced, showing the superstitious and idolatrous character of the Imperial government, and, by inference, the moral condition of its vast and varied population.

Lamaism (also called Shamanism), the form of Buddhism which prevails principally in Thibet and Mongolia, has representatives at the capital, as has been remarked. Chinese Buddhism, or the form of Buddhism which is so popular in Southern China, has not a few adherents in Peking. Tauism, or Chinese Rationalism, abounds there more than in the south of the empire.

Roman Catholic missionaries being established and protected there in the exercise of their religious and ecclesiastical functions, is it anything more than fair and equal that Protestant missionaries should be stationed and protected at the capital in the exercise of their religious privileges and duties? Is it not as important that the Christianity of Protestant England and America should have its defenders and its teachers at Peking, as that the Christianity of Roman Catholic France should have its defenders and its teachers there?

Peking is the political and the literary centre of an empire which contains one-third of the human race. Officers of high rank, from all parts of the eighteen provinces, receive their commissions from Peking; and many of them are obliged to visit the capital in person before they are eligible to the highest offices of government in the provinces. Candidates for the third and higher literary and military honours are also required to "ascend" to Peking from even the remotest portions of the remotest provinces before they can compete for these honours. The Imperial college, the Hanlin, is located at Peking, having for its inmates some of the successful competitors before the Emperor, coming from each of the eighteen provinces, and waiting there, in the discharge of various literary duties, until they shall be called to enter upon the mandarinate somewhere in the empire. Now, is it not highly important that these classes of influential and intelligent men should have access to Christian scholars from Western lands, and to the Christian literature originally from Western lands, teaching them " the truth as it is in Jesus," regarding God and the Saviour, the soul and eternity ?

THE END.